Diversity, Equity, and Inclusion in Sport

Ellen J. Staurowsky, EdD
Ithaca College

Algerian Hart, PhD
Missouri State University

Editors

Library of Congress Cataloging-in-Publication Data

Names: Staurowsky, Ellen J., 1955- editor. | Hart, Algerian editor.
Title: Diversity, equity, and inclusion in sport / Ellen J. Staurowsky, EdD, Ithaca College, Algerian Hart, PhD, Missouri State University.
Description: Champaign, IL : Human Kinetics, [2023] | Includes bibliographical references and index.
Identifiers: LCCN 2021055003 (print) | LCCN 2021055004 (ebook) | ISBN 9781718207264 (Paperback : alk. paper) | ISBN 9781718207271 (ePub) | ISBN 9781718207288 (PDF)
Subjects: LCSH: Sports for people with disabilities. | Physical education for people with disabilities. | Diversity in the workplace. | Sports administration--Moral and ethical aspects. | BISAC: SPORTS & RECREATION / Cultural & Social Aspects | BUSINESS & ECONOMICS / Workplace Culture
Classification: LCC GV709.3 .D589 2023 (print) | LCC GV709.3 (ebook) | DDC 796.04/56--dc23/eng/20220405
LC record available at https://lccn.loc.gov/2021055003
LC ebook record available at https://lccn.loc.gov/2021055004

ISBN: 978-1-7182-0726-4 (print)

The web addresses cited in this text were current as of January 2022, unless otherwise noted.

Acquisitions Editor: Andrew L. Tyler
Developmental Editor: Melissa Feld
Managing Editor: Anna Lan Seaman
Copyeditor: E before I Editing
Proofreader: Leigh Keylock
Indexer: Nan N. Badgett
Permissions Manager: Dalene Reeder
Graphic Designer: Sean Roosevelt
Cover Designer: Keri Evans
Cover Design Specialist: Susan Rothermel Allen
Photograph (cover): Maddie Meyer / Getty Images
Photo Asset Manager: Laura Fitch
Photo Production Manager: Jason Allen
Senior Art Manager: Kelly Hendren
Illustrations: © Human Kinetics, unless otherwise noted
Printer: McNaughton & Gunn

Printed in the United States of America 10 9 8 7 6 5 4 3 2 1

The paper in this book is certified under a sustainable forestry program.

Human Kinetics
1607 N. Market Street
Champaign, IL 61820
USA

United States and International
Website: **US.HumanKinetics.com**
Email: info@hkusa.com
Phone: 1-800-747-4457

Canada
Website: **Canada.HumanKinetics.com**
Email: info@hkcanada.com

E8348

Tell us what you think!
Human Kinetics would love to hear what we can do to improve the customer experience. Use this QR code to take our brief survey.

CONTENTS

PART II FORMS OF DIVERSITY IN SPORT

FOREWORD

In the early 1880s, the face of 19th century baseball, Cap Anson, refused to have his championship Chicago team play a game against an embryonic club from Toledo. His reason? The Toledo side employed as catcher a Black man, Moses Fleetwood Walker, and Anson declared he "won't play never no more with the nigger in" (Husman, n.d.).

Toledo eventually acceded to Anson's ultimatum, and all of baseball followed his lead in subsequent seasons. By the end of the 1880s, Walker and the few other major league baseball players of African descent were gone. Baseball became an all-White purview. And as it grew, ironically, into what we anointed America's pastime, most every other sport in post-Reconstruction Jim Crow America followed suit. For generations well into the 20th century, American sport was segregated by race. As late as 1990, professional golf planned to play one of its championships at an all-White male country club (Staff Writer, 1990).

And through it all, American sport somehow garnered a reputation as a place of meritocracy in American society. Few things are further from the truth.

Even 20 years into a new millennium, the remnants of segregation, inequity, and exclusivity in sport remain, manifest particularly in mostly homogenous ownership and management dominated by White men. The National Football League continues to be predominated by Black men as athletes—but Black men are vastly underrepresented as coaches and executives. African Americans and Afro-Latinx individuals, who make up a third of Major League Baseball's rosters, comprise only a fifth of the game's managers and less of its general managers and operations presidents. Even the Women's National Basketball Association, thought to be a paragon of progressivism, has far fewer women of color as coaches, executives, or franchise officers (www.tidesport.org/racial-gender-report-card).

Sports media, which so often points a collective finger at sport's diversity deficiency off its fields and courts of play, is more representative of the inequity in the games it covers than not (Lapchick, 2018).

In total, modern sport, just as early sport, is a grand site of exclusionary practices. Today's discriminatory practices are less overt than in the 1880s, but they are still present.

Against that backdrop, *Diversity, Equity, and Inclusion in Sport*, edited by Ellen Staurowsky and Algerian Hart, is an important and timely text. It underscores the mythology of sport, highlights its reality, and, unlike many writings before it on fairness in sport, offers solutions.

Through chapters by various authors on race, sexual orientation, religious identity, disability, sport as social change, and other topics, Staurowsky and Hart remind us how important sport is in everyday lives, producing and sustaining inequalities at the same time it influences people. And they suggest how sport, for the same reasons, can be leveraged for positive action.

The text doesn't suggest it is as simple as having an individual break a barrier—after all, sport has long lauded itself for its arrangement with Jackie Robinson to reintegrate baseball after 60 years of segregation. It isn't as easy as painting Black Lives Matter on basketball court baselines or in a football field's endzone. Instead, as Staurowsky observes in chapter 2, Engaging in Difficult Dialogues About Diversity, Equity, and Inclusion in Sport, it requires a deep dive into "how institutions and the people who work for them perpetuate values and beliefs that can promote or undermine the creation of inclusive and equitable environments that embrace and celebrate diversity." As new managers and leaders enter the sport administration world, they need to be adept at holding productive and meaningful conversations about DEI topics "such as privilege, the three components of bias (stereotypes, prejudice, and discrimination), and the concepts of social identity and intersectionality."

Far more often than not, sport has been a laggard on progress, playing by reprehensible rules of society rather than shattering them. It has usually only lived up to its much-celebrated ideals of meritocracy under pressure, or threat, or outright embarrassment. The Washington National Football League franchise, with an 80-year-old name that mocked Indigenous people, refused to listen to aggrieved Native American people and drop that name until the tsunami of racial reckoning in the wake of the police murder of George Floyd washed over the team as it did the rest of our institutions (Whyno, 2020).

It is time that sport earns what heretofore was fabricated credit from the media as being in the vanguard of social change and justice. *Diversity, Equity, and Inclusion in Sport* provides a blueprint on how to do so.

Kevin Blackistone
Professor of the Practice
Philip Merrill College of Journalism, University of Maryland
Panelist at ESPN
Columnist at the *Washington Post*

PREFACE

Since the 1960s, a focus on diversity has been a part of management approaches for corporations, communities, military organizations, higher education, and sport entities. It appears in value statements, principles for decision making, policy documents, and strategic plans. Over time in the United States, the expanse of that focus has changed from one that narrowly addressed gender awareness in the 1970s to a much broader focus on age, disability, ethnicity, gender identity and sexuality, political affiliation, race, religion, and social status and economic class.

The motives behind programming around diversity and inclusion have shifted from consciousness raising and awareness anchored in social justice to defensive posturing to protect against civil rights lawsuits to the need to harness the power of diverse workforces to improve work environments and increase productivity (Vaughn, 2007). In later years, the term *diversity* would be paired with the term *inclusion* to emphasize the need for action in addressing individual attitudes, barriers, biases, and prejudices and their manifestation in institutional forms of oppression such as racism and sexism. In effect, it wasn't enough to acknowledge difference without tackling the power dynamics emanating from a White patriarchy that held majority control over decision making, media, money, and the political structure.

As ubiquitous as the terms *diversity* and *inclusion* have been over the past 60 years in the United States, the underlying causes of oppression escaped and eluded substantive and lasting change. As surface conversations about diversity and inclusion were promoted, the gap between rich and poor in America grew at alarming rates; people of color struggled to gain access to education, health care, safety, and security; incarceration rates of men of color rose at staggering rates; and injustice flourished.

The systemic failures of societal institutions to help Americans engage in difficult dialogues about forms of oppression in the United States have led to a country in turmoil. Women and their allies have mobilized for the past five years under the banner of #MeToo, a movement grounded in the work of Tarana Burke, who founded an organization to assist sexual assault victims in 2006 (Nicolaou & Smith, 2020), and to protest the enduring equal pay gap for women across gender and racial and ethnic groups (Sheth, Gal, & Hoff, 2020). The Black Lives Matter movement and the calls for racial justice in the aftermath of police killings of Eric Garner, Michael Brown, Tamir Rice, Walter Scott, Alton Sterling, Philando Castile, Stephon Clark, Breonna Taylor, and George Floyd have led to calls for meaningful and lasting change in service to a fairer and more humane society (BBC, 2020).

While some people point to sport as a place where barriers that separate people melt away by virtue of a prevailing meritocracy that sees only human character, possibility, and talent, sport in fact is an integral part of society, reflecting fault lines that are found throughout society at large. Problems in the larger society about the mistreatment of segments of the population have been manifest in sport as well. Emerging awareness that sport is not a safe place for athletes has been revealed in sex abuse cases involving hundreds of female and male athletes at the youth, high school, college, Olympic, and professional levels, with school authorities and sport executives having failed to act to protect athletes. A new form of athlete activism has grown in a time of social media to reveal deeply entrenched racism in the exploitative practices of college athletic programs and professional sport entities.

There is much work to be done in educating future and current leaders about how to work toward meaningful change, creating accountability mechanisms to measure change, and addressing systemic issues that perpetuate long-standing prejudicial attitudes and biases. This book is a timely response to this moment. It differs from others in that the book itself includes the voices of a group of experts in their respective fields. No single author can or should tackle such a large project; this work requires collaboration and engagement across a number of areas of expertise. In our approach to this project, we have tried to be mindful of that reality, bringing authors to the project who can contribute to a book that will aid teachers and students, practitioners, and others interested in these issues in moving the conversation forward.

ACKNOWLEDGMENTS

When working on a project of this magnitude, which involved 17 authors and 15 sport leaders who are working on diversity, equity, and inclusion (DEI) issues in a variety of ways, there aren't enough words to express the level of gratitude and appreciation we feel for the gift of their intellectual talent, professional commitment, and generosity of spirit. At the time we undertook this project, the United States and countries around the world were in the throes of confronting the challenges of the COVID-19 pandemic and the shock waves emanating from racial unrest, economic disruption, and growing political divisiveness and rancor.

For our wonderful and tireless authors who agreed to take on the work of writing a chapter for this book while serving their students and institutions in the midst of an unprecedented time in American higher education, we are profoundly moved by your efforts. We know the sacrifices made in diminished time with family, fewer hours of sleep, and increased stress. To our authors and their institutions, recognized here in the order of their contributions in the body of the book, you hold our highest esteem and respect: Kevin Blackistone (University of Maryland); NaRi Shin (University of Connecticut); Jeff Montez de Oca (University of Colorado, Colorado Springs); Beau Houston (Bridges Lane Center for Student Athletes); Amira Rose Davis (Pennsylvania State University); Luca Maurer (Ithaca College); Kiera Duckworth (Erie County Medical Center Corporation); Mary Hums (University of Louisville); Eli Wolff (Brown University); Tim Mirabito (Ithaca College); Robin Hardin (the University of Tennessee); Amanda Paule-Koba (Bowling Green State University); Michael Sachs (Temple University); Billy Hawkins (University of Houston); Ketra Armstrong (Michigan State University); and Akilah Carter-Francique (San Jose State University).

At a personal level, a note of thanks is extended to faculty colleagues and administrators at our respective institutions, Ithaca College and Missouri State University, for their support of this project. That said, it is to the thousands of students who have graced our lives over many years that we reserve a special note, for their good humor, creative energies, and fierce convictions. They inspire us every day and have remained uppermost in our thoughts as we put this book together.

A personal note of thanks goes out to Dr. Frederick Becker and Tina Miller as well as the team of healers at Penn Medicine—including Dr. d'Entremont, Dr. Tchou, Dr. Chen, Dr. Jones, Dr. Kucharczuk, and their staffs—for extending my [Dr. Staurowsky's] shelf life and making this work possible.

And finally, to our endlessly patient and incredibly skilled editors and staff at Human Kinetics, Andrew L. Tyler, Melissa Feld, and Anna Lan Seaman, we offer our deepest thanks for helping us to develop this project and bring it across the finish line.

With the utmost respect and admiration,
Ellen J. Staurowsky, Ithaca College
Algerian Hart, Missouri State University

PART I

FOUNDATIONS OF DIVERSITY, EQUITY, AND INCLUSION IN SPORT

Peyton Williams/UNC/Getty Images

CHAPTER 1

Diversity, Equity, and Inclusion Within Sport Organizations

Algerian Hart and Ellen J. Staurowsky

LEARNING OBJECTIVES

- Define the terms *diversity*, *equity*, and *inclusion*.
- Cultivate a professional understanding of diversity, equity, and inclusion within the sport industry.
- Become familiar with shifting racial and gender demographics in the United States.
- Consider how the changing nature of work influences dialogues about diversity, equity, and inclusion.
- Reflect on how the relationship between employees and employers is changing.
- Become familiar with the value of diversity and return on investment (ROI) as it applies to inclusion.
- Develop an appreciation for the difference between deep-level and surface-level commitment to diversity.
- Become familiar with the concept of social identity and dynamics of inclusion.

In September of 2020, Martin Luther King III published an essay in *Rolling Stone* reflecting on how a new era of African American athlete activists were using their celebrity and notoriety for the purpose of promoting positive social change. The tradition of athlete activism is a long one in the United States and one that is intertwined with the nation's history. Athlete activists such as Colin Kaepernick, the former NFL football player who took a knee on the sideline to protest racial injustice and police brutality, share a history with athletes from the Civil Rights era, including Hank Aaron, Muhammad Ali, Tommie Smith, John Carlos, and so many others who joined King III's father, Dr. Martin Luther King Jr., in the 1960s in advocating for a more just and peaceful democratic society free of racial discrimination.

Upon Dr. King's death at the hands of an assassin in 1968, professional baseball was inclined to continue business as usual. Under the leadership of the great right fielder and noted humanitarian Roberto Clemente, however, the Pittsburgh Pirates refused to take the field. In explaining their decision to honor King and note the national tragedy that his death represented, Clemente, along with White teammate Dave Wickersham, issued a statement that read, "We are doing this because we white and Black players respect what Dr. King has done for mankind" (King III, 2020, para. 2).

The action of Clemente and Wickersham, according to Martin Luther King III, was wholly in keeping with the vision his father had for the society at large. He wrote that his father had once said, "We have to be together before we can learn how to live together" and that sport provides the kind of communal gathering space where interracial cooperation can occur. King III concluded by noting that as had happened in his father's generation, African American athlete activists in 2021 were speaking truth to power at a time when American values were under unprecedented assault:

> *Their continued commitment can help light the way forward to a new era of hope and healing for our country, when every citizen can feel safe and secure from racial violence. With our support, every stadium can become a "field of dreams," a place where brotherhood and sisterhood can one day prevail and help shape a better future for all Americans. (King III, 2020, para. 13)*

In this chapter, we will be situating discussions about diversity, equity, and inclusion in sport within the context of events occurring in the United States following the killing of George Floyd in May of 2020, which sparked a racial reckoning, and the COVID-19 pandemic, which highlighted the significant gaps that exist across our society in terms of **diversity, equity, and inclusion (DEI)**. This period of time has been marked by scenes of despair, sorrow, tragedy, and hope. Signs of the need for profound and meaningful change have been passionate, dramatic, and sometimes horrific: the swell of voices speaking out about sexual harassment, video evidence of police violence against Black individuals, and resulting protests and social media campaigns such as #BlackLivesMatter, #ADayWithoutImmigrants, and #WomensMarch. Diversity, equity, and inclusion issues drive much of the national conversation.

In the United States, shifting demographics have led to a dramatic increase in racial diversity. The traditional gender binary and the conventional family structure are being challenged. Prominent politicians have taken aim at racial and ethnic minorities, women, and the LGBTQ and immigrant communities. Women's voices have exposed sexual harassment in Hollywood and the technology industry. Diversity issues are dominating headlines. As the United States and other nations around the world undergo these demographic and cultural changes, sport leaders are called upon to help navigate difference, to recognize its value, and to foster inclusion. Some organizations have badly misfired when trying to reach diverse consumers across the United States. Diversity issues cause brand pain for those who do not get it right (Williams, 2013).

In the moment, some sport organizations are working to ensure that their workforces are representative of the wider society and groups they serve, that they provide fair and equitable treatment to all stakeholders (athletes, coaches, staff, and fans), and that they offer safe and supportive environments where people can thrive. If this moment has taught us anything, it is that work around diversity, equity, and inclusion is a central concern for every social institution, including sport. As such, the work we focus on in this book has short-term significance and long-term meaning for your future as a leader and change maker in the sport industry. In this chapter, we begin with defining *diversity*, *equity*, and *inclusion*. We move on to answering the question of why there should be an emphasis on diversity, equity, and inclusion within sport organizations. We then explore the distinction between deep-level and surface-level commitment to diversity, and we discuss the concept of social identity and the dynamics of inclusion.

Defining Diversity, Equity, and Inclusion

The concept of **diversity** encompasses a wide range of qualities and characteristics that distinguish people from one another. *Diversity* is used broadly to refer to demographic attributes such as sex, race, ethnicity, sexual orientation, class, ability, age, national origin, religious beliefs, and education. Sport is a diverse arena that includes individuals from different cultural and racial backgrounds.

Sport diversity, equity, and inclusion (DEI) is an important topic for a number of reasons. First, being exposed to diverse voices allows a person to view issues and problems from multiple perspectives, derived from distinct experiences, perspectives, knowledge, and connections. Rather than viewing the world from a single-focus lens, the person is able to expand their views and consider multiple options. Second, diversity can move people beyond their ethnocentric points of view, to learn not only about others' experiences and backgrounds but also more about themselves.

Equity is the recognition that we do not all start from the same access level; we must acknowledge imbalances within sport entities, make adjustments to address those imbalances, and intentionally cultivate access and opportunities for historically underrepresented populations. To use the analogy of a coach addressing the needs of a team, sport equity is not simply giving all players the exact same cleats but is providing all players with shoes of their size that fit. Sport equity is about recognizing inequalities and taking steps to address them. It is about changing the culture and structure of sport in pursuit of accessible spaces and opportunities to everyone across society.

Inclusion is the DEI glue, demonstrating intentionality by providing equal access to opportunities and resources for people who might otherwise be excluded from an organization or group structure. Inclusion in sport is about access and the removal of all forms of exclusionary practice that prevent individuals from participating (see figure 1.1).

FIGURE 1.1 Equality versus equity.

Cultivating a Professional Understanding of Diversity, Equity, and Inclusion in Sport

Sport in all of its forms exists within the larger society. In this part of the chapter, we explore reasons why sport leaders and those aspiring to work in the sport industry need to be conversant in and attendant to diversity, equity, and inclusion issues. To do so, we look at the shifting demographics in the U.S. population, the changing nature of work and the workforce, and changing relationships between employees and employers. The threads of what we discuss here will be expanded on throughout the rest of the text.

Shifting Demographics in the U.S. Population by 2030

At the beginning of 2020, the U.S. population numbered just over 331 million people, making the United States the third largest nation on earth (behind China, with 1.5 billion people, and India, with 1.46 billion). By 2030, it is expected that the U.S. population will increase by approximately 18.6 million (United Nations, 2019). Beyond the fact that the U.S. population and world population are growing, there are also several trends in the patterns emerging that are worth noting.

According to demographer Dudley Poston (2020) from Texas A&M University, the U.S. population is getting older. Whereas in previous generations people under the age of 18 comprised a larger percentage of the population than older Americans, this will no longer be the case in another 20 years as people live longer. More people than ever before will be living past 100 years of age. As that shift occurs, there will be economic issues associated with health care, the age at which people retire, and how we all live together.

Another shift that has been going on in the demographics of the United States for several decades, and will continue into the future, is in overall racial composition (figure 1.2). While non-Hispanic Whites comprised the majority race in the United States in 2020, representing 59.7 percent of the population, the representation of Whites has been dropping since the 1950s and is expected to continue into the decades ahead. It is expected that by 2045 non-Hispanic Whites will comprise less than 50 percent of the population. When considered across age and

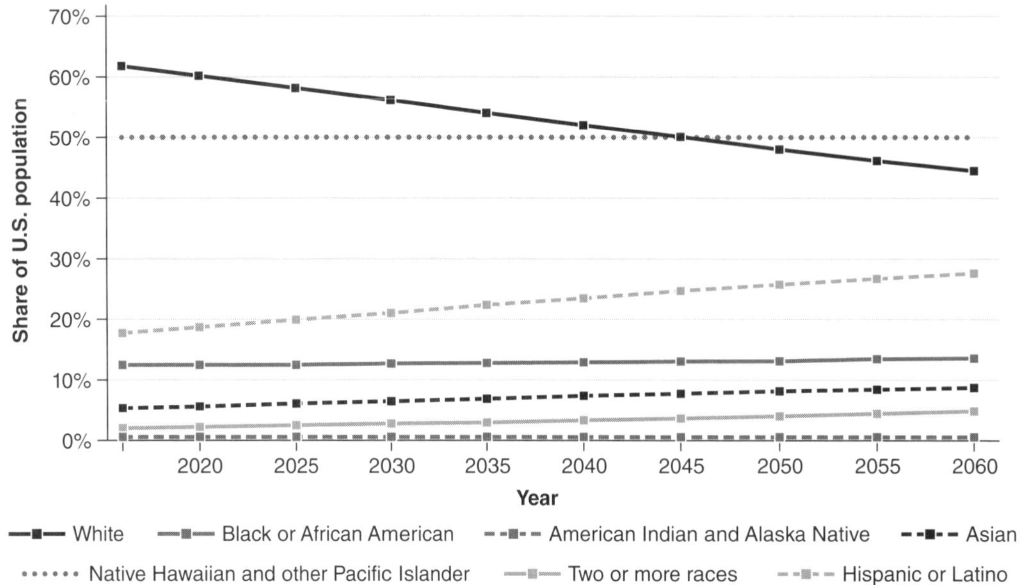

FIGURE 1.2 The projected race/ethnicity breakdown for the U.S. through 2060.

Reprinted from D.L. Poston, Jr., "3 Big Ways That the US Will Change Over the Next Decade, *The Conversation (2002)*. Distributed under the terms of the Creative Commons Attribution CC-BY-ND.

race, "on the first day of 2020, whites under age 18 were already in the minority. Among all the young people now in the U.S., there are more minority young people than there are white young people" (Poston, 2020, para. 21).

The Changing Nature of Work and the Workforce

Even before the COVID-19 pandemic, the nature of work across all sectors was changing due to technology, e-commerce, and the increasingly connected world. In sport, those changes manifest in myriad ways, including the growth in sectors such as wagering and esports, efforts to find more ways to engage fans through fantasy sports, ever-evolving niche markets emerging in the delivery of sport content to new audiences, and the intersection of technology and athlete performance (e.g., wearable technology or even Fitbit devices). And any of us who are in education—students and faculty alike—are well aware of how technology affects our experience, whether it is operating on learning management systems such as Blackboard, Canvas, or Sakai; learning in a virtual setting; or using ebooks and open access resources.

During the course of the pandemic, the shift to remote work carried forward as the nation started to recover. According to a Gallup poll conducted in September of 2021, "two-thirds of employees in white-collar jobs (67%) reported working from home either exclusively (41%) or some of the time (26%)" (Saad & Wigert, 2021, para. 2), while remote work was less prevalent among people working in education (48%) and health care (35%).

The shift to remote work has had an effect on employee expectations and their relationships with their employers. The same Gallup poll (Saad & Wigert, 2021) found the following:

- Ninety-one percent hoped that work from home would continue as an option after the pandemic ended.
- Thirty-three percent of full-time workers indicated that if their company eliminated the opportunity to work remotely, they would look for another job.
- Two-thirds of full-time workers indicated that they believed working remotely would have a positive or neutral effect on work culture.

The support for remote work stems from a reduction in the time and cost of commuting, greater flexibility to manage work and home life, and overall well-being. As Gould and Shierholz (2020) point out, however, framing remote work as something that "everyone" is doing ignores the fact that "less than 30 percent of workers can work from home, and the ability to work from home differs enormously by race and ethnicity" (para. 1). From a socioeconomic perspective, "Higher-wage workers are six times as likely to be able to work from home as lower-wage workers" (Gould & Shierholz, 2020, figure B).

While some predict that the disruption in the workplace that occurred during the pandemic will continue into the future, others are not quite as convinced. Those uncertainties are evident in the thinking of sport executives about the future of work in their organizations. On one hand, the pandemic inspired innovation in the sport space, with sport broadcasters no longer traveling to games and calling games from a studio or even their homes. "While tech companies like Facebook and Twitter have vocalized their efforts at maintaining a work-from-home option for their thousands of employees, no professional sports organization has made similar proclamations" (Moran, 2020, para. 4).

The Great Resignation and Changing Relationships Between Employees and Employers

In the fall of 2020, as the economy started to reopen after the pandemic-caused shutdown, the U.S. workforce did not rebound; millions of workers did not return to work. This trend, which came to be known as "the Great Resignation" or "the Big Quit," left positions unfilled and a worker shortage in certain sectors, especially in the service sector, hospitality, and production. As the United States opened up following the shutdown, employers had a difficult time retaining workers and hiring new ones. While a large percentage of employees who decided not to return to work were people age 55 and older who opted to retire early, jobs in areas such as hospitality and the service sector were being passed over by potential employees (Fox, 2021).

While the sport industry is a highly attractive sector for workers and has not, overall, suffered from the worker shortage trend seen in the Great Resignation, it has been a showcase for another trend: a shift in the relationship between employees and employers, where employees are wielding more power and influence (at least in this moment). Before the pandemic, the stage was being set for this with the 2019 campaign for equitable pay by the U.S. women's soccer team and with the efforts of players such as Malcolm Jenkins, then with the Philadelphia Eagles, who cofounded the Players Coalition in 2018. The Players Coalition, led by Jenkins and Anquan Boldin, persuaded the NFL to commit $89 million to social justice causes (Thomas, 2018).

The willingness of players to challenge the environment they work in—such as when LeBron James called out fans who directed inappropriate comments and gestures at him during a game, resulting in their ejection from the arena, and when WNBA players campaigned to oust one of their owners, Kelly Loeffler, from her U.S. Senate seat over racial justice issues (Buckner, 2021)—demonstrates that players are not going to passively go along and that athletes expect their employers to work with them to change abusive and discriminatory cultures.

How the changing nature of work will play out for women at this time is particularly interesting to track in the broader society and in sport. Some have credited women with leading the way in the Great Resignation, at a time when the percentage of women participating in the workforce was at the highest levels ever recorded (Fox, 2021). In 2019, just before the pandemic hit, 57.4 percent of women were in the workforce, compared to 69.2 percent of men, a figure that has remained relatively stable over time. Women's rise in the workforce parallels the increasing numbers of women going to college and earning college degrees from 1970 to 2019 (U.S. Bureau of Labor Statistics, 2021). In terms of the overall workforce, going into 2020, women comprised just over half of all U.S. workers, primarily because of the large representation of women in jobs in health care, retail, and education. Concerns that have long existed for working women—low wages and issues with child care and elder care—are believed to have contributed to women's participation in the Great Resignation.

The question of how the Great Resignation may or may not be affecting the sport industry is an interesting one to contemplate. While the past two decades have seen an unprecedented rise in the sheer number of women working in the sport industry—from the ticket office to the broadcast booth to the executive suite (Staurowsky, 2016; Staurowsky et al., 2020)—women as a whole, and non-White women in particular, remain significantly underrepresented throughout the industry.

Illustrative of this is the status of women in college coaching and leadership positions. When Title IX was passed in 1972, women represented over 90 percent of the coaches of women's university teams and 2 percent of the head coaches of men's teams (Acosta & Carpenter, 2014). According to the NCAA Gender and Race Demographic Database, in 2020 to 2021, females were underrepresented in the coaching ranks in two ways. Among head coaches of women's teams across all divisions, 41 percent were female and 59 percent were male. When considered within the context of all head coaches of men's and women's teams, 75 percent were male and 25 percent were female. What this means is that roughly 7 or 8 out of every 10 head coaches working in an NCAA college athletic program are male. The gender breakdown for college athletic directors was nearly identical (76% male to 24% female) (National Collegiate Athletic Association, 2022). It may take a few years removed from the pandemic before the full impact on the sport industry workforce can be fully assessed. A consciousness about the gender and race dynamics in the workforce should, however, be prompting an evaluation of talent recruitment, hiring, and retention practices to assess areas of sensitivity and vulnerability.

The Value of Inclusion and Return on Investment in Inclusion

Emblematic of the attention sport leaders within the industry are paying to DEI is a partnership between the National Association of Collegiate Directors of Athletics and an organization called Return on Inclusion. The National Association of Collegiate Directors of Athletics (NACDA) is an association that provides professional development support to college sport administrators and oversees 16 affiliate associations representing athletic staff who handle everything from budgets to compliance to marketing to athlete development and student services. In November of 2021 NACDA entered into a partnership with Return on Inclusion (ROI), an organization founded by Nevin Caple, a former women's basketball player at Fairleigh Dickinson and long-time equity advocate and educator. Through in-person trainings as well as content delivered online, it is the mission of ROI to help educate athletic department staff about how to create more inclusive cultures within athletic departments. In explaining the importance of the partnership with ROI, NACDA chief executive officer Bob Vecchione said, "Diversity, equity & inclusion education is far and away the number one topic across our Affiliate Associations that we are continuously looking to enhance" (NACDA, 2021).

The name of Caple's program, Return on Inclusion, answers in the affirmative a question that has historically been raised about DEI efforts—namely, whether **social returns on investment (SROI)** actually result from them. By naming her company ROI, Caple is signaling the value of an investment in developing an organizational culture that creates avenues for people to bring the best of themselves to their work—unburdened by stigmas, biases, or perceptions that hold them back—and that foster better collaborative environments. Such an investment results in many benefits to sport organizations and the people who work in them.

The social return on inclusion has been found in the positive impact that such investment has in the way people experience their work

The social return on inclusion has been found in the positive impact that such investment has in the way people experience their work environments and their productivity.
Luis Alvarez/DigitalVision/Getty Images

environments and their productivity. Antonio Viscaya Abdo, the general secretariat manager for the Federación Mexicana de Futbol Asociación, has noted that organizations that lead their industries in adopting DEI initiatives have benefited in numerous ways according to several performance metrics (Viscaya Abdo, 2020):

- *Profitability:* 25 to 36 percent more likely to outperform on profitability
- *Innovation:* up to 20 percent higher rate of innovation and 19 percent higher innovation revenues
- *Decision-making:* up to 30 percent greater ability of spotting and reducing business risks
- *Employee engagement:* statistically significant causal relationship with engagement and retention, for all employees

Researchers have examined how underrepresentation in coaching and leadership positions in sport has emulated the broader society—specifically, a male-dominated leadership profile with limited attention to demonstrating diversity and inclusion. One study that analyzed approximately 600 business decisions made by 200 different business teams in a wide variety of companies over two years found that all-male teams made better business decisions than individual decision makers 58 percent of the time, but gender-diverse teams made better decisions 73 percent of the time (Larson, 2017). Teams with diversity across gender, age, and geography made better decisions 87 percent of the time. Diverse organizations and teams with inclusion-centered practices fared best of all.

A report published by Gartner, a global research and advisory firm headquartered in Stamford, Connecticut, predicted that "through 2022, 75 percent of organizations with frontline decision-making teams reflecting a diverse and inclusive culture will exceed their financial targets" (Sakpal, 2019). Further, a 2020 study by JND Legal Administration concluded that the inherent value and benefits of diversity on employee well-being and organizational culture are generally understood; however, its impact on work performance is less frequently discussed or embraced. To compete in today's market and meet the demands of an increasingly diverse consumer pool, prioritizing inclusivity in the workplace is vital to success. Takeaways from the study are that diverse teams make better decisions, diversity fosters innovation, teams with diverse leadership generate more revenue, and diversity attracts and retains top talent.

While the value of diversity, equity, and inclusion efforts has been well documented, such initiatives often have to be nurtured by leaders who understand the distinction between simply talking about DEI and having a strategic DEI approach that permeates the organization. In the next section, we review this notion of a deep-level commitment versus a surface-level commitment to diversity.

Deep-Level Versus Surface-Level Diversity: The Signal From the Noise

From large global companies to small business entities, all organizations must recognize that they operate in a **polycultural** world. The strategic landscape requires organizations to differentiate the signal from the noise. Sport organizations can develop media, marketing, human resources, community engagement, education, and social responsibility approaches that recognize the impact, influence, potential, and returns on investment that emerge from diverse communities.

This is differentiating the signal from the noise—a concept akin to Cunningham's (2019) notion of deep-level versus surface-level diversity. The "signal" is the value of being aware, informed, thoughtful, and strategic, setting an authentic course of action that will make lasting change in diversity and inclusion measures. The "noise" is where an organization can get lost in shallow, tone-deaf attempts that are not representative of today's cultural landscape (Williams, 2013). Organizations can rise above the storm of diversity crisis and the lack of visible representation of diversity. The organizations and companies that actively pursue the **cultural competencies** required to navigate today's complex environment are organizations that develop culturally relevant strategies that accurately reflect the way America looks today.

An organization that has made modest progress in distinguishing between the signal and the noise is the National Football League (NFL). Their significant financial investment is an example of how they are signaling the value of investing in meaningful DEI initiatives. At the same time, the NFL has also been caught up in the noise, as evidenced by the dynamics surrounding a policy known as the Rooney Rule.

On the surface, the Rooney Rule was presented as an effort to address the racial imbalance that exists in the hiring of coaches and front office personnel in a league in which 70 percent or more of the players are not White. Discussions leading to the Rooney Rule emerged out of a moment in 2002 when two of the NFL's Black coaches, Tony Dungy (Tampa Bay) and Dennis Green (Minnesota), were fired from their respective positions, despite considerable success. Civil rights attorney Cyrus Mehri and criminal lawyer Johnnie Cochran teamed up and commissioned a study to be done of Black head coaches in the NFL and how they fared in relationship to their White counterparts (O'Connell, 2021a).

The author of that study, Dr. Janice Madden, found that Black coaches were being held to a higher standard in terms of winning: Black coaches averaged 1.1 more wins compared to White coaches. And when Black coaches were fired, they were not being given second chances. Threatening to file a lawsuit alleging racial discrimination in hiring, the issue rose to the attention of Art Rooney, owner of the Pittsburgh Steelers, who had long sought to encourage diversity within the NFL. Working with Mehri, Cochrane, and John Wooten, a former player and then highest ranking African American executive in the NFL, Rooney eventually argued successfully for the adoption of a rule that, at the time, required clubs with a head coach vacancy to interview at least one non-White candidate before extending an offer to someone (O'Connell, 2021a).

Over the years, the Rooney Rule has been expanded as a policy to cover other open positions, including general manager as well as coordinator and front office positions. In November of 2020, the NFL also moved to revise the policy to reward teams with draft picks if they demonstrated that they "worked toward diversity," a decision that Yahoo Sports columnist Shalise Manza Young described as "sort of insulting." Young went on to query, "Why do you need to be rewarded for developing Black men?" (O'Connell, 2021b, para. 13).

After 18 years in effect, the Rooney Rule had not affected the level of diversity at the highest levels of leadership in the NFL. As Harrison and Bukstein's (2020) report on the occupational mobility patterns in the NFL concluded, "Since the inception of the Occupational Mobility Report, there have been incremental advances in professional opportunities and growth for minorities that spark glimmers of hope. However, those tiny sparks have yet to foster a flame toward reaching the ultimate objective of a fair and open process for all" (p. 5).

The lack of a deep-level commitment to diversity at the NFL has been called out by the Fritz Pollard Alliance (FPA), a group of NFL coaches, scouts, and front office staff who are committed to educating the public about equal opportunity in sport. In January of 2020, the FPA issued a statement that described the NFL's system of hiring and promoting talent into upper levels of management as flawed because it was not embraced or enacted consistently across all franchises. The statement went on to note, "We cannot expect fairness if business remains status quo. Our focus must shift from counting emblematic victories each year to calling for measurable initiatives that support sustainable progress" (Florio, 2020, para. 3).

Sport organizations must adapt along with the polycultural social evolution. It will be uncomfortable. It will require honest reflection, hard questions, willingness to receive feedback, and forthrightness about not having all the answers. We need to lean into the discomfort rather than shy away from it. The organizations that approach DEI from a surface level or get lost in the noise will be left behind, making way for those that have more cultural intelligence, an understanding of how diversity is imperative to their SROI, and greater authenticity.

NFL Accused of Racial Discrimination by Former Head Coach Brian Flores

On the first day of Black History Month (February) in 2022, former Miami Dolphins Head Coach Brian Flores filed a class action lawsuit against the National Football League and its 32 franchises alleging race discrimination in its hiring, evaluation, and retention practices. Flores was fired from the Dolphins in January 2022 following back-to-back winning seasons, something that had not been achieved in Miami since 2003. In the lawsuit (*Flores v. National Football League et al.*, 2022), Flores alleged his dismissal stemmed from his unwillingness to engage in improper conduct at the request of owner Stephen Ross, most specifically throwing games to improve Miami's position in the draft and violating the NFL's tampering rules.

Once out on the job market, Coach Flores recounted that while he had been contacted by the New York Giants to interview for their head coaching vacancy, he learned through an email exchange with Patriots Head Coach Bill Belichick that his scheduled interview was nothing more than a sham to satisfy the requirement of interviewing a Black candidate under the NFL's Rooney Rule. Flores came to learn through his communication with Belichick that the Giants had already hired Brian Draboll and made that decision known to others outside the Giants organization even as they were interviewing Flores (*Flores v. National Football League et al.*, 2022).

As the complaint documents, this was not the first time that a franchise had invited him to interview in circumstances where they had no intention of hiring him. When he arrived in Colorado to interview with Denver Broncos executives John Elway and Joe Ellis, they arrived late to the meeting and appeared to have been out drinking the night before.

At the time the lawsuit was filed, and nearly 20 years after the Rooney Rule was adopted, there was only one Black head coach in the NFL while 70 percent of the players were Black (and nearly 90 percent of the starters were Black). A similar deficiency was found when looking deeper into the coaching ranks (*Flores v. National Football League et al.*, 2022, p. 3):

- Only 8 of the NFL's 32 teams (25 percent) employed a Black special teams coordinator.
- Only 3 of the NFL's 32 teams (9 percent) employed a Black quarterback coach.
- Only 6 of the NFL's 32 teams (19 percent) employed a Black general manager.

In the aftermath of the lawsuit being filed, John Elway released a statement through Adam Schefter countering Flores' description of the meeting, stating that he took Flores' candidacy seriously and that he was very engaged in the interview process. Elway went on to offer an explanation that his seemingly disheveled appearance was due to a late night flight that was taken in order to be back in Denver for the interview. Both John Elway and Stephen Ross characterized Flores' claims as defamatory.

The NFL, after initially calling Flores' claims meritless, launched an investigation into allegations that executives in both Miami and Cleveland may have offered to pay coaches to steer their teams to lose in an effort to gain access to better draft picks.

Four days after Flores filed the lawsuit, NFL Commissioner Roger Goodell issued a memo to franchise executives and club presidents announcing that the league would not be waiting for the lawsuit to run its course but would initiate its own external review to "reassess and modify our strategies to ensure that they are consistent with our values and longstanding commitment to diversity, equity, and inclusion" (Goodell, 2022, para. 1). Flores' legal team viewed the NFL's announcement of an external review as mere public relations given the history of racial discrimination within the league (Espinoza, 2022). This case, as of the date of publication, moves forward even as Brian Flores was hired by the Pittsburgh Steelers in the weeks following the lawsuit being filed (D'Abate, 2022).

Social Identity and the Dynamics of Inclusion

For most people, social identity is a big part of who they are. Social identity is that part of a person that comes from their membership in different groups, such as family, athletic teams, the school attended, a band or club, or a local church. Despite a tendency to think of one's self as an independent being, everyone is intimately connected to and influenced by the groups that they seek membership in. A sense of belonging in the social world can be a source of pride as well as self-esteem.

As Hogg and Abrams (1988) explain, access to social groups is influenced by categories connected to hierarchical systems of power, status, prestige, and social class. Power dynamics paired with stereotyping result in the creation of in-groups (a production of emphasizing and exaggerating similarities) and out-groups (a production of emphasizing and exaggerating differences). It is thought that there are three mental processes associated with the evaluation of individuals leading to the organization of in-groups and out-groups (separating into "us" and "them"): social categorization (*which groups do I fit in with?* and *which groups see me as fitting in?*), social identification (adopting the mannerisms and look of the group we belong to), and social comparison (making judgments about which groups are favorable and which are rivals) (McLeod, 2019). As McLeod (2019) elaborates, "the central hypothesis of **social identity theory** is that group members of an in-group will seek to find negative aspects of an out-group, thus enhancing their self-image" (para. 5). An appreciation of the dynamics that produce in-groups and out-groups is essential to DEI work because it helps us understand the forces that foster both inclusion and exclusion.

To illustrate this, consider Cunningham's (2019) examination of diversity within intercollegiate athletic departments, where he found that common in-group identity had a significant influence on group effectiveness. The propositions in Cunningham's (2019) model are based on tenets of social identity and social categorization theory that suggest individuals have an innate need to maintain high self-esteem. People make social comparisons to others in their environment to ensure high levels of esteem are achieved. Important to the purpose of Cunningham's (2019) work is the contention that in order to make social comparisons individuals must classify themselves, and others, into groups. As described by Ellemers, Kortekaas, and Ouwerkerk (1999), identification is a broad multidimensional construct of perceived inclusion with the group (self-categorization), evaluation of membership in the group (collective esteem), and emotional involvement with the group (commitment).

For inclusion to become infused in sport, there is a shift that becomes empowered by **cultural capital**. Cultural capital, a concept that originates from the work of Pierre Bourdieu (1984), is a form of currency that allows us to navigate a world that is socially stratified. Family income, parental educational levels, and parental occupations have profound impacts on the paths available to their children as they go through life, largely because of cultural capital. According to Paul Ingram, a business professor at Columbia University, "A person's social class origins leave a cultural imprint that has a lasting effect, even if the individual gains money or status later in life" (Ingram, 2021, para. 4). He conceives of social class as the forgotten dimension of diversity, pointing out that "people of lower social-class origins . . . through the conditions of birth and upbringing have had relatively less access to money, to contacts who promote their upward mobility, and to the cultural know-how necessary to get ahead in schools and companies" (para. 3).

An understanding of cultural capital, how it is accumulated, and how it influences social mobility is key to diversity, equity, and inclusion efforts. As Ingram poignantly notes, "The real deficit that workers from lower social-class origins suffer in school is not intellectual but cultural: They know less than those from higher class origins about what the pathways to education are and how to make the most of them" (para. 7). This ultimately translates to the workplace, where workers who have lower class origins are 32 percent less likely to become managers than workers who have upper class origins.

Ethical Considerations in Support of DEI Initiatives in Sport

Today's sport organizations must view ethics and morality as critical ingredients in the sport environment. As discussed by DeSensi and Rosenberg (2020), "It is not so much that there may be too many abuses in sport, but that the magnitude, severity, and far-reaching influence of these ills are staggering." From bribery in the International Olympic Committee (IOC) to fraud and money laundering in the Fédération Internationale de Football Association (FIFA), ethical wrongdoing dramatically disturbs the foundation of the inclusive ideals of sport. Sport not only reflects a society's ethical standards but also contains its own moral qualities that influence societal structures and institutions. Sport organizations must confront general and unique ethical problems in the administration and governance of sport, such as discrimination, harassment, unethical accounting, abuse of leadership authority, nepotism and favoritism, and the health and safety of athletes.

Organizations must remain intentional to foster sport as a vehicle and platform that can promote DEI. Understanding the possibilities and probabilities for the future of sport will help leaders in the sport industry anticipate trends in the years ahead and empower them to make informed decisions regarding the ethical organization of sport (table 1.1). For this to happen, sport organizations must take personal, moral, and social responsibility embedded in DEI. Accountability will be required, but doing what is right and inclusive may involve risks and controversy. The quality of organizational courage is one important characteristic that enables future sport leaders to continue toward an established, sustainable, and ethically inclusive sport industry.

Creating a Robust Workforce

Elevating the value of inclusion and belonging is vital to sport organizations if the goal is to create a workforce culture change. In particular, reimagining hiring practices and policies that are more equitable is essential to the sustainability of an organization's investment in DEI. Leaders of sport organizations must consider the different lived experiences of their employees to connect with their communities both externally and internally, which can help their workforce achieve their full potential. Growing a diversity footprint can start with these actions (Skonicki, 2021):

1. Identify particular actions with imagination and an appreciation for inquiry.
2. Stimulate diversity by celebrating, valuing, infusing beliefs, and promoting behaviors that acknowledge inclusion.
3. Elevate the priority of equity and provide resources that support opportunities for intentional access within the organization.

TABLE 1.1 Ethical Considerations for the Management of Sport Organizations

Consideration	Description
Professionalism	Treating employees and consumers with honor and respect, leading to credibility and promoting a feeling of trustworthiness
Equity	Distributing resources appropriately for employees, taking individual needs into account
Personal concerns	Engaging in the types of actions that let employees know that they are vital and cared about as individuals
Legal and financial management	Protecting marginalized populations and combating legal issues that have prevented their upward mobility within sport
League and franchise issues	Fostering inclusive spaces that benefit the local economy that are essential to communities where a sport organization can enhance civic identity
Social justice matters	Supporting and promoting equitable economic, educational, and workplace opportunities that enhance cross cultural well-being
Diversity, equity, and inclusion	Nurturing proactive behaviors that encourage cultural diversity, promote women's upward mobility in sport, and enhance ethnic minorities' (and others') opportunities
Spaces for belonging	Furthering the discourse where people's deeper needs are valued and members of society are encouraged to connect

Sport Industry Leader Profile

A'dja D. Jones

Title: Chief Diversity Officer for Athletics and Director of Student-Athlete Development and Community Relations at Missouri State University

Education: BA in history and a master of science in student affairs in higher education from Missouri State University

A'dja became a part of the Missouri State University Department of Athletics in June 2012 as a graduate assistant. She has climbed through the ranks and is now serving in a leadership capacity at MSU.

Current Diversity Agenda

In the summer of 2021, Jones helped construct the Bears Unite program after a robust dialogue about bias and **microaggressions**. These conversations spoke to the need to create an educational framework that establishes a baseline of foundations on identity, history, understanding others, and advocacy. Bears Unite builds a network that supports and nurtures the matriculation of non-White athletes navigating a predominantly White institution collegiate experience.

Jones also helped to form the unity council for the MSU Department of Athletics administrative and support staff, which supports programming that enhances DEI and positively impacts the athlete journey beyond the field of play.

One of the significant challenges A'dja has encountered in her roles of working in DEI is getting people to understand the challenges associated with finding spaces that uplift women of color within the arena of sport while addressing the value of belonging and gender equity. A'dja has nurtured partnerships in the community where allies have assisted her with supporting and building pathways that highlight the importance of DEI work both on and off campus.

Think of the limited number of non-White individuals serving in positions of power across the landscape of sport.

- Among the 40 teams that make up Major League Baseball, 40 percent of the players are people of color. But there are only 5 managers, just 1 team president, and no general managers or head coaches who are people of color.
- Within the 30 teams of the NBA, 83 percent of the players are people of color. Yet among NBA executives, there are only 12 team presidents, 10 general managers, and 9 managers or head coaches who are not White.
- In the NFL, 70 percent of the players are people of color, but leadership and ownership are primarily White. Among the 32 NFL franchises there are only 2 team presidents, 2 general managers, and 5 managers or head coaches who are not White.
- The NCAA Football Bowl Series' 130 colleges and universities, where 65 percent of athletes are people of color, 30 athletic directors and 18 football coaches are not White men.

How do we change this? These proportions present an opportunity for reflection in the sport business as the nation grapples with issues of social justice and equity.

Organizational diversity is a game changer, and sports organizations and leagues like the WNBA and NBA are paving the way where social change and access tangibly intersect. The sport landscape presents extensive opportunities to bring women and ethnic minorities into leadership. Doing so requires a collective obligation of cross-sport leaders to prepare our future sport practitioners, sport leaders, and sport organizers to work and live in a diverse society.

As described by Renee E. Tirado, former vice president of talent acquisition and head of diversity and inclusion in Major League Baseball, "We often say, 'We are the sport of Jackie Robinson.' We hold that responsibility very close to our hearts in the diversity department. We have to walk the talk that he did" (Footer, 2019).

Sport Industry Diversity Initiative

SPORT AND COMMUNITY LEADER: IT STARTS AT THE TOP

Dr. Lyle Q. Foster, university professor (Missouri State University), diversity trainer, and community entrepreneur, discusses the leadership potential of sport organizations when the pressure of societal change is on full display.

"I think what we're experiencing today seems to suggest that we're in a little different place now than before. I've noted over time [that] there are some sport organizations that [have] really taken some steps to do things in a different way. I think one of the things that has been learned is that diversity is invaluable. The bottom line is, if you have a more diverse workforce, you tend to have better retention." Foster says, "If you are invisible, how can anyone value you?"

Often it is in the team's best interest to adapt to the changing demographics of the community. A diverse community of sport fans live, work, and raise their families near sport teams. This affinity with a sport team can be better achieved if a team has a diversity of players who culturally, ethnically, or socially resemble the fan base. However, an organization that is not inclusive and does not provide opportunities for fans to feel valued can be left in a position that is not socially or financially sustainable.

Dr. Foster also says research indicates that sport organizations experience better productivity when teams have more diverse backgrounds. "It all stems from the commitment at the top. If the boss is all in . . . then those workers who want to succeed are going to want to be there as well. So you lead by example, and I think there's a lot of room for corporations, big companies here and elsewhere, to take up the mantle and start thinking about how we're going to look to our customers if they come in and they don't see diversity—or [don't see us] involved in programs that are going to make a difference."

SUMMARY

Engaging the call to action for increased diversity, equity, and inclusion within sport organizations goes beyond just that of talent attraction; it also affects a company's bottom line. The collective leadership across the sporting landscape must continue to urge sport organizations to strengthen their existing commitment to racial equity and access for marginalized populations. We cannot fix the scourges of discrimination, bigotry, and sexism if we deny their existence. We cannot welcome active and sustainable inclusive change without addressing structural racism. It is our responsibility to prepare our future sport practitioners, sport leaders, and sport organizers to work and live in a diverse society.

Today, diversity in sports organizations is readily recognized. Athletes of various ethnicities, cultures, genders, and sexual orientations often compete together on the same teams and come together to work on community initiatives. Although the degree of diversity in sports organizations today is much improved from decades past, moving toward a goal of equity and inclusion has additional barriers to overcome. As society has evolved, access and opportunity through sport has been a beacon of hope.

CRITICAL THINKING EXERCISES

1. Review a current or recent event involving a sport organization taking a stance against racial inequality, such as the Minnesota Timberwolves and the Minnesota Lynx standing firm for social justice reform.
2. Research the Tucker Center for Research on Girls & Women in Sport and #disruptHERS. Discuss what you find.
3. Explore the Words to Action section of the Institute for the Study of Sport, Society and Social Change (ISSSSC) website. How does the ISSSSC celebrate and empower athletes to use their platforms to advocate for social change?

REVIEW QUESTIONS

1. Why is promoting the values of diversity, equity, and inclusion so important to sport organizations?
2. What is social return on investment (SROI) in sport?
3. What is cultural capital, and why is it important?
4. What is social identity theory, and how does it support sport organization inclusion?
5. Does a polycultural perspective view culture as static?

Ronald Martinez/Getty Images

CHAPTER 2

Engaging in Difficult Dialogues About Diversity, Equity, and Inclusion in Sport

Ellen J. Staurowsky

LEARNING OBJECTIVES

- Explore the dynamics of power and privilege embedded in the hierarchical organizational structures that define the sport industry.
- Understand the nature of bias and its components (including stereotypes, prejudice, and discrimination) in sport.
- Reflect on the concepts of social identity and intersectionality.
- Explore the difference between equality and equity.
- Review guidelines for facilitating conversations about diversity, equity, and inclusion.
- Develop an understanding of the nature of allyship.

"The eyes of Texas are upon you." So go the words to the University of Texas' alma mater, set to the tune of "I've Been Working on the Railroad." When played by a 375-member marching band, capacity crowds of more than 100,000 at the Darrell K. Royal stadium have historically risen to their feet, waved along to the beat with the "hook 'em horns" hand sign, and repeated words adapted from an admonition from the former commander of the Confederate States of America army, General Robert E. Lee. After the Civil War ended, Lee took over as president at what was then Washington College (now Washington and Lee College), where he sought to remind his students that "the eyes of the South" were upon them (Young, 2020).

One of those students, William Prather, passed those sentiments along to his own students as president at the University of Texas (UT) in the early 1900s, adjusting the language to resonate and align more specifically with their state and school loyalties. Prather's students turned those words into a song that was popularized by White performers wearing blackface in varsity minstrel show performances on campus and at football games. Played at alumni gatherings, social functions running the gamut from christenings to funerals, and all manner of life events in between, the song has served as the ubiquitous soundtrack for one of Texas' leading institutions of higher learning. In its most modern iteration, the football team is expected to stand in front of alumni, students, and other Longhorns after games and join them in singing the alma mater (Levin, 2020; Young, 2020).

In the aftermath of the death of George Floyd at the hands of Minneapolis police in May of 2020, followed by a national response calling for an end to police brutality targeting non-White people and institutional racism, UT athletes from the sports of football, basketball, and track joined with other anti-racist activists calling for the athletic department and university to not only decry racism and other forms of injustice but to actively take steps to address problems on the University of Texas campus. Threatening to refuse participation in recruiting and fundraising efforts, the players demanded greater recognition of Black student contributions to the university, greater emphasis on educating the community about its racial history, and removal from buildings of the names of former university leaders who were known to hold racist beliefs or were avowed segregationists. Many of the players' demands were met, including initiatives to rename four campus buildings; permanently honor UT's first Black student, Heman M. Sweatt; install a statue representing the first Black football letterman at UT, Julius Whittier; rename the football field in honor of UT's Heisman Trophy winners, Earl Campbell and Ricky Williams; and allocate 0.05 percent of the athletic department's $200 million operating revenue to the Black Lives Matter (BLM) movement and Black organizations (Justin, 2020).

When it came to the players' demand that "The Eyes of Texas" no longer be used as the alma mater (a demand shared by other constituencies on the UT campus such as the marching band), they were met with resistance from alumni, donors, and administrators. Following a loss to Texas Christian University in October of 2020, the entire team, with the exception of quarterback Sam Ehlinger, left the field before the playing of the alma mater, provoking the creation of a petition calling for players to be required to participate. While head coach Tom Herman reportedly supported players on the team who wished to opt out of the ceremony, a position some believe may have led in part to his firing, athletic director Chris Del Conte overruled the coach, siding with donors and saying that the team should at least stand together while the song played (Young, 2020). In the face of denials from Conte about coercing players to remain on the field, players maintained their accounts after the season ended (McGee, 2021).

In the days and months following that event, efforts were made to clarify that Ehlinger was not the only player still on the field when the alma mater was sung although it remains unclear if any other players participated in the ritual (Levin & Maisel, 2021). And a committee charged to review the history of the song pursued their work even as University of Texas President Jay Hartzell made it clear that the Eyes of Texas would continue to be sung. The report itself, released in March of 2021, does not reach a conclusion but is put forward for community members to read and make their own determinations. The report noted that facts unearthed in its historical investigation:

> *add complexity and richness to the story of a song that debuted in a racist setting, exceedingly common for the time, but, as the preponderance of research showed, had no racist intent in that it was intended to parody the famous phrases of the university president. However, systemic racial intent existed in the setting and culture where the song debuted. The exclusion of Black students at that time presents an opportunity to think about how they and other communities of color have fought for inclusion and the work that remains to ensure all members of our community feel they belong. (Reddick, 2021, p. 2)*

This case illustrates how difficult the conversations that emanate out of long-standing racial beliefs can be and the subtle and overt ways that power is exerted over individuals with less status. It also serves as a window into the dynamics at play when issues of diversity and inclusion arise. We can wonder why administrators and members of the board of regents at the University of Texas are willing to take the names of racists off some of their academic buildings but resist taking action on a song that has a problematic racialized history. We can critically assess what it means for an athletic director to rationalize the continued use of such a song on the basis of the need to keep donors happy and contributing to the university, an athletic director who denies taking that position but is believed to have taken it by players, and a perception that the head coach was fired, in part, because he did not have control over his team when they declined to participate in a school tradition. And we can ponder what the impact is on a team made up of an estimated 62 percent non-White men who are expected to participate in a tradition that is racially offensive to them and their teammates.

In this chapter, we explore how institutions and the people who work for them perpetuate values and beliefs that can promote or undermine the creation of inclusive and equitable environments that embrace and celebrate diversity. We will also be examining key concepts that sport leaders need to be familiar with in order to engage in productive and meaningful conversations about diversity, equity, and inclusion, such as **privilege**, the three components of **bias** (**stereotypes**, **prejudice**, and **discrimination**), and the concepts of **social identity** and **intersectionality**. We will also be introduced to the differences between **equality** and **equity**; guidelines for fostering conversations about diversity, equity, and inclusion in sport; and the importance of **allyship**. This chapter is broad in scope to provide you with an overview of concepts and terms. In the upcoming chapters, you will learn more about each of the ideas broached here and have a chance to explore them further.

Sport Organizations, Power, and Privilege

A foundational concept when discussing diversity, equity, and inclusion in sport is privilege, defined as "the unrecognised advantage positioning certain people in a favoured state and systematically conferring power on groups of people in specific contexts" (Crevani, 2019). Culturally, in callouts on Twitter and in media commentary, we hear expressions such as "check your privilege." But what is it, really, and how does it work?

At a personal level, privilege emanates from social systems that confer advantages on members of certain **in-groups** based on an array of factors or characteristics that have historically been used to divide, separate, oppress, or marginalize people on the basis of age, class, economic background, ethnicity, gender, race, religion, and a host of other things. The system of privileging some at the expense of others has been likened to a 100-meter race where some runners with certain characteristics carry heavy weights while others have obstacles cleared out of their way without even being aware that there were obstacles to begin with. From a racial perspective, others have described White privilege as an invisible knapsack with special privileges that aid White people in navigating the world (McIntosh, 2003) and a luxury that allows White people to be ignorant of the ways in which their individual and collective experience differs from that of Black people (Wise, 2011). Sociologist Elizabeth Clifford (2020) describes privilege as "literally part of the air we breathe—just as invisible, and just as impossible to avoid the effects of" (p. 72).

Interestingly, Crevani (2019) refers to privilege as the undetected "upside" of discrimination and oppression, meaning that systems of inequality hide the advantages gained from discrimination, inequity, exploitation, mistreatment, and profiteering by making them appear to be earned fairly and without a negative cost to other people. Hidden advantages associated with privilege gained by those who benefit from discrimination and oppression are often rationalized through a myth of **meritocracy**, a pretense that everyone is treated the same and the people who work the hardest and are the most talented are rewarded accordingly because they rightly earned their position and place. This seemingly elusive and distant idea is one that is manifested in any number of ways in sport.

In writing about what he called the "Great Sports Myth," noted sport sociologist Jay Coakley (2015) observed that an unshakable and uncritical acceptance of sport as inherently good has resulted in the transfer of significant amounts of public money to the private sector. In critiquing sport megaevents such as the Olympic Games, Coakley (2015) noted that of the US$50 billion allocated to support the 2014 Winter Olympic Games in Sochi, Russia, US$20 billion went directly into the pockets of Russian oligarchs; at the same time, workers building venues for the event went unpaid and at least 25 died due to unsafe work conditions.

One of the reasons it is so uncomfortable to talk about privilege in sport is that it is on a collision course with meritocracy. Staff at the University of Michigan College of Literature, Science and Arts (2020) explained the problem of privilege this way:

> *Privilege, simply put, is societally granted, unearned advantages accorded to some people and not others. Generally, when we talk about privilege, we are referring to systemic or structural advantages that impact people based on identity factors such as race, gender, sex, religion, nationality, disability, sexuality, class, and body type. We might also include level of education and other factors of social capital under the umbrella of privilege. (para. 5)*

Consider the controversy that arose from a string of college admission fraud cases that came to be known as Varsity Blues. In total, 57 celebrities and prominent businesspeople were charged with federal crimes after bribing athletic department personnel (coaches and administrators) to designate their children as recruited prospects, thus increasing the likelihood of them being admitted (Kasakove, 2021). Former Georgetown University head tennis coach Gordie Ernst is alleged to have taken $2.2 million between 2012 and 2018 in fees from families, falsely designating them as "consulting fees" on his tax returns. In exchange for those fees, Coach Ernst listed 12 students as athletic recruits, including some who had never played tennis competitively (Das, Tracy, & Myers, 2019).

The Varsity Blues scandal showed a spotlight not just on how admission preferences for athletes could be manipulated but also how the college admission system, more broadly, is subject to influence by those with money and power. Parents seeking to influence admission decisions on behalf of their children without breaking the law may donate large sums to an institution without repercussion. As an example, embattled U.S. postmaster general and chief executive officer of the U.S. Postal Service Louis DeJoy, whose appointment to the position in June of 2020 was widely viewed as political favoritism, was found to have donated

$737,000 to Duke University in the months just prior to his son being accepted as a member of the men's tennis team as a walk-on in the fall of 2014. From the time his son started his career at Duke until it ended in 2018, DeJoy donated a total of $2.2 million to the institution and athletic department (Whistle, 2020).

Scholar Lucia Crevani (2019) points out that organizational practices perpetuate privilege for some at the expense of others within sport organizations. Big-time college football and its most elite conferences, referred to as the Power Five (Atlantic Coast Conference, Big Ten, Big Twelve, PAC-12, and Southeastern Conference), along with independents such as the University of Notre Dame, have long been criticized for demonstrating preference for their own programs over more worthy and deserving opponents when matchups for postseason bowl games are selected. Pointing to a Power Five bias that worked against a fair consideration of teams for the College Football Playoff (CFP) in the fall of 2020, longtime *Sports Illustrated* reporter Pat Forde alleged that the selection committee afforded the Florida Gators football team undue consideration after a loss to Louisiana State University late in the season. As Forde (2020) reported it, "If you thought the College Football Playoff selection committee gave outrageous preferential treatment to members of the Power 5 conferences last week at the expense of the outsiders, we have an update: They doubled down on the favoritism this week" (para. 2).

Writing about the lack of fairness in the selection of top college football teams for postseason bowls, sports journalist John Feinstein (2020) wrote that "The bowl system is so completely broken and corrupt that it needs to be blown up from top to bottom. Not tweaked. Not recalibrated. Blown up" (para. 6). He noted that in the seven years since the CFP system started, 5 of the top 65 schools eligible to be selected have dominated. Enumerating bids to play in the CFP, those schools included Alabama and Clemson (six each), Oklahoma and Ohio State (four each), and Notre Dame (two). When asked in 2020 to explain why the undefeated University of Cincinnati team (9-0) was ranked lower than teams that had multiple losses, namely the University of Oklahoma (8-2) and the University of Florida (8-3), the spokesperson for the CFP selection committee, Iowa athletic director Gary Barta, explained that Cincinnati's "résumé" was not as good. From a privilege perspective, it is instructive to note that Cincinnati was blocked from playing teams that would have enhanced their résumé if not for the ways that the scheduling rules were developed in 2020 (Feinstein, 2020).

Bias in Its Various Forms: Stereotypes, Prejudice, and Discrimination

In recent years, the sport industry has gone through a historic wave of firsts through the hiring of women into positions thought until recently to be reserved for men only. In September 2020, a National Football League (NFL) game featured women coaching on both sidelines, with the Cleveland Browns' chief of staff, Callie Brownson, and the Washington Football Team's full-year coaching intern Jennifer King taking the field. In that game, Sarah Thomas worked as a member of the officiating crew (McCarriston, 2020). In November 2020, the Miami Marlins announced the hiring of Kim Ng, the first woman and first East Asian American to be hired as a general manager of a Major League Baseball (MLB) franchise (Kepner & Wagner, 2020). Part of what makes these hirings historic is that we are witnessing in our time changes in a social institution shaped around a bias or an attitude that has privileged men by assuming that women were not capable of playing, coaching, or running the sports of football and baseball (figure 2.1).

Such bias rests on stereotypical thinking that influences perceptions about gender and gender identity and what roles people can play in particular sports. **Systemic discrimination** has operated to exclude half of the human race, namely women, from careers in football. From the youth level on, the sport has historically been coded as male, with calls for boys to sign up for Pop Warner football while girls signed up for cheerleading. Old ideas about female frailty have been used to preserve football's

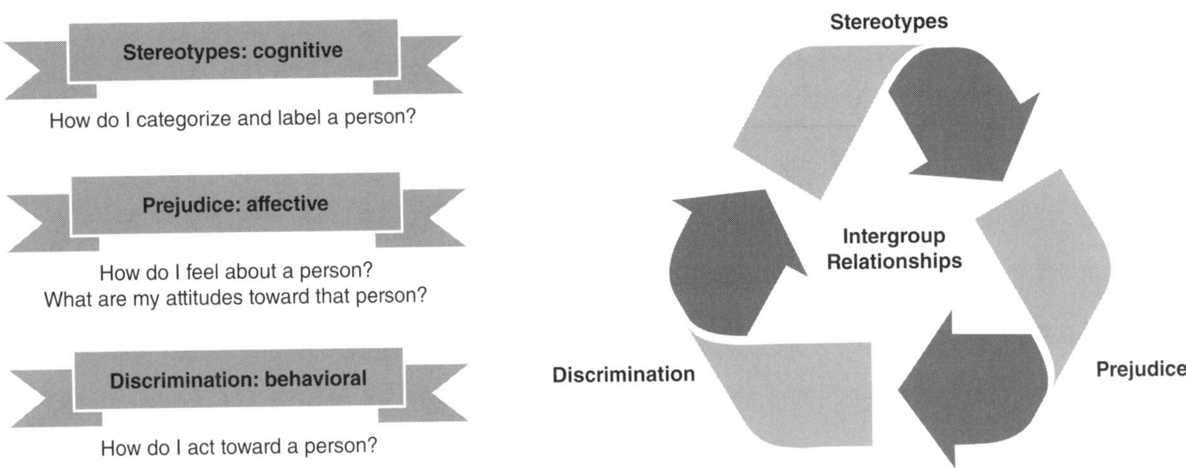

FIGURE 2.1 The three dimensions of bias.

status as a "contact sport" that receives an exemption from Title IX requirements for sex-integrated playing opportunities (Staurowsky, 2016). In effect, a seemingly benign argument that female athletes were protected from getting hurt by being prevented from playing the game appeared to be a reasonable course of action while grounding the logic in false assumptions designed to create a barrier to access (Staurowsky, 2016). Furthermore, football authority has been constructed in such a way that experts are considered to be those who played rather than those who have the requisite skill sets and acumen to run a business.

The end result has been a prejudice (a prejudgment) that women were disqualified from playing and working in the sport by virtue of the fact that they were female. Throughout the sport system, this connection between stereotype, prejudice, and discrimination has affected marginalized groups in countless ways that negatively affect access to opportunity and deprive the sport system of the talents of members from those excluded groups.

Social psychologists have conceptualized the relationship between stereotypes, prejudice, and discrimination as fitting with the principle of what is called the ABCs, or affect, behavior, and cognition (figure 2.2). The tendency to overgeneralize about a particular group on the basis of certain characteristics employs cognition (thinking) and is referred to as *stereotyping*. Prejudice takes that overgeneralization and pairs it with feeling or affect that distills into attitudes and is held in the absence of fact or in disregard of fact. Those attitudes have the potential to fuel behavior or actions targeting members of certain groups in discriminatory ways (Jhangiani & Tarry, 2014).

Stereotyping and Stereotype Threat

Research focusing on various sectors of the sport industry provides insight into how bias, whether **implicit** or **explicit** sometimes referred to as *unconscious* or *conscious bias*, affects marginalized groups in sport. Interviews with female sport management majors ($n = 17$) revealed barriers to their ability to be successful in a male-dominated environment, with male peers, faculty, and sport industry professionals subjecting them at times to sexism and sex discriminatory behavior (Sauder, Mudrick, & DeLuca, 2018). Numerous scholars have examined the gender stereotypes that have influenced hiring practices in sport and that

FIGURE 2.2 The ABCs of social psychology.

have supported ideas that men make better leaders in sport (Sabo, Veliz, & Staurowsky, 2016; Burton et al., 2009). Those stereotypes favoring men in hiring for sport positions have persisted despite evidence showing that women basketball players in the Women's National Basketball Association (WNBA) and NCAA Division I women's basketball perform well whether coached by men or women (Darvin, Pegoraro, & Berri, 2018).

In an examination of how women's sports were framed on the Instagram accounts for four major sports networks, specifically ESPN, Fox Sports, NBC Sports, and CBS Sports, between July of 2015 and July of 2016, sex stereotyping was prevalent. Of the 1,587 posts reviewed, 91 percent featured male athletes and men's sports issues. When women's sports and female athletes were included, they were represented in what have historically been more socially acceptable sports for women (tennis, golf) and in passive shots (Romney & Johnson, 2020). Even in settings where there is an appearance that stereotypical views of female athletes are disrupted, as in the circumstance where **male practice players** work out with top female college basketball players, male players still position themselves to maintain their privilege (Fink, Lavoi, & Newhall, 2016).

Gender is not the only factor that serves as a basis for stereotypes that affect perceptions of what sports people play, how sports are covered, what sports people invest in, and what kind of jobs they get in sport. Semi-structured interviews with five Paralympic swimmers, for example, demonstrated the tensions of a sport serving to provide a vehicle for self-realization, where the athletes described their experience in swimming as one allowing them to strive for goals, feel a part of a larger group, and feel more fully who they were meant to be while outsiders (parents, sport authorities, journalists) projected stereotypes onto them (Pack, Kelly, & Arvinen-Barrow, 2017). And in an examination of trends in coaching during a timeframe that captured 11 seasons between 2007-2008 and 2017-2018 across all NCAA sponsored sports (*n* = 2,450 teams; 625,119 coaches), gendered racial stereotypes were found to influence hiring. Black women coaches were more represented on men's teams when compared to Asian American women coaches and White women coaches were more likely to coach women's teams (Cunningham, Wicker, and Kutsko, 2020). Racial stereotypes were also found to influence perceptions in comparisons of Black and White quarterbacks. In a study with 274 White participants presented with background information about Black and White quarterbacks, participants did not apply stereotypes to the White players but drew upon long-standing stereotypes of Black athletes as being "naturally gifted" to explain why they were successful (Ferrucci & Tandoc, 2017).

While stereotyping refers to the perceptions that people have of others, **stereotype threat** "occurs when a person is worried about behaving in a way that confirms negative stereotypes about members of their group" (Hopper, 2019, para. 1). It is a form of negative self-talk or self-doubt that can adversely affect performance by creating an added layer of stress or pressure. College athletes are confronted with the stereotype of the dumb jock, with its attendant beliefs that they are underprepared for college-level intellectual work, are intellectually lazy, or are not as bright as other students. And college athletes live in environments where their nonathlete peers believe that athletes will not perform as well as other students and that professors have lower academic expectations for athletes (English & Kruger, 2020; Wininger & White, 2015). As Comeaux (2018 and others have noted, that general negative impression of athletes' academic abilities gets amplified when applied to African American athletes and combines with long-standing racial and gender stereotypes about African Americans being intellectually inferior.

For sport leaders, an understanding of stereotypes and how they become lenses through which human potential is amplified or muted is important. Seeing through and past stereotypes to the core of who someone is has the potential to open up opportunities and to identify where people can best contribute to the larger collective. Finally, the power of stereotypes to affect not only the way people are viewed by others but also how they see themselves is instructive for unlocking barriers to success.

Prejudice

Prejudice, the second dimension of bias, deals with attitudes, beliefs, and feelings people hold for members of their own group and for others. When leaders express support for certain forms of prejudice, there is a greater likelihood that followers will express those prejudices, as well. For example, in an experiment where subjects were exposed either to a statement made by Republican candidate Donald Trump during the 2016 U.S. presidential campaign that characterized Mexicans as drug traffickers, criminals, rapists, and generally "not good people" or to a statement from his Democratic opponent, Hillary Clinton, condemning those comments, exposure affected response (Schaffner, 2018). Later in the study respondents were asked to express their views of various groups of people. Those exposed to Trump's statement were more likely to write derogatory things not only about Mexicans but other racial and ethnic groups. In contrast, those exposed to Clinton's condemnation of Trump's language were less likely to express negative views (Schaffner, 2018). Similarly, in a study of explicitly racist and inflammatory language about citizens by political elites in the United States, those who hold prejudiced attitudes and beliefs are emboldened to give expression to them and to act on them (Newman, Merolla, Shah, Lemi, Collingwood, & Ramakrishnan, 2020).

During the COVID-19 pandemic of 2020, as anti-Asian sentiment increased and hate crimes targeting Asian Americans rose, due in part to the characterization of the virus as the "China virus" by President Trump and other leaders (Chen, Trinh, & Yang, 2020), Jeremy Lin, the first Taiwanese American basketball player to win an NBA championship (with the Toronto Raptors), wrote about this dynamic.

No stranger to living in a culture where his "otherness" as an Asian American male basketball player was the focal point for opposing fans, players, and in one instance, a coach, Lin was all too familiar with hearing disparaging comments about Asian people, comments that referees ignored or failed to address (Youngmisuk, 2017). In the sport of men's basketball in the United States, the inclination for some opposing fans to refer to Lin as Yao Ming, the 7'6" Chinese player who played for the Houston Rockets for seven seasons, epitomizes how Asian Americans born in the United States are often stereotyped as perpetual foreigners (Chen, Trinh, & Yang, 2020). In the midst of the pandemic, the rising tide of animosity directed toward Asian people prompted Lin (2020) to draw the connection between words and action:

> *As the tension and anxiety in the U.S. has gone through the roof, we're seeing that there's a real darkness beneath the words. It's not just trash talking or trolling or hateful speech. Asian Americans are being spit on, yelled at, and physically attacked in their own country.*

Discrimination

The third dimension of bias is discrimination, the enactment of prejudicial attitudes and stereotypical ways of thinking through decisions and policies that typically affect access to opportunity and fair treatment. Federal, state, and local laws, and the regulations designed to implement them, serve to shape antidiscrimination efforts in the sport industry. Title IX of the Education Amendments of 1972, the law that discourages sex discrimination in schools that receive federal funding, has been credited with creating the impetus for the substantial growth of women's sport in the United States over the past five decades.

In NCAA member institutions, for example, "women's sport participation opportunities increased by more than 1565 percent, from 29,977 in 1971-1972 to 499,217 in 2018-2019" (Staurowsky & Rhoads, 2020, p. 383). Despite increases in athletic opportunities for female athletes over time, there is widespread agreement among Title IX experts that there remain significant gaps in resources distributed to support women's sports and that female athletes and their coaches are not treated equitably in the system (Staurowsky & Rhoads, 2020). In 2017-2018, male athletes in NCAA Division I and II received $240,435,504 more in athletic scholarship assistance than female athletes (Staurowsky et al., 2020).

Just as the rights of female athletes are protected by law to ensure that they have an equal opportunity to participate in sport and to be treated fairly while playing, so too do athletes with disabilities. Officials from the U.S. Government Accountability Office conducted a review of the nation's elementary and secondary schools and found that athletes with disabilities did not have an equal opportunity to pursue their sports, signaling that school administrators were failing to comply with requirements under Section 504 of the Rehabilitation Act of 1973 and the Americans with Disabilities Act. In recent years, and in the aftermath of that report, momentum has been building to nationalize championships for athletes with disabilities at the college level under the umbrella of the NCAA (Comerford, 2018).

Beyond the playing field, antidiscrimination laws also cover a range of issues affecting people working in sport. Sports fans the world over were reminded of this during the 2019 Women's World Cup as awareness grew that while the U.S. Women's National Team was competing for its fourth championship win, they were also battling for equal pay and equal treatment (Staurowsky et al., 2020). In another sport, more than 60 former and current University of Iowa football players testified to having experienced or witnessed bullying, disparate treatment, racial discrimination, and threats they were subjected to by the coaching staff, all violations of Title VI of the Civil Rights Act of 1964 (Wadley et al., 2020).

These laws provide an avenue for people who have been deprived of their rights to hold individuals and institutions accountable when discrimination occurs. They also provide a framework to help sport leaders and institutions educate their constituencies about what is expected under antidiscrimination laws, to monitor and assess the kind of environment that people are subjected to in athletic departments and sport organizations, and to develop plans to ensure that they are being vigilant in abiding by the prohibitions on discriminating against people on the basis of sex, ability, race, or other protected categories.

Social Identity and Intersectionality

You may be familiar with the phrase "the whole is more than the sum of its parts." When we think about the roles that people play, we begin to appreciate what this phrase is getting at. Students are more than the grades they earn on exams; athletes are more than their performances; and employees are more than their job titles. As human beings, we have much to offer the world that goes beyond the boundaries of our capacity to check off tasks on a list or to be described and defined by a list of demographic characteristics.

So too is our identity shaped by the mix of social statuses and personal attributes that are a part of who we are and how those in the world view us as a result (figure 2.3). Our experience in the world is further influenced by where we are situated within organizations and political structures that marginalize certain groups on the basis of ability, age, class, education, ethnicity, family, gender identity, gender, nationality, political affiliation, race, religion, or sexuality (Barak, Krane, Ross, Mann, & Kaunert, 2018; Harrison & Coakley, 2020; LaVoi, McGarry, & Fisher, 2019; McDowell & Carter-Francique, 2017; Zenquis & Mwaniki, 2019).

Illustrative of this are criticisms made by White Fox News host Laura Ingraham about African American NBA players LeBron James and Kevin Durant for discussing politics and then–President Donald Trump in the course of a wide-ranging interview with ESPN

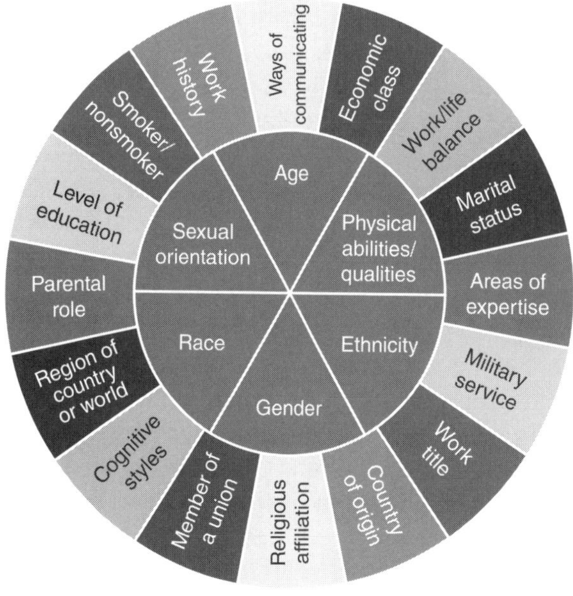

FIGURE 2.3 Intersectionality: the way we see ourselves and how others see us.

SportsCenter anchor Cari Champion (Sullivan, 2018). Ingraham (2018) framed her commentary about James and Durant as a "dumb jock alert," describing their views about President Trump's offensive racist comments as "barely intelligible not to mention ungrammatical."

She attempted to support her remarks with the inaccurate characterization of James as a high school dropout who pursued his professional career at the expense of his high school education. In her reporting, Ingraham ignored the fact that James had an estimated net worth of over $450 million at the time; was founder of a production company (Springhill Productions) and a media company (The Uninterrupted); had just opened his first I PROMISE School to serve the educational needs of underserved children in Akron, Ohio, with a pledge to invest an additional $41 million from his foundation; and had competed for the United States in three Olympic Games (winning two gold medals and a bronze). Instead, she concluded, "It's always unwise to seek political advice from someone who gets paid $100 million a year to bounce a ball. Must you run your mouth like that. Keep the political comments to yourselves. . . . Shut up and dribble" (Ingraham, 2018).

In theoretical terms, the dynamic at play in Ingraham's racist characterization of James—as an overpaid Black male athlete who should perform for majority White audiences but remain silent—is explained through a concept known as *intersectionality*. Legal scholar Kimberlé Crenshaw developed the term in the 1980s, seeking to encourage a better understanding of the limits of what is called "single issue" civil rights litigation. Her focus was on Black women who did not fit into a single issue civil rights framework, meaning Black women may experience not just race discrimination but sex discrimination as well. Out of that effort the term "intersectionality" came to describe "how race, class, gender, and other individual characteristics 'intersect' with one another and overlap" (Coaston, 2019).

In the case of Ingraham's "shut up and dribble" comment, we see intersectionality at work. James is not the target just because he is Black but because of his family roots, his educational background, his choice of occupation, and his political affiliation. Ingraham, in turn, operates from a position of Whiteness, out of an Ivy League educational background (she went to Dartmouth undergrad and law school at the University of Virginia), from a politically and religiously conservative point of view, and within the context of a major media outlet (Fox News).

According to Moore (2017), "Intersectionality is important to consider as a part of understanding issues of diversity and inclusion. . . . It provides a vital insight into where and how exclusion can be challenged, as well as identifying real opportunities for meaningful access to sport."

Achieving Fairness Within Difference: Equality Versus Equity

Achieving fairness while being conscious of difference requires a consideration of the frameworks of equality versus equity. In a nutshell, treating people equally means treating everyone the same. Treating people equitably means treating people fairly with an eye toward the outcome as well as the opportunity. In 2015, the City for All Women Initiative in Ottawa, Canada, used an example of what happens when three fans of different heights try to watch a baseball game and confront a solid fence that prevents them from seeing the game to illustrate the difference between equal versus equitable treatment (City for All Women Initiative, 2015).

In an equal treatment scenario, each of the fans is given the same size box to stand on. While each is treated fairly, because they are given help to overcome the barrier, the two taller fans benefit from standing on the box, but the shorter fan is still not able to see the game. In a scenario where the factor of difference in height is taken into account, the height of the box is adjusted to allow each of the fans to look over the fence to see the game. This adjustment creates equal access for each fan to watch the game. In a third scenario, where the fence is changed from a solid material to metal mesh material, there is no need for the fans to look over the fence because they can stand naturally and watch through the fence (see figure 1.1).

The takeaway is that the more directly the barrier to access is addressed, the more fans can enjoy the game and not have to adjust their behavior in order to watch it. This presents a fourth scenario to be considered. If you remove the barrier completely, that opens up even more opportunities for those fans to enjoy the game because they are not having to look through a fence.

There are also other assumptions to take into account. For example, the preceding scenario assumes that the fans can stand and watch the game. But how would a barrier be addressed if one of the fans was in a wheelchair or was not able to watch the game but could only listen to it? How would equity be achieved?

One of the ways we see this distinction between equity and equality playing out in the sport industry is in student access to internships. In a study released by the National Association of College Employers in 2019, racial disparities were found among students who completed paid versus unpaid internships. According to the report, White students were overrepresented in paid internships, multiracial students were overrepresented in unpaid internships, and Hispanic American students were overrepresented in terms of never having had an internship (Wood, 2020). In a study published by the University of Massachusetts' chief diversity officer and associate professor Nefertiti Walker and her colleagues (2020), interviews with 17 sport management majors revealed that there was a need for sport industry leaders to become more aware of "how unpaid internships disadvantage students from less privileged backgrounds and may, therefore, result in a less socioeconomically diverse workforce in the sport industry" (p. 1).

Even though all students appear to have an equal chance to apply, in reality many are prevented from applying due to inequity-caused economic circumstances. In effect, for students who can't afford to stop working for a paycheck in order to meet their financial obligations, what appears to be an opportunity is out of reach.

Guidelines for Facilitating Conversations About Diversity, Equity, and Inclusion

As a general observation, conversation about issues in sport abounds. Airwaves and the digital world are filled with passionate and lively discussion about fairness and equity in sport. Whole departments within sports marketing firms, franchises, leagues, athletic departments, gambling enterprises, and broadcast entities are devoted to engaging people in conversation about whether referees, umpires, and officials made the right call on any given play; whether ownership and management made the right decision about a player trade; whether one player versus another deserves to be considered a GOAT (greatest of all time); whether coaches and athletes violated rules to get a competitive advantage; or whether the health and well-being of athletes are being provided for and protected. From the proverbial water cooler to the chat box of a Zoom meeting, sports talk emanates out of a fundamental investment that justice should be served.

However, reflective of the larger society, talk about sport matters is shaped as much by the subjects that are avoided, ignored, or overlooked as it is by what is discussed. Sometimes there is a reluctance to discuss or even recognize key issues that emanate out of inequity because they are too difficult to talk about or the atmosphere is just too unsafe. We've all had those moments at one point or another in our lives when we wanted to ask a question or express a viewpoint that we thought would not be received well. We remained silent out of fear of retribution, awkwardness and uncomfortableness, anxiety at the prospect of appearing ignorant or stupid, threat of being labeled a troublemaker or not a team player, pressure to "say the right thing," or a desire not to offend. All of these things can discourage engaging around issues that need to be discussed in order to foster understanding and appreciation for people's differences.

A starting point in facilitating conversations is to acknowledge that there is economic value in promoting diversity and inclusion.
10'000 Hours/DigitalVision/Getty Images

So, how do we proceed? As sport leaders, how do we approach conversations about ageism, gender and racial inequality, religious bigotry, political power, athlete exploitation, intolerance, and a host of other issues? A starting point is to acknowledge that there is economic value in promoting diversity and inclusion, legal reasons to ensure that those working in and competing in sport are not discriminated against, and moral imperatives to treat athletes, colleagues, and peers with respect and dignity.

Experts who work in the area of diversity and inclusion report that open, sincere, and productive conversations do not happen by accident or magic. Rather, consideration needs to be given to establishing ground rules, cultivating empathy, and helping people understand why these conversations are important to their work as leaders and citizens. According to the CoachDiversity Institute (2020), there are 10 strategies or practices that can help facilitate difficult conversations:

1. Set the stage. When having conversations about bias and discrimination in the workplace, in a classroom, or on a team, make those who will be participating aware of what the topic is in advance. Give thought to how the discussion is going to be framed and explain to those participating what the purpose of the discussion is.

2. Establish discussion guidelines. These should be developed by the facilitator or put together in conjunction with the group to promote an environment that is safe and respectful. The Anti-Defamation League (ADL, 2020) recommends that discussion guidelines include a consideration of "listening and interrupting, how to deal with strong emotions, establishing trust, confidentiality, sharing 'air time' and dealing with differences or disagreements." Another key consideration is "making room for mistakes" and acknowledging in an explicit way that "because we are products of a biased society, students may not be cognizant that everyone has biases and holds stereotypes" (ADL, 2020).

3. Shape discussions around questions that participants can brainstorm and problem-solve. If appropriate, such questions could include an examination of an existing program and its effectiveness. (For example: Do we have a plan to ensure fair and equitable hiring? How effective is that plan?)

4. Set the expectation that there will be different viewpoints, and encourage humility.

There are numerous approaches to fostering open dialogue, one of them being establishing an understanding of the differences between a debate (where each side is arguing to be right, setting up a point/counterpoint) and a dialogue (where the emphasis is on listening, being collaborative, and being supportive) (Hastwell, 2020).

5. Listen more than you speak. Take a pause before responding; ask questions to clarify what was said. Defer judgment and speculation about motive.

6. Encourage curiosity and questions. Create a space where genuine understanding can occur when questions are asked and answered in a nonthreatening environment.

7. Check your privilege. Ask participants to consider how their advantages in life affect their perspective, experience, and worldview on issues.

8. Be mindful that the climate of the discussion is one where people are safe to express themselves, with an understanding that they will not be shamed or humiliated. Genuine dialogue can reveal naïveté, ignorance, strong emotions, and frustrations. Figuring out how to keep an open dialogue can be both challenging and rewarding.

9. Anticipate that roadblocks to progress will happen. Conversations about difference occur over time, and it is likely that there will be setbacks, resistance, or hesitancy to tackle certain subjects.

10. Recenter and refocus the conversation back to the purpose. It can take a conscious effort to work together toward equity and inclusion and the benefits of being aligned with those values (CoachDiversity Institute, 2020).

Skills learned from participating on teams are transferable to conversations about diversity and inclusion. The following are skills that are reinforced in athletic settings and can be drawn upon and relied on in conversations designed to foster diversity, equity, and inclusion in sport settings.

1. Stay focused when others are speaking.
2. Pay attention to body language.
3. Be aware of the goal.
4. Be invested in the success of the group and in bringing out the best in everyone.
5. Be supportive of others.

Becoming an Ally and the Nature of Allyship

Writing about the importance of athletics administrators becoming allies for college athletes who are marginalized, Jen Fry (2018) wrote that athletics administrators needed to "pay attention to the bigger pictures and the smaller details" (para. 5). The role of an **ally** requires a critical examination of the environment in which the ally plays, lives, and works, with sensitivity to what others around them (and sometimes who they are responsible for) are experiencing. As Fry (2018) explained, when athletics administrators take the time to provide and protect the interests of athletes with marginalized identities, they create a culture and climate that benefits all athletes. Stated another way, "Allyship represents a conscious strategy or set of actions that individuals in a dominant group can take to create social change" (Heffernan, 2018, p. 16).

Interviews with both female and male sport leaders ($n = 17$; 65 percent of whom were male) who worked in a variety of sport organizations, from professional franchises to nonprofit college athletic departments to media entities who engaged in gender allyship, revealed several things. First, their allyship started with an awareness that women are underrepresented in many sectors of the industry and that consciousness regarding the male-dominated environment they walk into warrants thoughtful management to ensure optimal conditions for women to be successful. Second, gender allyship is demonstrated in hiring processes, and when more women are hired, there is a shift within the organization that eventually distills into everyday interactions (Heffernan, 2018).

As individuals with multiple identities, "checking in" on the source of our own privilege provides a pathway to understanding how to exercise influence as an ally. For example, during the summer of 2020, LGBTQ+ athletes

Sport Industry Diversity Initiative

HASHTAG SPORTS AND INTEL SPORTS' INDUSTRY-WIDE DIVERSITY AND INCLUSION INITIATIVE

In June 2020, Hashtag Sports and Intel Sports announced an initiative designed to challenge the sport industry to hire more women and members of underrepresented groups in senior leadership positions. While the gender gap has been decreasing in the area of athletic participation, those in positions of setting strategy and envisioning the future of sport do not represent the diversity of fan bases, viewing audiences, and consumers. Recognizing that goals around diversity and inclusion require a consistent and ongoing commitment across every sector of the industry, the rationale for this initiative notes that 21st century sports fans include women and people with many cultural backgrounds, so it is important that creators and marketers reflect those demographics (Black, 2020a).

The initiative is overseen by the Committee on Diversity and Inclusion under the Engagement Academy of Sports × Entertainment, "a society of sports media, marketing, and entertainment professionals whose mission is to inspire creative talent of all ages while championing diversity, inclusion, and new ideas that galvanize the sports and entertainment industries" (Black, 2020a, para. 8). Established sport marketing executive Sandra Lopez (vice president and general manager, Intel Sports) leads the initiative and is joined by colleagues from AT&T, Bleacher Report, Instagram, NASCAR, NFL, Nike, the Familie V2, Turner Sports, Twitter, and Yahoo Sports (Apollo Global Management).

According to chief executive officer and founder of Hashtag Sport Anthony Caponiti, "The Engagement Academy's working committee will advocate for the industry to proactively build organizations that represent all genders, backgrounds, and voices and to do so with purpose and accountability. It's challenging yet simple—executive leadership, content creators, and marketers should look and think like their fans" (Black, 2020a, para. 12).

One of the first efforts undertaken by Hashtag Sports as part of the initiative was the launch of the Creators of Color program, a program designed to amplify the impact of work done at the intersection of sport, entertainment, and content by creatives who identify as Black, Indigenous, and people of color. A cohort of 30 young professionals working across eight creative specialties (video production; social media; podcasting; marketing and revenue; storytelling and editorial; on-camera talent; design and art; and photography) will be selected annually (Black, 2020b). Hashtag Sports hosted an inaugural summit for its initial class of Creators of Color in November 2021, focusing on providing support for underrepresented and marginalized voices in the industry space that intersects with sport, content creation, and entertainment while also fostering talent pipelines for sport entities seeking to hire people of color.

were prominent in lending their support to calls for a national reckoning on race in the United States. In explaining his activism on human rights issues, Adam Rippon, the first openly gay American athlete to win a medal at an Olympic Games, commented that he was well aware that his experience as an LGBTQ+ man was not comparable to being Black, but the sense that he had of being on the outside and not belonging informed his approach to speaking up about injustice. Similarly, when WNBA players participated in activism calling for racial justice, Israeli American WNBA player Sue Bird said, "As a White athlete, of course I'm gonna stand by my teammates, and wear these T-shirts in support. And a lot of people refer to that as being an ally. But now I think, as a White athlete, it has to go further than that. It can't just be that you show up, wear the T-shirt, and say you support. . . . What are you gonna do after that?" (Bushnell, 2020, para. 25).

There are factors that influence athletes taking up the banner of allyship on different issues. In a study of 159 college athletes, Toomey and

"Checking in" on the source of our own privilege provides a pathway to understanding how to exercise influence as an ally.
Abbie Parr/Getty Images

McGeorge (2018) found that there were three distinct profiles: More than half did not consider themselves to be LGBTQ+ allies, approximately a third considered themselves engaged on LGBTQ+ issues but not visible; and 7.5 percent were highly engaged and visible on LGBTQ+ issues. Coaches were found to influence athlete engagement as LGBTQ+ allies. Athletes who perceived their coaches as being supportive of LGBTQ+ people were more likely to be highly engaged and visible while athletes who perceived their coaches as less supportive were more likely not to consider themselves LGBTQ+ allies. Furthermore, athletes with a commitment to social justice were more likely to be highly engaged compared to those who were engaged but not visible (Toomey & McGeorge, 2018).

Allies and allyship should not be confused with an athlete or sport official speaking up on issues of equity and fairness on certain issues or taking a stance on a particular issue. In a study of allyship in elite women's sports, researcher Sarah Teetzel (2020) examined the complications associated with allyship when four highly successful retired female athletes (Martina Navratilova, tennis; Sharron Davies, swimming; Kelly Holmes, athletics; and Paula Radcliffe, marathon) publicly expressed opposition to trans female athletes competing on women's teams in 2019. Teetzel (2020) argued that there is a danger in requiring athletes to be allies, pointing out that "being mandated to act as an ally, without full commitment, does more harm than good" (p. 432). She further concluded that athletes should be supported in expressing their views but it is essential that those in leadership positions within sport organizations be responsible for educating their athletes about "the science and ethics of trans athlete inclusion" (Teetzel, 2020, p. 432).

Sport Industry Leader Profile

David Gould, MPA

Title: Chief Diversity and Impact Officer, Harris Blitzer Sports and Entertainment

In September 2020, Harris Blitzer Sports and Entertainment (HBSE) hired David Gould to serve in a newly created position to oversee the implementation of a $20 million racial equity plan. In the role of chief diversity and impact officer, Gould provides the vision and leadership for HBSE's internal and external diversity standards, programs, and initiatives across the wide portfolio of programs under the organization's umbrella, including two professional sport franchises (New Jersey Devils, Philadelphia 76ers), the Prudential Center, HBSE Real Estate, HBSE Ventures, and multiple esport properties. Collaborating with HBSE's human resources office and its diversity and inclusion advisory board, Gould works with the company's executive leadership to implement a comprehensive company-wide strategy that affects workplace culture (employee development programs); integrates with public-facing aspects of the business (marketing and community relations for building key partnerships and relationships); adopts best practices to encourage the growth of minority-owned businesses; and ensures that HBSE properties are contributing positively to the communities in which they operate (NBA, 2020). In establishing priorities, Gould focuses on "buying more from diverse businesses, promoting and marketing underrepresented entrepreneurs, recruiting and growing diverse talent within our company, and investing in communities of color."

Prior to his appointment as HBSE's chief diversity and impact officer, Gould served as the executive director of the Sixers Youth Foundation, where he worked with Philadelphia city authorities to refurbish basketball courts, provide safe basketball camps for the city's youth, and organize the distribution of lunches to thousands of children in underserved communities around the city.

SUMMARY

The purpose of this chapter was to introduce selected basic foundational concepts that will aid in understanding material covered in the remainder of the book. In the upcoming chapters, you will be able to explore more deeply some of the ideas presented here and expand on your thinking about how you would apply this material to discussions about ongoing issues in the sport industry that deal with diversity, equity, and inclusion.

As we wrap up this chapter, let's revisit where we started with fresh eyes, thinking about the University of Texas football team and the question of whether the alma mater, "The Eyes of Texas," should be replaced. Examining the tradition of playing that song in light of the two forms of discrimination discussed in the chapter, we encounter an interesting thought exercise. We can ask if subjecting players and other students to a song with a problematic racial history presents a barrier to their full access to their education. We can also ask if the policy requiring players to stand with the team while the song is playing results in a form of discriminatory treatment because players may feel that they will lose their scholarships and place on the team if they do not comply. We can reflect on whether the insistence that the song continue to be played is a form of White privilege designed to maintain a power base that marginalizes members of racial minority groups.

Before joining HBSE, Gould established himself as a key figure in undertaking significant work as the deputy director for community engagement and communications for Philadelphia Mayor Jim Kenney's Rebuild initiative. That initiative was designed to revitalize community spaces and promote local business growth in the city's low-income neighborhoods through an investment of more than $400 million. As a member of the leadership team, Gould contributed to efforts to revitalize community parks, recreation centers, and libraries, as well as create jobs for women and people of color. His work with the mayor's office was aided by work he had done at the William Penn Foundation, where he focused on community development and impact investing.

A Philadelphia native who grew up in the Germantown section of the city, Gould received a bachelor's degree in economics and political science at the University of Rochester while playing on the men's basketball team. He also holds a master's degree in public administration from the university. He has taught graduate-level courses at Penn's Weitzman School of Design.

In explaining what motivates him to do the work he does around diversity and inclusion in sport, Gould said, "I believe that sports—especially the business of sports—has an incredible opportunity to promote more awareness and equity within our society. Not only is sports an industry that generates a significant amount of economic activity—which has the potential to provide economic opportunity to underrepresented people and businesses—but it is also an industry that includes powerful brands and highly visible platforms . . . that can be leveraged to promote empathy, education, and awareness around issues of systemic inequity." In discussing what makes Harris Blitzer's focus on diversity and inclusion unique within the industry, Gould notes, "Our focus is unique because we tailored it specifically to what we do well. We [have] two tremendous brands in the 76ers and Devils and operate an arena. We are focused on how we leverage that platform and business to do good—whether it be speaking out on important issues, amplifying the experiences of underrepresented communities, or [promoting] diverse businesses. There are so many different ways we can have an impact and, over time, we hope to continue to find more ways to leverage every part of our business for good."

We can also consider how to best move forward with an agenda for change, engaging constituencies in conversations designed to educate and empower while creating alliances with individuals who will use their platforms and positions to aid in the effort.

CRITICAL THINKING EXERCISES

1. The criteria used by sport organizations to honor athletes and administrators and the way in which the accomplishments of athletes are memorialized in sport organizations should reflect the diversity, equity, and inclusion goals of the organization. Conduct an audit of a sport organization's hall of fame, including the criteria for selection, the membership composition of the selection committee, and the representativeness of those who have achieved hall of fame status.
2. Who do you consider to be an ally in sport? In your response, include the definition of *ally* and give enough background to support your view that the person chosen is an ally.
3. Thinking about your own experience in sport, as an athlete, coach, fan, administrator, or journalist, identify at least three stereotypes that you have encountered. Explain the context and the impact of each on individuals or on the larger sport system.

REVIEW QUESTIONS

1. Why did University of Texas athletes, students, and faculty object to the song "The Eyes of Texas"?
2. Sport sociologist Jay Coakley has written about something called the Great Sport Myth. What is the Great Sport Myth and what does it reveal about sport?
3. The concept of a meritocracy is that people are rewarded for doing what they are supposed to do and for working hard. Rewards within a meritocracy are distributed on the basis of merit. In effect, if there are five slots on a team, and you are one of the five best players to try out for the team, you should make the team. What does the Varsity Blues scandal show about meritocracies?
4. Who is David Gould, and what is his job?
5. What discussion guidelines would you develop for a class or a group you are working with to promote an environment that is safe and respectful? (List at least 5 to 10.)

PATRICK T. FALLON/AFP via Getty Images

CHAPTER 3

Social Class and Economic Status

NaRi Shin

LEARNING OBJECTIVES

- Understand the concept of social mobility and its subconcepts.
- Identify the conditions under which sport participation is most and least likely to lead to upward mobility and occupational success.
- Explain how social class and stratification intersect and influence participation in sport.
- Explore the implications of social class in youth and children's sport participation and how sport participation varies by race and ethnicity.
- Understand the concept of social capital and its three types: bonding, bridging, and linking.
- Identify how social capital can be developed through sport-based intervention programs.
- Discuss opportunities and challenges international athletes have in the U.S. sport field.

Many people in the United States consider sport a field where people from low-income or poor backgrounds can achieve upward social mobility (Green & Hartmann, 2012). The role of sport as a vehicle for social advancement has been evidenced by athletes who had the opportunity and fortune to play at the highest levels of sport leagues, such as Major League Baseball (MLB) and the National Basketball Association (NBA). Eisen and Turner (1992) argued that sports, as a social institution, are some of the most powerful agencies in changing lives, especially of young people. This is not only the case in the United States but all over the world. Serge Ibaka from the Republic of Congo, Albert Pujols from the Dominican Republic, and Manny Pacquiao from the Philippines are three athletes who grew up impoverished but made their way to sporting success and built a better future.

Serge Ibaka was born in the Republic of Congo as one of 18 children. Although he was introduced to basketball at a young age thanks to both of his parents' basketball careers, his family struggled due to the country's political situation. His mother suddenly died and his father was incarcerated during the Second Congo War, and Ibaka played basketball to cope with the hardship. Later, he and his family fled the country to France, where Ibaka joined a second-division basketball team. Then he moved to Spain and played with a second-division club, where he showed outstanding performance. In 2008, he participated in several international recruiting events, one of which was the Reebok Eurocamp, where he was selected as the Most Valuable Player. He caught the attention of NBA scouts. In the 2008 NBA draft, the Seattle SuperSonics (now the Oklahoma City Thunder) selected Ibaka as the 24th pick. He signed a two-year contract at $19 million with the Los Angeles Clippers in 2020, making him the sixth-highest-paid player on the team in 2021.

Albert Pujols plays baseball for the Los Angeles Angels. Pujols was born and raised in Santo Domingo, Dominican Republic. His father was a former softball pitcher. In pursuit of the American Dream, he and his grandmother and father immigrated to New York in 1996, when Pujols was 16. Pujols remembers his early immigrant life as difficult—he barely spoke English when he arrived. His family moved to Independence, Missouri, to stay with relatives a few months after they arrived in New York. It was there that Pujols started playing baseball in high school. His athletic performance earned him a baseball scholarship to Maple Woods Community College, where he played for one season. After a successful first year on the team, he decided to enter the MLB draft and signed with the St. Louis Cardinals. His current contract with the Los Angeles Angels is for 10 years and $240 million.

Manny Pacquiao is a Filipino boxer turned politician currently serving as a senator of the Philippines. Pacquiao was born and raised in the Philippines as the fourth of six siblings. He was introduced to boxing at the age of 12. His parents separated when he was 13, and he was raised by his single mother. Due to extreme poverty, he was not able to finish high school. With talent and training, he became the best junior boxer in the southern Philippines by the age of 15. Then he moved to Manila, the capital city, to make his professional boxing debut. Pacquiao became the first boxer to win the lineal championship in five different weight classes and has won 12 major world titles. He was eighth on Forbes' list of richest athletes of the decade, earning $435 million between 2010 and 2019 (CNN Philippines, 2019).

These three athletes share the commonality that their sporting success helped them escape impoverished backgrounds. Ibaka used an athletic career to escape civil unrest and immigrate to the United States. Pujols, as an immigrant from Central America, successfully achieved the American Dream through his baseball career. Following international success as a professional boxer, Pacquiao became a high-ranking politician back in his home country. Such stories lead many young people in poverty to think of sports as a promising tool that presents "the prospect of escape into a better world, at least a lift out of the direct poverty" (Walvin, 1995, p. 122).

As evidenced by the three stories, sports have long been viewed as a great equalizer in providing pathways to upward mobility and success. **Social mobility** refers to "the movement of individuals or groups between different positions within the system of social stratification" (Spaaij, 2011, p. 19). More specifically, it can be explained as "changes in an individual's social position which involve significant alterations" (Spaaij, 2011, p. 19) in their social environment and living conditions.

According to Sorokin (1959), there are two principal types of social mobility: horizontal and vertical. **Horizontal social mobility** is the transition of an individual from one social group to another on the same socioeconomic level, while **vertical social mobility** indicates a significant improvement in or degradation of the social position. Vertical social mobility can be upward or downward. Upward social mobility is demonstrated when individuals rise from a lower social position to a higher one.

Sorokin (1959) highlighted two distinctive types of social mobility: intergenerational and intragenerational. **Intergenerational mobility** indicates the difference between individuals' social positions at particular points in their lives and those of their parents, where **intragenerational mobility** refers to the more short-term mobility within a single generation. In this chapter, we focus on both, because a strong relationship has been identified between the social positions of parents and the positions their children occupy (Giddens & Diamond, 2005).

Sport and Social Mobility: The Research

The idea that participation in organized social activities, such as sport and physical activities, prevents deviance and promotes upward social mobility through enhanced social and cultural capital is central in many societies (Vilhjalmsson & Thorlindsson, 1992). Sport scholars have studied the relationship and interaction between sport and social mobility, with a particular focus on vertical upward mobility within a single generation. So far, two sociological models have dominated the research on the effect of sport participation on social mobility (Mackin & Walther, 2011): the **zero-sum model** and the **developmental model**. The zero-sum model argues that when individuals spend time on sport, it takes away the time they spend on academics, hindering performance in school and ultimately their social mobility (Coleman, 1961; Howell et al., 1984). On the other hand, the developmental model argues that participation in sport contributes to the improved performance of athletes in school and on the field. Scholars who support the developmental model have suggested that sport participation has a positive effect on the acquisition of human, social, and cultural capital (Broh, 2002; Rees & Sabia, 2010; Spaaij, 2009).

Sack and Thiel's (1979) early study examined the social origins and career mobility of college football players who graduated from the University of Notre Dame between 1946 and 1965. They started from the widespread belief that college football is an effective avenue for upward social mobility. Before their study, others argued that sport involvement in high school generally enhanced athletes' chances of attending college and further upward social mobility later in life, with few considerations paid to the athletes' individual factors. However, in contrast, Sack and Thiel (1979) found that within the team, members' rank had a marked impact on income mobility in later life. Athletes who played on the "first team," the highest rank within the team, experienced greater income mobility than athletes who played on the "second team" or reserves. The first-team athletes' upward mobility resulted from their celebrity status and ability to thrive in highly competitive settings.

Sport can have a different impact on the social mobility of minority athletes. May's (2009) study of a Georgia high school basketball team over many seasons found that sport participation propelled many young African American male students toward graduating from high school and avoiding deviant behavior. A high school diploma can lead to more educational achievement. Mackin and Walther (2011) added to this result that a high level of sport participation increased the likelihood of African American men earning a college degree. Sport involvement was also found to contribute to Hispanic male students' probability of earning a college degree. Sport participation, particularly high-level involvement, contributes to the educational achievement of athletes from racial minorities. Considering that education is a significant factor that influences upward social mobility, it is clear that involvement in sport is closely related to individuals' mobility across different social classes.

Social Class and Stratification

The two major factors that influence socioeconomic position when studying social inequalities are **social class** and **social stratification**. Upward social mobility is moving up from one social class to another. Social class is defined as "categories of people who share an economic position in society based on their income, wealth (savings and assets), education, occupation, and social connections" (Coakley, 2016, p. 256). Individuals have differing levels of social and economic resources and social rankings that are the result of the structure and organization of society (Kraus & Park, 2017). People in higher social classes, on average, have more abundant economic resources, influential networks, and connections that provide them with better opportunities. On the other hand, people in lower social classes have fewer resources and connections with powerful groups and are more frequently exposed to social or environmental threats such as discrimination, food insecurity, underemployment, and reduced health coverage.

Social stratification refers to the "ranking of individuals along a continuum of economic or cultural attributes such as income or years of education" (Muntaner et al., 2003). It is also defined as "structured forms of economic inequalities that are part of the organization of everyday social life" (Coakley, 2016, p. 256). Social class, on the other hand, means the differences in groups of people by income level, occupation, education, and cultural

Social mobility through sport may differ across different racial and ethnic groups.
Xavierarnau/E+/Getty Images

values. These differences are created through social stratification—the hierarchies or rankings of social groups within a society. Social stratification results from systemic and structural inequalities that have been established through social institutions over time. Because most countries are based on capitalist economic systems, including the United States, the social class structure is largely based on socioeconomic status. Socioeconomic status is a combined measure that includes income level, educational status, and occupation.

In the past few decades, economic inequality in the United States has increased more rapidly than in other countries. The share of national income earned by the top 10 percent of earners in the United States in 1980 was approximately 35 percent, but it increased to 47 percent by 2016. In Europe, the percentage was similar in 1980 (34%) and only increased to 36 percent. In the United States, less than 1 percent of people born into the bottom income quintile can move to the top quintile during their lifetime (Kraus & Park, 2017). Less than 3 percent of the students who attend four-year colleges and universities come from the bottom income quintile (Carnevale & Rose, 2003). As economic inequality increases, upward social mobility decreases due to the interactive relationship between economic status, educational opportunity, and social mobility. Another important determinant of social class is race and ethnicity. Many racial and ethnic minority families continue to experience limited access to educational and economic opportunities (Richeson & Sommers, 2016).

Social Class and Sport Participation

In U.S. society, social class and stratification influence who can play what sport and also whether an individual can play sport at all. Patterns of sport participation are closely associated with money, power, and privilege (Coakley, 2016), because "the class divisions that arise in economic life are liable to spill over" (Roberts, 2001, p. 21) into other areas of people's lives, such as sport and physical activities (Green et al., 2005). Active sport participation, attendance at sport events, and buying sport-related goods are positively correlated with an individual's income, education, and occupational status. Generally, the higher the social class, the greater the involvement in sport; sport participation occurs in the context of social class.

Over time, economic inequality has produced class-based lifestyles that involve particular forms of sport, because availability of financial resources is an important determinant of access (Falcous & McLeod, 2012; Stempel, 2006; Wheeler, 2012). For example, upper- and upper-middle-class groups' sport participation is more likely to include golf, tennis, skiing, and swimming. These sports often involve expensive equipment, facilities, and travel. Participants also need jobs that pay them enough money and to have lives in which they have the spare time and control over their time to participate. On the other hand, the lifestyle and sport participation patterns of middle- and lower-class groups tend to involve more public activities—free and open to the public, publicly funded, or available in public schools.

As middle- and lower-class groups and families rely on public activities funded by local, state, and federal governments, they are more likely to lose access to sport facilities and programs when subsidies are cut. Publicly funded sport programs have been reduced or eliminated in many U.S. communities. For example, varsity teams in low-income school districts are being eliminated (Kelley & Carchia, 2013). Wealthy neighborhoods and communities often have more tax revenue that can be used to build and maintain sport facilities, manage sport programs, and hire quality coaches and staff, while poor neighborhoods and communities often experience the opposite.

Economic Inequality and Sport Participation

When it comes to organized youth sports, the influence of family's social class on children's and youths' sport participation is important because participation in club sports, for example, requires a financial commitment and parental support. According to a national survey of parents by the Aspen Institute's Project Play initiative and Utah State University's Families in Sport Lab (2020), youth between ages 6 and 18 from low-income families quit sports because of the financial costs at six times the rate of children and youth from high-income families. The survey results also reinforced the idea that family income, which mostly determines the family's social class, shapes the sport that children and youth play. Children from high-income families were at least twice as likely to play field hockey, lacrosse, and tennis or to participate in skiing and snowboarding as children from low-income families were. Not only did children from high-income families play more expensive sports, but they also had more options. Parents from high-income families who participated in the survey reported that their child regularly plays more than two sports (2.07) on average. It was higher than low-income families, whose parents reported an average of 1.93. Parents from high-income families (upper- and upper-middle social classes) are more able to invest in their children's sport participation, which may translate to further class advantage in the children's future (Lareau, 2002; Wheeler & Green, 2014).

As evidenced by the Aspen Institute's survey, children and youth in lower- and working-class families often lack the support and consistency characterized by organized youth sport that involve established facilities, coaching staff, administration systems, and parental support.

Children and youth in upper- and upper-middle-class families often have more resources and safe (i.e., private) places to participate in sports. Girls are more affected by family income and social class than boys. Girls in low-income families often face the greatest barrier to sport participation because oftentimes family members consider their sport participation less important than boys' participation. In contrast, boys and girls in high-income families seldom face constraints that interfere with participation in after-school and summer programs, camps, and leagues. Family structure affects youth sport participation, as well. Single-parent families face more structural constraints, such as lack of transportation, time, and money.

Race, Ethnicity, and Sport Participation

The impact of social class on sport participation also varies by race and ethnicity. In a project for the Women's Sports Foundation, Sabo and Veliz (2008) found that race was an important factor that predicts children's involvement in organized youth sport. White children showed the highest levels of involvement in organized

Each sport requires different resources.
Nattrass/E+/Getty Images
Phynart Studio/E+/Getty Images

sport, particularly in high-status sports such as swimming and soccer (Mirehie et al., 2019). In contrast, a high level of participation by certain racial groups in particular types of sport (e.g., African American male students playing basketball) can be due to structural factors, such as a social class that is formed based on socioeconomic status or residential neighborhood (Goldsmith, 2003). A more affluent neighborhood provides better and more structural support for youth to participate in high-status sport, while families living in less affluent neighborhoods have less access to organized sport programs. Racial segregation in residential areas affects the different resources and access to youth sport programs and broadens the participation gap between different racial groups (Edwards, 1986; Quarmby & Dagkas, 2010).

In another report commissioned by the Women's Sports Foundation (Staurowsky et al., 2020), a comparison between White and African American girls revealed that White girls had three times the access to sports sponsored by private organizations that African American girls (21% to 7%) did. In turn, "African American girls were more likely to participate in programs offered through schools (65% of African American girls, compared to 50% of White girls)" (Staurowsky et al., 2020, p. 16). The differences in the rates at which African American and White girls participate in physical activity and organized sport stem from African American girls attending schools with fewer resources and in communities with higher poverty rates (Staurowsky et al., 2020).

Latinx youth in the United States have been known to be less likely to participate in sport compared to other racial groups, largely due to socioeconomic factors (McGovern, 2021). According to scholars in Latina/o studies, Latinx families are overrepresented in the lowest socioeconomic brackets. Therefore, financial obstacles to youth sport participation are especially pressing for U.S. Latinx families (Flores et al., 2017). Financial obstacles are interrelated with time, parental involvement, and transportation availability for Latinx youth who want to and are participating in youth sport (Adams et al., 2006; Borden et al., 2006). Low-income Latinx youth are less likely to take part in school sports than their high-income peers, even though school sports are typically free (Peguero, 2011). Many Latinx youths whose families reside in underfunded school districts are required to provide their own transportation to games and equipment for participation, which makes youth sport more difficult to access (Flores-Gonzälez, 2000).

Increasing Social Capital in and Through Sport

Scholars have argued sport can be a useful apparatus to develop and enhance social capital. For example, sport-based intervention programs are based on the ideas and beliefs that sport has the potential to promote certain societal outcomes, such as enhanced social connections, networks, and community involvement (Spaaij, 2009). Enhanced social capital helps individuals have upward social mobility. The idea of using sport as an intervention was adopted by the United Nations in the early 2000s, after which many local and global organizations started using sport for social and community development.

What Is Social Capital?

Several scholars have suggested different definitions of **social capital**. In this chapter, we use the work of Robert Putnam, U.S. sociologist (Putnam et al., 1993; Putnam, 2000). In his book *Bowling Alone: The Collapse and Revival of American Community*, Putnam (2000) presented data about the changing behavior of people in the United States and showed how they have become increasingly disconnected from one another. Putnam's (1995) definition of social capital is the "features of social organization such as networks, norms, and social trust that can facilitate coordination and cooperation for mutual benefit" (p. 66). So, for him, social capital is conceptualized as consisting of trust, reciprocity, and network. Among these factors, he specifically emphasizes social networks as being central to the building of social capital. Increased social networks (i.e., social connectedness) foster greater social solidarity and social cohesion (Welty Peachey et al., 2013).

Putnam (2000) conceptualized two types of social capital: **bonding social capital** and **bridging social capital**. Welty Peachey et al. (2013) summarized the two social capitals' definitions and the differences between the two:

> *Putnam positions bonding social capital as the value assigned to social networks between relatively homogenous groups of kin, neighbors, and close friends, where the ties, interaction, and familiarity are strong, and which produces resources for an individual to "get by" or cope. Bridging social capital, on the other hand, is conceptualized as relationships developed with individuals different from oneself, between socially heterogeneous groups, where social ties and bonds may be looser and more diverse. . . . These bridging networks provide individuals with the potential to leverage a broader set of resources. (p. 22)*

From this perspective, sports can provide an anchor and environment for relationship development between and within communities that will lead to an increase in social capital (Sherry et al., 2011; Smith & Westerbeek, 2007). Sports foster social inclusion and, as described earlier, provide social mobility for disadvantaged people because individuals get access to opportunities to make friends and develop networks, consequently reducing social isolation (Jarvie, 2003; Sherry, 2010; Spaaij, 2009). In sum, sports provide connections between diverse and different groups and social networks (Burnett, 2006). People play sports to make friends, be a part of a community, establish community bonding, and maintain their social network. Sport participation provides a chance for people to develop networks that can further contribute to their social and economic success, which provides people with upward social mobility.

In addition to bonding and bridging social capital, sport participation can foster **linking social capital** (Woolcock, 2001). While bonding and bridging social capital are about horizontal relationships (i.e., bonding within a homogenous group and bridging between heterogeneous groups within a relatively similar hierarchy), linking social capital refers to "vertical connections between different social strata, including those entirely outside the community" (Coalter, 2010, p. 1384). When an individual develops linking social capital, it means that they have relationships with people in positions of influence within formal institutions (Schulenkorf, 2013). They can draw resources, ideas, and information from formal institutions. Thus, linking with supportive people in positions with institutional power helps them achieve upward social mobility. By linking social capital, people can access wider networks and the potential for leveraging a wider range of social, cultural, and financial resources. If an individual participates in team sport, they develop networks within the team (bonding), and with that network, they get a chance to interview for a better-paying job (linking), then we can say they developed linking social capital because their sport participation led them to a better opportunity.

Sport for Development and Peace: Increasing Social Capital Through Sport

As sports have been recognized as a useful tool to increase the social capital of participants and provide upward social mobility, the idea of sport-based intervention programs was adopted by international institutions and organizations such as the United Nations (UN). In the last several decades, a great number of **sport for development and peace** (SDP) initiatives have worked to facilitate positive social outcomes (Schwery, 2003).

> *Sport for development is defined as the use of sport or physical activity—often community-based team sport—as a means to meet development objectives, particularly youth development, health promotion, gender equity, social inclusion, and conflict prevention. Sport in this context is a vehicle or a catalyst for the wider development objective. The positive mental and physical effects of sport itself are useful by-products. (Prescott & Phelan, 2008, p. 5)*

As such, many programs and initiatives have been working to enhance the social capital of participating individuals. One of the representative initiatives in the United States is Street Soccer USA, a nonprofit organization that uses soccer to help youths and adults overcome homelessness through upward social mobility (Welty Peachey et al., 2011). The initiative provides a support system for people experiencing homelessness to make positive life changes (Welty Peachey et al., 2013). Street Soccer USA was founded by Lawrence Cann in Charlotte, North Carolina, in 2005, with a mission "to fight poverty and empower underserved communities through soccer" (Street Soccer USA, n.d.). Through serious participation in soccer, Street Soccer USA attempts to achieve three major goals for its participants: (1) build community and trust through sport; (2) require participants to set three-month, six-month, and 12-month life goals; and (3) empower individuals by coupling clinical services, such as job searching or financial education, with sport programming and providing access to educational and employment opportunities (Street Soccer USA, n.d.).

Over the years, Street Soccer USA has expanded into 14 cities across the United States to serve youth in poverty, adults and families experiencing homelessness, and people in recovery from addiction. These populations have traditionally been difficult to reach through governmental programs, and they face recurring barriers to reentering housing and employment. In providing comprehensive services, Street Soccer USA has partnered with HELP USA, a nonprofit organization that provides shelter and support services to people experiencing homelessness. So far, Street Soccer USA has served over 15,000 youth and adults by creating positive change in their lives—most importantly, upward social mobility. Street Soccer USA has taught life skills and created a social safety net in the communities they serve. With improved self-esteem and self-efficacy, participants have reconnected to housing, employment, or further education or enrolled in rehabilitation programs.

Sport for development programs help participants develop social capital.
Ilya S. Savenok/Getty Images for Street Soccer USA

Sport Industry Diversity Initiative

INCREASING SOCIAL CAPITAL IN SPORT: UNIVERSITY OF CONNECTICUT STUDENT-ATHLETE SUCCESS PROGRAM (SASP)

The Student-Athlete Success Program (SASP) at the University of Connecticut recognizes the unique needs of the athletes and provides an individualized, holistic approach to supporting their efforts to reach their full academic, personal, and athletic potential during their time at the university (SASP, n.d.). It is a comprehensive support program that works with all athletes to provide individualized academic support, skill and career development, and community service and leadership opportunities. The program has established its reputation across the nation based on its achievements, such as graduation rates of both men's and women's sport teams. Statistical evidence shows that SASP has especially contributed to sport teams with athletes from racial minority backgrounds, such as men's football and basketball and women's basketball, which a greater proportion of African American athletes play.

Although the National Collegiate Athletic Association (NCAA) has suggested that the overall graduation rates of athletes have increased over the years, more detailed statistical data show that there is still a gap between the graduation rates of African American and White athletes. For example, the NCAA's 2000 report on graduation rates revealed that nearly twice the percentage of White athletes as African American athletes graduated from college over the past year (Anderson & South, 2000; Singer, 2005). Another study, conducted by Richard Lapchick at the Institute for Diversity and Ethics in Sport at the University of Central Florida, analyzed the graduation rates for Division 1A college football teams that made it to postseason play during the 2004-2005 season. He found that less than half of the African American athletes graduated at 39 out of the 56 colleges (Lapchick, 2003). It was also revealed that 63 percent of White football players versus only 47 percent of African American football players graduated from the 117 Division 1A colleges (Singer, 2005).

To tackle this issue, SASP has worked with the University of Connecticut community to help their athletes, especially those of color, as they begin studies at the university, progress through their coursework, receive their diploma, and move on to succeed in graduate school, the workforce, or professional competition. The primary goal of the program is to assist athletes from all backgrounds in reaching their educational goals while competing in intercollegiate athletics. Academic and social support programs, such as counseling, preadvising, tutorial, and life skills programs, are provided. With this variety of support programs, SASP is considered a model program of academic support in the United States.

The program's achievement shows its dedication toward teams that traditionally have more African American athletes. For example, the University of Connecticut football program had the highest NCAA graduation success rate (GSR) for African American athletes among state univer-

Sport-Based Opportunities for International Athletes

Athletes use sport as a tool for immigration and, ultimately, a professional career in the U.S. sport industry. Many players who compete in the Ladies Professional Golf Association (LPGA) Tour are not from the United States but from other countries like South Korea, New Zealand, Thailand, Australia, Germany, China, and Sweden (LPGA, n.d.). MLB is famous for its high number of foreign players among the top professional sport leagues in the United States, with many players from Asian countries (e.g., Japan, South Korea, and Taiwan) and other countries in the Americas (e.g., Dominican Republic, Cuba, Mexico, and Venezuela). In other cases, children of immigrants make successful careers in professional and elite level sport, such as Albert Pujols, who was introduced earlier in this chapter. Michelle Wie, a professional American golfer, is a second-generation Korean immigrant.

sities that participated in a bowl game following the 2008 season. Reported in 2009, the GSR for African American athletes in the University of Connecticut football program was 83 percent, which placed it seventh among the 68 schools playing in bowl games in 2008; third among public institutions, behind Army and Navy; and first among public state institutions. In 2019, the university's football and men's and women's basketball teams performed above the required NCAA academic progress rate (APR). With the structural support provided by the SASP, the men's basketball team posted a perfect 1,000 single-year APR score in the 2017-2018 year. The football team also had a steady improvement in its multiyear APR score over the previous five years.

Ellen Tripp, director of SASP, emphasizes that having a holistic view and philosophy with college athletes is important. Counselors at the program understand the support every athlete needs, particularly that support of Black athletes could be different from White athletes. Academic support provided by the SASP includes regular communication with the college athletes' professors through its academic center. The academic center also functions as a place for college athletes to receive individualized academic support, as well as a place where they can learn, grow, and celebrate their successes. The program emphasizes that athletes are empowered to become independent, successful, and active learners.

SASP has partnered with the Savings Bank of Manchester Charitable Foundation to hire a community service and student development coordinator. With support from the foundation and the coordinator, college athletes are offered the opportunity to participate in community service activities within the university and neighboring towns. Another partnership, with Morgan Stanley, provides financial education workshops for athletes. According to *Sports Illustrated*, approximately 78 percent of NFL players are either bankrupt or under financial stress within two years of retirement. Approximately 60 percent of NBA players become financially unstable within five years of retirement. Providing financial education workshops is particularly helpful for athletes in these sports.

Since research in college athlete success consistently shows that demographic variables such as race, gender, and ethnicity significantly influence their academic performance and graduation rates (Reynolds et al., 2012), the role of programs like SASP is of great importance. Research by Snyder (1996) and Palmer (1994) showed that African American athletes have false athletic dreams and overwhelming ambitions about using sport as a springboard to become rich and famous. Not only do the programs help athletes from all demographic groups excel academically, but they also help them dismantle false fantasies.

Sports are an effective method of upward social mobility for such athletes.

According to the NCAA, over 20,000 international college athletes are enrolled in and competing at NCAA schools (NCAA, n.d.-a). The NCAA provides guidelines for international college athletes that are mainly prepared by the International Student Records Committee (ISRC). The committee comprises international academic experts from NCAA member institutions. According to the NCAA (2020):

> *The ISRC provides knowledge and expertise regarding the international educational system to establish supplemental initial-eligibility policies and procedures, as stated in [the] Guide to International Academic Standards for Athletics Eligibility, which complements the NCAA Division I and II bylaws. Only the Eligibility Center international academic certification staff has authority to determine crediting and academic timelines. As part of this process, staff may review professional resources*

(e.g., NARIC), published information from the appropriate issuing body or government (e.g., ministry of education), and/or other information on a case-by-case basis. (p. 4)

The NCAA established these guidelines and eligibility standards to effectively and systematically recruit talented international athletes to U.S. institutions. Although each institution is responsible for recruiting, the NCAA maintains the guidelines and provides resources and administrative support (e.g., document processing, accreditation) for international athletes. In other words, the NCAA has established an institutional foundation for both U.S. institutions and international athletes. More specific supports provided by the NCAA include non-English language resources for future college athletes. Several NCAA documents have been translated into languages like French, Portuguese, and Spanish to help international athletes, their families, and others involved. The NCAA also provides country-specific information on its website (NCAA, n.d.-b) where the NCAA's initial eligibility information specific to more than 150 countries can be accessed.

According to the NCAA's report on trends in the participation of international athletes in NCAA Divisions I and II (NCAA, 2021), the proportion of international athletes has increased from 10.3 percent (2,720) to 12.9 percent (3,585) in Division I and from 6.6 percent (1,862) to 7.0 percent (2,112) in Division II since 2015. In Division I men's sport, 61 percent of tennis players were international, followed by 39 percent in ice hockey, 37 percent in soccer, and 24 percent in golf. In Division I women's sport, 59 percent of tennis players were international, followed by 44 percent in ice hockey, 35 percent in golf, 27 percent in field hockey, and 24 percent in water polo. The top 10 home countries by the number of first-year Division I international athletes were Canada, United Kingdom, Germany, Spain, Australia, Sweden, France, Netherlands, New Zealand, and Norway.

Among Division I men's sports, football and basketball were the top two for their change in the number of international athletes. Division I men's football had 24 international athletes in 2014, but the number increased to 55 in 2019 (129% increase). Division I men's basketball had 125 international athletes in 2014, but the number increased to 189 in 2019 (51% increase). Among Division I women's sport, track, cross country running, and soccer had the top three increases in the number of international athletes. What the international athletes in NCAA schools have in common across different sports and home countries is that their athletic talent helped them be recruited by top Division I and II schools. In many cases, these athletes are eligible for scholarships, which gives them a better chance to focus on academic and athletic performance. Some of them often achieve further professional success through being recruited and playing at major professional leagues. For example, Yan Kuznetsov and Artem Shlaine, ice hockey players at the University of Connecticut originally from Russia, were selected in the 2020 National Hockey League (NHL) draft.

Many foreign players have been competing in major professional sport leagues in the United States (i.e., NBA, NHL, MLB, NFL, and Major League Soccer). For example, in 2020-21 NBA season opening-night rosters, 107 international players from 41 countries were included (NBA, 2020). Thirty-four of the 107 international players participated in Basketball Without Borders (BWB) before starting their NBA careers. The BWB program, which is a partnership between the NBA and the International Basketball Federation (FIBA), is a "global basketball development and community outreach program that has seen 76 former campers drafted into the NBA or signed as free agents since 2001" (NBA, 2020). For the 76 former campers, basketball gave them a chance to be recruited by the biggest professional basketball league in the world and achieve sporting and economic success. This group included Joel Embiid (Philadelphia 76ers; from Cameroon; participated in BWB Africa 2011), Jamal Murray (Denver Nuggets; from Canada; participated in BWB Global 2015), and Pascal Siakam (Toronto Raptors; from Cameroon; participated in BWB Africa 2012).

Sport Industry Leader Profile

Sen Han

Title: Global Liaison and Chinese Liaison at IMG Academy

Education: BS in Biology, Beijing Institute of Technology, China; MS in Sport Management, University of Florida, United States

Sen Han has been a Chinese liaison with IMG Academy's Global Liaison Program for three years. Before his current role, Han served for three years as a student mentor for international and Chinese students at IMG Academy, a preparatory boarding school and sport training institution in Bradenton, Florida. Han, who was born in China and grew up in Japan and China, speaks Chinese, Japanese, and English. In 2016, when he was visiting a former classmate from the University of Florida at the IMG Academy, Han's friend introduced him to a manager at the Academy, who hired him. IMG Academy operates various programs at multiple levels, including tennis, football, soccer, baseball, basketball, golf, lacrosse, and track and field, and cross country running. Since its opening in 1978, IMG Academy has trained many Olympic and professional athletes, including those who were and are in major professional sport leagues, such as the NBA, NFL, MLB, Major League Soccer, Association of Tennis Professionals, Women's Tennis Association, Professional Golf Association Tour, and LPGA Tour.

The following is a summary of his career development, education, responsibilities at work, and insights as a professional in the global sport industry.

What was your career path?

When describing how I ended up in my current position, it should be noted that I was born in China and moved to Fukuoka, Japan, until I was 11, when my family moved back to Beijing, China. While growing up in Japan, I was able to learn Japanese, which helped me speak three languages—Chinese, Japanese, and English. After graduating from high school, I went to the Beijing Institute of Technology and majored in biology. It was in my college years that I became extremely interested in tennis. Before I started playing tennis, I participated in various sports, particularly racket sports, which helped me improve my tennis skills in a short amount of time. I joined the university's tennis club and competed at multiple events. Gradually, my interest switched to sport management when I became the captain of the tennis team and began to organize the team's training and competition schedule.

My passion for tennis led me to change my career to sport management. After graduating from the university, I applied for a sport management graduate program at the University of Florida. I chose the United States because of the size and level of the sport industry. While I was pursuing my MS degree at the University of Florida, I was able to make meaningful connections with sport industry professionals and alumni who helped me work in my current position. Because it is difficult for international students in sport management to be hired by any U.S. professional leagues, teams, or organizations, I did not imagine myself to be where I am now. I was visiting my colleague from the graduate program who was an alumna of IMG Academy. She was hired by the Academy, and she introduced me to her supervisor. At that time, the Academy was looking for an individual with an international background and an ability to speak Chinese or Japanese, due to the growing number of students from those countries. Because I speak Chinese and Japanese, I was immediately hired by the Academy.

I first started as a student mentor for international athletes, mostly from East Asian countries. They had been raised and educated in a different cultural background before they came

> *continued*

Sport Industry Leader Profile *(continued)*

to the Academy, which often made them stressed and led to a hard time adjusting to the new environment in the United States. My responsibility was staying with the international athletes in their dorms, mentoring them, and letting their parents know how their children were doing at the Academy.

While I was working as a mentor, I realized the need for the Academy to be more culturally inviting and inclusive for international athletes and their families. Since international athletes come from different cultural backgrounds, it was not feasible to try to fit them into the U.S. mainstream culture, so I proposed the Global Liaison Program. The goal of the program and the position of the global liaison was to be an intermediary between the Academy and the international athletes and their families. I became the first Chinese liaison of the Academy and have been working in the position since. I communicate with the parents of international athletes, listen to international athletes' concerns, and organize inclusive cultural events for the Lunar New Year and Mid-Autumn Festival. I want to continue to contribute to the training and learning experiences of our international athletes. I see myself as a global citizen who can provide a passage of cultural communication and development through sport. In the long term, I would like to connect different countries and continents through sport.

Athletes at IMG Academy, both international and domestic, are recruited in various ways. They are from diverse backgrounds in terms of socioeconomic status, race, ethnicity, nationality, and culture. Because the Academy's tuition is very high, regular students tend to be from upper- and upper-middle classes, but we also recruit extremely talented athletes at a young age whose families may not want to or cannot afford the Academy's tuition. Several partnerships maintain this recruiting system. For example, there are several Japanese junior tennis players at the Academy. They were recruited by the Morita Fund, a private charity and foundation in Japan managed by the founder of the Japanese conglomerate Sony. The foundation has been recruiting talented tennis players in Japan and financially supporting them so that they can train at our Academy. We also organize international training camps in multiple places worldwide. One of our athletes was recruited by our basketball coach while he was at a training camp in Australia. With his exceptional athletic talent, he trained at our Academy, and he now plays in the NBA. We have many similar cases of international athletes who were recruited based on their athletic talents and made their way to a successful professional sport career in the United States.

Although many international athletes have been successful in the U.S. college and professional sport, their experiences are not without challenges. For the athletes in NCAA-affiliated universities and colleges, the biggest challenge comes from the cultural, academic, and administrative differences between their home and the U.S., which includes language barriers (Robertson et al., 2000), perception of time (Pritchard & Skinner, 2002), administrative hurdles (Rodriguez, 2014), and homesickness (Lee & Rice, 2007). Often, students from Asian, Latin American, and African countries face stereotyping and discrimination in addition to the existing challenges (Lee & Opio, 2011). Professional players in the U.S. sport leagues face career-related challenges in addition to the cultural adjustment. The challenges include immigration and citizenship issues such as obtaining work permits, visas, and permanent residency on time, issues with salary and benefits, and social isolation (Rockwell, 2019; van Bakel & Salzbrenner, 2020).

SUMMARY

The purpose of this chapter was to introduce selected basic foundational concepts for the understanding of social mobility and sport. Sports have long been viewed as a "great equalizer" in providing pathways to upward social mobility and success in the United States and global societies. Sports can and may contribute to the development of horizontal, vertical, intergenerational, and intragenerational social mobility. Sport's contribution to upward social mobility may cross social class, race and ethnicity, and gender. Resource availability, parental support, gendered perceptions, and racial and ethnic background influence the sports and physical activity in which both adults and youth can participate.

With sport's potential for upward social mobility, sport-based intervention programs have been developed to promote positive social outcomes, such as enhanced social and cultural capital. Individuals, through participating in sport-based intervention programs that include educational and financial support, can build social networks and obtain opportunities that will make their lives better. SDP (sport for development and peace) is an institutionalized form of a sport-based intervention program. With the UN's endorsement, SDP has been flourishing as a major example of using sport for diverse purposes, including for upward social mobility. One of the exemplary cases we visited in this chapter was Street Soccer USA, a program through which many homeless individuals built social networks and reentered society.

In this chapter, we also discussed how sports have provided opportunities for both professional and collegiate international athletes. The number of international players and athletes in the U.S. sport industry will continue to increase. Therefore, it is important to think about how to make the industry more inclusive and welcoming to those with different backgrounds.

CRITICAL THINKING EXERCISES

1. Research shows that social class is positively correlated with sport participation and attendance at sport games and events across all categories of people. Conduct an audit of an estimated budget of a family of four attending a sport game (e.g., professional [major], professional [minor], intercollegiate, or high school). Include every aspect on which the family needs to spend money—tickets, transportation, concessions, purchase of memorabilia, accommodation, etc. Compare the estimated budget with an average household income in the United States and explain how social class is related to access to sport. Use your own experience to give comparative examples that either support or contradict your argument.
2. You have been hired by the NCAA to create guidelines that athletic departments, coaches, and staff of affiliated universities and colleges can use to support and expand developmental opportunities for their incoming international athletes. One of the goals is to help international athletes maximize their postgraduation career success in the U.S. sport industry. List the top five guidelines in your report and explain why each is important to the overall development of these international athletes at U.S. universities and colleges.
3. Think about your own experience in sport participation and identify three types of social capital you were able to develop through the experience. In your response, include the definitions of social and cultural capital and give enough background to support your answer.

4. When designing sport-based intervention programs for underserved populations, it is important to consider the ways the programs can foster three types of social capital—bonding, bridging, and linking—to further produce upward social mobility. Identify three exemplary program elements that you believe should be included in program design. Each program element should serve each of the three types of social capital.

REVIEW QUESTIONS

1. Define the concept of social mobility and identify the four subtypes of social mobility. Then discuss how sport participation can influence the four subtypes.
2. Between the zero-sum model and the developmental model, explain which model should be used by coaches, teachers, and parents and why.
3. In U.S. society, social class and sport participation are closely correlated. Identify the challenges in tackling this correlation and the strategies to make sport participation more accessible to all social classes.
4. Identify a sports for development program or organization, then explain how the program or organization uses sport programming to help participants develop social capital.
5. Review support systems or programs for international athletes at U.S. colleges and universities, as well as foreign players in U.S. professional leagues, and determine the ways the system or program helps athletes and players adjust and be successful.

PART II

FORMS OF DIVERSITY IN SPORT

CHAPTER 4

Race Matters in Sport

Joseph N. Cooper

LEARNING OBJECTIVES

- Describe how the sport industry reproduces racism.
- Outline four distinct levels of racism and examples of each level in the sport industry.
- Present six race-conscious theories from critical sport scholarship: critical race theory, systemic racism, internal colonization, settler colonialism, world-systems theory, and race-centric ecological systems theories.
- Provide anti-racist recommendations for improving the sport industry.

Imagine you are a new employee with a sport organization. The first observation you make when you walk in the building is that the images of all current and previous leaders of the organization are White males. Next, in your orientation training, you notice there is no mention of race, racism, diversity, equity, or inclusion, but rather the primary focus is on entertainment, revenue generation, profit margins, and performance in sales. The third observation, when reviewing the organizational calendar, is the recognition of holidays such as Columbus Day and St. Patrick's Day, among other Eurocentric events with no consideration of the offensiveness of some of these holidays. Nor does the calendar identify holidays that reflect cultural diversity and inclusion. This scenario reflects the experiences of Black, Native, Latino, and Asian American people who work in sport organizations in the United States, where racism and cultural erasure is institutionalized to the point that it is natural to most people working in these spaces.

Racism is a founding principle of the United States. From the land theft and genocide of Native Americans to the intergenerational enslavement and dehumanization of Black people of African descent to the exploitation and marginalization of Latinos to the stigmatization of and discrimination against people of Asian descent, U.S. history can be synthesized as the imposition of racial oppression (violent and nonviolent) against all groups deemed non-White[1] (the concept of **settler colonialism** is discussed later in the chapter) (Horne, 2017, 2020). The insidious ideology of White racism has influenced all U.S. institutions (e.g., political, economic, legal, education, health care, religion) and cultural practices (e.g., music, art, sport) (Coakley, 2017; Feagin, 2006; Sage, 1998; Sage & Eitzen, 2009). In 2013, five years after the election of the first Black president in the United States, the Black Lives Matter (BLM) movement emerged as a global social justice movement aimed at redressing prevailing racial injustices. Inspired and affected by the broader BLM movement, athletes began using their platforms to draw attention to the need for societal change, most notably Colin Kaepernick in 2016, when he chose to kneel during the national anthem before National Football League (NFL) games to protest police brutality and the oppression of racialized and economically disadvantaged groups in the United States. In 2020, following the highly publicized deaths of George Floyd, Breonna Taylor, and Ahmaud Arbery, sportspersons[2] across all races participated in calls for racial equity in society including in sporting spaces (Cooper, 2021).

Historically, the culture of sporting spaces has mirrored the ideologies and arrangements within the broader society in which it exists (Coakley, 2017; Sage, 1998; Sage & Eitzen, 2009). In terms of race, mainstream sport opportunities have historically only been available to those who were deemed as White. For example, in the late 19th and early 20th century, Blacks were relegated to subservient roles within the sports of boxing and horseracing (Wiggins & Miller, 2003). Interracial boxing matches were selectively arranged to demonstrate White superiority over Blacks, but even in instances where Blacks were victorious (e.g., Tom Molineaux's match versus Tom Cribb in 1810), Whites sabotaged the bouts to preserve their racist ideals (Aycock & Scott, 2011). With horseracing near the end of the 19th century, Blacks were relegated to the role of jockeys, which was viewed as a menial role, whereas Whites owned and trained the horses (Sage, 1998). In the 20th century, White-controlled professional and college sports did not fully racially desegregate until the early 1970s (Harris, 2000). Another example of racism in sports is the long-standing objectification, commodification, and dehumanization of Native Americans via the co-optation of their images as mascots. Staurowsky (2007) explained how the imper-

[1] This summary is not intended to exclude the class oppression intertwined with capitalism and colonization.

[2] The term *sportspersons* refers to athletes, coaches, administrators, media, spectators, and all who are connected to sport (Cooper, 2021). This term is intended to emphasize a broad range of individuals, groups, institutions, and organizations connected to sport who engage in activism.

missible use of Native Americans as mascots in a society where massive land theft and genocide was imposed on this group reinforces White colonization and imperialism. In 2020, the former mascot of the Washington Football Team of the NFL was finally discontinued, but this change only came after decades of protests, lawsuits, and threats of sponsorship removals. The lack of adequate Native American land acknowledgments, historical reckonings via land ownership shifts, and corresponding financial allocations from sport organizations (and state and federal governments) reflects the prevalence of settler colonialism in sport and society (Chen & Mason, 2019).

Despite changes such as the discontinuation of most Native American mascots, racism remains prevalent in the 21st century sport industry in the United States. For example, during the 2020 football season, nearly all members of the University of Texas (UT) football team, led by a group of Black players, chose to exit the field after their game against the University of Oklahoma when the university's alma mater song titled "The Eyes of Texas" was played (McGee, 2021). The song lyrics glorify anti-Black and pro-Confederate (read: pro-slavery) sentiments dating back to the Civil War era. As such, the players' protest signified their growing racial and sociopolitical consciousness during the BLM era. Similar to protests at schools such as the University of North Carolina at Chapel Hill (activists' removal of the Confederate Silent Sam statue) and Clemson University (activist efforts that led to the discontinuation of the honors college being named after former Confederate politician John C. Calhoun), there was growing discontent among anti-racist advocates and activists toward the need for these institutions to remove all vestiges of racist symbols including statues, songs, and honors. Researchers have highlighted how many college sport facilities are named after individuals or events that supported the enslavement of African people (later referred to as Black Americans or African Americans) and the colonization of Native Americans, which reflects the normalization of racial oppression in sporting spaces (Turick et al., 2019).

Notwithstanding this evidence, from its inception to the modern day, mainstream U.S. sports promote a colorblind racist and functionalist ideology (Coakley, 2017; Sage, 1998; Sage & Eitzen, 2009). According to Coakley (2017), the functionalist approach of mainstream U.S. sports posits that these activities foster social

In 2020, following the highly publicized deaths of George Floyd, Breonna Taylor, and Ahmaud Arbery, sportspersons across all races participated in calls for racial equity in society including in sporting spaces.
Mike Ehrmann/Getty Images

harmony (particularly cross-culturally), character development, and readiness for productive citizenship. Similarly, Hartmann (2019) outlined how the cultural dimensions of sport in the United States emphasize competition and skill development, a seemingly apolitical posture, individualism, and achievement through motivation. A major flaw with these presumptions is the disregard for how and why sports across all levels serve as hegemonic ideological outposts whereby social stratification and broader societal inequities are reinforced (Coakley, 2017; Sage, 1998; Sage & Eitzen, 2009). Within this chapter, I will outline the various ways in which sport reproduces the foundational ideology of White racism, distinct levels of racism, race-conscious theories for decolonizing sport, and anti-racist recommendations for enhancing equity and inclusion in and through sport. The framing of this chapter is grounded in a critical approach. More specifically, I employ what Sage (1998) described as a critical sensitivity (also referred to as critical theory [Coakley, 2017; Sage & Eitzen, 2009]) approach to examining sport whereby taken-for-granted meanings of the contexts can be reflected upon, challenged, and ultimately debunked. This approach conveys to the reader how and why race and racism matter in sport, but more importantly how and why anti-racism can matter more and transform these spaces from sites of exploitation, marginalization, exclusion, and stratification to equity, diversity, multiculturalism, inclusion, and empowerment.

Multilevel Racism in Society and Sport

To understand how race, racism, and sport intersect, it is important to operationally define key terms. The first key term to understand is race. Renowned social psychologists Omi and Winant (2015) offered the following definition of **race**:

> *A social construction and not a fixed, static category rooted in some notion of innate biological differences . . . It involves "othering," which is used to justify subordinate status, unequal treatment, to structure oppression and exploitation in numerous ways. (p. 12)*

Hence, from its inception, the concept of race was intended to foster division and mythical hierarchies based on desires for domination by Europeans and disguised in phenotypical differences. Relatedly, as opposed to a psychological or primarily a micro-level concept, scholars have asserted that the concept of **racism** (henceforth also referred to as racialized social systems) is best understood as a manifestation of multiple interlocking systems. Bonilla-Silva (1997) defined **racialized social systems** as "societies in which economic, political, social, and ideological levels are partially structured by the placement of actors in racial categories or races" (p. 469). As a multidimensional concept, Ray (2019) explained how racial structures[3] operate on three levels: (1) substructure (i.e., mental models or one's way of making sense of the world), (2) structure (i.e., rules and resources), and (3) superstructure (i.e., racial ideology). Similar to the problematic consequences of race, racialized social systems and racism inherently involve domination, oppression, exploitation, objectification, and dehumanization. Moreover, Scheurich and Young (1997) outlined four distinct levels of racism including **individual racism**, **institutional racism**, **societal racism**, and **civilizational racism**:

1. *Individual racism* (overt and covert) involves interpersonal racially biased acts of prejudice that cause harm to an individual or groups.
2. *Institutional racism* refers to institutions or organizations reinforcing racialized hierarchies via policies and practices (e.g., racial bias in hiring, evaluation, retention, and promotion).
3. *Societal racism* refers to embedded systems of racist cultural norms across and within a given geopolitical context (e.g., a nation or state).
4. *Civilizational racism* refers to the prevalence of multiple societies reproducing racist beliefs, laws, rules, structures, institutions, and treatment toward groups deemed as subordinate based on their race.

[3] See Ray (2019, figure 1, p. 33).

Table 4.1[4] provides societal and sport-specific examples of the four distinct levels of racism.

Racialized social systems also foster racial socialization in sports. Martin (2015) posited that racial socialization in the U.S. society has resulted in the establishment of White sports and Black sports. More specifically, Martin (2015) said racial socialization in sports is "the process by which blacks and whites learn what is expected of them to maintain the racial status quo and the myth of white supremacy and black inferiority" (p. 9). Within the United States, Blacks are socialized to participate in sports such as football, basketball, track and field, and boxing because success in these sports reifies racist stereotypes about their genetic predispositions of possessing fast-twitch muscle fibers, being aggressive, and engaging in activities that are viewed as less "intellectually" challenging (Sailes, 2010). This intellectual inferiority stereotype is also a primary reason for why Blacks are under-represented in sport leadership positions. The Institute for Diversity and Ethics in Sport (TIDES) has tracked hiring and retention rates along racial and gender lines across major sport organizations in the United States for the past four decades (TIDES, 2021). Since the initial publication of the Racial and Gender Report Cards, TIDES' reports have consistently revealed that Black, Latino, Asian, and Native Americans continue to be underrepresented in sport leadership positions across the intercollegiate and professional levels.

In an examination of the underrepresentation of African American coaches in college sport, Cunningham (2010) employed a multi-level systems analytical approach. The author

TABLE 4.1 Four Distinct Levels of Racism in Society and Sport

Distinct level of racism	Societal example	Sport example
Individual	Latino Americans being referred to as aliens or illegals (Solórzano & Yosso, 2002)	Jeremy Lin (professional basketball player) being called "coronavirus" during a 2021 G-League game (Levenson, 2021)
Institutional	The persistent underrepresentation of Black males as educators and administrators in K-12 school systems and concurrent overrepresentation of White females and males in these roles (Howard, 2014)	The long-standing structure of the NCAA that economically exploits football and men's basketball players via the amateurism principle and the economic marginalization of HBCU athletic departments (Cooper et al., 2014; Hawkins, 2010)
Societal	Racial wealth gap, police brutality, mass incarceration of Black Americans, health disparities, and systemic educational resource gaps along racial lines in the United States (Alexander, 2012; Carter & Welner, 2013; Darity & Mullen, 2020)	The underrepresentation of Black, Latino, Asian, and Native Americans in sport leadership positions at the professional and intercollegiate levels in the United States due to the White good ol' boys network (e.g., ownership, management, coaches, etc.) (Cunningham, 2019; Rosner & Shropshire, 2011)
Civilizational	The intergenerational impact of White European settler colonization on every continent in the world (e.g., land theft, genocide, environmental violence, religious persecutions, lynchings, sexual violations, family separations, cultural erasure, etc.) (Horne, 2017, 2020)	The intergenerational marginalization of the Global South within the structure of international sport organizations such as the International Olympic Committee (IOC) and Fédération Internationale de Football Association (FIFA) (Boykoff, 2016; Hylton, 2010)

[4] See Oseguera (2010) for a similar table focused on Black male college athletes.

described how macrolevel (e.g., institutionalized practices, political climate, and stakeholder expectations), mesolevel (e.g., prejudice, discrimination, leadership stereotypes, and organizational culture), and microlevel (e.g., head coaching expectations and intentions, turnover intentions, and relationships among multilevel factors) influences contributed to lower hiring and retention rates of African American head coaches (Cunningham, 2010). These same multilevel factors explain why Whites are consistently overrepresented in these roles; hence, reinforcing the racial social system of sport in the United States. In 2021, the NFL had seven head coaching vacancies and before the playoffs had ended, all positions were filled with White male hires (Armour, Freeman, & Schad, 2021). Despite pressure from the Fritz Pollard Alliance, several talented and qualified Black coaches such as Super Bowl champion offensive coordinator Eric Bieniemy were overlooked once again. This reality is a part of a legacy of exclusion. Collectively, these realities and scholarly research highlight how race and racism matters at multiple levels of society and sport beyond the interpersonal level. As such, any efforts seeking to redress racism must include a multilevel systems approach.

Key Foundational Terms and Theories for Understanding Racism and Decolonizing Sports

When race matters, terms such as equity, equality, diversity, inclusion, and anti-racism are commonplace. Equity refers to the fulfillment of fairness or justice within a given context (Espinoza, 2007). In the context of human relations, equality refers to providing the same treatment to all people regardless of their identity characteristics (e.g., race, gender, age, etc.) particularly the protection of their inalienable rights (UDHR, 1948). Harrison, Price, and Bell (1998) delineate diversity into two categories, surface-level and deep-level. **Surface-level diversity** refers to "differences among group members in overt, biological characteristics that are typically reflected in physical features" (Harrison et al., 1998, p. 97). Common surface-level diversity characteristics include heterogeneity in race, gender, and age. Within sports, the TIDES (2021) Racial and Gender Report Cards are useful tools for assessing progress or a lack thereof regarding surface-level diversity in sport leadership (see sidebar on Dr. Carla Williams).

Beyond surface-level analyses, it is important for sport leaders, managers, and practitioners to focus on enhancing deep-level diversity. Harrison et al. (1998) defines **deep-level diversity** as "differences among members' attitudes, beliefs, and values" (p. 98). Relatedly, Scott (2014) delineated the concepts of **organizational culture** and **climate**. **Organizational culture** refers to core values and assumptions promulgated by an organization, and these are deemed as being metaphorically under the surface—whereas **organizational climate** refers to procedures, policies, and practices, which are considered metaphorically to be on the surface. Contemporary sport leaders, managers, and administrators often focus more on changing culture through equity-minded rhetoric, symbolic gestures, and surface-level diversity efforts but evade the more challenging work of changing the climate and fostering more deep-level diversity. One result is the prevalence of hostile workplace climates for racialized groups and women (Cunningham, 2019; McDowell & Carter-Francique, 2017).

Hence, I posit that **inclusion** occurs when **deep-level diversity** is embedded within an institution and organization to the extent that all diverse groups seeking harmonious coexistence feel safe, welcomed, valued, embraced, and supported. In order to truly embody equity and inclusion, individuals, groups, institutions, and organizations must actively challenge realities grounded in oppressive ideologies such as racism, sexism, classism, ageism, and ableism, to name a few. One such approach involves the adoption and implementation of the ideology of **anti-racism**. Kendi (2019) described **anti-racism** as any action that views social problems as a result of racist policies (as opposed to individual or group behaviors) and promotes racial equality and equity through concerted policy replacement efforts (as opposed to reform).

Sport Industry Leader Profile

Courtesy of University of Virginia.

Dr. Carla Williams: 21st Century Trailblazer

Title: Athletic Director, University of Virginia

In 2017, Dr. Carla Williams became the first Black woman to be an athletic director at a Division I Power 5 Football Bowl Subdivision (FBS) school when she was hired at the University of Virginia (UVA) (Virginia Sports, 2021). In a multibillion-dollar college sport industry where White men occupy nearly every prominent leadership position, Williams' presence and success is noteworthy and groundbreaking. Williams' background includes being a former Division I college athlete, coach, and administrator at the University of Georgia (UGA).

During her second year as athletic director at UVA, she earned the 2019 Women Leaders in College Sports' Administrator of the Year for Division I FBS schools (Virginia Sports, 2021). In the same year (2019), the UVA men's basketball team won its first National Collegiate Athletic Association (NCAA) championship and the men's lacrosse team won its eighth NCAA title. These accomplishments among others resulted in UVA being awarded the coveted Capital One Cup for men's sports in 2019. Academically, under Williams' tutelage the Cavaliers had a record-breaking number of college athletes earn Atlantic Coast Conference (ACC) honor roll for high grade point averages. The NCAA acknowledged UVA for its high academic progress rates, which reflects the athletic department's commitment to supporting college athletes toward graduation (Virginia Sports, 2021).

As a visionary leader, Williams has devised a $180 million master plan that includes capital projects and increased support for college athlete scholarships (Virginia Sports, 2021). Most recently, Williams was among the leaders on the NCAA's solutions group that examined the history and proposals for reform to the bylaw on college athletes' rights to their name, image, and likeness (NIL). Williams' transformational leadership style is laudable. She has defied the challenges associated with racism and sexism in college sports by excelling as an athletic director at the most competitive and financially lucrative level in the United States. In a 2018 *Good Morning America* interview with Robin Roberts, Williams described the essence of her legacy when she said, "I'm living proof that you can do anything" (Miller & Thorbecke, 2018, p. 1).

Several race-centric theories undergird the ideology of anti-racism:

1. Critical race theory
2. Systemic racism
3. Internal colonization
4. Settler colonialism
5. World-systems theory
6. Race-centric ecological systems theories

Critical Race Theory

In the post–civil rights era, there was a growing cadre of legal scholars who noted how the perceived racial progress in the U.S. judicial system was not as seamless as the activists of the previous era predicted (Bell, 1980, 1992). Grounded in these realities, critical race theory (CRT) emerged as an analytical framework to understand how race and racism are foundational to the national identity of the United States and its social institutions, particularly the legal system. The initial tenets of CRT were racial realism (also referred to as the permanence of racism) and Whiteness as a property norm (Bell, 1980, 1992; Delgado & Stefancic, 2001). Bell (1980, 1992) argued racism is not only embedded in U.S. policies and practices, but it is also a permanent feature of this society. Understanding this reality enables one to avoid believing that the systemic nature of racism can be addressed through good intentions, meaningful interpersonal relations, or even the passage of antidiscrimination laws. Within sport in the 21st century, Bell's (1980, 1992) thesis has been proven accurate; despite widespread diversity, equity, and inclusion rhetoric and antidiscrimination policies in sport, racialized arrangements and inequities persist (Cooper, Newton, Klein, & Jolly, 2020; TIDES, 2021). According to Harris (1993), the Whiteness as property norm posits that Whites in the United States are empowered to exercise disposition, status property, and the right to exclude over those who are deemed as non-White. Since the country was founded upon Black dehumanization (and the oppression and genocide of Native Americans), Whites who fund big-time college and professional sports internalize the notion that the players (a majority of whom are Black in the sport of football and basketball at the professional and big-time college levels) are their property (Hawkins, 2010; Singer, 2020; Smith, 2009). The right to possession is one of the primary ways White racism manifests itself in sport, for example through ownership of Black athletic labor (exploitation), Native American land (theft), and identities (unauthorized objectification of mascots) (Chen & Mason, 2019; Hawkins, 2010; Staurowsky, 2007). In terms of the right to exclude, the underrepresentation of Blacks in leadership positions within the NCAA and among Power 5 Division I FBS athletic departments, along with the concurrent marginalization of historically Black colleges and universities (HBCU) athletic departments, reflects how Black exclusion is normalized without penalty (Cooper, Cavil, & Cheeks, 2014; Cunningham, 2019; TIDES, 2021).

Additional tenets of CRT include interest convergence, critique of liberalism, centrality of experiential knowledge, and intersectionality (Bell, 1980, 1992; Crenshaw et al., 1995; DeCuir & Dixson, 2004; Solórzano & Yosso, 2002). Interest convergence asserts that any gain by a disadvantaged group only occurs insofar as it benefits a privileged group. Numerous CRT sport scholars have noted how the increasing number of Black athletes in mainstream sporting spaces only occurred because the economic and public relations benefits of having this surface-level diversity yielded positive outcomes for Whites who were controlling these spaces (Hawkins, Carter-Francique, & Cooper, 2017; Singer, 2020). The critique of liberalism tenet emphasizes how objectivity, neutrality, and liberalism are myths and all aspects of the U.S. society involve subjectivity and power dynamics; hence, persisting conflicts are grounded in racist realities (Crenshaw et al., 1995). Those who organize sport claim these spaces are color-blind liberalist in orientation, but in reality, the same racialized stratification in the broader society manifests itself in sporting spaces in overt (e.g., racial differences in sport participation patterns) and covert ways (e.g., lack of culturally inclusive policies and practices in mainstream sports) (see Martin, 2015, for an extensive discussion on racialized socialization in sports). The centrality of experiential knowledge tenet refers to the significance and necessity of prioritizing the voices of those who have been the most adversely affected by systemic racism and related oppressions (Crenshaw et al., 1995; DeCuir & Dixson, 2004; Solórzano & Yosso, 2002). Intersectionality refers to the cumulative and distinct impacts of multiple oppressive ideologies (e.g., racism, sexism, and classism) on individual and group outcomes. Within sport, Black women experience distinct oppressions as athletes (Carter-Francique, 2017) and administrators (McDowell & Carter-Francique, 2017) as a result of their race and gender, as well their other intersecting identities.

Systemic Racism

In his seminal text, *Systemic Racism: A Theory of Oppression*, Feagin (2006) explained how the distinctiveness of the United States lies in the fact that it is the only modern-day economic superpower in the Western Hemisphere that was "explicitly founded on racial oppression" (p. 2). After the abolition of slavery (this assertion is questionable given the modern-day mass incarceration complex in the 21st century; see Alexander, 2012, for an extended analysis), legal segregation and other forms of racial oppression were introduced and enforced (e.g., vagrancy laws, Black codes, separate and unequal educational institutions, etc.) (Feagin, 2006). Systemic racism manifests itself in three distinctive, yet overlapping ways—material, social, and ideological (Feagin, 2006). Materially, Whites have controlled the means of production across industries and acquired intergenerational wealth. These material acquisitions such as access to money, land, healthcare, and legal protection, to name a few, have resulted in improved life outcomes for this racial group compared to Black, Latino, Asian, and Native Americans. In sport, Whites control the multibillion dollar leagues, governing organizations, teams, corporate sponsors, and facilities, which reflect a myriad of material benefits (Smith, 2009).

Socially, Whites have created networks that exclude Black, Latino, Asian, and Native Americans and established Eurocentric ways of doing, being, and thinking as normal and preferred and all non-Eurocentric cultural styles as abnormal and undesirable. Social networks have been cited as the primary source for new hires in sport leadership positions and this good ol' boys network (grounded in racism, sexism, and classism) has historically and contemporarily been largely exclusive to White males (Cunningham, 2019). Ideologically, Whites have promoted the idea that they constitute the highest form of humanity and all non-White groups are inferior (Feagin, 2006). The use of the amateurism principle within big-time college sports and its disproportionate impact on Blacks, who are already systemically deprived economically in the U.S. society, illustrates the ideology of White racism (Cooper, 2012). The promulgation of material, social, and ideological privileging and concurrent disadvantaging of different groups manifests in what Feagin (2006) describes as unjust enrichment and unjust impoverishment. Whites have unjustly enriched themselves through the imposition of violence against and exploitation of Black, Latino, Asian, and Native Americans (e.g., settler colonialism, imperialism, and capitalism) (Feagin, 2006; Horne, 2017; Horne, 2020). The latter groups have experienced unjust impoverishment that has resulted in lower quality of health and less access to wealth among a plethora of other negative life outcomes albeit to varying extents (e.g., anti-Black racism resulting in disparately negative life outcomes for Black Americans) (Alexander, 2012; Cooper, 2012; Feagin, 2006).

Another clear example of how systemic racism remains prevalent is with the gross disparities between the salaries of prominent Power 5 Division I FBS coaches (nearly all of whom are White), the revenues generated by the top earning athletic departments at historically White institutions (HWIs) (who are members of a White neoliberal and neocolonial NCAA), and the total revenues generated by athletic departments at HBCUs (see tables 4.2

TABLE 4.2 Highest Paid College Basketball Coaches

Coach	Race of coach	School	Racial institution type	Annual salary
John Calipari	White	University of Kentucky	HWI	$8.1 million
Mick Cronin	White	University of California, Los Angeles	HWI	$5.5 million
Chris Beard	White	University of Texas	HWI	$5 million
Rick Barnes	White	University of Tennessee	HWI	$4.7 million
Jay Wright	White	Villanova University	HWI	$4.4 million
Tom Izzo	White	Michigan State University	HWI	$4.1 million
Chris Mack	White	University of Louisville	HWI	$4 million
Bill Self	White	University of Kansas	HWI	$3.9 million
Bob Huggins	White	West Virginia University	HWI	$3.9 million
Buzz Williams	White	Texas Agricultural and Mechanical (A&M) University	HWI	$3.8 million

Note: See Hawkins (2010) for similar tables (1-3). The data cited reflects salaries of active college basketball coaches as of September 2021. Retiring coaches such as Mike Krzyzewski ($7.2 million salary) and Roy Williams ($4.1 million salary) were excluded from this list.

Data from G. Malone, *The Highest-Paid College Basketball Coaches in America* (AOL, March 28, 2021). https://www.aol.com/highest-paid-college-basketball-coaches-160048250.html.

TABLE 4.3 Highest Paid College Football Coaches

Coach	Race of coach	School	Racial institution type	Annual salary
Nick Saban	White	University of Alabama	HWI	$9.3 million
Ed Orgeron	White	Louisiana State University	HWI	$8.9 million
Dabo Swinney	White	Clemson University	HWI	$8.3 million
Jim Harbaugh	White	University of Michigan	HWI	$8 million
Jimbo Fisher	White	Texas A&M University	HWI	$7.5 million
Kirby Smart	White	University of Georgia	HWI	$6.9 million
Lincoln Riley	White	University of Oklahoma	HWI	$6.2 million
Gary Patterson	White	Texas Christian University	HWI	$6.1 million
Dan Mullen	White	University of Florida	HWI	$6 million
Ryan Day	White	Ohio State University	HWI	$5.6 million

Data from R. Gates, (2021, June 6). *College Football's 25 Highest Paid Coaches* (247 Sports, June 6, 2021). https://247sports.com/LongFormArticle/College-football-25-highest-paid-coaches-Nick-Saban-Dabo-Swinney-Ed-Orgeron-166204490/#166204490_16

TABLE 4.4 Top Revenue Generating Historically White Institution (HWI) Athletic Departments in 2018-2019

School	Conference	Total ranking in revenue among Division I athletic departments (out of 300)	Annual total revenue
University of Texas	Big 12	1	$223.8 million
Texas A&M University	Southeastern Conference (SEC)	2	$212.7 million
Ohio State University	Big Ten	3	$210.5 million
University of Michigan	Big Ten	4	$197.8 million
University of Georgia	Southeastern Conference (SEC)	5	$174 million
Penn State University	Big Ten	6	$164.5 million
University of Alabama	Southeastern Conference (SEC)	7	$164 million
University of Oklahoma	Big 12	8	$163.1 million
University of Florida	Southeastern Conference (SEC)	9	$159.7 million
Louisiana State University	Southeastern Conference (SEC)	10	$157.7 million

Based on "NCAA Finances," *USA Today* (2020). https://sports.usatoday.com/ncaa/finances/

TABLE 4.5 Top Revenue Generating Historically Black Colleges and Universities (HBCU) Athletic Departments in 2018-2019

School	Conference	Total ranking in revenue among Division I athletic departments (out of 300)	Annual total revenue
Prairie View A&M University	Southwestern Athletic Conference (SWAC)	147	$19.7 million
North Carolina A&T University	Mid-Eastern Athletic Conference (MEAC)	175	$15.8 million
North Carolina Central University (NCCU)	Mid-Eastern Athletic Conference (MEAC)	185	$14.6 million
Delaware State University	Mid-Eastern Athletic Conference (MEAC)	189	$14 million
Norfolk State University	Mid-Eastern Athletic Conference (MEAC)	192	$13.9 million
Alabama State University	Southwestern Athletic Conference (SWAC)	193	$13.4 million
Texas Southern University	Southwestern Athletic Conference (SWAC)	204	$12 million
Tennessee State University	Ohio Valley Conference (OVC)	208	$11.5 million
Florida A&M University (FAMU)	Mid-Eastern Athletic Conference (MEAC)	211	$11.2 million
Morgan State University	Mid-Eastern Athletic Conference (MEAC)	213	$10.8 million

Based on "NCAA Finances," *USA Today* (2020). https://sports.usatoday.com/ncaa/finances/

through 4.5) (Hawkins, 2010; Smith, 2009). In concert with Feagin's (2006) systemic racism theory, HWIs have benefited from unjust enrichment (including the legacy of slavery, legal segregation, and contemporary racial oppression) while HBCUs have suffered from intergenerational unjust impoverishment (Cooper et al., 2014).

Unjust impoverishment is reflected in the fact that the combined salaries of the top three highest paid college football coaches (Nick Saban of University of Alabama, Dabo Swinney of Clemson University, and Ed Orgeron of Louisiana State University) ($26.5 million), all White men, is higher than the total revenues generated by the top earning HBCU athletic department at Prairie View A&M University ($19.7 million) (Gibson, 2020; *USA Today*, 2021). In addition, the top revenue generating HWI athletic department, the University of Texas ($223,879,781), generates roughly $87 million more revenue than the top 10 revenue generating HBCU athletic departments combined ($136.9 million) (*USA Today*, 2020).

Moreover, Black football and men's basketball players at the Power 5 HWIs are subjected to athletic labor exploitation (Hawkins, 2010; Huma & Staurowsky, 2020; Smith, 2009). In a market-base study of big-time college sports, Huma and Staurowsky (2020) presented the following finding:

> *The average Division I FBS football and basketball player is denied approximately $208,208 and $370,085 of their fair market value, respectively. Over a four-year career, the lost value for the average football and basketball player is $832,832 and $1,480,340, respectively. After accounting for the value of college athletes' athletic scholarships between 2017-2020, approximately $10 billion in generational wealth will have been transferred from college football and men's basketball players, the majority of whom are athletes of color, to coaches, athletics administrators, and college administrators who are predominantly White or to institutions and programs that serve majority White constituencies. (p. 3)*

Black males constituted 55 to 56 percent of the teams at Power 5 HWIs listed in tables 4.2 to 4.5 (Harper, 2018). Along with their non-Black peers in these sports, they do not receive market-based value for their talents. Meanwhile, the majority of the White coaches at this level earn hundreds of thousands to millions of dollars for their services (see tables 4.2 and 4.3) not to mention the HWIs and corporate sponsors who profit handsomely from this arrangement as well. This racialized arrangement reinforces systemic racism via unjust enrichment and unjust impoverishment (Feagin, 2006). In addition, these inequitable arrangements in sport reflect the broader racial wealth gap in society, which illustrates the magnitude of White racist ideological hegemony in the United States (Sage, 1998). For example, according to renowned stratification economists, Hamilton et al. (2015) found in 2011 the difference in median family wealth between Blacks ($7,113) and Whites ($111,740) was $104,627. In the same report, the researchers noted how Black families with a head of household who graduated from college had 33 percent less wealth than White families whose head of household dropped out of high school (Hamilton et al., 2015). Thus, the racial economic deprivation in sport mirrors the broader U.S. society (Cooper, 2012).

Internal Colonization

In his seminal book, *The New Plantation: Black Athletes, College Sports, and Predominantly White Institutions*, Hawkins (2010) explained the applicability of the internal colonial model (Fanon, 1961/2004) for the examination of the racialized structure of big-time college sports in the United States. The internal colonial model consists of the following key components: (1) *colonizer* and *colonized* relationship, (2) *economics*, (3) *politics*, (4) *racism* (individual and institutional), (5) *social*, and (6) *cultural* (Hawkins, 2010). The interconnectedness of these components results in the perpetual exploitation of Blacks. The new plantation analogy positions the NCAA and its member institutions as the colonizers and Black male athletes as the colonized, which illustrates the prevailing economic and power arrangement that was established early in U.S. history with chattel slavery (Hawkins, 2010). Hawkins (2010) explained the central feature of the system when he said, "Race binds the colonized to a world constructed by the colonizer, which prescribes their worth and value based on their output or ability to produce" (p. 120).

Furthermore, within this model, Hawkins (2010) also explicated how Black athletes as a colonized group have lifestyles similar to oscillating migrant laborers. As oscillating migrant laborers, they experience marginality, labor exploitation, and rotation between their home communities and the campuses where they work (Hawkins, 2010). At the end of his book, Hawkins (2010) offered a plan for decolonization to counter the internal colonial relationship between the NCAA, its member institutions, and Black athletes. Specifically, he describes the process of **decolonization** as a collection of emancipatory strategies that empower athletes and provide them with resources needed to be competitive academically and athletically (Hawkins, 2010). The benefit of using the internal colonial framework, the plantation analogy, and a decolonization approach is that it enables advocates and activists for racial justice in sport to better understand the sociohistorical connection between Blacks who were unjustly enslaved and who labored during chattel slavery to the colonized oscillating migrant laborers of the 21st century (Black college athletes) who currently exist under the NCAA's exploitative collegiate model of athletics. This foundational understanding is critical for identifying and executing effective decolonization strategies.

Settler Colonialism

In an article titled "Making Settler Colonialism Visible in Sport Management," Chen and Mason (2019) offered a critique of the field of sport management that perpetuates Indigenous invisibility through the pervasiveness of neocolonial epistemologies. Often, the discussion of race and sport is discussed within a Black and White binary, which negates the experiences of racial, cultural, and ethnic groups outside of these categories. For example, prior to the enslavement of Black Africans on U.S.

soil (also referred to as Black Americans or African Americans), Indigenous peoples of the Americas (also referred to as Native Americans) experienced land theft, genocide, and colonialization. Acknowledging, confronting, and redressing these realities is essential for scholars and practitioners who assert that race matters. More specifically, Chen and Mason (2019) explained the importance of adopting a **settler colonialism** analysis toward sporting institutions and practices in the United States, Canada, Australia, and New Zealand:

> *If we take into consideration the material and epistemic dimensions of settler colonialism, we can also see its presence and impact on the social institution of sport in settler societies. First, the appropriation of land from Indigenous peoples . . . multisport and international events like the Olympics and the Commonwealth games take place on Indigenous land. . . . Indigenous sportspersons continued to face discrimination, marginalization, and limited access to resources in sport organizations . . . mainstream sport organizations have historically appropriated Indigenous cultural symbols. (p. 383-384)*

Chen and Mason (2019) examined how Indigenous people not only experience multilevel oppression, but these conditions have been perpetuated and exacerbated intergenerationally. Turick and colleagues' (2019) study of 18 Division I FBS basketball and football facilities illustrated the ongoing impact of settler colonialism in the U.S. sporting milieu. The authors found each facility was named after individuals who embodied racist beliefs toward Black Americans and/or Native Americans, which corresponds with racist views conveyed by the donors affiliated with the University of Texas mentioned in the introduction. The pervasiveness of neocolonial and Confederate nostalgia embedded in U.S. social institutions, particularly sport and education spaces, signifies what Bell (1992) described as racial realism within this geopolitical context. The settler colonialism theory is vital for understanding the foundational sources of modern-day racist arrangements and outcomes and enables the analysis of race to extend beyond the Black and White binary.

World-Systems Theory

In the U.S. capitalist culture, the idea of the American Dream is a deeply rooted principle. For years, sports have been viewed as a viable method of attaining the American Dream. In his book *Race, Sport, and the American Dream*, Smith (2009) explored how sports have adversely affected the African American community economically and educationally. Using Wallerstein's (1974) world-systems theory, Smith (2009) contextualizes racism in the United States within a broader transnational context. For example, Smith (2009) describes the athletic industrial complex in the United States as an extension of the global expansion of capitalism. The athletic industrial complex refers to the interdependent economic and political relationship between big-time professional and college sports in the United States and various social institutions such as the hotel, entertainment, construction, retail, restaurant, and tourist industries, to name a few (Smith, 2009).

According to the world-systems theory (Wallerstein, 1974), there are three levels of social, political, and economic engagement: (1) core, (2) semi-periphery, and (3) periphery. Globally, the core refers to imperial and colonizing countries or entities that militarily and economically dominate periphery countries through violence and resource extraction (Wallerstein, 1974). The semi-periphery refers to countries or entities that possess characteristics of both the core (economic exploitation of periphery countries) and periphery countries (exploited by core countries). Periphery countries or entities are those that are forced to submit labor and other resources to support the economic sustainability of the core countries (Wallerstein, 1974). Within Smith's (2009) application of world-systems theory to the U.S. context, the NCAA constitutes the core, the member institutions of the NCAA are the semi-periphery, and African American college athletes represent the periphery. The core has constructed a structure to exploit African American college athletes for their labor while monopolizing the intercollegiate athletic market. The infusion of a global theory that encompasses both racial and economic exploitation is beneficial for understanding how and why racist conditions in the United States connect to oppressive systems internationally.

Race-Centric Ecological Systems Theories

Several scholars have recommended critical ecological and sociological analyses for redressing systemic, cultural, institutional, and interpersonal racism within sporting spaces (Cooper, 2019; Cunningham, 2010; Martin, 2015; Oseguera, 2010; Sage, 1998; Sage & Eitzen, 2009). For example, Sage (1998) explained the recursive relationship between ideologies (e.g., White racism, capitalism, neoliberalism, etc.), social institutions (e.g., political, economic, educational, and religious), and cultural practices (e.g., sport, music, and art) that result in perpetual social inequalities. Specifically, Sage (1998) described how the ideologies of capitalism or classism, racism, and sexism in the United States are embedded in social institutions and reproduced (and celebrated) in the structure of sports across all levels (youth, interscholastic, intercollegiate, and professional). Thus, recognizing how ideologies influence institutions and cultural practices is foundational to identifying and creating new realities that disrupt and replace these ontological norms rather than reify them.

Challenging previous sport research that examined its intersection with race at the micro-level, Martin (2015) recommended studying the racial socialization of sports through a multidimensional lens. Several propositions reflect Martin's (2015) critical demography of athletic destinations:

1. Racism is a central feature of American social systems.
2. Racism is institutional.
3. Institutions, and the groups and individuals that make them up, reproduce these systems through social practices and policies.
4. Members of the dominant group receive unmerited privileges, while members of the subordinate racial minority groups receive unequal treatment.
5. Racism remains part of our social system, changing in form but not function (p. 18).

More recently, Cooper (2019) presented a race-centric ecological systems framework to analyze the racialized experiences of Black male athletes in the United States. Within this theory, it is argued that in order to understand modern-day racialized outcomes in sport, one must analyze the interplay between chrono (time and space), macro (ideological), exo (institutional), meso (interpersonal), and micro (individual) systems in society. Cooper (2019) also outlined the sub-system in the ecological systems framework, but this level is omitted from the current analysis to focus more on the five levels presented in the chapter. For Blacks in the United States, understanding the history of race-centric social movements over time, such as the Black Liberation Movement through Reconstruction (also referred to as the abolitionist movement) (early 1600s to late 1800s), New Negro Movement (late 1800s to early 1950s), Civil Rights Movement (mid-1950s to late 1960s), Black Power Movement (mid-1960s to 1970s), Black Feminist Movement (late 1960s to 1970s), Hip-Hop Movement (1980s to 2000s), and BLM movement (2010s to present), is essential for examining their access (or lack thereof) to privileges such as sport participation and leadership positions therein (Cooper, 2021; Cooper, Mallery, & Macaulay, 2020). These social movements and the historical context when they manifested constitute the chronosystem.

The macrosystem refers to the influence of ideologies such as White settler colonialism, racism, and capitalism (WSCRC) on political, economic, social, and culture power usurpation in sport. The exosystem refers to the influence of social institutions such as mass media and corporate sponsorships (among others) that have an indirect influence on individual and group experiences and outcomes. The mesosystem refers to the interactions between an individual and those within their immediate environment (e.g., family, school, community, athletic teams, etc.). The microsystem refers to individual schemas (e.g., identities) and actions (e.g., behaviors). The framework posits the interplay between these systems, particularly the prevalence of WSCRC in the

United States and its influence on the structure of sport and the experiences and outcomes of powerful groups subjected to intersecting oppressions (Cooper, 2017), which in many instances involves holistic underdevelopment, exploitation, and marginalization. Although Cooper's (2019) theory focused on gendered racism against Black males, the general framework can be adapted to examine the racialized experiences of various groups facing oppressive realities such as Black people who are not men (women, non–gender conforming, and trans), Latino, Asian, and Native Americans in sport and beyond.

Table 4.6 provides a summary of the anti-racism theories for decolonizing sport discussed in this section.

From Race-Avoidant to Race-Conscious Sporting Spaces

In order to redress the prevalence of racism in sports, there is a need for a paradigm shift from race avoidance to race consciousness. In his book titled *Racism Without Racists: Color-Blind Racism and the Persistence of Racial Inequality in the United States*, Bonilla-Silva (2018) outlined four frames of color-blind racism:

1. Abstract liberalism
2. Naturalization
3. Cultural racism
4. Minimization of racism

TABLE 4.6 Anti-Racism Theories for Decolonizing Sport

Theory	Key tenets	Notable sport scholars
Critical race theory	• Permanence of racism • Whiteness as property norm • Interest convergence • Critique of liberalism • Intersectionality • Counter-storytelling	John N. Singer Kevin Hylton Ben Carrington Akilah Carter-Francique Albert Bimper Joseph N. Cooper
Systemic racism	• Material • Social • Ideological • Unjust enrichment • Unjust impoverishment	John Singer Anthony Weems Justin Garner
Internal colonization	• Colonizers/colonized relationship • Economics • Politics • Racism (individual and institutional) • Social • Cultural • Oscillating migrant laborers	Billy Hawkins
Settler colonialism	• Colonization • Material • Epistemic	Chen Chen Daniel S. Mason
World-systems theory	• Core • Semi-periphery • Periphery	Earl Smith
Race-centric ecological systems framework	• Chronosystem • Macrosystem • Exosystem • Mesosystem • Microsystem	George Sage Lori L. Martin George Cunningham Leticia Oseguera Joseph N. Cooper

Similar to the U.S. government, mainstream sporting institutions in this society perpetuate abstract liberalism by using terms such as equal opportunity and meritocracy. The abstract liberalist view emphasizes individual choice as a primary factor in one's outcomes in society irrespective of sociostructural and environmental conditions. Naturalization is akin to racist eugenics theories such as social Darwinism, which suggest the observable social order is largely determined based on biological preferences and differences rather than socially, economically, and politically contrived arrangements. Cultural racism refers to the use of stereotypes to define group outcomes, such as generalizing the views and behaviors of a group without considering sociostructural or sociohistorical factors. Last, the minimization of racism posits that we live in a post-racial society, especially since the passage of the landmark Civil Rights Acts in the 1960s. This view became magnified when Barack Obama was elected as the first Black president in U.S. history in 2008.

A major flaw in colorblind racist logics, embedded in mainstream U.S. sporting structures, is the inattentiveness to the role of policy in influencing racialized outcomes. Challenging colorblind racism, Kendi (2019) argued that **anti-racism** refers to the creation, promotion, and implementation of race-conscious actions and policies that seek to reduce and eliminate racial inequities. Rather than suggesting good intentions and antidiscrimination laws alone will create equal outcomes across racial lines, Kendi (2019) recommends individuals and institutions acknowledge that racial inequities are a byproduct of political, economic, and social policy decisions that have historically privileged some groups over others—namely, Whites over Blacks. As such, several anti-racist policy ideas are presented for sport leaders, managers, and administrators to consider adopting within their respective organizations to achieve equity and inclusion.

One recommendation for shifting the paradigm in sports is the adoption of the *Continuum on Becoming an Anti-Racist Multicultural Organization* framework (Crossroads Ministry, n.d.). Within this framework, the following six categories are outlined:

1. Exclusive (an exclusionary institution)
2. Passive (a club institution)
3. Symbolic change (a compliance organization)
4. Identity change (an affirming institution)
5. Structural change (a transforming institution)
6. Fully inclusive anti-racist multicultural organization (in a transformed society)

This typology provides organizations with benchmarks to assess the extent to which their efforts are fostering anti-racism, deep-level diversity, and racial equity versus reproducing racism, nominal or no surface-level diversity, and racial inequities. In addition, the authors of this framework delineate institutions based on whether they are monocultural, multicultural, anti-racist, or anti-racist multicultural (Crossroads Ministry, n.d.). The differences between these categories lie in the intentionality, depth, and impact of their missions, policies, composition, and practices. It is recommended institutions adopt this framework to engage in critical self-reflection on and concerted action with their policies and subsequent impacts.

Along the same lines, Fay and Wolff (2009) presented an organizational continuum of sport governance that examined the extent to which sport entities acknowledged and addressed ableism. The continuum included six classifications for organizational governance:

1. Exclusive club
2. Lip service to inclusion
3. Tokenism
4. Critical mass
5. Tolerating/accepting diversity
6. Valuing diversity

Monoculturalism is the least progressive approach, grounded in exclusion, and multiculturalism is the most progressive approach, grounded in inclusion (Fay & Wolff, 2009). Both frameworks serve as analytical tools for sport organizations to examine how and if they are reinforcing, resisting, or replacing prevailing ideologies (e.g., racism, sexism, classism, ageism, ableism, heterosexism, etc.). In addition, organizations can examine how they are consciously or unconsciously reflecting on the four central frames of color-blind racism (abstract liberalism, naturalization, cultural racism, and minimization of racism) (Bonilla-Silva, 2018). Connecting with racial justice–oriented organizations to assist with changing these behaviors is also recommended. Organizations such as the BLM, Color of Change, Boston University Center for Antiracist Research, Equal Justice Initiative (EJI), the People's Institute for Survival and Beyond (PISAB), and National Association for the Advancement of Colored People (NAACP) are a few of numerous possible partnerships that could be pursued.

A.R.C. of Justice

Another useful anti-racist framework is what I call the A.R.C.[5] of Justice (see table 4.7). Each letter of the acronym includes five components that are important for organizations to know, reflect upon, and activate on a consistent basis to foster anti-racism within their spheres of influence.

A.R.C. of Justice: A Components

The five components of A include *agency, advocacy, allyship, activism,* and *alliances*. *Agency* refers to "the use of personal choice and/or group actions to express a sense of individuality and/or sociocultural disposition within a specific context" (Cooper, 2021, p. 76). Sport organizations often sanctioned behaviors that violate ethical standards, but seldom do they incentivize anti-racist actions. As such, organizational cultures *and* climates that value and support racial justice–oriented agency are recommended. Equity-minded and anti-racist institutions create conditions that encourage agency grounded in social justice aims. *Advocacy* refers to "intentional actions taken by an individual or group to generate awareness of and galvanize support for addressing specific social issues and conditions" (Cooper, 2021, p. 86). Currently, sport organizations engage in corporate social responsibility, but an anti-racist approach would involve assessing the extent to which these advocacy efforts reduce racial disparities within society at large. For example, sport organizations could advocate for, and role model through their own efforts, the implementation of reparations for African Americans (see Darity & Mullen, 2020, for expansive discussion) and Native Americans (Chen & Mason, 2019). Beyond land acknowledgments, organizations can advocate for Native Americans by directly confronting the racialized consequences of settler colonialism (e.g., returning the stolen land that many sport facilities are currently located on and building authentic and sustainable partnerships with them) (Chen & Mason, 2019; Turick et al., 2019).

Allyship refers to concerted efforts to support an individual or group who identifies with a different identity than oneself. For example, when a person who identifies as White expresses dissent with issues that harm individuals and groups that identify as Black then they are engaging in allyship. Many sport organizations employ and serve largely White constituents. In addition to diversifying their organizations, these entities can partner with racial justice–oriented groups to learn about the most effective ways to engage in allyship. For

TABLE 4.7 The A.R.C. of Justice

A	R	C
Agency	Respectful relationships	Consciousness
Advocacy	Representation	Care to conviction
Allyship	Resources	Cross-cultural collaborations
Activism	Redress	Courage
Alliances	Results	Commitment

[5] Darity and Mullen (2020) offered a compelling case for reparations for African Americans and presented an A.R.C. framework that focused on acknowledgment, redress, and closure. The A.R.C. of Justice presented in this chapter is distinct, yet the focus on racial justice and reconciliation is an overlapping theme of both models.

Allyship involves concerted efforts to support an individual or group who identifies with a different identity than oneself.
Ira L. Black - Corbis/Getty Images

example, there are numerous Black student athlete-led groups at HWIs across the country (e.g., Texas Tech University, University of California at Los Angeles, The Ohio State University, and Louisiana State University to name a few). It would behoove these athletic departments to listen to and support these organizations to learn about ways in which institutional allyship for racial equity can be fostered. *Activism* refers to disruptive actions that challenge inequitable arrangements and seek to replace these conditions with more equitable ones (Cooper, 2021; Cooper et al., 2019; Cooper et al., 2020). In contrast to penalizing and stigmatizing activism by athletes and staff, sport organizations should work with various stakeholders (internally and externally) to promote activism that contributes to social justice. Discussing, strategizing, and executing different types of activism as outlined in the African American Sport Activism Typology (AASAT) is recommended (symbolic, scholarly, grassroots, mass mobilization, legal, economic, political/civic, media, music and art, and military). (For extended discussions of the AASAT, see Cooper 2021, Cooper et al. 2019, and Cooper et al. 2020.) *Alliances* refers to strategic partnerships grounded in racial and social justice. Currently, it is not uncommon for sport organizations to donate money to social justice organizations. However, an anti-racist approach would involve more in-depth collaborations between sport and social justice organizations to ensure the values of anti-racism, equity, diversity, and inclusion are optimized within and beyond sporting spaces. These alliances could focus on intersectional issues that extend beyond national boundaries.

A.R.C. of Justice: R Components

The five components of R are *respectful relationships*, *representation*, *resources*, *redress*, and *results*. *Respectful relationships* for all human beings across identity backgrounds are paramount for any justice efforts. As noted earlier, socially constructed human hierarchies were established to commodify and subordinate certain groups (e.g., African Americans) (Bell, 1980, 1992; Feagin, 2006). An anti-racist approach to respectful relationships would acknowledge that athletes are human beings deserving of the rights and privileges afforded to all U.S. citizens as well as their non-athlete peers. Thus, sport organizations seeking to engage in anti-racist respectful relationships would adopt Native American land acknowledgment statements, ban former Confederate/pro-slavery names from facilities, and celebrate the contributions of Black, Latino, Asian, and Native Americans to sport (Chen & Mason, 2019; Turick et al., 2020). *Representation* in anti-racist terms involves both surface-level and deep-level diversity. An example of an anti-racist policy in sport would build upon the NFL's Rooney Rule and establish inclusion hires whereby position descriptions include expansive preferred qualities that account for the lived experiences, skills, and perspectives possessed by people from diverse backgrounds (Cooper et al., 2020). Affirmative action plans should also be viewed as a form of restorative justice rather than perceived as reverse racism. Establishing racial equity plans that utilize resources such as the TIDES Racial and Gender Report Cards and the Advancement for Blacks in Sport (ABIS) reports (see Sport Industry Diversity Initiative sidebar) is recommended. The expansion and amplification of initiatives such as the NCAA's Dr. Charles Whitcomb Leadership Institute, whereby intentional pathway programs are established to increase readiness and representation in sport leadership positions across diverse backgrounds, is also recommended (Cooper et al., 2020).

Similarly, *resources* (tangible and intangible sources of empowerment) should be allocated with a race-conscious approach. Anti-racist resource approaches for sport organizations would involve reallocation of funds toward communities that have been historically underserved and exploited due to systemic racism (Hawkins, 2010). These communities can be identified based on connections to athletes associated within the organization as well as those located in the same cities, states, or regions as the teams themselves. For example, in a city such as Atlanta, professional teams could reallocate monies to neighborhoods in south and southwest Atlanta to promote economic growth, access to quality healthcare, and educational attainment (e.g., Bankhead, College Park, etc.). Related to resources, *redress* involves correcting a previous harm caused by an individual, group, institution, and/or organization. Thus, instead of engaging in ahistorical colorblind racist postures such as equal opportunity for all, anti-racist and race-conscious sport organizations acknowledge the harms caused by current and previous policies and seek to redress them (Cooper, 2016). For example, the NCAA could pass legislation accounting for the unjust impoverishment toward Black college athletes in profit generating sports (as well as their non-Black peers in the same sports) (Cooper et al., 2017; Feagin, 2006) and create economic repayment packages (Huma & Staurowsky, 2020). A similar effort could be issued toward HBCUs, Hispanic serving institutions (HSIs), and Native American Tribal institutions (NATIs) athletic programs

Sport Industry Diversity Initiative

ADVANCEMENT OF BLACKS IN SPORTS (ABIS)

Advancement of Blacks in Sports (ABIS) was founded in 2020 to pursue "equal rights and fair treatment of Black people by examining current institutional policies and practices in an effort to promote racial, social, and economic justice" (ABIS, 2021, p. 1). The organization consists of over 100 leaders in the sport industry—administrators, coaches, consultants, scholars, community advocates, and business leaders. ABIS produces research and reports to enhance public awareness of racial inequities and injustices in sport. ABIS also provides consultation to leagues, teams, and institutions seeking to promote racial justice through their policies and practices.

ABIS focuses on the following six areas of advocacy: (1) economic sustainability, (2) education, (3) grassroots and community outreach, (4) racial equity research, (5) athletes, and (6) voting and civic engagement (ABIS, 2021). This race-centric organization believes the status quo of exploiting and marginalizing Black athletes, coaches, administrators, and athletic staff must be addressed through sustained collective action. Its racial equity efforts include interventions at the youth, interscholastic, intercollegiate, and professional levels. Committees with ABIS address topics such as racial equity research, standardized tests, voter registration, student athlete internships, hiring practices, Black Lives Matter advocacy, and an education initiative on teaching African American history (ABIS, 2021). Building on the legacy of the now-defunct Black Coaches Association, ABIS seeks to change the landscape of sport by creating more racial equity and concurrently foster similar outcomes in society more broadly.

and conferences (Cooper et al., 2014). Historical and contemporary exclusion and marginalization could be redressed through racial equity plans that account for multilevel racism. Consulting with race-centric sport advocacy organizations such as ABIS is recommended. Replacing current sport organizations that were founded with racist origins and the creation of new ones that are grounded in anti-racism is also encouraged. *Results* refers to observable outcomes that reflect the effectiveness of policies and practices in fostering racial equity. Eliminating racial disparities and inequities should be the benchmark of success for sport organizations beyond intentions, symbolic gestures, revenue generation, profit margins, viewership, popularity, and championships.

A.R.C. of Justice: C Components

The five components of C are *consciousness*, *care to conviction*, *cross cultural collaborations*, *courage*, and *commitment*. *Consciousness* involves the cultivation of critical self, institutional, societal, and civilizational awareness of how inequities manifest through systems across time and space. Using the race-conscious theories, scholars, advocacy, and activist groups cited throughout this text could facilitate conscious raising in sport organizations. *Care to conviction* refers to the internationalization and expression of concern for people and specific issues accompanied by a deep feeling of obligation to engage in concerted actions to change the status quo. Specifically, care to conviction involves a focus on improving the holistic life outcomes for a particular group that has been subjected to unjust treatment (also referred to as restorative justice). The NCAA has implemented a presidential pledge focused on racial and gender equity. This is a step in a progressive direction, but institutional care to conviction would be reflected in incentives, penalties, and position descriptions for fulfilling these desired aims (Cooper et al., 2020). If sport organizations truly care about Native Americans and convicted to be race-conscious actors, the use of mascots referencing their cultures should never be considered and explicit apologies and retribution should be issued for previous usage. Artifacts/symbols, missions, values, policies, and practices should signify care for all groups and specifically those who have historically be oppressed by White settler colonialism, racism, and capitalism (WSCRC). *Cross-cultural collaborations* refer to the intentional partnering with groups from diverse racial and ethnic backgrounds to foster optimal experiences and outcomes across and within various geographical, social, economic, and political contexts. It is recommended mainstream sport organizations partner with institutions and organizations that champion racial equity, particularly those that represent groups who have faced (and continue to face) oppressive realities, to establish conditions that improve social justice within and beyond sporting spaces. *Courage* refers to the willingness to challenge the status quo to create more racial justice in society in spite of the presence of apprehension, fear, and dissent. Supporting and at times leading activism grounded in racial justice is an example of courage, which was typified by the Women's National Basketball Association (WNBA) during the Summer of 2020 with their BLM demonstrations (Cooper, 2021). Last, *commitment* refers to protracted engagement (lifelong in the case of individuals and intergenerational in the case of institutions and organizations) in racial and social justice efforts. In the spirit of anti-racism, commitment remains until the inequities are eliminated in perpetuity.

SUMMARY

The purpose of this chapter was to outline multilevel racism in sports in the United States and present a paradigm shift for fostering anti-racism, diversity (surface-level and more importantly deep-level), equity, and inclusion. The distinct levels of racism occur at the individual, institutional, societal, and civilizational levels. Key terms such as equity, equality, diversity, inclusion, culture, climate, and anti-racism are important to understand and appropriately infuse in organizational policies and practices. Scholarly theories such as critical race theory, systemic racism, internal colonization, settler colonialism, world-systems theory, and race-centric ecological systems theories are useful for sport leaders, managers, and practitioners seeking to optimize racial equity within their organizations and society at large. Finally, the chapter concludes with the presentation of a paradigm shift for the sport industry including recommendations for promoting anti-racism and highlighting current efforts achieving this aim.

CRITICAL THINKING EXERCISES

1. Review a current or previous event that involves a racial inequity or injustice in sport (e.g., the University of Texas "The Eyes of Texas" alma mater song example from 2021 cited in the introduction) and provide a reflection on this incident using key concepts from the chapter.
2. Review The Institute for Diversity and Ethics in Sports (TIDES) Racial and Gender Report Cards and select one theory from the chapter to analyze the findings.
3. Review the NCAA's (2021) Student Athlete Engagement in Activism and Social Justice Report from their website and use key concepts from the chapter to analyze the findings.

REVIEW QUESTIONS

1. What are the four distinct levels of racism?
2. What are the differences between equity, equality, diversity, and inclusion?
3. What is the difference between organizational culture and climate?
4. What are the six theories outlined in the chapter that could be useful in understanding racism and decolonizing sport?
5. What is the A.R.C. of Justice and its applicability to sport organizations?

CHAPTER 5

Power Play: Race and Ethnicity in Sports

Beau Manierre Houston and Jeffrey Montez de Oca

LEARNING OBJECTIVES

- Gain foundational knowledge for understanding intersectionality concepts and evidence of their impact on diverse and vulnerable populations in athletic settings.
- Consider social and cultural diversity as a means of facilitating conversations on race and ethnicity in sports.
- Understand how power intersects with racial identity development in adolescent athlete participants.
- Integrate inclusive excellence principles into sports management decision-making.
- Apply critical thinking skills to create strategies and illustrate sound judgment based on given resources and circumstances to achieve desired outcomes.

Sixteen-year-old Ghanaian-born Gertrude Lamb confronted the Tyler Independent School District school board in Tyler, Texas, to address the naming of Robert E. Lee High School. Controversy over the school's name followed the summer of 2020's racial reckoning led by the Black Lives Matter movement, which accelerated examination of societal and organizational symbols for expressions of racism (Lee, 2020). Gertrude's journey through adoption from an orphanage in Ghana at the age of 10 landed her in the comforts of a White American family. In a letter to the board, she wrote, "I am from Ghana, Africa, where slavery first began. I can't be playing sports, supporting, and going to a school that was named after a person who was against my people right here in the United States. I cannot bear it and will no longer wear his name on my race jersey." Lamb's story intersects global history with local schools and communities in the present, as well as the role of athletics in those communities.

Gertrude's concern stemmed from the ongoing veneration of Robert E. Lee, a member of the slaveholding aristocracy of the Confederate South, who justified slavery as a peculiar societal institution necessary to maintain order between the races (Gallagher, 2020). Renaming places named after Robert E. Lee was a topic of concern in the 1970s, during a period of racial integration, and in 2017 in response to the Unite the Right rally in Charlottesville, Virginia. In August 2020, Tyler Legacy High School became the high school's name, and the board approved a new policy preventing the district from naming a school after any person, whether they have served the school district or community or are a person who is viewed as a local, state, or national heroic figure (Frazier et al., 2020).

The experience of racial and ethnic discrimination is not limited to high school athletics. Asian American Olympic athletes widely report the experience of racial discrimination even as they compete for their nation (Silva, 2021). Snowboarder and Olympic gold medalist Chloe Kim has reported receiving racist and misogynistic abuse online across her career, but extenuated during the COVID-19 pandemic, simply because she is Asian American (Kim, 2021). Further, scholars have documented how the media tends to use dehumanizing and racist caricatures to describe Asian American athletes at the Olympics (Namkung, 2021). And when a *New York Times* reporter confused Marai Nagasu of Montebello, California, for an immigrant, it recalled the 1998 MSNBC headline that read "American Beats Out Kwan" in reference to Tara Lipinski winning gold over (American) Michelle Kwan of Torrance, California (Randall, 2018), because each invokes the racial stereotype that Asians are forever foreign.

These anecdotes illustrate how race, ethnicity, and sports often collide to etch out complexities associated with people, time, symbols, and geography across a range of sports organizations. Specifically, racialized minority groups face a raft of challenges from institutional discrimination and modern racism that often show up in athletic spaces (Healey & Stepnick, 2019). Not recognizing these types of collisions and the debris they produce widens the inequities marginalized minority groups navigate, further perpetuates their marginalization, and deepens the impact of negative responses, both intended and unintended, from those in power positions (American Psychological Association, 2012).

This chapter examines how the intersection of sports, race, and ethnicity affects discussions and understanding about social and cultural diversity of sports leaders and the communities they serve. We argue that to recognize the complexities created by race and ethnicity, sports leaders need to adopt an intersectional perspective, because taking a "color-blind" perspective on race simply makes people blind to racism (Bonilla-Silva, 2006). To do so, we will describe the value of using intersectionality as a framework of theory and praxis to understand how power and control affect racially and ethnically diverse and vulnerable populations, and the choice to couple **inclusive excellence** with strategic planning and sound judgment. We will further illustrate our argument by focusing on the diverse demographics of K-12 educational settings and the important position interscholastic athletic directors serve as sport leaders in their communities. We conclude by presenting an Athletic Power Play Framework that any sport leader can use for adopting an intersectional perspective when engaged in problem-solving.

Intersectionality

To better understand the relationships between racially and ethnically diverse participants in sports and to understand the depth of their lived experiences in these interactions, we lean on the analysis and praxis tools of intersectionality. **Intersectionality** describes the interconnected nature of social identities, such as race, class, and ethnicity, within overlapping and interdependent systems of discrimination or oppression (Crenshaw, 1989; OED, 2020). At its core, it is an analytical tool derived from critical race theory (CRT) discussed in chapter 4. CRT focuses on dominant legal claims of neutrality, objectivity, color blindness, and meritocracy as camouflages for society's powerful oppressive forces (Chapman, Dixson, Gillborn, & Ladson-Billings, 2013; Tate, 1997). The two themes that guide intersectional analysis combine an approach to understanding human life and behavior rooted in the experiences and struggles of disenfranchised people, and using it as an essential tool linking theory with practice that can aid in the empowerment of communities and individuals (Collins & Bilge, 2016, p. 36).

This foundation requires intersectionality to exercise two organizational focal points, critical inquiry and critical praxis, that function synergistically as a form of investigation, analysis, and response (Collins & Bilge, 2016).

Conceptually, intersectionality is useful for capturing and theorizing the simultaneity of identity-based oppression and is necessary to understand the relationships of race, ethnicity, and other combinations of marginalizing identities. Further, it helps to address populations not typically represented in the discussion of identity, social oppression, or social justice in sporting spaces (Simien, Arinze, & McGarry, 2019; Wijeyesinghe, 2012). Kimberlé Crenshaw (1989) coined the term "intersectionality" when she showed how laws intended to combat either racism or sexism in the workplace did not address how Black women can experience workplace discrimination. Black women and girls figure prominently in intersectionality theory since they are subject to forms of sexism and racism specific to their identities as Black and female (Simien, Arinze, & McGarry, 2019). The Black feminist movement of the 1960s, created to combat tension within social movements of the time (civil rights, Black Power, Chicano liberation, and Pan-Asian movements), confronted their equity differences related to gender, race, and class (Springer, 2005). The development of intersectionality has deep roots not easily organized by time or geographic location, but it includes groups like the Combahee River Collective and the National Black Feminist Organization, as well as Chicana writers and activists like Cherrie Moraga and Gloria Anzaldúa, who edited *This Bridge Called My Back*, a collection of writings by Black and Indigenous women and other women of color who were doing intersectionality before the term was coined (Collins & Bilge, 2020). Since then, intersectionality as a concept for analysis, established through social and political movements and expressed through various art mediums, has developed into a tool commonly used by social institutions to recognize the vulnerabilities of formerly excluded citizens and assess their organizations' responsibility to understand how power operates in those spaces.

Intersectionality provides a powerful understanding of the relationship between marginalizing identities, like race and ethnicity, in a sporting context because it calls attention to the texture and consequences of inequalities experienced by individuals and groups given their social membership, and it illustrates how their subjectivities are embedded within systemic dynamics of power (Rodriguez, Holvino, Fletcher, & Nkomo, 2016). First, intersectionality acknowledges that individuals can simultaneously inhabit positions of both privilege and marginality and that these social positions influence the experience of identity (Collins, 2015; Simien, Arinze, & McGarry, 2019). Second, intersectionality offers a way of understanding and analyzing complexity in the world, in people, and in human experiences. In particular, it provides the ability to call attention to and explore the intersecting power relationships vital for resisting social inequality (Collins & Bilge, 2016; Dill & Zambrana, 2009). Third, intersectionality operates as a social justice intervention by guiding initiatives that can create effective strategies for delivering equitable opportunity, security, and well-being to people historically marginalized and underserved (Wijeyesinghe, 2012). As a complex, multiuse concept, intersectionality allows researchers and practitioners to diagnose experiences of diverse groups and implement solutions that foster social justice.

Examining Sport With an Intersectional Lens

Using an intersectional lens to examine professional, professionalized, and youth sports has grown among scholars. It centers athletes' varied lived experiences and offers evidence to initiate multilevel change in teams, organizations, and leagues that govern them.

Professional Sports and Intersectionality

An intersectional perspective is necessary to understand professional and professionalized sports. Many scholars have noted how race, gender, and capital accumulation operate to create crisis and opportunity in the NBA. The emergent dominance of Black men in the 1970s created an image of the NBA as becoming too Black, which resulted in White viewership declining. Anxieties about Black masculinities in a space of White consumption triggered increased policing of players by league officials in order to maintain capital accumulation. Under Commissioner Stern, a project was undertaken to control how Black masculinity was presented on and off the court, or what Hughes (2004) calls "managing Black guys." Marston (2020) provides a clear example of this when describing rules changes that took place in the NBA between 1990 and 2006, including "the dress code." Marston shows that ongoing White fears of and desires for the power of Black male athletes created the need to exert visible controls over those bodies so that NBA basketball could remain a safe, comfortable space of White consumption. "NBA players constituted a community of hyper-visibly Black men . . . Onto their bodies were mapped ideas about violent, deviant Black masculinity" (Marston, 2020, p. 128). At the same time, racialized images of "the ghetto" connected to constructions of "authentic" Blackness have been crucial for branding and selling NBA basketball (Oates, 2020). So although in recent years the NBA has come to be seen as racially progressive, it is important to understand how race and gender can intersect in ways that undermine the goals of inclusive excellence.

Professional athletes engaging in protests against state violence in communities of color further illustrates the need for an intersectional perspective. The increasing circulation of images on social media of police and vigilante violence against unarmed Black citizens in the United States triggered waves of athletic protests. These protests were spearheaded by Black women in collegiate basketball and the WNBA; they would later spread to the NBA and the NFL and be crystalized in the protests symbolized by Colin Kaepernick (Montez de Oca and Suh, 2020). When Kaepernick received notoriety, the protests spread like a prairie fire and were enacted by athletes, coaches, and officials from professional to youth sports and a panoply of sports besides football (Montez de Oca and Suh, 2020). McDonald (2020) illustrated how histories of exclusion and oppression get mobilized during anthem protests when she analyzed the Indigenous music trio Asani's rendition of the Canadian national anthem before an NHL hockey game and Kaepernick's protest during the U.S. national anthem prior to NFL football games. The musicality of the protest taps into deep wells of emotions. Protests for racial justice demonstrate that athletes, coaches, officials, fans, and even artists bring diverse histories of oppression to athletics that sports leaders need to understand.

Moraga (2018) shows that intersectionality is not only important on the field, it is also important to the broader sports industry. Recognizing opportunities to profit from the growing Latinx sport fanbase, ESPN launched ESPN Deportes in 2004 to provide 24-hour, bilingual (Spanish and English) sport content. ESPN Deportes reveals contradictory tendencies of a commercial sport network that targets the Latinx market. On the one hand, its shows can educate White and non-White audiences on the heterogeneity of Latinidad, dispel damaging stereotypes, and celebrate a language often stigmatized in the United States. On the other hand, as a commercial venture, the critique of race and racism on the network is often limited. Discussing the Max y Marly podcast, Moraga writes, "for all its usefulness as a cultural text that responds to a set of sociohistorical issues rooted in discrimination, mainstream nativism, and sexism, the podcast also inevitably reproduces problematic ideals of racial capitalism" (Moraga, 2018, p. 489). Moraga shows us that an initiative claiming the goals of inclusive excellence, as does ESPN Deportes, without a careful, intersectional analysis may actually undermine achieving those very goals.

Collegiate Athletics and Intersectionality

Carter-Francique (2020) describes a multilevel intersectional approach that contextualizes competing constructs when responding responsibly to the historical and contemporary stereotypes that Black collegiate sportswomen experience and that affect their choices, experience, and outcomes. First, she suggests an initial account of structural intersections, or overlapping structures, at play and counter them with cultural competency and culturally relevant practices. Next, addressing political intersections requires a critical lens to precisely define intended and unintended legislative consequences when two subordinated identities (Black and woman) pursue conflicting agendas. Last, combating representational intersections involves identifying and challenging negative media images and overall representational lack while working to create new positive replacements. This holistic use of intersectional analysis is consistent with the theoretical foundation of rooting out power

Using an intersectional lens to examine college sports centers athletes' varied lived experiences and offers evidence to initiate multilevel change in teams, organizations, and leagues that govern them.
Rich Schultz/Getty Images

imbalance and providing and implementing solutions, a praxis necessity.

Anderson and McCormack (2010) examined the impact of Black and White racial categories and sexual identity for gay and straight athletic American men to focus on the interlocking categories of oppression that limit athletes who are both gay and Black. In this case, intersectionality proves the negotiation of visible (race) and invisible (sexuality) identities and the impact on elevated rates of discrimination through racism, overt prejudices like homophobia, and measures of masculinity through demonstrations of physical superiority or inferiority in competitive spaces. The intersection of racism and homophobia in education and athletic settings describes another example of **positionality**, the power inherent in a person's immediate respective social position that dramatically influences the difference in what individuals have access to in society (Misawa, 2006). Analyzing institutional and cultural oppression and their similarities of oppression across identity groups creates more inclusive spaces for which athletes, administrators, and spectators benefit (Anderson & McCormack, 2010), and it is the responsibility of schools to establish inclusive practices that recognize diverse and inferior-positioned students (Misawa, 2006).

In another example, Wilkins (2014) looked at gender, class, and race in the context of how identity processes and social integration affect the construction of satisfying adulthood pathways. The author found that for Black and first-generation White men entering and matriculating through higher education, educational experiences and high school identity strategies, defined as the cultural scripts used to facilitate their intersectional identity locations, matter for college identity experiences and influence how differently situated these students construct pathways to adulthood. In analyzing pathways into college, Wilkins recognized the role of interscholastic sports in adolescent and adult experiences. Sports participation helped curb interactions that resulted in a range of out-of-school trouble for both Black and White high school–aged men, but specifically sports for Black male athletes also bolstered their social status and popularity and provided a space to associate with Black masculinity and claim Black authenticity. However, these high school strategies were effective for White men but did not carry over to college success for Black men, which exemplifies how intersecting visible (race) and invisible (class) identities supported White men but challenged Black men's ability to convert athletic careers into success in college.

Finally, using intersectionality to examine ethnic and athletic identity illustrates the operation of racialized remarks, peer stigmas, and cultural obligations that prioritize family experienced by Latinx male athletes at NCAA Division I sports (Ortega, 2021). In this case, athletic identity is viewed as the second negatively stereotyped or marginalized identity for Latinx male athletes. Discriminatory language was directed toward Latinx male athletes when other teammates referred to the consequences of immigration in relation to athletic ability, taunting by spectators during competition in the form of racial slurs, and by ridicule for conversationally engaging in their primary Spanish language. The athletic identity also created contentions with nonathlete peer groups when athletics is prioritized over Latinx affinity student organization and viewed as a form of assimilation or "acting White" (Ortega, 2021). Ortega (2021) recommends intentional acceptance of diverse student groups through the use of ethnic studies courses for the good of the greater student body and counter-spaces to establish support groups that work to provide academic, athletic, and social enhancement opportunities. **Counter-spaces**, originally created by African American students at predominantly White institutions, are recognizable spaces where marginalized students can be intellectually and socially challenged and where an empowering academic racial climate can be established and maintained (Ortega, 2021; Solorzano & Yosso, 2001). These collegiate examples and recommendations are transferable to their younger counterparts and the administrators that serve them.

High School Sports and Intersectionality

Consider some of the following examples of intersectional approaches to interscholastic sports participants, which further highlight their complexity and depth. First, Dagkas (2016) used intersectionality to provide an effective platform for legitimizing "non-normative bodies" (diverse bodies) in health pedagogy and physical education and sport by recognizing that racism, sexism, classism, and other factors constrain Black and ethnic minority young people's access to holistic, meaningful, and empowering learning in formal and informal sport and physical culture. Dagkas (2016) found a need for two-way communication between schools and families regarding physical fitness and that stakeholders need education and training to incorporate greater awareness of social identities into formal and informal pedagogical contexts.

McGovern (2020) described the experiences of college-educated Latinas who played interscholastic high school sports in the United States to demonstrate that social class and nativity influence sport choices. The author's findings revealed that the daughters of middle-class and native-born families have resources to access organized sport and prioritize participation, beginning sport at an early age, and that they benefited from consistent support during their athletic careers. Lower-class and immigrant families place a lower value on organized sport and have fewer resources to access opportunities. Class and generation also intersect with gender, race, and ethnicity to influence when women join organized sports and how they make sense of their athletic participation.

Finally, Denham (2019) examined the extent to which adolescent sports participation associated with concern about the treatment of racial minority groups and worry about race relations in the United States. He found that Latinx female 12th-grade athletes expressed greater concern about minority treatment, while Black female participants indicated more significant worry about race relations. In the same study, Denham (2019) found that baseball and softball participants who were predominantly White expressed less concern about racially minoritized groups but did not differ from other athletes' attitudes toward race relations. Additionally, while Black adolescents competing in baseball, softball, and soccer worried about race relations at relatively high levels, those competing in basketball expressed significantly less concern. Denham's complex theoretical framework showed how concentrated effort in interscholastic sport led to shared experiences and goals that minimize difference and level power. This exhibits the essence of intersectionality in how it functions to describe how oppression exists in societal structures that identities determine, and how these structures perpetuate hierarchies and orchestrate arrangements of interaction and coexistence (Hahn, 2013).

Continuous examination of multilevel legislation is a minimum standard when considering the challenges faced by community members with vulnerable intersecting identities of all types. This review of policies requires legislation to be developed or revised to respond to ongoing systemic oppressions prevalent in scholastic athletics and inevitable conflicts emerging from societal change. Carter-Francique's (2020) analysis of political intersections is useful to understand the examples of political intersectionality in interscholastic sports. These political intersections emerge when individuals are situated within at least two vulnerable group identities that pursue conflicting political agendas, like race, gender, and ethnicity, and often result in tangible loss. Beginning at the federal level, there has been considerable progress in women's sport participation opportunities since enacting Title IX of the Education Amendments Act of 1972, a policy designed to promote gender equity and equality in education (Pickett, 2009). These opportunities have allowed women and girls to participate in sports at the primary and secondary school level and the collegiate level in considerable numbers. However, when Title IX intersects with the Civil Rights Act of 1964, it

Sport Industry Leader Profile

B. Elliot Hopkins, MLD, CAA

Title: Director of Sports, Sanctioning, and Student Services at National Federation of State High School Associations

Education: BA (Sociology), Wake Forest University; MA (Leadership Development), St. Mary of the Woods College

B. Elliot Hopkins is passionate about serving as the director of sports, sanctioning, and student services for the National Federation of State High School Associations (NFHS) and editor of the NFHS baseball and wrestling rule books and case studies. Hopkins is also the director of the NFHS student leadership summit. He speaks nationally to students about hazing prevention and sportsmanship, beginning a second term as a board member of the Hazing Prevention organization and contributing to the online NFHS course on creating a safe and respectful environment. Finally, he serves on the USA Baseball board of directors as board secretary, representing the NFHS, and is a long-standing committee member of the USA Baseball sports medicine advisory committee. The former Wake Forest University football player and 1975 Brian Piccolo scholarship recipient recognizes the role of interscholastic sports as a vessel for academic enrichment, community collaboration, and a gateway toward college athletic participation.

What Was Your Career Path?

As you can imagine, I have a passion for young people and use my time to support my community and their many organizations. I am originally from Chicago, Illinois, and work to embody the complete athletic and activities administrator's role in interscholastic spaces. My professional and community service experiences cover a broad spectrum of responsibilities that contribute to amateur athletes' development. I have coached both boys and girls in elementary and junior high school basketball programs in Harrisburg, Pennsylvania, and led as a private elementary school's former athletic administrator. Also, I am a former consultant

has been shown to disproportionately exclude Black girls from participation (Pickett, 2009; Theune, 2019). Although White female sport participation has soared since Title IX, public schools where Black females are the majority offer fewer sport participation opportunities to girls. This shows that interscholastic athletic access and participation opportunities for females are unevenly distributed along racial lines. The outcomes of Title IX illustrate how laws narrowly targeting gender progress do not advantage all women evenly, and why it is so important to be attentive to how racism and classism intersect with sexism.

Interscholastic Sports: A Case Study

Competitive high school sports in the United States reflect many of the challenges across the sports industry with management and participants' experiences of the relationships between race, ethnicity, and sports. With more than 23,000 high school athletic departments, approximately 300,000 administrators, coaches, and officials, and more than 7.9 million students participating in interscholastic competitions, careful consideration is required for the for the New Jersey Department of Secondary Education, an instructor within the Indiana Department of Education School Safety Academy, and the Kentucky Center for School Safety, a Kentucky School Boards Association division.

Currently, I am in my 22nd year with the federation, and my primary responsibilities are high school baseball, high school wrestling, sanctioning, and student services. Currently, I serve on the USA Baseball board of directors as board secretary representing the NFHS and continue to serve as a long-standing committee member of USA Baseball Sports Medicine Advisory Committee. I work for 51 different state associations, and those commissioners and directors are my bosses. I value and support the work of diversity, equity, and inclusion at NFHS despite being the only male person of color (we have one Black woman) the National Federation has ever hired as a rules director in its 100-year history. So, you could say I am like the Jackie Robinson of it. People watch us, and they look at us because we are the only one of our type. Our voice at NFHS has to be diverse, and we have to show the world that we look like the world.

I came to the federation through the Pennsylvania Interscholastic Athletic Association (PIAA), where I am a retired basketball official and was the assistant executive director for several years. I learned a tremendous amount in that role, since Pennsylvania is the eighth largest state regarding participation numbers, and we operated with a staff of three. My duties included management and organization of specific PIAA championships, and I created and implemented the state's first sportsmanship program, "Sportsmanship—The Only Missing Piece Is You!" As a member of the PIAA executive staff, I represented Pennsylvania as the chair of the NFHS sportsmanship, ethics, and integrity committee, served as cochair of the NFHS citizenship committee, and was a member of the NFHS sanctioning committee.

At NFHS, we are about athletics and activities, performing arts, speech, debate, cheer, and band—anyone that plays. That's the bulk of our 12 million young people who participate in high school sports activities, and I cannot stray too far from those things. Taking advantage of these opportunities gives you a sense of teamwork, which is essential to your development, requires you to learn some things about yourself and become determined not to give up. You also finish with some excellent time management skills. You learn you can accept defeat and win with grace.

experience and outcomes of those involved (Forsyth & Olson, 2013; NFHS, 2020). Interscholastic sports goals include helping adolescents enhance sport skills, physical fitness, self-discipline, sporting behavior, teamwork, time management skills, self-confidence, and mental toughness while promoting life skills and lessons and enhancing academic performance (Lumpkin & Stokowski, 2011). Students making the choice to participate in interscholastic sports expect a sense of belonging and involvement, a connection to the community, and opportunities to gain valuable life skills and lessons (Zayas, 2018).

Examining these factors using a critical lens illuminates power structures in interscholastic sports with regard to race, ethnicity, and social class and requires a closer examination of the demographics of the students and staff that make up these spaces.

Race, Ethnicity, and Social Class in Public Schools

According to the National Center for Education Statistics (NCES), the racial and ethnic diversity of public school students has increased over time (de Brey et al., 2019). Between 2000 and

2017, the percentage of U.S. school-age children who were White decreased by 11 percentage points to 51 percent, and the percent of Black students decreased 1 percent from 15 to 14 percent. The percentages of school-age children from other racial and ethnic groups increased. Latinx children's proportion grew from 16 to 25 percent, the proportion of Asian American children grew from 3 to 5 percent, and the proportion of children of two or more races went from 2 to 4 percent. The percentage of school-age American Indians/Alaska Natives remained at 1 percent, and the percentage of Pacific Islanders remained at less than 1 percent during this time.

Although schools have become more diverse, they also remain highly segregated, which leads to differentiated and unequal experiences. In 2015, schools with more racial and ethnic diversity in their student populations also tended to have more racial and ethnic diversity among teachers. The percentage of ethnic minority teachers was greatest at schools with 90 percent or more ethnic minority students and was lowest at schools with less than 10 percent ethnic minority students (de Brey et al., 2019). Also, approximately 30 percent of public school students attended public schools where the combined enrollment of ethnic minority students was at least 75 percent of total enrollment in fall 2015 (de Brey et al., 2019). The prevalence of racial and ethnic diversity is at the forefront of consideration for modernizing the approach to interscholastic sports and activities.

Social class is an additional characteristic that deepens the categorization of racial and ethnic groups. In 2016, the percentage of children under the age of 18 in families living in poverty was higher for Black children than Latinx children (31 and 26 percent, respectively), while for White and Asian children the numbers were much lower (10 percent each). Among Asian subgroups, however, the percentage of children living in poverty ranged from 6 to 37 percent (de Brey et al., 2019). Among Latinx subgroups in 2016, the percentage of children under age 18 living in poverty ranged from 11 to 38 percent. The intersections of race, ethnicity, and social class of family units and communities affects what sports are available and how they are offered in their schools. Schools with high levels of poverty are still substantially more likely not to offer any interscholastic sports when compared to wealthier schools (Women's Sports Foundation, 2020).

Research demonstrates that the race and ethnicity of teachers has an impact on ethnic minority youth (Smith et al., 2020). The potential pool of teacher-coaches, which refers to teachers who volunteer their time to coach sports teams or accept a stipend to lead their individual school athletic and activity teams, consists of a demographic made up of staff members who are 75 percent White and majority middle-class females (Camiré, 2015). This pool is important given that many athletic directors begin as teacher-coaches since state issued teaching and administrator licenses are usually required for this role. Despite the racially lopsided figures comparing students to staff, individuals who accept these roles have a great responsibility to create, develop, and maintain relationships with athletes based on closeness, commitment, and complementarity (Camiré, 2015; Jowett, 2007).

Awareness of the imbalance between majority White coaches and athletic administrators and their ethnically diverse students requires further understanding of how race and ethnicity affect sporting and educational experiences. Misunderstanding or ignorance can undermine the benefits of interscholastic sports as a teacher of fundamental life skills for students. Confronting Whiteness in sporting and education spaces is necessary for understanding identity in the context of inequalities by considering power evasiveness, normalization processes, and the majority demographic's expectations (Watson & Scraton, 2018). Using a "critical Whiteness" lens to consider positions of power and privilege elevates the conversation of racism beyond societal institutions like the government, economy, and education, and places it in the hands of people who can then choose to adopt or strengthen an anti-racist stance in their everyday problem-solving (Ahmed, 2004).

Schaefer (2009) used the metaphor of a kaleidoscope to describe the pluralistic racial and ethnic experiences of an ethnically rich and multiracial America because it suggests a complex, dynamic image of different color patterns. In educational settings, **cultural pluralism** is "a value based on an appreciation for and encouragement of cultural diversity through simultaneously acknowledging cultural distinctions, promoting cross-cultural relationships, and encouraging the maintenance of the unique cultural identities of subgroups" (Smith et al., 2020, p. 52). Therefore, awareness of the benefits and challenges of pluralism is critical to maturing in education-athletic leadership roles. One wrinkle in this cultural pluralistic lens is that of socioeconomic class, which often maps onto racially segregated landscapes. These segregated landscapes can diminish the general expectation of post-secondary educational mobility patterns of high school athletes, which are further differentiated by gender, race, ethnicity, and school location. Inequalities across different schools limit racial and ethnic minority students' access to post-secondary education, and that in turn concentrates the benefits of interscholastic sports participation for ethnic minority students to high school, whereas predominantly White male athletes are more likely to continue this growth after high school (Melnick & Sabo, 1994).

Students understand the complexity of identity more fully when they can develop relationships with individuals different from them. A part of this identity is rooted in culture. Working on teams with a common goal helps students gain knowledge about their own and others' cultural heritage, family background, and life circumstances, thereby connecting the individuals to the group; groups to society; and individuals, groups, and society to structures of power (Jones & Abes, 2013). Hallinan and Jackson (2008) define **cultural diversity** as "an evolving, value-laden concept that often articulates with other contested concepts such as difference, differentiation, and multiculturalism" (p. 2). The dynamic it creates in interscholastic settings can facilitate acknowledgment, advocacy, and celebration of diversity but also create urgency for protest and discord for those who oppose this stance (Hallinan & Jackson, 2008).

Hammond (2014) theorizes culture as operating on three levels. First, surface culture is

Students understand the complexity of identity more fully when they can develop relationships with individuals different from them.

FatCamera/E+/Getty Images

the visual and concrete elements like food, dress, and music. Second, shallow culture captures the unspoken rules around everyday social interactions and norms, such as courtesy and nonverbal communication, and this is the level where rapport and trust grow. Last, deep culture consists of tacit knowledge and unconscious assumptions that govern our worldview, like ethics and norms. Race and ethnicity do not exist in isolation, and thus, enhancing knowledge sharing and expanding ways of knowing requires the act of intersecting them both with other social, cultural, psychological, and organizational renderings (Armstrong, 2011). Ahmad, Thorpe, Richards, and Marfell (2020) explain that this level of awareness and respect for cultural diversity demands multicultural training initiatives across sports organizations to improve policy and practice and programs.

Intersectional approaches can also illustrate how religious practices and freedom intersect with dynamics of race and ethnicity. The Tennessee Secondary School Athletic Association had a rule for volleyball that stated, "Hair devices made of soft material and no more than 3 inches wide may be worn in the hair or on the head" (Elassar, 2021). However, Valor College Prep High School freshman Najah Aqeel, a practicing Muslim, wore a head covering that exceeded the three-inch standard. To avoid disqualification from competition, she opted out of participation. Supported by the American Muslim Advisory Council, Najah and her family worked with state officials to enact a rule

Sport Industry Diversity Initiative

YOUTH CELEBRATE DIVERSITY

Colorado's Youth Celebrate Diversity (YCD), a nonprofit organization dedicated to educating and empowering youth to advance inclusion and equity for all, believes that education is a fundamental human right and that change comes from within a community rather than originating through outside forces. One of the focus areas of YCD is supporting athletes to make their teams and groups more inclusive and welcoming for everyone's benefit.

Systemic exclusion is apparent in schools when considering that schools provide boys over one million more opportunities to compete than girls (Sabo & Veliz, 2008). When factoring in race, we see exclusions within exclusion. For instance, 65 percent of African American girls who participate in sport through school realize this exclusion often because of their tendencies to attend schools with fewer material resources, human resources, and programs that encourage play (Staurowsky et al., 2020). Similarly, three-quarters of boys from immigrant families participate in athletics, while less than half of girls from immigrant families do. We also see exclusions in U.S. youth sports participation according to income; sports participation among middle and lower-income youth is declining, while participation among wealthier children is rising. On average, families with kids who play sports spend approximately $700 a year on fees, equipment, and more, while some spend up to $35,000 (The Aspen Institute, 2018). More public schools also charge "pay to play" fees than used to that price some families out (The Aspen Institute, 2018).

The Youth Celebrate Diversity executive student team, consisting of athletes supported by an inclusive athletic administrator and an inclusive athletics academic researcher, prioritizes an intersectional approach when advocating for inclusive excellence in interscholastic spaces. Micah Porter, organizer of YCD's inclusive teen sports program, describes it as "a glue that brings people together out of their larger pockets because of their common interests, into an environment that enhances understanding and opens up perspectives. This creates a sense of empathy toward another's life-long experience." The flagship annual event, named the Summit, is built on YCD's model of bringing together students and teachers from diverse school settings and classifications, including public and private and also urban and rural of various sizes, to build community, create conversations, and demonstrate positive change and forward thinking in Colorado's schools and communities.

change that adopted greater inclusion for religious hair coverings (Elassar, 2021). This example demonstrates that what might be a stylistic or aesthetic choice for one student can take on a larger religious and cultural significance for another. Policies and decisions inattentive to diversity disproportionately affect individuals of nondominant races, ethnicities, religions, genders, or other protected classes, making it crucial for sports committees and administrators to have ongoing cultural training to serve the needs of their entire communities.

In September 2019, matters of intersecting race and ethnicity sparked a national discussion. A video went viral of a referee watching an athletic trainer cutting the dreadlocks off a wrestler from Buena High School in Ventura, California, to avoid forfeiture from the event (NFHS, 2020). Dreadlocks are symbolic expressions of whole beauty that are intertwined with stories of struggle and religious adherence to Leviticus 21:5, which forbids balding, shaving, and cutting of the head and face, and speaks to the might of the lion's crown or royal stature (Frank, 2007). Ignoring this significance creates social and psychological harms for students of color (Macon, 2014). The referee claimed the wrestler's dreadlocks violate an NFHS rule governing the length of an athlete's hair and the circumstances in which a high school athlete must wear a hair covering, which demonstrates how rules such as this act as a form of cultural discrimination by centering White norms and aesthetics (Macon, 2014).

The Summit revamped the original state-focused and in-person model to a national one that achieves a greater scope of diverse topics and perspectives. This approach uses technology and digital media to facilitate dialogue and create community among athletes that attend a diversity of schools across vast cultural regions and conflicting political landscapes. The idea is to create affinity spaces where athletes can take on leadership roles and YCD can offer continuous programming throughout the academic year. The Summit focuses exclusively on topics of interest to athletes, coaches, and extracurricular programs in an effort to make interscholastic sports, activities, and programs more inclusive across the country. As with all YCD conferences and events, the Summit is planned entirely by the student executive team, a geographically diverse group of students representing a wide variety of high schools and identities. Some of the topics discussed include the following:

- Access and social differences between club sports and high school sports
- Balancing student and athlete identities
- Adult influence on student participation in sports and activities
- Creating community through sports and activities
- Socioeconomic barriers and discrimination in teen athletics and activities
- Religion's role in student activities and sports

Colorado High School Athletic Association Commissioner Rhonda Blanford-Green, the first African American woman commissioner in the country, backs the effort of the Summit through positioning the association as a contributing sponsor and official partner, explaining that these are the conversations needed and the level at which they needed to occur. Porter says that having the governing body on board gives credibility by functioning as the inclusive work voice across the political, cultural, and geographic landscape. Finally, the YCD offers media resources that speak to intersectionality topics that include books for diverse audience needs, podcast recommendations to initiate conversations, and national organization partners (YCD, 2022).

Ethnic and Racial Identity Development in Adolescents

The importance of an individual's racial and ethnic group and the meaning attached to it can change, shift, and evolve, especially during the developmental period of adolescence (Chavous, Leath, & Richardson, 2015). Identity results from microlevel individual and internal processes that occur as individuals encounter macrolevel public policies and other external influences interpreted through the daily experiences of difference associated with marginalized identities, including race and ethnicity (Renn, 2012). Examples at the microlevel include social shame and microaggressions targeting cultural traditions, and psychological stressors related to presence and worth being constantly questioned (Mathews et al., 2019). Under-resourced schools and activities programs resulting from housing practices are examples at the macrolevel.

Erickson's (1968) psychosocial theory acknowledges the social environment's influence on personal and social identities. In education settings, we can measure this impact through campus climate and culture. Campus climate describes the attitudes, behaviors, and standards of employees and students relating to inclusion of and level of respect for individual and group needs, abilities, and potential (Rankin & Reason, 2008). At the same time, campus culture combines various cultures on campus created mutually by all persons and accumulated in the long-term practice of school-running (Shen & Tian, 2012). It consists of three aspects: material culture (external symbols of campus culture), institutional culture (orderly development of campus culture), and spiritual culture (core and spirit of campus culture). These work together to offer individuality within academic offerings and cultivate culture creators. Together, culture and climate intersect to affect ethnic and racial identity development (ERID), or "the objective and subjective nature of group representation within an individual's context, highlighting how the dimensions are always interrelated" (Syed, Juang, & Svensson, 2018, p. 8).

The process of ERID begins early in childhood through parental cultural socialization and deepens during early adolescence due to a greater cognitive capacity that encourages an understanding of the role of ethnicity and race in everyday life (Vélez et al., 2019). Further, ethnic and racial identity are recognized as strong and positive when viewed as having a great understanding of pride and active engagement with one's ethnic and racial group membership (Vélez, 2019). To better understand ERID, Syed and colleagues (2018) prioritize

1. *perspective* (the objective and subjective understanding of ethnic and racial settings),
2. *differentiation* (how the ethnic group of reference is defined in a setting),
3. *heterogeneity* (the degree of variation, or diversity, of different ethnic groups in the setting), and
4. *proximity* (the distance between the individual and the setting being assessed).

Combined, these variables describe the complexities rooted in ethnic and racial settings.

While ERID can be positively influenced by any combination of peer groups, social media, teachers, and coaches, in interscholastic sports, they can also be negative. Negative interactions that result in discrimination or racism can have equivalent but negative psychological consequences related to self-esteem, prosocial tendencies, and well-being, and they can initiate experiences of depression and anxiety. For example, stereotypes inform adolescents' ethnic and racial identities by activating a desire to avoid or resist becoming an ethnic or racial stereotype (Way et al., 2013). **Stereotypes** are widely held societal beliefs, expectations, and generalizations applied to individuals who share common characteristics or to a social group like ethnicity, race, social class, and nationality (Taylor et al., 2019). For instance, Martin, Harrison, Stone, and Lawrence (2010) and Oseguera (2010) separately found that African American athletes perceive different expectations for Black athletes versus their White peers based on stereotypes.

On the other hand, positive outcomes result in healthy choices, academic achievement, and social engagement (Vélez, 2019). Approaches to encourage positive ethnic-racial identity include surface-level socialization and cultural awareness and deeper internal reflection around affirmation, exploration, and resolution (Vélez, 2019). When considering how race, ethnicity, and sport intersect, one must remember that marginalization of either race or ethnicity affects youth of color on many levels (Mathews et al., 2019). Athletic directors can help strengthen racial and ethnic identity by creating relevant courses or contributing to strength-based and culturally-based school and community-based interventions.

Conceptual Framework: Athletic Power Play

As athlete demographics continue to change, we invite athletic administrators to employ the Athletic Power Play Framework (APPF) as a tool with which to responsibly modernize approaches to problem-solving. The APPF helps analyze policies practically for program development, facilitating more effective interventions and culturally relevant programs and promoting more inclusive advocacy specific to their resources and desired outcomes (figure 5.1). Conceptually, it accounts for athletic and identity intersections using the five interlocked Olympic rings as a symbolic foundation. The Olympic rings are among the most globally recognizable sports symbols, signifying internationalism and universalism (Adair, 2013; Olympic Rings, 2021). However, instead of interlocking rings, ring-shaped gears demonstrate the interlinking of processes, teams, strategies, and operations, and they symbolize the multiple and constantly working intersectional principles outlined by Hankivsky (2014).

Power

First, the metaphor of a cog in the wheel describes the individual's presumed minor position in the significant societal structures in which they exist. The cogs of the gear create an interlocking relationship among the principles present. A gear's function indicates the constant presence and transmission of power within these systems of societal constructs they support. Power is a relational tool operating within the interpersonal, disciplinary, cultural, and structural domain (Collins & Bilge, 2016). These domains shape categories like race and ethnicity while extending the ability to affect society's decision-making process, influence others, pursue and protect one's self-interest, and achieve one's goals (Hankivsky, 2014; Healey & Stepnick, 2019).

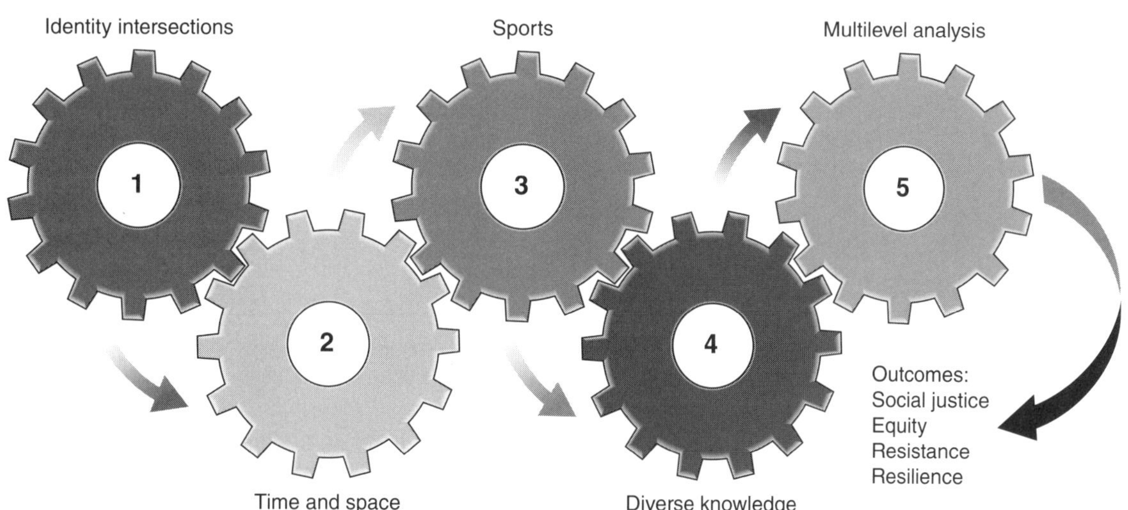

FIGURE 5.1 Athletic Power Play Framework.

Identity Intersections

Second, the identity intersections gear symbolizes the multiple and competing identities of the stakeholder. In addition to our discussion on race and ethnicity's visible identities, the Canadian Research Institute for the Advancement of Women (CRIAW, 2009) includes invisible identities like class, citizenship status, and religion. Collins and Bilge (2016) name necessary implications for contemplating identity in this intersectional approach. They require viewing identities as strategically essential (performing multiple different identities from one context to the next), as de facto coalitions (creating space for coalitional possibilities among individuals, as well as new directions for understanding groups), and as transformative identities (being formed within and also shaping broader social phenomena). Hankivsky and Cormier (2011) explain that it is the effect of identity intersections constituting and creating unique social locations important in analysis.

Time and Space

Third, the time and space gear connects with the identity intersections gear to emphasize the relationship created depending on when and where one lives; its interaction provides context for conditions and evidence for those conditions' consequences (Warf, 2008). Thinking about time and space also helps define strategies to strengthen efforts for demonstrating multicultural representation and understanding its value (Carter-Francique, 2020). For example, the presence and leadership of a coach of the same race or ethnicity can positively affect an athlete's attitudes, motivation, and achievement. Racially underrepresented coaches may have more positive expectations for racially underrepresented athletes' achievement than nonminority coaches (de Brey et al., 2019; Giving Compass, 2020). Challenges to specifically achieving the goal of coaching are evident at the macro (systemic), meso (process), and micro (group) levels. Cunningham (2020) explains that at the macrolevel, institutional racism, political climate, and stakeholder expectations affect hiring choices. At the mesolevel, a decision-making bias exists because of stereotypes, prejudices and discrimination, organizational culture, and organizational policies. These macro- and mesolevel challenges, along with barriers created by a lack of personal capital investment, personal identities, and self-limiting behaviors, become burdensome for the individual at the micro or individual level. Cunningham (2020) suggests that a multilevel approach is required for enhancing racially and ethnically diverse representation of coaches and administrators like how certifications are awarded and how personal lived experiences are valued.

Diverse Knowledge

The APPF calls for diverse knowledge from the people most often excluded in decision-making through a combination of qualitative, quantitative, empirical, and interpretative data analysis to describe more resonant and realistic narratives (Hankivsky, 2014). Teferra, Powers, and Fischman (2018) also emphasized referencing diverse researchers' scholarship to influence and provide the theoretical perspective for problems and provide practical implications for solving them. Finally, we couple Hankivsky's (2014) call for reflexivity with this diverse knowledge because it calls for truth telling from within the organization and continuous listening on behalf of the organization by the voices typically excluded from expert roles.

Multilevel Analysis

The final gear calls for multilevel analysis (MLA), a requirement for outcome response and direction, and therefore connects the larger bottom gears of identity intersections and sports. MLA involves considering effects across and between the macrolevel, mesolevel, and microlevel and requires addressing inequity and differentiation across the structure, identity, and representation to establish relational needs, determine transformative processes, and identify select interactions (Choo & Ferree, 2010; Houston, 2019). Strategies set forth by Cunningham (2020) for the microlevel require communication aimed to address uncomfortable subject matter that creates deeper intergroup connections. At the mesolevel, committing to inclusive excellence through principles, policies, and programs attracts allies. Finally, sports organizations function within communities and are therefore required to respond socially and politically in the interest of the members they serve.

Outcomes

Outcomes from the APPF are expected to lead to social justice, equity, resistance, and resilience (Hankivsky, 2014). Collins and Bilge (2016) connect these outcomes by underscoring the role intersectionality plays in addressing educational equities' complexities and the pipeline programs they market as forward-thinking initiatives. We accept their claim that critical education is the key to critical praxis and advocate for the investigation of the interaction between sports structures, other institutions, and athlete's cultural attributes that develop there.

Social Justice and Equity

Social justice comprises the fair distribution of society's resources and decision-making procedures that determine their distribution in an equitable manner (Tyler, 2000). When these dimensions of equity distribute vertically, and according to society's ascriptive identities like race, ethnicity, and religion, it creates the unequal treatment of people in different ranks, which serves as a basis for awarding privileges and disadvantages (Stone, 2012). Fairness in this process requires participation (contribution toward conflict resolution), neutrality (honesty, impartiality, and objectivity by authority), the trustworthiness of the authority (assessment of the motives of the third-party control), and treatment with dignity and respect (having regard shown for their rights and status within society) (Tyler, 2000). Organization directors can respond to this call for action similarly to one organization found at the collegiate athletics level. The Southeastern Conference (SEC) established a council on equity and social justice to respond to social injustices and inequities. Its efforts concentrate on increasing racial and ethnic minority representation, improving education on racial and social issues, deepening commitment within respective campus communities, and raising awareness for these and related topics (SEC, 2020). Councils like this provide the platform for resilience and a launching pad for resistance.

Resistance and Resilience

Resistance and resilience are means of disrupting power and oppression and challenging marginalizing norms and values. Various forms of resistance include creating or participating in coalitions and conferences, protests, and symbolic activism (Hankivsky, 2014). Historically, athletes have used their elevated platforms to demonstrate resistance to racism and other social oppressions to bring awareness to and advocate equitable practices in the most basic civil rights and equal protection under the law (Fitzgerald, 2014).

We reference George-Williams' (2019) Black Athlete Activist Leadership as the model for athletic administrators to consider when understanding the position of activism for disenfranchised athletic activist populations. George-Williams defines activism as "efforts and behaviors in which individuals or groups seek to make a change to the status quo for the benefit of oppressed groups" (p. 49). George-Williams accounts for individual actions, collective tactics, campaigns, and social movements as activism forms. The Black Athlete Activist Leadership model begins by looking at athletes as natural leaders and then considers the multiple identities they bring to a platform of advocacy. Simultaneously, the complete campus climate is evaluated, and holistic support that is intentional and prioritizes emotional health and wellness is offered.

SUMMARY

This chapter explored the complexities of race and ethnicity when they intersect in sports, with a case study on interscholastic sports. Education as a setting to these interactions reveals consequences of advantage, access, and multilevel power when it comes to leadership and governance. In response to these advantages, we advocate for athletes by encouraging their growth in ethnic and racial identity development and experiences. The Athletic Power Play Framework is offered for sport leaders to reference. Together, this research contributes to inclusive excellence by illuminating the need for context when describing sports' benefits and recognizes how certain identities result in individuals being disadvantaged, socially excluded, and targets of discrimination, intentionally and unintentionally. Responding to the intersections of race, ethnicity, and sports reveals challenging social inequalities and demands more inclusive sports spaces that resonate with participants who are holistic, multifaceted people.

CRITICAL THINKING EXERCISES

1. List at least eight identity classifications in interscholastic sports settings. Include both visible and invisible identities as well as emerging organizational categories of difference (e.g., linguistic fluency). Why is it important for an athletics administrator to consider these identity classifications when they are assigned or chosen?
2. Write an inclusive job posting for the high school's athletic director position. Include a description of the community your high school serves; the experiences required; knowledge, skills, and abilities required; and the general qualities of an ideal candidate.

REVIEW QUESTIONS

1. Describe the origins of intersectionality theory.
2. List three reasons an intersectional approach is useful in understanding sports.
3. How do cultural pluralism and cultural diversity compare and differ? How does this help to understand processes and dynamics within sports organizations better?

© Morgan Engel/NCAA Photos via Getty Images

CHAPTER 6

Sports as a Gendered Space

Amira Rose Davis

LEARNING OBJECTIVES

- Understand how gender shapes participation, access, and investment in sports.
- Explore the gendered dynamics of sport and reflect on how sports themselves are gendered.
- Consider how sports maintain or challenge traditional ideas about gender.
- Consider the challenges to gender binaries in sport.
- Identify ways to address gender disparities in sport.
- Discuss opportunities to make sports more gender inclusive.

"I got something to show y'all . . ."

Sedona Prince, a redshirt sophomore at the University of Oregon, was initially just relieved to be at the NCAA's postseason tournament in March 2021. The basketball player had finally recovered from a long injury, and despite the COVID-19 pandemic, the tournament was scheduled to proceed. The men's college basketball teams headed to Indianapolis for their March Madness tournament, while Prince and the rest of the women settled into San Antonio. The relief at being at the tournament was soon joined with another, more unsettling, feeling: a growing sense of frustration for what little the women athletes were provided.

Prince was not the only one taking notice. Ali Kershner, the strength and conditioning coach with Stanford women's basketball, was particularly concerned about the weight room. Kershner had seen the sprawling facilities the men were using in Indianapolis, but when she walked in to prepare to train her team, all she found was one rack of dumbbells and a pile of yoga mats (Killion, 2021). Kershner snapped a picture and uploaded a side-by-side comparison of the weight rooms. The image went viral, prompting the NCAA to say that the disparity was due to a lack of space at the women's tournament. For Sedona Prince, however, the matter was far from over.

"I got something to show y'all," Prince said into the camera as she began recapping the weight room debacle. As she showed the lonely weight rack and the pile of yoga mats, Prince told viewers about NCAA's claim that there was no space for a full women's weight room—and then dramatically swung her phone around to reveal a huge room with empty space (Brassil, 2021). "If you're not upset about this problem," concluded Prince, "you are a part of it."

Overnight, Prince's video went viral, from hundreds of thousands of retweets to national media asking for her to do interviews (Brassil, 2021). The issue of gender equality in college basketball was heating up. Over the course of the tournament, players, coaches, media, and fans drew attention to other troubling signs of disparity. From food and gifts to COVID tests and revenue-sharing, the increasing list painted a troubling but undeniable picture: Women athletes, their coaches, their fans, and their tournament did not matter to the NCAA.

Despite the outrage, there was very little shock. "While I appreciate the outrage, the fact that there is a huge disparity between men's and women's sports is hardly breaking news," commented retired Notre Dame coach Muffet McGraw. "This is an issue that women have been battling for decades. . . . We have been taking the crumbs from tables we don't even have a seat at" (Brennan, 2021). The idea that gender would influence the resources or investment in sport was accepted and, in many ways, expected. Women in sports have learned how to feast on crumbs. But how did we come to believe this disparity is natural? How have ideas about gender shaped—and continue to shape—the investment in or consumption of sports?

In this chapter, we explore how sports are gendered and how ideas about gender influence what sports and what athletes are valued and seen as normative. The viral discourse about the women's tournament prompted many people to ask why Title IX, the educational amendment that was pivotal in increasing the opportunities for girls and in women in sport, did not apply to the situation (Mertens, 2021). In this chapter we tackle that question as we discuss efforts that have been made to address gender disparity in sports and their limitations. Ideas about gender and sports go beyond the field and extend to coaches, administrators, sports journalists, and fans. This chapter examines how gendered ideas about bodies and minds shape the landscape of sports from the youth to the professional level, with particular attention to the media, marketing, and management of sports. We consider the rigid gender binary that exists in sports and grapple with the fact that it remains one of the most gender-segregated spaces in society. The chapter concludes by discussing how strict gender binaries erase nonbinary or trans people and by highlighting the ways people have disrupted sporting binaries—and in doing so challenged the foundational presumptions about sport and gender altogether.

Gender as a Social Construct

You may be familiar with the phrase "gender is a **social construct**," or perhaps you have heard a similar phrase about race. But what do people mean when they talk about social constructions? The idea of social constructions challenges the notion of the inevitable and argues that qualities such as race and gender that might seem fixed, biological, or natural are actually built by human knowledge and shifting shared understandings (Gergen, 2001). Race is not actually the color of your skin but, rather, the value and meaning society assigns to it. This is illustrated by how, historically, groups like the Irish in the United States were not considered White but became understood as White over time when ideas and boundaries about race shifted (Ignatiev, 1995). As historian Nell Irvin Painter asserts, "Race is an idea, not a fact" (Painter, 2010).

Gender, however, can feel more innate and harder to understand as a construct because it is so embedded and deep-rooted in our society. Even before birth, gender reveals or baby shower gifts follow color-coded markers to make a yet-to-be-born child's gender known. When the child is born, their reproductive organs mark them as biologically female, male, or intersex. That is one's **sex**. When the baby gets wrapped in a blue blanket, welcomed home with blue balloons, and placed in an animal, truck, or sports-themed nursery, it signals that he is a boy. And being a "boy" comes with meanings, values, and ideas that display the expectations of society. That is gender. Of course, the relationship between sex and gender is tightly woven because reproductive organs have been used to assign gender identity. As Judith Lorber notes, "Sex categories become gender status through naming, dress and other gender markers" (Lorber, 1994). Gender then becomes the overarching framework for understandings of **masculinity** and **femininity**—the set of attributes, behaviors, and roles associated with men or with women, respectively. Sociologists and gender theorists like Michael Kimmel, have demonstrated how these constructions are relational—that is to say, they are formed in opposition to each other (Kimmel, 1987).

Gender is bound up with and inextricable from social constructions such as race, class, and sexuality. Black women theorists such as Patricia Hill Collins and Kimberlé Crenshaw provide intersectional frameworks centered on Black women's navigation of "interlocking systems of oppression" to demonstrate that womanhood is not experienced the same way (Crenshaw, 1990; Collins, 2009). For instance, the midcentury expectation that women should stay at home to cook, clean, and raise babies, famously railed against in Betty Friedan's *The Feminine Mystique*, largely applied to White middle-class women, and not the women of color and working-class White women who already labored outside of their homes. In these overlaps and gaps, we can see how gender is racialized and race is gendered (Ferree, Lorber, Hess, & Altamira, 1999).

Gender markers can switch and evolve, affected by other identities and shifts in society, ever changing how individuals can "do" or "perform" their gender (West & Zimmerman, 1987). Not simply passive recipients of gender ideologies, people constantly produce and reproduce gender by "behaving in the ways they learned were appropriate for their gender status or resisting or rebelling against these norms." Yet rebelling against gender norms has altered, but not radically shifted, ideas about gender. In sports, this is especially true. While the last few decades have seen expanded ideas about gender leading to increased access for women, the foundational ideas about gender and sports still largely structure the entire sports landscape, from the backyard pickup games to the corporate meeting rooms stacked with industry professionals.

Making of Modern Sports: Reproducing and Rebelling Against Gender Norms

Sports have long played a pivotal role in society. The games that people play, watch, control, or even scorn are infused with meanings that go far beyond the sport itself. In some ways, sports are a mirror to society. They reflect the larger context around them. For example, as technology developed, modern sports reflected and incorporated these trends. Instead of listening to a game on the radio, the invention of TV allowed people to watch it. Yet, sports have also been a social laboratory of sorts. Instead of simply reflecting society, they have also changed it. When television became more accessible, modern sports began to use the emerging media to sell their leagues. The commercialization of sports ushered in new markets and created televised sports media that in many ways became a model for other forms of media. Consider how much political news content resembles ESPN, for example.

Understanding modern sports as both a mirror and a laboratory is useful for considering the ways sports affect and reflect ideas about identity, culture, politics, and more. The same way sports reflected and transformed modern technological gains can help us understand how sports do the same thing for less tangible ideas about race, class, and gender.

In this section we track the rise of modern sports alongside shifting ideas about gender. We pay attention to the ways in which sport reflects social gender norms, as well as how they affect, change, or challenge ideas about gender.

Gender and the History of Sport

According to Shari Dworkin and Michael Messner, sport has been one of the "key institutional sites for the study of the social construction of gender" (Scraton & Flintoff, 2002). The history of sport shows evidence that it has indeed been a crucial place where affirmations of and challenges to gender identity are transmitted. The foundations of modern gender norms can be located in the mid to late 19th century, where a sense of rugged masculinity paired with health and moral spirit developed into the ideal notion of manhood. Emphasizing qualities such as competitiveness, strength, power, speed, and domination, athletics was a place where a boy could "cultivate masculinity and achieve manhood" (Cahn, 2015).

Athletics became even more important in the early 20th century when urbanization, industrialization, and migration vastly changed the American way of life. If manhood had been bolstered by taming the wilderness, manual labor, and war, then the absence of that, along with the rise of middle-class society and a leisure class, created a crisis of masculinity. Educators, politicians, clergymen, and other societal leaders began to emphasize the need for the strenuous life. The idea of muscular Christianity paired respectable morals and mental fortitude with rigorous activity. Organizations like the YMCA institutionalized such ideas and offered robust athletic programming across the nation, while the development of college athletics "offered the metaphor of harsh competition" to teach young men to work hard, take command, and in the words of Oliver Wendell Holmes, "strain every nerve and muscle . . . to feel the passion of life at the top" (Gorn, 2010; Putney, 2009).

While sports became a laboratory for producing the strong masculine leaders of tomorrow, they also provided a space to challenge ideas of White masculine superiority. At a time when eugenicists and scientific racism asserted the inferiority of Black Americans, athletes like Jack Johnson disrupted such ideas. Gail Bederman begins her foundational study *Manliness and Civilization* with the Jack Johnson–Jim Jeffries fight of 1910. Johnson's defeat of White men in the boxing ring showed a strong Black manhood that terrified White America so much that they searched for "the great white hope" to vanquish Johnson and prove the dominance of White men (Bederman, 2008). The anxieties, national attention, and gendered and racialized implications of this boxing match underscored how central sports were to the development, performance, and proliferation of ideas about gender.

If sports were a space that made men, where did that leave women? Women's athletic participation created what Cahn (2015) calls a "conundrum." As girls and women pushed to play sports, their very presence troubled the prevailing ideas about gender. If sports provided a laboratory that made men, would women athletes become more masculine? Or would they make sports feminine? If they could also run and jump and dominate, what would stop them from eroding other "masculine spaces" and challenging the supposed superiority of men?

These fears over women in sports resulted in constant battles over the regulation and control of women's athletics. Some people argued that women needed gentle, noncompetitive play that made them fit for motherhood and other feminine duties but did not overwork them. In fact, many doctors argued that overexertion would lead to damaged reproductive abilities. They sought to thread a fine needle between promoting women's physical fitness to produce strong children and protecting women's perceived fragility, which formed through misguided ideas like a soccer ball to the stomach making one infertile or too much jumping leading to a uterus falling out (Elsey & Nadal, 2019; Davis, 2021).

These ideas led to calisthenics classes and "play days" instead of leagues. When women were able to play, they often played in hyperregulated and modified sports like girls-rules basketball that allowed six on the court, prohibited dribbling, and frowned upon any real exertion. Certain sports, such as tennis, golf, and swimming, were seen as elite and respectable. These clubhouse sports coincided with ideas about femininity, allowed for tennis dresses or golf skirts to be worn, and conveyed an upper-class sensibility—and therefore did not directly threaten gender norms.

Women who played sports, who loved competition, who were muscular, or who were especially high achieving had their gender constantly scrutinized. Early sporting pioneers and

Babe Didrikson, an early sporting pioneer and multisport athlete, was scrutinized for her body hair, chest, weight, muscles, and body type.
Getty Images

multisport athletes Babe Didrikson and Ora Washington both had many columns written about their appearance, scrutinizing their body hair, chest, weight, muscles, and body type (Cahn, 2015; Grundy, 2003). The more a woman excelled in sport, the more her femininity was questioned—underscoring the prevailing belief that athletics were inherently male and to succeed in them required masculine qualities.

Gender Norms and Modern Sport

In many ways these foundational concerns still linger around modern sports. As sporting opportunities for women have expanded, researchers have turned their attention to what sports are considered feminine or masculine and the ways in which the sports themselves become gendered (Koivula, 2001; Hardin, 2009). This **gender-typing** of sports results in certain sports like football and ice hockey being seen as masculine sports while field hockey or softball are seen as feminine sports. As Koivula demonstrates, masculine sports are associated with strength, speed, commercialism, and competition, while feminine sports are connected to aesthetics, advanced skills, and cognition (Koivula, 2001).

Like their historical predecessors, athletes in feminine or gender-neutral sports, and especially in sports whose uniforms are tight-fitting or include skirts, are not considered disruptive to gender norms about femininity (Jones & Greer, 2021). However, women playing "gender-inappropriate" sports continue to experience scrutiny about their body in ways that reassert muscles and strength as masculine traits. It is not just women who come under scrutiny for playing in "the wrong" sport. Men who play volleyball or field hockey, for example, and especially male cheerleaders, face scrutiny about their masculinity and sexuality (Sobal & Milgram, 2019; Tagg, 2008).

Playing a "gender-appropriate" sport does not always mean an athlete is viewed as acceptable or normative. Indeed, Black women athletes in sports traditionally considered feminine or respectable have still experienced racism and **sexism** that dismisses their bodies as "manly." Venus and Serena Williams have constantly dealt with comments deriding them as "the Williams brothers" or drawing upon dehumanizing stereotypes about Black women that describe them as "beastly" or animalistic while fetishizing their bodies as nonnormative others (Schultz, 2005; McKay & Johnson, 2008).

Sex-segregating and gender-typing sports do not merely have rhetorical consequences; they also affect access to athletics. The durability of the idea that men are inherently stronger than women resulted in sex-segregated sports from "4-year olds playing soccer . . . to senior bowling leagues" says law professor Nancy Leong (de la Cretaz, 2018; Leong and Bartlett, 2018). On top of sex-segregating sports, the gender-typing of sports can create restrictions for participation. Consider Rye High School in New York for instance, where students must file an application to play an "opposite-gender" sport and undergo a physical fitness test. In the fitness test, "girls must prove they're skilled, strong and fast enough to play with boys," while boys must prove that they are *not* "too skilled, strong, or fast to play with girls" (Haggerty, 2015). One student came face-to-face with this policy after applying to play field hockey. The student had moved from the Netherlands, where field hockey is a gender-neutral sport. Indeed, male youth athletes, such as this field hockey player, often face more restrictions on sports participation in "gender-inappropriate" sports because their presence is seen as inherently unfair (Messner, 2011), while a girl playing hockey or football can be dismissed as a nonthreatening anomaly.

Rather than challenge the essential presumption of athletic ability, second-wave **feminism** ushered in Title IX and greatly expanded sporting opportunities for girls while actually reinforcing the sporting binary. Michael Messner argues that the uncontested ideas about gender difference and sport "precluded a strategy of [gender] desegregation of youth sport," when fighting for access, and instead prompted the "creation of a kind of 'separate-but-equal' ideal" for youth sports (Messner, 2011).

In 1974, the National Organization for Women sponsored a civil rights claim against Little League Baseball so that girls could play the sport. In response to the legal mandate that they had to provide equal access, Little League established softball for girls (Ring, 2015). While softball is a great sport, it is also different from baseball, and many girls still want to play baseball. Despite this, girls in baseball get "squeezed out" or tracked into softball. Girls who remain on baseball teams report not getting fair playing time, taunts from opposing teams and their own teammates, and hearing boys say that the ultimate humiliation is getting beaten by a girl. These microaggressions transmit learned ideas about who belongs in a sport. They also work to police the boundaries of sex-segregated sports. Organizations such as Girls Travel Baseball try to address this by fielding a nearly all-girls travel baseball team. They compete across the country and hope that they can provide girls with an opportunity to play baseball "until [they're] not allowed to play anymore" (Luther, 2017).

Sam Gordon is a former internet sensation who gained fame as a nine-year-old when she was dominating youth football leagues. Gordon continued to play football but grew tired of playing on boys' teams. Gordon started a girls' tackle football league and later sued Utah school districts to argue that being able to play on a boys' football team was not equal access, instead pushing for the creation of girls-only football teams. While the district claimed there was not enough interest to do this, Gordon's legal team pointed out that "there was no amount of interest that girls could express and no mechanism for them to express it" that would be sufficient for the school district (Stubbs, 2020).

These examples demonstrate that even as athletes have pushed for access to sport and disrupted gender norms regarding what sports they can play, they have also reinforced the binary foundation and sex-segregation of athletics. Leong, though, makes a salient point about the perceived benefits of single-sex sporting spaces, noting that we cannot ignore the context of the sports landscape that can make coed sporting spaces inhospitable. "How much of it is about not wanting to play with boys," Leong asks, or is it "not wanting to play with people who don't treat you as an equal part of their team?" (de la Cretaz, 2018).

Power Plays: Gender and the Fight for the Control of Sports

Gender not only shapes athletes' participation in sports, but it also shapes who controls the games. From coaches to athletic administrators, the fight to define, structure, and control sports is tangled with ideas about gender. In this section we briefly look at some early battles of women athletic administrators, before turning our attention to the pivotal Title IX legislation and the continued gender-based struggles in the management of athletics.

Early Opportunities in Women's Sport

As college sports, early professional leagues, and amateur sports emerged and developed over the course of the 20th century, women always had their own ideas about athletic participation and control of their own games. Notably, women of color and ethnic White women, who were often working-class immigrants, found more expansive opportunities to participate in athletics. This is partly because their womanhood was already seen as outside the bounds of the ideal woman. Black colleges, industrial leagues, and YWCAs fostered early competitive athletic opportunities.

These early Black women athletic administrators in the 1920s and 1930s argued that "women should control women's athletics" (Davis, 2021). Women like Sadie Daniels at Fisk University and Maryrose Reeves Allen at Howard expressed an alternative vision for college athletics that emphasized health and community over competition and commercialism. By the 1940s, however, these women were pushed out when Black men took over all aspects of college athletics and implemented robust competitive opportunities for women. These pivotal points offer the opportunity to see how alternative sporting structures were possible at moments and then ultimately unable to take root. The power plays for control of sports at HBCUs (historically Black colleges and universities) in the mid 20th century foreshadowed similar national battles that would emerge by the 1970s.

On the heels of the civil rights movement, many marginalized groups looked to the legislative victories and blueprint that the movement had produced. Second-wave White feminists joined with Black women and other feminists of color to mount legal challenges to the gender-based discrimination they experienced. By far, the most transformative legislation was **Title IX of the Education Amendments of 1972**.

Title IX

Title IX is just 37 words.

> *"No person in the United States shall, on the basis of sex, be excluded from participation in, be denied the benefits of, or be subjected to discrimination under any education program or activity receiving Federal financial assistance."*

Title IX was a broad legislative victory that did not mention or take direct aim at sports. Yet legislatures quickly worried about the impact on public schools and universities and their football programs. Senator John Tower introduced the Tower Amendment to try to prevent Title IX from being applied to athletic departments. When this failed in 1974, a massive transformation of sports was underway. At the start of the 1970s, fewer than 300,000 girls were playing high school sports—just 5 percent of scholastic athletes. By the early 2000s, over 2.5 million girls were playing, now making up 56 percent of high school athletes (Acosta & Carpenter, 2006).

Despite anniversary celebrations and positive associations with the transformative nature of Title IX, researchers have shown that the media coverage and framing of the law has been negative and embedded with hegemonic ideas about gender and sports (Hardin, Simpson, Whiteside, & Garris, 2007). For instance, Ellen Staurowsky's work demonstrates that media coverage of Title IX used words like "fight" and other war metaphors to paint an adversarial picture of the legislation (Staurowsky, 1998). This framework pushed blame on women for daring to encroach on a perceived masculine space. As Staurowsky notes, it pitted women's athletic interests against the existing institutions, leading to a combative approach to gender equity instead of a collaborative one. Lane's (2018) study similarly showed that much of the discussion around Title IX was focused on how it would affect or harm men's sports and "confirmed the role of women in sports as that of trespasser rather than rightful participant."

Gender and Athletic Administration

While Title IX opened many doors to athletic participation, it also closed off possibilities of

Title IX has resulted in a massive transformation of sports with a huge increase in the participation of high school girls.

athletic governance and coaching for women. At the time of Title IX, women's college sports were governed by the Association for Intercollegiate Athletics for Women (AIAW). The AIAW, similar to the early Black women administrators, articulated a distinct vision for women's sports. While a variety of opinions existed within the organization, the AIAW as a whole was open to and interested in creating athletic programs that did not focus on profit or even necessarily on winning. Leaders of the AIAW made clear that the hegemonic sporting culture was unabashedly male, created and maintained by men, and that perhaps it did not suit the needs or wants of girls and women in sport (Hult, 1999).

What does a feminist sport look like? What are other possibilities of athletic governance? What might an alternative sporting culture look like? These questions, for a short moment in time, floated in the air. As debates raged across the country about Title IX, its implementation, and its consequences, women athletic directors like Donnis Thompson lamented the fact that people had "no imagination" when it comes to women's sports. She had a "vision and a dream" about what women's college sports could be (Davis, 2021). Yet Messner's work remains instructive here. Even as people considered new and innovative frameworks for sports, the fundamental ideas about gender still structured and constrained every conversation.

Despite not wanting to manage women's sports, and in fact attempting to legally get off the hook, the NCAA ultimately moved to take full control of women's athletic administration. By 1982, the NCAA had crushed the AIAW and halfheartedly shoehorned women's college sports into their existing structure. As women's college sports came under the control of the NCAA, the women who comprised a great majority of women's athletic directors and coaches soon found themselves pushed out of sport. They were replaced by mostly White men. When Title IX was passed, women made up over 90 percent of coaches and administrators of women's sport. In 2020, those numbers have dropped to 42 percent and 15.9 percent, respectively (Hruby, 2021; Davis, 2021).

Studies have shown that gendered ideas about sporting knowledge, constrained upward mobility, and institutional dead ends have contributed to the barriers for women coaches and athletic directors (Knoppers et al., 1991; Cooky & LaVoi, 2012; LaVoi & Baeth, 2018). Many opportunities exist as senior women's administrator, the highest-ranking administrative position traditionally focused on diversity, equity, and inclusion. This position has been like quicksand, holding women candidates in one place, unable to parlay that into a professional stepping-stone. Despite being more likely to have played college sports, to have coached, and to hold advanced degrees, athletic administrators face gender bias related to their ability to manage football programs and to court donors, among other things. This is especially true for Black women, who in addition to having playing and coaching experience are far more likely to hold a PhD yet remain on the margins of athletic governance (Carter-Francique & Olushola, 2016; Davis, 2021).

Gender and Coaching

Coaching opportunities are slightly less elusive. These jobs are almost always coaching women's sports, while men are perceived as allowed to coach both women's and men's sports. Studies have examined the perception of sporting knowledge, prior athletic experience, motivational ability, and prevailing ideas about a lack of trust or response to women's leadership or dominance as factors that affect the gender disparity in coaching (LaVoi and Baeth, 2018; Kane, 2016).

In recent years there have been a few women hired to coach men's sports, most notably in basketball, where former WNBA players have found some traction as assistant coaches in the NBA. Despite the anticipation, a woman has yet to be named head coach of an NBA team (Dator, 2021). While the high profile hires of Becky Hammon or Teresa Weatherspoon have spurred hope, the overall landscape is still bleak. In college basketball for instance, women make up 0.01 percent of men's team coaches. Recent studies that surveyed male coaches, women coaches, college students, and athletes, continued to show that ideas about gender and bias about women in sport dominate the evaluation of women coaches (Walker, Bopp, & Sagas, 2011; Walker & Sartore-Baldwin, 2013).

When discussing Title IX and the disparities in the numbers of women coaches and administrators, it is important to use an intersectional lens. **Intersectionality**, as defined by Kimberlé Crenshaw, means that Black women face the overlapping burdens of racism and sexism. The data on coaching disparities demonstrate why this lens is needed. While women were pushed out of coaching positions after Title IX, Black women coaches have particularly struggled to find opportunity.

Consider women's basketball, for example. A field study from the Global Sports Institute analyzed coaching patterns and demographics in women's college basketball from 1984 to 2020. The study found that while Black women make up over 50 percent of Division 1 basketball players in the Power 5, Black women coaches account for under 15 percent. Similar to Black women athletic administrators, Black women coaches also have more experience as players and higher degree attainment than their non-Black counterparts. For instance, 98 percent of Black women coaches played Division 1 college basketball themselves, compared to just 23 percent of White male coaches in the Power 5. Getting a job is hard, but retaining it is another challenge. Black women also had the shortest average head coaching tenures and were the least likely to receive a second head coaching job at a comparable level. White women were twice as likely as their Black peers to be offered another comparable job (Gerretsen et al., 2021).

Ideas about race and gender create these disparities. **Treatment discrimination** based on ideas of what "good coaching" looks like or what leadership entails plays a pivotal role in limiting opportunities for advancement. Many women get stuck as assistant coaches in charge of recruiting or tasked with managing the social-emotional aspect of team building because of perceptions that women have natural caretaking ability and are not strategic thinkers. Moreover, for men the traditional rewarded and celebrated coaching style is one that leads by force, whereas women—in and out of sports—are socialized to lead by relationship building and team development (Davis, 2021; Cunningham, Wicker, & Walker, 2021; Strauss, 2020). These foundational ideas can also have harmful and tangible impacts.

How Ideas About Gender and Coaching Frame Perception of Abuse in Sports

In 2018, a young football player at University of Maryland, Jordan McNair, died after suffering heatstroke and seizures at a football practice where he was being pushed beyond his limits. An investigation later revealed that under head coach D.J. Durkin, a culture of abuse thrived, from forced feedings of players to forcing them to watch graphic videos of serial killers or eye dissection. Yet Durkin is still being applauded and offered jobs by his peers to continue coaching. His tactics have been dismissed as "just a bit overboard" but largely seen as acceptable means for the end goal of making men. It is the idea that young men should just "take it" to make themselves stronger, tougher, and more formidable, and that it's in pursuit of masculinity and winning.

On the flip side of that, women coaches exhibiting abusive behavior can often go unnoticed. Recent studies have shown a rise in reported abuse in women's sport, with athletes documenting how they have been bullied or manipulated (Dodgson, 2020). The abuse often centers around body-shaming, name-calling, food restriction, and sexual harassment. Gender assumptions already make society less inclined to see women as abusers, and women coaches are no exception to that trend. Furthermore, no matter the gender of the coach, the overall lack of attention to women's youth and college sports makes it particularly easy for abusive cultures to thrive.

For men coaching women's sports, ideas about gender also structure the perception of their tactics and public image. The idea that male coaches will toughen girls up but also play a fatherly role has afforded male coaches of women's sports particular power in sporting structures. The assumption that a male coach is using women's sport as a stepping-stone

Sport Industry Diversity Initiative

WeCOACH

Well aware of the declining numbers of women coaches at the collegiate level, Celia Slater, Judy Sweet, and Ann Salerno went to the NCAA and requested support for a program aimed at helping women coaches. Soon, the NCAA Women Coaches Academy launched. Open to women coaches across all sports and NCAA divisions, the academy functions as a site where women coaches gather and talk about the unique barrier they experience.

As the academy grew larger, many coaches wanted to expand the conversation beyond college sports. In 2011, Slater and Sweet officially started the Alliance of Women Coaches. This parent organization invited women from all sports at all levels to network, share their experiences, consider future job opportunities, and help strengthen and expand the number of women coaches.

Now known as WeCOACH, the organization describes its mission as follows:

> *The new name and icon depict everything that our organization stands for: a strong, vibrant, and unified community. It represents powerful role models, leaders within individual sports who come together with collective voices stronger than their own, and those who are continually exhibiting resilience on and off the field of competition.*

WeCOACH continues to offer a coaches academy for women at NCAA schools. The multiday event fosters a coaching community, mentorship, and networking. WeCOACH has expanded to include a virtual two-day conference for women coaches at the high school level. This important expansion is the first conference of its kind in the nation. WeCOACH hopes to foster a pipeline of coaches at all levels and influence gendered perceptions of coaches and who can be coaches. It is especially important to do this work at the youth sports level.

WeCOACH has also been mindful of the unique experiences of women of color in coaching. WeAMPLIFY is a program to drive institutional change and facilitate conversations around barriers faced by women of color in the profession.

Most recently, WeCOACH has partnered with Hudl to offer the BreakThrough Summit, a digital leadership summit that highlights, celebrates, and unites women coaches across levels and sports. This event brings in speakers, hosts panels, gives out awards, and operates as the de facto public facing arm of the organization. Through the BreakThrough Summit, along with these other initiatives, WeCOACH is helping to support women coaches and change the game.

to their real goal of coaching men's sport is evident every time people ask coaches like UConn's women's basketball coach Geno Auriemma if he plans to finally make the "leap" to coaching men. The fact that he does not plan to coach men serves to bolster the inherent perception that he is a good guy because he could be coaching men but chooses to "stay in the women's game" (Jacobs, 2018).

However, the idea that men coaching women's sports is inherently good (almost as if it's doing charity work) can also result in a profound lack of oversight and accountability. Recent cases in the National Women's Soccer League, for example, have seen multiple coaches, most notably Paul Riley, finally be held accountable for years of abusive behavior and toxic work environments. Reports are that the league looked the other way when it learned of the abuse. Players said one deterrent from speaking out was the idea that a scandal or ousting of a prominent male coach could be detrimental to the league while it was fighting for stability and growth (Linehan, 2021).

Examining the way gender disparities exist at the coaching and administrative level in sports expands our understanding of sports as a gendered space. It is important to pay attention to how ideas about gender not only affect who coaches or plays but also how sports are governed and what behaviors are affirmed or ignored—even when they create harmful or toxic sporting environments.

Sports are more than just athletes, coaches, and managers, however. Sports media and fans make up a huge piece of the sports landscape. And our framing and consumption of sport are just as structured by ideas about gender.

Shrink It and Pink It: Gender in Sports Media, Marketing, and Fandom

The previous sections addressed the ways in which gender can affect the playing, coaching, and administration of sports. Let's consider these the internal ring in a concentric circle of sports. The external ring wrapping around those experiences includes watching, analyzing, reporting on, selling, and cheering (or jeering) the happenings in the inner circle. These rings work in tandem with each other. Fan pressure can result in a coach getting fired. A brand endorsement or marketing campaign can elevate an athlete to new heights. An investigation can reveal abuse, and sports media can downplay or ignore harm in pursuit of a "good story." Ideas about gender are transmitted not only through playing and coaching sports, but also through watching, consuming, covering, and marketing them. In this section we examine the role media, marketing, and fandom play in maintaining gender norms around the perimeters of sport.

Media

There are huge gender disparities in sports media. Women account for just 10 percent of sports editors and 11.5 percent of sports journalists and media professionals (Aykroyd, 2021; Lapchick, 2021). Women's sports only garner about 4 percent of coverage in dominant sports media platforms. These statistics help paint a bleak picture: The way sports is covered is largely mediated through a male—often White male—lens.

Jenn McClearen offers important considerations when regarding how feminism operates and is invoked in sports media. McClearen and others document some shifts in the approaches to covering women's sports—much of this change led by the few women in media spaces. Many of these shifts are certainly indebted to feminist organizing, but are feminist frameworks being used to cover and market women's sports? McClearen's work would indicate that the answer is no. Pointing to emerging popular marketing strategies like "#girlboss in a jersey," McClearen shows that the marketability of women athletes, even in this framework, only serves to reinforce gender norms, commodify a few women athletes, and profit (McClearen, 2018; Antunovic & Whiteside, 2018).

How might a feminist framing of sports stories change how sports are written about or documented? Male sports writers who covered the Brock Turner assault case and included his swimming times in the articles drew much criticism; it was an example of what Jessica Luther notes as a continued failure to cover gendered violence in any careful or thoughtful way (Luther, 2021).

The way that gender frames discussion around male athletes is also apparent when we look at the way sports media celebrates athletes who play through injury as "tough" or "warrior-like." Similarly, male athletes who play after personal loss or family events are applauded. The message is that they are the strongest type of men not to let pain or other priorities distract them from winning at all costs. It also means that players who choose to prioritize their health, safety, or family over a game find themselves under ridicule that doesn't just question their athletic ability but also their manhood. For example, when baseball player Dan Murphy missed the first two games of the season due to the birth of his first child, storied radio sports personality Mike Francesca ranted about it on the radio. "You're a major league baseball player. You can hire a nurse," Francesca railed. "What are you gonna do, sit there and look at your wife in the hospital bed for two days?" (Alter, 2014).

Considering the role of gender in sports media invites us to examine the ripple effects of such disparity in reporting and coverage. As many scholars have shown, the lack of coverage of women athletes connects to the lack of investment in their leagues and opportunities. Moreover, the athletes who do get celebrated or focused on often serve to reinforce hegemonic standards of femininity and masculinity (Bruce, 2015; Cooky, Messner, & Musto, 2015; Kane, LaVoi, & Fink, 2013).

Marketing

The logic of sport marketing is closely tied to prevailing ideas about gender—from the commercials shown during sporting events to the way leagues and individual athletes are promoted. To understand the gender politics of sports marketing, we examine three distinct facets of the industry: the way sports are marketed, the products that are marketed within sports, and the marketing of athletes themselves.

Branding Men's Sport

The marketing of men's professional sports is more about branding than it is about selling the idea of sport itself. Indeed, the notion of men playing sports for the entertainment of others is a long-accepted and popular facet of American society. Instead, the challenge for men's sport leagues is in how they infuse meaning into their product. While battles over amateurism versus professionalization of sports raged across the 20th century (and continue today in the realm of college sports), the commercialization of professional sports has risen exponentially since the late 20th century on. How do leagues draw distinction from each other? What does their specific sport mean and what experiences and ideas are they promising to fans?

Boxing, for instance, was initially viewed as a low class and ruthless sport in the 19th century until the Victorian era "crisis of masculinity" had Americans looking for ways to recapture some rugged masculinity. Boxing promoters and sports journalists in the early 20th century began branding boxing as the ultimate "manly art" where controlled brutality, grit, and strength affirmed the manhood of both those who fought and those who watched (Gorn, 2010; Bederman, 2008). This framing of the sport brought it into national prominence alongside baseball and later basketball.

When the National Football League was still young, in the 1950s and 1960s, it was competing with the big three Bs—boxing, baseball, and basketball—for attention. By the time we entered the 21st century, professional football was the most prominent and lucrative sport in America. And like boxing's rise decades earlier, ideas about masculinity contributed to the construction of the league's image.

In *Brand NFL: Making and Selling America's Favorite Sport*, sociologist Michael Oriard said that football's controlled brutality and "sanctioned savagery . . . provided an antidote to a civilization grown soft through prosperity" (Oriard, 2010). Leaning into this gladiator-like image, the NFL went heavy into entertainment and commercialization. These athletes did not have to be saints or role models or brainiacs, they just had to entertain. Using the fast-growing television industry, the NFL created a marketing model that would become the envy of all other professional sports leagues.

Embracing large TV revenues and massive tax-subsidized stadiums, commercializing every second of games and using sports media and the entertainment industry to bolster the NFL brand created a sporting spectacle deeply wedded to expressions of manhood. The prominence of cheerleaders (not simply as a game day gesture, but on calendars and as visible representations of franchises), the celebration of "big hits," the constant beer and car commercials, and the rhetoric invoking war and battle all contribute to the deeply gendered spectacle that professional football continues to sell—and that the nation continues to buy.

Mariah Burton Nelson's seminal book, *The Stronger Women Get, the More Men Love Football: Sexism and the American Culture of Sport*, argues that this intensely masculine space became an important site for men who were feeling challenged by the gains women were making in other parts of society. Even as women's professional sports took off in the 1990s, football remained a largely homogeneous gendered space. Recent work by Thomas Patrick Oates brings this analysis forward to the present, where increasing numbers of women write about, report on, watch, play, referee, coach, and manage football. Oates argues that things like fantasy sports and videos are new marketing tools and brand engagement that also serve to quell "deep anxieties in white masculinity" among men who feel that football is no longer a protected space due to shifting racial demographics and (very modest) gains in gender and sexual diversity (Oates, 2009).

Selling Women's Sport

While men's professional leagues figured how to brand themselves, women's professional sports had to contend with selling their very existence in the first place. Unlike men's professional leagues, women's sport challenges conventional gender norms. Understanding sport as a masculine space makes men's leagues feel like a natural feature of the athletic landscape. Women's professional leagues have to justify themselves. Marketing of burgeoning women's sports leagues in the 1990s tried to attract spectators that would be invested in and inspired by commercialized "girl power."

Women's sports were hardly framed as entertainment; rather, it was a matter of morality and social responsibility. Ad themes like Nike's "if you let me play" underscored this depiction, featuring girls rattling off statistics tied to the benefit of playing sport. One young girl on a swing says, "If you let me play I will be more likely to leave a man who beats me" (Dworkin & Messner, 2002). The impact of this framing still lingers today. It fostered a narrow marketing framework in which women's professional sports had to be both inspiring and nondisruptive to prevailing gender norms. When women's teams are too dominant, they are "ruining the sport" and not "playing nice," a charge rarely leveled at the celebrated dynasties in men's sport (Carpenter, 2018).

As women's sports struggled for stability, there was a profound lack of investment in their leagues. Soon, a narrative of failure emerged surrounding women's professional leagues, and despite marketing efforts, the lack of coverage from sports media proved to be a considerable challenge. In 2018 when the *Boston Globe* reported that the Boston Breakers, a team in the National Women's Soccer League, was folding, some were quick to point out that it was one of the few stories the *Globe* had written about the Breakers (Springer, 2018). Sports media cites lack of viewership as justification for lack of coverage yet ignores the fact that people cannot view games that are never aired or otherwise impossible to find. In fact, recent years have demonstrated that if you put women's sports on TV, the audience will come. In 2020, with new media deals in hand, viewership for the WNBA and NWSL grew 68 percent and 500 percent, respectively (The Fan Project Report, 2020).

Despite proving their worth constantly, women's sports still face indignities such as a WNBA team being pushed out of their home arena during the *finals* because of a Disney on Ice show and a *preseason* NBA game. When coverage is provided, it is often limited strictly to the game itself; postgame interviews and analysis are rare. Men's professional sports have leaned on this pre- and postgame coverage to spin narratives and build stories about athletes and teams. The coverage increases interest in the game and investment in the product. Similarly, the minimal availability of merchandise is a continued issue. After the 2019 Women's World Cup, there was a 500 percent increase in demand for jerseys, a demand Nike was unprepared for and unable to meet. As Kurt Streeter argues, "Merchandise is a metaphor, a signpost of something else: cultural capital . . . The signal sent when gear is so hard to find and so rarely seen? Women remain an afterthought" (Streeter, 2021).

Recent work by the Fan Project has demonstrated that women's sports are poised to be one of the most lucrative investments in the future of the sports industry. However, to capitalize and fully promote women's sports, marketing needs to rethink its foundational logic, much of which is tied to hardened gender norms and assumptions. "Rather than simply 'lifting and shifting' traditional [marketing] models, sports properties, brand and media can learn from agile women's sports . . . and embrace new monetization models" (the Fan Project, 2020).

Marketing Athletes

Perhaps the clearest way to observe how gender affects sports marketing is by looking at the sponsorship and marketing of individual athletes. Athletes are seen as particularly profitable if they perform in gender-appropriate ways. As scholars like Nicole LaVoi, Janet Fink, and Mary Jo Kane have demonstrated, sex appeal and an emphasis on physical appearance over athletic ability have typified the branding of women athletes. Market logic rewards and promotes narrow blueprints for sports marketing success.

The perceived physical attractiveness of women athletes is understood through familiar expressions of femininity, Whiteness, and heterosexuality. Despite the women of color and queer women prominent in professional sports, the faces of the leagues have historically been White, conventionally attractive women who could be read as heterosexual. These narrow frameworks limit the visibility and earning potential of women athletes who fall outside these parameters. As LaVoi, Fink, and Kane argue, women athletes cannot "define themselves in ways that fundamentally alter men's ideological and institutional control of sports" (Fink, Kane, & LaVoi, 2014).

Consider for instance, that Serena Williams, who has outplayed her opponents and dominated her sport, has struggled to make as much in endorsement and sponsorships as her White competitors. In 2015, she had won 20 grand slams and was ranked number one in the world, drawing in roughly $11 million in endorsements. That same year, Williams' media-framed rival and five-time grand slam champion Maria Sharapova was set to earn over $22 million dollars in endorsements—double Williams' amount. Williams held a 17-2 record against Sharapova, but the media seemed intent on framing them as a storied rivalry. In truth, it was the contrast between them—their bodies, appearance, and identity—that fueled this framing. It is also this juxtaposition that explains the huge disparity in earning power (Soong, 2015; Bain, 2015).

Still, Serena Williams plays an individual sport that affirms gender norms. Women in golf, tennis, ice skating, gymnastics, and, to a lesser extent, track and field have greater earning potential because their athleticism is not seen as inherently disruptive to concepts of womanhood. Sponsors and advertisers find it easy to market a young gymnast who may be muscular but is also wearing a sparkly leotard and a bow. Women athletes in other sports, especially ones that are seen as gender-inappropriate, struggle to find sponsors who are willing to invest in them.

When women's boxing was added to the Olympics in 2012, organizers wanted the athletes to wear skirts because they were afraid no one would know they were women. After successfully pushing back on this idea, the sport made its debut at the London Games. Claressa Shields, a Black teenager from Flint, Michigan, captured gold. She would defend her gold in 2016. After the Olympics, Shields watched as another young Black girl and gold medalist, gymnast Gabby Douglas, raked in endorsement deals. In a scene in the documentary *T-Rex: Her Fight for Gold*, Shields wonders why she cannot find the same support. The agents and representatives she is talking to assure her that they want to find those opportunities for her, but first they need her to stop saying she likes to hit people. It's not marketable for a woman. Shields responds, "But I'm a boxer?" Later, Shields said, "I wasn't the ideal woman. I wasn't the pretty girl who wears her hair straight.... I don't know. I guess I wasn't what they were looking for" (Cruz, 2016).

Recently, Shields has pivoted from boxing to mixed martial arts (MMA), citing greater earning opportunity. Jenn McClearen's 2021 book, *Fighting Visibility: Sports Media and Female Athletes in the UFC*, helps explain why emergent sporting spaces such as MMA have provided new possibilities for women athletes. McClearen details how the Ultimate Fighting Championship (UFC) has "branded difference" and leaned into gender and racial diversity as a part of their "millennial sports brand model." Using social media for promotion, rather than relying on traditional sports media, allowed the UFC to disrupt and rewrite narratives of women's participation in combat sports. While this model is not without its own challenges, it echoes the findings from the Fan Project that new frameworks with less restrictive gender expectations and intentional marketing can help elevate women in sports.

Fandom

So much of the marketing logic used to invest in athletes and leagues rests on gendered assumptions about sports fans. The expectation that men love sports while women don't understand them is an enduring idea from informal interactions to bars to lecture halls and locker rooms. The commercials that air during games and the sponsors of athletes underscore this.

Advertisers covet the 18- to 40-year-old sports fans that they assume to be middle-class White men. Lawrence Wenner and Steven Jackson (2009) argue that the prominence of beer in the sports marketplace "is driven by normative understandings of gender" that bind sports, beer, and masculinity together. One can expect to find commercials for cars, razors, and watches during a sporting event, the presumption being that the people watching are men. As people like David Berri have pointed out, however, the logic hardly reflects the fact that 45 percent of sports fans are women—and 47 percent for the NFL (Berri, 2006).

Recognizing these shifts, leagues and franchises have attempted to reach out to their expanding fanbases. Yet too often their attempts underscore the persistent belief that women do not understand sports. Take, for example, the women fan clubs many NFL teams sponsor. Teams like the Tampa Bay Buccaneers, who announced their RED program for women by noting they would teach them "everything they need to know about the X's and O's of football," including the "term of the week" such as "play clock." The RED program also promised to help "educate attendees on how to incorporate their passion for the Bucs into their other lifestyle interests like . . . home entertaining" (Macur, 2015).

Similarly, leagues continue to struggle when it comes to offering merchandise for women fans. Clinging to the "shrink it and pink it" logic propels teams to offer small, pink jerseys, regardless of the colors of the club, as the only merchandise offering in women's sizes. Women have continued to note that it's not the color that is offensive, but the lack of options.

As some leagues and sponsors tentatively move away from male-centric marketing logic, new realms of possibility open. The Glossier campaign is the first beauty product line to partner with the WNBA. (Given that the league was so focused on asserting that they were athletes but still feminine, it seems curious that such a partnership had not occurred before.) Copying and pasting a marketing model from men's sport has led the sponsorship and industry partners to broker deals between the WNBA and shoe companies, sports drinks, and the like. The emergent partnership with Glossier, along with Diva Cup (and for soccer, Luna Bar), indicates that brands and franchises are expanding their understanding of who sports fans are. It remains to be seen if these new frameworks will be able to infiltrate sporting spaces still gendered as male. It is one thing to see a commercial for sport tampons when watching women's sports, but when it airs during an NFL game, reflecting that yes, people who have periods are also watching football, it will be the next step in reimagining gender in the sporting landscape.

Beyond the Binaries: Disrupting Gender Dichotomies in Sport

Almost as soon as kids start playing organized sport, they are separated by sex. The gender segregation is fueled in part by persistent ideas about gender and athletic capabilities. However, at young ages, before kids have even gone through puberty and developed the hormones that supposedly account for athletic differences, they are being sorted into gender-specific leagues. Messner argues that even as gains have been made for girls in sport, the discourse around youth sports reinforces the idea that sports are the expected domain of boys. Moreover, in advocating for girls in sports, advocates have adopted language about girlhood and womanhood that enforces ideas of natural gender difference (Messner, 2018).

Indeed, one of the most prevailing ideas about gender that sports transmit is that gender is binary, fixed, and biological. Sport remains one of the most rigidly sex-segregated places in American society. Yet a new generation of disruptors continues to push against gender norms in sports by challenging the rigid gender dichotomies that sports reinforce.

Athletes who are **nonbinary**, **intersex**, and **transgender** are drawn to leagues that are modeling gender-integrated sporting spaces. Trans youth participation in and access to sport has become a major battle in the ongoing culture wars. Nearly half of the anti-trans bills fielded in state legislatures in 2020 and 2021 have targeted trans athletes. The resulting battles have revealed how rigid understandings of gender continue to structure sports *and* how sports is a key cultural site for the transmission and maintenance of such ideas.

Intersex Athletes and the Excluding Binary of Biological Sex Determination in Sports

In 2009, the governing body of international track and field forced middle-distance runner Caster Semenya to undergo **gender verification testing**. Tests to determine whether someone is "really a woman" have been used in international sport since the 1940s. Gender verification is exclusively aimed at policing the boundaries of womanhood. The presumption is that anyone who is "not truly a woman" would possess an unfair advantage over women competitors (Schultz, 2012). In the 1960s, these tests became routine practice in the Olympics and were administered as invasive genital examinations. Athletes would receive a card proclaiming them sufficiently female for competition.

By the time Semenya was subjected to testing, compulsory testing had stopped. Instead of widespread testing, global track and field governance now only tested those women whom people "suspected" of not being a woman. Semenya's gender presentation, race, and success drew scrutiny and has resulted in nearly a decade of testing, court cases, and competition bans (Nyong'o, 2010; Cooky et al., 2013). Semenya's case renewed public and organizational conversations about gender, sports, and fairness. It also demonstrated the limits of binary sporting structures.

Scholars like Lindsay Parks Pieper and Katrina Karkazis have demonstrated how sporting organizations' continued attempts to use "medico-scientific technologies" to engage in sex determination have only served to impose a false binary on biological sex while discriminating against those who do not fit into rigidly defined categories (Pieper, 2016; Karkazis et al., 2012). Semenya is intersex, which itself is an expansive category. In fact, nearly one in 100 births falls under the umbrella of "differences of sexual development." As Karkazis and Rebecca Jordan-Young (2019) point out, there are at least six markers of sex, including genitalia and hormones, and none of these markers exists on a binary. There are many ways in which someone can exist outside of the binary categories of female or male.

Athletic organizations like the International Olympic Committee have justified gender verification testing under a concern about men masquerading as women to gain advantage in athletic competition. Labeling such concerns under the umbrella of fairness has historically grouped sex testing in with drug testing. Yet decades of testing have only served to exclude intersex athletes, sending a message that by their very existence, in their natural state, they have an unfair advantage that would disrupt the competition. It is a curious argument when one considers that athletes who are tall or swimmers with webbed feet never trigger such concerns about mythical fairness (Luther, 2020). Although some people have argued hormones like testosterone may not even produce an advantage, in sports we assume it does (Karkazis & Jordan-Young, 2019). The fact is that sports continue to insist on a rigid binary at the exclusion of people who fall outside boundaries of the male/female dichotomy. Organizing sports in this way, from the youth level on up, severely limits athletic opportunities for intersex people. How fair is that?

Beyond reinforcing a problematic binary, the one-sided scrutiny on the boundaries of women's sport transmits the idea that girls and women are naturally athletically inferior to men. There is no gender verification testing in men's sports because of the idea that there is no advantage to anyone who is not truly male trying to compete in men's sports. While Semenya's case demonstrates the limits of binary categories on biological sex, scrutiny of trans athletes highlights the constraints of a binary view of *gender*.

Trans Athletes and the Politics of Participation

The increasing visibility of trans athletes has complicated the neatly drawn gender boxes in and around sports. At the Olympic level, the International Olympic Committee issued the Stockholm Consensus in 2003 that affirmed the right of trans athletes to compete after surgical changes, multiyear hormonal therapy, and legal sex change. In other words, as McClearen notes, "Trans inclusion in sport is only possible for those who have selected physical alteration that adheres to medically sanctioned categories of male and female" (Fischer & McClearen, 2020).

In 2015, trans cyclist Chris Mosier challenged the IOC to remove the surgical requirement from its policy. As a result, IOC updated its bylaws to say that trans men (those who transition from female to male) were eligible to compete without restriction. Trans women also no longer were required to have surgery; however, conditions for hormonal levels and consistent testosterone monitoring were imposed. A year later, in 2016, Mosier would become the first trans athlete to compete internationally under the new policy. No trans athletes qualified for the 2016 Olympics. However, the 2020 Games (held in 2021) had three trans athletes, Laurel Hubbard, Quinn, and Chelsea Wolfe.

McClearen and other scholars highlight how trans inclusion in sports relies on medical scrutiny, testing, surveillance, and the maintenance of binary gender categories. This hyperpolicing

Laurel Hubbard, one of the first openly transgender Olympians, at the 2020 Tokyo Olympics.
Wally Skalij /Los Angeles Times via Getty Images

of gender is tied to the previously discussed notions of biological sex and athletic advantages. Sport is very visibly a sex-segregated space, and thus it has become the epicenter of public discourse around trans inclusion, gender policing, and public policy.

While Olympic and professional athletes like Mosier certainly garner attention, the bulk of conversation around trans athletes has been occurring at the youth level. Trans youth sports participation has become a central political battleground of the ongoing culture wars in the United States. Trans youth have few hormonal or surgical pathways, in part because many kids are not old enough to qualify. Therefore, trans youth policies often center on either respecting and affirming a child's gender identity or using birth certificates and biological sex as fixed identity markers.

In 2020, Idaho passed HB 500, a bill requiring youth in scholastic sports to participate according to their birth certificate and not in accordance with their gender identity—effectively banning trans youth from athletics all together. Since then, similar legislation has been introduced in 30 states, with five states passing similar bans within the 2020 and 2021 legislative years (Barnes, 2021b). When signing the ban into law, the governor of West Virginia noted that he was unaware of any athlete the policy would even currently apply to. So how does a bill get passed that addresses a purported problem for which there is not a single example?

As it is with NCAA and Olympic policy, much of the focus on trans youth athletes has been centered on the threat of trans girls, particularly trans girls of color like track stars Andraya Yearwood and Terry Miller. A trans boy, Mack Beggs, also became a national story when his home state of Texas continued to require him to compete with girls despite beginning testosterone treatment. His competitive success became a key rallying point for those wanting to restrict gender-affirming participation. The common denominator in these spotlighted stories is winning. Like with Caster Semenya, athletic success invites scrutiny. When the focus is shifted to trans or intersex athletes who disrupt these dichotomies but *lose*, it undercuts the arguments around fairness and competitive advantage.

In youth sports, the bans and restrictions to limit trans participation are rhetorically positioned as a defense of youth in sports, particularly of girls in sports. The exclusion of trans youth is seen as a necessary means to the end goal of maintaining gender-segregated sporting space. Remember that part of the idea behind this status quo is that sports benefit youth and that getting girls into sport helps their self-esteem, body issues, and confidence. Rarely however, are trans youth given similar consideration. "By focusing so much on biology and physiology, the impact is the dehumanization of those kids. You take away their personhood by boiling them down to their body parts and hormones—things that especially don't matter for prepubescent athletes," writes journalist Britni de la Cretaz (2021). Many scholars, policy advocates, and psychologists point to the benefit of sports participation for trans youth, noting that it is and could be an affirming space that combats isolation, stigma, depression, and more (Morris & Van Raalte, 2016).

The discourse around trans athletes utilizes sport and its myths of meritocracy, its perceptions of fairness, and its visibility as a sex-segregated social site to drive larger cultural conversations. Trans athletes, particularly youth, who challenge existing sporting structures and attempt to create space for themselves are disrupting the gender binary that has been foundational to the way athletics are organized. Yet, the fact that including trans youth athletes in sports has become a political football and a culture wars litmus test demonstrates once again that sports does not simply mirror society and reflect gender norms, it also drives (and sometimes disrupts) prevailing ideas.

Breaking Out of Binaries: New Possibilities for Gender and Sport

The fight for participation by trans and intersex athletes has often required reinforcing and submitting to the binary structure of organized

Sport Industry Leader Profile

Renee Montgomery

Title: Part Owner of the Atlanta Dream

In her senior year at the University of Connecticut, Renee Montgomery led the storied women's basketball program to a national championship, capping off a 39-0 undefeated season. Shortly after that, Montgomery was selected as the fourth overall pick in the 2009 WNBA draft. For 11 years, Montgomery was a key player for the Minnesota Lynx, the Connecticut Sun, and the Atlanta Dream. However, when COVID threatened the 2020 season, Montgomery decided to sit out. That was not the main reason, however.

"After much thought, I've decided to opt out of the 2020 WNBA season," Montgomery tweeted. "There's work to be done off the court in so many areas in our community. Social justice reform isn't going to happen overnight but I do feel that now is the time and Moments equal Momentum. Let's keep it going!" Fueled by a deep commitment to social justice and motivated by continued issues of police brutality, Montgomery joined Maya Moore as another WNBA player who put career aside to focus on activism and reform.

Montgomery received lots of support for her decision and motivated a few other players to make a similar choice. "This is not a breakup from basketball. Don't think I won't be back. I'm still rooting for the Dream, I'm still rooting for my teammates. I'm still going to be attached to the WNBA," she wrote in the *Players' Tribune* before the season started (Montgomery, 2020). And as it was set to kick off, Montgomery cheered on her teammates and the rest of the league for dedicating the season to #SayHerName and #BlackLivesMatter. Montgomery also watched in rage as the owner of her team, Kelly Loeffler, a U.S. senator from Georgia, publicly attacked the players of the WNBA for their dedication.

sport. However, nonbinary athletes like basketball player Layshia Clarendon and soccer player Quinn have become visible and vocal examples of athletes who don't (and refuse to try to) fit inside one box or another.

When Quinn was selected to the Canadian women's soccer team for the 2020 Olympics, they became the first openly trans and nonbinary Olympian to compete. When Quinn helped their team capture the gold medal, even more barriers were broken. "I feel optimistic for change. Change in legislature. Changes in rules, structures, and mindsets," said the Olympic gold medalist (Thompson, 2021).

In the WNBA, veteran and leader Layshia Clarendon was also advocating for change. After a year of leading the WNBA in activism around Black Lives Matter and voting rights, Clarendon took a huge step in 2021 when she announced that she had top surgery during the off-season. Clarendon was worried about the reactions of WNBA teammates, but the announcement was met with love and affirmation, and it even led the league's social justice council to add trans and nonbinary advocacy efforts to its platform. "I feel very woman, and I feel very man. I feel both, and I feel neither, and I feel like all the gender expansiveness that exists in the world is in me," Clarendon said. For the first time they felt fully seen by teammates and fans alike (Barnes, 2021a).

Both Quinn and Clarendon are staunchly committed to using their visibility to increase access and inclusion in sports to youth who are

Loeffler was intent on publicly reproaching her team and the league, in part as a show of strength for the senate race she was in. For Dream players and across the WNBA, Loeffler's actions were attempting to draw them into a fight she would profit from. Together, they strategized a different response. The Dream endorsed Loeffler's opponent, emphasizing their shared values and wearing shirts of support at their game day warm-ups. In fact, they refused to even say Loeffler's name anymore.

The entire situation sparked a realization for Montgomery. "I started to think, the people that can enact the most change are the ones in those positions of power—the owners, the managers . . . that was the trigger in my mind to think, maybe I need to be there in those positions" (Hinchliffe, 2021). Montgomery began to speak publicly about getting into ownership, drawing support from people like LeBron James. When Loeffler lost the election and was bought out from the team, Montgomery was part of the new ownership group, becoming the first ever WNBA player to become an owner in the league.

The journey into ownership was unplanned and unconventional; however, Montgomery has long been a leader. "As a captain on the court and as a vet, we deal with many different personality types, and we have to function as a unit," she explained. "Good communication that gets through to people is essential off the court and in the front office. We have to be able to make decisions that best benefit the team and organization as a whole. It's a team mentality" (Oliver, 2021).

Now as part owner and team executive of the Atlanta Dream, Montgomery continues to change the game. She has innovative ideas for the franchise and hopes that her journey inspires other Black women and former athletes to get into athletic governance.

"The reason I chose my career path is because I've always enjoyed assisting people and also making them laugh along the way. I was a point guard my whole life so leading teams was a skillset I built over my career. I take it very serious that I'm one of a few Black women when it comes to ownership. The more successful I can be, the more doors I hope it opens for other Black and Brown women so I make sure if I'm going to be the example, that I set a good tone."

also nonbinary. "Athletics is the most exciting part of my life and it brings me the most joy. If I can allow kids to play the sports they love, that's my legacy and that's what I'm here for," said Quinn (Thompson, 2021). While their very presence compels reconsideration of the status quo, both athletes still play in leagues defined by gender, the *Women's* National Basketball Association and National *Women's* Soccer League, respectively. The wording highlights the limits of individual athletes within sporting systems with deeply gendered foundations. Some leagues, however, model new possibilities of gender-integrated competition.

Gender-integrated sporting spaces already exist within mainstream sports. Consider mixed doubles in tennis or mixed teams in curling. Recently, Olympic sports have introduced mixed relays in track, triathlon, and swimming. These gender-integrated events maintain ideas of fairness by mandating the same number of men and women competitors. It also leans into the spectacle of women and men competing together to draw fans to the sport.

Other nontraditional sporting spaces have provided models for what gender-inclusive sporting practices might look like. Ultimate Frisbee is a sport that embraces the tag line "anyone can play" and offers mixed competitions from the youth to the professional level. Scholars like Thornton and Crocket analyze the continued gender ideologies present in the sport, but new leagues are explicitly trying to disrupt hegemonic practices (Crocket, 2013;

Thornton, 2004). The new Premier Ultimate League, for example, set out to "push people to think beyond" binaries and "intentionally open up a space for people to feel like they had a home to participate in a professional sport," (Ahmed et al., 2019). The league intentionally used "womxn" to signal that it was gender expansive and deemed athletes eligible based on their gender identity alone.

Fletcher indicates that roller derby is another sport that is grappling with how to provide expansive gender-affirming experiences (Fletcher, 2018). While the sport has roots as a mixed-gendered competitive space, its resurgence in the early 2000s was fueled by feminists looking for a sporting space that would accommodate a range of femininities and sexualities. Male-identified athletes began to form their own leagues alongside these dominant derby spaces. Now, derby teams across the world are considering how a gender-expansive space has also reproduced sporting binaries.

One of the most intentional sports that has endeavored to disrupt gender binaries is one that many do not even know is really played: muggle quidditch, the sport adapted from the fictional game depicted in J.K. Rowling's Harry Potter series. Played in colleges and club teams across the world, muggle quidditch is a real thing and ever expanding. U.S. Quidditch introduced Title 9 and 3/4. Named for the platform that takes you off to the magical Hogwarts and for the pivotal Title IX legislation. The policy is aimed at gender equality and inclusivity by ensuring that genders are represented on the pitch.

Explaining why Title 9 and 3/4 is important, U.S. Quidditch (n.d.) writes:

> *When all genders are able to compete equally on the pitch, they will learn to respect and value each other's abilities regardless of gender identity. It is well researched that sports participation improves the lives of those who identify as or are perceived as female, and levels the "playing field" not only in sports but in every aspect of society. Quidditch takes those benefits a step further by promoting a sport that is truly free of gender-based restrictions, rather than evenly segregated between men and women (as it currently exists under Title IX). Title IX additionally continues to exclude those who do not identify with the binary gender system. Through Title 9 3/4, USQ is more inclusive to transgender individuals by using gender as opposed to sex in policies. We understand that the process of transition is a very personal (and expensive) decision, and is influenced by many factors, none of which are, or should be, because a sport requires it. USQ also hopes to be a positive example for other sport leagues as well as a way to positively influence how players view other genders.*

Perhaps it is telling that we must turn to a fictionalized sport made real to find some of the most expansive gender-inclusive policies. Gender norms still structure the foundation of almost all organized sport. Although the invention of new games is certainly one approach to gender equity in sports, individual athletes, leagues, and activists are continuing to fight for access, influence, and visibility in sports writ large. From the historic battles to get in the game to the continued way sports transmits and maintains gender norms, modern sporting practice is all bound up in ideas about gender. Creating gender equity in sports requires us to confront all of the ways that our ideas about gender structure how sport is played, governed, and marketed—even if it means troubling the very foundation on which our understanding of sports is built.

SUMMARY

The purpose of this chapter was to consider the ways gender structures the way we play, market, consume, and think about sports. Moreover, it outlines how sport itself has been and continues to be a key site for the maintenance of gender norms and ideologies by highlighting the explicit and implicit way sports reinforce hegemonic gender expressions and examining the barriers faced by those who disrupt them. Understanding gender as well as key terms presented in this chapter such as femininity, masculinity, gender-typing, intersectionality, and social construct, are important steps to making sport more equitable and accessible. Last, the chapter presents examples of the way innovative athletes, leagues, brands, fans, and media professionals are working to shift the sports landscape and how their work provides a blueprint for continued efforts of equity and inclusion.

CRITICAL THINKING EXERCISES

1. Considering your own relationship to sports, how has gender affected your participation, fandom, or career interests? Have you ever considered this before? Is it challenging to identify the ways it has affected your relationship to sports? Why or why not might that be?
2. It is sometimes challenging to imagine other possibilities in sport. However, more conversations are happening now about what a feminist sports culture or a gender-inclusive sporting space might look like. Consider some of the institutional barriers we have highlighted and offer up a solution that might address the issue.
3. Imagine you are a sports agent and your client is a rising athlete looking for sponsorship. Your client is uninterested in beer, cars, and music. What product might you bring to your client? How might you pitch it? Is your product gendered? Pay attention to your responses and discuss how you were able to disrupt or maintain gender norms as you were marketing your client.

REVIEW QUESTIONS

1. How do ideas about gender affect the structure of sporting opportunity and access? List and discuss three examples.
2. The pivotal Title IX legislation is nearly 50 years old. In what ways has Title IX changed the relationship of gender and sports? Consider the intended and unintended consequences of the legislation. How might you revise Title IX for the next 50 years?
3. Describe why it is important to consider intersectionality with regards to gender in sports?
4. How have rigid binaries been maintained in sports? Why do you think sport is a particularly rigid site of gender expression? How might we imagine a sporting future that is not structured by gender?

Stacy Revere/Getty Images

CHAPTER 7

Sexual Diversity, Sexual Orientation, and Sexual Identity

Kiera Duckworth and Luca Maurer

LEARNING OBJECTIVES

- Explore the sociocultural dynamics LGBTQ persons may confront while participating or working in sport.
- Understand ways to use best practices for inclusive language in sport.
- Understand microaggressions and how to interrupt when they happen.
- Explore policy implications on the LGBTQ communities.
- Review strategies to create more inclusion in sport for LGBTQ individuals.

Although there have been recent lurches forward toward inclusion for lesbian, gay, bisexual, transgender, and queer (LGBTQ) people in society, including a few high-profile athletes who have come out, when it comes to sport, the playing field is far from level. The National Sports and Society Survey (NSASS) found that a third of all respondents perceive that LGBTQ athletes are not welcome in sport, while half of LGBTQ respondents reported enduring abuse, insults, bullying, or discrimination when playing sports, discussing sports with others, or spectating (Knoester & Allison, 2021).

An example of the extent to which homophobia and sport are intertwined can be found within soccer, where there is a many-decades-long history of displays of overt anti-LGBTQ bias during games, in countries throughout the world. The practice of spectators shouting derogatory antigay chants, slurs, and songs from the stands and displaying signs and banners with homophobic slogans is long-standing. Attempts by nations and by sport governing boards to try to quell this rampant homophobia through education, legislation, or policy have resulted in backlash and actually increased homophobic behavior during games. Efforts in both France in 2019 and Concacaf (one of FIFA's regional governing bodies) in 2021 to intervene and reduce these behaviors backfired when fans ramped up their efforts in protest of the new rules (Rosman, 2019; Goff, 2021).

Fueling these practices is the faulty assumption that all people involved in sport—fans, athletes, coaches—are heterosexual and cisgender. This assumption then ignites a vicious cycle that creates sport environments in which people are more likely to publicly express anti-LGBTQ bias—and more comfortable with doing so.

Yet the NSASS also found that more than a third of gay and lesbian people are dedicated and enthusiastic sport fans. The impact of witnessing such abuse, whether in the stands or from the field, is significant and can extend from the immediate feelings that result all the way to deciding to avoid sports or to completely discontinue playing sports.

But sport is interwoven throughout U.S. society, as well as integral to many people's well-being. A Trevor Project study found better physical and mental health outcomes for LGBTQ people who played sports as compared to those that didn't (Trevor Project, 2020). Tired stereotypes and assumptions still lingering in sport harm everyone, regardless of sexual or gender identity. The data are clear that LGBTQ people benefit—just as heterosexual cisgender people do—from the ability to experience and enjoy sport, whether as a fan, as an athlete, or in other roles. More efforts are needed to effectively address anti-LGBTQ stigma and discrimination so that it is safe, welcoming, and affirming for all.

Overview of Sexual and Gender Diversity

While sexual and gender diversity have always been a part of the human experience, it is only in more recent history that terms and identity labels to describe this diversity have been created. Lesbian, gay, bisexual, transgender, and queer (LGBTQ) people use many different words to describe their lived experience and identities. In addition, the terminology LGBTQ individuals and communities use to self-describe themselves changes over time.

While recognizing the many different ways people self-identify, for the purposes of this chapter the term LGBTQ is used to describe people who experience same-sex attraction or who are somewhere on the gender identity continuum in a place not wholly congruent with the sex they were assigned at birth.

About Terminology and Language

There are many regional and community variations in the use of language and terminology when it comes to LGBTQ identity. Language is a living document, and words and their definitions change over time.

Many earlier terms for LGBTQ communities and individuals were inherently pathologizing because they were coined by the medical establishment. They were grounded in the belief that sexual and gender diversity was a disease to be cured or a disorder requiring medical intervention, rather than as expected variations across the human experience (American Psychiatric Association 1952, 1968, 1980, 1987, 1994, and 2013; Davies & Davies, 2020). This is part of the larger history of diagnosis, through which those with power and privilege exercised explicit and implicit bias over people with minoritized and marginalized social identities through medicine (Brown, 1990). In this way, diagnosis functioned as a tool of social control of nondominant groups. Although some of these approaches and diagnoses have long since been recognized as instances of prejudice rather than science, the beliefs and biases from which they sprang are still enacted today in legislation and policy against LGBTQ people in the United States and abroad.

Common Identifiers: Terms and Concepts

The following terms and definitions are central to this chapter. They are also frequently misunderstood or confused, even today. They are provided here as a fundamental basis for understanding, and to help readers contextualize this chapter and its implications for the field.

- *Sexual orientation*—To whom one is attracted (e.g., heterosexual, gay, lesbian, bisexual, queer). A heterosexual person is attracted to people of a different sex or gender. A gay or lesbian person is attracted to people of the same sex or gender. A bisexual person is attracted to people of different and the same sex or gender.
- *Gender identity*—A person's deep-seated, internal sense of who they are as a gendered being (e.g., cisgender, transgender, nonbinary, genderqueer). A transgender person has a gender identity that does not match the sex they were assigned at birth, or whose gender identity is different from the one society expects of them. A cisgender person has a gender identity that matches the sex they were assigned at birth. Nonbinary people have a continuum or spectrum of gender identities and expressions, often rejecting the assumption that gender is strictly an either/or option of male/men/masculine or female/woman/feminine based on sex assigned at birth. Some additional words that people may use to express their nonbinary gender identity include agender, bigender, genderqueer, and genderfluid.
- *Gender binary*—The idea that gender is strictly an either/or option of male/men/masculine or female/woman/feminine based on sex assigned at birth, rather than a continuum or spectrum of gender identities and expressions. The gender binary is often considered to be limiting and problematic for all people, and especially for those who do not fit neatly into the either/or categories. Words that people may use to express their nonbinary gender identity include "agender," "bigender," "genderqueer," "genderfluid," and "pangender."
- *Coming out*—A process with multiple layers that involves recognizing and accepting one's sexual orientation or gender identity and making decisions about how, whether, and when to share that information with others. Coming out is not a one-time event. Because heterosexuality and cisgender identity are majority experiences, many people are assumed to be non-LGBTQ. This means some LGBTQ people are engaged in the process of continually having to come out to others throughout their lives. On the other hand, some people are assumed to be LGBTQ, whether they share their identity with others or not. This is often because of other people's assumptions about gender presentation and sex stereotypes. So while some LGBTQ people are faced with decisions about coming out frequently, there are also LGBTQ people who never get the opportunity to decide, due to the assumptions of others.
- *Sex assigned at birth*—The sex (female or male) assigned to a child at birth. Sex is usually assigned based upon a cursory observation of the external genitals of the newborn. Although this is sometimes referred to as biological sex, birth sex, or natal sex, the process of assigning sex at birth, especially in the United States, is more fittingly contextualized as an administrative or governmental process because the corresponding gender marker is then entered on the child's birth certificate. Thus, it becomes part of the state's definition of an individual's

identity—even if the sex assigned at birth is inaccurate or does not correspond to the individual's gender identity. A birth certificate is a core identity document used throughout life for any number of other processes that have nothing to do with genitalia or gender identity (e.g., to establish citizenship status, age, or parental rights).

- *Sexual behavior*—The variety of different ways human beings engage in sexual activities. There are many different sexual behaviors one may choose to engage in or choose to abstain from. Some sexual behaviors can lead to pregnancy or sexually transmitted infections, while others do not. Sexual behavior and sexual identity are different dimensions of human experience. That is to say, despite persistent myths and stereotypes that purport that certain sexual behaviors are practiced only by individuals of specific sexual orientations, a significant body of research demonstrates that human sexuality is far more complex and varied. Sexual behavior and sexual identity are not the same thing.

Demographics

How many LGBTQ people are there in the United States? The Williams Institute (2019) estimates the adult population of the United States who identify as LGBTQ as 4.5 percent. An estimated 6 percent of the LGBTQ community self-identify as queer (Goldberg, Rothblum, Russell, & Meyer, 2020). An estimated 1.4 million American adults—0.6 percent—are transgender people (Flores, Herman, Gates, & Brown, 2016), although that number is also believed to be an undercount due to the impact societal stigma and discrimination have on reporting.

The Williams Institute also estimates that 37 percent of adults who identify as LGBTQ have had a child at some point during their lives, and that as many as six million American children and adults have an LGBTQ parent. For LGBTQ people under age 50, almost half of women and a fifth of men are raising a child under 18 years of age, irrespective of whether they are partnered (Gates, 2013).

Many estimates rely on data from the U.S. Census and the American Community Survey, which undercount LGBTQ people and families because they count only those people living together in relationships in a single household—and only those willing to report their status truthfully. It is not known how many people do not share their sexual identity because they are fearful or concerned about disclosing their sexual orientation. The U.S. Census does not include questions about respondents' sexual orientation or gender identity. Instead it asks only about the relationship status and gender (on the binary) of the members living in the household.

Historically, research about LGBTQ people has focused on a deficit approach, that is, on ways in which LGBTQ people's lives are difficult, dangerous, or risky as compared to cisgender heterosexual people. One of the most well-known and often researched conceptualizations about how LGBTQ people differ from non-LGBTQ people is centered on vulnerability to a host of negative situations and consequences due to societal discrimination, stigma, and hostility: isolation, stress, violence, depression, substance use, and suicide. But LGBTQ people are at particular risk not because of their LGBTQ status, but because of societal stigma and its effects (Mink, Lindley, & Weinstein, 2014).

Although White gay and lesbian people are the focus of most research and media representation (Bible, Bermea, van Eeden-Moorefield, Benson, & Few-Demo, 2018; van Eeden-Moorefield, Few-Demo, Benson, Bible, & Lummer, 2018), people who are Black, Latinx, or Indigenous are the most likely to be raising children among all LGBTQ people (Kastanis & Wilson, 2014).

Diversity and Variation

There is a great deal of diversity and variation within and across the experiences of LGBTQ people. And there are different norms and cultural values about sexual orientation and gender identity across the United States and around the world. In some places, LGBTQ people are persecuted (UN Office of the High Commissioner for Human Rights, 2012); in others, they are treated similarly to non-LGBTQ people (Ottosson, 2006), and in some cultures they are revered (Picq & Tikuna, 2019). The impact of colonialism has had lasting effects on peoples and cultures throughout the world. Many of the existing prohibitions against LGBTQ identity and the criminalization of same-sex relationships in nations around the globe have their roots in penal codes imposed by colonizing nations.

In the U.S., it is a complex picture. Many of the unique concerns of LGBTQ people have to do with their continued and often complex unequal legal status. Prior to 2015, LGBTQ partners lacked access to the economic benefits of marriage because it was illegal for them to marry in the United States. Partners and children of LGBTQ parents could not access federally provided resources or state-conferred rights of both parents, including employment benefits like dependent health care, family leave, and pension benefits; the right of both parents to make emergency medical decisions; access to family support programs such as Social Security; veterans' benefits; equal taxation; military service benefits; pathways to legal immigration; inheritance; and access to courts for matters such as wrongful death and worker's compensation (Defense of Marriage Act, 1996).

At least 1,138 federal rights and privileges were extended only to heterosexual married couples (United States Government Accountability Office, 2004), with hundreds more at the state level. It was not until 2003 that the Supreme Court ruled that consensual adult sexual behavior was protected under the Fourteenth Amendment, thus decriminalizing private consensual sexual activity between same-sex adults (*Lawrence et al. v. Texas*, 2003).

In 2015 the U.S. Supreme Court decision *Obergefell v. Hodges* (2015) extended marriage equality to same-sex couples nationwide. Though heralded as a panacea that would comprehensively end the unequal legal status of LGBTQ individuals and families in the United States, attempts to relegate LGBTQ Americans and their families to second-class citizenship are still very much alive today. Many new state laws and federal policies have been enacted post-*Obergefell* with the specific and sole purpose of further ensconcing anti-LGBTQ discrimination into everyday life to prevent LGBTQ people from fully participating in society. These include restricting adoption and fostering to different-sex married couples only, attempting to criminalize medically necessary treatment of transgender Americans, prohibiting transgender people from military service, restricting access to public restrooms, stripping away decision-making rights when a partner or child is ill, and limiting to heterosexual cisgender people federal rights to fair housing, homeless and victims services, and other health and human service services (Movement Advancement Project, 2020).

A confusing, difficult-to-navigate patchwork of inequity still exists. At the federal level, there is currently just one pro-LGBTQ law—the Matthew Shepard and James Byrd, Jr. Hate Crimes Prevention Act, signed into law in 2009. This expanded existing federal hate crimes legislation to include crimes motivated by the victim's sexual orientation, gender identity, or disability status. The most up-to-date maps illustrating the patchwork of state and local laws addressing LGBTQ people and nondiscrimination, foster care, adoption, and other issues, can be found at the Movement Advancement Project's website.

Currently there is also no federal law prohibiting discrimination against LGBTQ people nationwide. Until 2020, Americans could be fired or denied a job because of their sexual orientation (actual or perceived) in 28 states and because of their gender identity in 29 states (*Bostock v. Clayton County*, 2020; Movement Advancement Project, 2020). This means that prior to 2020 less than half the total LGBTQ American adult population lived in states prohibiting employment discrimination based on sexual orientation and gender identity.

Discrimination can play a significant role early, as LGB adolescents are also 40 percent more likely to be stopped or arrested by police, and they are more likely to be expelled from school and convicted by courts than heterosexual peers with the same level of misconduct (Himmelstein & Brückner, 2010). LGBTQ youth, particularly LGBTQ youth of color, are also overrepresented in the juvenile justice

Sport Industry Leader Profile

Marie Curran-Headley

Title: Athletic Director, State University of New York (SUNY) Cobleskill

Marie Curran-Headley was appointed director of athletics at the State University of New York College of Agriculture and Technology at Cobleskill in 2017. Curran-Headley oversees 23 varsity sports in addition to recreation and intramural sports and serves as the chair of the sport and exercise academic department.

An experienced and dynamic leader, Curran-Headley launched esports as a varsity level sport in 2020. Her bold vision of growth for the department has reinvigorated the athletes, staff, and alumni of SUNY Cobleskill and breathed new life into the institution. As the chair of the Department of Sport and Exercise, she oversaw the development of a four-year baccalaureate degree while establishing and maintaining viable channels of communication and working relationships with faculty, administration, and the student body. Her ability and willingness to serve her campus can best be demonstrated by the numerous campus committees on which she serves. She became an integral part of the COVID-19 return to campus committee and provided an invaluable service to her institution by operating the COVID-19 testing center on campus.

Curran-Headley is an active member of Women's Leaders in College Sports and serves on the NCAA National Softball Committee. She is pursuing her PhD in educational culture, policy, and society from the (SUNY) University at Buffalo.

Marie values the student experience that can be cultivated through athletics. As a former athlete who played for a hall of fame coach, she knew what her own college experience meant to her personal and professional development. Her collegiate coach was instrumental

system, with almost 40 percent of incarcerated girls identifying as LGB, while 85 to 90 percent of incarcerated LGBTQ youth are youth of color (Movement Advancement Project, 2017).

Historical Threads of Exclusion and Discrimination

From the 1970s, when baseball outfielder Glen Burke was traded from one team and then let go from his contract from another likely because team management believed he was gay (Inner strength, 1994), to the 1990s, when Penn State basketball coach Rene Portland's policy forbidding lesbians on her team was publicized (Sandomir, 2018), the history of sport is full of examples of ways power and privilege operate relatively unchecked. This results in significant effects, not only on individual athletes but throughout sport and on society at large. Power and privilege serve to demonize, other, and suggest that people with some social identities are less than fully human and not entitled to participate in sport or the public sphere. Further, many of these same themes are socially constructed: "Is one man enough (or woman enough) to compete?" Who is doing the gatekeeping? And for what ultimate goal?

The culture of sport perpetuates sexism, homophobia, and heterosexism under the assumption of the gender binary. While perpetuating these oppressive and limiting sysin the early stages of her coaching career. Athletics allowed for a multitude of conversations between members of diverse backgrounds. College exposed her to these conversations and also allowed her to be more open about her sexuality. For Marie, the driving focus of her work is providing a college experience that expands athletes' perspectives and gives them the tools to be successful after college.

Marie has worked at both Division I and Division III levels. These levels of student athletics have different goals, and her professional goals are most aligned with those at the Division III level. In her view, Division III athletes learn responsibility and leadership skills in different ways while balancing their studies and athletic pursuits. "I think we care about them as people and succeeding in life. If a player has to leave [their team] due to mental health reasons, we still take care of them and make sure they are doing okay outside of their sport. We want them to succeed with or without sports."

Asked why it is important to be out, openly gay, in her career, Marie replies, "Because Pat Griffin told me so." Marie recalls hearing author and coach Pat Griffin speak about her own experience in coaching athletes. Pat talked about her experience embracing her gayness and how athletes in her department did not have prior representation of a successful, lesbian woman. Just simply talking about her partner and their lives together shifted perceptions among Pat's athletes and allowed for more acceptance.

Marie is open about her wife and their life together. She says that this portion of her identity, a marginalized sexuality, can be a source of commonality between her and students of color. "It's another path to talk to our student-athletes about the minority or the marginalized position. I can relate to student-athletes of color due to the marginalization," she says. Marie also emphasizes that women in sport do not have enough representation in leadership roles, and she recognizes that her position as the leader of an athletic program can also serve as a powerful model for athletes in her program.

tems, the gender binary is further enabled and enacted. Homophobia, as defined by Osbourne and Wagner (2007), is "the negative thoughts, feelings, and/or behaviors an individual has in response to others who are perceived to be gay or lesbian." Homophobic expressions can take the form of verbal discourses, physical actions, or the atmosphere created among a team. Heterosexism, as defined by Ronald G. Morrow and Diane L. Gill (2003), "is a belief in the superiority of heterosexuals or heterosexuality evidenced by the exclusion, by omission or design, of non-heterosexual persons in policies, procedures, events, or activities." Allowing these behaviors and attitudes to manifest themselves in the sport world creates a difficult atmosphere to participate in. Not only is it detrimental to gay, lesbian, or bisexual athletes, but this environment also hinders a heterosexually oriented athlete as well.

Sabo (1994) lists the five ways in which homophobia reinforces hegemonic masculinity and heterosexist beliefs. First, the prevalence of homophobia in sport "hurts gay athletes who face the daily threat of stigma and discrimination." The second is it "serves to enforce conformity to traditional gender roles [which] reinforces male hegemony." The third way homophobia reinforces heterosexism is it "promotes the cultural devaluation of women." Fourth, it "hurts even women who aren't lesbians." Finally, the fifth way is to "distract public awareness from heterosexual misconduct in sports" (Sabo, 1994). These five ways limit and constrict all participants of sport.

If Sabo's five main reinforcements of sexual inequality are coupled with Morrow and Gill's list of the four most common sexist myths, then one can see the effects of perpetuating homophobia in sport. Morrow and Gill (2003) summarize these myths: "Sports are for men and not women; all male softball players are heterosexual while all female softball players are lesbians; gay men are delicate and nonathletic, whereas straight men are tough, strong, and athletic; homophobia is normal and healthy." These sexist beliefs contribute to the oppression of females and non-heterosexually oriented males in our society.

Heterosexually oriented athletes are in a difficult position, specifically female athletes, because they are assumed to be lesbian for merely participating in sport. The dismissal of their sexuality is oppressive to the specific individual in consideration. Due to heterosexist norms and the hierarchy that is in place in American culture, heterosexual males are the benefactors in this regard. The distribution of power in American society is clearly in favor of heterosexual males. In the sport world they can feel as if they are participating in an environment that is free of homosexual peers while also immediately assuming that female athletes are homosexually oriented. Thus, through the perpetuation of homophobia in one institution integral to the socialization of many individuals—sport—heterosexually oriented males retain their superiority in this hierarchy.

Sexism, Heterosexism, Homophobia, and Male Athletes

Male athletes, and men in general, are socialized and required by society to assert their heterosexuality or be subjected to ridicule and harassment. Sabo (1994) continues his argument by saying, "Some sports are inherently more masculine than others and promote homophobia among athletes," such as football, basketball, and lacrosse. If one cannot project or prove that they are heterosexually oriented, then they are immediately labeled as gay. As Messner states, "the extent of homophobia in the sports world is staggering. Boys (in sports) learn early on that to be gay, to be suspected of being gay, or even to be unable to prove one's heterosexual status is not acceptable" (Messner, 1995). The sport world is a sphere in which hegemonic masculinity can be reproduced and perpetuated.

Males in our society must emphasize and defend their masculinity throughout their daily lives. If male athletes cannot assert themselves as strong, aggressive, and tough then they will face ridicule from their peers. Jim Rome, a television and radio personality who reports news from the sport world, emulated this point during a 1994 interview with NFL quarterback Jim Everett. Rome, who was pushed out of his chair by Everett in retaliation, "taunted Everett by calling him 'Chris' [female tennis star Chris Evert], a veiled reference to the quarterback's . . . lack of toughness" (Nylund, 2004). This instance is an example of how hypermasculine the world of sport can be. Rome uses an insult by referring to a male athlete as a female, which is socially inferior in our society. Everett was compelled to defend himself while simultaneously reasserting his masculinity by using physical force against Rome. Again, Jim Everett is a professional football player. Football is regarded as the most masculine sport in our society, so for Rome to declare Everett as "no more than a woman" he is posing a harsh challenge to the quarterback.

Merely participating in some sports can alone label a male athlete as gay and thus inferior in society. For example, some sports are considered by society as less masculine, as mentioned above. Fencing and cheerleading are two sports where male participants can face ridicule by their peers, and this is where Sabo and Anderson focused their articles. Both sports require strategy, subtlety, and finesse, which are classified as feminine traits and therefore inferior to masculine traits. Femininity in male sports will not be tolerated, as illustrated by Anderson in his interviews with male cheerleaders who played football in high school but cheer in college. The collegiate cheerleader states, "Masculinity has nothing to do with sexuality. I have really flamboyant friends who are straight [like me]" (Anderson, 2005). A man transgresses the acceptable gender roles when he acts in an effeminate manner. Thus, the structure surrounding homophobia in sport keeps the rigid gender binary in place. Sabo makes this argument in his article by saying, "Homophobia serves as a vehicle for [keeping] social conformity to traditional gender expectations desirable and nonconformity something to be feared and distained" (Sabo, 1994). When young men are participating in sports such as fencing and cheerleading, they are seen as transgressing the gender roles. Therefore, they are feminine and have lost their status as a masculine man in society.

Anderson (2005) continues by arguing that homophobia even limits straight men in their sexual behaviors. He employs personal accounts in his study to argue that many heterosexually oriented men can have sexual interactions with other men when a woman is present (i.e., a threesome). However, they must conceal their same-sex sexual practices outside of their team boundaries because in our society there is a "one-time rule" in regard to homosexual actions. On one specific co-ed cheering squad, homosexual behavior is allowed when a woman is present but in other contexts it would be a major transgression of one's expected gender role. Anderson argues that in the greater culture many would label a man homosexually oriented if he has had sexual relations with the same sex. The frequency of such an occurrence would also not be of importance; if sexual relations happen with the same sex, even one time, then he is labeled as gay. Anderson furthers his analysis by saying, "homosexuality is acceptable [within this group] but the expression of femininity is not" (Anderson, 2005). Men on this particular team were socially allowed to transgress the sexual boundaries and expectations but they were not allowed to cast an effeminate persona. They were to remain as masculine as possible and to conform to the overall societal norms of masculinity.

Application of this limiting concept of sexual expression was also used by Laura S. Brown (2004). However, she related it to women and their lesbian identity. Brown argues that a "lesbian identity [is] primarily a self-ascribed definition. . . . This identity may or may not be congruent with overt behavior . . . and it may also be ascribed to a woman by others, even if she does not accept this definition" (Brown, 2004). An individual's sexuality is personal, but

Cheerleading and fencing are two sports where male participants can face ridicule by their peers, and the structure surrounding homophobia in sport keeps the rigid gender binary in place.
Jamie Schwaberow/NCAA Photos via Getty Images

some people must construct and define their identity around what others have assumed. It is difficult that in our society women in sport are ascribed the label of lesbian for being athletic.

Sexism, Heterosexism, Homophobia, and Female Athletes

Female athletes face pressures of homophobia in a very different light. According to societal expectations, females are already transgressing the gender norms by merely participating in sport. This has been the general societal stigma against female athletes since women were permitted to participate. The female athlete was generally looked at as a deviant individual and alone in her athleticism. As she excels in sport she is distinctly more deviant. Paul Willis observed this sentiment, saying, "To succeed as an athlete is to fail as a woman, because she has, in certain profound ways, symbolic ways, become a man" (Willis, 1982). Christine Griffin et al. (1982) echoed this thought in their article as well.

Female athletes as a whole have struggled to be taken seriously in the traditionally masculine arena of sport, but lesbians in sport are stigmatized continuously through homophobia. As stated previously, women in sport are immediately assumed to be lesbians for their mere participation in athletics. The perpetuation of homophobia in women's sport heavily relies upon sexism in the greater society. Pat Griffin discusses this idea thoroughly in her article titled "Changing the Game: Homophobia, Sexism, and Lesbians in Sport." She argues that there are six categories in which homophobia manifests itself in women's sport. They include "silence, denial, apology, promotion of heterosexy image, attacks on lesbians, and [the] preference for male coaches" (Griffin, 1992). These manifestations send a very clear and controlling message not only to lesbians in sport but to all women involved with sport. They have the power to control and stigmatize all female participants.

Kauer and Krane (2006) observed the promotion of the heterosexy image through their study of female collegiate athletes. Some players said that they were assumed to be lesbians when they did not adhere to traditional femininity. One athlete was quoted as saying, "Female athletes are degraded if they don't look the proper way: thin, shaved, and beautiful. People just think you're gay because you're not wearing make-up" (Kauer & Krane 2006). This player was clearly transgressing the gender binary because she was not displaying enough femininity in her everyday life. Many players interviewed said that they were harassed and assumed to be lesbians by men in general if they did not reflect the hegemonic femininity that our society demands.

Griffin explains the first manifestation of homophobia, silence, as "lesbians in sport [that] are treated like nasty little secrets that must be kept locked tightly in the closet" (Griffin, 1992). Women as a whole are trying to gain society's acceptance to participate in sport and keeping the silence about lesbians in sport may further this goal. If silence is not kept then many participants in sport will employ denial. For example, if a player is suspected of being a lesbian, those around her will deny that she is or not even acknowledge the fact that lesbians are in sport (Griffin, 1992).

Sabo echoes the third point that Griffin makes about homophobia in women's sport, the manifestation of homophobia that they refer to as apology. If a female sport figure does not appear to be "feminine enough" there is a stigma placed against her. There is a fear in women's sport that female athletes will look like lesbians. Griffin mentions that athletes are encouraged to attend classes about etiquette, personal appearance, and how to act "like a lady" in public (Griffin, 1992). She also discusses the cultural pressures that many coaches face in her book entitled *Strong Women, Deep Closets: Lesbians and Homophobia in Sport* (Griffin, 1998). These are perfect examples of how society is uncomfortable with the idea of bending the gender lines. Sabo recognizes this idea in his article entitled "The Politics of Homophobia in Sport." If lesbians in sport can remain "hidden" and can "conform to traditional gender expectations, they help to maintain the social and political dominance of elite males" (Sabo, 1994). This culture is traditionally male-dominated, and women are considered to be socially inferior to men.

Following this logic, since lesbians in sport are silenced, forced to deny, and act in an apologetic manner toward their sexual identity, they are expected to act out heterosexual roles. Hargreaves argues this point by stating, "lesbians are forced to . . . assume a heterosexual identity. [This] is usually passed off 'innocently' as a 'harmless' joke or innuendo" (Hargreaves, 2000). This is absurd to expect from an individual in exchange for participating in sport. If the cultural standards were reversed, would we as a society demand that all heterosexual athletes stay in their closet and assume a homosexual identity? It is unreasonable to demand this of someone, yet our society and the culture of sport expects this behavior constantly.

Although the articles are outdated, the observations are still valid and can be seen today in some aspects. The practice of sex testing some female competitors to prove they are not men masquerading as women in sport has a long history that continued throughout the 2021 Olympics, with intense scrutiny particularly upon Black women athletes who excel in their sport. Such scrutiny reflects the societal thought that if a woman is to succeed in sport then she must be a man because only men can excel in athletics.

Heterosexism, Bisexual Invisibility, and Bisexual Erasure

Research that specifically focuses on bisexual people in sport is profoundly lacking. Although many studies include the "b" for bisexual in their titles, their designs, discussions, and implications rarely speak to the experiences and needs of bisexual people and instead concentrate on lesbian women and gay men while frequently entirely overlooking bisexual people. This in many respects mirrors the state of bisexual invisibility and bisexual erasure in American society at large. One of the few notable exceptions in the literature attributes this lack of academic interest to the belief that to be defined as a gay man, especially in sport, one need only experience same-sex attraction once in their lifetime—thus rendering bisexuality impossible, by definition—and that interventions that reduce homophobia also reduce biphobia (Anderson & Adams, 2011). The absence of a substantial body of work exclusively focused on bisexual people then serves to contribute to and reinforce the absence of bisexual visibility within sport and society, in a self-perpetuating cycle.

Legislation and Policy Issues

During the first four months of 2021, more than 100 bills aimed at restricting the rights of transgender children, their parents, and their doctors, began moving through state legislatures in 33 states (Ronan, 2021). Many of these sought to prohibit transgender children from participating in sports. Others criminalized safe, evidence-based medical care for transgender children and young adults. A few reraised the issue of whether transgender people should be allowed to use public restrooms and other facilities (North Carolina signed the first such effort into law in 2016; it was later repealed), while Texas legislators sought to charge parents with child abuse if they were supportive of their transgender child (Munce, 2021).

At the time of this writing, laws banning transgender girls and women from sport have been enacted in Texas, Arkansas, and Mississippi, and more are moving quickly toward passage across the country (Krishnakumar, 2021).

Many of these bills also require some type of "proof" of sex in order to be allowed to play, which could result in girls being forced to have their genitals examined. This also means any athlete that someone else—coaches, competing team, spectators, parents—thinks does not appear sufficiently feminine enough, or who displays athletic performance that excels, could be challenged and disqualified unless they undergo a physical exam of their sexual anatomy (Srikanth, 2021).

The history of using policy and legislation to control who can fully participate in daily life and social and recreational activities, including sport (along with facilities often used in tandem like locker rooms, changing areas, and restrooms), extends far back from the present day. During other periods of American history, the focus of who is granted full humanity, who is deemed worthy of dignity and respect, has rested squarely on allowing or denying access to public facilities. Often such efforts deftly deployed myth and stereotypes to fuel moral panic to justify these actions (Sanders & Stryker, 2016). History contains other examples of public facilities as a focus of oppression and legislation against marginalized groups; often contextualizing these as necessary to "protect" dominant groups across lines of race, gender, and sexuality (Godfrey, 2003). Segregation, discussions to move forward the ERA and the Americans with Disabilities Act, attempts to curtail people living with HIV from society—all have been times when laws carved out access for some to have the right to use public facilities, while others did not.

Some of the same tactics used today to try to regulate and eliminate transgender people from participating in sport have been used against Black people, women, people with disabilities, LGBTQ people—in sport and in use of public facilities like pools, restrooms, and changing areas (Kafer, 2016; Adair, 2015). Before this latest round of antitransgender prejudice, there was discussion of whether lesbian and gay people should be allowed in locker rooms, echoing the historic roots of segregation and use of force and fear in the service of the status quo. Although it may appear as one new chapter of marginalization, this was never about locker rooms, bathrooms, or sports. It was about exerting power and control over marginalized bodies while at the same time heralding outstanding athletic achievement in White, cisgender men, not as an anomaly for intrusive examination and disqualification but as proof of their superiority.

In many cases the discrimination was overt, fueled by anti-Black prejudice and White supremacy, such as the intentionally segregated leagues in baseball and the history of college teams not being integrated nor White teams playing against Black teams until well past the midpoint of the 20th century (Barra, 2013).

In other cases, discriminatory misogynist practices and policies ensured some athletes' bodies would be subject to heightened scrutiny to gain the right to participate. The International Olympic Committee began requiring sex testing for all women athletes in 1968. At the time, the test consisted of a group of physicians who visually inspected the athletes while the athletes were undressed. The year prior, a race official tried to physically pull Kathrine Switzer off the Boston Marathon course. At the time, women were prohibited from participating, and medical professionals continued to reinforce the myth that running could affect a woman's fertility and do other long-term damage. In New York in 1972, marathon officials allowed six women to compete on the condition that they run separately from the men. And the first Olympic Women's Marathon didn't take place until 1984 (Moran, 1984). The Boston Marathon was also the first major marathon to include athletes using wheelchairs, in 1975 (Boston Athletic Association, n.d.).

In each of these, prohibiting some groups of people from participating has been framed either as necessary to provide protection from physical harm (e.g., to the individuals in the group from injuring themselves, or to protect other athletes from being injured by them) or that the mere act of their competing would give them an unfair advantage.

Contemporary examples of perpetuating the myth of an "unfair advantage" and of policing women's and girls' bodies can be found at the intersections of gender, femininity, and anti-Blackness. Caster Semenya, who is not a transgender person, has had her right to compete challenged at the international level several times over (Maese, 2019). Semenya, an accomplished runner, received attention because of her athleticism that ultimately led to her being compelled to undergo sex testing in order to retain her eligibility. Some sport governing bodies questioned her outstanding performance simply because she is so fast, and used this as grounds to challenge whether or not she is a woman. Semenya has been subject to various forms of chromosomal and hormonal testing throughout her career, and has been found to have naturally occurring levels of testosterone higher than average. For this reason, sport governing boards have stated they will require her to subject herself to medical measures to suppress her testosterone levels in order to be allowed to compete (Block, 2021). During the 2021 Olympics several additional women from Namibia and Burundi were challenged in similar ways to prove that they are women, simply on the basis of their dominance in their events (ESPN, 2021). While at the same time, White athletes who excel in their sport and whose appearance matches a more hegemonic notion of femininity, like Katie Ledecky, have not.

Unintended consequences also abound. For instance Mack Beggs, a transgender boy, was allowed to compete by state athletic rules only in the league corresponding to his sex assigned at birth. He ultimately won the annual Texas state girls' wrestling championship, twice (Boren, 2018). Laws and policies focusing on transgender athletes could have far-reaching effects that extend not only to whether transgender people will be able to be a part of public life, but also to the likelihood that cisgender girls' eligibility to participate will be challenged as a result. Yet at the time of this writing the NCAA has announced they may cancel and relocate events from states that have enacted legislation against transgender athletes (NCAA, 2021).

Actions for Equity and Inclusion

As mentioned earlier in this chapter, terms LGBTQ people use to describe their identities and experiences evolve and change over time. They also vary within and across LGBTQ communities and across generations and geography. The words used in publicity and promotional material are frequently examined by LGBTQ people to evaluate whether the event or offering is credible, safe, and inclusive. Therefore it is important to use appropriate terms, the names and pronouns individuals

Mack Beggs, a transgender boy, was allowed to compete by state athletic rules only in the league corresponding to his sex assigned at birth. He ultimately won the annual Texas state girls' wrestling championship, twice.

Michael Stravato/For The Washington Post via Getty Images

use for themselves, and inclusive language in all sport communications and settings (Chang et al., 2020). Although frequently framed as an issue specific to LGBTQ people, this should be practiced—and expected—in all professional contexts. Using inclusive language benefits not only LGBTQ people but all people of different lived experience, backgrounds, and family status. For instance, use terms like parents rather than mother and father; partner or spouse rather than husband or wife; and athletes, fans, scholars, students, or the team name, rather than gender-specific words like "guys," "girls," and gender qualifiers on team names such as "Lady Huskies" in coaching and teaching situations. Forms, documentation, websites, and social media content should model this as well.

Some professionals and peers concentrate a great deal of effort into knowing all the different terms and definitions used within LGBTQ communities. While this has its place, what is more important is being able to consistently demonstrate behavior that is affirming and inclusive: the willingness to be open to new concepts and ideas, especially about groups of which the person is not a part; the ability to identify teachable moments and to interrupt bias and stereotype; the capacity to model respect in all settings; and the cultural humility to accept that mistakes will happen and to readily offer a sincere apology when they do.

Using the names and personal gender pronouns people use for themselves is central to conferring dignity and respect. In addition to being the only respectful way to refer to people, using the lived or chosen name of adolescents (a name used by the person that is different from the one given them at birth) has been shown to significantly reduce depression, suicidal ideation, and suicidal behavior in transgender youth (Russell et al., 2018). Mypronouns.org is a comprehensive resource that covers what personal gender pronouns are, how to use and share pronouns, and additional links and resources. Another website, pronouns.minus18.org.au, functions as an app when used on a tablet or smartphone and offers the user the ability to practice using gender pronouns in a fun, interactive, and private manner.

On the macro level, each of these elements would ideally be included in policy documents regarding eligibility and nondiscrimination and in expectations for behavior or codes of conduct. When statewide or sport-specific policies don't yet exist or are due for review, model policies for LGBTQ inclusion can be found through a variety of sources, including GLSEN.org, LGBT Sport Safe, transathlete.com, and Athlete Ally.

Cultural Humility

The understanding and ongoing practice of cultural humility, already frequently used in interdisciplinary contexts (Mosher et al., 2017), is not only helpful but essential. Cultural humility focuses on learning from others, critically examining one's own cultural awareness, interpersonal respect, mutual partnership to change imbalances of power, openness, and being attuned to others with regard to receiving new cultural information. By starting from a place of cultural humility, practices, policies, and playing environments can be created that not only accept LGBTQ athletes but expect them.

Intersectionality

Intersectionality (Crenshaw, 1993) describes the cumulative ways power and privilege combine or overlap in the lives of individuals and groups, especially people with nondominant social identities, to produce multiple effects of marginalization and discrimination (e.g., racism, sexism, heterosexism). An athlete or sport professional who is LGBTQ, a person of color, and an immigrant experiences discrimination in ways that are compounded and complex. It is as if an exponent is placed on the level of discrimination and oppression one might face, as these intersecting experiences and identities overlap to produce societal marginalization.

Because some LGBTQ people, especially youth, are at risk for negative outcomes, sport professionals and sport opportunities can play a role in putting things into a more multidimensional context. Society is overtly hostile

Sport Industry Diversity Initiative

USA HOCKEY 2019 POLICY ON TRANSGENDER AND NONBINARY ATHLETE ELIGIBILITY

USA Hockey (2019) crafted a clear, concise, and comprehensive policy covering how transgender and nonbinary athletes fit within the range of USA Hockey programs offered, as well as acknowledging and providing meaningful inclusion steps to support diversity across the lived experiences of players.

USA Hockey prefaces the policy points with a clear and matter-of-fact explanation that the policy is grounded in their existing guiding principles of supporting equity and inclusion, and that the sport be one "where people of all backgrounds can contribute and play ice hockey, and to do so in a fair and safe manner." The introduction also demonstrates how this policy fits within the framework and foundation of the organization overall, within its goal of providing a healthy and respectful environment in which all athletes may play.

The policy has several components. It reiterates that many USA Hockey programs are not gender specific or gender segregated, and thus eligibility extends to all players regardless of gender identity, gender expression, or sex assigned at birth. It then sets out the criteria for transgender girls' eligibility on girls teams, and transgender boys' eligibility. The policy also specifically addresses gender nonbinary athlete eligibility and describes ways their participation is encouraged and protected under the policy. Additional sections address documentation and logistics for athletes wishing to change their gender marker in USA Hockey registration records, as well as respectful locker room behavior.

Similar to the introduction, the policy closes with respectful additional concrete recommendations and guidelines applicable to this specific topic that also dovetail with the guiding principles and goals of the organization overall.

to LGBTQ people (Meyer, 2003). Responding to stigma, stress, internalized oppression, the desire to fit in, managing family disapproval, and sheer survival all play a role in behaviors that may lead to increased risk. Sport educators and professionals can also help individuals, colleagues, and their communities transition from more traditional and common but outdated models that focus narrowly on preventing harm when it comes to LGBTQ youth, and shift to proactively promoting the well-being of LGBTQ youth (Greenspan et al., 2019; Ryan, 2014). Sport participation and opportunities for LGBTQ people of all ages can also address societally imposed stigma and improve gaps in health, belonging, and connectedness (Ceatha et al., 2019; Greenspan et al., 2019; Petty & Trussel, 2018). It is equally important that sport professionals address LGBTQ people and themes from a perspective that avoids reducing all LGBTQ people to one issue and thus risks further marginalization and stereotyping. Rather, honoring each individual in addition to recognizing the diversity across and within LGBTQ communities is central to success.

Universal Design

When it comes to LGBTQ people and themes, a number of principles, concepts, and strategies align uniquely for the purpose of inclusive and effective education of sport professionals. These include universal design, intersectionality, cultural humility, and critical thinking skills.

The conceptual framework of universal design—first utilized to support the needs of people who have disabilities—can be applied to improving LGBTQ inclusion and equity within sport, as well. From the physical design of spaces to the consideration of supports for learning, participation, and teaching, principles of universal design help to create physical and emotional spaces that foster respect and trust (Couillard & Higbee, 2018). Attitudinal barriers, addressing unequal access to facilities, inclusive and culturally competent data collection, marketing, and professional development can all play a role in designing sport events, sport programs, and professional training and coaching strategies that center on inclusion, dignity, and respect.

Critical Thinking

Engaging critical thinking skills is also essential (Dozono, 2017). Rather than perpetuate a continued focus on the perceived majority experiences (White, male, heterosexual, cisgender), support individuals in shifting to examine sport through the lens of people typically left out or "othered"—for instance, employing critical thinking to shift from focusing on LGBTQ individuals within society to how society has portrayed and responded to LGBTQ people. Similar to employing cultural humility toward furthering equity and inclusion, critical thinking skills are another means to discern and unpack which athletes and fans are centered, and which are overlooked or ignored.

Program Promotion

Effective promotion of programs that serve the needs of LGBTQ families, or families with LGBTQ members, must address several key themes. Efforts at transparency of purpose and philosophy, as well as specific and informed outreach, will be required.

LGBTQ visibility in sport is on the rise publicly but there are many individuals behind the scenes that are in positions to support someone coming out publicly. These folks can contribute to a positive environment that is inclusive of differing sexual and gender identities. In contrast, people in those roles might contribute to creating an unwelcoming, or hostile, environment that is not safe for an individual to come out.

A number of factors can be barriers to participation. LGBTQ people might not participate in sport programs or attend sport events because of fear of being outed by attending, concern about safety and respect issues related to LGBTQ identity, or skepticism that the sponsoring organization would be welcoming and inclusive of LGBTQ people. LGBTQ individuals and communities also contend with the legacy of being pathologized at best, vilified at worst. LGBTQ people may distrust sport programs and events until they demonstrate themselves to be inclusive, safe, and equitable for everyone. Sport professionals must take care, though, to avoid tokenizing or generalizing, while avoiding stereotypes as well.

Engaging with LGBTQ leaders in local communities and enlisting their input is another strategy for success. Collaborating or volunteering at existing events planned by and for LGBTQ people (e.g., local LGBTQ organizations initiatives, LGBTQ pride events) may contribute to a sense of credibility, commonality of purpose, and goodwill. In some areas, it may be challenging to engage with LGBTQ people if the overall climate is still stigmatizing or perceived to be unsafe.

In addition, the impact of microaggressions—pervasive everyday "brief verbal, behavioral, or environmental indignities, whether intentional or unintentional, that communicate hostile, derogatory, or negative slights and insults" (Sue et al., 2007)—must be actively examined and addressed (Nadal, 2019). The presence of microaggressions in the environment may lower participation rates and trust, whether the source of microaggressions is from sport professionals, from other participants, or from fans.

Allied members of sport organizations can play an important part in creating positive work environments for marginalized individuals. Allies—those that do not identify as a member of the LGBTQ communities but use their privilege to support and advance equality—greatly affect the culture of an organization. An ally's visibility within the organization, presence at competitions, and formal and informal support of LGBTQ individuals positively contribute to advancing a more equitable and positive environment for out and closeted members of the LGBTQ communities. Those in positions of privilege can take action to confront discriminatory or hateful language, challenge heterosexism and anti-LGBTQ bias, strive to use more inclusive language and correct pronouns, allow space to discuss LGBTQ issues in your area, and be knowledgeable about LGBTQ issues and concerns (Linley et al., 2016).

SUMMARY

This chapter explores the experiences of LGBTQ people who work and compete in sport, the limitations of a sport system designed around a gender binary, and the challenges people with marginalized and minoritized sexual orientations and gender identities experience in sport and sport workplaces. Historic challenges have included the impacts of misogyny, heterosexism, transphobia, and bisexual erasure, as well as individual organizational and institutional stigma and discrimination. The influence of pervasive structural racism has magnified and compounded the ways in which some athletes' bodies are scrutinized, too. Changing terminology, depathologization of LGBTQ identity, and changes in technology have also paved the way for more agency, autonomy, and self-determination, while sometimes serving as tools to restrict participation as well. Although barriers remain, there are also a variety of practices and tools at our disposal to extend equity to people of all sexual orientations and gender identities. A thorough understanding and operationalizing of intersectionality in the service of extending equity is necessary to address the confluence of overlapping factors that particularly impede the participation of Black women and transgender people. By employing critical thinking, practicing cultural humility, implementing universal design principles, using existing resources, and investing in thorough equity audits of existing programs and opportunities, sport can truly become a space for everyone.

CRITICAL THINKING EXERCISES

1. Watch one of the documentary films about LGBTQ people and sport listed below, and discuss. What were the themes of the film? What stands out most for you about the film? Did anything in particular resonate for you? Did anything come up that you'd like to learn more about? What does this film say about the state of LGBTQ people and sport? If you could take one action to improve the climate for LGBTQ people in sport, what would it be?

    - *Changing the Game* (2019) (high school athletes)
    - *Claiming the Title: Gay Olympics on Trial* (2009)
    - *Training Rules* (2009) (basketball)
    - *Out In the Line-Up* (2014) (surfing)
    - *Queens and Cowboys: A Straight Year on the Gay Rodeo* (2014)
    - *Game Face* (2015) (MMA and college basketball)
    - *Man Made* (2018) (bodybuilding)
    - *The Ice King* (2018) (skating)
    - *Alone in the Game* (2018) (professional athletes)
    - *Out for the Long Run* (2011) (high school and college athletes)
    - *Ring of Fire: The Emile Griffith Story* (2005) (boxing)
    - *Steelers: The World's First Gay Rugby Club* (2020)
    - *Out: The Glenn Burke Story* (2010) (baseball)
    - *100% Woman* (2004) (mountain biking)
    - *Walk Like a Man* (2008) (rugby)

2. Do an LGBTQ inclusion audit of the website of a major sport team. Is there a nondiscrimination statement that includes sexual orientation and gender identity? Can it be easily found? Are there regularly scheduled events that specifically welcome LGBTQ people, like a Pride Night or LGBTQ fan appreciation events? Is there information about inclusive facilities available at the sport venue, such as all gender restrooms or a policy affirming that individuals can use the restroom that corresponds to their gender identity? Is there a map or other specifics about where these are located? Are images and symbols that reflect LGBTQ people and communities included on and integrated across the site? Is it possible and relatively easy to find information about ways the organization is involved with, sponsors, or contributes to issues affecting LGBTQ communities, such as partnerships with local or national LGBTQ organizations, or actively engaging in the development and maintenance of LGBTQ affirming laws and policies? Is there information about the board of directors that indicates ways in which their professions, avocations, or service are representative of the needs and issues of LGBTQ people?
3. View some of the images and accompanying information about the college and high school athletes profiled by the Fearless project by Jeff Sheng at www.fearlessproject.org/about. Using this chapter as a resource and your own experiences in sport, what are examples of some of the types of challenges these athletes may have faced? What kinds of opportunities? In what ways might the athletes have been affected by these?

REVIEW QUESTIONS

1. What does an individual's *gender identity* encompass?
2. Provide some examples of patterns of discrimination and exclusion in sport programs and society at large when it comes to themes of equity and inclusion?
3. There is also lack of research that specifically focuses on bisexual people in sport. Explain the impact of this gap on individuals, within sport and within society.
4. What is the purpose of conducting an inclusion audit?
5. Describe three strategies to intervene as a bystander when you observe microaggressions or acts of marginalization.

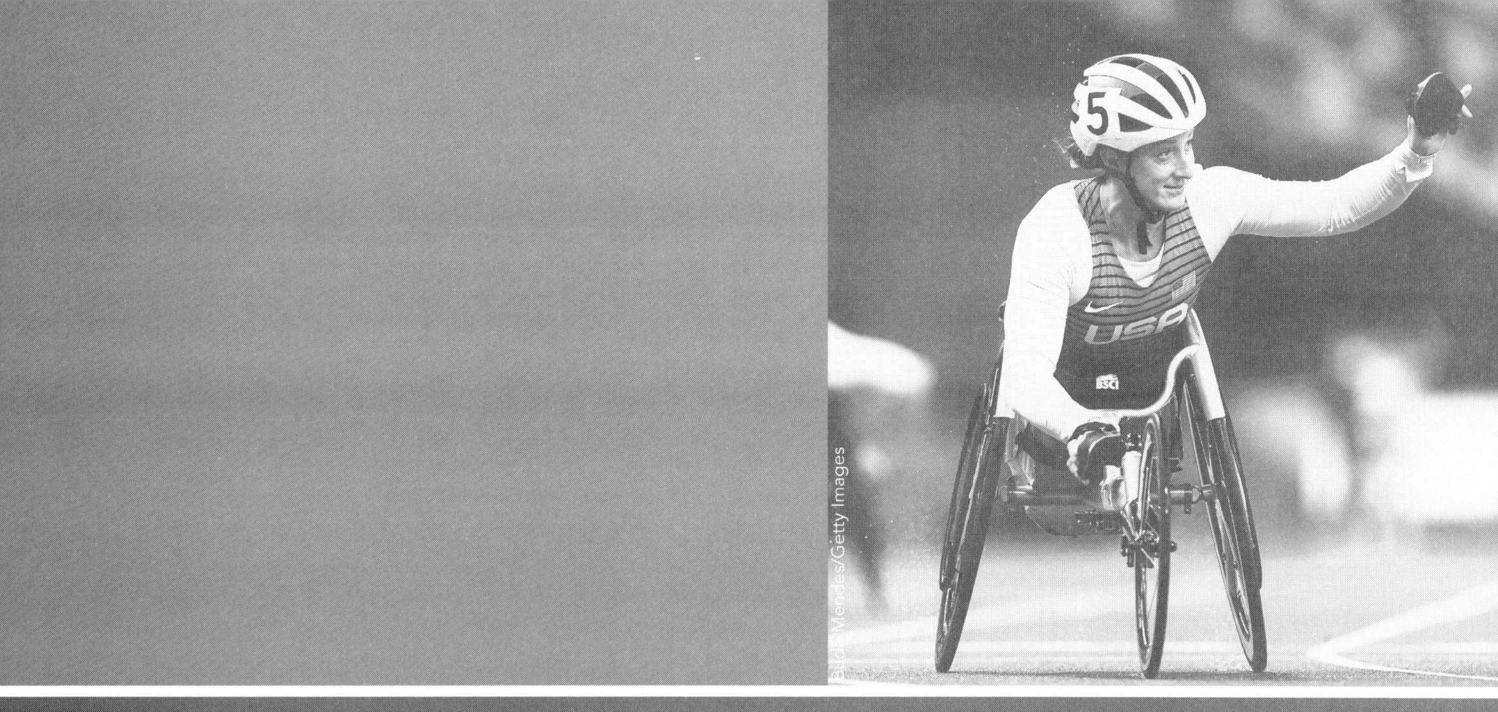

CHAPTER 8

Disability: Inclusion in Action

Mary A. Hums and Eli A. Wolff

LEARNING OBJECTIVES

- Establish the importance of including disability in the diversity, equity, and inclusion discussion.
- Learn to assess a sport organization's disability practices.
- Understand how best practices promote disability inclusion.
- Become aware of proper representation of athletes with disabilities, the need for more people with disabilities in sport management positions, and including disability in Olympic Movement language.

As a young girl, Tatyana McFadden was adopted after spending the first six years of her life in a Russian orphanage, and she arrived in the United States to a new world. Born with spina bifida, which limited her mobility, she was an active child and it soon became apparent to her family that physical activity and sport could be in her future. A sport that caught her interest early on was wheelchair racing—she was a fast and talented young athlete who got discovered and became a Paralympian at age 15, winning silver and bronze medals at the Paralympic Games in Athens in 2004. However, when the time came for her to compete as a member of her own high school's track team, she was met with great resistance. What are we to do with this girl in a wheelchair who wants to be on the track with her teammates? Does she pose a safety issue? Should she be included in meets and earn points for her team and if so, how, particularly when she would be "the only one"? Unable to find an equitable solution, Tatyana's family decided it was time to engage the legal system in order to create the opportunity for her, and other high school aged athletes like her, to be allowed to participate in high school sport. This legal undertaking eventually resulted in the passage of the Maryland Fitness and Athletics Equity for Students with Disabilities Act, and Maryland became the first state to require participation opportunities for students with disabilities. Thanks to her family's effort, we have now seen an increasing number of states offering participation opportunities for young athletes with disabilities. As for Tatyana, the young girl who just wanted to be a part of her high school track team has won 20 Paralympic medals and continues to be a role model for athletes both with and without disabilities.

While Tatyana McFadden's story is amazing, it does prompt a question: Must it take legal action for athletes with disabilities to simply be included in sport and physical activity? This chapter addresses this question, including looking at ways in which **sport managers** can guide their organizations in providing more opportunities for inclusion. We examine strategies and best practices to see how athletes with disabilities can have their fair opportunities to participate in sport and physical activity. We see how inclusion is not only possible but celebrated.

Sport and Physical Activity for People With Disabilities: Setting the Stage

Conversations about diversity in sport are becoming more commonplace. However, oftentimes **disability** is left out of diversity and inclusion in sport conversations, policies, and programs. It is important to recognize that we cannot truly strive for or achieve diversity and inclusion without disability as a central pillar. Disability must take a front row seat in diversity, equity, and inclusion in sport. Disability is not a separate issue or topic but one that fits directly into the diversity and inclusion conversation. As we strive for diversity and inclusion in sport, we must ensure that disability is included and equally valued in the sporting context.

In describing disability inclusion in sport, Nixon (2007, p. 419) writes "Inclusion is the final stage of integration of people with disabilities in a sport competition or organization, in which they are involved, accepted, and respected at all levels of the competition or organization." Disability inclusion can be implemented and prioritized into action in different ways. Some organizations give only lip service or achieve tokenism, whereas others are engaged toward accepting disability inclusion and moving toward valuing disability inclusion (Fay & Wolff, 2009). As we examine and discuss later in the chapter, sport managers can implement the **Criteria for Inclusion** framework within their sport organizations.

People with visible and invisible disabilities are present in all areas and aspects of the sports industry as athletes, managers, officials, coaches, media, and spectators. The sports industry has an opportunity to foster an environment inclusive of all people with disabilities, from athletes to decision-makers within the industry. Athletes with disabilities take part in sports in multiple settings, both mainstream settings alongside nondisabled peers and disability-specific settings alongside peers with disabilities (United Nations, n.d.). Recognizing the range of opportunities and settings for people with disabilities to engage and participate in sport is a critical aspect of valuing and including people with disabilities in sport in all settings.

Unfortunately, however, people with disabilities often run into an "ism" just like many people in other marginalized and minoritized populations. In this case, it is known as **ableism**. Mackelprang and Salsgiver (1999) have described the effects:

> *Ableism devalues people with disabilities and results in segregation, social isolation, and social policies that limit their opportunities for full societal participation. People with disabilities are also susceptible to internalizing stereotypes and negative beliefs. This process, which we call internalized ableism, is similar to internalized racism and sexism of other devalued people. (p. 1)*

People with disabilities should not experience stigma, shame, fear, or isolation in sport, and yet we know ableism is present in sport. For example, media coverage of sport for people with disabilities is not yet commonplace. Few athletes, even at the elite level, have substantial corporate sponsorships. And sometimes, athletes with disabilities are held out as inspirational figures not *because* of their success based on their athletic ability but rather for their success *despite* their disabilities. Sport managers can take actions to right these inequities, and examples of that are shown in this chapter.

Disability is in every corner of sport. Through the lens of diversity and inclusion, sport can embrace and make room for people with disabilities and can be a place that fosters

People with disabilities should not feel that they have to settle with a mindset that segregation and separation is the better option.
sot/Photodisc/Getty Images

opportunity and inclusivity for people of all disability backgrounds. People with disabilities should be able to express pride and joy in sport and with the progress, albeit slow at times, being made to create opportunities, policies, and pathways for the inclusion of people with disabilities in sport. People with disabilities should not feel that they have to settle with a mindset that segregation and separation is the better option. A diverse and inclusive sports environment is one that needs to fully embrace the value of including people with disabilities. One place where we can examine this is the language used to reflect disability.

As we know, over the years, the use of language changes, and this is true for terms referring to people with disabilities as well as race and gender. Words that were commonly used to describe people with disabilities (e.g., crippled, handicapped, impaired, suffering from) have slowly given way to more inclusive and less derogatory terms (people with disabilities, people living with a disability). The words we use shape the image of the world in which we live (Hums et al., 2020). A recent example of a sport organization using more inclusive language occurred with Major League Baseball (MLB). For many years, when a player was hurt, he was placed on what was called the Disabled List or the DL. MLB was the only major North American sports league to use the term "disabled" with their athletes. Other leagues used the word "injured." After almost 15 years of working to get that title changed, a group of disability advocates persuaded MLB to move from the Disabled List to the Injured List, which is a more accurate depiction of the players on the list (Hums et al., 2020). Billy Bean, MLB's vice president and special assistant to the commissioner, said the following:

> *In recent years, the commissioner has received several inquiries regarding the name of the "Disabled List." . . . The principal concern is that using the term "disabled" for players who are injured supports the misconception that people with disabilities are injured and therefore are not able to participate or compete in sports. As a result, Major League Baseball has agreed to change the name "Disabled List" to be the "Injured List" at both the major and minor league levels. All standards and requirements for placement, reinstatement, etc., shall remain unchanged. This change, which is only a rebranding of the name itself, is effective immediately. (Passan, 2019)*

This marked a solid example of positive use of inclusive language related to disability.

We have now established some of the theoretical background on the importance of including disability in diversity, equity, and inclusion efforts in the sport management arena. It is time to provide illustrations of what **best practices** look like. These can provide a map on which sport managers can model their organization's inclusion activities.

Strategies and Best Practices for Disability Inclusion

Given the importance of including disability in the diversity, equity, and inclusion discussion, sport managers need to decide what actions they can take in order to be truly inclusive of disability. But where should they begin? This next section provides several useful frameworks and includes numerous examples of successful strategies that sport managers are using to promote disability inclusion. These frameworks include the Criteria for Inclusion, universal design, and selected best practices across the sport industry.

Criteria for Inclusion

The Criteria for Inclusion framework (Fay & Wolff, 2009; Hums et al., 2019; Hums et al., 2009) lays out considerations for sport organizations to develop inclusion, specifically inclusion of people with disabilities. The model includes nine criteria (table 8.1), with explanations of what disability-inclusive organizations would look like.

1. Funding/Sponsorship

An example in funding and sponsorship for inclusion comes from an organization outside

TABLE 8.1 Criteria for Inclusion

Criterion	This criterion examines
Funding/sponsorship	The budget distribution to athletes with disabilities in sports organizations, as well as sponsorship money designated to people with disabilities.
Media/information distribution	The use of images of athletes with disabilities, as well as the advertising of events for people with disabilities.
Awards/recognition	Awards given by sport organizations to and for people with disabilities.
Governance	People with disabilities within the governance structure of sport organizations.
Philosophy	Whether and how disability is mentioned in mission and vision statements or other organizational documents addressing the philosophy and values.
Awareness/education	If and how the sport organizations are educating and training organizational members and constituents about disability.
Events/programs	How sport organizations are establishing specific events and programs for athletes with disabilities and also including athletes with disabilities in existing events and programs.
Advocacy	How sport organizations take a proactive role in promoting their work and initiatives related to sport for people with disabilities.
Management	If and how the sport organizations are employing people with disabilities as sport managers.

of sport that uses sport as a major sponsorship property—Toyota. The automobile company recently announced, "We're honored to support 17 U.S. Olympic and Paralympic athletes and 17 U.S. National Governing Bodies and High Performance Management Organizations on their journeys to the Olympic and Paralympic Games Tokyo 2020 and beyond" (Toyota, 2021, para. 1). The company is a sponsor of Team USA and features not just Olympians but also Paralympians Brad Snyder and Melissa Stockwell (paratriathlon), David Brown, Jerome Avery, and Jarryd Wallace (para track and field), Jessica Long (paraswimming), Oksana Masters (paracycling), and Steve Serio (wheelchair basketball). The Paralympians are listed side-by-side online with equal visibility as the Olympians.

2. Media/Information Distribution

Sport organizations rely heavily on web pages to present their face to the public, and so web content allows for a reflection of inclusion. When accessing the University of Illinois' Athletics home page, the featured banner photo can be more than just the typical football or basketball photo. Instead, athletes with disabilities sometimes appear first (University of Illinois, n.d.). The International Tennis Federation (ITF) website features images and information on tennis for people with disabilities, and its page on flagship events lists the Billie Jean King Cup, Davis Cup, Olympic Games, and Paralympic Games (ITF, 2021c).

3. Awards/Recognition

The ESPYs have traditionally been awarded to athletes in categories such as best male athlete, best female athlete, or best team. Early in the life of ESPN's awards program, the organizers added categories for "best male athlete with a disability" and "best female athlete with a disability." The ITF has a page titled "Honouring Outstanding Performance: Past Champions," and among those listed as most successful ITF champions are men's and women's wheelchair winners (ITF, 2021a).

Sport Industry Diversity Initiative

USA HOCKEY

USA Hockey, the national governing body for ice hockey in the United States, incorporates disability into its diversity, equity, and inclusion platform, and it provides opportunities for a range of disability populations under the umbrella of its disabled hockey program. USA Hockey has a disabled hockey committee consisting of each of the disciplines of disabled hockey and incorporates regional organizing and staff support (USA Hockey, 2021b). When we consider the Criteria for Inclusion, USA Hockey's disabled hockey activities and initiatives check the boxes for many, if not most, of the model criteria. Recognizing the challenges of supporting and serving a number of disciplines under the umbrella of disabled hockey, USA Hockey has done a good job to move the needle toward full inclusion. "USA Hockey is committed to fostering a welcoming environment for all by building a diverse, equitable and inclusive game. We celebrate every race, gender and background to unite as one community. We believe meaningful action can positively affect important change in our sport and carry over into our everyday lives" (USA Hockey, 2021c). USA Hockey takes into account the wide array of types of disabilities potential participants may live with. "USA Hockey's disabled hockey program provides playing opportunities regardless of a discipline. Currently, there are six disciplines recognized and supported by USA Hockey throughout the nation, including blind/visually impaired, deaf/hard of hearing, sled, standing/amputee, special hockey and warrior hockey." The national governing board offers a wide variety and levels of activities for participants:

> *In addition to its six disciplines, USA Hockey also oversees a number of events within its disabled hockey program, highlighted by its Disabled Hockey Festival, the largest hockey event of its kind. Other initiatives USA Hockey manages include the Disabled Hockey Workshop and USA Hockey Sled Classic, presented by the NHL. (USA Hockey, 2021a, para. 2)*

USA Hockey presents a good example of best practices in incorporating people with disabilities in their sport. Offering different levels of competition, combined with taking into consideration several different disability types, the organization is welcoming to all.

4. Governance

Representation by people with disabilities on sport organization boards is essential to making sure that their voices are heard in the governance structures. Since this is the level where policies and procedures are established, having a presence is imperative. The United States Olympic and Paralympic Committee (USOPC) includes Paralympic athletes on its Athlete Advisory Council (AAC) as required in the bylaws:

> *A. Sport Representatives. There shall be one Representative on the AAC from each sport/sport organization in the following categories:*
>
> 1. *Sport organizations recognized by the USOPC as National Governing Bodies ("NGBs") for Olympic or Pan American sports, which may also govern and/or manage sports on the Paralympic or Parapan American program.*
> 2. *Sport organizations recognized by the USOPC as Paralympic Sport Organizations ("PSOs") for Paralympic or Parapan American sports.*
> 3. *Sports on the Olympic/Paralympic/Pan American/Parapan American Games program that are governed and managed by the USOPC.*
> 4. *Sports on the Olympic/Paralympic/Pan American/Parapan American Games program that are governed by the USOPC, but externally managed by a separate*

> *sport organization, referred to as High Performance Management Organizations (HPMOs).*

> *B. General Paralympic Representatives. There shall be three (3) General Paralympic Representatives from NGBs recognized by the USOPC as the NGBs for Olympic or Pan American sports, which also govern and/or manage a sport on the Paralympic or Parapan American Program. (USOPC, 2020a, p. 1-2)*

5. Philosophy

An example of a sport organization that includes disability as part of its basic philosophy is FIFA. For example, "On the International Day of Disabled People, FIFA is proud to celebrate disabled footballers, officials and fans that form a key part of the rich diversity of the football family" (FIFA, 2020, para. 1). Another example here is the USOPC. Founded as the United States Olympic Committee, for many years the organization acted as both the National Olympic Committee and the National Paralympic Committee for U.S. international sport. This influential governing body's leadership recently made the decision to change its name to incorporate the word Paralympic (Allentuck, 2019). According to the USOPC (2019, paras. 2,4,7)

> *"This is a proud day for Paralympic and Olympic sport in the United States and a change that is representative of our organization's commitment to inclusivity," said USOPC Chair Susanne Lyons. "This change is about more than an organizational name."*

> *"To me this means that Paralympic athletes are fully included, embraced and celebrated by the USOPC," said four-time Paralympian Oksana Masters.*

> *"This is a historic moment for the Paralympic Movement in the United States," said Andrew Parsons, president of the International Paralympic Committee. "To see the USOPC make this inclusive statement by changing its name demonstrates the true parallel nature of the Olympic and Paralympic movements."*

6. Awareness/Education

When a host city is awarded the Olympic and Paralympic Games, the city's organizing committee also engages in educational programming that features both the Olympic and the Paralympic Games. For example, for the Rio 2016 Games, the Rio 2016 education program was taught in 162 city schools across Rio de Janeiro, Brazil. A major Games legacy, the program aimed to promote the Olympic and Paralympic values to young people (IPC, n.d.).

7. Events/Programs

The Commonwealth Games have long included events for athletes with disabilities on equal footing with able-bodied athletes' events. Unlike the Paralympic Games and other major sporting events, the para-sport program at the Commonwealth Games is fully integrated. This means there is no separate event or ticket for para-sport events, and a medal won by a para-athlete contributes to a nation's medal tally (Commonwealth Games Federation, 2020). The program for the 2022 Games in Birmingham shows the following events for people with disabilities: para swimming, para athletics, wheelchair basketball, para track cycling, para lawn bowls, para powerlifting, para table tennis, and para triathlon (Commonwealth Games Federation, 2021).

Major marathon events such as the Boston and New York marathons feature men's and women's wheelchair divisions, which are awarded for placement just like the able-bodied divisions. Events need not be international in scope, however, to be inclusive. Local road races that promote wheelchair divisions model inclusive behavior, as well.

8. Advocacy

As discussed, the Commonwealth Games offer a wide variety of sports for athletes with disabilities and have set themselves up as an example to other multisport events how to do so seamlessly. According to the website, "At the 2002 Commonwealth Games in Manchester . . . para-athletes were fully integrated into their national teams, making them the first fully inclusive international multi-sport

Games" (Commonwealth Games Federation, 2020, para. 2). The Commonwealth Games has consistently been a champion for and displayed public support for the inclusion of athletes with disabilities.

Until recently, the longtime chief executive officer for the federation was David Grevemberg, who joined the organization after years of work with the International Paralympic Committee. His leadership greatly influenced the organization's commitment to advocating for people with disabilities in sport and showed how advocates in sport organizations can make a difference.

9. Management

Some sport organizations occasionally employ people with disabilities for tasks in and around stadiums or arenas. While providing employment opportunities at any level for people with disabilities is a positive, this element as a criterion for inclusion refers to hiring people with disabilities in management-level positions. There have been a few football coaches with disabilities (e.g., Doug Blevins and Rob Mendez), but it is difficult to find sport managers with either visible or invisible disabilities. One notable person is Jen Armbruster, who is the inclusive recreation and fitness center coordinator at Portland State University. There is a need to increase the numbers here. A section later in the chapter addresses this issue in more detail.

The Criteria for Inclusion framework provides a useful tool to assess how inclusive sport organizations are of people with disabilities. Another strategy sport managers can use to promote inclusion is the concept of universal design.

Universal Design

All of us are no doubt familiar with the Americans With Disabilities Act (ADA) and all it has done to help people with disabilities navigate physical space. Ramps, elevators, designated parking spaces, automatic doors, and braille signage are now common in an arena, stadium, fitness center, swimming pool, ice rink, or ski area, and they are mandated by the law. While simply following the law ensures the basics of access are present, additional practices make environments not just accessible, but more welcoming (Hums et al., 2016). Here is where the concept of **universal design** comes into play. Ireland's National Disability Authority (2020, para. 1) provides the following definition:

> *Universal design is the design and composition of an environment so that it can be assessed, understood, and used to the greatest extent possible by all people regardless of their age, size, ability, or disability. An environment (or any building, product, or service in that environment) should be designed to meet the needs of all people who wish to use it. This is not a special requirement, for the benefit of only a minority of the population. It is a fundamental concept of good design.*

Those last two sentences reflect how universal design embodies inclusion. When it is implemented, places and spaces are accessible for everyone.

Universal design encompasses five distinct environments, including physical aspects of a facility or a space (built environment, information environment, and communication environment) as well as intangible aspects (policy environment and attitudinal environment) (Institute for Human Centered Design, 2011). The first three of these typically manifest themselves in conjunction with ADA, since they deal with physical elements. The other two intangible elements take a more expansive view. So what would these elements look like in practice? Let's use the example of a baseball stadium.

Physical Aspects

Assessing universal design in the built environment is relatively straightforward. Curb cuts, accessible washrooms, designated parking spaces for patrons with disabilities, and concourse aisles wide enough to facilitate open movement are standard. Next, the information environment lets patrons navigate the stadium with ease. Here we include signage for security, seating, luxury box locations, washrooms, concessions, and any health protocols such as social distancing floor spots. All of these need to be large enough, have sufficient color contrast for ease of reading, and should be located at the right heights for visibility.

The communication environment deals with how the stadium provides information to potential patrons prior to their arrival. For example, websites with proper-sized wording as well as audio options for listening should let people know where parking and seating sections for people with disabilities are located and whether or not a fan can bring in a bag of any size. Some people, for example, may prefer to sit on the first-base side, while others might want to be sure the seats are in the shade. Information on seating locations is essential when a person with a disability plans a trip to the ballpark.

Intangible Aspects

Beyond these physical elements, universal design goes on to address a few intangible elements that create a more welcoming environment for all patrons. The policy environment addresses issues such as service animals and health-related protocols, but also more general topics such as smoking policies or eligibility for use of seating in the sections designated for patrons with disabilities.

The "attitudinal" element refers to how people with disabilities are treated when they are at the stadium, and much of this is nested in employee training. Parking attendants, ushers, and concession workers all need to be briefed on how to respectfully interact with all patrons, of course, and particularly with patrons with disabilities. One very useful suggestion emanates from the training materials for the workforce at the 2015 Parapan American Games in Toronto, Canada. Workers were instructed to use the "just ask, just listen" approach, which gives respect and self-determination to patrons with disabilities (Toronto 2015 Pan Am/Parapan Am Games, 2015).

Sport managers who use the elements of universal design create a more welcome and user-friendly environment not just for people with disabilities, but for anyone who might be attending an event at their venue. Wide aisles, clear signage, useful information on the website, useful policies, and welcoming personnel all lay the groundwork for a positive and inclusive customer service experience. Everyone deserves to have a fun day at the ballpark.

Now that we have laid out strategies such as the Criteria for Inclusion and universal design, let's have a look at some best practices. While there are certainly a wide array of these, this next section provides selected examples from different segments of the sport industry.

Industry Segment Best Practice Examples

One way to understand and activate disability inclusion is to examine some best practices across different sport industry segments. Going segment by segment, we next lay out examples that illustrate how inclusion can be successfully achieved.

Intercollegiate Athletics

The University of Illinois is a longtime leader in inclusion of athletes with disabilities in intercollegiate athletics. For example, at the London Games in 2012, athletes from the University of Illinois brought home 10 of the USA's 28 medals (Kuzma, 2016). Although the program resides within disability services at Illinois, it does collaborate across the university, and the wheelchair basketball and track and field programs at Illinois have had tremendous success and nurtured numerous Paralympic-level athletes. At the 2012 Paralympic Games in London, 16 wheelchair basketball players from Illinois competed. This was followed by 11 in Rio in 2016 and 5 more in Tokyo (Lieberman, 2021; O'Brien, 2021). The oldest wheelchair basketball program of its kind, the team was a charter member of the National Wheelchair Basketball Association when it formed back in 1949. In 1972, the school established the first women's wheelchair basketball team. Star wheelchair basketball player Steve Serio summed up the Illinois experience in these words:

> *You could feel every day in practice that you were part of something bigger than yourself. . . . It was bigger than practice that one day because there were all these ties to generations before us who paved the way to give us the opportunities that we had present day. It made us work harder and meant more to be part of the wheelchair basketball program.* (Lieberman, 2021, para. 12)

The University of Illinois has produced a plethora of Paralympians in track and field. Names like Tatyana McFadden, Amanda McGrory, Kelsey LeFevour, Adam Bleakney, Sharon Hedrick, Jean Driscoll, Josh George, and Ann Cody are scattered among the school's Paralympic roster history, and there are so many more well-known athletes. The university has shown a solid record over time of committing resources to its athletes with disabilities.

Another example in intercollegiate athletics is present in a newer initiative—CUNY Adaptive and Inclusive Sports. In December 2017, the City University of New York Athletic Conference (CUNYAC) released a groundbreaking inclusive and adaptive sports platform to educate athletes with disabilities about the opportunities to play competitive sports within the city's five boroughs. Fifteen universities that comprise the CUNYAC are taking part in the initiative that includes swimming, track and field, wheelchair basketball, and tennis (CUNYAC, 2017). This initiative is consistent with the system's overall commitment to diversity and inclusion. According to CUNYAC executive director Zak Ivkovic:

> *CUNY Athletics has a long-term commitment to ensuring students with disabilities have the appropriate opportunities available to compete recreationally, on an intercollegiate athletic team or even in the Paralympics. We encourage the use of our accessible facilities throughout the university and the facilities made available by our partners in the tri-state area. Our goal is to grow our reach in the areas where our students feel the most comfortable and see as their best participatory fit. (CUNYAC, 2017, para. 7)*

Some initiatives like these are large, but universities can also take small steps to promote inclusion. For example, the bylaws requirements for election to the University of Louisville Athletic Hall of Fame make it clear that a Louisville student who competes in the Paralympic Games is eligible for induction just like Olympians (University of Louisville Athletics, 2021).

Professional Sport

In the world of professional sport, an example of inclusion comes from the National Hockey League (NHL). The NHL's Chicago Blackhawks[1] have a long history in the league; they were one of the original six teams to be welcomed into the league. While the NHL is a league often seen as conservative in its approach, in terms of disability inclusion it has actually done quite well. One example from the NHL is Chicago's AbilityLab Blackhawks Sled Hockey team (AbilityLab, 2021). Founded in 1999, and in cooperation with the AbilityLab Adaptive Sport Program, the team is open to anyone with disability. Players have opportunities for two different teams, "(a) a traveling competitive team for more advanced athletes; and (b) a developmental team for up and coming athletes who wish to learn and develop their sled hockey skills as well as hone their talents at area competitions" (AbilityLab, 2021, para. 3). The team's gear features a jersey bearing the Blackhawks traditional logo. The Blackhawks are also a founding member of the Midwest Sled Hockey League, which features two other teams that share the names of their NHL partners—the St. Louis Blues and Colorado Avalanche.

National Governing Body

USA Volleyball is associated with the USA's women's and men's national teams and their records and athletes at the Olympic Games. USA Volleyball, however, also oversees the men's and women's sitting volleyball teams and has been a leader in promoting the sport of sitting volleyball. USA Volleyball has worked to grow the sport around the country and created opportunities for individuals without disabilities to take part in sitting volleyball so that it is an inclusive sport. USA Volleyball has included sitting volleyball in their Get Out & Play Volleyball grassroots and school initiative that includes participants with and without disabilities (USOPC, 2020b). According to USA Volleyball, "Anyone can play sitting volleyball, and there are sitting volleyball divisions that allow able-bodied players to compete at the USA

[1]The Blackhawks present an interesting conundrum. On one hand, their work to promote disability inclusion is stellar. On the other hand, their continued use of the team name "Blackhawks" is problematic when considering issues with inappropriate use of names of Indigenous people. The team recently stated they "would commit to increasing awareness of Native American culture and the legacy of the famous Sauk leader who the team is named after, Black Hawk" and are "committed to raising the bar even higher to expand awareness of Black Hawk and the important contributions of all Native American people" (Fernandez, 2020, paras. 1, 3).

Sled hockey is a sport that has been promoted by the Chicago Blackhawks.

Volleyball Open National Championship each year" (USOPC, 2020b, Sitting Volleyball section).

International Tennis Federation

A visit to the ITF web page features not only information on the traditional women's and men's competitions, but also on the UNIQLO Wheelchair Tennis Tour.

> *Wheelchair tennis has been part of the Paralympic Games since 1992 and has been played at all four Grand Slams since 2007, while the BNP Paribas World Team Cup is the sport's flagship international team competition. Wheelchair has its own professional tour, the UNIQLO Wheelchair Tennis Tour, which boasts over 160 tournaments across 40 different countries in every region of the world. The tour offers over $3 million USD in prize money and culminates in the season-ending NEC Wheelchair Masters and UNIQLO Doubles Masters. (ITF, 2021b)*

Over the years, tennis has slowly embraced diversity by offering similar payouts for men's and women's championships. Their efforts in terms of inclusion of people with disabilities position them as a model to other international federations.

High School

Younger athletes with disabilities want their chance to participate, and so efforts are being made to provide opportunities for high school athletes. Ever since U.S. Paralympian Tatyana McFadden brought unfair treatment of high school athletes with disabilities to the forefront, more attention is being focused their way (Kuzma, 2021).

High school sport is a responsibility of the individual states, and so there is a wide variety in the offerings for high school athletes with disabilities, although they share a common goal. In 2016, Cody Porter, manager of media relations for the National Federation of State High

School Associations, reported "...inclusion is the ultimate goal of the 30 state associations currently offering a state championship/event in Adapted, Allied or Unified Sports (para. 6).

As an example of inclusion, the Illinois High School Association's (IHSA) state track finals for Division 2A lists wheelchair races alongside all the other scheduled events (IHSA, 2021). The IHSA hosts a state championship in wheelchair basketball, as does the Georgia State High School Athletic Association. The state of Ohio has Adaptive Sports Ohio, an organization that acts as a resource to help high school students with disability access sport opportunities. The organization provides opportunities in track and field, assisting high school students with equipment and coaching. They also work with school districts to offer wheelchair basketball for students in grades 1-12 (Adaptive Sports Ohio, 2021).

Another interesting partnership in high school sport is the Special Olympics program known as Unified Champion Schools. The program promotes social inclusion by using a model that "offers a unique combination of effective activities that equip young people with tools and training to create sports, classroom and school climates of acceptance" (Special Olympics, 2021a, para. 2). The program is fueled by inclusive sports, inclusive youth leadership opportunities, and whole school engagement, and it nurtures an environment where students with disabilities feel welcome and included.

Campus Recreation

Two examples of inclusive campus recreation programs come from the University of Iowa and Portland State University. The University of Iowa in Iowa City offers a campus recreation program featuring a strong selection of adaptive sport opportunities (University of Iowa, n.d.). Iowa makes it very clear that providing recreational opportunities for all makes for better recreational sport experiences for everyone—people both with and without disabilities. Program opportunities include adaptive rowing, aquatics programs, fitness programs, outdoor programs, tennis programs, and unified sports. In addition, Iowa's website provides information on available equipment and facilities in the Campus Recreation and Wellness Center. Adaptive equipment is highlighted on the website with locations around campus clearly identified for each. Braille descriptions on fitness machines, an upper body ergometer, cable crossover machines, and closed caption TV are offered. Building accessibility and accommodations are clearly noted for the various campus fitness locations.

At Portland State University, the campus recreation website encourages people to "play your way" and states:

> *Campus Rec celebrates diversity, inclusiveness, and authenticity in all of our programs. Our Inclusive Rec offerings demonstrate our commitment to creating holistic wellbeing and a welcoming community for all. Enjoy accessible spaces, programs, and equipment, including outdoor trips, adaptive climbing and swimming, wheelchair sports, goalball, open inclusive rec time, and youth events for the entire PSU community. (Portland State University, 2021, para. 1)*

The sport offerings for people with disabilities at Portland State present great variety. They include adaptive climbing, goalball, adaptive swimming, intramural leagues, open inclusive rec, outdoor trips, Unified Sports, and wheelchair basketball (Portland State University, 2021).

Recreational Sports

Special Olympics Unified Sports provides an example of a sort of inverse inclusion. Here, able-bodied athletes combine forces with Special Olympics athletes to form teams for competition (Special Olympics, 2021). Unified Sports joins participants with and without intellectual disabilities as teammates. The teams have players of similar ages and abilities, making for a fun and inclusive experience for all parties. Unified Sports programs are now active in over 4,500 elementary, middle, and high schools as well as more than 70 colleges and universities (Special Olympics, 2021). Beyond this, Special Olympics has now partnered with the United Nations High Commission for Refugees to take the power of sport to another vulnerable population, refugees. Its programming helps serve refugee communities by being more connected to local culture through sport (Special Olympics, 2021).

These examples of best practices illustrate how disability inclusion is not only possible but makes for a better environment for all participants. When sport managers make the commitment to disability inclusion, programming is strengthened and welcoming.

Inspiration Porn, Disability in Sport Management, and Principle 6

Beyond the day-to-day practice, there are still broader ongoing issues related to incorporating disability in the diversity, equity, and inclusion conversation. Some of these—appropriate use of inspiration, increasing the number of sport managers with disabilities, and including disability language in the Olympic Movement—are discussed here.

Inspiration: What Is the Message?

A high school–aged athlete with Down syndrome is allowed to suit up in uniform for the last game of his school football team's season. Near the end of the game, the coach puts the player into the game, and everyone knows in advance this will happen. The quarterback hands the ball off to the athlete and he starts to run. His teammates "block" for him as the players on defense either easily fall down or make halfhearted and often dramatic-looking flailing attempts to bring the runner down. Of course, he runs the length of the field and scores a touchdown while the crowd cheers wildly! A feel-good story that the media gladly picks up.

But wait—what message is being sent by all this? While onlookers might feel as if something inspiring has happened, what "inspiring" message does this communicate about people with disabilities in sport? The authors realize this stance might not resonate with all readers but an action such as this can be quite detrimental to the movement as a whole. The message is that people with disabilities in sport need "special" treatment, they cannot succeed on their own athletic merit, and their participation is seen only as inspirational and not ability based. Events like these are often referred to pejoratively as "inspiration porn." Although definitions of inspiration porn vary, "like actual pornography, Inspiration Porn provides kind of superficial pleasure and gratification for the viewer, while objectifying, often harming the mostly passive subjects being looked at" (Pulrang, n.d., para. 6). Inspiration porn is present when people with disabilities are portrayed in a way that elicits "sentimentality and/or pity; an uplifting moral message, primarily aimed at nondisabled viewers; or disabled people [are] anonymously objectified, even when they are named" (Pulrang, n.d., para. 4).

How do we avoid this in sport? Report stories on athletes with disabilities by focusing on their athletic ability. For example, a wheelchair basketball player can be admired for her ability to shoot three-pointers rather than seen as exceptional for playing basketball despite being, quote, "confined to a wheelchair" (an example of ableist phrasing that should never be used). As mentioned earlier in this chapter, language matters!

Increasing the Number of Sport Managers With Disabilities

While we are beginning to see an increase in the number of athletes with disabilities on different levels, the number of sport managers and coaches with disabilities remains quite low (Itoh et al., 2018). Sport managers with disabilities should not be limited to management positions in disability sport, just as female sport managers should not be limited to working only with women's sports. While the underrepresentation of other minoritized and marginalized groups has been well documented in publications such as the University of Central Florida's annual *Racial and Gender Report Card*, disability remains generally overlooked. This is a not a criticism of the University of Central

Florida's work. Gathering information on the numbers of people in sport management is quite difficult, because disability cannot be determined, for example, by looking at a photo roster of employees. Disability can take numerous forms, and many people live with invisible disabilities that they may choose not to disclose to their employers.

Perhaps in the sport industry, as in other industries, people think the costs associated with hiring a person with a disability would be onerous. Yet, according to Kennedy and colleagues:

> *Hiring people with disabilities need not cost any more than hiring someone without a disability. Accommodations for the majority of people with disabilities cost nothing. And when there is a cost involved with providing technology or other tools, it is usually less than $500, and there are tax incentives available to help. (2019, para. 4)*

So it appears cost is not the issue, but the perception of cost can be. This is an issue that needs more investigation.

Examining how sport for people with disabilities is included in university sport management programs would also be helpful, because this is the training ground for future sport managers. Teaching about disability in any discipline is important, as Ferguson (2006, as cited in Shapiro et al. [2012, p. 105]) points out.

1. People with disabilities are one of the largest and least understood minority groups in the United States.
2. Ignorance feeds discrimination and stereotypes.
3. To eliminate stereotypes, we first have to see them and challenge the assumptions behind them.
4. Familiarity breeds comfort, not contempt.
5. We should recognize the important contributions people with disabilities have made throughout history.
6. Disability is part of the diversity we should celebrate in society.
7. Our literature, art, and popular entertainment are full of imagery and portrayals of disabilities.
8. Race, gender, and disability are related throughout history.

According to the Global Sports Mentoring Program:

> *With the growth in prominence of the Paralympic Games and the increasing development of adaptive sport worldwide, the time is right to empower leaders with a passion and commitment for promoting equity and opportunity so that everyone receives the opportunity to get in the game. (2018, para. 4)*

Yet as Shapiro and colleagues (2012) go on to point out, more needs to be done to effectively infuse disability into the sport management university curriculum. The work must continue.

Principle 6 of the Olympic Charter

Principle 6 of the Olympic Charter, the Olympic Movement's public statement on diversity, inclusion, and nondiscrimination, reads as follows:

> *The enjoyment of the rights and freedoms set forth in this Olympic Charter shall be secured without discrimination of any kind, such as race, colour, sex, sexual orientation, language, religion, political or other opinion, national or social origin, property, birth or other status. (IOC, 2020, p. 12)*

As you can see, disability is not specified as one of the areas included within Principle 6. Although there have been Olympians with disabilities and people with disabilities have worked within the Olympic Movement, disability has mostly been an invisible topic, relegated to "other status." The growing awareness and understanding of disability as an integral part of diversity and inclusion brings hope that before long disability can be added and codified into Principle 6. "Even when one starts with the premise that disability *is* part of the fabric of the spirit of Olympism, more still needs to be done to further publicly advance disability inclusion within the Olympic Movement" (Wolff & Hums, 2021, p. 1). One way to advance would be to include the word *disability* in Principle 6 of the Olympic Charter.

Sport Industry Leader Profile

Stephanie Wheeler

Title: Head Coach, University of Illinois Women's Wheelchair Basketball Team

Stephanie Wheeler is the head coach of the women's wheelchair basketball team at the University of Illinois and was a Paralympic gold medalist and world champion in her career as a Paralympic athlete. Stephanie has been a leader and champion for disability inclusion, LGBTQ inclusion, and diversity in all areas of sport. Stephanie approaches her role as a coach and a leader from an educational perspective. She encourages her college athletes to succeed in sport, in the classroom, and in all areas of life.

Stephanie leads with a kind but firm approach not only at the University of Illinois, but also with the National Wheelchair Basketball Association and the United States Olympic and Paralympic Committee. Stephanie works throughout Olympic and Paralympic sport educating her peers on the value and importance of diversity and inclusion. She does not shy away from challenging and difficult conversations, and she ensures that the topics of ableism and homophobia, and the importance of their intersectionality, are examined. Through the leadership Stephanie displays, we can see that we all have multiple identities and perspectives and that we can be proud of who we are in every way. She provides hope that the future of diversity and inclusion in sport engages and embraces a wider view that includes people with disabilities, along with recognizing and valuing sexual orientation at the forefront.

Stephanie Wheeler is a role model for her leadership and her advocacy for diversity. Here is a list of features on her and her great work:

Athlete Ally. (2018). *Paralympian and coach Stephanie Wheeler: Sport moves society forward.* www.athleteally.org/paralympian-coach-stephanie-wheeler/

SBNation. (2021). *Stephanie Wheeler on coaching college athletes with disability, winning Paralympic gold.* www.outsports.com/2020/1/16/21061539/stephanie-wheeler-on-coaching-college-athletes-with-disability-winning-paralympic-gold

WeCOACH. (2018). *7 questions with Stephanie Wheeler.* https://wecoachsports.org/membership/coach-of-the-month/stephanie-wheeler/

SUMMARY

Including disability into diversity, equity, and inclusion goals and activities in sport is not a "maybe" but a "must." As we have seen in this chapter, disability is an emerging area within diversity and inclusion initiatives in the sports industry. Historically, diversity has prioritized race and gender, and we are now seeing this definition expanding to recognize that disability is essential to any work on diversity, equity, and inclusion in sport. This chapter illustrated methods for including people with disabilities in sport not only on the playing field but in all roles and areas of sports, as described through the Criteria for Inclusion and universal design. We shared concrete examples of sports like tennis, volleyball, and ice hockey that are advancing the role of promoting disability in sport. The time is now for people with disabilities to gain more visibility, respect, and inclusion in sport. Sports organizations and stakeholders should integrate disability into their diversity, equity, and inclusion strategies, programs, and policies, using the examples and resources we have shared throughout this chapter. We are hopeful for a future in sport where people with disabilities are a seamless dimension in the fabric of the sports industry.

CRITICAL THINKING EXERCISES

1. You are working for your university's athletic department and are developing a list of potential events to bring to your university. One of these events is the Wheelchair Rugby National Tournament. The event would be held at your university's basketball arena. You want to make sure that the arena is properly equipped to host the event. Using the five principles of universal design as a guide, write up an assessment of what the arena staff would need to do to properly host the event by addressing each principle. Make sure your assessment specifically addresses your arena and is not just general statements about universal design.
2. Choose one sport industry segment (professional sport, intercollegiate athletics, high school sport, international federations, etc.), and find an example of best practices for disability inclusion for each of those two industry segments. Explain why you chose your example. Also explain what sport managers could learn from each of these best practices.
3. Choose a sport organization you would like to work for someday. Go online and find information on how the organization is addressing diversity, equity, and inclusion. Does it include disability?

REVIEW QUESTIONS

1. Name and define the five principles of universal design.
2. Name and define the nine elements of the Criteria for Inclusion.
3. What is Nixon's definition of *inclusion*?
4. What is the definition of ableism? How is it similar to other "isms" such as racism or sexism?
5. Why does Principle 6 of the Olympic Charter need to be amended?

CHAPTER 9

Preserving Athlete Humanity in a Production Culture

Ellen J. Staurowsky

LEARNING OBJECTIVES

- Examine the nature of the sports industrial complex.
- Explore the relationship between athletic labor and management.
- Identify some of the systems that focus on the ranking and valuing of athlete bodies and performance.
- Consider how sport fans consume sport and examine the potential for sport fans to become desensitized to athlete humanity.
- Reflect on how sport, if not managed appropriately, can dehumanize athletes in service to profit motives.

On May 31, 2021, Japanese women's tennis player Naomi Osaka, who at the time was ranked number two in the world, withdrew from the French Open after being fined $15,000 for refusing to participate in a required press conference following her first-round win (Maine, 2021). In explaining her decision, Osaka issued a statement on Twitter noting that she "never wanted to be a distraction" and that she felt her withdrawal was the best thing for the tournament, other players, and her own well-being (Osaka, 2021).

Osaka had signaled on Instagram the Wednesday before the tournament that she was going to avoid press obligations and was willing to accept being fined. According to *New York Times* reporter Matthew Futterman, "She had watched too many players break down during news conferences and leave the dais in tears. She said the process felt to her like 'kicking a person while they are down'" (2021, para. 3). Osaka wrote:

> *If the organizations think they can keep saying, "do press or you're going to get fined," and continue to ignore the mental health of the athletes that are the centerpiece of their cooperation [sic] then I just gotta laugh. (Futterman, 2021, para. 4)*

When she failed to show up for the mandatory press conference at the French Open, the decision to fine her and also threaten further sanctions came not just from the French Tennis Federation (FFT) but officials representing the other three governing bodies that sponsor the four Grand Slam tournaments, including the All England Lawn Tennis and Croquet Club (Wimbledon), Tennis Australia (the Australian Open), and the United States Tennis Association (the U.S. Tennis Open) (Hrdlicka, Moretton, Hewitt, & McNulty, 2021). While expressing concern for Osaka's health, the Grand Slam tournament representatives emphasized that a player's responsibility to engage with the media benefited them, the media, and the fans, and it was a key element in promoting the growth of the game and the fan base. They also framed the requirement that players would participate in press events as part of participating in the tournament as one of fairness, noting that the regulations governing player conduct were designed to maintain a level playing field and eliminate the unfairness that would arise if some players met their obligations to the press while others did not (Hrdlicka, Moretton, Hewitt, & McNulty, 2021).

As the controversy surrounding Osaka's decision and the reaction from the governing bodies that control the sport continued, Osaka shared more about her own situation, explaining that she had suffered depression since the U.S. Open in 2018 and that she struggled with demands to meet with the press because she was unaccustomed to public speaking (Osaka, 2021). She wrote, "I am not a natural public speaker and get huge waves of anxiety before I speak to the world's media. I get really nervous and find it stressful to always try to engage and give you the best answers I can" (Osaka, 2021).

Osaka's case highlights the pressures athletes are under to perform and whether the personal sacrifices athletes make regarding their health and well-being are reasonable. In commenting on Osaka's decision to take time away, one reporter said, "She has the right to put her health and sanity above the unending demands imposed by those who stand to profit from her labors" (Korducki, 2021, para. 6). Sportswriter John Hermann (2021) noted that part of what came to light as a result of Osaka's decision was the expectations of athletes that come from their status as entertainers and celebrities. As he pointed out, Osaka had not declined to step onto the court and compete in her sport. She declined to speak to the press. It was only after tournament directors from all of the major tournaments threatened to sanction her and potentially ban her from other tournaments that she stepped away, raising questions of who has control over an athlete and how that control is exerted.

The reaction from tennis officials was further complicated days after Osaka announced that she was withdrawing not just from the French Open but the Berlin WTA 5000 Tournament (a tournament considered to be a tune-up before Wimbledon). Roger Federer departed after winning a third-round match, saying that he was leaving the tournament to protect his health but citing no specific injury. Gilles Moretton, the president of the same French Federation that fined Osaka, offered these thoughts about Federer's decision: "Everyone wants to see [Federer] play as long as possible. We know he will be 40 soon. It will be difficult. We can see it, and he knows it himself, and he needs to preserve himself" (Melero, 2021).

Osaka's case illustrates the complications associated with player relations and sport governing bodies. Athletes labor for their own livelihoods but also for the profit of sport organizations, their corporate partners, and their audiences. However, as executive director of the World Players Association Brendan Schwab (2017) notes, athletes are situated at an intersection between sport and human rights because of increasingly extraordinary regulations that are often difficult to defend either legally or morally.

The body plays a central role in conceptualizations of sport. Within the sport marketplace, bodies are assets, scrutinized for value, tracked for availability, and assessed a certain shelf life. In an age of ever-increasing surveillance, the bodies of athletes are regarded as tools of production and property to be traded or transferred; they are subject to shaming and material to be used as leverage. In this chapter, we explore the complications of athletes operating within a commercial marketplace and the protections that need to be in place to preserve the humanity of the athletes and those who seek to control them.

The Sports Industrial Complex

The sport industry is big business in the United States and worldwide. In a report produced by Research and Markets, taking into account the impact of COVID-19, the global sports market was expected to grow from $388.28 billion in 2020 to $599.9 billion by 2025 (Globe Newswire, 2021). According to one of the largest multinational professional services companies in the world, PricewaterhouseCoopers, the market for North American professional and college sports across four segments (gate receipts, licensed merchandise, media rights, and sponsorships) was projected to be in the vicinity of $83.1 billion by 2023 (McCaffrey et al., 2021).

While sport is often considered an activity (football, golf, soccer, swimming, tennis), as a social institution it is "as much a product of **capitalism** as the factory, the stock exchange, and the unemployment line" (Collins, 2013, front matter, para. 2). As a result, athletes who labor in what Kalman-Lamb (2019) refers to as professional and **high-performance sports** (e.g., college sports, Olympic sports) are commodities. At its most fundamental, what it means to refer to an athlete as a **commodity** within a capitalist system is the athlete (who can be paid or unpaid) selling their labor power to an employer for a wage, salary, or other form of compensation (e.g., an athletic scholarship). In turn, they work in what scholars and reporters have over the years referred to as the **sports industrial complex** (Maguire, 2004) or the **athletic industrial complex** (Smith, 2014). Sport as a business is intertwined with broader social and political systems in support of a profit-based economic system. What this means for athletes is that they are not just playing sports but are performing in a system that has broad social and political implications.

In theory, capitalism within a free society is designed to uplift members of every class. Competition exists to encourage the best leaders and visionaries to rise to the top and to be compensated accordingly for their contributions to society and the economy. Workers are treated fairly by their employers and valued for the work they do. The power differential between employers (owners) and workers is justified as necessary to the efficient running of the business. Inequities across classes exist as a result of merit, the logic being that those who work hard will reap the benefits of their labor.

Marxist analyses of capitalism, however, pinpoint the tensions that arise between the owners (the **bourgeoisie**) and the workers (the **proletariat**). In effect, while capitalism has the potential to positively serve the society, a tendency to put profit above the interests of employees, to undervalue their labor, to risk their health and safety, to entrap them in systems of oppression, and to engage in other abuses of power requires accountability and a counterbalance to the power that is centralized with those in charge. These tensions fuel labor movements in the United States and around the world.

These tensions also form the substance of concerns that emerge around how athletes are treated by coaches, administrators, and managers of professional leagues, college conferences, and other governing bodies, such as the National Collegiate Athletic Association (NCAA), the International Federation of Association Football (FIFA), the International Olympic Committee (IOC), and the United States Olympic and Paralympic Committee (USOPC). For professional teams that have players' associations, labor issues regularly arise from concerns that athletes are working harder while incurring greater risk for less than their fair share of compensation and in the absence of long-term health care protections.

In 2020, the National Football League (NFL) announced a plan to add a game to the regular season schedule, but only after players negotiated for an increase in their share of the league's revenue through their players association (the National Football League Players Association or NFLPA), in recognition that if they were going to assume more risk playing a longer season, they deserved greater compensation. The decision, however, was a narrow victory for owners, one that players agreed to reluctantly because of the continuing expansion of the season, the increasing number of games they are expected to play, and efforts to expand the NFL's global footprint by scheduling games overseas. While management argues that the decision came with a reduction in the number of preseason games (and a greater number of injuries occur during preseason) the players were concerned about the impact of a longer season on their health and safety (Belson, 2021). In the end, the NFL was the clear winner because the 17th game allowed them to negotiate for a new media rights deal totaling more than $100 billion, a figure that nearly doubled what the expiring contracts offered (Belson, 2021).

While athlete labor as a whole shares similar concerns as labor in other industries, including but not limited to fair wages, work conditions, health and safety issues, medical care, educational benefits, advancement opportunities, and retirement, the conditions under which athletes work presents additional avenues of concern. Because the sport industry is so intimately tied to media, athletes perform in the public domain, subjected to intense scrutiny from audiences. Owners in major league sports (NFL, NBA, WNBA, NHL, MLB) and athletics administrators, coaches, and conference commissioners in the NCAA and college conferences control what teams athletes play on and under what circumstances they can move to other teams. In entities like the Ultimate Fighting Championship (UFC), fighters are often bound by one-sided contracts that provide UFC president Dana White with the discretion to determine when and if a fighter will get a match (Happe, 2021). As the interest in legalized gambling on sport increases following the U.S. Supreme Court's reversal of the Professional and Amateur Sports Protection Act (PASPA) in 2018, there is a greater investment in the performance of athletes and a greater investment on the part of their employers in the gambling industry (Healy, 2020).

Ranking and Valuation of Athlete Bodies

From the time athletes enter into the sport system, they are ranked according to their performance and physical attributes. Athletes who evidence promise and the potential for a future in certain sports garner attention through a variety of public ranking systems. To illustrate, junior athletes in sports such as tennis and golf are ranked using point systems respectively established by the International Tennis Federation and American Junior Golf Association. Subscription based entities like Extra Inning Softball cover the spectrum of competition from high school to NCAA to Women's Professional Fastpitch (WPF), providing player and team rankings.

The more lucrative the sport, the more elaborate the tracking of player talent. For football and men's basketball, media entities support networks of websites such as 247Sports.com (CBS) and Rivals.com (Yahoo! Sports) that evaluate player talent in those sports and report on their recruitment, assessing the overall value of the recruitment efforts for top college football and men's basketball programs. In these ranking systems, a player with the highest ranking is referred to as a five-star recruit or prospect. Interest in prospective players is followed in terms of how many schools have expressed an interest in the player, the level of interest the player has in accepting an athletic scholarship offer from a particular school (otherwise known as a commitment), and the player's ultimate decision.

Media coverage of showcase camps such as the ESPN 300 Elite Underclassmen Camp demonstrates the investment leagues, college programs, and media entities have in fueling interest in prospects entering the pipeline of football talent and the numerous ways in which that talent is monetized (Brooks, 2021). Organizationally, these camps mirror the structure of player assessment in the NFL. In 2021, the entire ESPN 300 Elite Underclassmen Camp Series, sponsored by Under Armour, was scheduled in five locations around the country—Orlando, Houston, Los Angeles, St. Louis, and Charlotte—between mid-April and late May (UCReport, 2021). The camps are run as invitation only and designed to assess the top high school football playing talent in the United States. A report on each of the invited prospects is made available to the schools in the Power Five conferences (the top college conferences in the United States) and a total of 98 Football Bowl Series (FBS) schools (the top Division I football playing schools in the country) (UCReport, 2021).

At the professional level, the search for talented athletic labor in football has served as a hub for the evaluation of players, regulation of their entry and movement within the league, and marketing of both professional and college teams. In the 1930s, the NFL pioneered the concept of the player draft as a way of regulating how talent was distributed across teams. Those early efforts would lead to the creation of scouting services (e.g., BLESTO, National Football Scouting or NFS, Quadra Scouting) by the 1960s, with each running a camp where top prospects were invited. In 1985, the three camps were merged, and Indianapolis-based NFS was chosen to run the event. Thus was born the NFL Scouting Combine (National Football League Operations, 2021a).

In its most recent iteration, the NFL Scouting Combine (also known as the National Invitational Camp) limits the number of college seniors and underclassmen who declare for the draft to 335. An NFL committee sorts through lists of players under consideration by the 32 teams in the league and votes to determine which players will receive invitations to the Combine. Data on each player is gathered from existing game film and interviews with team representatives. Players undergo medical exams and tests, including drug testing, and height and weight are confirmed. The Wonderlic test, which measures cognitive aptitude and problem-solving skills under time pressure, is administered. Physical tests include bench press, 40-yard dash, vertical jump, broad jump, 20-yard shuttle, three-cone drill, and 60-yard shuttle; field drills that vary depending on position supplement these (Moriello, 2020; Football IQ Score, 2021).

While images of the Combine often feature a football player during a workout or in a press interview, the scrutiny players receive from a team of doctors outside of the public view demonstrates the level of pressure players are under and the degree of medical information kept for each player. As the NFL describes it, they work closely with the NCAA to "identify and groom" college players to compete at the next level if they have the requisite "talent, commitment, and dedication." Working through a medical advisory committee, data collection on invited athletes is available through an NFL/NCAA database that contains records posted by physicians, athletic trainers, and other specialists who have treated football players during their college careers. Review of

Information gathered from the Combine and other processes feeds into the valuation of players and decisions that are made in the selection of players by teams during the NFL draft.
Joe Robbins/Getty Images

player medical histories begins before players arrive at the Combine and is distilled into electronic medical records distributed to all 32 clubs by the NFL (National Football League Operations, 2021b).

When players arrive in Indianapolis for the Combine, those who have had injuries or currently have an injury are taken to an Indiana hospital for X-rays and MRIs. As orthopedic surgeon and sports medicine specialist David Geier (n.d.) describes it on his website, "Often players will have 3-4 sets of x-rays and 2-3 MRI's. I don't know the number of MRI's done for the Combine, but it must be staggering because MRI facilities in Indianapolis perform the tests around the clock that week" (para. 5). They are then taken in small groups where they are given a physical exam. The examining doctor then presents the player's case to a group of physicians and athletic trainers associated with other teams. After the doctor has presented the player's medical profile, the player is questioned by team medical personnel, who then rate the player (Geier, n.d.).

Information gathered from the Combine and other processes feeds into the valuation of players and decisions that are made in the selection of players by teams during the NFL draft. While baseline compensation and terms of employment for players are set through collective bargaining that occurs between the NFL and the NFLPA, the economic fate of players is determined by how much their services are valued by the teams that wish to hire them. Thus, the higher the player goes in the draft (in effect the earlier they are chosen by a team), the better off the players are financially.

The NFL draft and Scouting Combine evolved in tandem with an ever-evolving media landscape, raising the level of attention on players. In 1980, ESPN approached the NFL about televising what was then known as its annual player selection meeting. Covering it first as a news story, the NFL draft would, 40 years later, be one of the biggest events on the sports calendar (Ellenport, 2020). In 2019, the NFL draft Nashville reported attendance of 600,000 (Leimkuehler, 2019). According to the NFL, the three most-watched drafts yielded audiences of 6.2 million in 2019, 8.3 million in 2020, and 6.1 million in 2021 (NFL, 2021).

The college football television calendar nests next to and complements that of professional football. Conference media days take place in July before the NFL's preseason, the kickoff of the college season is timed to occur before the NFL's kickoff, the regular college season wraps up with the Army-Navy Game, bowl selections and the Heisman Trophy award ceremony just as the NFL playoffs get underway, and the new year starts with the College Football Playoffs, followed in a few weeks with the Super Bowl. The relative quiet of the spring is filled with the NFL Scouting Combine in March, college football spring games being televised in April a week before the NFL draft, and attention focused on high school prospects in May (Kercheval, 2021). When taken as a whole, it provides wall-to-wall coverage of football from high school through the pros.

Sport Consumption and Disintegrating Boundaries

There is a tacit understanding between sport leagues, teams, franchises, and sport media entities that the staged conflict that exists as part of a game or event draws divided crowds who cheer for one side or the other. Part of the marketing of sport and the calculus involved in getting people to "buy in" to what a sport entity is selling, whether it is the sport itself, the accomplishments and personalities of the players, or the demeanor of the coach, relies on a classic construction of "us versus them." In effect, audiences and those attending games are asked to pick a side and be loyal to it. Moving fans to feel for a team, to develop an affinity for it, and to invest in it pays psychological and spiritual dividends for the fan and profit for the owners.

From a capitalist perspective, we see sport not only serving as a product but the endless ways that spectator sport becomes a platform for product extensions, with the goal of expanding markets (Coakley, 2005). The status conferred by fandom is displayed through merchandise and enacted in a multitude of ways from pregame tailgates to the local philharmonic playing the team fight song to wearing team colors to work, school, church, hospital, funeral home, autobody shop, or grocery store. Prestige derives from closeness to the action—videos and images posted on social media bearing witness that fans were on site for a big game or grabbed a selfie with a player or team executive.

In the 20th century, the commercialization of sport was tied to the building of imposing stadiums and arenas and communication technologies. Sports sections in newspapers and magazines shaped the U.S. consciousness about sport and sport heroes using stories that focused primarily on men's sports. Those not fortunate enough to have the financial means or be near a major league or college game day experience could listen to games on the radio. The film industry framed the narrative around sports as being larger than life. And television made sport accessible and relatable to the masses.

By the dawn of the 21st century, all-day coverage of sports had been around for 20 years and was maturing. The digital age delivered the infrastructure for more channels devoted specifically to sports and for sport leagues and conferences to own their own networks. With the evolution of social media, the citizen journalist in the 2020s could offer their own views on the sports news of the day, and sport fans found avenues to express their own hot takes on whatever was happening with their teams or with sports in general. As the number of outlets covering sports increased, and as more avenues became available to share information about players and teams, there was an increasing demand for content. Performances of teams and players are parsed out in pieces in addition to the whole, driven by the proliferation of social media and the increasing influence of sport analytics, fantasy sports, and legal sports gambling, as well as the racialized dynamics surrounding the most popular televised sports in the United States. In this section we examine the impact of sport analytics, fantasy sports, and legalized sports betting on how athletic bodies are viewed by owners and fans, as well as the racialized dynamics that exist within major sport properties in the United States and the impact that has on non-White players.

Sport Analytics

In 2003, reporter Michael Lewis published a book called *Moneyball*, a story about Oakland A's general manager Billy Beane collaborating with economist Paul DePodesta to build a playoff-caliber team with limited resources by valuing statistical analyses of players or subjective evaluations (West, 2017). Although a preoccupation with facts and numbers has been a hallmark of the sport industry game recaps, box scores, team standings, and player rankings, this emphasis on relying on mathematical modeling and prediction took on a new dimension when applied to the sport industry in the early 2000s.

Refined film analysis allowed for frame-by-frame breakdowns of player performance. Optimal speed, power, exertion, and force could be calculated by taking raw data and distilling it into a performance algorithm. The methods of gathering data also changed. No longer were speed and effort being measured merely by external timing devices and how much a player lifted in a weight room, but shoe and apparel companies like Nike were marketing wearable technologies as a benign way of improving performance.

Wearable technologies expand the scope and methods for gathering what is known as athlete biometric data. The seeming attractiveness of these devices is the fact that real-time information can be gathered on an athlete without interruption, regardless of activity throughout the day. Heart rate, blood sugar levels, blood oxygen rates, body temperature, pulse, and sleep time can be measured and recorded through a sensor.

Marketed as an aid to performance, the pitch for using these devices is that athletes benefit from objectively knowing if they are working too hard or they need to scale back, coaches benefit because they can make more informed decisions about when to substitute players or hold athletes accountable if they are not performing up to a level where they should be, medical personnel have access to information that may signal the need for interventions sooner, and fans benefit because athletes and teams are putting in better performances.

As athlete performance is broken down into more and more categories and the surveillance of athletes and their bodies becomes increasingly cellular in nature (blood counts, rates of perspiration, muscle twitch counts), such mechanization prompts questions as to whether athletes are viewed by owners and fans as machines or as human beings, drawing comparisons to athletes as cyborgs (a hybrid person and machine) and raising questions about where the boundaries are for what stakeholders can expect of them and do to them.

As a case in point, consider how college sport officials have entered into agreements with wearable technology companies, gathering data on college athletes for the financial gain of athletic departments and the companies (Jessop & Brown, 2019). While athletes in the NBA, for example, have a players' association that has negotiated limitations on how and under what circumstances data can be gathered from players, with the stipulation that changes to any data gathering efforts are subject to collective bargaining, no such protections are in place for college athletes. Although college athletic departments claim that they allow athletes to opt in to any data gathering that is done through wearables, opting in is not the same as fully informed consent. Further, because athletes at the college level have historically been deprived of having advisers and representatives to help them raise questions about the agreements they are entering into, this population may not be informed enough to know what questions they should be raising or might not feel that they have the power to opt out. The bottom line is the more private information an owner or coach has about an athlete, the more control they have over them. As these kinds of controls become normalized, fans potentially become more comfortable seeing athletes as pieces of performers (as data, video clips) rather than as performers or as people.

Sport Industry Diversity Initiative

WORLD PLAYERS ASSOCIATION (WPA)

The World Players Association (WPA) was established in 2014 as an autonomous sector of UNI Global Union that serves 85,000 professional athletes across 100 player associations in over 60 countries. In 2017, the WPA made history when it published the Universal Declaration of Player Rights (otherwise known as the Declaration) (figure 9.1). WPA executive director Brendan Schwab explained the importance of the Declaration.

> *The Declaration fills a glaring gap. In the rule books of world sport there are thousands of pages detailing onerous obligations, but not one that coherently spells out the internationally recognized human rights of the athletes. The result has been the widespread and sometimes tragic violation of the rights of the world's players. The Declaration makes clear that the rights of players can no longer be ignored, and athletes must be able to quickly access justice to ensure their fundamental rights are protected, respected and upheld. (World Players Association, 2017, para. 4)*

As a foundational principle, the Declaration is based on a belief that sport organizations owe a duty of respect for the rights of others. For athletes, according to the WPA, those rights include access to sport, labor rights, personal rights, and legal rights (World Players Association, 2017).

In 2019, the WPA launched the first global study of its kind to delve into the childhood sport experiences of elite athletes, known as CARES (Census of Athletes Rights and Experiences). Through in-depth interviews ($n = 13$) and an online survey of 297 athletes conducted between December 2019 and June 2020, the WPA found that 61 percent of the athletes reported being subjected to emotional abuse at least once as children. While training or competing, one in three elite athletes who participated in the study indicated that they had been subjected to physical abuse. More than half of the athletes (51%) were not aware as child athletes that there were organizations like players associations or unions, and nearly 70 percent were not aware as children that working in sport brought with it any rights prior to the age of 18 years (Rhind, Musson, Florence, Gilpin, & Alford, 2021).

Like other players associations and unions, the WPA works to foster a more inclusive culture within the sport industry. During the critical year of 2020, in the midst of the COVID-19 pandemic, the IOC was criticized for delaying its decision to postpone the Tokyo Games. WPA's Schwab commented that the delay was due to the IOC's entrenched decision-making process that isolated it and cut it off in a way that did not serve its stakeholders. Schwab argued that the culture within the IOC needed to change from one that viewed decision-making as hierarchal to one of the greatest inclusiveness (Homewood, 2020).

FIGURE 9.1 Universal Declaration of Player Rights.

Reprinted by permission from World Players Association, UNI Global Union. https://www.uniglobalunion.org/news/world-players-association-launches-universal-declaration-player-rights and https://www.uniglobalunion.org/sites/default/files/files/news/wpa_udpr_portico_v3.pdf

Fantasy Sports and the Emergence of the Desensitized Fan

The global **fantasy sports** market is vast and is expected to grow by $6.2 billion between 2020 and 2024. The market caters to niche audiences whose interests are as diverse as auto racing, baseball, basketball, football, horse racing, soccer, and table tennis. Fantasy sport consists of "virtual teams made up of real players of professional sports, which fantasy players can pick and draft to their fantasy team. Players can pit their team against other virtual teams, and whether a team wins or loses depends on how the real players perform in actual games in a given day or week" (Chu, 2018, para. 7). A socially based activity that occurs online, players can participate in daily (select new players each week) or traditional forms of the game (select a team that competes with different teams each week). The survey company Statista reported that there are nearly 46 million people in the United States who participate in fantasy sports (Fantasy Sports & Gaming Association, 2020), 78 percent of whom play fantasy football and 39 percent of whom play fantasy baseball (Get Sports Info, 2021). The popularity of various fantasy sports shifts from country to country. In the United Kingdom, it is fantasy soccer; in India, it is fantasy cricket (Get Sports Info, 2021).

The fantasy sport space engages fans to make decisions about players, to follow performances of players intensely to see how that affects the standing of their fantasy teams. Some say that the greatest effect fantasy sports has had on fan engagement is the capacity it has to turn a casual fan into a fervent one. In talking about the effect of fantasy on the sport of football in the United States, the president of the Fantasy Sports and Gaming Association, Paul Charchian, said, "It has been a seismic shift in how the game is consumed and the level of interest. This created a whole new level of fandom that was never on the map before" (FSGA, 2019, para. 3).

The ecosystem that exists around fantasy sports includes sponsorships, draft parties, merchandise, actual game tickets, and brand marketing. Fantasy sport participation is linked to greater fan engagement that translates into watching or going to more games and following teams more intensely on a daily basis (Kilpatrick, Hathaway, & Milavec, 2016). However, as fantasy sport participation has become more entrenched, perhaps more mature as a fan option, there has been a subtle shift that some researchers are detecting in identification and loyalty. Those who play fantasy football may develop a dual identity, with loyalty to both the league and a team. Which one becomes the most important one (league versus team) could negatively affect teams because fantasy players might be less inclined to want to follow a specific team and be more engaged in their own fate related to what is happening throughout the league (Sleep et al., 2019).

As much as fantasy sports participants may be motivated by any number of considerations, including escaping from the pressures and demands of their lives, feeling the excitement of a competitive environment, engaging socially with others in a fantasy sport community, or questing for the potential financial rewards when wagering is added into the mix, fantasy sports have been referred to as "yet another example of how professional athletes have been dehumanized" (Larkin, Dwyer, & Goebert, 2020, p. 404). Citing the idea of **mechanistic dehumanization** (wherein people are treated as objects), fantasy sports create a context that economists and other social scientists have associated with dehumanization, that being the buying and selling of human beings (Harris et al., 2014). And while Larkin and colleagues (2020) found that fantasy sports participants tended to associate humanness more with fantasy football athletes than with fantasy-ineligible athletes, athletes operating in the real world have been targets of fan abuse and online hate.

Former Carolina Panthers player Jonathan Stewart, who played in the NFL for more than 10 years before retiring in 2019, commented that for the players "it's not a fantasy, it's real life. These are guys who have actual families. This is a job. It's not fantasy" (Rhoden, 2015, para. 2). Fantasy players react badly when "their" players get injured, upsetting "their" prospects for success in a daily or weekly fantasy pool. While fantasy sports are lauded

A draft party is just one part of the ecosystem that exists around fantasy sports.
Gabe Ginsberg/Getty Images

as a complement to traditional forms of sport consumption—and traditional forms of sport consumption are rife with their own set of troubled relationships between fans and athletes—these added layers complicate those relationships further.

Legal Sports Gambling, Impact on the Industry, and How Athletes Are Viewed

As much as fantasy sport has changed the way that fans engage with sport and athletes, changes in the legalized sports gambling space have resulted in an increase in interest in professional and high-performance sports, along with increased investment in them from media entities, corporations that want to reach audiences using sport platforms, and fans (Healy, 2020).

Sport media entities have changed the way they cover leagues and events by emphasizing gambling interests as part of the story line. Boundaries between leagues and events and gambling interests, such as sports books and casinos, have come down, leading to new partnerships. As a case in point, it was announced in April 2021 that Caesars, DraftKings, and FanDuel were "official sports gambling partners" of the NFL. As part of these agreements, the NFL's gambling partners are authorized to use NFL trademarks for the purpose of promoting online gambling. Gambling content will be integrated on NFL online platforms, and the NFL's gambling partners will have access to the NFL's official league data feed (Bemis, 2021).

Prior to 2018, major professional franchises and college sport properties in the United States had stayed away from Las Vegas because it is the largest sports gambling market in the country. They reversed after legalized sports gambling was voted in nationwide, leading to the NHL's Golden Knights, NFL's Las Vegas Raiders, and the WNBA's Las Vegas Aces all establishing a home there. The NCAA and college sport conferences have also responded to the changing landscape, encouraging preseason and end-of-season tournaments and championships to take place in Vegas, where the proximity to gambling interests used to be thought too risky and reputationally damaging (Stutz, 2021). As a matter of dimension, as more states legalize sports betting (as of this writing 22 states allow sports betting, with another five set to authorize it within the 2021 calendar year), the impact is felt across the industry. In the first two months of 2021 alone, sports betting revenues were up by 155.9 percent from the previous year, with $3.5 billion bet through sports books in February of 2021 (Stutz, 2021). To put it simply, more sports betting means more watchers and followers of sport; more sport watchers and followers means more opportunities for advertisers to reach audiences, which means more lucrative media rights deals; more lucrative media rights deals means more money for league owners.

While expanded opportunities provide for some people within the sport industry to make more money, the context within which players and their performances are valued has shifted. Although gambling has always had an influence on sport and has been viewed as a sport itself (World Championship of Poker, as one example), in an atmosphere where the parsing of athlete performance is normalized, opportunities to bet expand. Sports gamblers are not just betting on the outcome of the game or which team or athlete covers the spread but on the ongoing action that is occurring within a contest, otherwise known as proposition (prop) bets. Will a pitcher throw a strike in a certain situation? Will a soccer goalie prevent a score during a penalty kick? Will a tennis player double fault? Will a golfer double bogey on hole nine?

Athletes in professional and high-performance sports are already subjected to all manner of vitriol when they fail to deliver. Researchers have found that sport fans who identify more strongly with a team are more willing to endorse aggression directed at opposing coaches and athletes. They further found that fan attitudes toward the use of aggression against opposing coaches and athletes is similar among fans of professional and college sport (Hilliard & Johnson, 2018). In a study of 200 fans between the ages of 18-31, a majority of whom were male (65%) and White (77%), "53% and 45% admitted some willingness to trip a player or coach, respectively, whereas only 35% and 39% admitted some willingness to break the leg of a player or coach… 17% admitted a willingness to murder a player or coach" (Hilliard & Johnson, 2018, p. 314). While athletes are vulnerable to abuse from fans, activist athletes are particularly vulnerable to hate-filled backlash of contempt and scorn (Kaufman, 2008).

In April of 2021, sport governing bodies and leagues associated with English Football, including the English Premier League, the Football Association, the Women's Super League, and others united to boycott social media for three days to challenge social media companies to do more to respond to the ongoing racist and sexist abuse and harassment players have been subjected to (Ornstein, 2021). Consider the death threats Green Bay Packer Marquez Valdes-Scantling received after he fumbled a critical pass during a game against the Indianapolis Colts in November 2020 (Galluccio, 2020). Or the death threats and racist comments directed at college basketball players E.J. Liddell (Ohio State University), Kofi Cockburn (University of Illinois), and several members of the West Virginia University team (Emmitt Matthews, Taz Sherman, and others) after their teams lost during March Madness (Boren, 2021; Zaslau, 2021). Add fan disappointment to financial loss where there is a perception that fans "own" players, and the ingredients for this kind of fan behavior to escalate are evident.

Racial Dynamics of Major Sport Properties and Their Impact on How Athletes Are Viewed and Treated

In other chapters in this book (chapters 3, 4, and 6), Drs. Shin, Cooper, and Davis detail how the most lucrative sectors of the sport industry operate with predominantly Black and Brown athlete labor forces working for owners, athletics administrators, and coaches who are predominantly White. In 2020, the racial composition of players in the NFL included 57.5 percent Black or African American, 24.9 percent White, 9.4 percent two or more races, 1.6 percent Hawaiian or Pacific Islander, 0.4 percent Hispanic, 0.2 percent American Indian or Alaska Native, 0.1 percent Asian, and the remaining 5.9 percent undisclosed or other. In contrast, 28 of the 32 head coaches in the NFL were White (87.5%); 84.8 percent of chief executive officers or presidents of NFL franchises were White, 93.6 percent of general managers or directors of player personnel were White; 86.3 percent of vice presidents were White; 81.2 percent of senior administrators were White; and 75.4 percent of those working in professional administration were White (Lapchick, 2020) (figure 9.2).

Within this racialized environment, the practice of putting athletes out on display in public forums to further examine their well-established physical skills (these athletes have been playing in front of audiences and before cameras for years before they receive an invitation to the NFL Combine) for the purposes of determining their value (Runstedtler, 2018) conjures up the history of how slaves were treated in the United States. In writing about what he referred to as the "construction of the fantasy plantation," McGregor (2016) notes:

> *The [NFL Combine] event produces a cacophony of statistics that enable fans, scouts, and media to discuss a player by quantifying their value, effectively divorcing their talent from their humanness. The NFL Combine is in the business of dehumanizing players so teams can make unbiased comparisons and decisions, allowing them to focus on their value to a multibillion-dollar industry. (para 2)*

McGregor (2016) also points out that this increasing focus on fantasy, player statistics, and standings is taking place at a time when the safety of the game and the integrity of the NFL itself is under fire for its failure to acknowledge long-term health risks associated with playing the game and the resulting tragedy of former NFL players and their families living with, and dying from, chronic traumatic encephalopathy, other forms of cognitive illnesses (ALS, dementia, memory loss), Parkinson's, attendant psychological issues such as anxiety and depression, and myriad other health issues. He writes:

> *Thinking of athletes as real people forces us to address the tensions of watching real people participate in a violent sport, destroying their bodies, for our entertainment. Looking at them only as numbers, however, allows us to avoid the uncomfortable ethics of watching football or dealing with their off-the-field behavior. This is perhaps why fantasy football continues to grow in popularity amidst the increasing data pointing to the long-term danger of playing football. (para. 13)*

Whether readers feel comfortable with or see the parallels that McGregor draws upon in his analysis, there is no question that the NFL itself has a racialized view of how it deals with and responds to players. In 2021, it was revealed through court documents that the NFL was using different racial standards to assess cognitive damage suffered by former players as part of the NFL's settlement of concussion claims. Using a race-normed standard that was based on a belief that African Americans were not as intelligent as Whites, former Black players were facing the prospect of having to demonstrate greater cognitive impairment compared to White players in order to receive an equitable settlement (Belson, 2021). (See chapter 13 for the history of racial stereotyping of Black NFL players as intellectually inferior.)

This kind of approach to dealing with players is not found exclusively in the NFL. The NCAA, for many years, has compared college athlete labor to prison labor when defending itself against athletes seeking minimum wage under the Fair Labor Standards Act as employees (King, 2018). Relying on *Vanskike v. Peters*, a precedent setting case that has been used to deny hourly wages and employee status to prisoners under an exception in the 13th Amendment (the amendment that ended slavery except for those in involuntary service as "a punishment for a crime") (Kisiel, 2021), the NCAA has persisted in arguing that the conditions under which athletes work are similar to those of convicted felons (*Livers v. NCAA*, 2017). In 2018, in a rebuttal on behalf of former Villanova football player Poppy Livers to the

FIGURE 9.2 Comparison of NFL head coaches and players.
Based on Lapchick (2020).

Sport Industry Leader Profile

Ramogi Huma

Title: Executive Director, National College Players Association

Ramogi Huma is the embodiment of someone who witnessed an injustice and acted to make a difference. His journey as a college athlete advocate began when he was in his first year of playing football at the University of California, Los Angeles (UCLA) in 1995. He watched as one of his teammates, All-American Donnie Edwards, was punished with a one-game suspension because he accepted groceries valued at approximately $150 that had been delivered anonymously to his doorstep. Huma simply could not understand how an athlete who did not have enough money to eat was threatened by the NCAA after accepting a couple of bags of groceries. The NCAA defended its decision by arguing that NCAA rules expressly barred college athletes from receiving extra benefits that would not be available to students more generally (in effect, if students around campus are not receiving gifts of food from anonymous donors then athletes are prohibited from doing so; otherwise, they jeopardize their eligibility to play).

For Huma, the issue was much simpler. How could any entity like the NCAA, which was running a multimillion-dollar business, deny a hungry person food and punish them for accepting food when they were hungry? Over time, as Huma began to learn more as a player about the way the college sport system worked, he realized that the rules and regulations imposed on college athletes were unreasonably restrictive in some cases and neglectful in others. For example, at the time he was starting his work in the 1990s, the NCAA prevented colleges from paying medical expenses for injuries athletes suffered during summer workouts.

Moved to action, Huma initially created a student group to represent the interests of athletes on the UCLA campus. That group eventually became the National College Players Association (NCPA), and his advocacy has now become his life's work. Backed by the United Steelworkers, the NCPA has empowered thousands of college athletes from over 150 campuses to participate in actions in pursuit of improving the lives of college athletes.

NCAA, the plaintiffs wrote, "Defense Counsel's insistence that Vanskike be applied here is not only legally frivolous, but also deeply offensive to all Scholarship Athletes—and particularly to African-Americans. . . . Comparing athletes to prisoners is contemptible" (King, 2018, para. 9).

Athlete Labor as Social Reproductive Labor

Sociologist Nathan Kalman-Lamb (2019) has argued that to fully understand the importance of sport in a capitalist society, athlete labor should be understood to be a form of social reproductive labor. What this means in a nutshell is that as professional and high-performance sport appears laser-focused on athletes what the fans do with what they are confronted with leads to a social reproduction of the value of labor. In an economic system intent on suppressing labor value and increasing profit for owners and corporate stakeholders, fans play a role in aiding and abetting the dehumanization of athletes. This seems like such a distant concept when put on the page, and yet, the industry-specific ways in which athletes are monetized and valued, traded, and moved around like objects on a game board or in an electronic game, rated and ranked, stamped with a predictive expiration date, used, and then dismissed after their production value diminishes, is difficult to ignore.

Just a few days after Naomi Osaka announced that she was leaving the French Open early due

For more than 25 years, Huma has worked with countless athletes to address the range of issues they face in a college sport system that often does not protect their interests. Those issues include physical and sexual abuse, medical malpractice, unpaid medical expenses, and loss of athletic scholarships. He has also been a leading voice for change, promoting policy and regulatory reform through meetings with lawmakers and public policy makers. Over the years, he has testified before numerous committee hearings in the United States Senate and House of Representatives. He has worked with state legislatures to craft bills to protect college athletes' rights to educational benefits, fair compensation, fair treatment, healthy and safe work conditions, and medical coverage.

On the issue of compensating college athletes for the use of their names, images, and likenesses, Huma worked closely with California legislators and Governor Gavin Newsom to enact the Fair Pay to Play Act in September 2019. That effort has since led to the passage of similar bills in at least 26 states as of this writing, with 16 going into effect by the end of 2021, and others with effective dates ranging from 2022 through 2025 (Varsik, Hiegel, & Parry, 2021). Huma has served as a consultant on some of the most consequential lawsuits against the NCAA, including *White v. NCAA* (2006), *Agnew v. NCAA* (2012), *O'Bannon v. NCAA* (2015), and *Jenkins v. NCAA* (2021).

Huma has coauthored several studies with Ithaca College professor Ellen J. Staurowsky (formerly with Drexel University). Their 2020 collaboration, entitled "How the NCAA's Empire Robs Predominantly Black Athletes of Generational Wealth," estimated that the fair market value of FBS football and men's basketball players is approximately $208,000 and $370,000, respectively. Examining what that loss of compensation meant from a generational wealth perspective, they determined that the NCAA denies college athletes in the sports of football and men's basketball approximately $10 billion of their fair market value over the course of four years.

Huma holds a bachelor's degree in sociology and a master's of public health from UCLA. When he was competing, Huma was recognized as UCLA's Defensive Rookie of the Year. While he played for UCLA, the team won back-to-back conference championships in 1997 and 1998.

to the pressures of being under such intense media scrutiny, several incidents involving fans abusing NBA players occurred during playoff games. In Philadelphia, a 76ers fan poured popcorn on Washington Wizards guard Russell Westbrook as he left the arena with an ankle injury. Trae Young, who plays for the Atlanta Hawks, was spat upon by a New York fan in Madison Square Garden. And three Utah Jazz fans were removed from the arena following their harassment of the family members of Memphis Grizzlies guard Ja Morant (Abrams, 2021)

In recent years, athletes laboring in professional and high-performance sport, whether paid or unpaid, have been compelled following the way they have been treated to state explicitly that they are human beings. E.J. Liddell from Ohio State, for example, in responding to the online expletive-laced reactions he received following the Buckeyes' loss to Oral Roberts in the NCAA Division I Men's Basketball Tournament, one of the milder ones being "don't ever show your face at Ohio State. we hate you," responded, "Honestly, what did I do to deserve this? I'm human" (Jardy, 2021).

In understanding the ways in which athlete labor is different from that of labor in other industries, and the attendant pressures on athletes who serve the profit motives of sport owners and the corporate interests aligned with sport, a further distinction is revealed. Part of the tensions that arise around the fair treatment of athletes in professional and high-performance sports like college football and basketball (men's and women's) is that the exchange of value is not just for the service provided by the athlete but also their personhood (Kalman-Lamb, 2019). As a consequence, as sport becomes more deeply intertwined with other social and political institutions that serve a profit economy, there is an imperative to ensure that athletes have the representation they need through players associations to push back against their dehumanization and to work toward regulatory systems that are more inclusive.

SUMMARY

The purpose of this chapter was to introduce the idea that sport is not just an activity, but in some countries like the United States, the production of capitalism. The social, political, and economic forces shape what is known as the sports industrial complex, where athletes are viewed not only as performers but as commodities.

We went on to explore how such athletic systems that provide employment and opportunity for athletes and entertainment for the masses can also create tensions between athletic labor and management when profit motives overtake care and concern for workers. And while athletic labor shares many concerns in common with other industries, such as fair compensation, safe workplaces, medical care and insurance benefits appropriate to the occupation, and educational benefits, coverage from media that itself has a stake in the industry adds a layer of scrutiny to athletic labor.

Changing consumption patterns of sport fans, inspired by the growth of fantasy sports and legalized sports betting, introduce elements that can produce the mechanistic dehumanization of players, a phenomenon that occurs when human beings are bought and sold. Finally, the chapter explores why checks and balances in the system are so important in balancing the interests of owners, other corporate stakeholders, athlete labor, and fans.

CRITICAL THINKING EXERCISES

1. Select a player from one of the U.S. major professional sport leagues or major college athletic programs. Follow social media for a month and chart the number of abusive comments made online directed toward the player.
2. In light of all of the ways that elite athletes are assessed and evaluated, debate whether the NFL should consider stopping the Combine. What are the reasons to keep it? What would be the reasons to get rid of the practice?
3. Pick a sport that is not one of the top professional or college sports in the United States. Study the way players, athletes, or performers in those sports are ranked. Can you identify any systemic hegemony (meaning are the patterns of assessment the same but just not as visible because the teams are not as prominent due to less media coverage)? In what other ways can sport be dehumanizing and devalue athletes?

REVIEW QUESTIONS

1. Sport as a social institution is said to be as much of a product of capitalism as what other institutions or entities?
2. What is the sports industrial complex?
3. What does it mean for an athlete (professional or college) to be referred to as a commodity?
4. What concerns does athlete labor share with labor in other industries? What distinguishes athlete labor from other industries?
5. What is the NFL Combine and what do players go through during the Combine? What is the connection between the NFL Combine and the NFL draft?
6. Because college athletes do not have players associations or unions, what is problematic about the agreements college athletic departments reach with wearable technology companies?

CHAPTER 10

The Politics of Sport and the Political Forces That Shape Sport

Ellen J. Staurowsky

LEARNING OBJECTIVES

- Become familiar with the general concept of politics and its connection to power.
- Explore the interconnections between sport, politics, and power.
- Examine how sport organizations lobby for their political interests and court public and government favor.
- Identify the intersections between sport fandom and politics.
- Discuss how sport reflects the dominant values of national interest.

In June of 2021, female hammer thrower Gwen Berry made her second U.S. Olympic team by placing third at the U.S. track and field Olympic Trials. Controversy followed, however, when she turned away from the American flag as she stood on the podium during a medal ceremony, holding up a T-shirt with the words "Activist Athlete" (Jenkins, 2021).

According to Berry, she was moved to action by the playing of the national anthem at the ceremony. Although USA Track & Field (USATF) claimed the timing of the anthem was merely coincidental to the medal ceremony, in her words, Berry felt she had been "set up" to do something because she had been suspended back in 2019 for raising her fist in a demonstration against racial injustice at the Pan American Games. At the time, she expressed a sentiment that "The Star-Spangled Banner" was a song interwoven with racism and not representative of her experiences as an American. For that protest, she was subjected to a yearlong suspension imposed by the United States Olympic and Paralympic Committee (USOPC) for violating the International Olympic Committee's (IOC) Rule 50 policy, a policy that bars athletes from raising their fists in protests and wearing apparel with political messages (Kilgore, 2020). She believes that she lost as much as 80 percent of her sponsorships when the USATF Foundation reduced her funding and Nike refused to renew her contract (Kilgore, 2021).

Reactions to her protest were mixed. In calling for her to be removed from the U.S. team, Congressman Tom Cotton (R-AR) commented, "I don't think it's too much, when athletes are competing to wear the Stars and Stripes—to compete under the Stars and Stripes in the Olympics—for them to simply honor that flag and our anthem on the medal stand" (Takala, 2021, para. 2). Similarly, U.S. Representative Dan Crenshaw (R-TX) expressed a belief that as a minimum requirement for membership on the Olympic team an athlete should "believe in the country you're representing" (Takala, 2021, para. 4). U.S. Senator Ted Cruz (R-TX) characterized Berry as a "leftist" who hated America (Fischels, 2021).

A recipient of the 2020 Toyota Humanitarian Award, given to a USATF athlete who has established an outstanding record of community involvement, Berry herself made it clear that she cared deeply about her country, so much so that she felt compelled to use the platform she had to speak up about racial injustice. When the USATF announced Berry as the recipient of the award in December of 2020, CEO Max Siegel said, "Gwen Berry is a mother, an athlete and advocate for social change. She is using her platform to make societal change and we are proud that she represents our sport" (USATF, 2020).

When White House Press Secretary Jen Psaki was asked about President Joseph Biden's views on the appropriateness of Berry's conduct as an athlete representing the United States, she gave a statement:

> *I know [Biden] is incredibly proud to be an American and has great respect for the anthem and all that it represents. He would also say that part of that pride in our country means recognizing there are moments where we, as a country, haven't lived up to our highest ideals, and that means respecting the right of people granted in the Constitution to peacefully protest. (Fischels, 2021, para. 7)*

Color of Change is promoted as the U.S.'s largest online racial justice group; its mission is to "challenge injustice, hold corporate and political leaders accountable, commission game-changing research on systems of inequality, and advance solutions for racial justice that can transform our world" (Color of Change, 2021a, para. 1). The organization stepped in to sponsor Berry following the 2019 protest, working to help broker a deal between Berry and Puma so that she could continue competing and pressuring the USOPC to change its rules regarding athlete protests, which it did in 2020 (Color of Change, 2021b).

In the aftermath of Berry's protest at the Olympic Trials, Color of Change's sponsorship of Berry garnered media attention, with the organization being depicted as a threatening, "leftist" group aligned with militant and radical causes (Alexander, 2021). *Washington Post* reporter Sally Jenkins (2021) noted that the framing of Berry and her supporters in this manner is consistent with how Black activism has been treated in United States. Situating the reaction to Berry's actions within a larger historical context, Jenkins noted that efforts on the part of African Americans to address race issues and demand change, whether they are athletes or not, are often labeled as disloyal and unpatriotic. Dan T. Carter, a scholar from the University of South Carolina who has studied the history of civil rights in the United States, told Jenkins that "there is certainly a harsh, hard rhetoric that attempts to demonize them and cast them out of American society" (para. 12).

In Gwen Berry's case, she had violated no rule or law when she turned away from the flag. Her decision arose from her lived experience as a woman who grew up in Ferguson, Missouri, taking to heart the murder of fellow citizen Michael Brown, who was shot six times by police in 2014, and the fear she held for the safety and security of her own son. From Berry's perspective, "It's our sacrifice. It's our podium. It's our moment" (Jenkins, 2021, para. 19).

Gwen Berry's protests and the reactions to those protests are part of a much larger dynamic that helps us understand the intersection between sport, power, and politics. This case demonstrates how sport, along with those acting in relationship to it, is intimately tied to political institutions.

Notwithstanding the wishes of those who say that sport should be free of politics, sport is a production of political forces, and sport serves to influence political conversations. In this chapter, the concept of politics will be introduced. We will explore the interconnections between sport and politics, how sport organizations lobby for their political interests and court public and government favor, and how sport reflects the dominant values of national interest.

Politics as a Social Institution, Activity, and Process

Take a deep breath and just think for a moment about the term "politics." Some people major in it. Some people work in it. Some people report on it. Some people live for it and others have no patience with it. But what exactly is it? Good question.

Author Andrew Heywood (2013) says it can mean many things, from the exercise of power to the study of governmental entities to the allocation of resources to the manner in which decisions are made. Distilled to its essence, "Politics, in its broadest sense, is the activity through which people make, preserve and amend the general rules under which they live" (Heywood, 2013, p. 2). As people live, work, and strive to thrive together, the process of reaching agreement about those rules emerges from discussion and debate, and efforts are made to resolve conflicts that arise from competing ideas, diversity of opinion, the needs of various groups, and opposing viewpoints. The power that comes from collective action provides motivation to recognize the value of compromise and cooperation. Thus, politics deals with the "distribution and exercise of power within a society." A political institution is the entity through which that power is exercised and distributed.

Rooted in the Greek word *polis*, meaning city-state, the political arena is where we find the machinery or mechanisms of government, from local municipalities to statehouses to federal agencies being activated in service to specified public interests. The decisions made by public policy makers and politicians in that arena often have sweeping implications for large groups of people—or equalizing effects for groups of people marginalized by status, access to resources, or other social barriers. Lessons from the feminist movement, however, remind us that the personal is political—meaning that, for instance, it is one thing to generally understand that there is a gender wage gap, it is an entirely differently thing to try to pay your bills, help provide for your family, and get ahead when you are earning less simply because you are a woman (Lee, 2007).

A key feature of political entities (and effectively every social relationship) is power and power arrangements. Nineteenth century sociologist Max Weber conceived of **power** as the ability for one person or entity (e.g., organization, business, team, or nation) in a given situation to effectively get their way, even when confronted with resistance or opposition. This can happen peacefully, through subtle challenges, by subversive manipulation, or through outright coercive and violent means (University of Minnesota, 2016).

There are different types of power. Weber described legitimate authority as power that is exercised for justifiable and appropriate reasons as agreed upon by the people who are subjected to that authority. Sports examples include ceding authority to a league commissioner to handle disciplinary matters; having referees, umpires, and judges officiate games; and giving authority to mediators to resolve labor disputes between leagues and players. However, power can also be a matter of "soft" influence (**soft power**), where attitudes or preferences are shaped by persuasive messaging or arguments sometimes delivered by "charismatic" individuals (**charismatic authority**) whose personal stories or qualities compel attention (e.g., Rachael Denhollander, a former gymnast turned lawyer who advocated on behalf of hundreds of female athletes sexually assaulted by former USA Gymnastics and Michigan State University sports medicine physician Larry Nassar) (University of Minnesota, 2016).

With this overview of what politics is and the role that power plays in political organizations, we can begin to appreciate its relevance to exploring diversity, equity, and inclusion issues in sport. We can consider how sport figures engage in politics; the interconnections between sport, politics, and power; how political entities support or undermine sport as a social institution; and how sport becomes a vehicle for representing national interests.

Engagement of Politicians in Sport

As a cultural form that intersects with the political arena, politicians play a variety of roles in the spectacle of sport. Presidents, members of the U.S. Congress, those serving in state legislatures, mayors, and local politicians may make an appearance to throw out the first pitch on opening day at a ballpark. Friendly wagers between governors of states whose teams are competing in a National Football League (NFL) playoff game or college sport championship are regular occurrences.

White House Invitations to Sports Figures and Teams

The tradition of inviting sports figures and teams to the White House is symbolic of the changing role of sport in American society. A bipartisan tradition, the invitation to the "people's house" is predicated on celebrating a form of excellence (Stephens, 2017). In the case of U.S. leagues that span the Canadian border (the NHL and MLB), there has been precedent for inviting Canadian professional teams, as well. As early as 1865, baseball teams were invited to the White House. Reflecting the expansion of sport as a business and its growth at all levels of society, an occasional ceremony recognizing a particular sporting activity of the day, such as President Ulysses S. Grant hosting the first professional baseball club, the Cincinnati Red Stockings, in 1869, eventually gave way through the decades to a cycle of invitations recognizing champions from professional, college, and individual and team Olympic sports (Neumann, 2016). According to Hester (2005), starting with the Carter administration in 1977 and through the next 25 years, there was a steady increase in the number of times the White House hosted professional and college teams, averaging seven per year during that period of time.

White House invitations for athletic teams occur within the context of the presidential administrations that host them. And U.S. presidents have had their own preferences for sport and their own relationships to it (see table 10.1

for a sample of some U.S. presidents and their sport interests). Those interests create a context for the visits athletes and teams make to the White House.

As much as these visits are intended to be bipartisan, the invitations themselves reflect the political sensibilities of the presidential administrations that issue them. And athletes and team officials who are invited are not always willing to set aside their own viewpoints to participate in a ceremony with a president with whom they do not agree. In 2012, in recognition of the Boston Bruins winning the Stanley Cup a few months before, goalkeeper Tim Thomas, who identified as a member of the Tea Party, publicly declined. He wrote a formal statement to the press:

> *I believe the Federal government has grown out of control, threatening the Rights, Liberties, and Property of the People. . . This was not about politics or party, as in my opinion both parties are responsible for the situation we are in as a country. This was about a choice I had to make as an INDIVIDUAL. (Hardie, 2012, para. 4)*

Other athletes, including but not limited to Larry Bird (Boston Celtics) in 1984, Michael Jordan (Chicago Bulls) in 1991, Tom Brady (Boston Patriots) in 2015, Jake Arrieta (Chicago Cubs) in 2016, and Chris Long (Philadelphia Eagles) in 2018, have declined invitations to the White House.

As other authors in this text have noted (see chapter 13), there was a marked shift in the way White House visits were managed under the Trump administration, stemming from contentious relationships between President Trump, the National Basketball Association (NBA),

TABLE 10.1 Selected U.S. Presidents and Their Sport Interests

U.S. president's name	Term of office	Sport contributions or connections
Theodore Roosevelt	1901-1909	Credited with intervening in the violence occurring in college football in the early 1900s, President Roosevelt's contribution resulted in the creation of what would become the NCAA.
Franklin D. Roosevelt	1933-1945	Following the bombing of Pearl Harbor in 1941, FDR's advice was sought by MLB Commissioner Kennesaw Mountain Landis about the appropriateness of playing baseball. President Roosevelt responded by saying that it was best for the country to continue to play.
Harry S. Truman	1945-1953	In exchanges with the head of the U.S. Olympic Committee, Avery Brundage, President Truman expressed a view that it was imperative that the United States beat the Soviet Union at the Olympic Games in 1952. This was the first appearance of the USSR in the Olympics.
John F. Kennedy	1961-1963	It was under President Kennedy's administration in the 1960s that the President's Council on Physical Fitness was initiated. JFK's sister Eunice Kennedy Shriver became a leading figure in the creation of the Special Olympics.
Richard M. Nixon	1969-1974	President Nixon signed into law Title IX of the Education Amendments Act, reducing sex-based discrimination and ushering in a new era for women's sports.
Gerald R. Ford	1974-1977	President Ford was well known for having played football at the University of Michigan.

(continued)

TABLE 10.1 *continued*

U.S. president's name	Term of office	Sport contributions or connections
Ronald W. Reagan	1981-1989	President Reagan, a former actor, had portrayed Notre Dame football player George Gipp, who died from influenza, inspiring an expression, attributed to coach Knute Rockne, to "win one for the Gipper." Reagan's association with that iconic moment morphed with his political persona, where he was referred to as the Gipper and where his followers were encouraged to win one for him.
George H.W. Bush	1989-1993	President George H.W. Bush was well known for his baseball playing career at Yale. He was closely aligned with the NFL.
William (Bill) J. Clinton	1993-2001	In March 1994, President Bill Clinton was featured on the cover of *Sports Illustrated* extolling the virtues of his home state of Arkansas's men's basketball program. Described in an accompanying article as the "nation's first fan," Clinton was known for his love of golf and jogging and general enthusiasm for sports.
George W. Bush	2001-2009	President George W. Bush served as managing general partner of the Texas Rangers before leaving that position to run for governor of Texas.
Barack H. Obama	2009-2017	President Barack Obama's love for the game of basketball and his connections to a network of college and professional basketball teams and coaches (his brother-in-law is Craig Robinson, then an NCAA Division I men's college basketball head coach who would later become executive director of the National Association of Basketball Coaches) inspired ESPN to broadcast his March Madness selections live. First Lady Michelle Obama was committed to the nation's health, starting the "Let's Move" program.
Donald J. Trump	2017-2021	President Donald J. Trump had well-established and strong connections with the sport industry through multiple avenues. He was an avid high school athlete who often reminisced about his baseball career. An enthusiastic boxing fan, he owned several casinos, thus connecting him to sports gambling. He entered into numerous professional sport ventures, including performing alongside World Wrestling Entertainment (WWE) owner Vince McMahon, hosting wrestling events at his hotels, and owning wrestling properties such as Monday Night Raw. As a real estate owner and developer, he also owned several resorts and golf clubs.
Joseph (Joe) R. Biden	2021-	President Joseph Biden played football at the University of Delaware, is an active runner and cyclist, and has been an advocate on behalf of women athletes for decades.

the Women's National Basketball Association (WNBA), and some people in the women's sports community, resulting in questions about whether the tradition should or would continue in the future. As pointed out by Jerry Carino of the Asbury Park Press (2021), of 14 basketball teams that won major championships during the Trump administration, only one (the Baylor women's basketball team) visited the White House. In one case, the Golden State Warriors' invitation was revoked after Stephen Curry stated in an interview that he was not interested in going. The highly successful WNBA team the Minnesota Lynx, which has had a strong history of social activism, was not invited after winning the championship in 2017, while the University of North Carolina men's basketball team, after winning the NCAA men's championship in 2017, quietly declined the invitation. In a divided political landscape, where players are more publicly active on social issues, some players have questioned whether White House visits, once considered to be an honor, can achieve the goals intended. Others, however, point to the tone that is set by leaders in terms of the manner in which political discourse occurs. They hold out hope that there can be a return to less strident discourse that allows for greater tolerance of perspectives. Sport team visits to the White House may prove to be a barometer of how the nation is doing in that regard.

Sport as a Platform for Political Messaging

The appearance of a politician at a game can hold important resonance and meaning. In 2019, in the lead up to what would be a hotly contested presidential race, President Donald Trump was booed at a World Series Game featuring a matchup between the Washington Nationals and the Houston Astros. However, a few weeks later, while attending a college football game between the two top teams in the nation, University of Alabama and Louisiana State University, President Trump was widely cheered (Payne, 2019). The reception of the president at each of those events reflected the level of support he had in those different demographic areas. He had strong support in Alabama, with an approval rating of 63 percent at one point in 2018 (Kirby, 2018). In contrast, in Washington, DC, during Trump's reelection bid nearly 91 percent of voters supported Joseph Biden, compared to 5.8 percent support for Trump (FiveThirtyEight, 2020).

As much as sport can be a platform where political figures align their interests with those of the fans in the stands, it can also serve as a place for collective response to national tragedy. In the aftermath of the coordinated attacks orchestrated by al-Qaeda terrorists on September 11th, 2001, involving hijacking four planes and flying them into the World Trade Center, the Pentagon, and a field in Shanksville, Pennsylvania, life in the United States paused while the full magnitude of what had happened became clear. As the nation grieved for the loss of life and as citizens of a country whose mainland had never come under attack from a foreign entity dealt with the reality of what that attack meant, a nation of unsettled people looked to themselves and to their leaders for assurance. When sporting events resumed, people reported finding solace by going to games, whether they were sports fans or not. They wanted to be a part of the displays of patriotism at games, where ceremonies were staged to remember the victims who had died, their families, and the first responders and military personnel who were responding to the attack. As sportswriter Dan Wetzel (2011) described it, "Sports mattered the same: not as a game, as a gathering" (para. 17).

As immortalized in the film *Nine Innings from Ground Zero*, U.S. President George W. Bush would appear 49 days later in New York City, at Yankee Stadium, just miles from where rescue workers continued their work in finding those who had died in the attack on the World Trade Center. Two iconic New York teams, the Yankees and the Mets, were playing in Game 3 of the World Series. With the nation on high alert, and despite reservations from his Secret Service contingent, President Bush insisted on throwing out the first pitch. Striding to the mound, he calmly stood alone in a stadium with 55,000 people, open and vulnerable even with helicopters in the air space overhead and snipers on the turrets. After standing for a moment, he casually wound up and threw a perfect strike (Lavine, 2004). As online blogger Brad Callas (2017) noted, "In one moment, Bush picked up the pieces that was the nation's shattered confidence. Most importantly, it wasn't by way of a televised speech, but with an act that is as American as it gets—a first pitch on America's Pastime's biggest stage" (para. 7).

In discussing the power of sporting events following the September 11th attacks to fill a cultural need in response to the trauma and uncertainty that people were feeling, Brown (2004) wrote about the efforts of sports leagues to convey patriotic messages that reinforced unity and served as a reminder "that life must go on" (p. 41). He also pointed out, however, that the heavy military presence at those events and the unified chants of "USA" moved beyond contributing to the psychic healing of a nation to creating a subtle wave of unquestioning patriotism that signaled an endorsement of war (Butterworth, 2005).

Within a month of the attack, President Bush authorized Operation Enduring Freedom, the term used for the U.S. government's global war on terrorism. It began with air strikes targeting al-Qaeda and the Taliban in Afghanistan and lasted until 2014. The Bush administration received criticism three years later for misleading the American public about the death of former Arizona Cardinal football player Pat Tillman, a figure who had become a symbol of patriotism by turning down a $3.6 million dollar NFL contract to serve his country as an Army Ranger. Against his wishes, Tillman's story became part of a narrative of American heroism that was used in collaborative efforts between the NFL and the U.S. government to promote the merits of the war and to recruit soldiers to aid in it (Staurowsky, 2005). When news of Tillman's death was initially reported, the Army claimed that he had been killed by enemy fire. After a memorial service that was aired on major news outlets like CNN and ESPN, the family was told that Tillman's death was the result of friendly fire. In the months and years following, the Tillman family, investigative journalists, members of Congress, and others believed that the Department of Defense shared **disinformation** with the American public about the events of Tillman's death in order to protect the image of the military and government officials. His death remains a troubling chapter that has continued to prompt numerous investigations and unresolved questions (Devereaux, 2017; Fish, 2006).

Sport can serve as a place for collective response to national tragedy. President Bush was able to restore confidence to the country after the September 11th attacks by throwing out the first pitch at Game 3 of the World Series in 2001.

TIMOTHY A. CLARY/AFP via Getty Images

Interconnections Between Sport, Politics, and Power

There are certain spaces in society where the convergence between sport, politics, and power are clearly illustrated. In this section, we explore two of these: public financing of sport stadiums and facilities and the area of sport lobbying.

Public Financing of Sport Stadiums and Facilities

What would the sport system in the United States look like if sport as an institution really were **apolitical** and separated entirely from governmental entities and the political ecosystem? Consider the economic investment governmental entities have in sport facilities alone. From community recreational facilities that host youth sport leagues to high school gymnasiums and playing fields to local golf courses, ice rinks, tennis courts, and running paths, to university athletic complexes, to professional sporting arenas and stadiums, the public investment in sport is vast. Historically justified as a public good, public investment in sport teams, venues, and events take myriad forms, including the allocation of taxpayer dollars, the issuance of tax-free bonds, imposition of hotel and luxury taxes, tax incentives to draw professional teams from other cities or prevent professional teams from moving to other cities, free land, and other forms of subsidies.

In an ongoing Georgia State University study tracking taxpayer spending on professional sports stadiums, the taxpayer burden for the top 15 cities totals more than $7.5 billion (Rossi, 2021). The reason these kinds of projects are often supported with public financing or a combination of public and private financing is a "belief that new stadiums will create significant impact on the local community through increased jobs in the short-run and increased spending through tourism over the long-run" (*Berkeley Economic Review*, 2019, para. 2).

The public financing of sport facilities, however, is a tangle of wishful thinking, overoptimism, civic pride, and prestige-seeking balanced against financial returns that consistently fall short of projections and do not deliver on the promised positive economic impact. We can ask two questions. First, why are there financial shortfalls on publicly subsidized stadiums? And second, why do communities keep investing if economists have been reporting these problems for years? Let's start with the first.

There are several reasons cities do not realize the positive economic benefits they think they will when they make decisions to publicly support stadiums and arenas:

- Assessments of potential economic impact give little consideration to what is lost as a result of the priorities determined when a stadium project is adopted. If a community is spending on a stadium, it's not spending on something else, such as education or other economic growth areas. Thus, building a stadium may not produce the strongest return on investment compared to investing in education and job training programs, for example (Sanders, 2020).
- The gap between the projected construction costs when a stadium is approved and the actual cost of the project is great. Communities typically pay more than what they expect to pay.
- Taxpayers bear some or all of the burden of paying for ongoing facility maintenance and upgrades; public funds continue to support these privately owned sport franchises (Sanders, 2020). In effect, the obligation turns out to be much longer than taxpayers think it will be.

According to a poll of economic experts conducted by the University of Chicago in 2017, 57 percent of respondents agreed or strongly agreed "providing state and local subsidies to build stadiums for professional teams is likely to cost the relevant taxpayers more than any local economic benefits that are generated" (Cockrell, 2017, para 3). Only 2 percent of those economists who responded disagreed with that statement (12% were uncertain; 10% had no opinion) (Cockrell, 2017). Of course, not all value can be quantified by balancing columns on a spreadsheet (Johnson & Whitehead, 2000). Taxpayers may be willing to accept a less positive or even negative economic impact to have a professional team in their city because of its ability to bring people together and to give people something (quite literally) to cheer for.

Tensions around the level of tolerance citizens have for funding stadiums and paying the costs associated with professional teams can run high. Once a team is entrenched in a community and there has been an investment made, the questions become how much more a community will be asked to invest, what the payoff will be, and what the view of the professional team will be as a result. In May 2021, Major League Baseball announced that it had given the Oakland Athletics (Oakland A's) permission to relocate if they are unable to reach an agreement on a plan for a new ballpark (Katsuyama, 2021). Talk of relocation is often used by franchises and leagues in efforts to get favorable deals from the municipalities they are in. This is a particularly tender point for a city like Oakland, whose NFL franchise, the Raiders, did relocate to Las Vegas, where the new $1.9 billion Allegiant Stadium was completed in July 2020. Reportedly, Las Vegas contributed $750,000 to that project (Kudo, 2020).

In the case of Oakland, this is not just about a ballpark but the conversion of an industrial part of the city into a mixed-use area. As such, the A's proposal, known as the Howard Terminal development project, "would be one of the largest developments in the United States" (Reichard, 2021a, para. 3). Such a project raises questions about whether the city has the infrastructure to support it and what the project will do to existing business interests in the area. For those reasons, the project has drawn opposition from shipping and industrial firms that are concerned about the negative impact it could have on jobs and from fiscal analysts who question whether the project will cost far more than the $12 billion that is currently estimated. Contrary to MLB's characterization of the process as a protracted one, the process of the Oakland proposal has been streamlined by city and state officials (Reichard, 2021a). As of July 2021, the project was moving forward with a proposal that infrastructure needs would be addressed by creating two different tax districts, one for Howard Terminal and one for the general area. Interestingly, Oakland was also seeking a 45-year commitment from the Oakland A's that they would remain in the city if the stadium was built (Reichard, 2021b).

In addition to issues of impact on infrastructure and cost, stadium projects also raise profound questions regarding who the stadiums are for and the impact they have on those living in the areas where the stadiums are being built. Among the groups opposing the Howard Terminal plan proposed by the Oakland A's is the East Oakland Stadium Alliance, a group that estimates that thousands of living wage jobs would be eliminated if the project were to be authorized in its present form (Anthony, 2019). Those fears are not unfounded. Stadium-building for professional sport teams is often associated with **gentrification,** a process whereby construction projects are built in lower income neighborhoods, resulting in those living there being pushed out or displaced for projects that financially benefit the wealthy. The value of the real estate on which projects are built represents long-standing economic inequities, discriminatory housing policies, and **redlining** (a systematic denial of services to racial minorities) that push minority communities into certain sectors of cities while ensuring that those sectors remain financially deprived (Coleman, 2020).

Sport Lobbying

Behind the scenes, sport executives and administrators know they need to follow what happens in the political arena, not only the passage of laws, but also relevant court decisions and topics that public policy makers want to study on behalf of constituencies. An issue like the unsafe playing conditions in football, for example, is often brought to the attention of the American public and lawmakers by the mobilization of media, constituent outreach to legislators, and the work of groups like the Concussion Legacy Foundation. Founded by Dr. Christopher Nowinski, a former college football player and professional wrestler, the Concussion Legacy Foundation has supported research into chronic traumatic encephalopathy (CTE) in football players and other athletes, developed educational programs to create more awareness about concussive and subconcussive hits on the health and well-being of athletes, and created public policy proposals to make sport safer. Please see the Sport Industry Leader Profile for more information about Dr. Chris Nowinski.

As indicated earlier in the chapter, there is a large public investment in sport. At times, sport organizations seek assistance to have laws passed or amended that benefit their businesses; at other times the business practices sport organizations engage in may be exploitative or illegal, warranting government scrutiny. As a result, professional and college sport organizations hire lobbyists who are paid to educate politicians about issues and to advance legislative agendas that are favorable to their businesses.

According to Open Secrets, a group that tracks the money organizations spend to influence policy and elections, nearly $10 million was spent in 2020 on lobbying in the area of recreation. Organizations that qualify in that category are diverse, ranging from the Academy of Model Aeronautics to the Professional Golf Association to SeaWorld Entertainment. While the NFL appeared to lead spending in 2020 at $1,290,000, the combined spending of the NCAA, major college conferences (Atlantic Coast Conference, Big Ten, Big 12, PAC-12, and Southeastern Conference), and major college football championship organizations (College Football Playoff, Bowl Championship Series) was nearly twice as much as the NFL ($2,430,000) (Open Secrets, 2020).

In the case of college sport, which is aligned with the education sector, additional lobbying efforts may occur through national and state higher education associations. Further, in 2015, after the Northwestern football team signed union cards, the Division I athletic directors' association rebranded under the name of LEAD1 Association and hired Tom McMillen, a former professional basketball player who had served in Congress, to lobby for its own interests against college football players (Staurowsky, 2016). According to LEAD1, its mission is to influence how the rules of college sport are enacted and implemented. Representing 130 Division I athletic directors in the NCAA's top football playing tier of schools known as the Football Bowl Subdivision (FBS), LEAD1 organizes an annual meeting of its members every September in Washington, DC, using the occasion to brief lawmakers about its concerns. Emblematic of the power of **soft influence**, LEAD1 has hosted congressional luncheons on the Hill during its annual meeting. In 2017, at its first congressional luncheon, LEAD1 honored more than 50 members of Congress who were former college athletes, and in 2018, it ran a contest naming the top 25 former college athletes who were serving as congressional staffers (LEAD1 Association, 2018).

One of the reasons college sport entities spend so much money on lobbying efforts is the name, image, and likeness (NIL) issue. As lengthy legal battles over the NCAA's restrictive rules had been playing out in the judicial system without a response from the NCAA, a bill called the Fair Pay to Play Act passed in California in September of 2019. The bill allowed college athletes in California to receive compensation for endorsement deals under certain terms and conditions, along with allowing athletes representation to help them make those deals. As the NCAA delayed making a decision regarding whether it would relax its rule barring athletes from being able to earn money from such promotional activities as working at summer camps, signing autographs, making appearances at certain types of events, and promoting clothing lines and other products, similar bills were introduced in 37 states and eight federal-level bills pertaining to college athlete compensation were introduced in the U.S. Congress (as of July 6, 2021). Of the 37 state bills, 21 were passed (Saul Ewing Arnstein & Lehr, 2021).

Although each of the state laws regarding athlete compensation from use of their NIL have their own particular nuances, they include

- provisions for athletes to seek licensed, professional representation (agents),
- stipulations that prevent athletes from entering into contracts that are in conflict with agreements with an existing athletic team or department contract (such as a team contract with Nike, for example), and
- requirements that athletes report contracts they have entered into with a designated person on their campus.

Some of the laws also provide that schools and athletic departments are prevented from reducing or revoking an athlete's scholarship as a result of an athlete earning compensation from an NIL contract and from contracts that limit the ability of an athlete to use their NIL for commercial purposes (Saul Ewing Arnstein & Lehr, 2021). As the first of the state NIL laws went into effect in late June and early July of 2021, the NCAA passed an interim NIL policy,

Sport Industry Leader Profile

Chris Nowinski

Title: Cofounder and CEO, Concussion Legacy Foundation

Education: BS (sociology), Harvard University; PhD (behavioral neuroscience), Boston University

Dr. Chris Nowinski is a social entrepreneur leading a global conversation on concussions, CTE, and the future of sports. Dr. Nowinski is cofounder and CEO of the Concussion Legacy Foundation (CLF), a nonprofit organization leading the fight against concussions and CTE in the United States, Canada, the UK, and Australia. Dr. Nowinski is also the cofounder and visionary behind the acclaimed Boston University (BU) CTE Center and VA-BU-CLF Brain Bank, which has changed how the world views the long-term effects of head impacts in sports.

An academic All-Ivy Harvard football player turned WWE professional wrestler turned neuroscientist, Chris discovered the concussion crisis the hard way when a 2003 kick to the chin in a WWE match ended his promising career, causing postconcussion syndrome. At the time, Chris had already been the youngest Hardcore Champion in the history of the WWE and had been named 2002 Newcomer of the Year by *WWE Magazine*.

Dr. Nowinski's experience was the spark that inspired him to commit his life to serving patients and families who share similar experiences and ensuring a safer future for the next generation of athletes. Dr. Nowinski first wrote the investigative expose *Head Games: Football's Concussion Crisis* in 2006, cofounded CLF in 2007, and cofounded the Boston University CTE Center and VA-BU-CLF Brain Bank in 2008, where he serves as the outreach, recruitment, education, and public policy leader.

What was your epiphany moment? What led you to envision the Concussion Legacy Foundation?

My epiphany moment came on January 18, 2007, when we reported the findings of deceased former NFL player Andre Waters' brain study on the front page of the *New York Times*. I had been trying to get the world to care about concussions and brain trauma in sports through

which directs athletes to abide by their state laws and to seek advice from their institutions. It also states that NIL opportunities cannot be used to induce recruits to attend one school over another (Hosick, 2021). As college athletes continue to push for more change, they are facing the reality that they need to strengthen their own voice to counter the lobbying efforts of established college organizations that represent institutions and administrators, organizations like the NCAA, the conferences, and professional associations like LEAD1. While the National College Players Association has served that role (see chapter 9), a new organization created by current and former athletes called United College Athlete Advocates has emerged to help athletes organize (see Sport Industry Diversity Initiative sidebar).

Sports Fandom and Politics

In June 2021, Statista, the German company that serves as a source for marketing and consumer data, reported that nearly three-quarters of Americans self-identified as sports fans, with 25 percent being avid fans, 47 percent being casual fans, and the remaining 28 percent not writing the book *Head Games: Football's Concussion Crisis* in 2006. The book didn't capture hearts and minds, but through writing it I developed a plan to fix sports. What was missing was the concrete evidence to convince people the problem was real. Brain donation was the key to providing that evidence, and when news of the brain studies of our sports heroes could be shared directly with the public through the media, we could begin to open the public's eyes to the issue. The Concussion Legacy Foundation was initially launched with the vision of creating a brain bank to continue to study the brains of athletes and advance the science, then transform the findings into programs to keep the next generation of athletes safe.

What has been the primary inspiration for the work you do?

What inspires me has evolved over the last 15 years. Initially, I drew a lot of inspiration from my frustration with the NFL for their Big Tobacco–like "league of denial" approach to CTE. The league was using its extraordinary influence and resources not to help football players with problems created by playing football, but instead to mislead them about the risks so they could profit from their labor, leaving them to suffer alone or their wives and children to pick up the pieces. It was inhumane. As a football player myself, my parents and I had been misled when I signed up to play at 13, and I had brain damage because of it. I was inspired to end this cycle of exploitation of children and families with fewer resources and information. Now that we've forced the NFL to evolve, my inspiration comes from the amazing patients and families we work with who have been fighting the consequences of concussions and CTE. Through this work I've seen some of the worst of humanity, but today, working with a motivated staff, scientists, philanthropists, patients, and families, I feel I see some of the best of humanity.

What one thing would you recommend aspiring sport leaders need to know in working to continue to change the sports culture to make it safer for athletes?

Aspiring sports leaders need to understand what motivates the various constituencies that make up our sports culture to enact change. It's important to understand that your goals are not their goals, and their goals are rarely explicitly stated. If you can begin to see the problem from their point of view, you can understand the levers you need to pull to get them to change.

fans (Gough, 2021). Among the top-rated television series for 2020-2021, as measured for the adult 18-49 demographic, the NFL earned the top three spots for rating share and viewers (Schneider, 2021). Even during the first year of the COVID pandemic, or perhaps because of it, sports continued to dominate the linear television platform, increasing in importance because of its ability to draw viewers in a dispersed media landscape. According to Nielsen (2020), 8 of the top 10 single telecasts were sport properties (see table 10.2).

Given its highly mediated form and the magnitude of audience (the Super Bowl regularly draws an audience of 100 million viewers or more), there has historically been a strong economic incentive for stakeholders in the sport industry to ensure that they are apolitical, causing media entities and league ownership to reserve the right to reject certain types of advertising, for example. And apparently for good reason.

The NFL's Super Bowl LIV in 2020 was historic not only because of the fourth quarter comeback orchestrated by Kansas City quarterback Patrick Mahomes but also because of the airing of two 60-second national political ads purchased by the Republican Donald J.

TABLE 10.2 Top 10 Telecasts in 2020

Name of telecast	Originator	Average number of viewers (in millions)
Fox Super Bowl LIV	Fox	102,013
Fox Super Bowl post game	Fox	58,121
Fox NFC championship	Fox	43,625
Fox NFC Playoff-Sun	Fox	38,023
AFC wildcard playoff	CBS	31,828
AFC divisional playoff-SA	CBS	29,828
The Masked Singer	Fox	27,407
CFP championship L	ESPN	25,842
Fox NFC Championship—Post	Fox	24,335
The Oscars	ABC	24,316

Based on Nielsen, *Tops of 2020: Television* https://www.nielsen.com/us/en/insights/article/2020/tops-of-2020-television/ (Dec. 14, 2020).

Trump Campaign and the Democratic Michael Bloomberg campaign. The price of each ad was $10 million, far surpassing what corporations had paid previously. This signaled a marked departure from previous years. Going back as far as 1989 (when Ad Meter started to rank the popularity and effectiveness of ads aired during the Super Bowl), political candidates had not advertised during the national broadcast, although political figures over the years had purchased ad time at the state and local levels (Schad, 2020).

Surveys of Americans about the political content of Super Bowl ads reveal generally that they watch the game for reasons of escapism, to relax, to spend time with family and friends, and to enjoy the show, not to have to think about social and economic problems. As reported by the *Wall Street Journal*, a Morning Consult survey of 4,400 adults specifically asked respondents their views on the Trump and Bloomberg ads. Only 19 percent thought the Super Bowl was either "very" appropriate (6%) or "somewhat" appropriate (13%) for such advertising. When broken down by party affiliation, there was strong agreement from both Democrats and Republicans opposing the airing of ads for candidates from their own respective parties (56% of Democrats opposed the Bloomberg ad; 63% of Republicans opposed the Trump ad). Those findings were generally consistent with a survey conducted by Morning Consult the previous year, where two-thirds of Americans did not want advertisers to make political statements (WARC, 2020).

Sport and Its Fans Are More Political Than They Think

Thorson and Serazio (2018), however, make the case that "while partisan conflict may still be anomalous in professional sports, sports culture reinforces values that are relevant to—if not explicitly about—politics" (p. 392). The deeply embedded narrative within sport culture and media coverage that sport is a meritocratic undertaking that affords everyone the same chance to succeed through hard work—and that hard work will be rewarded with personal satisfaction, societal approval, and financial benefits—belies the fact that the American Dream in sport and elsewhere is often rarely so straightforward and eludes many people (Sage, 1998).

As one illustration, the meager amount of media coverage devoted to women's sport in televised news and highlight shows in 2019 was 5.4 percent, a figure that has effectively not changed since the 1980s despite an impression of linear growth in women's sport (Cooky et al., 2021). The lack of coverage, and the decisions made regarding coverage of women's sport, convey messages about the value and the status of women in sport (see chapter 6 for more details).

Sport Industry Diversity Initiative

UNITED COLLEGE ATHLETE ADVOCATES

On June 30, 2021, the same day the NCAA announced an interim policy that allows college athletes to profit from their names, images, and likenesses without jeopardizing their athletic eligibility, a nonprofit organization called the United College Athlete Advocates (UCAA) was launched with the purpose of creating a sustainable infrastructure to support college athlete efforts to improve the circumstances under which they compete and work. As they put it, they are working to "ensure our college athlete community is safe, educated, and compensated" (UCAA, 2021). Although the NCAA claims that athletes have an opportunity to influence policy through representation on NCAA committees, the UCAA addressed a letter to NCAA president Mark Emmert a day after it launched, pointing out that the NCAA issued its interim NIL policy after secret meetings including no athletes, that athletes have zero representation on the NCAA's Board of Governors (the center of its decision-making mechanism), and that athletes make up only 3 percent of representatives across the entire association's committees. The organization followed that with a statement that it believes the UCAA should receive 1 percent of NCAA revenues to invest in athlete-focused programs, including educational initiatives and other programs that drive progress on perennial problems (UCAA Letter to NCAA President Mark Emmert, 2021). The UCAA's letter received no response from the NCAA; however, in an initiative undertaken by the NCAA to revise its governance document (which they refer to as a constitution) in 2021, an athlete representative would have a seat on the NCAA's Board of Governors (Hackney, 2021).

Part of the impetus for the creation of the group was the protests that occurred in the summer of 2020 by the PAC-12 football players and other college athletes around the country, who were expressing concern about racial injustice and health and safety issues. Founded by seven current and former college athletes, the UCAA is an independent group of athletes operating outside of the structures of NCAA, conferences, and institutions. Its purpose is to elevate the voice of athletes in areas such as racial justice, gender equity, mental health, LGBTQIA+, and economic rights. Its goal is to shift the power dynamics within the college sport structure toward the players, rather than the institutions. In speaking about this imbalance, former Washington State cross country runner and UCAA cofounder Andrew Cooper explained that "the issues we deal with recycle each year. To me, the NCAA benefits a lot from that. They benefit from us not having a united community. They benefit from us not having a real voice, and they definitely benefit from us having no real power in the system" (Giambalvo, 2021, para. 4).

The UCAA provides support for athletes, starting with their teams and moving up through conference structures. When a majority of any team signs up with the UCAA, those players can then hold an election for a representative, who is then connected to representatives within their conferences (e.g., PAC-12 volleyball, SEC football). At the launch date, the UCAA was designed to accommodate athletes from the Power Five conferences (Atlantic Coast Conference, Big Ten, Big 12, PAC-12, and Southeastern Conference). There is an intention to expand into other conferences as their work continues. The overall structure of the UCAA is designed to support a college athlete movement through secure communication networks, impact coalitions, and democratic players' associations (UCAA, 2021).

Based on a survey of 1,051 sport fans conducted in partnership with Civis Analytics, Thorson and Serazio (2018) found that "sports and politics are closely intertwined," as seen in the positive associations sport fans have for the U.S. military and economic individualism. They further found that those who self-identify as being politically conservative are more likely to oppose what they perceive to be partisan politics in sport, a condition that arises when challenges are made to the status quo. They conclude that rather than being an entertainment form that provides for escape from social and economic problems, "ideological messaging is omnipresent in the sports culture" (Thorson & Serazio, 2018, p. 399).

Social Media Campaign for Hockey's Brianna Decker

As much as fans say they want sport to be separated from politics, and despite the reality that sport is intimately connected to politics, fans themselves regularly activate around political issues. Consider the reaction of NHL fans to Brianna Decker, a U.S. Women's National Ice Hockey Team player who was invited to participate in the NHL's all-star skills competition as a gesture of support for women's ice hockey. She registered the fastest time in the Premier passing event (1:06), beating the eight NHL players who were participating, but the $25,000 prize was given to NHL player Leon Draisaitl, who scored the fastest time among the male contestants (1:09) (Kaplan, 2019), prompting questions from fans. As the story evolved, the NHL claimed to have recorded a time for Decker that was slower than that of Draisaitl. Per an account from Canadian sports journalist Elliotte Friedman, the NHL said that Decker's time was around 1:12-13. As Jharveri (2019) noted, "It's unclear why the NHL waited until Saturday night [the night after the event] to release what they say is Decker's time" (para. 13).

Fans watching the event were unofficially clocking Decker's time. When they realized she had won, they took to Twitter, circulating a #PayDecker hashtag, expressing their views that Decker was being treated unfairly and drawing attention to the issue. One fan pointed out the disconnect between NHL Commissioner Gary Bettman talking about the importance of inclusion and supporting women's hockey and then the league not paying Decker when she won the event. One fan wrote, "Don't treat her like a mascot/cheerleader demonstrating a skill. She's a legit hockey player with the top skill!" (CBC Sports, 2019, para. 12). Another fan wrote "the largest NWHL [National Women's Hockey League] contract currently is $26,000. Leon Draisaitl makes 327 times that. #PayDecker" (Jhaveri, 2019, para. 6). The campaign led to the Canadian hockey equipment company CCM stepping up to pay Decker $25,000 for her performance and win (CBC Sports, 2019).

European Soccer Fans Mobilize to Oppose Creation of Super League

Fans will not only mobilize on social media to hold sport organizations accountable for abusing their power, but they will also take to the streets or engage in physical action to register outrage when the team they have invested in is going down a path that they believe threatens the sport, the industry, or their own view on how sport should be run. An example of this occurred in the spring of 2021 when the owners of 12 of the top European football (soccer) teams attempted to form a Super League in an act regarded by the fans as motivated by power and greed.

While executives with UEFA, the umbrella organization that oversees European football, were finalizing new rules and getting ready to announce those changes for the Champions League, a core group of team owners led by Florentino Pérez, president of Real Madrid, were working in secret behind the scenes to create a competing league made up of the most lucrative and powerful teams, closing out the others. Such a plan had the potential to destroy the professional football industry as it existed in Europe, preventing other teams from moving up through a process known as promotion and relegation (teams are moved or transferred within leagues depending on their performance, leaving the door open for an underdog team to compete against elite teams and for teams that are underperforming to drop down).

While European football has a decidedly international scope and scale, given that teams sign players from around the world and the fan base is truly global, the teams themselves have strong local fan followings. When the plans for a Super League were leaked, the response was swift and dramatic. In the absence of engaging their own team management, players, or fans in their plans, public outcry, especially in Great Britain, was fierce. Politicians, including UK Prime Minister Boris Johnson, French president

Fans will not only mobilize on social media to hold sport organizations accountable for abusing their power, but they will also take to the streets or engage in physical action to register outrage when the team they have invested in is going down a path that they believe threatens the sport, the industry, or their own view on how sport should be run.
OLI SCARFF/AFP via Getty Images

Emmanuel Macron, and even future heir to the British throne Prince William, went on the offensive, decrying the owners as self-serving and greedy.

In an interview on Sky TV that received 7.2 million views, former Manchester United player turned broadcaster and coach Gary Neville offered a searing assessment of the owners as impostors who failed to appreciate the culture of football in the UK, wrought from more than one hundred years of fans who lived for their teams and loved them. Pointing out that this was not the first time that owners from outside the country, including U.S. sport executives Joel Glazer (Tampa Bay Buccaneers and Manchester United) and John Henry (Boston Red Sox and majority owner of Liverpool FC), member of the royal family of the United Arab Emirates Sheikh Mansour bin Zayed al-Nahyan (Manchester City), and Russian billionaire Roman Abramovich (Chelsea), had tried to alter the structure of European football in service to their own profit at the expense of the game, Neville called for an independent regulator to create a system of accountability and transparency, stating:

> *I'm disgusted, absolutely disgusted. I'm disgusted with Manchester United and Liverpool most. I mean Liverpool, they pretend "you'll never walk alone"—"the people's club"—"the fan's club"; Manchester United—100 years—born out of workers around here and the breaking away of a league without competition that they can't be relegated from is an absolute disgrace, and honestly, we have to wrestle back the power in this country from the clubs at the top of this league and that includes my club. (Sky Sports, 2021)*

While Neville had the microphone, the fans had the street, and current players had their own platforms. Taking exception that owners advocating for the Super League were making this move during the COVID pandemic, when local teams were struggling and when health and safety rules were barring fans from going to games, fans' anger bubbled over. Two days after the announcement, hundreds of disaffected fans surrounded a bus carrying Liverpool players to a game with Leeds. Players stood with the fans opposing the breakaway, expressing solidarity by wearing T-shirts, posting their support on Twitter, and demanding meetings with management. Within 48 hours of the formal announcement about the Super League, starting with Manchester City and followed by Chelsea, Arsenal, Tottenham, Manchester United, and Liverpool, it had lost its foothold in Britain and had fallen apart (Panja & Smith, 2021).

The failure of the Super League illustrates how intertwined sport is with politics. It also illustrates the constant tensions that exist that require systems of checks and balances, because even in the aftermath of this very public failure, there were those warning that efforts to execute plans for consolidation will continue, not just in European football, as part of the ongoing globalization of the sport industry. As a writer from Sportico noted, part of the failure with the Super League was its miscalculation of the European football fan base, whose affinity for their favorite teams may "serve as a substitute for the loss of nation, state, or religion" (John-WallStreet, 2021).

Sport Fan Consumption and Inadvertent Exposure to Political News

Although there are multiple dimensions to fan engagement in politics, one less obvious one is the role televised sports media plays in inadvertently exposing fans to political news content. As news consumption undergoes a shift from more traditional forms of media, such as print, cable and network television, and radio to social media, with those in younger demographics (18- to 50-year-olds) relying more heavily on social media, there is a shift in how much news is consumed. A Pew Center study in July 2020 revealed that 18 percent of adult Americans were getting their news from social media sources. When compared to those who got their news from more traditional sources, those getting their news from social media sources knew less about the 2020 U.S. presidential election, less about the COVID-19 pandemic, and less about political news in general (Infield, 2020).

This notion of inadvertent exposure to political news happens when fans who might otherwise have little to no interest or engagement in political issues are introduced to it through sports coverage. This can happen in a couple of different ways. For example, in the lead-up to the start of the NBA season in 2021, conflicts arose between some players and the league's COVID-19 vaccination requirement, thereby introducing the political vaccination divide into sports news (Salvador, 2021). Or, when mega sporting events such as the Olympic Games are held in countries with histories of human rights violations, fans may be exposed to those issues for the first time because government officials call for greater accountability, advocates call for boycotts, and media express concerns regarding potential censorship (Myers, 2021).

In light of this changing landscape, media scholars Ryan Broussard and his colleagues (2021) explored the degree to which sports media coverage delivers political news to people who have stopped watching, listening, or reading about the news or who are partisan news consumers (individuals who may not be exposed to the full scope of news coverage on a particular topic). Through a representative sample of 1,493 adult Internet users, they found that sports media delivers low, but substantial, inadvertent exposure to news to those who follow sports. As news consumption continues to shift, and as more Americans follow sports, sports media may play an even larger role in shaping political views of sports fans.

Sport as a Vehicle for Representing National Interests

In the United States, citizens learn early that there is a connection between national interests and sport. From youth league through professional sport, displaying the American flag and singing the national anthem are as routine as announcing starting lineups or introducing who is competing. As Billings and colleagues (2015) point out, the singing of the national anthem is so embedded in the way we think about sport events that the act itself is not viewed as political:

> *Its presence is political because it defines a game in terms of nationalism, suggesting that a sporting event is an appropriate place to affirm principles that bind Americans together as a people. By contrast, its absence or a protest against its presence is political because it calls those very principles into question. (p. 163)*

Whenever U.S. teams take the field on the world stage in mega sporting events such as the Olympics and the Women's World Cup, the teams represent a national interest reflective of collective American values to the rest of the world while affirming to American citizens what it means to be an American. What stirs audiences to follow those teams and celebrate their successes is a shared **national identity** that resonates with common understandings about the values of freedom, democracy, and opportunity. According to Rowe (1999), sport is situated in a unique way to foster a sense of nationalism and national identity because it has the capacity to develop collective consciousness through its sheer span and reach.

The International Olympic Committee (IOC) says that the Olympic Movement is dedicated to building "a peaceful and better world by educating youth through sport practiced without discrimination" (IOC, 2021b, para. 2). It notes that in order for this to happen there needs to be "mutual understanding with a spirit of friendship, solidarity and fair play" (IOC, 2021b, para. 2). Insofar as the Olympic Movement has been associated with the idea of sport being used as a vehicle to bring people together from diverse backgrounds, historian Erin Redihan (2018) points out "the Games have long enabled global superpowers to enact their political and ideological conflicts in sport" (para. 1).

Positioning the U.S. within a global context, there is an expectation that American athletes will be among the best in the world. For more than 25 years, since the United States hosted the Summer Games in 1996, it has dominated the medal count (Wharton, 2021). In 2021, in the pandemic-delayed 2020 Tokyo Games, U.S. athletes earned a total of 113 medals (39 gold, 41 silver, 33 bronze), with the next two highest performing countries being the People's Republic of China with a total of 88 (38 gold, 32 silver, 18 bronze) and Russia with a total of 71 medals (20 gold, 28 silver, 23 bronze). The representation of the medal count itself is instructive in terms of how nations assess their success in the Games. In one accounting, Japan outperformed Great Britain if the analysis is based on gold medal count rather than total medal count, because Japan won 27 gold medals compared to Great Britain's 22. On the other hand, Great Britain won a total of 65 medals (gold, silver, and bronze) compared to Japan's count of 58 (IOC, 2021a).

The Olympic Games speak to the challenges associated with sport being apolitical or politically neutral. As broadcasters, media entities, and national sport governing bodies report what the medal counts are in any given Olympics, the IOC remains quiet about a ban on medal counts, grounded in Rule 6 of the Olympic Charter, which expressly emphasizes that competitions are intended to take place between athletes in individual and team sports and not between countries (Terraz, 2021). In a case of mixed messaging, in the IOC's guidelines for media organizations' editorial use of Olympic properties for the 2016 Games, the IOC states that it had no objection to the use of countdowns or medal tables as long as the "layout was considered" (IOC, 2016).

An argument can be made that the competition set in motion by the Olympic Games is not about political neutrality but the fostering of nationalism. The opening ceremony draws political leaders to witness it, and the parade of athletes is organized around nationhood. In that opening ceremony, the host nation has an opportunity to tell its national story through myth, history, and image. The medal ceremonies themselves emphasize the country where the champions are from with flag displays and the winner's country's anthem being played. And finally, events are framed as country versus country. Although the closing ceremony is designed symbolically to convey a message that boundaries have disintegrated as a result of the Games and athletes are unified through sport, it is notable that this is a flourish at the end of an ongoing narrative that has emphasized nationalism in the lead-up and during the Games themselves.

Given the magnitude of the corporate investment in the Games, where televised sport spectacle relies on the drama and suspense of competing countries and athletes from different parts of the world, there is an economic incentive in fostering the multiple national narratives that circulate through Olympic coverage. NBC Sports alone invested more than $12 billion in the rights to broadcast the Games through 2032 (Garcia, 2018).

The perspective that the Olympic Games are deeply influenced by and invested in political issues creates context to better understand our opening scenario involving U.S. hammer thrower Gwen Berry. As Terraz (2021) observes, "there seems to be a disparity in the Olympic Movement's approach to politics when it comes from athletes, where there is the potential for severe sanctions, compared to sport nationalism arising from medal tables, where it seems to have all but accepted their existence" (Terraz, 2021, para. 17). One wonders whether Berry or any other athlete competing in an international event would feel the need to protest if the Games were really about the athletes and not the countries they represent. Then again, if we accept that the personal is political, there would still be contested issues that would call out for challenges or responses, such as human rights violations, oppressive governmental regimes, and the influence of corporations in the global market.

SUMMARY

The purpose of this chapter was to become familiar with the concept of politics, its connection to power, and the various ways in which we see these connections manifest in sport. As part of our exploration of the intersection between sport and politics, we looked at how politicians engage with sport through the tradition of the White House visit, U.S. presidential interest in sport, and sport as a platform for political messaging. We further considered how sport is connected to political interests, as demonstrated in the public financing of stadiums and concerns citizens have about those financial arrangements, as well as efforts by organizations to cultivate relationships with governmental entities to influence public policy or encourage the passage of certain laws to make sport a better and safer space.

In this chapter we also explored the myth that sport can be apolitical or politically neutral, illustrating in a variety of ways just how intertwined sport is with politics. An understanding of politics and how it operates alongside and within sport provides insight into the abuses of power that lead to exclusionary and discriminatory practices in sport and the barriers that prevent equity and inclusion. Such understanding further provides an awareness of how public policy makers can be engaged to address issues in sport.

CRITICAL THINKING EXERCISES

1. In the opening scenario for the chapter, we were introduced to U.S. female hammer thrower Gwen Berry and her protests at the Pan American Games in 2019 and the U.S. Track and Field Olympic Trials in 2020. One of the things we learned is the USOPC, which had sanctioned Berry with a yearlong suspension for her 2019 protest, later changed its rules to permit athletes to protest during domestic events. After doing research on this topic, create a class debate on the question of whether the IOC's rule barring athletes from protesting (Rule 50) at its events should be changed.

2. Explore how athletic programs in your local high school are financed. Does your community fund high school athletic programs through tax dollars or through additional fees assessed for extracurricular activities? Can you figure out how much funding is provided through the school budget and how much is raised through booster clubs?
3. Choose your favorite professional team and research how its athletic facility is funded. Was the facility funded entirely by taxpayers? If so, when was the facility built? How long will it take for the taxpayers to pay off the construction costs associated with the facility? Are there ongoing discussions about facility upgrades? Has the franchise threatened to relocate elsewhere if they don't get the upgrades they need? Does the team have practice facilities? Who paid for those? The franchise or the community? Was there a private/public partnership? What economic impact studies have been done to determine whether the city or the state has recovered their investment? Are there local groups that have opposed the public funding of a private enterprise like a professional sport team?

REVIEW QUESTIONS

1. Who is Gwen Berry and what did she do that created controversy at the U.S. Track & Field Olympic Trials in 2021?
2. Describe the reactions of politicians to Gwen Berry's protest.
3. Describe what the term *politics* means or how it is defined.
4. Identify the forms that public investments in sport facilities can take.
5. What is the process of gentrification and why is it a concern when professional stadium projects are proposed and built?
6. How have sport team visits to the White House changed over time, and what might those visits say about the state of political discourse in the U.S.?
7. How does the IOC contradict its stance that competition at the Olympic Games should be played between athletes and not countries?
8. How does sports media coverage contribute to the inadvertent exposure of sport fans to news?
9. What percent of Americans identify as sports fans?
10. What was the significance of European football fans pushing back against the efforts of the owners of a small group of teams to create a super league?

KENZO TRIBOUILLARD/AFP via Getty Images

CHAPTER 11

Sport, the Influence of Institutionalized Religion, and Religious Identity

Timothy Mirabito and Robin Hardin

LEARNING OBJECTIVES

- Explore how religion is projected at the most visible levels of sport.
- Discuss the complexities of contrasting religious beliefs and the impact on sport.
- Raise the First Amendment implications posed by the intersection of sport and religion
- Examine the public perception of the intersection of sport and religious identity.
- Explore how religious beliefs are impacting sport governance and operations.

Tim Tebow, a former National Football League (NFL) quarterback, was publicly praised and similarly criticized for his unwavering outward display of his Christian faith when he was playing football. Tebow would typically begin public appearances by stating something like "I'd like to start by thanking my lord and savior Jesus Christ" and would conclude his interviews by saying, "God bless you" (Dodd, 2011b, para. 4). His evangelical Christian beliefs were displayed through biblical scriptures inscribed on his eye black, his repeated use of the terms "God" and "Jesus Christ," and even a popular trend referred to as "Tebowing," which was an enactment of genuflecting on one knee in a prayerlike position—something Tebow routinely did on and around the football field.

Tebow polarized fans because of his expressions of faith and because of his abilities as a football player (Dodd, 2011a; Goldman, 2011; Morrissey, 2011; Mirabito, Huffman, & Hardin, 2013). There were many supporters of Tebow, as well as many critics, and both revolved around his ability as a quarterback and his outspokenness of his Christian faith. Tebow was perceived as inept at quarterbacking and described as "grossly overrated" and "terribly flawed." His adversaries were said to be a "seething army of detractors" who openly opposed Tebow as a football player and as a religious devotee (Schwartz, 2011). Tom Krattenmaker, a columnist for *USA Today,* referred to Tebow as a "cultural warrior" and likened Tebow's "athletic, religious, and political visage" to that of a "saint" or even "God" (Krattenmaker, 2010, para. 9). After the Broncos lost in the playoffs to end their 2011 season, Krattenmaker (2012) wrote about Tebow:

> *The rises and falls of Tebow these past few months have provoked all manner of speculation about the theological significance of the Jesus-professing quarterback of the Denver Broncos, just as his exploits have stoked a vociferous proxy battle in the ongoing national argument over the public standing of the evangelical faith embodied by the Broncos' No. 15 [Tebow]. All of this has come at a volume that has made it hard for anyone to think straight. (para. 2)*

Evangelical athletes—and athletes of other denominations—have openly revealed their faith as part of their public persona since Tebow. But none have been part of the national discourse in the United States like the former Florida Gator who won two national championships and the Heisman Trophy. Tebow's role in the American lexicon of sport is a window into the relationship religion and sport have long fostered and provides important context about the convergence of these two social institutions.

The chapter will explore many of the complexities in the convergence of religion and sport; something that has at times revealed itself as unfair or inequitable. For instance, Colin Kaepernick's kneeling protest during the national anthem, which was optically similar to Tebow's genuflecting in prayer, was one of the biggest stories in the NFL in 2016. Kaepernick, who was falsely accused of converting to Islam shortly after his protests began, was positioned as an anti-American who displayed radical Islamic ideology because he would not stand for the national anthem (Peter, 2016). Fifty years earlier, Muhammad Ali, who was also portrayed as a "radical" Islamist, was exiled from boxing for refusing to enlist in the army and participate in the war in Vietnam (Saeed, 2002). The purpose of this chapter is to explore these intricacies and how they influence the current sporting landscape.

Religious Influence on the Foundation of Sport

The intertwinement of religion and sport is steeped not only in history but in ritualistic behavior, as well. Sundays are a day to practice religion and sport. Large facilities that house substantial crowds of people, idolatry of

Colin Kaepernick's kneeling protest during the national anthem and Tebow's genuflecting in prayer reveals the complexities between religion and sport.
Josie Lepe/MediaNews Group/The Mercury News via Getty Images
Ezra Shaw/Getty Images

mythic figures, and overlapping symbols and vernacular (e.g., "Hail Mary," "David versus Goliath," "prayer," "miracle") are just some of the intersecting characteristics. Scholars have analyzed not only the similarities (Price, 2001) and how they began (Parker & Weir, 2012), but what it means that they exist (Grano, 2017). This burgeoning field of study is still relatively new, while the coexistence of religion and sport is not (Bain-Selbo & Sapp, 2016). That, of course, has led to some notable disagreements about the veracity of the comparison (Carter, 2012) and the appropriateness of the association between the institutions (Wieting, 2015).

Sullivan (2010) contended that sport could not be viewed as a religion and the mere proposition was simply "ludicrous" (p. 10). However, he later conceded that observing a filled-to-capacity football stadium on a Sunday afternoon was sufficient evidence that many have *substituted* sport for religion. This argument is an extension of Higgs' (1995) staunch belief that sport and religion are socially and individually grounded, but not equal. He wrote, "They are not the same activities; they have different purposes and are carried out in different ways and usually at different times" (p. 1). Scholars like Bain-Selbo (2009) disagreed and argued that a sport like college football is a religion for many people in the South. This argument brings up one common agreement: There is a necessity for spiritual fulfillment in society. The coexistence of sport and religion, whether interchangeable or supplemental, has linked the two establishments together. Perhaps this explains the preponderance of prayer before and after sporting events, religious gestures by athletes while playing a sport, and the emersion of sport chaplains in college athletic departments across the country (Dzikus, Hardin, & Waller, 2012).

The chasm that exists between scholarly perspectives, specifically the roles that religion and sport are intended to play in society, is emblematic of the relationship the two have forged. Historically, sport has played a specific function in the way different religious groups celebrate their faith. Some facets of sport were a byproduct of religious initiatives that mirrored outcomes to that of athletics. Sport has attracted new followers of religion through the visibility of athletes displaying their faiths. Sport, for some people, has been adopted as a suitable replacement for religion. And, for some athletes, religion has served as a respite or a guiding influence for those playing sport. A foundational challenge surrounding this discourse is the divergent evolutions religion and sport have had. Most modern religions tend to be recognizable derivatives of their original iterations. Modern sport, however, tends to be much different from that of the Ancient Greeks or early Chinese, as Bain-Selbo and Sapp (2016) noted:

> *Part of the problem some have with calling sport a religion stems from an ancient practice of denying anything that seems new, the status of religion. While sport is, apparently, as ancient as human culture, the sports with which we are more familiar . . . were invented just recently. (p. 3)*

History of Sport and Religious Intersections

The collective moment of silence that has become commonplace at sporting events and in stadiums worldwide was rooted in early 20th century England. A nationwide minute of silence was held in the United Kingdom in 1910 out of respect for the death of King Edward VII (Foster & Woodthorpe, 2012). Since then, the moment of silence has evolved into a prompted moment of reflection and thought, which was often impelled by an event such as loss or death. A moment of silence has also been associated with prayer, which in part is a result of public schools seeking a daily moment of silence at the beginning of the school day to accommodate students who wished to pray before school (Kaminer, 2002). The moment of silence is one of many behavioral parallels drawn between sport and religion that has prompted comparisons between the two. Coakley (2009) analogized sport and religion as places for communal assembly, as emphasizing perfection of mind, body, and spirit, as having shared values that are demonstrated and often celebrated, and as a common place for heroes and heroic accomplishments. He also noted that "both can be used to distract attention from issues and thereby become 'opiates' of the masses" (Coakley, 2009, p. 533). These similarities have provoked debate among scholars on whether sport is considered a religion.

Muscular Christianity

The history of **muscular Christianity**, which formed in the 19th century, is riddled with complexities. The definition of the movement is sometimes oversimplified and characterized as a commitment to strengthening the Christian ethic, specifically as it pertains to the mind, body, and spirit (Rosen, 1994). Each of those characteristics tended to be foundational in the popular sports at the time, which included boxing, rugby, cricket, and football (American soccer) (Watson, 2007), which allowed for a natural association between Christianity and sport. When dissected further, however, the muscular Christian ascendency was framed by hypermasculinity and a White Anglo-Saxon Protestant perspective that marginalized entire swaths of the European and American populations (Hall, 1994). Charles Kingsley, an English novelist, social reformer, and Christian socialist, and Thomas Hughes, an author, politician, and Kingsley contemporary (Watson, 2007), were central figures in founding the muscular Christian movement. Their novels *Two Years Ago* (Kingsley, 1857) and *Tom Brown's School Days* (Hughes, 1857) are viewed as the doctrines that helped establish the manliness required to be a muscular Christian (Rosen, 1994).

Some scholars argue that Kingsley and Hughes' adaptation of King David and the perception that muscular Christianity promoted the exhibition of pure manliness was a mischaracterization of their work (Hall, 1994). Hall (1994) specifically noted that Kingsley "did not enjoy having the phrase 'muscular Christian' applied to him. But neither actively worked to quell those interpretations of their work, and the messages began to germinate quickly throughout England and the United States in the mid-19th century. Watson (2007) observed that the timing of Kingsley and Hughes' work was apt for three reasons.

1. The **Industrial Revolution** created more sedentary behavior, which was antithetical to the Victorian ideal of activity.
2. Emerging science related to human physiology made direct connections between mind and body.
3. England was subject to hostile threats from several European adversaries, which created a perception that the muscular Christian movement would aid in "produc[ing] leaders that were well educated and manly" (p. 81), in contrast to the early Victorian era depictions of a gentle and even "feminine" Jesus Christ that had been unacceptable for many White middle-class men.

YMCA

The **Young Men's Christian Association** (YMCA), originating in 1844 in England and 1851 in the United States, became an integral part of the muscular Christianity movement. The YMCA, which usually opened branches in highly populated urban areas, sought to enrich young men who aspired to exercise their faith and bodies in a Christian environment. This was important for men who were seeing an increase in discretionary time and had jobs that were requiring far less physical output due to automation (Ladd & Mathisen, 1999). The Industrial Revolution helped advance a growing middle class that largely benefited White men, a sizable number of whom were Protestants. It also eliminated many physically demanding jobs that had enabled Christian men to maintain their physical aptitude. The YMCA was an ideal supplement for those men who were looking for physically demanding activities. On its face, that exchange seemed both legitimate and wholesome. The reality, however, was the motivations of muscular Christianity during this time were more nefarious (Eschner, 2017). Perelman and Portillo (2013) noted that the aforementioned softness of the Victorian age was undesirable for many followers of muscular Christianity and was seen as a threat due to a burgeoning women's movement. The influx of immigrants from "lesser" European countries was also seen as a danger because many of the immigrants were occupying the physically demanding jobs the Anglo-Saxon population once held. Early strains of the eugenics that manifested in both Germany and the United States in World War II were observable during this time (Perelman & Portillo, 2013). In her article "When Jesus got 'too feminine,' white dudes invented muscular Christianity," Stephanie Buck (2017) wrote, "In the late 1800s, the YMCA introduced athletic competitions while championing its Christian principle of 'healthy mind, body, and spirit.' The organization's charitable underpinnings democratized the idea of masculine faith" (para. 17).

Despite the disreputable motivations that underscored some of the growth of muscular Christianity, the YMCA capitalized on the newly energized interest in sport to help shape some of the landscape that would become modern sport. Robert Roberts, the first physical education director at the Boston YMCA, coined the term "bodybuilding" in 1881 (Eschner, 2017). James Naismith, in coordination with Springfield College—a YMCA training school—famously used peach baskets to develop the first iteration of the game of basketball in 1891 (Ladd & Mathisen, 1999). Handball, racquetball, volleyball, and swimming lessons were all also rooted in the YMCA. The organization and its various contributions to the sporting landscape were given greater visibility in the United States at the turn of the century because of the support of Teddy Roosevelt, avid sportsman and 26th president of the United States (Lumpkin, 2010). Roosevelt's championing of programming that enhanced masculinization bolstered the YMCA's social relevance, but it also led to other organizations like the Boys' Brigade, the Knights of King Arthur, and the Boy Scouts of America (Ladd & Mathisen, 1999). The YMCA, however, served as the standard-bearer for sport-specific programming in the muscular Christian movement. It was a movement that reached its peak in the early decades of the 20th century but slowed significantly at the beginning of World War I (Putney, 2001). Several factors curtailed the growth of muscular Christianity, including the budding success of Jack Johnson, a Black heavyweight boxing champion, the migration of popular sport away from the Ivy League (Perelman & Portillo, 2013), and the Great Depression (Buck, 2017).

Fellowship of Christian Athletes

The prominence of the muscular Christian influence on sport waned in the years following World War I, but the popularity of modern sports increased exponentially. Sustained advancements in technology continued adding discretionary time and a capacity to engage with sport, notable athletes marketed sports to the populace, and urbanization in a post–World War II America increased the demand for youth sport outlets for children (Ladd & Mathisen, 1999). It was that appeal to youth sport programming that inspired Don McClanen to start an organization called the Fellowship of Christian Athletes (FCA) in 1954 (FCA, 2020). McClanen, with the help of several prominent college and professional sport figures, sought to reengage sporting culture as a conduit to Christianity and viewed FCA's role as a ministry that guided coaches to instill Christian values in their athletes. The FCA incorporated the familiar hypermasculine lens that shaped muscular Christianity and capitalized on a growing "hero-worship culture" to entice engagement (Demarest, 1960). The organization did, however, have a somewhat more inclusive structure than its predecessors and, like the YMCA, grew on an international level.

Athletes in Action

Dave Hannah founded Athletes in Action (AIA) in the mid-1960s, and it mirrored FCA's evangelical approach to spreading the values of Christianity throughout the world using the platform of sport. The two organizations are not associated with each other, despite the same ideological grounding and other notable similarities. AIA tends to be more mission-oriented, spreading its brand of Christian ideology throughout the world (KFA, 2018). AIA grew out of a larger Christian organization called the Campus Crusade for Christ (also referred to as "Cru"), which was started by Bill Bright in 1951 (AIA, 2020). AIA was considered the "athletic arm" of Cru and was integral in helping the larger organization reach 400 colleges in 52 countries by 1977 (Koppett, 1977). *The New York Times* published a profile of AIA that year after AIA's basketball team won the Amateur Athletic Union's national amateur championship in 1976. The organization had similar successes in cross country running and weightlifting, which raised the organization's national profile substantially. The article featured a quote from Hannah that offered his distinguishing characteristics of the AIA:

> *Our mission is to spread the Gospel, but there's a big difference between preaching and sharing. We don't say to people, this is how it is and this is how you ought to be; we just tell them what each of us has found out for himself, and how they can follow it up if they want to. (Koppett, 1977, para. 8)*

Hannah and others asserted AIA was less aggressive with their recruitment of fellow Christians, but observers noted FCA was less strict than AIA in asking their members to adhere to their brand of Christianity (KFA, 2018).

Christians in Sport

At the same time AIA was growing into prominence in the United States, a small group of Christians in the United Kingdom saw the opportunity to capitalize on the symbiotic relationship between religion and sport. Originally identified as the Christian Sportsmen's Outreach in 1975, the European version of evangelical Christian ministries came to be known as Christians in Sport (CIS) by 1976. Tennis was at the center of adaptation of CIS, which was conceived of by Reverend Alan Godson, tennis commentator Gerald Williams, Wimbledon tennis champion Stan Smith, and businessman Kenneth Frampton (CIS, n.d.). The impact FCA and AIA were having in the United States helped the modernized tenets of muscular Christianity proliferate in North America, but the European landscape was less enthusiastic about the movement early on (Parker & Collins, 2012). CIS, despite the slower growth in the UK compared to its American counterparts, has since realized the same rapid growth throughout the world. According to its website, CIS is in 150 countries worldwide, supports 10,000 Christian athletes, and partners with several other sporting ministries (CIS, n.d.).

FCA, AIA, and CIS, which are routinely grouped together when discussing contemporary derivatives of muscular Christianity, have expanded the Christian footprint in sport throughout the world. These organizations have diverted from the solely male-oriented programming that emphasized the "manliness" image of Victorian Christianity and have been more deliberate in focusing on the wholesomeness of modern Christianity. That said, they have had some persistent marginalizing approaches. Namely, these ministries have been widely criticized for their views of the LGBTQ community (Shea, 2014). Advocacy groups like Outsports, a subsidiary of sports blogging network SB Nation, have been particularly critical of the ministries, stating they are "rooted in homophobia" with a view that "to be a member of the LGBTQ community is to also be a sinner" (Nye, 2019, para. 8).

First Amendment Issues

Clemson University's football program has gone through a renaissance since Dabo Swinney, the school's head football coach, took over the program in 2008. The Tigers have vied for four national championships (winning two, in 2016 and 2018), have had 36 All-American players, and have produced 13 first-round draft picks in the NFL (as of 2019). He has turned the program into a perennial contender on the field but has also turned the staff and its players into a Christian organization off the field (Rohan, 2019). Swinney has had players baptized at practice, instituted "church days" for the entire team, quoted scripture to media, and made hiring decisions based on coaches' faith (Baumgaertner, 2019; Rohan, 2019). His outward commitment to his faith is well documented, earning him both praise and disdain, but it has also garnered some legal objections. The Freedom from Religion Foundation (FFRF) submitted a letter of complaint to the university in 2014 that cited Swinney and Clemson for violating the **First Amendment**, specifically infringing on the separation of church and state (Baumgaertner, 2019). Swinney denied any wrongdoing (Robinson, 2014) and the grievance never amounted to any specific litigation, but the accusation points to important questions regarding religion, public institutions, and Constitutional protections.

The legal consequences for actions that violate the separation of church and state are cloudy. The FFRF has submitted letters to several other institutions with little to no support from the legal community. The situation offers an interesting look at not only what the laws are, but how they are enforced.

The First Amendment to the United States Constitution is the preeminent doctrine when discussing the legality of religion in the United States. It says, "Congress shall make no law respecting an establishment of religion, or prohibiting the free exercise thereof." The oft-referenced "establishment clause," the first clause of the amendment, attempted to separate church and state in order to protect its citizenry's religious liberty (Gunn & Witte, 2012). The second part of the amendment, also known as the "free exercise clause," was intended to protect citizens' ability to practice religion without interference from the government. The genesis of these clauses, or this amendment holistically, was to protect citizens from an oppressive government that might exert its will on the people like the Crown and the Church of England did prior to the Revolutionary War.

Clemson's football team and Swinney represent the types of conflict that challenge the spirit of these laws and create litigation nightmares because of the ambiguity over what actions violate the First Amendment. The FFRF complaint certainly appears to have at least some merit, considering Clemson is a public institution and there are documented (and public) records of nonsecular religious practices. But public high schools and colleges like the University of Tennessee routinely hold public prayers prior to athletic events. There are even questions about whether moments of silence should be considered prayer; something that routinely happens at publicly funded arenas and municipalities. These are just some of the religious practices that contravene the laws and regulations.

College Football, Religion, and Pregame Prayer in Southern Culture

The intersection of sport and religion evokes a variety of emotions from fans, athletes, coaches, administrators, and other stakeholders. That is particularly true in Southern culture, where college football and religion are two prominent institutions. One common, and often the most visible, practice of religious expression is the act of prayer. Court cases have questioned the legality of public prayer at state institutions, but some public schools continue to pray at institution-sponsored events, including athletic contests. The practice of public pregame prayer hosted at a state institution may come as a surprise to some people, because the Supreme Court prohibited pregame public invocations in the 2000 decision in *Santa Fe Independent School District vs. Doe* (Matthews-Pillette, 2000). We have already touched on the Constitutional implications of not maintaining church and state boundaries. Further information regarding the separation of church and state can be found in the works of Batista (2002), Blackman (2010), Borden (2008, 2009), Gillentine, Goldfine, Phillips, Seidler, & Scott (2004), Hyndman (2005), Miller, Lee, & Martin (2013), Modrovich (2004), Santa Fe Independent School District (2000), and Speich (2001).

The intersection of college football, religion, and the culture of the Southeastern United States (the South) has been described as threads woven into the fabric of Southern culture (Bain-Selbo, 2012). The idea of place far exceeds the physical space associated with a town, region, state, or nation; it also includes "those living there" and "who they are and what that location means to them" (Bain-Selbo, 2009, para. 2). Southern society gravitated toward college football as a sense of pride in the early decades of the 20th century (Baker, 2007; Bain-Selbo, 2009, 2012). Barnhart (2000) suggested "nothing is more ingrained in the Southern psyche than the love of Southern college football—not as a game or a mere diversion, but as a way of life" (p. 1). Barnhart elaborated on the time-honored football traditions:

> *[Tradition is] the glue that binds the generations of Southern college football fans to one another and keeps them coming back to their beloved campuses year after year. People in the South take these football traditions very, very seriously. To many fans, the renewal of these traditions each fall provides all the physical and emotional comfort of a warm blanket on a cold winter's night. (p. 151)*

Some of the policies are based on circumstances such as region of the country or the legal issues surrounding the topic. For example, the FFRF, the same organization that cited Dabo Swinney's actions at Clemson, actively targeted high schools and colleges in Georgia, Mississippi, and Tennessee for leading prayers over the loudspeaker prior to games (Popke, 2012). A Mississippi district school superintendent named Brian Freeman received one of the FFRF letters and responded to the complaint by saying, "For generations, [pregame prayer] is a practice that's been followed throughout the South" (Popke, 2012, para. 3). Baylor University, as an illustration, continues to pray before its sporting events. The Lee County School District in eastern Alabama, conversely, ended its practice of praying before games in 2017 due to legal pressures. A statement from district administrators said, "The school system was facing litigation that we felt as though would not rule in our favor if we continued with prayer over our public address system" (Kennedy, 2017, para. 7).

Another prominent feature of the Southern culture is adherence to religious beliefs, particularly evangelical Protestantism (Association of Religion Data Archives, 2013). Religious practices share certain attributes. As Slusher (1967) says, "Both sport and religion employ intricate rituals which attempt to place events in traditional and orderly view" (p. 173). Specifically, prayer is a common religious expression that has been studied in the sport context primarily with athletes and coaches (Coakley, 2009; Czech, 2004; Leonard, 1998; Murray, Joyner, Burke, Wilson, & Zwald, 2005; Stevenson, 1991). Scholars argued there are rituals of the game day experience (e.g., pregame, during, and postgame) (Czech, 2004) that qualify it as religion (Bain-Selbo, 2008). Bain-Selbo concluded that college football fans in the South identify their game day experience as a fundamental element of their emotional and communal lives. This overlay of sport, prayer, and ritual provides unique insights on fandom in the South.

To repeat the metaphor, college football and religion are woven together, meshing into the fabric of Southern culture. Traditions have a unique way of promoting the game day atmosphere, fandom, and stakeholder satisfaction. However, when these traditions, particularly public prayer, move into the realm of ritualistic behavior, unintended consequences may ensue. Ritualistic traditions can be beneficial when they foster emotional attachment, but emotions can also fuel divisive, exclusionary, and alienating behaviors that are detrimental to the sporting experience and society as a whole. Athletic administrators must recognize that emotionally charged situations can cause conflict when it comes to religion and college football in the South. Public prayer is seemingly prevalent in the South whether one agrees or disagrees with invoking a public prayer in the context of an athletic event. Athletic administrators employed at public universities would be prudent to consider the implications associated with managing the religiously charged game day experiences and stakeholder satisfaction, particularly in Southern culture.

Chaplains' Role in Holistic Care

Holistic care grew out of the concept of holism, the idea that the whole is better than its parts (Smuts, 1926). Holism situates health as physical, mental, and spiritual well-being, and true care means attention to each aspect of the person (Waller et al., 2016; Zamanzadeh et al., 2015). Therefore, a physical injury cannot be fully healed without also healing the mental and spiritual impacts of the injury. In response, a reimagined concept of health care—in contrast to the traditional medical model—emerged. Termed *holistic*, *collaborative*, *interdisciplinary*, or *interprofessional* care, it is health care provided by a variety of professionals, including medical doctors, behavioral health specialists, psychiatrists, social workers, and dietitians, as well as chaplains (Burns et al., 2004; Raney, 2015; Waller et al., 2016). Models of holistic care have become a best practice in all aspects of health care due to the focus on the whole person, and chaplains are an integral part of that (Leung et al., 2018; Tjale & Bruce, 2007).

Good health is more than just being injury-free or disease-free; it is also having a sense of serenity and emotional well-being (World Health Organization, 1946). Ensuring the well-being of athletes means addressing depression, eating disorders, anxiety, violence, drug abuse, and suicide, as well as other emotional issues (Dodd, 2014; Zirin, 2014). For example, Josh Hamilton, the number one pick in the 1999 Major League Baseball draft, had the help of the MLB when he needed it. His drug and alcohol use kept him out of baseball from 2003 to 2005. He returned to baseball and was the American League MVP in 2010. He had a relapse in 2012, and the Texas Rangers hired a "handler" for him who also served as a hitting instructor with the team. Interestingly, the person charged with assisting Hamilton had served as a sport chaplain at the University of Alabama from 1996 to 1999 (Durrett, 2012).

Chaplains can be found throughout sporting organizations—collegiate athletic teams, professional teams, and national teams overseen by sport governing bodies. Chaplain is a term used to identify a member of the clergy who conducts religious services for an institution, such as a prison, hospital, or corporation. The term **sport chaplain** commonly defines the role and function of a lay or ordained member of the clergy who provides spiritual care for athletes, coaches, and sport administrators. One of the common duties of the sport chaplain is counseling and spiritual care for athletes, coaches, sport administrators, and, in some cases, their families. Counseling and spiritual care are often required in a crisis situation or, more routinely, to enable and empower the spiritual growth and development of athletes and coaches. Chaplains have thus become an integral part of the holistic care model for athletes.

A mounting body of research acknowledges that spiritual care correlates positively with self-esteem, coping (Harper, 2012), hopefulness (Waller, 2016), and the development of a "healthy" nonathletic identity (Stone, Harrison, & Mottley, 2012). Spiritual care can help with avoidance of deviant behaviors—drug addiction, alcohol addiction, criminal behavior (Duff, 2012; Yusko, Buckman, White, & Pandina, 2008), fewer instances of mental health challenges (Yoonas, 2009), educational attainment (Hodge, Harrison, Burden, & Dixson, 2008), and overall resiliency (Huffman, 2014). Spiritual care should be a part of the care of athletes due to the positive outcomes associated with spiritual health, and chaplains should be a part of the team providing holistic care to athletes. Spiritual health is an important component of an individual's well-being and an integral aspect of a holistic health philosophy. Spiritual health is vital to the overall well-being of individuals, and chaplains play an integral role on the holistic care team in this regard (Huffman, 2014; Waller et al., 2008). It is certainly difficult to gauge emotional, psychological, and spiritual stability on the surface. Therefore, having chaplains as part of the athlete support system is critical. The health of athletes is often focused solely on the physical health, but holistic care encompasses care for the complete person: physically, emotionally, and spiritually (Waller, Dzikus, & Hardin, 2008).

One of the common duties of the sport chaplain is counseling and spiritual care for athletes, coaches, sport administrators, and even referees.
Matt Cashore-Pool/Getty Images

Conflicts Between Sport and Religion

The *Marquette Sports Law Review* published a list of four categorical areas in which potential conflicts exist between religion and sport. These were (1) substantive aspects of sport, (2) scheduling of practices and competitions, (3) regulations of appearance and apparel, and (4) requirements of eligibility (Idleman, 2001).

The first category addresses the way the sport is played and how it may controvert religious beliefs. Idleman (2001) used the example of bowing in the sport of judo. A Shinto competitor would be prohibited from bowing toward another competitor, a core requirement of the sport. That is considered a substantive, or essential, aspect of the game. The other three categories are peripheral categories but cover a wide swath of potential issues. Examples of each are more pervasive than we may think and have occurred for decades.

The Judeo-Christian heritage of the United States, paired with the explicit objectives of muscular Christianity, have greatly influenced the landscape of modern sport. There are countless examples of other faiths, however, that have affected sport both internationally and in the United States. Judaism, for instance, like Christianity, experienced a period of "muscular Judaism," which employed sport as a medium to promote Jewish beliefs. However, the goal of muscular Judaism was "unlike muscular Christianity that sought to change Christian values to incorporate athletic achievement, (but) to prove that Jewish men were real men who excelled at sport" (Alpert, 2019, p. 140). Muscular Judaism was a byproduct of the Zionist movement and was established by Max Nordau in the late 19th century.

Members of the revitalized Jewish sports community were viciously attacked in the summer of 1972 in Munich, Germany, during the Games of the XX Olympiad. A subset of the Palestinian Liberation Organization (PLO) called Black September raided an Israeli apartment in the Olympic Village on September 5, 1972, and took 11 members of the team hostage. After a daylong standoff that was broadcast across the world, the athletes were murdered at the military airport of Fürstenfeldbruck in a botched rescue attempt by the German government. The Israeli–Palestinian conflict, rooted in Jewish and Muslim discontent, garnered more attention from this attack on the world's largest sporting stage than any other instance before or after, and the assault changed the course of international terrorism forever (Maslin, 2005).

Female Muslim athletes have been front and center in the realm of religious constraint. The male-dominated Muslim culture, especially in Middle Eastern countries, had long prohibited women from participating in sporting events. The Islamic Federation of Women's Sport, founded in 1991, attempted to address the dearth of athletic programming available to women. While the organization has been largely successful in providing opportunities for female athletes, discussion of hijabs—or head coverings—has persisted as a cultural point of contention (Harkness & Islam, 2011). FIFA, the international governing body for football (soccer), and the International Olympic Committee (IOC) were again at the forefront of the religious conflict in the early 2000s. Both governing bodies prohibited players from wearing hijabs during matches, which effectively forced the women to decide between their religion or their sport (Ahmed, 2018). FIFA and the IOC reversed their positions in 2014, but the juxtaposition of athletes being able to demonstrate the sign of the cross or point to the heavens after a good play versus not allowing headdresses was stark.

Emily Murdoch (2014), writing for *World Religion News*, reported on a similar circumstance with a wrestler at the (SUNY) University at Buffalo in 2014. She discussed Muhamed McBryde, a "devout Muslim" and talented wrestler whose faith prohibited him from shaving his face. The NCAA guidelines mandated that athletes be clean-shaven in order to participate, which essentially put him in a position—like his female counterparts—where he had to decide between his wrestling career and his faith (Murdoch, 2014).

Michael Sam, whom Murdoch also mentioned in her article, wanted to be drafted in the NFL as a defensive end. Sam, an All-American and the 2013 Southeastern Conference (SEC) Defensive Player of the Year at the University of

Sport Industry Leader Profile

Scott Barron

Title: President, Knoxville (Tennessee) Independent School League; Director of Athletics, Sacred Heart Cathedral

Education: BA in Economics, University of Tennessee

What role do you see religion playing in sport?

From the beginning of the ancient Olympic Games, sports have been rooted in religious festivals or traditions. Sport got its birth there, and now in the United States, people see sport as a religion. It is difficult to separate the two. I see sport as a platform to celebrate your faith and to promote our faith.

I have used my [Christian] faith when I coached and when I played athletics to give me strength. It helps keep things in perspective. I coached high school boys, and it is a strong developmental time for them. They depended on me. I used my faith to guide me in why we were doing things and what we were trying to achieve. Religion helps give focus to why you are doing what you are doing.

How important is the spiritual well-being of athletes and coaches?

It is the foundation of the identity for a lot of athletes. Tim Tebow is a fantastic example. You think of him, and you think of a religious athlete. It is how he identifies himself. He would much rather be known as Tim Tebow the Christian than Tim Tebow the athlete. It is really important for us that have a strong faith because that is how we define our happiness in general, our spiritual health.

How is the relationship between sport and religion in the South different from other parts of the country?

Sports is a religion in the South, and religion is huge in the South. It is how you identify yourself. I am a Catholic first, and then a Tennessee fan second. You are known by your faith

Missouri, was drafted in the seventh round of the 2014 draft. Sam came out as gay prior to the draft and was the first openly gay player to be drafted in NFL history (Belson, 2014). Evangelical groups, especially one led by Jack Burkman, a Washington lobbyist and ardent evangelist, openly threatened NFL organizations if they drafted Sam. Burkman was quoted as saying, "The NFL, like most of the rest of American business, is about to learn that when you trample the Christian community and Christian values there will be a terrible financial price to pay" (Blair, 2014, para. 5). Even though Sam was drafted by the St. Louis Rams, he was released by the team a week before the season started and never played in an NFL regular season game.

Expressing Religious Identities

The taxonomy of what are acceptable religious demonstrations in sports and what are not is complex and subjective. Athletes have made it routine to point to the heavens during games or wear jewelry adorned with religious symbols. Many athletes have acknowledged their belief in a higher power during media engagements or have gestured with the sign of the cross or similar symbols of prayer during play. Female athletes have recently been permitted to wear hijabs as an explicit compliance of faith, and moments of silence are routinely observed at tradition and which college team you follow. They are the cornerstones of life in the South, and the cornerstones of cultural experiences in the South. It is hard to escape one without the other because they are just so intertwined.

What is your perception of organizations like the Freedom from Religion Foundation intervening in public institutions' outward displays of spirituality?

That is one of the great things about our country. I can disagree with them, but I will go to war just to support the fact they can say that publicly. Schools cannot endorse or advance a particular religion, but they also cannot inhibit the expression of religious beliefs. I think that is where things hinge. Free thought comes into play even in the expression of religious beliefs. But in the end, nothing should be able to suppress a person's ability to express their religion. That's one of the reasons people came here to settle our country. That is part of the greatness of our country—we can actually disagree without fighting.

What role do you see FCA and AIA playing in the promotion of Christian values in athletes?

I think they are good because they help organize the athletes and coaches who have a desire to be spiritual. These organizations give them a roadmap and direction on how to do that. They are invaluable in that way. It is also an age someone may be afraid to say, "Hey, I am a Christian." If you are part of the FCA, you are surrounded by a number of other athletes, and it really gives you confidence and courage to say, "Yes, I'm a Christian; I'm a practicing Christian." They really give direction and focus.

What role do you see the outward display of religion playing in sport?

My perspective is our country was founded on the belief that you can just be who you are and who you want to be. We were founded on the belief of tolerance. It also has a trickle-down effect on younger people who know it is okay to say, "I am a faith-based person." To have the ability to express our religion in a time of more secular society is really important.

arenas around the world. But there are places where these demonstrations are not allowed, as well. For instance, the NFL and NCAA adopted rules that prohibit athletes from putting messages on their eye black. Those rules were established after Tim Tebow made the practice popular at the University of Florida, routinely putting Bible verses below his eyes. The St. Louis Cardinals, similarly, banned players from etching crosses into the dirt on the back of the pitcher's mound at Busch Stadium after fans observed the symbols in 2013 (Matthews, 2013). And, while many organizations have loosened their headwear policies, it is still not universally accepted for women to wear headdresses in all sports.

The distinction between permissible and impermissible religious actions seems to be influenced, at least in part, by a utilitarian perspective of inclusivity. For instance, the American South, which is monikered the "Bible Belt," has been more steadfast in maintaining the convergence of religion and sport (Bain-Selbo, 2009). The relative homogeneity of Christian faith prevalence may be a factor. In other places, institutions of sport tend to distinguish allowable activities based on how secular it is—or even how explicit the display is.

Religious identity, in this arrangement, is almost an overgeneralized appropriation of a specific religion's routines that sets expectations for how sport actors are to behave.

Sport Industry Diversity Initiative

INTERFAITH EFFORTS FOR INCLUSIVITY

Interfaith services on college campuses have increasingly allowed for more diverse and collaborative religious environments at these institutions. Loyola Marymount University, for instance, announced a partnership with the Academy for Jewish Religion–California that will begin in 2021. The merger between these programs is intended to advance interreligious discourse that will enrich the separate community stakeholders under a shared facility. It is a venture similar to others at Georgetown University, University of Pennsylvania, and Boston College.

University of California–Davis hosted what they called the "Davis Interfaith Games" in 2017, which was an event that allowed faith-based student organizations to play competitive events against one another. The initiative was used to promote fellowship under the umbrella of religion, which organizers intended to use as a platform to promote inclusivity.

The college programming that exists around this topic, however, appears to be relegated to the general student population; it is not typically incorporated into athletics departments. Team chaplains, who may either be on the school's payroll or be a volunteer, are typically of a specific denomination, which is naturally less inclusive. This constraining cultural dynamic is even more obvious at religiously affiliated schools such as University of Notre Dame and Baylor University, where team chaplains are exclusively Christian.

For instance, if a player is Muslim, there are assumptions of how that player may look, act, or even think based on the associations other people make of their faith. In some cases, that identity is embraced and overtly celebrated by players. In other cases, the player may be constrained by the expectations bestowed upon them based on a single facet of their life. The range of religion and spirituality is an interesting starting point in this conversation.

Religion and Spirituality

The nuanced differences between religion and spirituality, terms that are often used interchangeably, have notable implications for this conversation. Religion is an institutionalized belief system aimed at congregating people of the same values and principles that center on an "ultimate reality" (de Blot, 2011, p. 11). The ultimate reality is typically a higher power like God or Allah and the systems are often a consequence of a doctrine (e.g., Bible, Torah, Quran). Spirituality, on the other hand, is a less rigid, more ambiguous relationship with a set of beliefs that involve an individual's connection to meaningful ideologies, values, or beings absent of a specific structure. "Spirituality is related to the same Ultimate Reality but takes a more secular approach, while religion's point of view is more sacral" (de Blot, 2011, p. 11). Religion requires a belonging, while spirituality simply requires effort, which has an impact on inclusion efforts. In order for religion to realize inclusivity, the stakeholders must share that same faith. Spirituality, however, does not mandate membership and allows for multiple perspectives and denominations.

The distinction helps to create space where certain practices find shelter under the categorization of spirituality rather than religion. For instance, moments of silence may imply that participants are praying, but it is a secular activity that anyone can participate in. The same can be said of pointing to the heavens after hitting a home run or scoring a goal. The gesture is benign enough not to signify any specific religion but does demonstrate some spirituality on the actor's part. The balance, of course, is establishing practices that are inclusive while simultaneously allowing athletes and coaches the autonomy to demonstrate their individual religious identity. The remaining sections focus on various religions.

Christianity

Christians are the largest religious population in the world (Hackett & McClendon, 2017) (figure 11.1). Christianity is a monotheistic religion that began shortly after the death of Jesus Christ, whom followers believe is the son of God. Jesus, himself a follower of Judaism, looked to reform the Jewish faith through his ministry (*Judaism*, 2022). Christianity, largely born out of the death and resurrection of Jesus, spread quickly after the first decades AD (Latin for *the year of our lord*). Early power struggles and political pressures created a splintering among followers, and born from the Great Schism and eventual Reformation were distinct Christian faiths: Catholicism, Eastern Orthodox, and Protestant (Cohen, 1998). The doctrine that guides Christianity is the Bible, which unites the separate ideologies under the Holy Trinity: God, Jesus (son of God), and the Holy Spirit. Christians are also united in believing that the Messiah will return and that if you follow Jesus' teachings you can inherit eternal life (URI, 2020).

The cross, which signifies Jesus' persecution, is the most common symbol of Christianity seen in the sport complex. Athletes will often touch their head, chest, left shoulder, and right shoulder as a sign of the cross. The sports that allow jewelry also tend to see Christian athletes wearing crosses as pendants demonstrating their faith. A number of teams have adopted Christian-based nicknames like the Saints, Friars, Crusaders, Quakers, and Knights. And, of course, evangelical athletes like Tim Tebow and Stephen Curry regularly invoke praise for God and Jesus Christ during media appearances. The symbolism of Christianity is certainly present in a multitude of ways and, like the muscular Christianity era, the athletes themselves are integral vehicles for the promotion of faith. Those athletes include Russell Wilson, Philip Rivers, Kurt Warner, Reggie White, Gabby Douglas, Allyson Felix, Lolo Jones, Clayton Kershaw, Derek Fisher, Dwyane Wade, Manny Pacquaio, and many others.

Islam

The Muslim faith is the second largest and the fastest-growing religion in the world (Hackett & McClendon, 2017). Like Christianity, Islam is monotheistic, and there are divergent factions of believers, predominantly Sunnis and Shiites. The Islamic higher power is referred to as Allah. Muslims acknowledge the existence of figures found in Christianity and Judaism, like Abraham, Jesus, and Moses, and have a holy doctrine called the Quran. The prophet Muhammad, who was born in AD 570, is viewed as the originator of this faith through his conversations with Allah and his work spreading the teachings of Allah through his ministry (*Judaism*, 2022). Muhammad was born in Mecca, Saudi

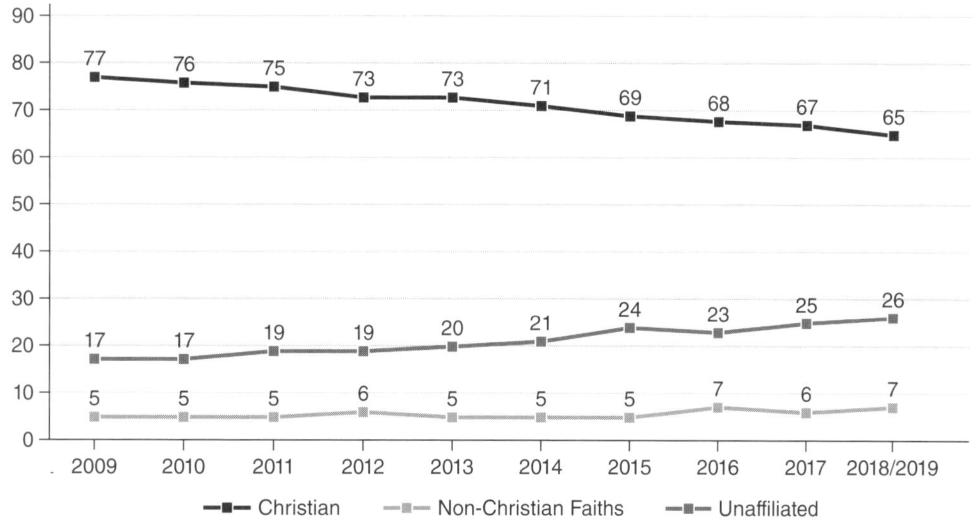

FIGURE 11.1 Pew Research reports nearly 30 percent of U.S. adults identify as religiously unaffiliated.
About Three-in-Ten U.S. Adults Are Now Religiously Unaffiliated, G. A. Smith, Pew Research Center, Washington, D.C. (2021). https://www.pewforum.org/2021/12/14/about-three-in-ten-u-s-adults-are-now-religiously-unaffiliated/

Arabia, which is considered a holy land among Muslims, many of whom believe a pilgrimage to the city is a requirement of faith. Unlike Christianity, Islam is not laden with symbols like the cross to signify its followers.

The lack of symbolism is certainly a reason that there are so few explicit examples of Islam in sport. The number of Muslims in the United States (3.5 million) compared to Christians (205 million; Hackett & McClendon, 2017) is another reason. But the dissonance experienced by Muslims participating in sport is an additional important factor (Mackintosh & Dempsey, 2017). Many Muslims believe that Allah strictly prohibited any activity that may be harmful to the mind, body, or spirit of an individual. That belief would certainly limit sport participation in a modern context. Add that Muslim women are routinely discouraged from participating in sport, as mentioned earlier, and you have a recipe for limited engagement. The most visible Islamic representation in sport has historically been the athletes themselves, specifically through the Nation of Islam, which was thrust into the American lexicon through the growth in popularity of Muhammad Ali. Born Cassius Clay, Ali publicly converted to Islam in 1964 and became a vocal activist in the plight of Blacks and Muslims in the United States (Eig, 2017). A number of famous athletes followed in Ali's footsteps, including Kareem Abdul-Jabbar, Mahmoud Abdul-Rauf, Mike Tyson, and Bernard Hopkins. There, of course, were other athletes who were born into the Muslim faith who achieved success in sport as well. Zinedine Zidane, Hakeem Olajuwon, Imran Khan, and Naseem Hamed are just some of those notable athletes.

Kansas City Chiefs defensive back Husain Abdullah, a Muslim, knelt on both knees after scoring a touchdown in a 2014 game (Stampler, 2014). The gesture was emblematic of the Muslim tradition of bowing toward Mecca. Abdullah was assessed an unsportsmanlike penalty for the move. There are many similar examples of individual celebrations of faith or sport being a venue for religion.

Judaism

Judaism was born out of a belief that God communicated with Abraham, a prophet recognized in Christianity, Islam, and Judaism, and that God would continually be revealed through prophets (*Judaism*, 2017). The holy text in Judaism is the Torah, which is encapsulated in the Tanakh. The Jewish place of worship is called a synagogue, and religious leaders are referred to as *rabbis*. Like the previous two monotheistic religions, the Jewish faith has different factions: Conservative Judaism, Orthodox Judaism, and Reform Judaism (MJL, 2018). Reform Judaism is the most progressive—and popular—classification of the religion in the world. Orthodox Judaism, conversely, is the most rigid form of Judaism, with great emphasis placed on the rituals and practices of the faith. Shabbat, the Jewish tradition of prayer and rest roughly analogous to the Sunday Sabbath in Christianity, starts at sunset on Friday and continues until sundown on Saturday. The most ardent Jewish followers will avoid all technology and nonprayerful activities. That includes participating in sports.

Sandy Koufax, one of the most famous baseball players in Los Angeles Dodgers history and a devout Jewish athlete, famously opted to miss important games throughout his career when they were scheduled during Jewish holidays. For instance, he did not pitch Game 1 of the 1965 World Series because it was scheduled on Yom Kippur, the Jewish day of Atonement, which is considered the most important holiday on the Jewish calendar (Rothenberg, 2017). Koufax is one of many famous Jewish athletes, and Judaism, like Islam, is mostly represented by athletes who publicly share their faith. Some noteworthy Jewish athletes include Ian Kinsler, Morgan Pressel, Amar'e Stoudemire, Hank Greenberg, Julian Edelman, Sue Bird, Aly Raisman, Dara Torres, and Mark Spitz.

The Pittsburgh Steelers temporarily redesigned their logo, which traditionally has three hypocycloids inside of a circle, to include the Star of David as one of the hypocycloids in the triad for one game in 2018 (figure 11.2). The change was an effort by the organization to show solidarity after a gunman killed eight people inside the Tree of Life Synagogue in Pittsburgh the day before a game (Chamberlain, 2018).

Other Faiths

Mormons are among the most prominent religions that have not been discussed. Part of the challenge that Mormon athletes face is that their faith requires that they go on a year-long mission when in their late teens. The Church of Jesus Christ of Latter-day Saints, the institutional face of Mormonism, is dedicated to this cause, which happens to occur during important developmental years for aspiring professional athletes. Basketball players Jabari Parker and Jimmer Fredette, as well as baseball player Jeff Kent, are some of the more noteworthy Mormons in contemporary sports.

Venus and Serena Williams, two of the most successful tennis players in American history, are Jehovah's Witnesses. Hinduism (Mohini Bhardwaj), Buddhism (Tiger Woods), and even Scientology (Jason Lee) are part of the sport and religion landscape.

FIGURE 11.2 After the mass shooting at the Tree of Life Synagogue in Pittsburgh, the Pittsburgh Steelers temporarily redesigned their logo to include the Star of David.
Mark Alberti/Icon Sportswire via Getty Images

SUMMARY

The entangled relationship religion and sport have forged is complicated. The value-driven principles that religion purports to employ are somewhat parallel to the character-driven outcomes sport intends to support. Each of those takeaways, of course, is subjective and ultimately not universally realized. Religion is laden with personal biases and fraught with contentiousness that has marred humanity for centuries. Bias against Muslims, Jewish persecution, and discriminatory practices based on any faith are all rooted in society's acceptance of varying religious ideologies. Sport, similarly, has had issues with race, gender, sexual orientation, socioeconomics, and, of course, religion throughout its history. So, merging the two creates natural challenges. It also creates opportunities. Sport can serve as a venue to practice those values instrumental in the construction of religion. Morality and ethics are foundational, albeit overgeneralized, concepts that are routinely associated with athletic success. They are also cornerstone structures used to frame the desired outcomes of religion.

The evolution of muscular Christianity is an example of these complexities. On its face, the movement was intended to address a societal need to literally strengthen a population using a symbiotic approach to religion in sport. The theory was grounded in important intrinsic and extrinsic rewards. The practice, however, was found to be more duplicitous and also reinforced tragically discriminatory behavior that inhibited growth among marginalized groups for decades. There are still traces of that behavior today. Perhaps, the most important takeaway from this relationship is that the discourse surrounding sport and religion is continuing. That common space that sport and religion can occupy concurrently is important to understand, and scholarly exploration of the topic continues to emerge.

CRITICAL THINKING EXERCISES

1. *Athletics Director Scenario.* Divide the class into four different groups (dependent on class size). Each group is a team that has been installed as the athletic leadership of a Division I athletics department and one of their first tasks is how to resolve the department's handling of spiritual leadership. The first group is told they are hiring a full-time chaplain to service all of the religious and spiritual needs of all athletes. The second group is told they must hire several different religiously affiliated personnel part time to address the spiritual and religious needs. The third group is tasked with allowing individual teams to choose religious or spiritual leaders to fulfill those needs. Finally, the fourth group is told that they cannot bring in anyone officially to be a religious or spiritual leader. Each group should list the positives and negatives of their scenarios and choose which alternative situation they would have preferred.
2. *A Worthy Tradition.* A small Midwest town's Christian Community Youth Organization (CCYO), which sponsored the most competitive youth women's basketball program in the area, was forced to disband due to a lack of funding. Several coaches consolidated members of the league into four teams and joined a local city league in a neighboring town. Each team that was previously a member of the CCYO decided to continue the tradition of praying before each city league game began. After the first game, parents of the opposing teams began to complain, with the general thesis of their grievances being that the games were played in a municipal facility and public prayer was not allowed. Divide the students into equal groups and ask them to gather a possible response from the perspective of the players of the former CCYO league.
3. *Religious Headwear.* A high school state association has strict uniform guidelines in what is acceptable and allowed to be worn during basketball competitions. One of those rules is that no headwear of any kind can be worn during competition except for headbands or similar items to aid in perspiration absorption. A participant on a girls' basketball team wants to wear her hijab during competition in adherence to her Muslim faith. The coach tells her the rules do not allow this but says he will seek guidance from the state association to determine whether an exception can be made. Is there any recourse for the athlete besides opting out of participating?

REVIEW QUESTIONS

1. The former college and professional quarterback, Tim Tebow, is an evangelical Christian. What does this term mean, how did Tebow express his faith, and how did people react?
2. What is your take on whether sport can be thought of as a religion, as a substitute for religion, or is merely aligned with sport because people of various faiths participate in sport and bring their values and perspectives to the sporting arena with them?
3. What is muscular Christianity and how has it influenced the development of sport from the mid-1800s into the early 1900s?
4. What is a sport chaplain, and what role(s) can they play in relationship to a team?
5. What is the distinction between religion and spirituality?

DANIEL LEAL/AFP via Getty Images

CHAPTER 12

Coming of Age and Aging Out in Sport

Ellen J. Staurowsky, Amanda L. Paule-Koba, and Michael Sachs

LEARNING OBJECTIVES

- Discuss how conceptions of age and aging affect the way that we think about sport.
- Explore the range of sport opportunities across the span of a lifetime.
- Become familiar with athlete prodigies and issues regarding early sport participation, including policies determining when and where they are permitted to play.
- Examine athlete retirement processes and career transitions.
- Identify the ways that discrimination on the basis of age is manifest in sport.
- Become aware of how we see ageism in sport and how age microaggressions are manifest in sport.

The image immediately captivates. A pint-sized four-year-old boy named Nate balances with confidence on a surfboard as he rides wave after wave to shore. Seemingly born to the sport, he stands atop a floating polyurethane and fiberglass board that he grunts and strains to move once the ride ends. On the beach, that same board would flatten him under its weight if he could lift it.

When he is surfing, his stance is classic, one foot in front, the other behind, his upper body in sync with the movement of the board and the currents. He is "regular footed," meaning that he balances with his left leg forward. Lacking the height and weight he needs to maneuver the boogie board, his father provides the power to get out in the ocean at a far enough distance to catch a wave. As he paddles to get into position, lying belly first on the board, his hands just reach the water. Feeling a wave coming, he readies to accelerate, pushing up onto his feet and into position.

On his face is a mix of joy and subtle calculation, manifest in the adjustments that are made to keep going until he tumbles off, disappears for a moment, and resurfaces, cork-like as he gets his bearings. Having already mastered the high-level skill of "hanging 10," where a surfer balances while all 10 of their toes are curled around the edge of the board, Nate has been described as a prodigy (McCarthy, 2020).

After video of Nate circulated online and the publication of a news story about him in September of 2020, Nate's accomplishments as a young surfer garnered both acclaim and concern, illustrating the centrality of age in discussions about athletes, their access to sport, and expectations about athletes (McCarthy, 2020). For athletes, there is no escape from issues around age, the beliefs that others have about age and athletic performance, and the stereotypes that arise when athletes are viewed through the lens of age.

Nate's case drew attention in part because it challenged perceptions of when athletes should be encouraged to enter sport and under what conditions, what the obligations of parents and authorities are to allow athletes to compete at certain levels, and whether the interests of athletes are served if they are pushed too quickly to develop. Hidden within those areas of concern are others about what happens to athletes who are injured and have to retire early and identify so strongly with their sport participation that they have difficulty when they retire. Furthermore, just as Nate represents a "novelty," challenging assumptions of how young athletes may be to exhibit athletic excellence and proficiency, how good can athletes be—and for how long?

In this chapter, the multiple dimensions of how the sport system engages with age will be considered. We explore age as a factor that influences access to sport opportunity and the way sport is organized; the complexities associated with athlete prodigies and when and where they are permitted to play; athlete retirement processes and career transitions; sport opportunities across the span of a lifetime; and discrimination on the basis of age for athletes and those working in the sport industry.

In Sport, Age Matters

In sport, age is not just a number. It is a defining characteristic that shapes the structure of sport from youth through senior leagues; the identity of athletes from rookie to veteran; and the policies that govern access to participation through age limitations and restrictions (Atkinson, 2009). Age is used to signal readiness and maturity to take up sport and its challenges. It can also predict when an athletic career is likely to peak and when it is over.

This stream of awareness about age within the context of sport reflects a broader understanding of aging over the course of one's life. This section of the chapter deals with age as a factor in sport; age limits and restrictions at the youth level, relative age effects and delayed puberty, sport-specific age restrictions, gifted athletes, age and the eligibility clock at the college level, and age restrictions in professional sport.

Age as a Factor in Sport

Experts in human development have described stages that people go through in their lives, from infancy through old age. Educational systems are set up to usher students through various stages of cognitive, psychological, and social development. Each stage along the way is intended to build on the previous one and to expand skills and competencies to help prepare students to be productive citizens, good financial providers, and supportive family members. Longevity in professional life mirrors a similar understanding of human development and is marked by the signifiers of early, mid, and late career, suggesting a maturation process that is linked in no small part to age.

In sport, the terms are different but the trajectory is the same. Younger athletes are referred to as rookies. Athletes who have been playing longer are referred to as veterans. In turn, masters-level athletes are typically those aged 35 years or older who continue to train and participate in competitions for older athletes (Tayrose, Beutel, Cardone, & Sherman, 2015). By design, the infrastructure of the sport system is built to acknowledge the necessity for fostering sport participation within the context of age. Questions regarding when athletes are old enough to participate and when athletes are too old to participate loom large and are reflected in the way that sport is organized.

Age Limits and Age Restrictions in Sport

Consider nearly any sport you can think of to see how notions about age affect how and when athletes access sport opportunity. As an example, Little League Baseball and Softball offer support for youth athletes (ages 4-16 years) in baseball, softball (girls and boys), and an adaptive baseball program for individuals with physical and intellectual challenges. Each league that Little League Baseball offers is organized into divisions based on player age. Little League provides a calculator to help parents and local officials determine if an athlete meets the age eligibility requirement, along with age charts for each league and program. For baseball and softball, the divisions are sorted as shown in table 12.1.

For Little League's adaptive baseball program, called Challenger, there are two divisions, and players between the ages of 4 and 18 are eligible to play, with exceptions made to accommodate individuals who are as old as 22 if they continue to be enrolled in school. Those who are 15 and above may be selected for a senior division (Little League, 2021).

Age requirements, limits, and restrictions would not be embraced as uniformly across the sport industry if there were not strong justifications to do so. At a cognitive level,

TABLE 12.1 Little League Baseball and Little League Softball Division Breakdown by Age

Name of division	League age (as determined by calculator)	Brief description
Tee ball	4-7 years	Introduces players to basics of the game
Minor league	5-7 years	• One year of tee ball • Coach pitch or machine pitch
Minor league	7-12 years	• Player pitch, coach pitch, machine pitch • Local officials may decide age cutoffs
Major league	9-12 years	• Players selected for this division • Local officials may restrict teams to an age range of 10-12 years or 11-12 years
Intermediate 50/70 division	11-13 years	Local officials may restrict teams to an age range of 12-13 years
Junior league	12-14 years	Local officials may restrict teams to an age range of 13-14 years
Senior league	13-16 years	Local officials may restrict teams to an age range of 13-14 years

Based on Little League (2021).

sports across the spectrum rely on higher order thinking skills to grasp strategy and game play. Any observer of the "beehive" phenomenon in youth team sport settings (picture five-year-olds swarming around one ball) knows it is a process for athletes to learn that running into open spaces where the ball can be passed advances the ball down the field faster. Such moves require conceptual understanding of triangles. For team sport athletes, it takes time to think in multiple dimensions and consider what is happening on either side, behind, and in front as they focus on the target ahead. Interpersonally, they confront the necessity of sharing. They further discover the trust that needs to exist among teammates to move away from the ball, knowing that it will be passed back. And they learn the benefits of collaboration as they engage in the give and take of the game. All of these processes speak to the need to take the emotional, intellectual, and physical maturity of athletes into account and to empower athletes to be successful by introducing experiences when they are ready for them.

Regulations governing the ages for athletes to compete consider how best to create environments for athletes to thrive and grow. In community and school-sponsored sport programs for youth athletes, for example, a balance is expected to be struck between supporting advanced participation and providing opportunity for those less skilled or less experienced. This balancing of interests is reflected in policy, as seen in the statement made in the National Federation of State High School Associations Handbook on age eligibility in athletics. According to the policy, each state high school association must adopt an age limit requirement that

> *provides commonality between student-athletes and schools in interscholastic competition; inhibits "redshirting"; allows the participation of younger and less experienced players; enhances the opportunity for more students to participate; promotes equality of competition; avoids overemphasis on athletics, and helps to diminish the inherent risk of injury associated with participation in interscholastic athletics. (Howard, 2020, p. 19)*

Age requirements, limits, and restrictions are embraced in sports due to changing cognitive skills demonstrated by the beehive phenomenon in youth soccer where players aren't yet developmentally ready for higher-level play.

Relative Age Effects and Delayed Puberty

The sorting out of youth athletes by age has long-term consequences for athlete performance due to something called the **relative age effect (RAE).** Research has found that athletes who are born closer to the start of a specified age band tend to be more physically mature, exhibit greater coordination, and generally have greater success in their sport. Let's say that in order to be eligible for a particular sports team, the age clock starts on January 1 and runs through December 31. The athletes who are born earlier in the first quarter of that year (with birthdays in January-February-March) get an earlier start compared to those with birthdays in the fourth quarter (October-November-December). First identified in the sport of ice hockey in the 1980s, RAE has been found in a variety of sport settings, including soccer and track (Joyner, et al., 2020). The effects of RAE have been found in athletes representing many sports, affirming that early differences in physical and emotional maturity can carry over into adulthood. In a study of 44,000 Olympic athletes born between 1964 and 1996, the relative age effect influenced elite level performance (Joyner et al., 2020).

The phenomenon of RAE offers a window into the intersection that exists between physical development (the body), athletic identity, ability, and social factors. A relatively older athlete who benefits because they are more physically and emotionally mature by virtue of the timing of their birth may or may not be more talented athletically than others in their age cohort. However, they receive competitive advantages in the form of access to coaching and attention from coaches, teams, and playing opportunities, as well as support and reinforcement from peers and family members. In addition to whatever hard work and physical talent a youth athlete brings to their experience, the social environment they are in contributes to increased levels of self-confidence and optimism about their future in sport.

Another age-related issue that can affect athletes, the sport they play, and their persistence in certain sports is the age at which they reach puberty. For athletes who experience **constitutional growth delay (CGD),** otherwise referred to as delayed puberty, their athletic identity can be disrupted because their physical maturity is out of sync with their peers. Pediatric endocrinologist Dr. Joel Hahnke explained this in an interview about young people with delayed puberty: "Basically it means your body is programmed to have puberty develop later than average, and it's a variation of normal development" that typically runs in families (Brenneman, 2019, para. 12).

As late bloomers, athletes face difficult decisions about their careers. Some will become discouraged and stop participating entirely. Others will shift sport interests and move from team sports to individual sports. Others may reassess their fit for certain positions. And still others will persist in the hope that not only will they catch up with their peers but their efforts to do so will put them ahead in the long run. Experts on youth sport development note that coach understanding about talent assessment is important in ensuring that athletes are treated fairly and not simply dismissed from the sport system on the basis of age or age-related conditions when they are still developing (Brenneman, 2019; Deffenbach & Thompson, 2020; Duffek, 2017; Gray & Plucker, 2010).

Sport-Specific Age Restrictions to Protect Young Athletes From Abuse and Injury

Age regulations and policies also take into account the specific demands of particular sports. The sports of women's gymnastics and football offer interesting case studies in how age restrictions evolve and the implications if those restrictions are too lenient or too strict.

Women's gymnastics became an Olympic sport in 1956, and in absence of an age restriction, it began to focus on young female gymnasts who adhered to expectations of femininity but were skilled in acrobatics. The result was the emergence of international female gymnast sensations such as Olga Korbut and Nadia Comaneci, who were petite and girlish but completely captivating and thrilling.

By 1971, the influx of preadolescent competitors in women's gymnastics prompted the International Gymnastics Federation to institute its first minimum age requirement that set the mark at 14 years to compete internationally. Even with that effort, the ranks of elite level women's gymnastics continued to be dominated by young female athletes, resulting in a culture where girls with little power and world experience were being coached by authoritative adults in hypercompetitive situations. The minimum age requirement was raised to 15 in 1981 (Kerr, Barker-Rutchi, Schubring, Cervin, & Nunomura, 2015).

News reports in the 1990s about the endangerment of female gymnasts who were suffering from overtraining, delayed physiological development, debilitating and sometimes fatal injuries, and coach abuse led to the minimum age requirement being raised to 16 in 1997, a standard that is currently in effect. As the age to compete in international competition has been raised, there is a growing emphasis on how to coach female gymnasts postpuberty and an awareness of the challenges female gymnasts face trying to stay in the sport as their bodies change (Dolski, 2016).

The 2018 revelations that hundreds of female athletes, including a large number of female gymnasts, were victims of sexual abuse perpetrated by former U.S. women's gymnastics team doctor Larry Nassar prompted calls for the minimum age requirement in the sport to be raised to 18 years of age for senior international competition. The reasoning was that 18-year-olds would be less vulnerable to targeting by abusive coaches and affiliated staff because of greater life experience and emotional development (Cervin, 2020). As of this writing, however, the minimum age to compete internationally remains at 16, the number set nearly 25 years ago.

In the sport of football, discussions about age restrictions in recent years have focused on the question of when and under what circumstances youth athletes should be subjected to tackling and being tackled, with some questioning whether the sport poses a uniform health risk that argues for tackle football to be abandoned entirely. The tragic deaths of several current and former National Football League and college players; the high profile lawsuits of players and their families alleging negligence on the part of organizations from Pop Warner through the National Football League in their failure to inform participants of the long-term and potentially fatal risks associated with head trauma precipitated by the concussive and subconcussive hits sustained in the game; the work of investigative journalists uncovering troubling information about the football industry withholding information from players; and increased research on head injuries in football and conditions such as chronic traumatic encephalopathy (CTE) have prompted medical authorities, educational associations, family members who have lost loved ones to CTE and related illnesses, public policy makers, and sport governing bodies to explore age restrictions in the sport.

In 2015, the American Academy of Pediatrics' Council on Sports Medicine and Fitness issued a report exploring arguments for and against age restrictions for tackle football. Some argue that athletes should not participate in tackle football until high school because when the brains of youth sport participants are developing in the earlier years, they are more susceptible to the traumatic consequences of physical contact. However, there is no uniform agreement within the medical community about the appropriate or optimal age to allow youth athletes to participate in football. Others argue that waiting to teach athletes how to tackle and how to absorb the impact of a tackle until football players are in high school may subject them to higher risk because they have not had years of practicing a critical skill among athletes who are stronger and more coordinated (Meehan & Landry, 2015).

The Concussion Legacy Foundation, an organization that is involved in advocacy, policy development, and research to advance understanding about the health consequences of head and neck injuries sustained in sport, most particularly CTE, issued a white paper calling for tackle football to be banned for children under the age of 14 years (Nowinski & Cantu, 2019) (see chapter 10 for the sport leader sidebar on Concussion Legacy Foundation founder, Chris Nowinski). Citing the "bobble head effect," the authors of the Concussion Legacy Foundation position, former college and pro athlete Chris Nowinski and longtime sports medicine physician Robert Cantu (2019) point out that a child's body is not designed for tackle football, with head-to-body ratios that are disproportionate to those found in adults. Children's heads are simply more vulnerable to the negative effects of the kind of physical contact that occurs in tackle football, something that has been recognized in other sports such as ice hockey, where checking is prohibited until 13 years of age. They further argue that there is growing scientific evidence to show that tackle football is simply not good for children. They note, "In the pre-adolescent and adolescent years (age 8 to age 13), the brain undergoes dramatic changes and maturation that are responsible for the transition from child to adult brain function" (p. 4). Disruption to blood flow, blows to the body that cause a whiplash effect, and other traumas that interrupt the development of neural pathways and brain structure set the stage for cognitive and behavior issues both during and after playing careers (Nowinski & Cantu, 2019). While sport governing bodies such as U.S. Youth Soccer, USA Hockey, and U.S. Lacrosse have adopted age restrictions to bar young players from contact with other players through physical checking (hockey, lacrosse) or through contact with the ball through heading (soccer), the sport of football has been slow to implement similar measures. As a consequence, efforts are underway to propose legislation to protect the health and safety of youth football players (Nowinski & Cantu, 2019).

Gifted Athletes and the Sport System

In sport, and in other areas of life, efforts to regulate according to chronological age come up against the inevitable challenges associated with the variability of human experience. To illustrate, athletes who are ready to run a fast break in basketball rely on the readiness of teammates to fill three lanes, to pass and catch on the run, and to successfully execute a layup once they are down court. A skilled basketball player is going to be held back if they are playing with teammates who have not yet mastered running and dribbling at the same time.

And herein lies the limit of age limitations, because human potential defies such neat arrangements insisted upon by organizing athletic development around age as defined by birth dates. Not all athletes are best served by age restrictions, and the restrictions themselves become barriers to success, slow down growth, and impede the ability of some athletes to achieve their full promise.

Thus, at the youth level, age eligibility regulations serve as well-intended, albeit imperfect, controls to mediate the vast differences that can exist in coordination, emotional maturity, skill, and strength across groups. At a practical level, in terms of differences that exist within groups, there will be some children who will be bigger or smaller for their age group. As a case in point, six-year-old football player Aiden Smith received national media attention in the fall of 2020 while playing in a 6U (six and under) league in Texas because of his towering presence. Standing at 5'1" and 130 pounds, a seeming giant among children, Smith's physical presence and skills far surpassed those of his teammates and opponents (Walker, 2020).

Athletes who exhibit remarkable proficiency in their sports at young ages have been called **athlete prodigies**. These athletes learn the skills associated with their sports more rapidly than other children in their age range (Winner & Drake, 2018). Elizabeth Winner, a developmental psychologist, describes as a distinguishing feature of a child prodigy their consuming focus on the activity in which they excel. In her words, "One often cannot tear these children away from activities in their area of giftedness. These children have a powerful interest in the domain in which they have high ability, and they can focus so intently on work in this domain that they lose sense of the outside world" (Hambrick, 2015, para. 6). Recent research suggests that environmental factors and genetics influence the performance of child prodigies (Hambrick, 2015).

Athletes such as top high school boys basketball recruit Dior Johnson pose dilemmas for school administrators and officials from sport governing bodies who recognize that not every athlete fits neatly into the lockstep system created by eligibility requirements that are based on age. In Johnson's case, at the age of 13 years, through an exception in New York State high school eligibility rules, he was permitted to play on the varsity team at Saugerties High School as a seventh grader (Interdonato, 2017).

Based on his performance, it is clear that he had the physical talent to compete at that level and emerge as the best player not just on his team but as one of the best players in the country. In his first year on varsity during the 2016-2017 season, he recorded multiple 30-point games, scoring 15 points in the fourth quarter of a game against Washingtonville. By the time he was in his second varsity season at Saugerties, as he grew from 5'9" to 6'3", he recorded a 53-point game against Burnt Hills–Ballston Lake in December 2018. He also became the youngest player in New York State to score 1,000 career points, in his 40th career game while still in eighth grade (Interdonato, 2020).

Johnson's case offers a window into the challenges an athlete with significant gifts encounters as they pursue opportunities and find the place that best allows them to continue to grow and flourish. According to his bio on recruiting site 247 Sports, he went on to attend, for varying lengths of time, six different schools while also competing on Nike Elite Youth Basketball League (EYBL) teams. A five-star rated ESPN top 25 recruit for the high school class of 2022, Johnson originally committed to Syracuse University but later changed to Oregon (Borzello, 2020a; Mumm, 2021).

Described as a household name in basketball circles, Johnson's quest to play with other top recruits has rendered him an itinerant. As he tweeted at the time he announced his verbal commitment to Syracuse, he wrote, "Through blood, sweat and tears, late nights staying in the gym working on my craft, I've learned no matter what, you have to make decisions where you see yourself thriving the most" (Interdonato, 2020, para. 4). For a time he played on the same Nike EYBL youth team as Bronny James (ranked at 25 for the 2023 class as of this writing) and he has also played with five-star prospect Joshua Christopher at Mayfair High School (Borzello, 2020b).

After spending two months with the high-powered basketball program at Oak Hill Academy in Virginia in the fall of 2020, Johnson left there and enrolled at Corona Centennial High School in California. About the unique situation Johnson has been navigating, his head coach at Centennial, Josh Giles, commented, "I think he's been forced into a situation that most kids don't experience until they're maybe 17 or 18, if they're really good. He's been forced to experience that since he was like 12 or 13" (Curtis, 2020, para. 14).

What does such a disrupted lifestyle do for a teenager who feels the pressure to make the right decisions to find an optimal environment to realize his gifts? Within a two-year span of time he attended schools in New York, Georgia, Florida, Virginia, and two different towns in California. A lingering question about Johnson—or any athlete who has demonstrated a gift for learning their craft and hitting performance milestones early in their career—is whether they are better off seeking out playing environments that appear to provide the challenges necessary to ensure continued growth or could the environment in his own backyard in New York have been sufficient? This is not a question that offers an easy answer.

Malcolm Gladwell (2008), a journalist who has written about individuals he called "outliers" (people who are successful but whose accomplishments fall outside of what is thought of as normal), writes that early success does not necessarily predict future success. Innate ability and genetic predispositions account for some measure of success, but social and environmental factors contribute, as well.

Researchers also caution that athletes who are regarded as exceptionally talented may actually be better learners, early bloomers, or individuals who have practiced more. Thus, they caution that a more refined view of what is meant by giftedness or prodigiousness in sport is recommended (Gray & Plucker, 2010).

Speeding Up and Slowing Down the Eligibility Clock in College

As athletes prepare for and enter the college sport system in the United States, outright age limits are replaced with athlete eligibility regulations that provide for four years of playing within a five-year window of time. There are six different scenarios where eligibility calendars aligned loosely with age can be adjusted to give athletes more time to develop physically, qualify academically, recover from injury, or respond to a host of other issues (Sports Engine, 2018).

Legend has it that the practice of speeding up, stopping, or slowing the eligibility clock for athletes in college started in 1937 with a University of Nebraska football player named Warren Alfson. Following his first year on what was then called the freshman team, Alfson sought permission from school authorities to take a year to practice with the team but not suit up for games so that he could get into better shape, increase his playing time by waiting for older athletes ahead of him on the roster to graduate, and preserve his eligibility. The term "redshirting," which has come to be associated with adjusting the eligibility clock, was coined when Alfson was given a red shirt without a number, signifying his decision to delay competing on the varsity squad. There is now a color wheel of shirts designating different eligibility statuses for college athletes (Myerberg, 2016). Table 12.2 has a description of each.

Age Restrictions and Access to Professional Careers in Sport

The dilemmas that a high school basketball player like Dior Johnson face are not ones confronting all young athletes who have the potential talent to play professionally, but they are created, in part, by the way the U.S. sport system has been integrated into the educational system. In other parts of the world, including Europe, Canada, and Central and South America, the avenues for pursuing elite and professional athletic careers are through local and professional clubs. Through the creation of football (soccer) academies run by professional teams, athletes as young as 10 years old are recruited, given free room and board and access to local schools, and developed for professional careers in soccer (Miller, 2020).

The sport of ice hockey in North America has had a similar system to that of the European model. In Canada, high school teams are run as intramural programs for athletes who have an interest and enthusiasm for the game. The focal point of talent development is centered in three Canadian Hockey Leagues (CHL)—the Ontario Hockey League, the Western Hockey League, and the Quebec Major Junior Hockey League. For youth players, those leagues are the pinnacle of hockey, where players focus on being drafted by National Hockey League (NHL) teams or going on to play on athletic scholarship at U.S. universities. Notably, in the NHL drafts from 2014 to 2019, nearly 50 percent of the players drafted had spent time playing in the Canadian Hockey Leagues, with an additional 10 percent coming from Sweden, a country that runs their ice hockey talent development program in a manner similar to the European football (soccer) academy model (Miller, 2020).

Major League Baseball has also adopted the development of academies outside of the United States, specifically in the Dominican Republic (DR) and other areas of Central and South America. The result has been an increase from 1 percent of international players on Major League Baseball (MLB) teams in 1980 to a third of the league, with most of those players coming primarily from the DR and Venezuela. Players can sign at the age of 16 with an MLB club, with signing bonuses to attend an academy in the DR averaging $5,000 to $10,000. Controversially, youth players are represented by street agents, or buscones, who typically take 40 percent of a player's signing bonus (Miller, 2020).

Concerns about age restrictions denying younger athletes who may be in the prime of their careers opportunities to play and to benefit financially from their success have also been raised about female athletes. While U.S. tennis player Coco Gauff made history in 2019 by becoming the youngest player to qualify for a Wimbledon singles draw and the youngest player to qualify for a Grand Slam tournament main draw at the age of 15, she was held back from fully competing because of the Women's Tennis Association's (WTA) age restriction policy. Under that policy, female athletes under the age of 13 are not permitted to play in professional tournaments, even if

TABLE 12.2 Types of Eligibility Status for College Athletes

Type of eligibility status	Description	Reason
Blueshirt	• Makes unrecruited athletes eligible to receive an athletic scholarship at the start of first-year practice • Allows athletes to practice with the team but not play in varsity contests	Indicates an "unrecruited" athlete (someone who has not had an official visit to a university hosted by the athletic department under NCAA rules, has not had a coach visit their home, has not signed a National Letter of Intent, and was not offered an athletic scholarship)
Grayshirt	• Occurs when there are too many recruits and not enough scholarships to give to them • Typical athlete in this scenario starts school without a scholarship either as a part-time student or at a two-year institution • For athletes who will begin their enrollment full-time on scholarship the next semester	• Provides coaches with the flexibility to deal with athletes who committed to their programs but whom they were unable to fund in the first semester • Due to the part-time status of athletes in this situation, they are not eligible to practice or work out with their teams
Greenshirt	Typically an athlete who graduates from high school in December and starts college in the spring semester	• Allows athletes in fall sports to get adjusted to college early without the pressure of being in season • Provides an opportunity to participate in spring practice activities
Pinkshirt	• Provided to athletes who become pregnant • Permitted to retain athletic scholarship under the terms of the award (prevents an athlete from having her scholarship immediately taken away if she becomes pregnant, but it does not provide a guarantee of a one-year award being renewed)	• Provides an additional year of eligibility • Regards pregnancy as a temporary disability
Redshirt	• Eligible to receive an athletic scholarship • Access to practice, strength and conditioning, and other services such as academic tutoring • Not eligible to participate in games	• Provides additional year of physical development • Used for recovering from an injury
Redshirt (academic)	• Eligible to receive an athletic scholarship • Access to practice, strength and conditioning, and other services such as academic tutoring • Not eligible to participate in games	Indicates the athlete does not meet all academic requirements
Redshirt (Division I football) (instituted in 2018)	Athletes can play up to four games or 30 percent of their season and still have four years of eligibility	• Reduces pressure on athletes to play when hurt • Increases opportunities for athletes to get playing time without using up a whole year of eligibility • Gives coaches flexibility in how they use their player personnel

they qualify. Female players ages 14 to 17 are restricted to eight events per year, with only three of those with prize money more than $60,000 permitted. When a player reaches the age of 17, she is permitted to participate in 16 events. There is an exception that players who are under these restrictions may receive a limited reprieve through something called a merited increase (Carroll, 2019; Tandon, 2019).

In the United States, college programs as de facto developmental leagues for the professional sports of basketball and football have produced ongoing controversies. In basketball, the National Basketball Association's (NBA's) age restriction requires that players be at least 19 years old and one year removed from the date of their high school graduation to qualify to play in the league. Some high school players choose a different route: MarJon Beauchamp opted to bypass college and spend time training with a private company, and LaMelo Ball chose to play for a team in the Australian League. The NBA policy's impact on the basketball system has resulted in a phenomenon at the college level called "one and done" (O'Donnell, 2019).

While players who commit to a college program and then exercise their right after a year to stand for the NBA draft have been criticized for prioritizing basketball over their educational interests and being disloyal to programs that invested time and resources in their development, the market is what drives their behavior. With lucrative contracts on the line and keen competition for only a few professional playing opportunities each year within the NBA, players have to make decisions based on the options available to them. The industry itself has placed a value on younger players in the draft. Since the age policy went into effect in 2006, the top player in the draft has routinely been a first-year player coming out of the college ranks. That in itself argues that the longer a player stays in college, the lower their value in the draft becomes (Stark-Mason, 2018).

As legal analyst and senior sport law reporter for Sportico Michael McCann points out, "These eligibility rules are uniquely limiting" (2020, para. 6). While teenage athletes might face age limitations, in professional leagues such as the NHL, MLB, professional tennis, and other pro leagues they do have pathways to work as professional athletes. McCann illustrates the unusual impact the NBA's age restriction policy has on basketball players in the United States through the example of Dallas Mavericks star Luka Dončić. Originally signed with Real Madrid at the age of 13, "He went on to play five years of pro hoops before joining the NBA as a rookie" (McCann, 2020, para. 6).

While the NBA has yet to remove the age restriction, the loss of players overseas and the increasing financial stakes that prompt high school players to consider alternatives to college (because the college system fails to fairly compensate players) have prompted the NBA to invest more in its developmental league. In 2020, a top high school player like Jalen Green from California found it attractive to bypass the college game in favor of the NBA's G League, a league that offers the possibility of elite players earning as much as $500,000 a year and receiving access to top-level coaching and training facilities (Givony & Wojnarowski, 2020).

Sport and Age Discrimination

A reasonable person might ask why restriction policies that limit or prevent younger athletes from working as professionals do not constitute age discrimination policies. The National Football League (NFL) does not have a minimum age for being hired to play in the league, but there is a requirement that football players must be out of high school for three years before they are eligible to play. As a consequence, a football player who graduates from high school at 18 is not eligible to participate in the NFL until age 21. The restrictions preventing players going straight from high school to the NFL were challenged in 2003 by former Ohio State football player Maurice Clarett, who completed his first year and then opted to prepare for the NFL draft instead of returning for a second year of playing at the college level. Clarett alleged that the rules violated federal antitrust law that prohibits competing businesses (NFL franchises) that benefit economically from conspiring to prevent younger players from being hired if not for those rules. Michael McCann, who represented Clarett, described the case:

> *As a collective, teams support older eligibility rules so that young players can develop their skills, and become more marketable, on someone else's dime—namely, American colleges. Colleges welcome this arrangement because they earn off those young players' labor and name, image and likeness. (2020, para. 9)*

Although Clarett prevailed in federal district court, he lost in the U.S. Court of Appeals for the Second Circuit. The judge in the case, Sonia Sotomayor (who is now a U.S. Supreme Court justice) reasoned that since the National Football League Players Association (NFLPA) had agreed to the rule, antitrust law did not apply, despite the fact that Clarett and other affected younger players could not be members of the union and the NFLPA's members stood to gain by protecting their own jobs at the expense of younger players (McCann, 2020).

Sensibly, one could ask if there is no remedy for younger players who are denied employment simply because they are young. We might expect that the federal law that prohibits employees from being discriminated against because of their age, the Age Discrimination Employment Act of 1967 (ADEA), would apply. However, the ADEA expressly applies to individuals who are 40 years of age or older. The specificity of the law emerges out of the circumstances that led to its passage, when individuals between the ages of 40 and 65 were particularly vulnerable in the 1960s to being let go by employers who would try to increase profit margins by reducing labor costs (Lovell, 2012; Wrady & Michel, 2015). While some state **age discrimination** laws cover a greater number of people, unless the ADEA were to be amended to recognize that younger workers may also experience discrimination based on age, there are actually few avenues of legal recourse for athletes whose futures are affected by age restrictions.

From time to time, athletes and their parents may believe that age has been used to improperly justify an athlete being cut from a team. As a case in point, in *Jane Doe, next friend of John Doe v. Ladue Horton Watkins High School* (2018), a male soccer player alleged that his rights under the Age Discrimination Act of 1974 (a federal law that applies to individuals of all ages) were violated after being cut from the school's boys soccer program. According to the complaint, the coach explained that while the player was "on the bubble" in terms of making the varsity team, he ultimately was not considered because of some "gaps" in his skill set. When the boy's stepfather asked why his son could not play junior varsity, the response was that the junior varsity program was reserved for first years and sophomores to give them time to develop. While the player and his parents believed that he had been cut because he was a junior, the judge found the coach's explanation that the decision was based on an assessment of skill and not the player's age or grade. The judge further found that because participation in interscholastic sport is a privilege and not a right, the boy had no recourse.

These kinds of cases illustrate how difficult proving a case of age discrimination can be. Some will argue, for example, that policies based on grade are not age-specific policies. Others will argue that there is a need to balance the interests of all students. In the above case, 48 athletes tried out for 24 spots on the varsity team. If, in theory, all of those cut from the varsity and put on the junior varsity were juniors and seniors, there would be no opportunity to develop talent coming up from the lower grades. But what is a player like the son of *Jane Doe* to do? He was allegedly told to "man up" and work on his game. His father claims that his son did exactly that, working with a private coach and improving to the point where he had been a leading scorer on the junior varsity the year before (Collins, 2018). In a meritocracy, that kind of effort should be rewarded and yet, with new talent coming up each year, how are the interests of all players to be balanced with limited resources, personnel, and opportunities to play?

Beyond age discrimination faced by athletes is age discrimination experienced by those working in the sport industry. According to the AARP report (2019), **ageism**, or prejudice based on age, is rampant in workplaces in the United

States, with 25 percent of workers over 45 years old indicating that they have heard negative comments about their age; three in five workers having seen or experienced age discrimination; and 76 percent of older workers fearing that their age is an impediment to finding another job. Several recent examples illustrate how this is experienced in the sport industry.

First, when NBA commissioner Adam Silver announced in June 2020 that the league would return to play following an interruption of its season during the COVID-19 pandemic, he also said in an interview on TNT that "some older coaches may not be able to be the bench coach in order to protect them." As well-intentioned as that statement was, it drew criticism because of the **age microaggression** (an indirect, unintentional expression of prejudice) embedded in the assumption that older coaches, by virtue of their age, needed to be protected. By pointedly keying off age as a factor in who would be courtside and who would not, the NBA ran the risk of violating the ADEA (Goetzel, 2020).

Second, three men's basketball officials filed a lawsuit against the NCAA and numerous Division I conferences (*Barker, Allocco, & Pilla v. NCAA*, 2020) alleging that a policy decision to encourage the hiring of younger officials without regard to documented performance evaluations constitutes discrimination under city and state human rights laws in New York. According to the lawsuit, "The Alliance and the NCAA have made it clear that they favor young referees and that older experienced referees like Barker will no longer receive the most lucrative assignments to Division I basketball games" (*Barker, Alloco, & Pilla v. NCAA*, 2020, p. 6).

Sport Opportunities Across the Lifespan

As much as there is a preoccupation with the age athletes can turn professional and under what circumstances, there is also a preoccupation with how long athletes will continue to compete. With an ever-increasing emphasis on athlete production (the work output that athletes generate while playing) as a result of a reliance on analytical data in judging athlete performance, some people predict that athletes will age out of professional sport at younger ages (Leitch, 2019). And yet, "older" professional athletes are challenging perceptions of how long athletes can continue to compete at the highest level.

After becoming the oldest golfer to win a major championship, in 2021, 50-year-old Phil Mickelson was characterized as an anomaly, his accomplishment described by ESPN as "stunning" (Pietruszkiewicz, 2021). Despite increasing scrutiny and calls for their retirement, athletes like NFL quarterback Tom Brady (who won his seventh Super Bowl in 2021 with the Tampa Bay Buccaneers at the age of 43) and Serena Williams (considered to be the greatest female tennis player in the history of the game and who was ranked eighth in the world by the WTA in 2021 at the age of 39) represent a new generation of athletes who are breaking ageist stereotypes. Some people have argued that an athlete's longevity has proven in recent years to be an asset rather than a detriment. As Jeff Bercovici (2018) points out, new efficiencies in training techniques and a better understanding of human physiology and the human body's response to aging have greatly expanded expectations for how long athletes can compete and at what levels.

Older athletes are categorized as "masters athletes." According to Tayrose and colleagues (2015), "The masters athlete is typically defined as older than 35 years (as this is the age at which cardiovascular issues tend to become a greater cause of morbidity) who either trains for or takes part in athletic competitions often specifically designed for older participants" (p. 270). The number of masters athletes in the United States has steadily increased, due in part to a growing population of baby boomers (people born between 1946 and 1964), and a sport-obsessed culture (Tayrose et al., 2015). Increases in the number of masters athletes are also due to a growing appreciation for what science has revealed about aging, "that staying active is perhaps the best way we know to defy the aging process and add years to one's life span" (Crouch, 2019, para. 3).

There are lessons to be learned from some of the world's oldest athletes, for whom age,

Older professional athletes are challenging perceptions of how long athletes can continue to compete at the highest level. NFL player Tom Brady won a seventh Super Bowl at age 43.
Todd Kirkland/Getty Images

as the saying goes, is no barrier. They take up their chosen sports for a variety of reasons, including wanting the benefits of feeling better, participating in an active lifestyle, taking on new challenges and competing, learning new things, discovering newfound talents and capabilities, dealing with depression and stress, and cultivating friendships (Godwin, 2019).

Triathlete Edwina (Eddie) Brocklesby became the oldest British woman to complete the Ironman (a grueling competition that calls on athletes to swim 2.4 miles; bike 112 miles; and run a 26.2 mile marathon) at the age of 72 years. Known as the Irongran, she did not begin her athletic career in earnest until she trained for her first marathon when she was 52 (Godwin, 2019). Centenarian Ida Keeling (106 years old as of this writing), who set numerous world records in the 60-meter and 100-meter dash after she was 95 years old was encouraged to begin running when she was 67. Keeling became the first woman in history to complete a 100-meter race at the age of 100 years. She got into running as a way to deal with grief following the deaths of her husband and two sons. At the urging of her daughter, they trained together for a 5K run, and the rest was history. Fauja Singh, who ran his first marathon when he was 89 years old, continued to run in road races until he was 104. Even in his "retirement" at 108 years old he walks five miles a day (Godwin, 2019).

Athlete Retirement Processes and Career Transitions

An athletic career, no matter how great the athlete is, can only last for so long. One day, whether that day comes at the end of high school, college, professional league, or somewhere in between, the individual will transition from athlete to former athlete. When that day comes, it is vital that the athlete has a plan for the next step in their future.

Sport Industry Diversity Initiative

NATIONAL SENIOR GAMES ASSOCIATION

The National Senior Games Association (NSGA) was founded in 1985 for the purpose of promoting healthy lifestyles for adults through education, fitness, and sport. The NSGA hosts the largest multisport event in the world for seniors. Known as the National Senior Games, the event is a biennial event for athletes 50 years and older with 20 events (NSGA, 2021). Like other sport entities that have attempted to refer to their event as the Olympics, the National Senior Games was once known as the Senior Olympics. Following objections in 1990 from the United States Olympic Committee (now the United States Olympic and Paralympic Committee), the organization abandoned use of the term and adopted the term "Senior Games."

The emergence of the Senior Games reflects growing recognition of the aging population in the United States. According to the Administration for Community Living (2021), adults aged 65 years of age and older numbered 54 million in 2019 (the most recent reporting year available), representing just over 16 percent of the U.S. population. By 2040, older adults (aged 65+) are expected to comprise nearly 22 percent of the U.S. population. As older adults live full and active lives, they pursue opportunities to compete in sport, continue to participate in sport activities they love, or take up new sports motivated by the same passions and motivations that all athletes feel, from the thrill of victory to the fulfillment that comes from taking on challenges to being around people who share common interests.

Athletes qualify a year in advance by participating in Senior Games sponsored at the state level or through National Veterans Golden Age Games or the Canada Games. When the Senior Games kick off in Pittsburgh in 2023, it is expected that approximately 14,000 athletes will be competing (Gewirtz, 2021). The performances of athletes in the Senior Games have defied ageist stereotypes that depict the elderly as frail and inactive. Dottie Gray, who did not take up running until she was 54 years old, continued to run 5K races almost every weekend in her 90s. Over the years she has set numerous world records at national and international senior competitions (Petrin, 2016).

During its 30th anniversary in 2017, NSGA recognized a number of athletes, including Hazel Hassen Bey, a bowling champion who had attended every Senior Games event during those three decades. After receiving a bowling ball as a gift from her late husband over 60 years ago, Hazel bowled despite living with rheumatoid arthritis, which affected her legs more than her hands. Regardless of the challenges that life has presented, her attitude has been that the Lord gave her a bowling ball and she was determined to use it (Moon, 2017).

The notion of transition emerged out of crisis theory (Lindemann, 1965), because when a crisis ends, the transition process starts (Parkes, 1971; Weiss, 1976). Transition is the process of change from one state or place to another. According to Schlossberg (1981), "a transition can be said to occur if an event or non-event results in a change in assumptions about oneself and the world that requires a corresponding change in one's behavior and relationships" (p. 5). For many athletes, the transition process of leaving their sporting experience behind is a difficult one (Barcza-Renner, Shipherd, & Basevitch, 2020; Grove, Lavallee, & Gordon, 1997; Hart & Swenty, 2016; Lally, 2007; Smith & Hardin, 2018; 2020; Stokowski, Paule-Koba, & Kaunert, 2019; Warehime, Dinkel, Bjornsen-Ramig, & Blount, 2017; Wylleman, Alfermann, & Lavallee, 2004). For many athletes, a profound sense of sadness occurs when the journey of being an athlete is over and they have to move into "a new social environment and into the workplace" (Smith & Hardin, 2018, p. 62). The degree to which the athlete struggles to move on to the new role is partially dependent upon whether the transition is normative or nonnormative and how strong the individual's athlete identity is.

Sport Industry Leader Profile

Jonathan T. Orr

Title: Executive Director at Athlete Transition Services and Program Director at NPower

Jonathan Orr was born and raised in Detroit, Michigan. After high school, Jonathan earned a football scholarship to the University of Wisconsin (UW). During his time at UW, he earned a bachelor's degree in community leadership and nonprofit management. While at Wisconsin, Jonathan also found success on the football field, which led to him being drafted by the Tennessee Titans. His time in the NFL was short-lived, lasting only two seasons before he was released from the Oakland Raiders.

Shortly after the end of his football career, Jonathan found himself facing significant personal struggles. He did not know who he was without football or what to do with his life. Eventually, Jonathan developed a plan for transitioning into the next season of his life. This plan included using the transferable skills and strengths he had acquired from his athletic experiences, identifying his gifts and talents, and setting value-based goals. Jonathan returned to school and earned a master's degree in organizational leadership from Trevecca Nazarene University and has since worked in positions of leadership for various nonprofit and educational organizations.

In 2014, Jonathan started Athlete Transition Services, an organization that helps athletes prepare for life after sports. Through workshops and life coaching services, Jonathan and his team educate and equip athletes with the information, tools, and strategies needed to facilitate their overall growth and development. Since its conception, ATS has provided services for college athletes at over 20 universities across the country, including Alabama, Clemson, Florida State, Florida, Utah, Virginia Tech, and Wisconsin. In 2018 Jonathan released his first book, *Game's Over Life's Not: The Athlete's Guide for Transitioning*. Jonathan and his team have experienced a great deal of personal and professional success, and it is his passion to help other athletes do the same.

Normative and Nonnormative Transitions

Normative transitions are planned and are often voluntary in nature, whereas nonnormative transitions are unexpected and end with involuntary retirement from sport (Stoltenburg, Kamphoff, & Lindstrom Bremer, 2011). Examples of a normative transition would include Barry Sanders' or Andrew Luck's voluntary retirements from the NFL at the peak of their careers, each of Michael Jordan's retirements from the NBA, or a collegiate athlete's choice not to pursue a professional athletic career upon graduation. Examples of a nonnormative transition include an athlete who is involuntarily cut from a team, a career-ending injury, or even the cancellation of a current season or loss of an upcoming season due to the COVID-19 pandemic. Nonnormative transitions are generally more traumatic in nature due to the unexpected or sudden occurrence of the end of the athletic career. Whether an athlete's athletic career ends via a normative or nonnormative reason, they will have to undergo a transition process as they move into their new role in life and try to move past their athletic identity.

Jonathan Orr's personal struggles with transitioning into life after sports are what motivates him to help current athletes. As a Black male who grew up in the inner city, he placed "all of his eggs in the athletic identity basket." He describes his early identity as being a football player, and that identity stuck with him through his time in the NFL. However, once his football career came to an end, he struggled, and he noticed others in similar situations felt the same way. He contends that he, and athletes like him, "were not exposed to a lot of options" regarding different careers and "the opportunities to explore our other interests, our passions, our gifts, and talents."

Once he found his way in life both professionally and personally, he reflected on his transition struggle and wanted to help others navigate their own path as well. He began informally coaching his peers through the process of transitioning and he noticed transition issues were "more and more prevalent" in athletes at all levels. His personal experience coupled with his passion to help others led to the creation of Athlete Transition Services.

Athlete Transition Services "provides empowering workshops and 1 on 1 life coaching services to college and professional athletes to assist with their transition to life after sports and to help facilitate their overall growth and development" (2021). The types of programming ATS has for athletes and athletic departments include workshops on personal development, athlete identity, self-discovery, career paths, financial literacy, and creating a game plan.

Jonathan believes that one thing that could be changed now that would make a difference in fostering diversity and inclusion in the sport industry is to have earlier intervention and support athlete development. He says you usually hear about it in college, if at all. He believes programming in youth sport should emphasize developing the total person and not just the athlete, so that athletes then have an easier time transitioning to life after sport when their playing days are over.

If he could offer advice to young professionals wanting to make a difference in the sport industry it would be to never lose sight of the fact you are serving human beings. Often, athletes are placed upon a pedestal, and if they make a mistake they are sometimes demonized. Jonathan urges all practitioners to remember that athletes are more than what they do and to help the athletes develop their whole self.

Jonathan lives in Canton, Michigan, with his wife, Heydie, and their children, Carsyn, Catheryn, and Owen.

Athletic Identity

Athletic identity is the level to which the individual self identifies with the role of an athlete from cognitive and social perspectives (Horton & Mack, 2000). Athletic identity has been shown to be a contributing factor to how an athlete transitions to life after sport. If an athlete has a high athletic identity, it can often lead to trouble transitioning to new experiences or accepting their new role in life (Blinde & Stratta, 1992; Grove et al., 1997; Kidd, Southall, Nagel, Reynolds II, & Anderson, 2018; Lally, 2007; Lavallee, 2005; Lavallee & Robinson, 2007; Smith & Hardin, 2018; 2020; Stokowski, Paule-Koba, & Kaunert, 2019; Stoltenburg, Kamphoff, & Lindstrom Bremer, 2011). Transitioning out of sport is more challenging for those with a strong athletic identity because often the athlete's entire social circle, free time, and support system are wrapped up in their sport participation (Blinde & Stratta, 1992; Grove et al., 1997; Rohrs-Cordes & Paule-Koba, 2018; Stoltenburg, Kamphoff, & Lindstrom Bremer, 2011). Additionally, these athletes have often neglected other aspects of their life or identities, such as education or internships, in order to maintain their high athletic identity.

A high athletic identity does not only lead to transition problems for collegiate athletes. Grove, Lavallee, and Gordon (1997) found that athletic identity had a positive correlation with former elite athletes' anxiety about making decisions regarding planning for the future or assessing career paths for retirement after sport. However, anxiety was negatively correlated with career planning prior to their retirement.

Athlete Transition Out of Sport

Retirement from sport, whether normative or nonnormative, can have implications for future planning and post-athletic life. The trouble with creating a plan to help is that the retirement experience is diverse and contains many variables for the athletes and the individuals supporting them. To ease the transitional adjustment out of sport for athletes, it is important to shift the athlete's focus to other positive areas in their life while simultaneously minimizing the negative effects of the sudden identity change (Cosh, Crabb, & LeCouteur, 2013). Athletes with high athletic identity rely on social support to help them make the emotional, physical, and psychosocial adjustments necessary to successfully transition out of sport (Grove et al., 1997; Rohrs-Cordes & Paule-Koba, 2018; Stokowski, Paule-Koba, & Kaunert, 2019; Stoltenburg et al., 2011).

Athlete retirement interventions have become a way to help athletes at all levels prepare for the inevitable end of their playing career. These programs focus on career transition and life skill programs that strive to provide support, education, and resources to retiring athletes (Barcza-Renner, Shipherd, & Basevitch, 2020; Hansen, Perry, Ross, & Montgomery, 2018; Wylleman, Alfermann, & Lavallee, 2004). Examples of these programs include the U.S. Olympic and Paralympic Committee's Athlete Career and Education program (2019) and the NCAA's After the Game (2018), both of which offer athletes education and support before and during the sport retirement process.

SUMMARY

The purpose of this chapter was to consider the way that age, and conceptions of age, affect the access individuals have to sport and the experience they have while competing and working in the sport system. For an athlete prodigy like Nate, our young surfer with his whole future ahead of him, being mindful of the responsibility associated with creating environments where athletes can grow and thrive, regardless of age, is the worthiest of projects. Lack of sensitivity regarding age can lead to microagressions that reflect subtle prejudices. In Nate's case, assuming that he is too small or vulnerable to harm might create barriers to his development. As Nate's identity becomes entwined in his athletic pursuits, attention may need to be given to broadening his horizons so that he will have multiple interests. If he persists in the sport of surfing, Nate may find that he is on course to participate in the Olympics. Interestingly enough, the sport of surfing is one of the few sports that does not evidence a relative age effect (RAE) (Redd, Fukuda, Beyer, & Oliviera, 2018). What we know about athlete identity is that as Nate continues on his journey through the sport system he will benefit from broadening his horizons and balancing out his athlete identity, anticipating that his career will be marked by transitions. For Nate as well as other athletes and those working in the sport system, greater consciousness about the constant presence that conceptions of age play from entry through retirement is key to healthy transitions and to reducing or eliminating age discrimination.

CRITICAL THINKING EXERCISES

1. An age microaggression is the expression of a prejudice based on age. Think about your own experience in the sport system. Identify at least five age microaggressions you have observed or heard about.
2. After reading the section about the way age influences how sport is organized, reflect on your own experience in the sport system. How have age and age restrictions affected your own journey through the sport system?
3. Europe has academies for younger athletes who want to pursue professional careers in football (soccer), while the United States has relied heavily on school-based programs to develop talent for professional leagues like the NFL and the NBA. Research sport academies further and consider the pros and cons of creating an academy model in the United States.

REVIEW QUESTIONS

1. What are the justifications for age limits in sport?
2. What is relative age effect and how does that affect athletic performance?
3. What should coaches know about constitutional growth delay (CGD)?
4. Why has the Concussion Legacy Foundation called for tackle football to be banned for players under the age of 14 years?
5. How does the NFL avoid charges of age discrimination in its limit on younger players participating in the league?

PART III

CREATING AND SUSTAINING DIVERSE, EQUITABLE, AND INCLUSIVE SPORT ORGANIZATIONS

Bettmann/Getty Images

CHAPTER 13

When They See Us: Sport Leaders Moving Beyond Bias

Billy Hawkins

LEARNING OBJECTIVES

- Discuss the institutional oppression exhibited in the forms of institutional racism and institutional sexism.
- Identify additional ways decolonization can be employed in the sport industry.
- Explain how sport can be an emancipatory institution for racial justice.
- Discuss the role of sport as a site of resistance for racial injustice.
- Identify specific examples of athletes or sporting events that have demonstrated the power of sport as a site of resistance to racial injustices.
- Apply critical thinking skills to a problem involving racial injustice in the sport industry.
- Discuss the opportunities and challenges facing sport leaders who are seeking to achieve diversity and inclusion initiatives.

The quarterback (QB) position in football is held as the definitive intellectual position on the roster. It is the leadership position where a premium is placed on cognitive skills, creative thinking ability, confident poise, and the ability to command and lead under pressure. These characteristics have typically been associated with White men, specifically, and seen as shortcomings among Black male athletes. The Black male athlete is perceived to be more physical or athletic and ill-equipped to lead or execute to achieve a desired outcome. Although Black athletes have played the QB position in their segregated experiences, once the desegregation of sports occurred, this position was reserved for "Whites" only because, again, Black athletes were seen as lacking in the abilities to "run an offense." Thus, remnants of the historical stereotype of the intellectually inferior Blacks prevails in the sporting context.

The 1988 Super Bowl XXII in San Diego provided a stage to challenge this belief of racial intellectual superiority. The Washington football team was competing against the favored Denver Broncos. The Broncos were led by the star QB John Elway, who epitomized the supposedly ideal QB: White, pocket passer, poised, reader of defenses, and ability to lead. The Washington team was led by Doug Williams, whose football pedigree was the antithesis to his opponent's: product of a historically Black college, dual threat runner or passer, and, most importantly within the context of the ideal QB, he was Black. Could Williams destroy years of racial ideologies and the hegemonic racist practices that prevailed in professional football? His presence alone was a challenge to the dominant social order and historical conventions of the National Football League (NFL) and a revolution to the belief in the inferiority of people of African descent.

Williams' performance is considered one of the best Super Bowl performances of all times. In the 42-10 upset of the Broncos, he finished the game completing 18 of 29 passes for 340 yards with four touchdowns. His performance was a significant blow to the myth of the intellectually inferior Black athlete, especially as it relates to the QB position. It took this stellar performance for many football fans, coaches, and owners, who once held the belief that Blacks were unfit to be QBs, to question this previously held belief. Williams' presence and performance also contributed to the long legacy of Black QBs that came before him (e.g., Fritz Pollard, the first Black NFL QB; Joe Lillard, George Taliaferro, Willie Thrower, Marlin Briscoe), and it was a catalyst for the increase in Blacks in QB positions, especially in major college football and the NFL. For example, in 2020, 10 of the NFL's 32 starting QBs were Black. Collegiate and professional coaches and general managers are moving beyond seeing the Black QB as an option QB or additional running back but as a viable leader and an offensive threat as a pocket passer.

One way of decolonizing the mind from believing in the myth of Black intellectual inferiority, which suppresses Black leadership in the NFL, is high visibility of Blacks excelling in leadership positions in sports as managers, athletic directors, and commissioners, similar to how they have and are overcoming this myth on the playing fields. The ultimate way of decolonizing the mind is the deconstruction of the myth of White supremacy. The verdict White supremacy has cast upon Black people, which judges them to be incapable or intellectually inferior, creates a lifestyle of having to prove one's capability and legitimacy—a burden of Blackness in a system of White supremacy. Therefore, the path to overcoming racial biases for Doug Williams was a process of working against racist ideologies by proving them false, intentionally or unintentionally.

This pattern of destructing myths has often been replicated in sport leadership positions, whether it is in coaching winning percentages, winning at the championship games, or in being an effective administrator. The deconstruction of racist and sexist ideologies has in part rested upon marginalized group members' abilities to overcome barriers and prove themselves capable despite oppositional beliefs. Just like Doug Williams' performance cemented his legitimacy as a QB, sport leaders of color, including women, have a similar lived experience of fighting for access and legitimacy.

The system of **patriarchy** has created opposition for women to express themselves fully in sporting practices. Women's trajectory in sport has followed the path symbolized in Doug Williams' Super Bowl performance. Women have had to overcome misconceptions, myths, and beliefs about physical abilities and leadership capabilities to gain access in this industry. Again, a way of generating the process of **decolonizing** the mind from believing in the myth of male superiority is visibility of women who have excelled in sports leadership positions as managers, athletic directors, and coaches. Similarly, the ultimate way of decolonizing the mind from the infection of patriarchy is the destruction of the myth of male superiority.

This chapter explores how sport can be used to address the need for decolonizing the mind of racial and patriarchal beliefs to address systemic and institutionalized oppression. Sport has proven to be a site of resistance to gain access and legitimacy and to achieve equity and equality for marginalized groups. It will also address where and how truth and reconciliation need to occur in sport.

White Supremacy in the Post–Civil Rights Era

Having a Black or Brown face in a high place does not justify or guarantee racial progress. Cosmetic changes in the racial demographics of leadership have canvased this nation, reaching the highest office with the two-term presidency of Barack Obama. His presence, passion, and persistence toward change provided significant symbolic empowerment, but his presidency did not move the needle much in terms of substantive change in decreasing anti-Black racism. As a matter of fact, according to the FBI's 2018 hate crime statistics, this nation has seen a 17 percent increase in reported incidents of hate crimes, where 46 percent of these incidents were motivated by anti-Black racism (U.S. Department of Justice, 2018). In 2019, according to an FBI report, hate crimes increased nearly 20 percent under the Trump administration (figure 13.1). We have also witnessed the radicalization and weaponization of White supremacy as demonstrated by recent police murders of over 215 Black people, comprising 28 percent of people killed by police while making up only 13 percent of the population (Mapping Police Violence, 2020) (figure 13.2).

The eight years of hope that 44th President Barack Obama engendered was torn from this nation with the four-year presidency of #45. During #45's reign as president, this country witnessed an increase in marginalized groups expressing their frustrations through protest and organizing. The #MeToo movement, originally created by Tarana Burke in 2006 to seek justice for issues of sexual harassment and sexual abuse, saw a resurgence in 2017. The Black Lives Matter movement was birthed after the repeated murders of unarmed Black men and women by police officers or Whites posing as guardians of White neighborhoods (e.g., George Zimmerman and the murder of Trayvon Martin or the murder of Ahmaud Arbery by Travis McMichael). The four-year reign of #45 radicalized White male supremacy and exposed festering wounds this country has ignored. His reluctant departure from the White House, accompanied by the internal terrorist attack on the U.S. Capitol by White and

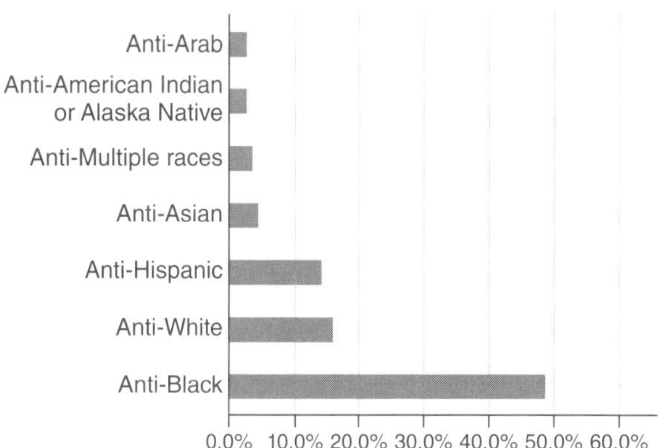

FIGURE 13.1 Hate crimes increased nearly 20 percent under the Trump administration.

Adapted from Federal Bureau of Investigation, *FBI Releases 2019 Hate Crime Statistics* (2019). https://www.fbi.gov/news/pressrel/press-releases/fbi-releases-2019-hate-crime-statistics; https://ucr.fbi.gov/hate-crime/2019/topic-pages/incidents-and-offenses

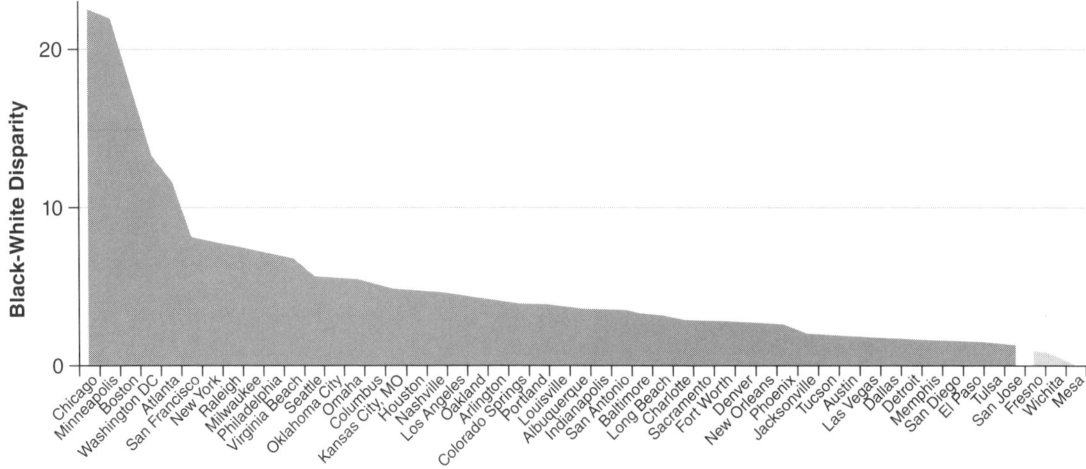

FIGURE 13.2 Black people make up 28 percent of people killed by police while making up only 13 percent of the population.

Reprinted by permission from Samuel Sinyangwe (2022). https://mappingpoliceviolence.org.

male supremacists and supporters of making America "great again," highlights a segment of this nation's population that refuses to accept change.

Sport is a microcosm of society that reflects and reinforces its dominant ideologies, and sport leadership continues to face challenges of advancing, accepting, and promoting diversity, equity, and inclusion. Especially at the professional and collegiate levels and in the sports of football and men's and women's basketball, where Blacks make up a significant percentage of the athletic labor force, there is inertia in diversity, equity, and inclusion materializing. Undeniably, the **Civil Rights Act of 1964** and **Title IX of the Education Amendments of 1972** laws have moved the moral compass of this nation. Each has had its impact on improving racial and gender equity conditions in the institution of sport. However, legislating morality is only part of the equation of advancing this nation toward reaching its potential in recognizing and accepting that all people are created equal, with inalienable rights. Thus, there is plenty of room for improvement in sport and the broader society.

The decolonization of sport leadership spaces has involved the relinquishing of power by White males, specifically, as a result of people of color fighting for access and legitimacy. Remnants of **colonization** linger where power is centralized into the hands of a few. It has taken these forms of legislation to shift the power dynamics and challenge various forms of institutionalized oppression within the institution of sport.

Institutional Oppressions: Institutional Racism and Sexism

Carmichael and Hamilton (1967) provide examples of how these concepts operate in the following scenario:

> *When white terrorists bomb a black church and kill five black children, that is an act of individual racism, widely deplored by most segments of the society. But when in that same city—Birmingham, Alabama—five hundred black babies die each year because of the lack of proper food, shelter and medical facilities, and thousands more are destroyed and maimed physically, emotionally and intellectually because of conditions of poverty and discrimination in the black community, that is institutional racism. When a black family moves into a home in a white neighborhood and is stoned, burned or routed out, they are victims of an overt act of individual racism which most people will condemn. But it is institutional racism that keeps black people*

Legislating is only part of the equation of advancing this nation toward reaching its potential in recognizing and accepting that all people are created equal, with inalienable rights.
Jim Davis/The Boston Globe via Getty Images

locked in dilapidated slum tenements, subject to the daily prey of exploitative slumlords, merchants, loan sharks and discriminatory real estate agents. The society either pretends it does not know of this latter situation or is in fact incapable of doing anything meaningful about it. (p. 4)

Institutional racism is a product of White supremacy and operates at the macro or systemic level to oppress, in this case, Black people, whereas overt racism manifests at the micro-level. Both have negatively impacted the entry and persistence of non-White people in sport leadership positions.

Hiring practices in collegiate and professional sports are examples of institutional racism, where White men are predominantly represented in leadership positions on and off the field. The Institute for Diversity and Ethics in Sport under the leadership of Dr. Richard Lapchick has provided data in the form of Racial and Gender Report Cards since the early 2000s that track the racial and gender demographics in collegiate and professional sports (TIDES, 2021). The numbers of Black head coaches and administrators in collegiate and professional football and basketball remain dismally low despite the fact that these sports are heavily populated with Black athletes.

Another form of institutional racism in sport can be found in the historical practice of stacking, or position centrality, where certain racial groups, in the sport of football for example, have dominated certain positions based on preconceived racial beliefs and ideologies. Much of the research on stacking dates back to the '70s and '80s and focuses on football, basketball, and baseball. The premise of stacking is that certain positions can be classified as either "thinking" or "nonthinking" positions. The thinking positions are generally the leadership positions in the sport, such as quarterback in football (see opening scenario sidebar) or pitcher in baseball. The nonthinking positions are positions that are more reactive, require less cognitive skill, and place a premium on physicality, such as running back in football or outfielder in baseball (Leonard, 1987). The root of this practice is grounded in colonial ideologies about race and racial abilities, specifically the racial beliefs about the intellectual superiority of White people and the intellectual inferiority but physical superiority of Black people or people of African descent. This form of institutional racism has ultimately had an impact on Black people getting into leadership positions beyond the field as coaches and administrators, because a sport's thinking positions generally lead to the sport's leadership positions.

Similarly, as a product of male privilege, **institutional sexism** limits opportunities for women in sport leadership positions and in positions of power and leadership in the broader society. This nation has finally elected its first woman vice president in Kamala

Sport Industry Diversity Initiative

RACIAL RECKONING IN INTERCOLLEGIATE ATHLETICS

In an effort to address the dismal representation of non-White people in leadership positions, the National Collegiate Athletic Association (NCAA) created a presidential pledge in 2016, intended for presidents and chancellors at colleges and universities to show "the pledge and commitment to promoting diversity and gender equity in intercollegiate athletics" (NCAA, 2020b, para 1). According to NCAA's demographics database for 2018-2019, Whites comprise 85 percent of directors of athletics and head coaches in men's sports across all three NCAA Divisions (NCAA, 2020a). A need exists to increase racial and gender diversity in leadership positions throughout NCAA divisions.

The NCAA positions this pledge as a shared value statement for member institutions and the presidents and chancellors who sign on, and each higher education official signing it "pledges to specifically commit to establishing initiatives for achieving ethnic and racial diversity, gender equity and inclusion, with a focus and emphasis on hiring practices in intercollegiate athletics, to reflect the diversity of our membership and our nation" (NCAA, 2020b, para 1). As of September 2020, most member institutions have presidents and chancellors who have signed the pledge: Division I, 82.8 percent; Division II, 73.8 percent; Division III, 75.8 percent (NCAA, 2020b). Those who sign on have access to a toolkit of best practices and "other resources to assist in their diversity and inclusion efforts" (NCAA, 2020b, para 6).

The NCAA is a member-led organization, where it purports that its member institutions create the rules and policies that govern college sports. Therefore, this "pledge and commitment to promoting diversity and gender equity" was a creation of its members. The challenge of adhering to this pledge and commitment depends on many of these institutions being able to overcome their storied histories rooted in slave profiteering, segregation, and the denial of educational access and opportunities to African Americans, specifically. The challenges include deconstructing the "good ol' boy" system where White male masculinity has been the premium in leadership positions. Power Five conferences like the Southeastern Conference (SEC) or Atlantic Coast Conference (ACC), each with several schools in former Confederate states, are finally increasing the number of Black people in the athletic directors' positions. As of 2021, for example, Dr. Carla Williams is athletic director at Virginia, Candice Storey Lee at Vanderbilt, Nina King at Duke University, and Allen Green at Auburn. The first Black athletic director in the SEC was not hired until 2003, with David Williams at Vanderbilt and Damon Evans at Georgia in 2004.

The path to fulfilling this pledge and commitment will be challenging for some of the NCAA members and smoother for those institutions that have sought to embrace a culture of diversity, equity, and inclusion for their highest levels of administration, for faculty and staff, and their student body.

Harris. The time it has taken to accept and elect a woman to this office speaks to the power institutionalized sexism has had in restricting women's access to the position of the second highest executive branch officer in the U.S. federal government. Vice President Kamala Harris has persisted against institutionalized sexism to become the highest-ranking woman in this country's history. Also of significance is that she is the first person of African and Asian descent to become vice president.

In the context of intercollegiate sport, despite Title IX legislation, institutionalized sexism is prevalent. According to Acosta and Carpenter's (2014) 37-year longitudinal national study, 90 percent of women's teams were coached by women prior to Title IX legislation. By 1978, this percentage had dropped to 58.2 percent, and by 2014 only "43.4 percent of the coaches of women's teams are females" (Acosta and Carpenter, 2014, p. 18). A similar pattern is seen with women in athletic director positions. Acosta and Carpenter (2014) illustrate that during the year Title IX was enacted, 90 percent of athletic directors over women's programs were women, whereas in 2014, women only represented 22.3 percent of athletic directors. Despite the increase in women's participation in sport, women's presence in leadership has not mimicked their participation patterns.

Several theoretical explanations undergird hegemonic masculinity, which creates barriers to leadership for women in college athletic leadership positions. In summary, they are homologous reproduction, social role theory, role congruity theory, and **intersectionality**.

- *Homologous reproduction* is "the tendency for the dominant group to preserve that dominance by 'systematically reproducing themselves in their own image'" (Stangl & Kane, 1991, p. 50).
- *Social role theory* is "the idea that society has different expectations for men and women" (Buzuvis, 2015, p. 276).
- *Role congruity theory* "explains why jobs deemed to require communal characteristics are seen as more appropriate for women, while jobs seen to require agentic characteristics are deemed appropriate for men" (Buzuvis, 2015, p. 276).
- *Intersectionality* informs how "stereotypes about race and sex orientation intersect to magnify the barriers to entry experienced by those who are or are perceived to be minorities in additional ways than sex" (Buzuvis, 2015, p. 276).

These theoretical explanations are only a few of the lenses scholars have used to view hegemonic masculinity's manifestations in creating barriers for women in sport leadership. They also provide insight into the challenges women in sports leadership positions have overcome to obtain and maintain a presence in athletic leadership positions. Both institutional racism and sexism are products of historical ideologies of non-White people and women. Despite these oppressive institutionalized practices, sport has been, to some degree, an emancipatory structure and a site of resistance to dominant forms of institutional oppression.

Sport as a Site of Resistance and Reconciliation

It has been over 100 years since the ratification of the 19th Amendment, which gave women the right to vote, and 50 years since the passage of Title IX legislation, which is still working to improve both racial and gender conditions within educational institutions receiving federal aid. It has been over 150 years since the 13th Amendment was ratified to abolish slavery and the passage of the 15th guaranteed voting rights to African American men. As alluded to earlier, the election of former president Barack Obama was a monumental first in placing a Black face in the highest office in the United States. In the context of sport, in 2020, the Washington NFL team hired its first African American president, Jason Wright, and the National Hockey League's Florida Panthers hired its first African American assistant general manager in Brett Peterson. In 2021, Houston, Texas, one of the most diverse cities in the United States, has three Black men as head coaches of three of the city's professional sports teams: David Culley with the Texans (NFL), Stephen Silas with the Rockets (National Basketball Association [NBA]), and Dusty Baker with the Astros (Major League Baseball [MLB]). There has been a similar pattern of an increase in racial diversity in intercollegiate athletics, where there is an increased representation of Black men in head coaching positions, athletic directors, and as conference commissioners in Power 5 conferences.[1] For example, in January 2020, Kevin Warren became the first Black commissioner of a Power 5 conference—the Big Ten Conference.

We are also witnessing many firsts for women moving into leadership positions and positions that have been held exclusively by men in the industry of sport, specifically, and in the broader society, in general. African American women and women of other non-White races are moving into spaces of power previously dominated by White men. In sport, Sarah Thomas became the first woman to referee in an NFL Super Bowl. Several women are coaching in the NBA (e.g., Jenny Boucek with the Dallas Mavericks, Lindsay Gottlieb with the Cleveland Cavaliers, Teresa Weatherspoon with the New Orleans Pelicans[2]); a total of 14 women have coached or are currently coaching in the NBA as of 2021. Six women have made history by becoming part of an NFL team's coaching staff. Another first is Kim Ng's employment as a general manager for MLB's Miami Marlins and the employment of several women on coaching staff for MLB teams. The NFL's Washington Football Team hired its first African American female coach in Jennifer King, and Maia Chaka has become the first African American female referee in the NFL.

This is only a sample of how sport is a site of resistance against forms of institutional oppression. Progress against institutional racism and sexism is being made at various levels. This progress has to be viewed both in terms of the excellence exhibited by the overcomers and the institutional obstacles they have and continue to overcome. Sport has and could continue to be a beacon signaling the potential for other social institutions' ability to resist social injustices and progress toward diversity, equity, and inclusion—a space for reconciliation and truth to prevail.

The nature of sport, where collective effort and teamwork are required in both individual and team sports, makes it ideal for a social justice study at the intersections of class, race, sexual orientation, religious preferences, and other marginalized identities. For example, multiracial team sports are confronted with the necessity of conformity and social interaction to achieve a desired outcome. Sport is a space where multiple social identities can converge in a team or within an athletic department, yet that does not adversely affect the unity to achieve a desired goal. Thus, unity is not disrupted by multiple social identities. Therefore, at the individual level, we can have an athletic team or athletic department consist-

Kim Ng, general manager for MLB's Miami Marlins, is Major League Baseball's first female general manager.
Michael Reaves/Getty Images

[1]The Power 5 conferences are also known as the Football Bowl Subdivision and are the highest level of collegiate athletics. They are made up of the following conferences: ACC, Big Ten Conference, Big 12 Conference, Pac-12 Conference, and the SEC.

[2]Becky Hammon was a coach with the San Antonio Spurs but in 2022 was hired as the head coach of the WNBA's Las Vegas Aces.

ing of a multiplicity of expressions, such as race, ethnicity, and socioeconomics, united to achieve one goal and win championships. At the community level, we can have, for example, a predominantly Black athletic team, cheered on by a predominantly White audience, at an institution with a history of segregation, united around a common interest. This practice is repeated at the state and national levels, where multiplicity does not trump unity in the context of sport. This is the beauty of sport and its power as a space of and for reconciliation. This is the truth of sport, and this is the message that must prevail.

Sport Industry Leader Profile

Niya Blair Hackworth

Title: Director of Inclusion at the NCAA Office of Inclusion

Education: BA in English, University of Central Arkansas; MEd in education (with an emphasis in higher education) from the University of Arkansas. Blair Hackworth is pursuing a doctorate of education in organizational leadership at Abilene Christian University.

Niya Blair Hackworth became a part of the NCAA Office of Inclusion team in August 2019 after spending over a decade working at institutions of higher education. As the director of inclusion, Blair Hackworth leads, partners, and assists in diversity and inclusion related initiatives, focusing on race and ethnicity and college athletes with disabilities, for member institutions and the national office staff. Before joining the NCAA, she served as the inaugural director of the Center for Diversity and Inclusion at the University of Houston, where she provided leadership, strategic vision, organization, and administrative oversight of campus-wide initiatives, training, and programs in the areas of diversity, equity, and inclusion. Blair Hackworth has also worked at three other institutions of higher education in the areas of social justice, diversity, leadership, and minority male programs. She presents at national and regional conferences and for campus and community organizations in the areas of inclusion, intercultural competence, and leadership. Blair Hackworth is a qualified administrator of the Intercultural Development Inventory, a tool that measures intercultural competence (Office of Inclusion, 2021).

Blair Hackworth's passion for working in diversity and inclusion has been to advocate for marginalized people by using her voice for those who have been deemed voiceless. She finds her current role invigorating because she is an advocate for college athletes. She says this is stimulating and challenging because athletes express multiple identities, not just an athletic identity, and their voices should be recognized. Her role stretches across three divisions (NCAA Divisions I, II, and III) among a variety of institutions with varying missions and philosophical approaches. In this capacity, Blair Hackworth also works with college athletic staff and coaches to further their understanding of diversity, equity, and inclusion through educational opportunities and initiatives. Blair Hackworth is the primary liaison to the NCAA Minority Opportunities and Interests Committee.

One of the significant challenges she has encountered in her work has been getting people to understand the value and importance of diversity and inclusion. This "buy-in" is critical to the realization of any diversity and inclusion initiatives. Thus, her passion lies in advocating for the marginalized and educating stakeholders of the values associated with working toward achieving diversity, equity, and inclusion in their respective organizations.

SUMMARY

White supremacy and male privilege manifested as institutional sexism and racism have prevailed throughout U.S. history, leaving their imprint through institutionalized practices of oppression. These practices seek to secure the posterity of White men, in general, by any means necessary. The manifestation of these systems of oppression in the United States is part of a larger global scheme of imperialism where Brown- and Black-skinned people have been colonized and their land extracted of its resources, and then their labor has been exploited by Europeans and their descendants. They have also worked to marginalize women and maintain their dominance of women's bodies and labor. Decolonization has been an ongoing global process where political and economic power is shifting from the hands of the powerful into the hands of the powerless. This process is not without resistance, but through protest and legislation, progress has been made.

Within the United States, there has been a resurgence of White supremacy due to its weaponization. Movements like Black Lives Matter, #MeToo, and other forms of activism have launched resistance to forms of oppression that have objectified and abused women and terrorized and murdered people of color, especially African Americans, Latinos, and Asians. These movements are descendants of the slave abolitionists, women's suffragists, civil rights activists, and Black Power activists, which span the historical landscape of the United States. They have been necessary in moving this country toward its potential of being a just and equitable nation, where all can actualize their inalienable rights of life, liberty, and the pursuit of happiness.

The history of U.S. sport has reflected and reinforced patterns of oppression. Sport history, like U.S. history, is illustrative of how women and non-White people have had to fight to gain access, legitimacy, equity, and equality as athletes and in the roles of coaches and administrators. Despite its history of aligning with the racist and sexist precepts of this country, sport in the United States has also been a site of resistance to these forms of oppression. Sport has shown its potential to be a great social experiment, where equity and equality can be fully expressed. This chapter has attempted to provide a minuscule glimpse of this possibility being fulfilled. Undoubtedly, as we move toward reaching our potential and actualizing all possibilities through the continual process of decolonizing the mind and decentering Whiteness as the indicator of superior leaders, when they see us, i.e., non-White people, women, and other marginalized groups, they will not see an anomaly or a diversity hire, but legitimate candidates and capable leaders.

CRITICAL THINKING EXERCISES

1. In considering the process of decolonizing leadership positions for women in sport, there have been structural changes due to the passing of Title IX legislation, which are fostering ideological changes, i.e., the way we think about women in sport leadership positions. Choose five examples of women in sport leadership positions and discuss common characteristics that illustrate how structural changes have fostered ideological changes.
2. In considering the process of decolonizing leadership positions for non-White people in sport, there have been structural changes due to the passing of the Civil Rights Act of 1964 legislation, which are fostering ideological changes (i.e., the way we think about non-White people) in sport leadership positions. Choose five examples of non-White people in sport leadership positions (e.g., coaches, sport administrators, general managers) and discuss common characteristics that illustrate how structural changes have fostered ideological changes.
3. When examining the concepts of institutional sexism and racism, give examples of each and discuss how sport has been a site of resistance for each.

REVIEW QUESTIONS

1. List and explain the four theoretical explanations for barriers women face upon entry into leadership and coaching positions in collegiate athletics. Give examples of how women are making strides in leadership, coaching, and other administrative roles in collegiate sports.
2. Visit the Office for Civil Rights website and list the three-prong test and discuss its purpose.
3. Identify three examples where women and three examples where non-White people are still the "firsts" in entering into sport leadership positions or positions of authority once dominated by White men.
4. Reviewing the Acosta and Carpenter (2014) 37-year longitudinal national study, discuss the changes in women teams coached by women head and assistant coaches since the passing of Title IX legislation.
5. Reviewing the Acosta and Carpenter (2014) 37-year longitudinal national study, discuss the changes in women athletic directors since Title IX legislation was passed in 1972.

Toni L. Sandys/The Washington Post via Getty Images

CHAPTER 14

Creating a Vision to Ensure Diversity, Equity, and Inclusion Within Sport Organizations

Ketra L. Armstrong

LEARNING OBJECTIVES

- Identify the various elements of culture that affect human behaviors.
- Define organizational culture and the elements that comprise it.
- Explain the various ways in which sport organizations create subcultures of exclusion.
- Discuss the reasons for failed diversity, equity, and inclusion initiatives.
- Explain the role of leadership in ensuring the vision of diversity, equity, and inclusion in sport organizations.
- Describe the steps in the process of creating a strategic plan for achieving diversity, equity, and inclusion in sport organizations.

"Number one, we're never going to change the name of the Washington Redskins." This is how Daniel Snyder, owner of the National Football League (NFL) franchise located in the nation's capital, responded to a question posed to him on October 2, 2001, about changing the name of his franchise and eliminating the Native American caricature depicted as its mascot. To Snyder, the name was their tradition (since 1933); it represented competitiveness and honor, and it was not meant to be derogatory to Native Americans. However, the more prevailing sentiment was that the name and imagery were an incredibly offensive, dehumanizing, racially derogatory, and disparaging racial slur that perpetuated stereotypes of Native Americans. They were demeaning to the cultural heritage of Native Americans, and the misappropriated mascots and branding (Whitinui, 2020) dishonored their traditions and cultural expressions. Consequently, some NFL referees refrained from working the team's games, some media professionals refused to use the name (Kilgore & Allen, 2020), and some fans discontinued their patronage of the team. But, for the most part, the organization and its consumers and other constituents continued with business as usual.

The intensity of the controversy (e.g., protests, moral challenges, and litigation) over the name and derogatory racial epithet associated with it ebbed and flowed for nearly five decades (Kilgore & Allen, 2020). As Kilgore and Allen said in the *Washington Post*, "change happens slowly, then all at once." The "all at once" change was precipitated by the racial reckoning and heightened Black Lives Matter movement in 2020 to address systemic racism. The Washington's owner faced mounting pressures from investors and sponsors (Federal Express, Nike, and PepsiCo) demanding that the word and visuals be removed. On July 12, 2020, after decades of resisting, the organization announced the removal of the name and imagery. It would later be named the "Washington Football Team." The change was met with mixed emotions, resulting in the loss of support from some of their loyal consumers (Jenkins, 2020). However, the BBC reported that Ray Halbritter, Oneida national representative and founder of the Change the Mascot campaign, commented: "This is a good decision for the country—not just Native peoples—since it closes a painful chapter of denigration and disrespect toward Native Americans and other people of colour. Future generations of Native youth will no longer be subjected to this offensive and harmful slur every Sunday during football season" (BBC, 2020). Deb Haaland, who, at the time, was one of the only Native American women in the U.S. Congress and is now serving as the U.S. Secretary of the Interior stated: "About time. It shouldn't take a huge social movement and pressure from corporate sponsors to do the right thing, but I'm glad this is happening" (BBC, 2020).

Although a critically important action, changing its racist name and imagery were not the only elements that needed changing in this franchise—it also needed an internal cultural change. There were widespread reports of sexual harassment, mistreatment, and verbal abuse of women in the organization. As one of the women reported of the harassment, "At the Washington Football Team, I felt like it was institutionalized. The ownership, or the leadership of the company, I don't think they respect women. And I don't think they saw it as a problem" (Bumbaca, 2020, n.p.). Following an extensive investigation and detailed report, the organization was fined $10 million for toxic workplace culture and was required to implement a number of protocols to improve the company culture and its treatment of women (Ushe, 2021). As the National Organization for Women commented, "Washington's football team thinks it can erase decades of racism by changing its name, and decades of sexism by firing a few executives. But women—who are pro football's fastest growing demographic—won't settle for window dressing. The toxic culture has to change—today" (NOW, 2020). For the Washington football, changing their name *and* changing their culture are imperatives for changing their organizational "game."

Creating workplaces where differences are celebrated and everyone feels valued, respected, and a sense of belonging is a challenge for many sport organizations. Although removing culturally insensitive images and artifacts and firing individual offenders are important parts of the process of ensuring organizational diversity, equity, and inclusion (DEI), sustainable change must go beyond performative measures of window dressing and requires changing toxic workplace cultures. Herein lies the primary focus of this chapter. It will equip you with the knowledge to combat and refrain from engaging in the practices that perpetuate racial denigration and sexual harassment that were endemic in the culture of the Washington organization and that also pervade other sport organizations. This chapter addresses what sport organizations need to do to create workplace cultures that enable and support the ideals of DEI. It provides an overview of the various elements of personal and organizational culture and illustrates their impact on workplace inclusion and exclusion. It discusses some ways in which sport organizations have sought to address DEI, and it highlights the role of sport leadership in DEI success. This chapter concludes with an overview of a process for creating a strategic plan to integrate and ensure a vision of DEI within sport organizations.

Diversity, Equity, and Inclusion in Sport: New Playing Field, New Rules, New Game Plan

Diversity (the variation of individual differences—demographics, ideologies, experiences, social and cultural characteristics, and others), **equity** (the fairness and justice in individuals' treatment, access to opportunities, experiences, and outcomes), and **inclusion** (an environment where everyone feels authentically accepted, valued, respected, connected, embraced, and supported, with full access to opportunities) have attained a new level of prominence in sport. The importance of diversity, equity, and inclusion (DEI) was heightened during summer 2020 with protests and demonstrations that amplified demands for social justice. On the heels of intensified social unrest, many sport organizations were pressured with demands from their various constituents (athletes, coaches, staff, consumers, and sponsors) to acknowledge and address the social injustices in society that also permeated their organizations.

However, as illustrated in the opening scenario about the Washington Football Team (now known as the Washington Commanders) and as will be revealed in Abigail Eiler's profile later in this chapter, not all sport constituents agree that social injustices exist in sport, and thus not all are supportive of sport organizations' active involvement in DEI endeavors. For instance, the Dallas Stars of the NHL reportedly lost season ticket holders—both individual and company accounts—over their support for Black Lives Matter (Ortiz-Lytle, 2020). However, the Dallas Stars' CEO and president stated that the organization stood by its decision to publicly support the Black Lives Matter movement and supported their players 100 percent. The Dallas Stars' interim coach said, "We're all against the social injustice and racial discrimination that's going on around the world. If our players think that this is the best way that they can support that, then they have our full support, and we are proud of the stance that they have taken" (n.p.).

The Dallas Stars were not the only sport entity facing this challenge; mixed support for sport organizations' involvement in DEI and social justice was and has been expressed by a number of internal and external constituents of various sport organizations (high school, collegiate, professional, and international), raising the stakes and risks of DEI involvement. Consequently, some sport organizations proceeded carefully and cautiously in their DEI responses (Jhaveri, 2020). Others actively responded to the social injustice crises by releasing statements professing their values, beliefs, and commitment to social justice and the fundamental ideals and principles of DEI. Words and images related to DEI were prominently communicated and displayed throughout the institution of sport. For instance, many sport teams were adorned in clothing and game uniforms that communicated DEI slogans and branded messages. DEI images and words were also displayed through sport organizations' social media outlets and in sport stadiums and arenas, such as on the courts of nationally televised National Basketball Association games, in NHL arenas, on the scoreboards of Major League Baseball, on soccer fields, and at various other sport venues. Advertisements and promotions for and during sport events also contained DEI related messages.

Notwithstanding some opposition and hesitancy, it seemed as though a real movement was afloat in sport for DEI. Moreover, the demands for sport organizations' involvement in DEI came from voices and actions of multicultural and multigenerational sport constituents. Be it based on their free willingness to do so or a result of pressure from internal or external constituents, sport organizations, which heretofore had largely been silent on matters of social injustice, began to acknowledge social injustices in society and within their organizations. Many of them spoke loudly and boldly about DEI through public and visible means and mediums. Without question, sport organizations' engagement in social justice activism represented a marked improvement, particularly considering their previous silence, invisibility, and lackluster involvement in the DEI space. However, although sport organizations' performative and symbolic gestures in support of DEI are notable, ensuring a vision of meaningful and lasting change requires that DEI is intentionally and strategically embedded into their systems, structures, functions, people, and places. DEI must be infused into the genetic code of sport organizations and threaded in the fabric that characterizes their ways of being and ways of doing.

We have surpassed the social-cultural-political tipping point in our world where fully embracing DEI was merely an *option* only for

Following the protests and demonstrations that amplified demands for social justice, DEI images and words were also displayed through sport organizations' social media outlets and in sport stadiums and arenas, such as in NHL arenas.
Jeff Vinnick/Getty Images

Sport Industry Leader Profile

Abigail Eiler

Title: Chief Diversity Officer at the University of Michigan Athletics Department

Education: BS, MSW, LMSW–Clinical, QMHP; Social Work, University of Michigan

Abigail Eiler is a former athlete in water polo at the University of Michigan (UM). She is now UM Athletics' chief diversity officer and director of athletic counseling, and she is a member of the Big Ten Conference's Equality Coalition. She is a licensed clinical social worker and educator with more than 15 years of experience working in tribal and nontribal communities across the U.S. and Canada. She is also a clinical assistant professor of social work at UM and teaches in Community Action and Social Change. Abigail utilizes an anti-racist framework in her work to address privilege, oppression, diversity, and social justice. In the interview, Abigail shares her insights, experiences, and perspectives as a DEI leader in sport.

What are your responsibilities as the chief diversity officer in Athletics at the University of Michigan?

As the chief diversity officer (CDO), I am responsible for facilitating and participating in consensus building activities to help develop and implement a comprehensive DE&I strategic plan for the Department of Intercollegiate Athletics at the University of Michigan. When I was asked to serve as CDO in September 2020, I inherited an existing strategic plan. The plan was meaningful but was not evoking the changes that I believed were possible in a large, diverse organization such as ours. I engaged in consensus building with existing members because it offered an opportunity for everyone to share their ideas and visions. The consensus building discussions led to newly assigned roles and responsibilities, improved steps to address existing problems with our current structure, and included a full agreement among the participants involved. This has increased individual and collective investment in the plan and has enhanced our community by improving the culture of our department. The following are other responsibilities I have as the CDO of UM Athletics:

- Overseeing and approving the athletic director's DEI initiatives
- Providing monthly updates to the athletics leadership team on DEI activities (e.g., upcoming events and resources and talking points for program or unit discussions)
- Working closely with units across campus to help create policies, programs, and professional development opportunities for our staff and college athletes
- Serving as an adviser for our student-sponsored DEI-related organizations, specifically our Wolverines Against Racism organization
- Consulting, supporting, and advancing our college athletes' health and wellness initiatives, recognizing that DEI is part of wellness and has an impact on health outcomes
- Researching and evaluating recruiting and retention practices to promote healthy engagement for college athletes from underrepresented communities
- Working with HR to explore hiring practices (e.g., unconscious bias training for hiring)

> *continued*

Sport Industry Leader Profile *(continued)*

Is it really necessary to have a strategic plan to ensure DEI in sport organizations? Why or why not?

YES!! It is important to assess what is working and what is not working. Creating a strategic plan through consensus building increases investment in the DEI goals that have been identified together—as a team. While the world is ever-changing and flexibility is important, benchmarking goals and objectives helps us determine if "what we are doing [is] helping improve our system—are we creating a more diverse, equitable and inclusive environment?"

How did you develop your strategic DEI plan? Who was involved in the planning process?

Everyone in the UM Athletics Department was invited, and 26 people participated. The plan was reviewed by our leadership team and signed by the athletic director, general counsel, and CDO. College athletes' voices were heard through focus groups, and their recommendations were included in our plan.

How do you determine the vision and values that will be included in the plan?

We did a values exercise with the participants. We used the values identified to create our goals and objectives, as well as the mission statement for our DEI plan.

What are the main elements or components of your DEI plan?

Awareness (education); hiring and recruitment; community culture (with an emphasis on breaking down silos and coming together), and respect.

What types of DEI activities or initiatives are most successful or effective?

There are a number of our programs that I am really proud of.

- We have "unity calls." This is when our college athletes, staff, and coaches come together to talk about their experiences, listen to each other, and support one another (in the good times and the difficult ones) to promote change within our community.
- We established a Women Uplifting Women network and mentorship program for our college athletes with our female alumnae.
- Our training programs—professional development and educational opportunities—have really helped people to learn about themselves and others.
- We hosted some staff visioning activities and discussions (in which 77 staff members attended) to gather more feedback, to engage in transparent and meaningful conversations, and to develop more meaningful relationships across our different programs (e.g., communications, development, medicine, coaching).
- We have created spaces for open dialogue—we want everyone to have a place where they can be heard, share information, and grow as a *team*.
- Last, we have regular DEI meetings. We meet twice a month and the meetings are open to everyone.

How do you engage the college athletes, coaches, and other administrators in your DEI initiatives?

As the CDO, I am present; I show up at meetings, practice, and competitions—not once, but as much as I possibly can. I am committed to developing relationships with our college athletes, coaches, and administrators. I rely on my cultural beliefs and values, as well as my formal social work education that fosters cross-cultural skills, such as harnessing empathy, being genuine and authentic, and meeting the individual or team where they are.

What factors are most responsible for DEI plans being successfully integrated into a sport organization's workplace (including employee policies and practices)?

A culturally inclusive environment requires mutual respect, effective relationships, clear communication, explicit understanding about expectations, and critical self-reflection.

What are the challenges of implementing and integrating DEI plans into a sport organization's workplace (including employee policies and practices)?

Not everyone believes that diversity matters or that inequities continue to exist within our current systems. DEI is not given the same priority or space as winning a game in sport organizations. Many people are too uncomfortable to engage in a conversation because they feel unprepared, uninformed, or worried about what others may think. The stigma related to anti-racism efforts continues to affect the level of change and support that is received, and it is a barrier to reaching the change that is possible. Organizations still have a way to go to reach cultural and linguistic competency and establish a space where everyone feels respected and included. Sports is still heavily led by men—there needs to be more balance and inclusion of women and nonbinary people making decisions. Putting a focus on DEI and the creation of DE&I positions will hopefully create more opportunities for minorities to get their foot in the door and a seat at the table.

What advice would you give others who are currently working in a sport setting and struggling with addressing DEI in their workplace?

Go to people who won't come to you—build up relationships. Make sure that your strategic plan is known, and create space (educational opportunities and discussions) to explore it. Make it interesting—we often make everything very, very serious—is there something that can be a celebration to increase involvement?

What advice would you give to others who are aspiring to hold a similar position related to DEI in sports (like chief diversity officer, director of DEI, etc.)?

Build your network, promote your niche, and be willing to embrace conversations that lead to change—we do not always hear ideas we agree with, but do we listen? And when we listen, do we respond in a way that accepts the wider scope of beliefs and attitudes? Remember that acceptance is not always about approval; it is also about reality, and that looks different for people. We will not always agree, but we can be respectful and find common areas to work on together that improve who we are individually and collectively.

Is there anything else you would like to share about ensuring a vision of diversity, equity, and inclusion within sport organizations?

Continue to show up—every day. Continue to create opportunities—every day. Continue to have hope—every day.

forward-thinking sport organizations. Instead, fully embracing and achieving the ideals of DEI is a *requirement* for any sport organization that wants to succeed within the social, cultural, economic, and political milieu in which sport operates. The profound impact of recent social movements dramatically challenged and changed the way in which sport organizations must operate. What is more, the importance of DEI will continue to increase, given the increased diversity of sport constituents (i.e., its workforce, athletes, consumers, communities, and host of business partners), and society's increased appetite and demands for diversity, equity, and inclusion. Sport organizations now find themselves on a new and different playing field. They are required to play a new game with new rules. As such, there is a critical need for a new game plan. And, in the new game plan, a successful DEI program is what *winning* looks like.

Culture: It's About People and It's About Places

Embarking on the type of process that Abigail Eiler described to successfully integrate DEI within sport organizations requires a fundamental understanding of culture. Culture is a complex phenomenon and a dynamic processing system. Hall (1981) professed that there is not one aspect of human life that is not touched, influenced, or altered by culture. He concluded that culture is the medium through which humans live. I profess that culture is also the medium through which successful DEI initiatives must be realized.

Culture Is Personal

Personal culture is broadly defined as a way of life; an accumulation of learned behaviors that distinguish members of a society, that represent groups they identify with, and that include the group's symbolic expressions and what the group thinks, values, says, and does (Carr-Ruffino, 2009; Park & Huang, 2010; Testa & Sipe, 2013). We are all products of our learned culture through our cultural heritage. The reference groups to which we belong (based on our race, ethnicity, tribe, gender, sexual orientation, age, education, social class, religion, ability, nationality, and other identifiers) influence our culture. We live and express our lives through cultural nuances, and we often see the world not as *it* is, but as *we* are—through the lenses of our culture.

One way in which elements of culture have been explained is through the visual image of an iceberg, illustrating that there are visible and invisible elements of culture (figure 14.1). The tip of the iceberg pertains to the surface elements of culture (i.e., food, clothing, hairstyles, language, and physical appearance) that are visible and readily discernible. On the underside of the iceberg is a mass of cultural differences and dissimilarities unseen, unheard, unwritten, and unspoken (e.g., our values, attitudes, motivations, beliefs, perceptions, ideologies, assumptions, orientations). Be they seen or unseen (the tip of the iceberg or the mass underneath), culture exerts a pervasive impact on our lives.

Culture shapes our collective programming, serves as our mental map, and offers lenses through which we view reality. Therefore, it influences us in wide-ranging ways: our thoughts and perceptions; what we think is important; how we associate with others; how we play; what we value; our priorities; how we communicate; how we act, behave, and express ourselves; and more. Culture also directs our attention, influences our ideologies, activates our cognitive structures, shapes our consciousness, is motivational, is emotional, elicits affect, and energizes and directs our behavior (Cox, 1994; Park & Huang, 2010). Different cultures have different values, beliefs, expectations, assumptions, orientations and ways of operating in the world.

Carr-Ruffino (2009) surmised that "culture hides much more than it reveals, and what it hides, it hides most effectively from its own members" (p. 29). Oftentimes we are not aware of the extent to which our culture influences our lives, including those hidden effects that pertain to how we approach our work. It is often not until we are in conflict with the norms, customs, and traditions of someone from a

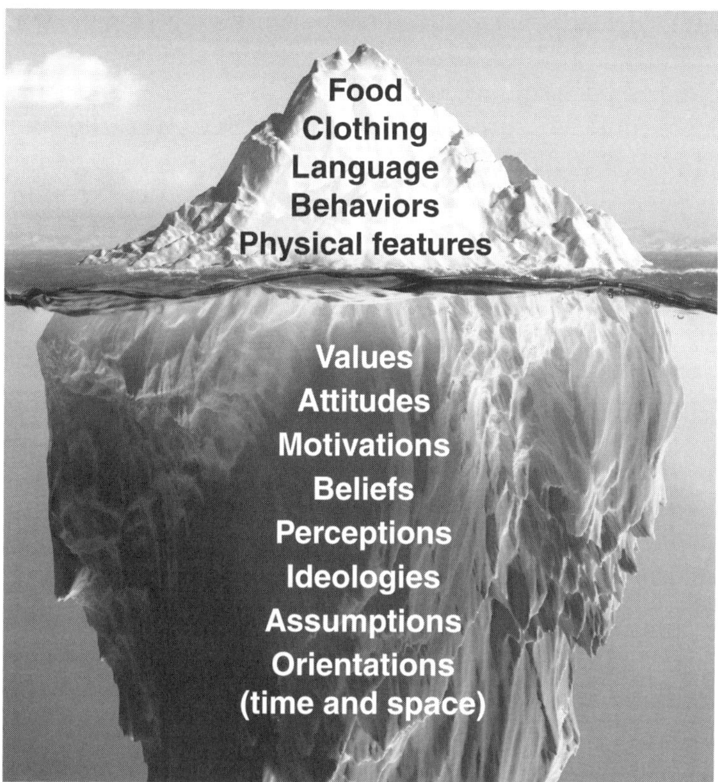

FIGURE 14.1 Elements of the cultural iceberg.

different culture that we become more mindful of the uniqueness of our own culture. We have long been taught the Golden Rule, to treat others as *you* would like to be treated. But a new lexicon is required, and we are now asked to instead practice the Platinum Rule: Treat others as *they* would like to be treated. Successfully integrating DEI into sport organizations requires individuals to have a self-awareness of their personal culture and a willingness to understand how culture affects others.

Culture Is Organizational

Although culture is personal, culture is also crystalized in organizations (Carr-Ruffino, 2009). Moreover, culture is posited as something an organization *has* and something an organization *is* (Testa & Sipe, 2013). Although there are many varied definitions of **organizational culture,** it is posited here as the collective norms, values, expectations, behaviors, belief systems, and artifacts (images, symbols, narratives, etc.) that define or represent the charisma or personality of an organization. Deal and Kennedy (1982) identified five aspects of organizational culture:

1. The organization's business environment
2. The values or norms of behavior shared by members of the organization
3. The individuals identified by the organization
4. The rites and rituals employed by the organization to reinforce the values and norms of behavior
5. Communications and the management of the cultural network that sustains the organization's culture

In sum, organizational culture is the collective imagery, interaction, and integrative environment created by people, policies, practices, principles, products, and place.

As discussed previously, every person is a product of their culture. Individuals do not customarily leave their culture outside the door of their workplaces. Instead, their culture enters with them and informs and influences their workplace aspirations, performance, and overall job satisfaction in subtle and profound ways. Thus, be it expressed or implied, the cultural penchants of individuals comprising an organization influence the cultural pulse of their respective organizations. Because organizations consist of "cultured" individuals, it stands to reason that the cultural values, norms, and expectations of individuals in positions of power and influence become reproduced, reified, normalized, collectively shared, and codified in the different policies, practices, principles, assumptions, and procedures that govern the organizations. Therefore, organizations serve as a cultural repository and a portal for the collective human culture of individuals therein.

Schein (1992) also offers an apt description of organizational culture.

> *[Organizational culture is] a pattern of shared basic assumptions learned by a group as it solved its problems of external adaptation and internal integration which has worked well enough to be considered valid and therefore, taught to new members as the correct way to perceive, think, and feel in relation to those problems. (p. 12)*

Schein's definition amplifies the role of assumptions as fundamental to an organization's culture. It addresses the collective belief systems and values that lead to assumptions about how an organization works and how its internal systems operate. As Testa and Sipe (2013) suggest, assumptions made by an organization help to clarify its culture because they communicate and convey the sentiments of "the way we do it" or "how things are done here." Assumptions of culture are dispersed, expressed, and implied in various demographic and ideological ways. Moreover, elements of culture are deeply entrenched at the micro (individual), meso (group), and macro (system or institutional) organizational levels.

Organizations often codify and objectify their culture in branded symbols, images, and narratives (be they visual or auditory) that represent and convey salient elements of their cultures. For sport organizations, this is often accomplished in the imagery and meanings conveyed in team names, mascots, slogans, and logos as objective markers and representations of their culture (Armstrong, 2013). For instance, the Washington Redskins logo and the NASCAR Confederate flag elicited and evoked sentiments of racial hatred and denigration, and they were branded elements that were associated with those respective organizational cultures. Ensuring the integration of DEI within sport organizations must therefore consider the various tangible and intangible narratives, symbols, and markers that convey and communicate culture. However, managing the personal, human elements of culture as situated within an organizational context is the most critical element of DEI success, and is the primary focus of this chapter.

The presence of **cultural homogeneity** (preponderance of cultural sameness) or **cultural plurality** (preponderance of cultural difference) throughout an organization creates an **organizational climate** (the metaphoric temperature of an organization relative to how it feels to work there—e.g., warm and accepting or cold and unwelcoming). Organizations that reflect limited cultural diversity are considered **monocultural** (the normalizing of one common culture), whereas those that represent various forms of cultural diversity are considered **multicultural** (the normalizing of multiple diverse cultures). Organizational cultures become brand markers in and of themselves, and they are often the defining characteristics of organizational workplaces. You may recall from the opening scenario in this chapter that a "toxic organization culture" was a defining feature of the Washington Football Team. Successfully integrating DEI within sport organizations requires a cultural responsiveness to create respectful multicultural workplaces that celebrate cultural plurality. This is the most important and most challenging feat to actualizing DEI.

Working While Cultured

The cultural issues and tensions in society are also present in sport organizations. Thus, sport workplace settings are microcosms of a multicultural society. Personal and organizational cultures intersect in work environments and influence how sport organizational practices often challenge the cultural orientations of the employees and how individuals experience their workplace cultures. Cox (1994) offered some functional ways personal and organizational culture intersect to affect the workplace experiences:

- *Time orientation:* Some individuals in an organization prefer linear time (such that time occurs in phases of past, present, and infinite future). Others prefer circular time (time does not stretch into the future but is in the past and present, occurring in repeated cycles), while others prefer procedural time (in which time itself is treated as irrelevant because the behavior is activity-driven and takes as much time as needed for its completion). Individuals' time orientation influences various workplace practices such as the scheduling of appointments, adherence to fixed start and end time to meetings, and approach to long or short-range planning.
- *Space orientation:* Space orientation involves physical space (such as physical location of office, workplace spatial arrangement, the presence of walls, and workplace architecture) and personal space (such as personal norms of touching, closeness, and privacy). As Cox indicated, violation of space norms can cause individuals psychological discomfort at work.
- *Leadership style orientation:* Some people prefer a task-oriented leader (where accomplishing the task is the primary focus of the leadership style), while others prefer a relationship-oriented leader (which is leadership with an emphasis on relationship building). Some cultures prefer a democratic leadership style (which is more participatory in nature and involves multiple individuals in the process), while others prefer an autocratic leadership style (which is more authoritarian in nature with one individual controlling organizational decisions). Incongruence rooted in different cultural orientations for expected and preferred leadership styles may affect workplace performance.
- *Individualistic and collectivist orientations:* Employees with an individualistic cultural orientation prefer to work in a manner that is autonomous and self-reliant and that allows them some independence at work. On the other hand, individuals with a collectivist cultural orientation are likely to be more group-oriented (focusing on the needs and goals of the group), and desire interdependent work settings. These cultural differences affect workplace performance and the manner in which teamwork and individualism are preferred, embraced, and rewarded in a workplace.
- *Cooperative and competitive orientations:* Although individuals from some cultural groups prefer a cooperative approach, others are more competitive. This affects their approaches to tasks and their interactions with others in the workplace. It also affects how they value their work and how they want it valued.
- *Locus of control orientations:* Individuals from different cultures have different orientations that allow them to make sense of their life and work experiences. While some believe that the locus of control for their accomplishments and opportunities for advancement is external, others believe it to be internal. This affects their expectations, motivations, work ethic (the energy and effort they exert), and overall level of job satisfaction.
- *Communications style:* Individuals from different cultures have different styles of expressing and communicating information. Such differences are manifested verbally and nonverbally and in communications delivery, responsiveness, meanings conveyed, and interpretations. Miscommunications due to cultural misunderstandings dramatically affect the quality and nature of individuals' organizational experiences.

These are just a few ways in which cultural orientations in sport organizations may lead to workplace conflicts. Although individuals are often more readily judged in their workplaces by elements of their surface culture (race, gender, age, appearance), I hope it is clear how and why it is actually the elements of culture on the underside of the iceberg where the substantive challenges of ensuring a vision of DEI lie. Successfully integrating DEI into an organization requires a keen understanding of the myriad subtle and profound ways in which culture affects workplace dynamics, processes, and procedures. It is therefore important to keep in mind that organizations are "cultures at work." Additionally, personal values are typically greater motivators of people than organizational values (Izzo & Vanderwielen, 2018). Because the workplace is such a meaningful personal-professional space, successfully integrating DEI requires that artifacts, styles of engagement, and other personal modes of expressing culture are recognized and encouraged as long as they are not in violation of sport organizations' core values, principles of integrity, codes of conduct, and workplace civility; and do not adversely affect performance. For instance, while an employee may have a procedural time orientation as an element of their culture (where a project has no definite end date), organizational effectiveness may require a definite timeline for project completion. In this case, the employee will need to adapt their cultural orientation to time for organizational success.

Cultural Exclusion: I'm Out

> *We all live under the same sky, but we don't all have the same horizon.*
>
> *Konrad Adenauer*

As illustrated in the previous section, cultural diversity may lead to different and often conflicting ways of experiencing an organization's workplace culture. When cultural differences are not well understood or appreciated, they lead to cultural clashes; relationships, experiences, and encounters that are unfair, unpleasant, stressful, and unhealthy; and stereotypical thinking, prejudicial feelings, and discriminatory actions (Carr-Ruffino, 2009). Since we often fear the unfamiliar or that which we do not understand, the complexity of the cultural diversity individuals bring to a sport organization is often met with rejection, creating inequity and sub-cultures of workplace exclusion. Consequently, employees from culturally underrepresented groups often experience a range of culturally derived personal oppressions, leading to marginalizing workplace encounters. Structural and systemic organizational cultural exclusion also leads to occupational exclusion and a lack of access to information and networks that affects career mobility, opportunities, and experiences:

- *Glass ceiling:* The invisible barriers that keep culturally underrepresented individuals underrepresented and in lower level management positions (Bartol, Martin, & Kromkowski, 2003; Davis & Maldonando, 2015; Ng & Sears, 2017).
- *Glass cliff:* The overrepresentation of culturally underrepresented individuals in risky, underperforming, and/or precarious positions (e.g., low salaries, limited opportunities for promotion, low authority) that perpetuate negative stereotypes and discrimination (Cook & Glass, 2013).
- *Glass escalator:* The process by which individuals from the majority culture benefit from workplace advantages that allow them to be overrepresented in leadership positions in organizations that are widely populated by individuals from the underrepresented culture (Williams, 2013; Wingfield, 2009). For instance, while women who work in male-dominated sport organizations (such as the NFL) often experience a *glass ceiling* that prevents their ascension to top leadership positions, men who work in predominately women's sport settings (such as the WNBA) often benefit from the *glass escalator* allowing them to climb (or escalate) to top leadership ranks.

There are instances when individuals may **culturally mask** (covering or hiding stigmatized aspects of their authentic cultural identity, cultural orientations, lifestyles, values, or behaviors) to conform to organizational cultural norms or to attain the attributes needed to feel included in the mainstream organizational culture. Thus, cultural exclusion may be variable or transient. For instance, individuals can change their food or music preferences to fit the cultural preferences of their colleagues. Individuals can also change their orientation to time, or their preference for task-oriented or relationship-oriented leadership to fit the broader organizational culture. However, in other cases, the sources of cultural exclusion are fixed, unchangeable, unattainable; they cannot be masked or covered. The exclusion is more permanent. For example, individuals cannot/do not change their race, ethnicity, sex, or religion to fit the predominant culture of their organization.

Moreover, feelings of inequity and exclusion in an organizational workplace culture are often devastating because it is a setting individuals do not have the freedom to avoid. Thus, the consequences of systemic inequity and organizational cultural exclusion are often distressing because they affect individuals' livelihood and overall well-being. Although under the same "workplace sky," individuals from underrepresented cultural groups often have a very different view of their "workplace horizons." Ensuring a vision of DEI within sport requires abolishing the issues, structures, and systems of inequity and exclusion clouding workplace possibilities.

Cultural Inclusion: All In

> *We need to give each other the space to grow, to be ourselves, to exercise our diversity. We need to give each other space so that we may both give and receive such beautiful things as ideas, openness, dignity, joy, healing, and inclusion.*
>
> *Max De Pree*

Sport organizations that are committed to DEI must realize and appreciate the vibrancy that cultural diversity allows. Brown (2016) recounted an inspirational commentary she read from a blogger who defined this vibrancy.

> *Diversity is about going for the awesome in life instead of settling for what you're comfortable with. Diversity is about each individual maximizing their impact on the world, instead of trimming their personal stories—the traumas, the talents, the struggles—down to fit some imagined mold. (p. 40)*

If you think of diversity as referring to *who* is allowed to maximize their impact in an organization, then think of equity and inclusion as referring to *how* the organization is supporting the "awesomeness" of each individual (with access and opportunity, voice, feeling of belonging, and sense of connection to maximize their potential without cultural masking) that the blogger referenced. It is important that **equity** (the fair and just treatment for all to eliminate existing disparities) is not used interchangeably with **equality** (the same treatment for all, while not acknowledging existing disparities). Inclusion should also not be mistaken for the concept of **assimilation**. Assimilation is the process in which members of an underrepresented group or culture adopt and accept the values, behaviors, and beliefs of the culture of the majority group, often at the expense of their cultural distinctiveness (Pless & Maak, 2004). In contrast, inclusion recognizes, appreciates, and leverages the individual differences that cultural diversity boasts.

As Cox (2001) surmised, "the challenge of managing diversity is to create conditions that minimize its potential to be a performance barrier while maximizing its potential to enhance organizational performance" (p. 4). When cultural differences are understood and respected, the result is effective cross-cultural relationships that (1) widen and deepen individuals' perspectives, offering them alternative worldviews, and (2) foster more productive individuals and teams (Carmeli & Spreitzer, 2009; Carr-Ruffino, 2009). Thus, equity and inclusion make the composite whole greater than the sum of its diverse parts. In fact, when equity and inclusion are achieved, the organizational whole is greater *because* of the sum of its diverse parts.

Regarding inclusion, Ferdman (2014) encouraged us to see inclusion in a broader sense beyond the individual level. He offered a multilevel framework that also posited inclusion as

- an interpersonal behavior (concerning interrelations among and between people in the organization);
- a group-level dynamic (i.e., group norms, organizational collaborations, and collective group experiences);
- leadership (i.e., the roles, responsibilities, and behaviors of leaders that create inclusion); and
- organizational attributes (i.e., the organizational policies and practices that foster, cultivate, and celebrate a climate of inclusion).

Successfully integrating DEI requires its entrenchment throughout the multilayered ecosystem of sport organizations. Please refer to the sidebar "Every Voice Is Heard and Everybody Belongs" for an illustration of how one sport organization, the Dallas Mavericks, sought to entrench DEI throughout their organization.

Diversity, Equity, and Inclusion in Sport: Leadership Matters

It is important to understand the manner in which organizational dynamics influence leadership; however, as the sidebar on the Dallas Mavericks illustrate, it is also important to recognize the role of leadership in shaping and influencing organizational dynamics. **Leadership** is an interpersonal and behavioral process whereby an individual influences and motivates others to achieve certain goals (Northouse, 2004). Leaders play a critical, vital, and essential role in fostering, encouraging, and promoting a diverse, equitable, and inclusive organizational culture (Cox, 2001; Ferdman, 2014, Pless & Maak, 2004). Leaders are responsible for

- setting an organizational vision and agenda that prioritizes DEI;
- allocating resources for DEI;
- creating policies, practices, and accountability for DEI; and
- creating overall organizational culture to support DEI success.

Cox asserted that "leadership is the most essential element for change; without it nothing happens" (p. 18). Sport leaders have approached DEI in numerous ways, with varied degrees of success.

Cultural Myopia

A traditional way in which sport leaders have addressed efforts to promote fairness and equality was through a lens of **cultural myopia** (i.e., a narrow-mindedness, shortsightedness, inability, and/or unwillingness to acknowledge elements of culture). The premise was to "not see" cultural differences. After all, if sport leaders did not acknowledge seeing cultural differences, they would not have to confront the challenges of uniquely addressing them. Moreover, the prevailing mantra in the spirit of team or group cohesion was that of the melting pot metaphor. In this metaphor, different cultures were expected to melt into the pot or dissolve their cultural differences into one blend (much like the concept of assimilation), removing the visibility of individual cultural uniqueness.

Under the premise of a culturally-myopic (and thus, a culture-neutral) leadership approach, conversations about culture were muted, and individuals from underrepresented or marginalized cultural groups were encouraged and expected to mask or cover their authentic cultural identities to blend into the dominant organizational culture. This was perceived to be an equal, safe, and inoffensive approach to addressing cultural differences in the workplace. However, this is not an effective way to address diversity, equity, and inclusion, because it encourages erasure of cultural diversity. The DEI goal of sport organizations should be to see culture so that workplaces may be more

- culturally centered instead of culturally censored,
- culturally authentic instead of culturally artificial, and

Sport Industry Diversity Initiative

EVERY VOICE IS HEARD AND EVERYBODY BELONGS

The Dallas Mavericks of the National Basketball Association (NBA) were among the sport organizations highlighted at the 2021 *Sports Business Journal* conference "All In: Investing in a Culture of Representation, Equity, and Action," for the manner in which the organization has created a workplace environment where (as the slogan states) "every voice is heard and everybody belongs." However, the Mavericks did not arrive at this celebratory place organically. Instead, for decades it was a sport entity ravished with an organizational culture that was marred by gender inequity, sexual harassment, racism, misogyny, and blatant discrimination and disrespect, notably for women and people of African, Asian, Hispanic, and Native American descent. As one of the Mavericks employees commented to Deadspin sports blog: "It's a culture that's been around that long and with employees that have been around that long, it's gonna take a lot to scrub it clean." (Moskovitz, 2018, n.p.). In no uncertain terms, despite its wins on the basketball court, this was a sport organization that was losing in the game of diversity, equity, and inclusion, and it was forced take a full "time out." This was not an organization where every voice felt heard, nor was it an organization where everyone felt they belonged.

Cleaning up the cultural toxicity in the Mavericks' environment required a transformational organizational change and a redefinition of its values and expectations. It also required the people involved with the team to reimagine a new vision for ensuring DEI within and throughout the organization and extending to their various stakeholders and partners. In 2018, they boldly proclaimed that their organization would set the NBA standard for diversity and inclusion. Since then, they have been unapologetically determined with intentionality and commitment to strategically achieve this feat.

To begin, the Mavericks had to acknowledge and name the sources of toxicity that were permeating their organizational culture. They had to take full ownership of the negligence and disarray that traumatized many of their employees and adversely affected their workplace opportunities and experiences. Next, they gathered necessary information to more accurately define the nature and extent of the problems. To do so, they hired an external entity to provide an unfiltered picture of their workplace culture. After identifying the problems, they had to empower the appropriate people with the appropriate resources and authority to address them.

Enter Cynthia Marshall (an African American woman, former senior vice president and chief diversity officer at AT&T, and award-winning human resources expert) as the newly named chief executive officer (CEO). Marshall was hired by owner Mark Cuban to transform the Mavericks after *Sports Illustrated* exposed a "corrosive workplace culture" at the organization. Although she had not previously worked in a sport capacity, this was not a deficit in her professional portfolio. A more important attribute was her pedigree as a change agent with a wealth of experience with DEI and a solid record of success. These skills would prove to be invaluable when applied to the human resources initiative she would undertake in sport for the Dallas Mavericks.

Among the initiatives Marshall implemented were hiring a vice president of diversity, equity, and inclusion; instituting a zero-tolerance policy for abuse and harassment; starting a hotline for employees to report misconduct; hiring an ethics and compliance officer; establishing counseling for staffers traumatized by the toxic work environment; and developing a hiring plan that increased the number of women in senior leadership from zero to 47 percent. The changes Marshall implemented went beyond diversity and also addressed the underlying cultural issues that led to the inequity, harassment, and inappropriate conduct.

Under Marshall's direction, the Mavericks have made notable progress, guided by a clear vision and supported by a strategic DEI plan. As Marshall stated on the Mavericks website boasting about their DEI efforts: "Our inclusion strategy efforts are ongoing throughout the organization and in our community as we focus on our key DEI pillars: Customer, Reputation, Agenda for Women, Family (work, home, community), Talent, Suppliers and Sponsors. We are committed to develop training, education and recruiting through a DEI lens." Marshall's leadership is an empowering testament illustrating real and effective organizational cultural change—where "every voice is heard and everybody belongs."

- culture celebrating instead of culture surrendering.

> *Not everything that is faced can be changed. But nothing can be changed until it is faced.*
>
> *James Baldwin*

Framing the Issue . . . But Missing the Picture

To advance beyond the culturally-myopic approach, a number of other "well-intended" attempts to address DEI have been implemented. Some of them have backfired, heightened cultural tensions, hindered success, and exacerbated the problem (Thomas & Ely, 1996). However, Ely and Meyerson (2000) offered an insightful summary of some framed approaches that appeared to support gender equity: "fix the woman," "value the feminine," "create equal opportunities," and "challenge the system."

Shaw and Frisby (2006) applied these frames to sport organizations and extended Ely and Meyerson's frame of "challenging the system." They acknowledged the need to contest the deeply held assumptions, values, and practices embedded in sport organizational cultures that systemically privileged and empowered certain groups. They also addressed the need to concurrently recognize the intersections at which gender-related oppressions occur within sport organizations and called for a challenging of the narratives that position gender equity and organizational effectiveness as competing interests.

Shaw and Frisby's (2006) application of Ely and Meyerson's (2000) frames for achieving gender equity in sport are akin to and, thus, appropriate lenses for critiquing approaches to DEI in sport organizations more broadly. Therefore, I have relabeled and adapted the essence of the frames to address cultural marginalization in sport organizations.

1. *Frame one: Fix the culturally marginalized.* In this approach, sport organizations posit cultural differences as skill set deficits. Therefore, the solution is to "fix" individuals who are culturally marginalized with training and skills to emulate the cultural majority. It presumes that the skills of the cultural majority are the most desired skills.

2. *Frame two: Value the culturally marginalized.* In this approach, sport organizations appear to recognize cultural differences by celebrating the traits of individuals from culturally marginalized groups. However, this approach is based on false overgeneralizations and further marginalizes people into what is deemed "culturally acceptable" (i.e., culturally appropriate) roles.

3. *Frame three: Create equal opportunities.* In this approach, sport organizations seek to address structural constraints and create equal opportunities for culturally marginalized groups. Title IX (for gender equity), the premise of affirmative action policies (for racial equity), and other legal mandates are the bases for these practices. However, such approaches—albeit laudable in attempt—have yielded very little DEI success because the policies alone are not enough to change structural conditions.

4. *Frame four: Challenge the system.* In this approach, sport organizations seek to address DEI by dismantling the underlying imbalances of cultural power that lead to cultural oppression and marginalization. In this approach, systems and assumptions that reinforce cultural dominance and perpetuate cultural marginalization are challenged and contested. This process would also address the intersections at which cultural oppressions occur within sport organizations and challenge the narratives that position DEI and organizational effectiveness as competing organizational interests.

While frames one, two, and three appear to support DEI, in actuality they undermine the premise of what they purport to accomplish. Frame four—challenging the system and power structure that perpetuates and sustains cultural marginalization—is the frame from which DEI should be integrated in sport organizations.

Adler (1986) also offered some approaches to DEI. Each of these has also been evident in sport organizations, to varied extents:

- *Parochial:* Cultural differences and their impact on the organization are ignored ("My way is the only way").

- *Ethnocentric:* Cultural differences are noticed, but the ways of others are seen as inferior and are viewed as only causing problems ("My way is the best way").
- *Synergistic:* Members believe that a combination of various approaches is best ("My way and their way differ, and we can learn from each other"). This is the ideology needed to support the integration of DEI within sport organizations.

Cox (2001) found that there were three main factors as underlying reasons DEI programs failed or yielded disappointing or ineffective results.

1. *Misdiagnosis of the problem.* The lack of representation in an organization by individuals from a particular sociocultural identity and the lack of sensitivity to those identities were often considered the problems DEI needed to address. While these factors were contributors to the problem, the more significant issue was that the organizational culture was often a toxic and troubling environment that would not support and sustain a diverse and inclusive culture.

2. *Employing the wrong approach.* Given that the problem of DEI has generally been diagnosed as insufficient diversity, the approach to solutions has largely focused on increasing diversity representation by changing what Cox referred to as "inputs to the system." However, as Cox asserted, since elements of the systems within an organization are interrelated, changing the inputs (i.e., recruiting for more diversity among the workers) without changing other corresponding elements of the system (e.g., policies, practices) will do very little to promote real and sustainable DEI change. As Brown (2016) proclaimed, "Companies can hire voraciously to fix their lack of representation, but an inclusive culture that embraces all differences is the way that organizations can actually keep that talent . . . diverse talent . . . will not stick around to be excluded" (p. 73).

3. *Misunderstanding of the learning curve.* An organization's failure to understand the process, evolution, and shape of the learning curve for leveraging DEI work was the third cause Cox (2001) identified for failing to meet the challenges of DEI. Obtaining the necessary knowledge and skills to master DEI work (i.e., the dynamics of culture and the complexity of human behavior) requires a patient, sustained, and methodical effort. Cox also opined that many organizations have a naive notion of the process required for obtaining the necessary competencies to institutionalize DEI and change the organizational culture accordingly.

Creating a vision to bring about DEI within sport organizations requires a careful diagnosis of the problems to derive appropriate solutions. Although it may feel as though they are racing against the clock regarding integrating DEI, sport organizations must invest the time, energy, learning, and resources to obtain the necessary capacity and commitment required for real and sustained DEI changes.

Transformational Leadership: An Imperative for Sport Organizational Change

> *It's easy to get duped into thinking that the only important moments of purpose congruence are the big ones, those that directly affect the course of project, produce, service, or company's overall goodwill. . . . But day-to-day, moment to moment, it is the small ways we lead and operate that show who we are, what we believe, and how we support our purpose. . . . it is in these moments that a culture is shaped.*
>
> *Izzo & Vanderwielen, 2018, p. 77*

Thomas and Ely (1996) long contended that there is a distinct way to unleash the power and benefits of DEI in a workplace. I contend that the distinction lies in leadership. Leaders must be at the fore of the metamorphic changes required to integrate DEI within sport organizations. Pless and Maak (2004) affirmed that leadership for DEI is a social process and a relational and interactive task. Leaders must be inspirational and aspirational in their approach. The type of leadership employed to ensure DEI in sport organizations will play a vital role in its success.

Two broad classifications of leadership are transactional and transformation. **Transactional**

leadership focuses on the exchanges (such as rewards and punishments, and informational, personal, physical, and financial resources) that occur between the leaders and their followers (Lussier & Kimball, 2014; Northouse, 2004). **Transformational leadership** refers to the process whereby a leader engages with members of the organization and creates connections that inspire and raise the level of motivation and morale among the leader and the followers (Northouse, 2004). Moreover, transformational leadership is a process defined by personable, affective, and visionary leadership. It affects individuals at a deeper and more emotional, spiritual, and value-laded level (Lussier & Kimball, 2014; Northouse, 2004).

Transformational leaders are genuinely concerned with developing their followers to perform to their fullest potential. Northouse (2004) identified four factors defining transformational leadership:

1. Charisma or idealized influence (a quality that makes individuals want to emulate and follow them)
2. Inspirational motivation (their high expectations and symbolic appeal that inspires and motivates the commitment and high achievement among their followers)
3. Intellectual stimulation (their encouragement of followers to be creative and innovative)
4. Individualized consideration (the creation of organizational climates that support the needs of the followers)

Compared to transactional leadership, transformational leadership has resulted in higher aspirations, greater effort, performance beyond expectation, lower turnover and absence, and greater job satisfaction (Lussier & Kimball, 2014; Northouse, 2004). Moreover, transformational leaders empower followers and nurture them through change and raise the consciousness of their followers to transcend their own self-interests for the sake of others and for the good of the group or organization (Northouse, 2004).

Northouse (2004) also noted that transformational leaders are "social architects. . . . They make clear the emerging values and norms of the organization. They involve themselves in the culture of the organization and help shape its meaning" (p. 183). Furthermore, transformative leadership may also lead to transformative learning, which includes

- altered frames of reference,
- critical reflection and dialogue,
- new understandings, and
- taking action (Mezirow, 1997).

Due to their individualized consideration of the needs of their followers, transformational leaders are also more likely to exhibit the **cultural competencies** (the cultural intelligence inventory—knowledge, skills, attitude, agility, sensitivity, and humility to respond in culturally appropriate ways) necessary to promote cultural equity and inclusion.

The overarching goals of celebrating human differences, treating individuals fairly and justly, and fostering a collective sense of belonging make DEI a transformative process that requires transformative learning. While various approaches to leadership may be effective in creating and ensuring a vision of DEI, it is my contention that transformational leadership holds the highest potential for success. Traits of transformational leaders are the traits that are most likely to facilitate trust, connectedness, engagement, and commitment necessary for DEI success within sport organizations.

Thriving With Culture: DEI Is What Winning Looks Like

Inclusivity means not "just we're allowed to be there," but we are valued. I've always said: smart teams will do amazing things, but truly diverse teams will do impossible things.

Claudia Brind-Woody

The business (i.e., economic or profit-driven) case for diversity and inclusion has long been used to justify the need for organizations to engage in DEI initiatives. However, the real business case of sport should be the utilization of its most valuable resources—the talents of its people—respectfully, effectively, and efficiently. This is enough, in and of itself, to justify the importance of DEI. However, there is a performance benefit as well that should not go unnoticed. **Thriving** is what happens when individuals feel a sense of purpose, excitement, and vitality for their work, leading to job satisfaction and workplace innovation (Carmeli & Spreitzer, 2009).

Individuals are more readily motivated to identify with and work in an organization they perceive as a place where they are treated fairly, belong, and can thrive as the cultured being they are. If, on the other hand, the organizational culture is one that is marred by a lack of diversity, unfair treatment, and pockets of exclusion where people experience stereotypes, prejudice, and biases, it is an organization that welcomes *surviving* instead of *thriving*. Carmeli and Spreitzer (2009) revealed that feelings of connectivity mediated the relationship between a sense of trust and thriving in organizations. They also revealed that thriving mediated the relationship between connectivity and innovative work behaviors. Individuals who are not included in the organizational culture or are required to mask their cultural identity to fit into an organization are not likely to experience the trust and connectivity that leads to thriving.

Successfully integrating DEI within sport organizations requires that organizations (1) welcome and nurture a culturally diverse talent pool; (2) inspire them with a transformational purpose and strategic vision; (3) create an equitable and inclusive organizational culture that welcomes and facilitates cultural belonging, cultural connectedness, cultural liberation, culturally authentic awesomeness; and (4) cultivate inclusive excellence. See figure 14.2.

Think of it this way. The overall goal of leaders is akin to that of a symphony orchestra conductor. The different people in the orchestra bring the essence of themselves to the stage, playing their own unique instruments with styles that only they can. The task of the conductor is to embrace the different and unique gifts and talents assembled and create a harmony in a rhythm of musical oneness. This musical oneness is the sound of the orchestra thriving. Such is also the task of sport leaders. People bring their cultured selves (as instruments) to sport organizations. The goal of the leader (as the conductor) is to create an environment where all of the collective talents within the organization (packaged *in* different people and packaged *as* different people) can thrive—to a rhythm of oneness, as inclusive excellence doing amazing and impossible things.

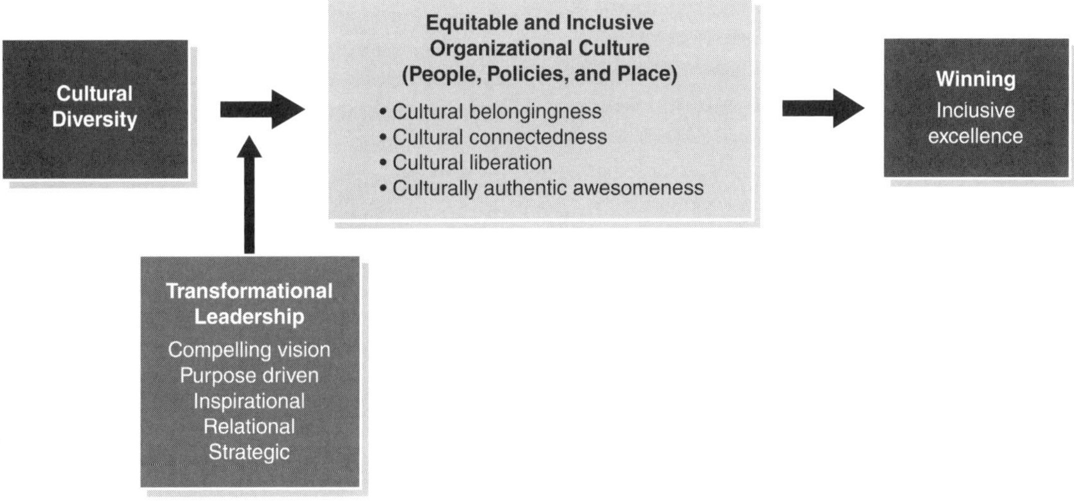

FIGURE 14.2 Winning with diversity, equity, and inclusion: Cultivating inclusive excellence.

Game On: Creating a Vision to Ensure DEI

Everyone starts a business with passion, but not everyone starts it with enough planning.

Pooja Agnihotri

So far, I have presented you with an overview of background and foreground information necessary to engage in the process of creating a vision to ensure DEI within sport organizations. Now, it is time to turn our attention to how sport organizations should use such understanding to integrate DEI into their workplaces. As Brown (2016) noted, leading cultural change requires skill and will. I would add to the front of this list the related concept of *courage*—embracing the task in spite of the likely fears. For instance, it takes courage at the outset to (1) be present in this journey of discovery, (2) fully engage in this complex and emotion-laden adventure, (3) contest long-held assumptions, (4) embrace the fear of the unknowns, and (5) acknowledge the inconvenient truths and discomfort of social and cultural injustices that DEI seeks to address. It also requires unique technical and human relations *skills* to address the harms suffered due to social injustices in the workplace, and to confront the hidden privileges that some enjoy that are denied to others. And yes, given the arduous nature of this task, it also requires a strong *will*—unwavering determination—to boldly challenge and meaningfully change organizational traditions and workplace norms that have prevented the realization of DEI.

Integrating DEI within sport organizations to celebrate differences and create conditions where everyone can thrive requires a continuous effort that is systemic, strategic, and intentional. Developing a DEI **strategic plan** (a dynamic document or framework containing analyses, strategies, and tactics addressing where an organization is, where it wants to go, and how it plans to get there) exponentially increases the likelihood of DEI success. There are various elements in a DEI strategic plan, and they may differ based on the nature of the sport organization. However, generally, most successful DEI programs engage in the following processes while creating a DEI strategic plan.

Establish DEI Leadership

As discussed previously in this chapter, leadership is critical to ensuring DEI success. Therefore, establishing DEI leadership is one of the first steps in creating a plan to ensure the integration of DEI within sport organizations. This begins with appointing an individual to lead the DEI initiatives. It is important that the title of the DEI leader conveys the power and prestige equivalent to leaders of other organizational departments or units. The DEI leader should be a part of the organization's C-suite or executive team—where critical organizational discussions take place and decisions are made. In addition to identifying a leader, the organization should create and determine the structure of a DEI office, define the roles and responsibilities of the DEI personnel, and determine the personal, informational, physical, and financial resources needed.

Determine Organizational Vision for DEI

Having a clear vision for DEI lays the foundation for supporting DEI efforts. Actualizing the vision requires an understanding, application, and integration of concepts discussed throughout this chapter. This process requires sport organizations to (1) acknowledge the need for DEI; (2) develop a compelling vision that illustrates the values of DEI; (3) socialize and facilitate the acceptance of the vision of DEI; and (4) engage in practices to manage the actualization of DEI. See figure 14.3 for a summary of the process of ensuring a transformative vision (Pless & Maak, 2004) of DEI within sport organizations.

Convene a DEI Planning Team

DEI requires a comprehensive team effort. Moreover, convening an inclusive planning team is the most effective way of securing

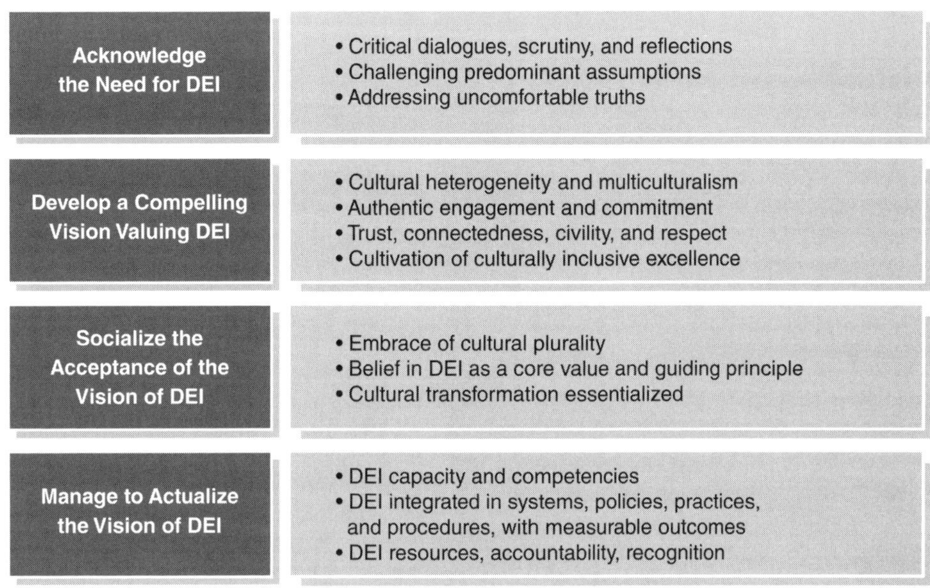

FIGURE 14.3 Ensuring a transformative vision of diversity, equity, and inclusion within sport organizations.

institutional buy-in to the vision, support for the process, and mobilization of the workplace community for DEI success. The DEI team members should include representatives from various constituent groups such as top, middle, and entry level managers; staff; coaches; athletic support personnel; athletes; alumni; and others.

Gather and Analyze Data

The DEI plan should be based on comprehensive data about the sport organization's constituents, its internal culture and climate, and its external environment. This is the most important aspect of the planning process, and it may be accomplished in a variety of formal and informal ways. Such data may be obtained via surveys, interviews, focus groups, and a cultural audit, along with critically reviewing internal data (such as policies, handbooks, reports, consumer data, sales data, and other data within the organization). Data may also be obtained from informal conversations, town hall meetings, and listening tours with various constituents.

The data collection process should yield some important information and valuable insight to help develop the DEI plan. It should offer plausible answers—and perhaps even generate more plausible questions—to the following questions:

- What does DEI look like in our organization?
- What should DEI look like in our organization?
- What are the sources, patterns, and overall nature of diversity defining our organization?
- What groups or identities are well represented throughout our organization and why? What groups or identities are underrepresented and why?
- Where is DEI present in our organization and where is it invisible (which departments, units, positions)?
- What systems, policies, and practices are supporting DEI, and which ones are challenging or contesting DEI?
- Which voices and experiences are empowered and elevated in our structure? Which ones are silent and marginalized?
- How does it feel to work here?
- What are we doing right? What are we doing wrong? What needs improving?

The data collection process should culminate in an analysis of the strengths (internal conditions that are favorable to successfully integrating DEI within the organization), weaknesses (internal conditions that are unfavorable to successfully integrating DEI within the organization), opportunities (external conditions in the environment that are favorable to successfully integrating DEI within the organization), and threats (external conditions in the environment that are unfavorable to successfully integrating DEI within the organization). This process is referred to as a **SWOT analysis**. The DEI plan should be designed to maximize the strengths and opportunities and minimize the weaknesses and threats, for successful integration of DEI within the organization. The results of the data gathering process and the SWOT analysis should be summarized in the plan.

Develop Strategic Actionable Items

Specific DEI goals and objectives to determine the strategic thrusts guiding the planning process should be developed. **Goals** pertain to the broad statements regarding what the organization hopes to achieve relative to DEI. **Objectives** are specific, measurable, achievable, realistic, and time-bound action items that propel the organization toward the stated goals. The DEI strategic plan should contain action items that state (1) the overall goal and strategic DEI objective, (2) measures of success, (3) specific action item(s) to accomplish the objective, (4) person(s) responsible, (5) resources needed, and (6) time for completion. Table 14.1 shows a sample section of a DEI strategic plan for inclusive staff recruitment and inclusive communications.

The action items are the heart and soul of the DEI strategic plan. Successful DEI plans include a combination of structural, functional, symbolic, and performative action items. The following are some DEI planning principles:

- *Integration:* Every unit within a sport organization must be accountable for contributing to achieving the DEI goals and objectives and upholding the organizational values of DEI. DEI plans should contain action items for various systems, networks, units, and functional areas within the sport organization (e.g., marketing, communications, finance and business operations, facilities and event management, human resources, development, athlete support services). DEI plans should also address the various workplace structures, policies, and procedures that create inequities (such as hiring practices, promotion processes, performance reviews, salary inequities, family and child care allowances, climate micro and macroaggressions).
- *Segmentation:* DEI plans should not be designed as one-size-fits-all. Instead, they should be customized to address the unique needs of segments of their constituents. For instance, some action items should be specifically developed for athletes, coaches, staff, and administrators, for new or longer termed employees, and for alumni.
- *Education:* To help create capacity and widespread engagement in this process, and to flatten the steep learning curve, DEI plans should include required participation in educational and training endeavors (workshops, seminars, speaker series, etc.) to support organizational learning and promote shared understanding.
- *Affiliation:* The creation of intraorganizational support (e.g., job shadowing and mentorship programs) and affiliated networks should also be a part of DEI plans. Cultural affinity, ally, and advocacy groups are also unique ways to create community to support DEI success.
- *Celebration:* Although DEI plans should address the critical areas that need attention, they should also build in some fun activities for individuals in various stages along the DEI continuum to learn about and celebrate DEI.

Approve, Socialize, and Market the Plan

Once the DEI plan is created, it should be reviewed by the organization's legal office to ensure that the items it contains are legally permissible. After approval is obtained, the

TABLE 14.1 Sample Excerpt of Strategic Diversity and Inclusion Action Plan

Goal and strategic objective	Measures of success	Action items	Person(s) accountable	Resources needed	Time of completion
Goal: Inclusive staff recruitment Objective: Progressively increase the diversity represented among our current staff	Measurable increase in diversity representations in staff application pools	Require search committees to participate in unconscious bias training prior to search process Require search committees to report on the action items engaged in to secure a diverse applicant pool	• Human resources • Search committees • DEI leaders/staff • Others TBD	Dates, times, costs, and registration logistics for available unconscious bias trainings Access to HR best practices manual for search committees	Continuous, for each position of hire within the organization
Goal: Inclusive communication Objective: Remove any organizational communications that are culturally insensitive or inappropriate	All organizational print, electronic, and material artifacts are free of culturally inappropriate or culturally insensitive content, images, narratives, and inferences	Review all print and electronic communications (brochures, reports, website, social media, audio broadcasts, etc.) to ensure they contain no culturally insensitive or culturally inappropriate images, narratives, and inferences Perform a cultural audit throughout our workplace's settings and physical spaces to review all signs, images, and material artifacts to ensure there are no culturally insensitive or culturally inappropriate images, narratives, or inferences	• Marketing director • Sports information director • Facility manager • DEI leader/staff • Others TBD	Access to all print and electronic marketing and communications materials and organizational artifacts Access to all organizational workplace settings and physical spaces	Continuous review Constantly monitored

plan should be socialized (via presentations, meetings, events, etc.) among the organizational members to familiarize them with the elements of the plan and to build consensus for supporting the plan. Lastly, DEI should have a significant visible presence and should be marketed and promoted widely throughout the organization (e.g., on the website, in print and electronic materials, in the signage and artifacts in the buildings and physical spaces, etc.). Many sport organizations have elevated their positioning of DEI in their organizations by branding it on premium items and with unique slogans, images, and apparel that represent their DEI value statement. See figure 14.4 for a branded DEI example.

FIGURE 14.4 University of Michigan Athletics' branding of DEI (equality)
David Berding/Getty Images

Implement the Plan

DEI plans should clearly identify the resources (personal, financial, informational, physical, or otherwise) needed to implement the action items. They should also address how the success of the action items will be determined, who will be responsible for leading the endeavor, including how accountability will be ensured, and a timeline by which the action item should be completed. The DEI planning team should constantly monitor the implementation process and make any needed adjustments. However, implementing the DEI plan should not be the responsibility solely of the DEI planning team, but it should involve everyone in the organization, integrated into their regular roles and responsibilities.

Evaluate the Plan

The DEI plan should undergo constant and continuous evaluation for feedback, to make necessary revisions, and to monitor its progress. Sport organizations should engage in formative evaluations (throughout the year) and summative evaluations (annually, at the end of the year). Diversity-driven, equity, and inclusive behaviors and contributions should be acknowledged and rewarded (Pless & Maak, 2004). Given the challenges of transforming an organizational culture, mistakes are bound to happen. As such, it is important to recognize the missteps along the way. Meaningful apologies, humility, and honesty for mistakes made during this process are critical to long-term DEI success.

Although the elements in the DEI strategic planning process are presented in a linear manner here, they do not have to occur sequentially. For instance, positioning, evaluating, and promoting the plan occurs continually throughout the process. Moreover, the objectives and action items and the resources needed must be flexible and responsive to organizational situations and environmental conditions. Last, the plan should not be considered fixed but should be a living document—iterative, dynamic, and amenable to necessary change.

SUMMARY

"Being able to recognize and promote the uniqueness of different groups of a diverse workforce is not only acknowledged as instrumental in improving performance, but also an imperative that organizations can no longer choose to ignore" (Vohra & Chari, 2015, p. 324). So, what does it take to successfully integrate DEI into sport organizations? As this chapter has conveyed, it requires an acute and discerning understanding of personal and organizational culture and their intersecting impact on workplaces; a mindfulness of the challenges and misstep approaches to DEI; inspirational, aspirational, and visionary transformational leadership; and a DEI strategic plan.

The features in this chapter—the professional profile of Abigail Eiler, the chief diversity officer at UM, and the sidebar about Cynthia Marshall, the CEO of the Dallas Mavericks—are illustrations of DEI success. Both cases elucidate (1) a fundamental understanding of personal and organizational culture; (2) the importance of correctly diagnosing DEI problems and devising appropriate solutions; (3) the role of transformational leadership; (4) the need for systemic integration of DEI throughout the organization; (5) the importance of consensus building, having critical dialogue, and training; and (6) the necessity of having a strategic plan.

We know that the world needs sport (for social, cultural, psychological, and economic reasons). And sport needs leaders who have the courage, skill, and will to (1) acknowledge the myriad ways in which sport organizations convey their culture internally and externally, (2) recognize cultural exclusion in the workplace, (3) eradicate workplace injustices, (4) promote employees' cultural empowerment, and (5) foster transformative sport organizational cultures that embody the ideals of diversity, equity, and inclusion.

CRITICAL THINKING EXERCISES

1. Discuss why "under the surface" elements of culture present the greatest challenges to DEI success.
2. Discuss four ways in which personal and organizational cultures intersect in a sport workplace.
3. Select a sport team or organization. Try to find out whether it has a DEI plan. If so, what are the components of the plan? Does the plan appear to be integrated throughout the organization? Are the DEI measures both performative and structural? How would you assess the overall nature of the plan? Why?

REVIEW QUESTIONS

1. List three surface elements of one's personal culture.
2. Discuss what cultural masking is in the context of DEI.
3. Discuss some of the reasons for failed or unsuccessful DEI programs.
4. Compare and contrast how transactional and transformational leaders may embrace the task of ensuring a vision of DEI within sport organizations.
5. List and discuss the steps in creating a DEI strategic plan.

CHAPTER 15

Using Sport as a Platform for Lasting and Significant Social Change

Akilah R. Carter-Francique

LEARNING OBJECTIVES

- Define and understand social change in the context of sport and society.
- Describe power and how sport organizations have used it to promote marginalization.
- Discuss the purpose and benefits of critical theory and social change.
- Define the three sensitivities and explain ways they can be employed to promote diversity, equity, and inclusion and social change.

In the spring of 2020, the world was met with the incredible challenge of change with a historical series of events. The coronavirus (which causes COVID-19) pandemic led government officials to order local communities, cities, states, and countries to shelter in place and stay at home, an action that disrupted societal norms, daily routines, and personal interactions (World Health Organization [WHO], 2020). Then, on May 25, 2020, 46-year-old George Floyd, an African American man, was killed in Minneapolis, Minnesota. His death was preceded by his arrest for allegedly using a counterfeit bill (Maxouris, Hanna, & Almasy, 2020). Derek Chauvin, a White police officer with the Minneapolis Police Department, knelt on Floyd's neck for what was found to be 8 minutes and 46 seconds after Floyd was already handcuffed and lying face down. Chauvin's actions led to Floyd's death and the subsequent resurgence of the Black Lives Matter movement. Activists, organizations, and businesses responded with renewed efforts toward diversity, equity, and inclusion (DEI) (Lankes, 2021; Le Poidevin, 2020; Taylor, 2021).

The confluence of events forced change. Our greater society viewed and experienced, in real time, a shift in daily routines, a reallocation of energies, and the necessity to navigate social spaces with caution. Sport as a microcosm of society was also forced to change. Sport participants, sporting spaces, and professional sport managers had to adjust to state, federal, and international guidelines and mandates while simultaneously challenged to provide the service of sport—fueled by public demands and situated in its elevated significance within capitalism and the global economy.

Athletes demonstrated that they are more than athletes. They demonstrated that they are viable members of society with knowledge, networks, and the financial means to bring forth aid and relief. New Orleans Saints football player Malcolm Jenkins said the following:

> *There's a lot of need and I think as athletes we have the ability to advocate for people. . . . Some people want to keep sports simply about sports and that's that, but there's also a consciousness behind it that sports have a larger responsibility to society that feeds it. . . . That mentality needs to switch and that starts with league leaders and our country's leaders to be able to come together not only with a national plan but a way to really galvanize people and give hope. (LoRé, 2020)*

Jenkins' sentiment was shared by many athletes and supporters who view sport as more than merely play and entertainment, but also as a viable institution to promote social change.

In this chapter we will demonstrate the ways that sport can serve as a platform for lasting and significant social change. Throughout this chapter, definitions will guide our understanding of social change complexity, theoretical frameworks will be shared to discuss organizational change and social change, and the concept of sociological imagination will be explored to identify how athletes and others can serve as advocates and activists in the promotion of social change.

Social Change, Critical Theory, and Power

> *Not everything that is faced can be changed, but nothing can be changed until it is faced.*
>
> *James Baldwin*

James Baldwin, an American essayist, novelist, playwright, poet laureate, and activist, recognized that facing the realities and problems of our society is necessary for change to be possible (Peck, 2016). As a cultural critic in the 1960s, 1970s, and 1980s, Baldwin used his pen, paper, and voice to amplify his analysis of society. Sport managers, professionals, and scholars should face realities and think critically when broaching the conception of diversity, equity, and inclusion within sport organizations.

Social Change

Invoking a critical perspective is important to promote social change. **Social change**, in the field of sociology, is defined as "the alteration of mechanisms within the social structure, characterized by changes in cultural symbols, rules of behavior, social organizations, or value systems" (Wilterdink & Form, 2021). These cultural symbols, rules of behavior, social organizations, and value systems serve to develop and maintain change within social structures. But social structures are institutions consisting of human beings who interact with each other and operate in their environments.

In sport, social change is viewed conceptually as change with intersecting factors. Slack and Parent (2006) describe the concept of change as an internal and external negotiation of area factors that include structure and systems, products and services, technology, and people (figure 15.1). Structural and systemic change in a sport organization consists of "modifications to areas of a sport organization such as its division of labor, its authority structure, or its control systems." *Products and services* are "the addition, deletion, or modification of other areas." *Technological change* is the "production process, the skills and methods it uses to deliver its services, or its knowledge base." *People* means the "modification to the way people think and act and the way they relate to each other" (Slack & Parent, 2006, pp. 239-240). Akin to social change, these four factors play a role in the culture, values, and norms of sport organizational change.

Furthermore, change is viewed as a paradox based on its developmental aspirations and capitalistic competitiveness (Peters, 1990; Slack & Parent, 2006). Slack and Parent (2006) describe sport organizations and their business practices as a management paradox in that certain aspects of management must remain constant and unchanged (output, cost, workforce) while their efforts to identify new markets and innovation efforts must evolve with the times. Thus, there is a need to identify balance in their consistency and change. Several theoretical frameworks and conceptual models explain change processes within a sport organization. For example, theoretical approaches such as institutional theory (Zucker, 1983, 1987), population ecology, resource dependence theory, life cycle approach (Kimberly, 1980) and contextual approach (Pettigrew, 1980, 1987) each address sport organizations' business of change. People are one of the factors that contribute to change,

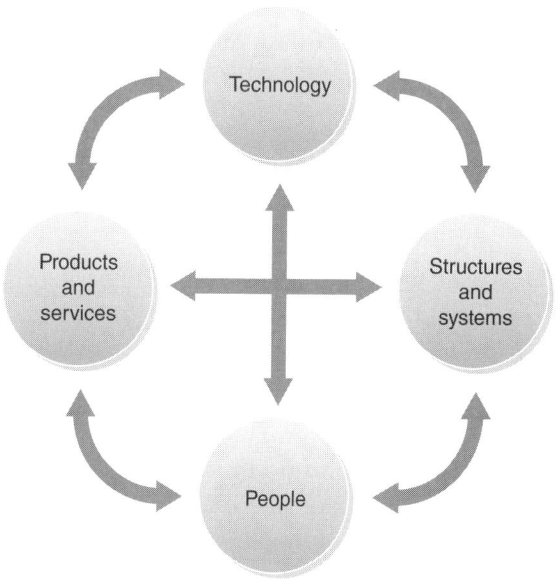

FIGURE 15.1 Potential areas of change in sport organizations.

Reprinted by permission from T. Slack and A. Thurston, "Organizational Change in Sport," *Understanding Sport Organizations: Applications for Sport Managers*, 3rd ed., edited by T. Slack, with T. Byers and A. Thurston (Champaign, IL: Human Kinetics, 2021), 317.

but the theories are limited in their ability to speak to *social* change. In the quest to promote diversity, equity, and inclusion, sport organizations need to employ theories that consider power dynamics and promote fairness and impartiality (Agyemang, Singer, & Weems, 2020; Cunningham, Dixon, Singer, Oshiro, Ahn, & Weems, 2021; Kaufman & Wolff, 2010).

Critical Theory

In 1982, Comstock ascertained that a host of theoretical frameworks (e.g., exchange theory, phenomenological approaches) have the potential to address power dynamics within organizations. Ultimately, he declared that **critical theory** had the greatest ability to examine power dynamics and the most comprehensive approach to remedying power imbalances.

> *[Critical theory] assumes that the power distributions we observe are the consequence of a dialectic between historically changing power structures and collective understandings, values, and motives. Fundamental changes in power relations occur as a result of the unintended consequences of political action. These lead to contradictions between social structures and understandings and new power structures. The critical approach retains the concepts of human intentionality and choice while recognizing the constraints of socially preformed structures and understandings. (Comstock, 1982, p. 139)*

Critical theory, a social and political movement steeped in the philosophical ideology of Karl Marx and Sigmund Freud, emerged from the Frankfurt School (Germany) in the 1930s. Critical theory, as coined by Max Horkheimer, is influential in the fields of history, literature, law, and other social sciences. It has also influenced perspectives on the role of technology, the monetization of culture, the major corporations that dominate society (e.g., monopolies, cartels), capitalism, and the decline of individualization. Through its critique and influence, critical theory seeks to explain and transform the human experience.

Critical theory consists of two central components. First, research and analysis will illuminate the truths of social phenomena. Second, research and criticism of the social structures should give reverence to the individuals' and groups' desired culture, values, and morals. Critical theory can be viewed narrowly or broadly, depending on individual interpretation. Critical theory must be simultaneously explanatory, normative, and practical. Critical theory must be explanatory to clarify what is inequitable in society. It must be normative to provide social norms for critique. And it must be practical to identify achievable goals and responses for social change. Knowledge is power; and once an individual or group (e.g., athletes) knows about its inequities, they can take action (Agyemang, Singer, & Weems, 2020; Armstrong & Jennings, 2018; Kaufman & Wolff, 2010).

Power

Indeed, knowledge is one aspect of power and within sporting structures. Sport's evolution into a social structure is meaningful because it is holistic and relational (Coakley, 2017; Sage, 1998). The relational patterns displayed within sport reflect sport's communication potential both within organizations and among people, organizations, businesses, and technology (Slack & Parent, 2006). There are multiple definitions of power. Broadly, **power** is defined as "legal or official authority, capacity, or right" and "possession of control, authority, or influence over others" (*Merriam-Webster*, n.d.). Adopting Michael Parenti's (1995) definition, power is "the ability to get what one wants, either by having one's interest prevail in conflict with others or by preventing others from raising their demands" (p. 4).

Power can also be defined as "the ability to influence others and impose one's beliefs," noting that "all power is relational, and the different relationships either reinforce or disrupt one another" (Race Equity Tools, 2020). Arguably, power is operational and can be "unequally distributed globally and in U.S. society. . . . Some individuals or groups wield greater power than others, thereby allowing them greater access and control over resources" (Intergroup Resources, 2012). Power accrues to those with economic wealth, dominant social identities (e.g., race, gender, sexual orientation), favored citizenship status, or higher levels of education. Power thrives by valuing resources that treat as "other" those persons who are without dominant and valued identities, economic means, or access to resources. Based on these definitions and hegemonic characteristics, an individual might ask how power operates in sporting spaces or how a person can promote equitable access and positive treatment without power.

Power is connected to the attainment of resources. Parenti (2011) has further comments about power:

> *Power belongs to those who possess the resources that enable them to shape and influence the actions and beliefs of others, such resources as jobs, organization, technology, publicity, media, social legitimacy, expertise, essential goods and services, organized force, and—the ingredient that often determines the availability of these things—money. (p. 4)*

In sport, power appears in organizational leaders (e.g., race and gender exploitation and hiring; see Racial and Gender Report Cards for analysis and interpretations; TIDES, n.d.), financial distribution and academic engagement (e.g., economic exploitation of college athletes; see conferences, peer-reviewed journals, *Journal of Issues in Intercollegiate Athletics*, and reports that examine issues; College Sport Research Institute, 2021; see Athlete Rights, Positions and Issues at the Drake Group, 2020), access and inclusion opportunity (i.e., athletes, historically marginalized individuals; see Sport Conversations for Change, educational toolkits at the Institute for the Study of Sport, Society and Social Change, 2021; see Redefining Disability Podcasts and Move United Magazine at Move United, 2021; see Tucker Center Talks, Distinguished Lecture Series, #SHECANCOACH Project at the Tucker Center for Research on Girls & Women in Sport, 2021; see Unified Champion Schools at Special Olympics, 2021), and policies (e.g., lesbian, gay, bisexual, transgender, queer+ [LGBTQ+]; see Athletic Equality Index at Athlete Ally, 2016). Identifying these aspects of sport participation, leadership, management, and affiliation and how power is disrupted and dismantled is of interest when instituting diversity, equity, and inclusion within sport and using sport to promote social change.

Power and Addressing Social Change With a Sociological Imagination

The concept of diversity, equity, and inclusion is defined and discussed throughout this book. This place of this concept in the management of sport, its organizations, its events and programs, and its personnel and participants is vitally important to the institution of sport and its relationship to social structures and social change. Social structures influence institutions and sport is a microcosm of society and its social structures. Critical theory can be of aid through its explanatory, normative, and practical response. Other theories also reflect a critical theory framework, like sociological imagination.

Sociological Imagination

Sociological imagination is the ability to shift from one mindset to another. It is the ability to identify the connections between an individual's personal troubles and society's public issues. In 1959, C. Wright Mills conceptualized this idea to bring forth awareness and challenge dominant sociological perspectives. *The Sociological Imagination* is a seminal reading in the field of sociology.

> *[Sociological imagination] enables its possessor to understand the larger historical scene in terms of its meaning for the inner life and the external career of a variety of individuals. It enables him to take into account how individuals, in the welter of their daily experience, often become falsely conscious of their social positions. Within the welter, the framework of modern society is sought, and within that framework the psychologies of a variety of men and women are formulated. By such means, the personal uneasiness of individuals is focused*

> *upon explicit troubles and the indifference of publics is transformed into involvement with public issues. (p. 12)*

In other words, it provides an opportunity to consider rich histories and individual and group biographies and then to find the relationships between them and contemporary society. The goal is to identify how an individual's personal troubles (e.g., cancer, unemployment, racial discrimination) are related to public social issues (e.g., morbidity rate categories, pay inequity, stereotypes).

Mills' (1959) concept eventually found a following outside of sociology, in academic disciplines, career fields, and other social and cultural institutions like sport. In *Power and Ideology in American Sport: A Critical Perspective*, George Sage (1998) welcomed a host of scholars from a range of disciplines to explicate the interplay between personal and public. In doing so, Sage (1998) illuminates how Mills' sociological imagination is relevant to a critical perspective on the role of sport and sport institutions. Sage framed the sociological analysis as (1) historical sensitivity, (2) comparative sensitivity, and (3) critical sensitivity.

Historical Sensitivity

First, **historical sensitivity** is the ability to identify historical truths, biographies, and events in order to attain a more informed understanding of contemporary issues. Employing Mills' (1959) concept of historical sensitivity is key when examining the notion of **equity**. People must examine, study, and contextualize past events to gain historical sensitivity. Identifying these histories can be beneficial in all sporting professions and roles. A participant's knowledge of social and cultural history is useful. For example, in February of 2018 after winning the NBA championship game series, the Golden State Warriors basketball team were invited to the White House for a ceremonial, celebratory visit. Coach Steven Kerr along with team members inclusive of Steph Curry and Klay Thompson did not embrace Trump's invitation and thus were disinvited. However, a mixed-race (e.g., Black, White) team lead by a White coach chose to go to Washington D.C. and visit the National Museum of African American History and Culture (NMAAHC) instead. During their visit, they took advantage and engaged with the featured exhibitions (e.g., Slavery and Freedom, A Changing America), learned stories (e.g., Artifacts of the Tulsa Race Massacre, Testimony as Literature), viewed and accessed the Curator Chat Series (e.g., Sports Leveling the Playing Field), and learned the skills and strategies when Talking About Race as characterized their experience as a fulfillment of the team's DEI initiatives (see NMAAHC, n.d.; Allen, 2016; Tracy, 2017; Estrada, 2018; Hill, 2018). While for sport managers, a knowledge of history can aid in the production and dissemination of knowledge via multimedia platforms (pamphlets, websites, social media platforms such as Facebook or Instagram) and organizational welcome centers and museums (e.g., College Football Hall of Fame, Women's Sports Museum, Wimbledon Museum), these efforts have practical use in the promotion and marketing of a team or organization to diverse cultures, education of fans and students (high school, undergraduate, and graduate students) from diverse economic classes, and solicitation of philanthropic endeavors. In alignment with Boring (1963), having a historical sensitivity is necessary because "attention to history is valuable not to predict the future, but to understand the present better" (Sage, 1998, p. 7).

Comparative Sensitivity

Second, **comparative sensitivity** is the willingness to learn about a culture and society other than your own. This sensitivity is similar to Gloria Ladson-Billings (1995, 2008) culturally relevant pedagogy in K-12 education or Larry Purnell's model of cultural competence in nursing and health care (2000, 2016). Comparative sensitivity promotes diversity awareness, a broad understanding of the human condition in other countries, and an appreciation of sport across national and global cultures. Sage (1998) contends that a comparative sensitivity "allows us to break free of ethnocentrism, or our tendency to believe that the modes of social organization and behavior in our society are somehow superior to all other cultures" (p. 7). To embrace comparative sensitivity, individuals need to look inward and acknowledge their intersectional identities. This form of analysis encourages self-awareness of intersectionality (e.g., race, sex, religion, ability) and of individual moral values, cultures, and traditions, in addition to inequitable experiences. Reflection and awareness can aid those in positions of power to consider the significance of change. Coakley (2017) intimates that "the future emerges in connection with social change, and social change is driven by the actions of people who create a reality that fits their visions of what life should be like" (p. 514). To achieve an equitable, fair, and culturally relevant future in sport and society, individuals and groups need to consider "others," or individuals and groups that have been historically disenfranchised and pushed to the margins of society based on their identity (e.g., race, ethnicity, sex and gender, sexual orientation, social class, religious affiliation, language, age, mental and physical ability, geographic residence).

Critical Sensitivity

Third, **critical sensitivity** is an inherent task of a social critic; it seeks to deconstruct social structures, social institutions, and social processes. Scholars and thought leaders have taken up this charge through their writings and texts, op-eds, books, and, following the 2020 coronavirus-influenced shift to online interaction, through virtual workshops, webinars, and conferences. The increase in virtual engagements during the pandemic has served as an opportunity to share perspectives and years of thought in a new way (i.e., moving from academic journals and member-only conferences to free, open access, no-to-low-cost registration) to individuals from diverse races, ethnicities, ages, sexualities, political perspectives, and languages. Information and insider perspectives that were once inaccessible became accessible for individuals experiencing or advocating for others with personal troubles to learn, understand, and take action. Sage (1998) deduced that critical sensitivity "empowers us with a willingness to think and act critically, to problematize conventional definitions of reality, thus ferreting out falsehoods and contradictions when they exist" (p. 8).

A challenge in cultivating a sociological imagination for diversity, equity, and inclusion can be recognizing ways to promote social change. Employing a critical lens, Mills' (1959) three-pronged analysis poses specific questions for people to learn about and understand each sensitivity (table 15.1).

Take a moment to review and analyze the series of questions. Do they support attaining the information needed to critique an individual brand, an organization, or an institution? Are there other questions of interest that can add to our contemporary understanding in the respective categories based on history, notable influencers, and events since Mills' (1959) conception of a sociological imagination? Are there additional questions that could be proposed given what we understand today about the institution of sport, its participants, its organizations, and the current state of diversity, equity, and inclusion in sport and society?

This effort of reflection (both personal and public), or audit, is a healthy activity for all sport entities, both to acknowledge change and to increase engagement, service, and profits (Slack & Parent, 2006). The proposed questions provide a starting point for the process of social change. However, organizations have resisted the process of social change to achieve diversity, equity, and inclusion. This resistance is rooted in a lack of understanding and trust, self-interest, conflicting assessments of change, and anticipated costs of change from individuals and groups.

Scholars have delineated many approaches toward the management of organizational change. In 1967, Greiner suggested a six-stage model toward organizational change (pressure and arousal, intervention and reorientation, diagnosis and recognition, invention and commitment, experimentation and search, and reinforcement and acceptance) (Greiner, 1967). Lorsch (1986) identified four steps in an organization's experiential change process that included awareness, a period of confusion, new leadership and vision, and experimentation. Archetypes (Greenwood & Hinings, 1988) and tracks (Kikulis, Slack, & Hinings, 1992) are other approaches. Several methods toward achieving

TABLE 15.1 Questions to Promote a Sociological Imagination

Sensitivity	Questions
Historical	• Where does this society stand in human history? • What are the mechanics by which it is changing? • What is its place within and its meaning for the development of humanity as a whole? • How does any particular feature we are examining affect, and how is it affected by, the historical period in which it moves? • What are the period's essential features? • How does it differ from other periods? • What are its characteristic ways of history making?
Comparative	• What is the structure of this particular society as a whole? • What are its essential components, and how are they related to one another? • How does it differ from other varieties of social order? • Within it, what is the meaning of any particular feature for its continuance and for its change?
Critical	• What varieties of people now prevail in this society and in this period? And what varieties are coming to prevail? • In what ways are they selected and formed, liberated and repressed, made sensitive and blunted? • What is the meaning of "human nature" of each and every feature of the society we are examining?

Note: See Mills (1959) chapter "The Promise" in *The Sociological Imagination* for the listing of the questions.

Based on Mills (1959).

organizational change consist of one or a combination of the following (Slack & Parent, 2006):

- Education and communication
- Participation and involvement
- Establishing change teams
- Idea champions
- Facilitation and support
- Negotiation
- Manipulation
- Cooptation
- Coercion

These managerial responses to change are valuable in planning for resistance to organizational change and still support the transition of an organizational culture.

Resistance and Social Change

Organizational change and social change are different. Social change in sport is historically promoted by outside agitators through advocacy and activism (Cooper, Macaulay, & Rodriguez, 2019; Edwards, 2018; Sage, 1998). Because social change is met with such resistance, radical change is often required to disrupt the status quo and the tradition of social injustice, inequality, and inequity that permeate sport organizations and societal institutions.

Sport participants, athletes, and sport leaders have used their platform for social change through advocacy and activism. **Advocacy** is a declaration of support or recommendation for a specific policy or cause. Often, support or recommendations carry only limited risk of jeopardizing professional or personal affiliations. **Activism**, on the other hand, is the "engagement in intentional actions that disrupt oppressive hegemonic systems by challenging a clearly defined opposition while simultaneously empowering individuals and groups disadvantaged by inequitable arrangements" (Cooper et al., 2019, p. 154-155). Examining how sports interact with public and social issues will reveal a threat of high risk and high cost to the individuals' and group's professional and personal affiliations.

Sport Industry Diversity Initiative

CONDUCT A DIVERSITY AUDIT

A diversity audit is a process to understand, identify, and provide a comprehensive review of an organization's diversity, equity, and inclusion efforts. This unbiased and reflective exercise is an important opportunity to review the mission, vision, goals, demographics, policies, programming, and services efforts inside and outside the organization.

The diversity audit can be singular, focusing on one aspect of diversity like race and racism, or comprehensive, focusing on multiple aspects of diversity that include race, social class, sex, sexual orientation, religion, ability, language, and nationality analysis. The purpose of a diversity audit is to provide the leadership and staff with information and feedback on the strengths, weaknesses, opportunities, and threats (a.k.a. SWOT analysis) of its organizational diversity. Identifying areas of strengths and weakness and the feelings of stakeholders can pose financial and personnel benefits. Financial benefits can manifest through consciously positive and mindful reactions, as well as approaches toward social issues. For example, when a social issue emerges or a social tragedy erupts, how an organization and its stakeholders respond to the issue (e.g., statement release, program action) could directly or indirectly affect the organization's financial bottom line.

The diversity audit can be a large or small undertaking depending on its size, scope, and frequency. Once the scope is identified, the areas of diversity analysis are as follows:

- *Data:* Baseline quantitative and qualitative statistics of physical representation, experiences, and perspectives of leadership, staff, and internal (e.g., sponsors, donors, service providers) and external stakeholders (e.g., participants, members, fans).
- *Policies:* Rules created to direct and reflect the mission, the practices, the strategic goals, and the culture of the organization and management at all levels of operation (e.g., hiring committees, promotion standards, acknowledgment of local, state, or federal mandates and legislation).
- *Practices:* Methods or programs that were created to promote diversity and support inclusion for staff, such as creating employee resource groups for those with marginalized identities (race, gender, sexual orientation) and activities for outside stakeholders, such as program development for low income youth or Indigenous communities.
- *Culture:* Standard that respects and reflects the presence of diverse people and groups in society as well as their interests, talents, and skill sets.

Organizations and institutions may conduct and deliver a diversity audit on their own initiative; there are ample surveys available for self-study. However, employing an independent agency that has expertise, an unbiased perspective, and no conflict of interest is a best practice to encourage. Several organizations outside and inside of the sport context specialize in this service and process. For example, an organization wanting to address a single issue like race should visit Racial Equity Institute at www.racialequityinstitute.com. For sexual orientation, see Athlete Ally at www.athleteally.org. For a comprehensive diversity audit, see Beloved Community at www.wearebeloved.org.

History of Athlete Activism

One could argue that the notion of athlete activism was birthed out of the concept of a sociological imagination based on athletes' ability and willingness to use their platforms to amplify the connection of personal troubles to public issues. Through athletes' activism actions, you can see efforts that seek to simultaneously explain their purpose, concretize social issues by sharing specific cases and data, and make the issues practical, understandable, and accessible. Often, their personal experience is a data point within the social issue. Historical accounts of athlete

Sport Industry Leader Profile

China Jude

Title: Vice President for Diversity, Equity and Inclusion at the Denver Broncos

China Jude was a collegiate volleyball player at Alabama A&M University, a historically Black university in Huntsville, Alabama. After completing her athletic eligibility and graduating with a bachelor's degree in broadcast journalism, Jude went on to obtain her master's degree in sport administration from the United States Sports Academy. During her educational journey, Jude acquired work experience in historically Black colleges and universities (HBCUs) and historically White higher education institutions' departments of athletics. Her work experiences include assistant and head volleyball coach, senior women's administrator, assistant athletic director, senior associate athletic director, and athletic director. Jude focuses on providing support for athletes' developmental needs and encouraging career development of staff members and coaches.

In 2017, Jude earned a doctorate of education in sport administration from Northcentral University. Her dissertation, entitled *A Quantitative Study of Motivations Behind Athletic Alumni Financial Giving in a HBCU* illuminates the benefits of diversity, equity, and inclusion (DEI) and cultural understanding within profit-driven organizations, fundraising efforts (e.g., encouraging giving, seeking donations). Her analysis illustrates the value of employing a critical lens in combination with a sociological imagination to understand how to encourage alumni giving and donations to HBCU institutions. Jude's DEI efforts do not end at her research skills. In 2020, she achieved certifications in employment law and in diversity, equity, and inclusion from Cornell University.

Dr. Jude's qualifications and expertise led to her appointment as the vice president for DEI for the NFL's Denver Broncos in 2021. The role is to "work closely with football, business and community leadership on diversity, equity and inclusion (DEI) strategy" (Denver Broncos, 2021). The role also involves working with departments for human resources and community development, "focusing on recruitment, hiring processes, overall workplace environment and external outreach" (Denver Broncos, 2021). The multi-interfacing role of vice president for diversity, equity, and inclusion is important for best practices for implementing DEI within sport organizations. Jude's role is also to be an advocate and activist, "leading the organization's overall DEI strategy and representing the team as an external ambassador on social justice initiatives" (Denver Broncos, 2021).

activism show that athletes represent diverse identities. They use their platforms at the professional, Olympic, collegiate, and high school levels to serve as advocates and activists. They make the personal public through protests on a host of issues (Carter-Francique, 2022; Davis, 2019; Whitener, 2021; Wulf, 2019).

- Racism (Major Taylor, Muhammad Ali)
- Jim Crow segregation (Leonard Bates)
- Gender equality (Wilma Rudolph, Chris Ernst, Kathrine Switzer, Sanya Tyler, Gregg Popovich)
- Identity and sexual orientation (Chris Kluwe, Michael Sam, Brittney Griner)
- Pay equity (Billie Jean King, Megan Rapinoe, and the United States Women's National [Soccer] Team)
- Mental health and illness (Michael Phelps, DeMar DeRozan, Kevin Love)
- Sexual abuse (The Fierce Five—Gabby

Douglas, McKayla Maroney, Aly Raisman, Kyla Ross, Jordyn Wieber)

- Racism and police violence toward Black people (Colin Kaepernick, Eric Reid, Ariyana Smith, Evander Kane, National Basketball Association, Women's National Basketball Association, Major League Baseball, Major League Soccer)
- Political ideology (Eroseanna Robinson, Mahmoud Abdul-Rauf, Gwen Berry, Race Imboden)
- Criminal justice reform (Maya Moore)

These issues of change represent a few of the social issues that athletes respond to with activism. Take some time to review the histories of these athletes, their respective sports, and their connection to the issues. Through critical analysis you may find patterns of athlete activism that encompass a time period, a certain type of organizational structure, a particular legislative policy, and a local or global experience that affects the access and treatment of participants in sport and society.

Scholars and journalists have identified various patterns of sport activism. For example, in *Race and Resistance: A Typology of African American Activism*, Cooper, Macaulay, and Rodriguez (2019) identified patterns of Black athlete activism and use of athletic platforms to promote social change. They identified five typologies:

1. *Symbolic activism:* Social awareness and structural change in the areas of economic, education, politics, and social engagement
2. *Scholarly activism:* The promotion of critical awareness through the transmission of ideas and theoretical analyses to provoke thought and understanding and to influence policy reform within oppressive systems
3. *Grassroots activism:* Broad social uplift efforts that counter hegemonic notions of engagement and that aim toward short-term goals
4. *Sport-based activism:* Actions taken by athletes to challenge or alter a specific rule or law that maintains oppressive systems, associations, or culture
5. *Economic activism:* Actions by individuals or groups to promote fiscal empowerment and social uplift in historically marginalized communities

Activism and the Olympic Games

Athlete activism has been recorded since before the first modern Olympic Games in 1896 (Blackburn-Dwyer & McMaster, 2018; Wulf, 2019). The Olympic Games have continued to serve as a space of influence and an athletic backdrop of activism and social change. (See 1906 Athens Intercalated [Olympic] Games, 1936 Berlin Olympics, 1964 Tokyo Olympics, 1968 Mexico City Olympics, 1972 Munich Olympics, 1980 Moscow and 1984 Los Angeles Olympics, 2008 Beijing Olympics, 2020 [2021] Tokyo Olympics.) This context is important for understanding how athletes have connected personal experience to social issues toward advocacy, activism, and social change.

Individual Activism

For many people, Muhammad Ali serves as a blueprint for athlete activists. His successes in the boxing ring nationally in the United States and internationally at the Olympic Games gave him the opportunity to use his platform to speak about realities, inequities, and atrocities worldwide. There are texts, films, websites, awards, and centers that give reverence to Muhammad Ali. Because of his athletic talent, long career, fame, and travel, he was able to view the invisible communities (e.g., historically Black colleges and universities [HBCUs] through donation with the United Negro College Fund [UNCF], 1967; South Africa during apartheid, 1975) and hear the silent voices (Palestinian refugee camp, 1974, "Operation Let Freedom Ring" for missing prisoners of war and missing in action, 1994) in societies and political regimes that marginalized, disenfranchised, and oppressed them. Ali knew that being a Black athlete in sport held great social power, and as the greatest of all time, the GOAT, he had the latitude, the platform, and the irresistible charisma to amplify personal troubles and their corresponding social issues (Bryant, 2019; Edwards, 2018; Montville, 2017; Zirin, 2005, 2007). Because of his continued successes and domination in the boxing ring, the media captured his performances, shared his messages, and informed the masses. In 1967, after he converted to Islam, Ali was eligible for the U.S. military draft and service in the Vietnam War. However, as a Black Muslim and conscientious objector, he protested the Vietnam War and refused to enter the military. As a result, Ali was arrested, convicted (but not imprisoned), stripped of his boxing title, and unable to obtain a boxing license in the United States for three years while his case was under appeal. At the age of 25, Ali endured extreme criticism, hatred, and ostracizing by politicians, media, sport associations, athletes, and peers both White and Black (Calamur, 2016). He won his appeal, but Ali's protest came with great cost.

Athletes before Ali and those who followed in his activist footsteps (e.g., Tommie Smith, John Carlos, Peter Norman, Mahmoud Abdul-Rauf, Colin Kaepernick, Race Imboden, Gwen Berry, Raven Saunders) sacrificed and endured personal and public pain; lost financial opportunities ranging from professional sponsorships and endorsements to basic nine-to-five employment; suffered disconnection from family, friends, and the athletic team; and faced disregard for their state of mental health (e.g., anxiety, depression, suicidal ideation) and physical health (e.g., loss of fitness, injury). For an athlete to utilize their platform to influence and promote effective social change, they have to hold some level of prominence in their sport, and either their ability or the event at which they are competing must draw the attention of a mass audience. All these components coalesced at the 1968 Mexico City Olympic Games and thrust a group of committed athletes into history.

Group Activism

While Muhammad Ali is deemed the embodiment of an athlete activist, the mid 20th century Olympic Project for Human Rights is deemed the embodiment of group, or collective, activism. The organization, which was not affiliated with the International Olympic Committee (IOC), was birthed at San José State University and nurtured in classrooms, corridors, athletics facilities, and homes (Edwards, 2017; Hartmann, 2003). Dr. Harry Edwards, former college athlete turned professor, recognized the power of sport and the analytical tool it offered to serve as a transformational agent of social change. Edwards' experiential oppression, critical analytical foresight as a sociologist, and coordinating abilities led him, Ken Noel, and a group of Black athletes to form a strategic union to demand institutional change.

The purposes of the Olympic Project for Human Rights were "to (1) stage an international protest of the persistent and systematic violation of Black people's human rights in the United States, (2) expose America's exploitation of Black athletes as political propaganda tools in both the national and international arenas, (3) establish a standard of political responsibility among Black athletes vis-à-vis the needs and interests of the Black community, and devise effective and acceptable ways by which athletes could accommodate those responsibilities, and (4) make the Black community aware of the substantial, hidden, dynamics and consequences of their sports involvement" (Edwards, 1979, p. 2).

Edwards realized that athletes have the potential to threaten the status quo and disrupt dominant society's efforts to exploit and discriminate. One result of the collective effort was the iconic, black-gloved fists of a first place Tommie Smith and a third place John Carlos atop the men's 200-meter medal ceremony in 1968 Olympic medalist podium, along with the allyship of second place Australian medalist Peter Norman. Their stance was (and would still be now under IOC Rule 50) deemed disrespectful and opposed to the values of the IOC and the Olympic Games (Athlete 365, 2021). As a result, Smith and Carlos were ejected from the games and sent back to the United States (Carlos & Zirin, 2011; Smith & Steele, 2008). Their position of raising awareness of social inequities was not fully recognized for its **social justice** standpoint until 50 years later (Shinn, 2019). Their athletic activism was anchored in civil and human rights and guided

Raven Saunders is an example of athlete activism.
Ryan Pierse/Getty Images

by five imperatives—robust commandments to take collective action and operationalize social change. Edwards' five imperatives (2017, pp. xiv-xv) propose that activists need to obtain and identify

1. a substantial and organically sustained pool of aggrieved plaintiffs seeking redress;
2. a relentless and expanding demand for change, legitimized not only by aggrieved populations but also by collaboration with "outside" interests and even, knowingly or not, by some detractors;
3. a threatened "establishment interest" that makes the changes demanded more reasonable and appealing to the establishment in terms of cost–reward outcomes than maintaining the status quo;
4. substantively factual arguments and supporting ideological "scaffolding" and framing to successfully surmount and overcome characteristically employed adversarial ploys; and
5. a sustaining ideology beyond that professed by adversaries, one that legitimizes the goals and the means that enable vigorous pushback against tendencies toward hegemony and retrenchment of the necessary changes.

Operationalizing activism is imperative for athlete advocates and activists to recognize the value and the transformative power in how their personal actions can influence social issues and identify the ways that their quest for social justice can promote social change.

(Re)imagined Athlete Activism

Present-day athlete activists employ collective activism in the spirit of revolutionary change. Their efforts include a thoughtful reflection and reverence toward history; a comparative awareness of social and political norms with time, context, and issues; and a critical understanding of the dynamics between power and oppression. Looking at history through a critical lens and a sociological imagination unveils a sense of repetition and urgency for social change during an individual's lifetime.

In *It Is Time: From Protest to Policies, Programs, and Progress*[1], Edwards (2018) analyzes the athlete activism of LeBron James, Dwyane Wade, and the Miami Heat's "I Can't Breathe" campaign in response to the death of Eric Garner in 2012; college basketball player Ariyana Smith's protest in response to the death of Michael Brown in 2014 (Zirin, 2014), and Colin Kaepernick's season-long kneeling in response to the deaths of Black and Brown individuals by the police force in 2016. *It Is Time* describes the cyclical pattern of athlete activism through an analytical observation of social movements. A **social movement** is defined as a loosely organized but sustained campaign in support of a social goal, typically either the

[1] In 2018, Edwards' paper *It Is Time: From Protest to Policies, Programs, and Progress* was posted on the Institute for the Study of Sport, Society and Social Change (ISSSSC) website. Edwards founded the ISSSSC in 2017 at San José State University with the goal of promoting research, analysis, and programs at the intersection of sport and society.

implementation or the prevention of a change in society's structure or values. Although social movements differ in size, they are all essentially collective. This collective composition may be to carry out, resist, or undo a social change. In *It Is Time*, Edwards (2018) summarized the challenges faced by athlete activists of the present, using as his primary thesis a call to action to athlete activists to "move beyond protests in the arena."

As the architect, consultant, and resident expert for professional athletes and national and international teams, Edwards understands fully the need for and power of protests. Edwards' (2017) concept of the five imperatives includes a next step, after the protests. Edwards (2016) contends that social movements, including protests, come in waves and have an average 10-year life span before their proverbial expiration date. Activism, in any form or degree, requires a level of endurance that necessitates strategic transition of phases to move toward sought-after social change. He explains that athlete activists should connect with a foundational organization to provide support, maintain stamina and forward momentum, and minimize the effects of institutional retaliation and protest fatigue. Edwards' (2018) call to action reads as follows:

> *It is time for all parties involved to both "beat the clock" and get out ahead of the dynamics that history tells us are already well on this side of the sports–political horizon. It is time to move on from a focus on protests to the formidable task of working directly with the people in their communities, with helping to craft policies, develop programs, and set standards of progress. It is time to move protesting, speaking, and otherwise messaging about the people and their circumstances to standing and working directly with the people and whatever other interests or potential allies that might be earnestly willing and committed to working with dedicated athlete activists in achieving the goals of greater justice for Black people and other peoples of color and their communities.*

These next steps, whether realized or not, have aided individuals' and groups' ability to achieve social change, both small and large.

Sport as a vehicle for social change continues to be driven by individual athletes, teams, and groups that employ the organizing practices, incorporate strategic directives, recognize the power of collaborative politics, and encompass the use of technological advances. Creating or promoting social change through the guise of sport is a complex reality in which athlete activism is one aspect within sport that can be used as a vehicle for social change. Extant literature reveals that sport activism is a powerful method to ignite social change (Cooper, Macaulay, & Rodriguez, 2019; Cooper, Mallery, & Macaulay, 2020; Edwards, 2010, 2016, 2017; Hartmann, 2009; Haslett & Smith, 2019; Hoffman, 2020); and there are multiple methods to make significant social change. That stated, present-day athlete activists are leaning on the experiences of past athletes to understand the contexts. They are comparing the patterns of athlete engagement and are critically examining the social and political contexts to identify the best ways to leverage their platforms to amplify the issues and promote social change. Continued analysis of athlete activists' efforts reveals that they are engaging in Cooper and colleagues' (2019) typologies (symbolic activism, political activism, scholarly activism, grassroots activism, and economic activism). Furthermore, such activism methods as legal activism, media activism (e.g., social media), music and art activism, and military activism (Cooper, Mallery, & Macaulay, 2020) support efforts to use sport as an institutional example to promote social change.

Becoming a Change Agent

Sport is a site for social change, and athlete activism is valuable to society as a method to promote social change. Using sport as a site of resistance presents the institution of sport as being influential in culture and politics. Sage (1998) reminds us that individual and group resistance have addressed race, gender, class, and political inequalities. Sage also says that resistance against power dynamics yields transformation and social change—and promotes diversity, equity, and inclusion in sport and society.

This chapter and other chapters in this text have shown historical and contemporary examples of individuals' and groups' use of activism to promote social change. Yet readers may still have questions. "What are the processes for becoming an activist?" "How can I use my platform to promote social change?" Not all athletes are activists, just like not all activists are athletes. Advocacy and activism are intentional processes beyond the scope of sport participation, yet sport can serve as a viable opportunity and platform. Athletes, scholar activists (Carter-Francique, Gill, & Hart, 2017), sport journalists (Agyemang, Singer, & Weems, 2020), lawyers and legal activists (Hoffman, 2020), and sport entities (Cavil, 2015) utilize their respective platforms to promote social change in sport and society. The incorporation of a sociological imagination in sport has allowed issues pertaining to diversity, equity, and inclusion to be imagined and (re)imagined (Cooper, 2012; Theberge & Donnelly, 1984). In *Sport and the Sociological Imagination* (Theberge & Donnelly, 1984) scholarly writings provide insight on how a sociological imagination can (re)imagine the diversification of sporting spaces, best practices, and policies in reference to race, gender, social class, ability, age, culture, family interactions and relationships, and retirement and transition status.

In the resurgence of the Black Lives Matter social movement, athlete activism rushed to the forefront of international consciousness, using televised media and social media to inform, engage, and mobilize audiences. The use of **technology**, or scientific knowledge to facilitate practical goals through developed machinery or equipment, is a modern-day strategic tool that centers the athlete's voice and narrative. Jackson (2017) discusses social media:

> *We're in an era now substantially dominated by the impact and pervasive influence of social media and the Internet, where instantaneous communication has put a premium on clarity and validity of perspectives and analysis. Sport is particularly significant in this environment because of the stature and status of the athlete, owing principally to their ability to express themselves over social media.*

This perspective affirms sports' influential role in society locally, regionally, nationally, and internationally.

Technology, particularly social media, broadcasts a counternarrative and an unfiltered display of the relationship between personal troubles and public issues. Whether they know it or not, the engagement methods athlete activists use are championed by the Anti-Defamation League (ADL) and include actionable and empowering methods to educate others, advocate for legislation, run for office, protest and demonstrate for an issue, create a public awareness campaign, conduct a survey and share the results on an issue, raise money for a cause, write a letter to a company or organization, participate in community service, or get the press involved.[2] The significance of sport as a social change institution may be greater than we can fully understand as a society, and without obtaining and analyzing quantitative and qualitative data, we may never truly know. Thus, until then it is of benefit to continue to engage, encourage, and empower the sociological imaginations of athletes and all individuals, groups, and sport entities that choose to use sport to create a more equitable society.

SUMMARY

The purpose of this chapter was to present the multiple ways that sport can serve as a platform for lasting and significant social change. Sport, as a cultural and social institution, can reflect cultural morals and values, as well as resist situations that do not welcome balance, fairness, and civil liberties. Identifying how power dynamics contribute to social equity and inequity, knowing about social justice, and delineating the ways that critical theory can support the analysis help us understand social change. An analytical framework is an important foundation for strategies to enact change. Critical theory addresses social, political, and cultural norms and can lead toward practical and goal-driven methods of engagement.

[2] Founded in 1913, the ADL seeks to "stop the defamation of Jewish people and to secure justice and fair treatment for all" (ADL, 2021). The ADL addresses discrimination and threats through programming, policies, and skill development to reveal deficiencies and combat intolerance.

Individuals, groups, and leaders need the capacity to acknowledge history, the ability to compare and contrast social contexts, and the consciousness and willingness to critique the experiences and established policies and practices. Moreover, steps to success involve building a sociological imagination that encompasses understanding individual and group contributions to social movements, the use of technology, and encouraging athletes to use their platforms to uplift and support a transformation toward inclusion.

CRITICAL THINKING EXERCISES

1. Select one of the following films to watch as an individual or group. Identify the organization and the core social issue(s).
   - *League of denial: The NFL's concussions crisis* (2013) (117 minutes)
   - *Life without basketball: The life of a female Muslim athlete* (2019) (89 minutes)
   - *Not just a game: Power, politics, and American sports* (2010) (62 minutes)
   - *Rising phoenix* (2020) (106 minutes)
   - *The weight of gold* (2020) (60 minutes)
2. Throughout this chapter, the concept of collective action was described as one approach toward advocacy and activism. Identify three national organizations and three local or regional groups that could aid the athlete(s) should they desire to advocate for themselves.
3. Identify a sport organization of interest to you. Create a timeline of societal issues that have taken place since the sport organization's inception. Then, using the organization's website(s), social media, and news articles, identify their response to these issues (e.g., 9-11, #MeToo, mental health, COVID-19) and reactions of their members, athletes, fans, and sponsors. Provide constructive criticism on the adequacy of the response. Consider the timing, wording, method of response, and any additional action(s) to acknowledge and contextualize the organization's reaction.
4. As you have learned in this chapter and book, athletes have the potential to promote social change through their advocacy and activism. Identify an athlete of your choice. Develop a marketing strategy or campaign plan that highlights the athlete and their social change platform. Describe how the athlete's efforts connect with or add to the branding of their respective sport organization affiliation or their national or international team affiliation.

REVIEW QUESTIONS

1. What is social change? How can sport as a social entity contribute to social change?
2. What is the definition of power?
   - In what ways can power be used to hinder social change?
   - In what ways can power be leveraged to promote social change?
3. How does critical theory contribute to our understanding of social change through the institution of sport?
4. Define sociological imagination. List and describe the three sensitivities as described by Mills and Sage.
5. How are advocacy and activism similar? How are advocacy and activism different?

REFERENCES

Foreword

Husman, J. (n.d.). Moses Fleetwood Walker. Sabr. Retrieved from https://sabr.org/bioproj/person/fleet-walker/.

Lapchick, R. (2018, May 2). Making waves of change: The 2018 Associated Press sports editors racial and gender report card. Scribd. Retrieved from https://scribd.com/document/510096226/7d86e5-9dca4bc2067241cd-ba67aa2f1b09fd1b.

Staff Writer. (1990, June 22). No Blacks policy at PGA site. Los Angeles Times. Retrieved from https://www.latimes.com/archives/la-xpm-1990-06-22-sp-236-story.html.

Whyno, S. (2020, July 13). Washington's NFL team drops 'Redskins' name after 87 years. APNews. Retrieved from https://apnews.com/article/nhl-mlb-sports-general-nfl-north-america-b6f6919292f5a3c94cb23d92b-de21a54.

Preface

BBC. (2020, June 26). *George Floyd: Timeline of black deaths caused by police*. BBC . www.bbc.com/news/world-us-canada-52905408.

Nicolaou, E., & Smith, C. (2019, October 9). A #MeToo timeline to show how far we've come—& how far we need to go. *New York Times*. www.refinery29.com/en-us/2018/10/212801/me-too-movement-history-timeline-year-weinstein.

Sheth, S., Gal, S., & Hoff, M. (2020, March 31). 7 charts that show the glaring gap between men's and women's salaries in the US. *Business Insider*. www.businessinsider.com/gender-wage-pay-gap-charts-2017-3.

Vaughn, B.E. (2007, Spring). The history of diversity training & its pioneers. *Strategic Diversity & Inclusion Management Magazine*, 1(1), 11-16.DTUI.com Publications Division.

Chapter 1

Acosta, V., & Carpenter, L. (2014). *Women in intercollegiate sport: A longitudinal, national study, thirty seven year update: 1977-2014* [Unpublished manuscript]. www.acostacarpenter.org.

Armour, N., Freeman, M., & Schad, T. (2021, January 14). Why do some NFL teams never hire people of color as GMs and coaches and others do? *USA Today*. www.usatoday.com/story/sports/nfl/2021/01/14/nfl-coaches-best-and-worst-nfl-teams-when-hiring-people-color/6653774002.

Barber, M.C. (2021). Racial inequity and the law: How racial bias influenced legal systems. Department of History, Missouri State University.

Bennett, T., Gayo-Cal, M., Savage, M., Silva, E., Warde, A., & Wright, D. (2009). Culture class, distinction. *The British Journal of Sociology*, *60*(4), 851-858.

Bourdieu, P. (1984). *Distinction: A social critique of the judgement of taste*. Cambridge, MA: Harvard University Press.

Bryan, A., Pope, S., & Rankin-Wright, A.J. (2021). On the periphery: Examining women's exclusion from core leadership roles in the "extremely gendered" organization of men's club football in England. *Gender & Society*, *35*(6), 940-970. https://doi.org/10.1177/08912432211046318.

Buckner, C. (2021, February 26). Kelly Loeffler sells stake in WNBA team after clashing with players over Black Lives Matter. *Washington Post*. www.washingtonpost.com/sports/2021/02/26/kelly-loeffler-senator-sells-wnba-atlanta-dream

Burton, L.J. (2015). Underrepresentation of women in sport leadership: A review of research. *Sport Management Review*, *18*(2), 155-165.

Burton, L., & Leberman, S. (2017). *Women in sport leadership: Research and practice for change*. New York, NY: Routledge.

Claringbould, I., & Knopper, A. (2007). Finding a "normal" woman: Selection processes of board membership. *Sex Roles*, *56*(7), 495-507.

Cunningham, G. (2019). *Diversity and inclusion in sport organizations: A multilevel perspective*. New York, NY: Routledge.

D'Abate, M. (2022, February 19). Brian Flores to join Steelers' coaching staff, ending speculation of Patriots return. *SI*. Retrieved from https://www.si.com/nfl/patriots/news/brian-flores-to-join-steelers-coaching-staff-ending-speculation-of-patriots-return.

DeSensi, J., & Rosenberg, D. (2020). *Ethics and morality in sport management*. Morgantown, WV: FiT Publishing.

Ellemers, N., Kortekaas, P., & Ouwerkerk, J.W. (1999). Self-categorisation, commitment to the group and group self-esteem as related but distinct aspects of social identity. *European Journal of Social Psychology*, *29*(2-3), 371-389. https://doi.org/10.1002/(SICI)1099-0992(199903/05)29:2/3<371::AID-EJSP932>3.0.CO;2-U.

Espinoza, J. (2022, February 5). Brian Flores's attorneys suspect Roger Goodell's memo was a "PR ploy." *Complex.com*. www.complex.com/sports/brian-flores-attorneys-say-roger-goodell-memo-pr-ploy.

Flores v. National Football League et al. (2022). Complaint filed in the United States District Court Southern District of New York. Case 1:22-cv-00871. https://s3.documentcloud.org/documents/21195065/flores-v-nfl.pdf.

Florio, M. (2020, January 13). Fritz Pollard Alliance slams NFL hiring practices. *NBC Sports*. https://profootballtalk.nbcsports.com/2020/01/13/fritz-pollard-alliance-slams-nfl-hiring-practices.

Footer, A. (2019, April 12). Trailblazer girls soak up Jackie's legacy. *MLB*. Retrieved from https://mlb.com/news/trailblazer-series-girls-tour-dodger-stadium.

Fox, M. (2021, November 17). Women are leading the way in the "Great Resignation". Here's what it means for employers and job seekers. *CNBC*. www.cnbc.com/2021/11/17/women-are-quitting-at-higher-rates-than-men-during-the-great-resignation.html.

Goodell, R. (2022, February 5). Memorandum to chief executives and club presidents. National Football League. https://twitter.com/TomPelissero/status/1489980373815726092?ref_src=twsrc%5Etfw%7Ctwcamp%5Etweetembed%7Ctwterm%5E1489980373815726092%7Ctwgr%5E%7Ctwcon%5Es1_&ref_url=https%3A%2F%2Fwww.complex.com%2Fsports%2Fbrian-flores-attorneys-say-roger-goodell-memo-pr-ploy.

Gould, E., & Shierholz, H. (2020, March 19). Not everybody can work from home: Black and Hispanic workers are much less likely to be able to telework. *Working Economics Blog*. www.epi.org/blog/black-and-hispanic-workers-are-much-less-likely-to-be-able-to-work-from-home.

Harrison, K., & Bukstein, S. (2020, February). *Occupational mobility patterns: An examination of leadership, access, opportunity, social capital, and the reshuffling effect within the NFL*. National Football League. https://operations.nfl.com/media/4229/2020-nfl-diversity-and-inclusion-report.pdf.

Hogg, M.A., & Abrams, D. (1988). *Social identifications: A social psychology of intergroup relations and group processes*. Taylor & Frances/Routledge.

Ingram, F. (2021, January-February). The forgotten dimension of diversity: Social class is as important as race or gender. *Harvard Business Review*. https://hbr.org/2021/01/the-forgotten-dimension-of-diversity

Jones, W. (2021). Finally, pay equity in big-time women's college basketball? A Kitagawa-Blinder-Oaxaca decomposition. *Journal of Issues in Intercollegiate Athletics, 14*, 461-482.

King III, M.L. (2020, September 4). This new era of athlete activism can help fulfill MLK's dream. *Rolling Stone*. www.rollingstone.com/culture/culture-commentary/martin-luther-king-black-athlete-activism-mlk-dream-1055187 (Reprinted from "New era of athlete activism can help fulfill MLK's dream," 2020, *Sportico*, www.sportico.com/personalities/people/2020/mlkiii-guest-editorial-1234612702).

Larson, E. (2017, September 21). New research: Diversity + inclusion = better decision making at work. *Forbes*. www.forbes.com/sites/eriklarson/2017/09/21/new-research-diversity-inclusion-better-decision-making-at-work/?sh=7ec3d2894cbf.

McCord, M.A., Joseph, D.L., Dhanani, L.Y., & Beus, J.M. (2018). A meta-analysis of sex and race differences in perceived workplace mistreatment. *Journal of Applied Psychology, 103*(2), 137-163. https://doi.org/10.1037/apl0000250.

McLeod, S. (2019). Social identity theory. *SimplyPsychology*. www.simplypsychology.org/social-identity-theory.html.

Messner, M., & Sabo, D. (1990). *Sport, men, and the gender order: Critical feminist perspectives*. Champaign, IL: Human Kinetics.

Moran, E. (2020, June 8). NACDA. (2021, November 1). Roundtable: Sports executives on the future of remote work. https://frontofficesports.com/future-of-remote-work-sports/.

NACDA and Return on Inclusion announce groundbreaking partnership. https://nacda.com/news/2021/11/1/nacda-nacda-and-return-on-inclusion-announce-groundbreaking-partnership.aspx.

National Collegiate Athletic Association. (2022). NCAA gender and race demographic database. www.ncaa.org/about/resources/research/ncaa-demographics-database

O'Connell, J. (2021a, February 5). The true origins of the Rooney Rule: Part 1. *Global Sports Matter*. https://globalsportmatters.com/listen/2021/02/05/the-true-origins-of-the-rooney-rule-part-1.

O'Connell, J. (2021b, February 11). The true origins of the Rooney Rule: Part 2. *Global Sports Matter*. https://globalsportmatters.com/listen/2021/02/11/the-true-origins-of-the-rooney-rule-part-2.

Perras, C. (2020). Moving toward equal pay for professional female athletes: What we can learn from equal pay legislation in Iceland. *Indiana International and Comparative Law Review 30*, 319-348.

Poston, D. (2020, January 2). 3 big ways that the U.S. will change over the next decade. *The Conversation*. https://theconversation.com/3-big-ways-that-the-us-will-change-over-the-next-decade-126908.

Saad, L., & Wigert, B. (2021, October 13). Remote work persisting and trending permanent. *Gallup News*. https://news.gallup.com/poll/355907/remote-work-persisting-trending-permanent.aspx.

Sakpal, M. (2019, September 20). Diversity and inclusion build high-performance teams. https://www.gartner.com/smarterwithgartner/diversity-and-inclusion-build-high-performance-teams#:~:text=Diversity%20and%20inclusion%20drive%20financial,by%2050%25%2C%20on%20average.

Shaw, S., & Hoeber, L. (2003, October). "A strong man is direct and a direct woman is a bitch": Gendered discourses and their influence on employment roles in sport organizations. *Journal of Sport Management 17*(4), 347-375.

Skonicki, K. (2021, March 16). Powerful options for putting the REAL framework into action to achieve workplace diversity. *Lewisu*. Retrieved from https://lewisu.edu/experts/wordpress/index.php/powerful-options-for-putting-the-real-framework-into-action-to-achieve-workplace-diversity/.

Staurowsky, E.J. (2016). *Women and sport: Continuing a journey from liberation to celebration.* Champaign, IL: Human Kinetics.

Staurowsky, E.J., Watanabe, N., Cooper, J., Cooky, C., Lough, N., Paule-Koba, A., Pharr, J., Williams, S., Cummings, S., Issokson-Silver, K., & Snyder, M. (2020). *Chasing equity: The triumphs, challenges, and opportunities in sports for girls and women.* New York, NY: Women's Sports Foundation.

Staurowsky, E.J. (2021). Pay equity and the Tokyo 2020 Olympics. *Olympics Analysis.* https://olympicanalysis.org/section-5/pay-equity-the-tokyo-2020-olympics.

Thomas, L. (2018, May). The radicalization of American football. *The Atlantic.* www.theatlantic.com/magazine/archive/2018/05/malcolm-jenkins-philadelphia-eagles/556886.

Turner, K. (2017). The rights of school-employee coaches under Title VII and Title IX in educational athletic programs. *American Bar Association (ABA) Journal of Labor & Employment Law, 32*, 229-253.

United Nations. (2019). *World Population Prospects 2019, Volume 1.* United Nations, Department of Economic and Social Affairs. https://population.un.org/wpp/Publications/Files/WPP2019_Volume-I_Comprehensive-Tables.pdf.

U.S. Bureau of Labor Statistics. (2021, April). *BLS report: Women in the labor force: A databook.* www.bls.gov/opub/reports/womens-databook/2020/home.htm.

Vizcaya Abdo, A. (2020, December 5). Inclusion + diversity = better performance. How sports organizations can create greater value through I&D. *LinkedIn.* www.linkedin.com/pulse/inclusion-diversity-better-performance-how-sports-can-vizcaya-abdo.

Walker, P. (2022, February 3). Broncos' John Elway responds to lawsuit, issues formal statement in wake of Brian Flores's allegations. *CBS Sports.* www.cbssports.com/nfl/news/broncos-john-elway-responds-to-lawsuit-issues-formal-statement-in-wake-of-brian-flores-allegations.

Williams, D.A. (2013). *Strategic diversity leadership: Activating change and transformation in higher education.* Sterling, VA: Stylus.

Chapter 2

ADL: Anti-Defamation League. (2020). *How should I talk about race in my mostly White classroom.* www.adl.org/education/resources/tools-and-strategies/how-should-i-talk-about-race-in-my-mostly-White-classroom.

Banks, C.A., Pliner, S.M., & Hopkins, M.B. (2013). Intersectionality and paradigms of privilege. In K.A. Case (Ed.), *Deconstructing privilege* (pp. 102-114). New York: Routledge.

Barak, K.S., Krane, V., Ross, S.R., Mann, M.E., & Kaunert, C.A. (2018). Visual negotiation: How female athletes present intersectional identities in photographic self-representations. *Quest, 70*(4), 471-491. doi:10.1080/00336297.2018.1461661.

Black, E. (2020a, June 15). *Hashtag Sports & Intel Sports announce industry-wide diversity inclusion initiative* [Press release]. www.prnewswire.com/news-releases/hashtag-sports--intel-sports-announce-industry-wide-diversity--inclusion-initiative-301076573.html.

Black, E. (2020b, December 16). *Hashtag Sports announces game-changing annual recognition program for minority content creators.* Salamanca Press. www.salamancapress.com/news/state/hashtag-sports-announces-game-changing-annual-recognition-program-for-minority-content-creators/article_296d0023-15d8-5853-a3b4-4262a73927e4.html.

Burton, L.J., Barr, C., Fink, J.S., & Bruening, J.E. (2009). "Think athletic director, think masculine?": Examination of the gender typing of managerial subroles within athletic administration positions, *Sex Roles 61*: 416-426.

Bushnell, H. (2020, June 19). *Lessons in anti-racism allyship from LGBTQ athletes who know first hand how important it is.* Yahoo Sports. www.yahoo.com/lifestyle/lessons-in-antiracism-allyship-from-lgbtq-athletes-who-know-firsthand-how-important-it-is-180507302.html.

Chen, H.A., Trinh, J., & Yang, G.P. (2020). Anti-Asian sentiment in the United States—COVID-19 and history. *American Journal of Surgery, 220*(3), 556-557. https://doi.org/10.1016/j.amjsurg.2020.05.020.

City for All Women Initiative. (2015). *Advancing equity and inclusion: A guide for municipalities.* www.cawi-ivtf.org/sites/default/files/publications/advancing-equity-inclusion-web_0.pdf.

Clifford, E. (2020). One day I went for a run: Presenting a new metaphor for teaching about privilege. *Transformations: The Journal of Inclusive Scholarship and Pedagogy, 30*(1), 72-78. doi:10.5325/trajincschped.30.1.0072.

CoachDiversity Institute. (2020). *Ten strategies for holding difficult conversations about diversity.* https://coachdiversity.com/blog/ten-strategies-for-holding-difficult-conversations-about-diversity.

Coakley, J. (2015). Accessing the sociology of sport: On cultural sensibilities and the great sport myth. *International Review for the Sociology of Sport, 50* (4-5), 402-406.

Coaston, J. (2019, May 29). *The intersectionality wars: When Kimberlé Crenshaw coined the term 30 years ago, it was a relatively obscure legal concept. Then it went viral.* Vox. www.vox.com/the-highlight/2019/5/20/18542843/intersectionality-conservatism-law-race-gender-discrimination.

Comeaux, E. (2018). Stereotypes, control, hyper-surveillance, and disposability of NCAA Division I Black male athletes. *New Directions for Student Services, 2018*(163), 33-42. https://doi-org.ezproxy2.library.drexel.edu/10.1002/ss.20268.

Comerford, D.M. (2018). A call for NCAA adapted sports championships: Following the Eastern College Athletic Conference's lead to nationalize collegiate athletic opportunities for athletes with disabilities. *Marquette Sports Law Review, 28*(2), 525-551.

Crevani, L. (2019, June). Privilege in place: How organizational practices contribute to meshing privilege in place. *Scandinavian Journal of Management, 35*(2). www.sciencedirect.com/science/article/pii/S0956522117300647.

Cunningham, W., Wicker, P., & Kutsko, K. (2020). Gendered racial stereotypes and coaching intercollegiate athletic teams: The representation of Black and Asian women coaches on U.S. women's and men's teams. *Sex Roles, 84,* 574-583. https://doi.org/10.1007/s11199-020-01186-2.

Darvin, L., Pegoraro, A., & Berri, D. (2018). Are men better leaders? An investigation of head coaches' gender and individual players' performance in amateur and professional women's basketball. *Sex Roles, 78*(7-8), 455-466. https://doi-org.ezproxy.ithaca.edu/10.1007/s11199-017-0815-2.

Das, A., Tracy, M., & Meyers, N.J. (2019, March 12). The coaches connected to the college admissions fraud case. *New York Times.* www.nytimes.com/2019/03/12/sports/sports-college-admissions-scam.html.

English, J., & Kruger, A.C. (2020). I am not only a student-athlete: Investigating social identity complexity as a stereotype threat mitigation strategy to reduce barriers to academic engagements. *Journal of Issues in Intercollegiate Athletics*, Fall, 29-55. http://csri-jiia.org/wp-content/uploads/2020/09/SI_2020_01_02.pdf.

Equality v. Equity. (2019). Diffen.com. www.diffen.com/difference/Equality-vs-Equity.

Feinstein, J. (2020, December 21). Army got its bowl game at last, but this broken system needs to be blown up. *Washington Post.* www.washingtonpost.com/sports/2020/12/21/army-bowl-game-opponent-jeff-monken.

Ferrucci, P., & Tandoc, E.C. (2017). Race and the deep ball: Applying stereotypes to NFL quarterbacks. *International Journal of Sport Communication, 10*(1), 41-57. https://journals.humankinetics.com/view/journals/ijsc/10/1/article-p41.xml.

Fink, J.S., LaVoi, N.M., & Newhall, K.E. (2016). Challenging the gender binary? Male basketball practice players' views of female athletes and women's sports. *Sport in Society, 19*(8/9), 1316-1331.

Forde, P. (2020, December 15). Selection committee doubles down on favoritism in penultimate rankings. *Sports Illustrated.* www.si.com/college/2020/12/16/selection-committee-power-5-bias-playoff-rankings.

Fry, J. (2018, June 28). *Allyship for athletic administrators.* Medium. https://medium.com/@jenfry/allyship-for-athletic-administrators-9278262fc0e3.

Harrison, C.K., & Coakley, J. (2020). Hip-hop and sport: An introduction: Reflections on culture, language, and identity. *Sociology of Sport Journal, 37*(3), 166-173. https://journals.humankinetics.com/view/journals/ssj/37/3/article-p166.xml?content=pdf-6970.

Hastwell, C. (2020, December 23). *The difference between debate, discussion, and dialogue.* Great Place to Work. www.greatplacetowork.com/resources/blog/the-difference-between-debate-discussion-and-dialogue.

Heffernan, C. (2018, August). *Gender allyship: Considering the role of men in addressing the gender-leadership gap in sport organizations* [Unpublished dissertation]. University of Minnesota. https://conservancy.umn.edu/handle/11299/201034.

Hopper, E. (2019, February 18). *What is stereotype threat? The negative effects of worrying about confirming a stereotype.* Thoughtco.com. www.thoughtco.com/what-is-stereotype-threat-4586395.

Ingraham, L. (2018, February 28). Jocks on politics [YouTube]. *The Ingraham Angle.* www.youtube.com/watch?v=8sNWpmR14W4.

Jhangiani, R., & Tarry, H. (2014). *Principles of social psychology* (1st int'l ed.) Adapted from Dr. Charles Sangor's original work. Creative Commons. https://pressbooks.bccampus.ca/socialpsychben.

Justin, R. (2020, June 12). UT-Austin football players demand school rename buildings named after racist figures, donate to Black Lives Matter. *Texas Tribune.* www.texastribune.org/2020/06/12/ut-austin-football-players-buildings-racism.

Kasakove, S. (2021, October 9). The college admissions scandal: Where some of the defendants are now. *New York Times.* www.nytimes.com/2021/10/09/us/varsity-blues-scandal-verdict.html

Kepner, T., & Wagner, J. (2020, November 18). Kim Ng has been ready for years. *New York Times.* www.nytimes.com/2020/11/18/sports/baseball/kim-ng-miami-marlins.html

Lavoi, N., McGarry, J., & Fisher, L. (2019). Final thoughts on women in sport coaching: Fighting the war. *Women in Sport and Physical Activity Journal, 27*(2), 136-140. https://journals.humankinetics.com/view/journals/wspaj/27/2/article-p136.xml.

Levin, J. (2020, June 17). The damning history behind UT's "The Eyes of Texas" song. *Texas Monthly.* www.texasmonthly.com/the-culture/ut-austin-eyes-of-texas-song-racist.

Levin, J., & Maisel, I. (2021, May). Behind the scenes of UT's 'The Eyes of Texas' controversy. *Texas Monthly.* www.texasmonthly.com/news-politics/behind-the-scenes-of-uts-the-eyes-of-texas-controversy/

Lin, J. (2020, April 20). The darkness has not overcome it. *The Players Tribune.* www.theplayerstribune.com/articles/jeremy-lin-darkness-has-not-overcome-it.

McIntosh, P. (2003). White privilege: Unpacking the invisible knapsack. In S. Plous (Ed.), *Understanding prejudice and discrimination* (pp. 191-196). Boston: McGraw-Hill.

McCarriston, S. (2020, September 28). *NFL history made: Two female coaches and a female official on field for the same game in Cleveland.* CBS Sports. www.cbssports.com/nfl/news/nfl-history-made-two-female-coaches-and-a-female-official-on-field-for-same-game-in-cleveland.

McDowell, J., & Carter-Francique, A. (2017). An intersectional analysis of the workplace experiences of African-American female athletic directors. *Sex Roles, 77* (5-6), 393-408.

McGee, K. (2021, March 3). UT-Austin football players say they were forced to stay on field for "The Eyes of Texas" to appease angry donors and fans. *Texas Tribune.* www.texastribune.org/2021/03/03/ut-austin-eyes-of-texas-donors/

Moore, M. (2017, May 12). The question of intersectionality in women's sports. Michelle Moore [Website]. http://michellemoore.me/the-question-of-intersectionality-in-womens-sport/.

NBA. (2020, September 16). *Harris Blitzer Sports & Entertainment names David Gould chief diversity and inclusion officer* [Press release]. www.nba.com/sixers/harris-blitzer-sports-entertainment-names-david-gould-chief-diversity-and-impact-officer.

Newman, B., Merolla, J., Shah, S., Lemi, D., Collingwood, L., & Ramakrishnan, S. (2020). The Trump effect: An experimental investigation of the emboldening effect of racially inflammatory elite communication. *British Journal of Political Science, 51*(2), 1-22. doi:10.1017/S0007123419000590.

Pack, K., Kelly, S., & Arvinen-Barrow, M. (2017). "I think I became a swimmer rather than just someone with a disability swimming up and down:" Paralympic athletes' perceptions of self and identity development. *Disability and Rehabilitation, 39*(20), 2063-2070. https://doi.org/10.1080/09638288.2016.1217074.

Reddick, R. (2021, March). The Eyes of Texas history committee report. Austin, TX: University of Texas at Austin. http://utw10957.utweb.utexas.edu/eot-report/Eyes_of_Texas_Report_3.2021.pdf

Romney, M., & Johnson, R.G. (2020). The ball game is for the boys: The visual framing of female athletes on national sports networks' Instagram accounts. *Communication & Sport, 8*(6), 738-756.

Sabo, D., Veliz, P., & Staurowsky, E.J. (2016). *Beyond X's & O's: Gender bias and coaches of women's college sports*. New York: Women's Sports Foundation.

Sauder, M.H., Mudrick, M., & DeLuca, J.R. (2018). Perceived barriers and sources of support for undergraduate female students' persistence in the sport management major. *Sport Management Education Journal, 12*(2), 69-79.

Schaffner, B.F. (2018). Follow the racist? The consequences of Trump's expression of prejudice for mass rhetoric. www.ashford.zone/images/2018/09/followtheracist_v2.pdf.

Staurowsky, E.J., & Rhoads, A. (2020). Title IX athletics coordinators in NCAA Division I institutions: Roles, responsibilities, and potential conflicts of interest. *Journal of Issues in Intercollegiate Athletics, 13*, 381-404.

Sue, D.W. (2015). *Race talk and the conspiracy of silence: Understanding and facilitating difficult dialogues on race.* Hoboken, NJ: John Wiley & Sons.

Staurowsky, E.J. (2016). *Women and sport: Continuing a journey from liberation to celebration.* Champaign, IL: Human Kinetics.

Staurowsky, E.J., Watanabe, N., Cooper, J., Cooky, C., Lough, N., Paule-Koba, A., Pharr, J., Williams, S., Cummings, S., Issokson-Silver, K., & Snyder, M. (2020). *Chasing equity: The triumphs, challenges, and opportunities in sports for girls and women.* New York, NY: Women's Sports Foundation.

Sullivan, E. (2018). *Laura Ingraham told LeBron James to shut up and dribble; He went to the hoop.* NPR. www.npr.org/sections/thetwo-way/2018/02/19/587097707/laura-ingraham-told-lebron-james-to-shutup-and-dribble-he-went-to-the-hoop.

Teetzel, S. (2020, August). Allyship in elite women's sport. *Sport, Ethics, and Philosophy, 14*(4), 432-448.

Toomey, R.B., & McGeorge, C.R. (2018). Profiles of LGBTQ ally engagement in college athletics. *Journal of LGBT Youth, 15*(3), 162-178. https://doi-org.ezproxy.ithaca.edu/10.1080/19361653.2018.1453428.

University of Michigan Literature, Arts, & Sciences Staff. (2020). An instructor's guide for understanding privilege. Ann Arbor, MI: University of Michigan. https://sites.lsa.umich.edu/inclusive-teaching/wp-content/uploads/sites/853/2021/02/An-Instructors-Guide-to-Understanding-Privilege-FINAL-2.pdf

Wadley et al. v. University of Iowa. (2020). www.courthousenews.com/wp-content/uploads/2020/11/iowa-football.pdf.

Walker, N.A., Agyemang, K.A., Washington, M., Hindman, L.C., & MacCharles, J. (2020). Getting an internship in the sport industry: The institutionalization of privilege, *Sport Management Education Journal, 15*(1), 1-14. https://journals.humankinetics.com/view/journals/smej/aop/article-10.1123-smej.2019-0061/article-10.1123-smej.2019-0061.xml.

Whistle, W. (2020, September 3). The Varsity Blues admissions scandal continues. *Forbes*. www.forbes.com/sites/wesleywhistle/2020/09/03/the-varsity-blues-college-admissions-scandal-continues/?sh=21941a7271cb.

Wininger, S.R., & White, T.A. (2015). An examination of the dumb jock stereotype in collegiate student-athletes: A comparison of student versus student-athlete perceptions. *Journal for the Study of Sports and Athletes in Education, 9*(2), 75-85.

Wise, T. (2011). *White like me: Reflections on race from a privileged son.* New York: Soft Skull Press.

Wood, S. (2020, September 9). *Report finds disparities among students earning paid internships.* Diverse Education. https://diverseeducation.com/article/189784/.

Young, S.M. (2020, October 22). *With roots in racism, "Eyes of Texas" should be banned. So why isn't Texas listening to its Black students?* Yahoo Sports. https://sports.yahoo.com/eyes-of-texas-tom-herman-athletes-song-battle-005335387.html?src=rss.

Youngmisuk, O. (2017, May 10). *Jeremy Lin says racist remarks he heard from opponents were worse in NCAA than NBA.* ESPN. www.espn.com/nba/story/_/id/19353394/jeremy-lin-brooklyn-nets-says-heard-racist-remarks-more-frequently-college-nba.

Zenquis, M.R., & Mwaniki, M.F. (2019). The intersection of race, gender, and nationality in sport: Media representation of the Ogwumike sisters. *Journal of Sport and Social Issues, 43*(1), 23-43. doi:10.1177/0193723518823338.

Chapter 3

Adams, L., Baskerville, K., Lee, D., Spruiell, M., & Wolf, R. (2006, March 22). *The Hispanic community and outdoor recreation.* UCLA Anderson School of Management Applied Management Research Program for the Outdoor Industry Association. https://outdoorindustry.org/wp-content/uploads/2017/03/ResearchHispanic.pdf.

Anderson, A., & South, D. (2000). Racial differences in collegiate recruiting, retention, and graduation rates. In D. Brooks & R. Althouse (Eds.), *Racism in college athletics: The African-American athlete's experience* (pp. 155-169). Fitness Information Technology, Inc.

Aspen Institute Project Play. (2000, January 14). *Survey: Low-income kids are 6 times more likely to quit sport due to costs.* www.aspenprojectplay.org/national-youth-sport-survey/low-income-kids-are-6-times-more-likely-to-quit-sports-due-to-costs.

Borden, L.M., Perkins, D.F., Villarruel, F.A., Carleton-Hug, A., Stone, M.R., & Keith, J.G. (2006). Challenges and opportunities to Latino youth development: Increasing meaningful participation in youth development programs. *Hispanic Journal of Behavioral Sciences, 28*(2), 187-208.

Broh, B.A. (2002). Linking extracurricular programming to academic achievement: Who benefits and why? *Sociology of Education, 75*(1), 69-96.

Burnett, C. (2006). Building social capital through an active community club. *International Review for the Sociology of Sport, 41*(3-4), 283-294.

Carnevale, A.P., & Rose, S.J. (2003). *Socioeconomic status, race/ethnicity, and selective college admissions.* Report for the Century Foundation.

CNN Philippines. (2019, December 26). *Pacquiao among highest-paid athletes of the decade—Forbes.* CNN. www.cnnphilippines.com/sport/2019/12/26/Manny-Pacquiao-highest-paid-athlete-Forbes.html.

Coakley, J. (2016). *Sport in society: Issues and controversies.* McGraw-Hill.

Coalter, F. (2010). Sport-for-development: Going beyond the boundary? *Sport in Society, 13*(9), 1374-1391.

Coleman, J.S. (1961). *The adolescent society.* Free Press of Glencoe.

Edwards, H. (1986). The collegiate athletics arms race. In R. Lapchick (Ed.), *Fractured focus: Sport as a reflection of society* (pp. 21-43). Lexington Books.

Eisen, G., & Turner, D. (1992). Myth & reality: Social mobility of American Olympic Athletes. *International Review for the Sociology of Sport, 27*(2), 165-174.

Falcous, M., & McLeod, C. (2012). Anyone for tennis? Sport, class and status in New Zealand. *New Zealand Sociology, 27*(1), 13-30.

Flores, A., Lopez, G., & Radford, J. (2017). *2015, Hispanic population in the United States statistical portrait.* Washington: Pew Research Center. www.pewresearch.org/hispanic/2017/09/18/2015-statistical-information-on-hispanics-in-united-states/.

Flores-Gonzälez, N. (2000). The structuring of extracurricular opportunities and Latino student retention. *Journal of Poverty, 4*(1-2), 85-108.

Giddens, A., & Diamond, P. (2005). *The new egalitarianism.* Polity.

Goldsmith, P.A. (2003). Race relations and racial patterns in school sport participation. *Sociology of Sport Journal, 20*, 147-171.

Green, K., & Hartmann, H. (2012). Politics and sport: Strange, secret bedfellows. *The Society Pages.* http://thesocietypages.org/papers/politics-and-sport/.

Green, K., Smith, A., & Roberts, K. (2005). Social class, young people, sport and physical education. In K. Green & K. Hardman (Eds.), *Physical education: Essential issues* (pp. 180-196). Sage.

Howell, F.M., Miracle, A.W., & Rees, C.R. (1984). Do high school athletics pay? The effects of varsity participation on socioeconomic attainment. *Sociology of Sport Journal, 1*, 15-25.

Jarvie, G. (2003). Communitarianism, sport and social capital. *International Review for the Sociology of Sport, 38*(2), 139-153.

Kelley, B., & Carchia, C. (2013, July 11). "Hey, data data—swing!" The hidden demographics of youth sport. *ESPN The Magazine.* www.espn.com/espn/story/_/id/9469252/hidden-demographics-youth-sport-espn-magazine.

Kraus, M.W., & Park, J.W. (2017). The structural dynamics of social class. *Current Opinion in Psychology, 18*, 55-60.

Ladies Professional Golf Association. (n.d.). *Players ranking: Top 100 money list.* www.lpga.com/players.

Lapchick, R.E. (2003). *Racial and gender report card.* The Institute for Diversity and Ethics in Sport, University of Central Florida.

Lareau, A. (2002). Invisible inequality: Social class and childrearing in black families and white families. *American Sociological Review, 67*, 747-776.

Lee, J., & Opio, T. (2011). Coming to America: Challenges and difficulties faced by African student-athletes. *Sport, Education and Society, 16*(5), 629-644.

Lee, J., & Rice, C. (2007). Welcome to America? International student perception of discrimination. *Higher Education, 53*(3), 381-409.

Mackin, R.S., & Walther, C.S. (2011). Race, sport and social mobility: Horatio Alger in short pants? *International Review for the Sociology of Sport, 47*(6), 670-689.

McGovern, J. (2021). Are Latinx youth getting in the game? The effects of gender, class, ethnicity, and language on Latinx youth sport participation. *Latino Studies, 19*, 92-113.

Mirehie, M., Gibson, H., Kang, S., & Bell, H. (2019). Parental insights from three elite-level youth sport: Implications for family life. *World Leisure Journal, 61*(2), 98-112.

Muntaner, C., Borrell, C., Benach, J., Pasarin, M.I., & Fernandez, E. (2003). The association of social class and social stratification with patterns of general and mental health in a Spanish population. *International Epidemiological Association*, *32*(6), 950-958.

National Basketball Association. (2020, December 22). *NBA rosters feature 107 international players from 41 countries: A record 17 Canadian players and a record-tying 14 African players are rosters this season*. www.nba.com/news/nba-rosters-feature-107-international-players-from-41-countries.

National Collegiate Athletic Association. (n.d.-a). *International student-athletes*. https://www.ncaa.org/international.

National Collegiate Athletic Association. (n.d.-b). *International country-specific information*. www.ncaa.org/student-athletes/future/africa.

National Collegiate Athletic Association. (2020). 2021-2022 *Guide to international academic standards for athletics eligibility*. http://fs.ncaa.org/Docs/eligibility_center/International_Information/International_Guide.pdf.

National Collegiate Athletic Association. (2021). *Trends in the participation of international student-athletes in NCAA Divisions I and II*. https://ncaaorg.s3.amazonaws.com/research/demographics/2021RES_ISATrendsDivSprt.pdf.

Palmer, T. (1994). The athletic dream and the Black male student: Primary prevention implications for counselors. *The School Counselor*, *41*(5), 203-210.

Peguero, A.A. (2011). Immigrant youth involvement in school-based extracurricular activities. *Journal of Educational Research*, *104*(1), 19-27.

Prescott, D., & Phelan, J. (2008). *Shared goals through sport: Getting a sustainable return for companies and communities*. International Business Leaders Forum. www.sportanddev.org/sites/default/files/downloads/27__shared_goals_through_sport_getting_a_sustainable_return_for_companies_and_communi.pdf.

Pritchard, R.M.O., & Skinner, B. (2002). Cross-cultural partnerships between home and international students. *Journal of Studies in International Education*, *6*, 323-354.

Putnam, R.D. (1995). Bowling alone: America's declining social capital. *Journal of Democracy*, *6*, 65-78.

Putnam, R.D. (2000). *Bowling alone: The collapse and revival of American community*. Simon & Schuster.

Putnam, R., Leonardi, R., & Nanetti, R.Y. (1993). *Making democracy work: Civic traditions in modern Italy*. Princeton University Press.

Quarmby, T., & Dagkas, S. (2010). Children's engagement in leisure time physical activity: Exploring family structure as a determinant. *Leisure Studies*, *29*, 53-66.

Rees, D.I., & Sabia, J.J. (2010). Sport participation and academic performance: Evidence from the National Longitudinal Study of Adolescent Health. *Economics of Education Review*, *29*(5), 751-759.

Reynolds, L., Fisher, D., & Cavil, J.K. (2012). Impact of Demographic Variables on African-American Student-athletes' Academic Performance. *Educational Foundations*, *26*(Summer-Fall), 93-111.

Richeson, J.A., & Sommers, S.R. (2016). Toward a social psychology of race and race relations for the twenty-first century. *Annual Review of Psychology*, *67*, 439-463.

Roberts, K. (2001). *Class in modern Britain*. Palgrave.

Robertson, M., Line, M., Jones, S., & Thomas, S. (2000). International students, learning environments and perceptions: A case study using the Delphi technique. *Higher Education Research and Development*, *19*, 89-102.

Rockwell, G. (2019). Educating Latin American baseball players: How MLB should protect their players for after their careers. *Pepperdine Policy Review*, *11*, Article 5.

Rodriguez, A. (2014). International student-athlete and stress: Implications for American universities' administrators. *Journal of Academic Administration in Higher Education*, *10*(2), 39-47.

Sack, A.L., & Thiel, R. (1979). College football and social mobility: A case study of Notre Dame football players. *Sociology of Education*, *52*(January), 60-66.

Sabo, D., & Veliz, P. (2008). *Go out and play: Youth sport in America*. Women's Sport Foundation.

Schulenkorf, N. (2013). Sport for development events and social capital building: A critical analysis of experiences from Sri Lanka. *Journal of Sport for Development*, *1*(1), 25-36.

Schwery, R. (2003). *The potential of sport for development and peace. Bulletin no. 39*. Biel: Swiss Academy for Development (SAD). www.icsspe.org.

Sherry, E. (2010). (Re)engaging marginalized groups through sport: The Homeless World Cup. *International Review for the Sociology of Sport*, *45*(1), 59-71.

Sherry, E., Kang, A., & O'May, F. (2011). Social capital and sport events: Spectator attitudinal change and the Homeless World Cup. *Sport in Society*, *14*(1), 111-125.

Singer, J.N. (2005). Understanding racism through the eyes of African American male student-athletes. *Race Ethnicity and Education*, *8*(4), 365-386.

Snyder, P.L. (1996). Comparative levels of expressed academic motivation among Anglo and African-American university student athletes. *Journal of Black Studies*, *26*(6), 651-667.

Smith, A., & Westerbeek, H. (2007). Sport as a vehicle for deploying corporate social responsibility. *Journal of Corporate Citizenship*, *25*, 43-54.

Sorokin, P. (1959). *Social mobility*. Free Press.

Spaaij, R. (2009). Sport as a vehicle for social mobility and regulation of disadvantaged urban youth: Lessons from Rotterdam. *International Review for the Sociology of Sport*, *44*, 247-264.

Spaaij, R. (2011). *Sport and social mobility*. Routledge.

Staurowsky, E.J., Watanabe, N., Cooper, J., Cooky, C., Lough, N., Paule-Koba, A., Pharr, Williams, S., Cummings, S., Issokson-Silver, K., & Snyder, M. (2020). *Chasing equity: The triumphs, challenges, and opportunities in sports for girls and women*. New York, NY: Women's Sports Foundation.

Stempel, C. (2006). Gender, social class and the sporting capital-economic capital nexus. *Sociology of Sport Journal, 23*(3), 273-292.

Stephens, N.M., Markus, H.R., & Fryberg, S.A. (2012). Social class disparities in health and education: Reducing inequality by applying a sociocultural self model of behavior. *Psychological Review, 119*(4), 723-744.

Street Soccer USA. (n.d.). *Mission—Model—Impact*. www.streetsoccerusa.org/mission-model-impact/.

UConn Student-Athlete Success Program. (n.d.). *SASP overview*. https://uconnhuskies.com/sport/2018/6/12/sport-sasp-spec-rel-counseling-program-overview-html.aspx.

van Bakel, M., & Salzbrenner, S. (2020). Going abroad to play: Motivations, challenges, and support of sports expatriates. *Thunderbird International Business Review, 61*(3), 505-517.

Vilhjalmsson, R., & Thorlindsson, T. (1992). The integrative and physiological effects of sport participation: A study of adolescents. *Sociological Quarterly, 33*(4), 637-647.

Walvin, J. (1995). *Passion of the people? Football in South America*. Verso.

Welty Peachey, J., Cohen, A., Borland, J., & Lyras, A. (2011). Building social capital: Examining the impact of Street Soccer USA on its volunteers. *International Review for the Sociology of Sport, 48*(1), 20-37.

Welty Peachey, J., Lyras, A., Borland, J., & Cohen, A. (2013). Street Soccer USA Cup: Preliminary findings of a sport-for-homeless intervention. *ICHPER-SD Journal of Research in Health, Physical Education, Recreation, Sport & Dance, 8*(1), 3-11.

Wheeler, S. (2012). The significance of family culture for sport participation. *International Review for the Sociology of Sport, 47*(2), 235-252.

Wheeler, S., & Green, K. (2014). Parenting in relation to children's sport participation: Generational changes and potential implications. *Leisure Studies, 33*, 267-284.

Woolcock, M. (2001). The place of social capital in understanding social and economic outcomes. *Canadian Journal of Policy Research, 2*(1), 11-17.

Chapter 4

ABIS. (2021). *Home page*. Advancement of Blacks in Sports. www.weareabis.org.

Alexander, M. (2012). *The new Jim Crow: Mass incarceration in the age of colorblindness*. New York, NY: The New Press.

Armour, N., Freeman, M., & Schad, T. (2021, January 14). Why do some NFL teams never hire people of color as GMs and coaches and others do? *USA Today*. www.usatoday.com/story/sports/nfl/2021/01/14/nfl-coaches-best-and-worst-nfl-teams-when-hiring-people-color/6653774002/.

Aycock, C., & Scott, M. (2011). *The first Black boxing champions: Essays on fighters of the 1800s to the 1920s*. Jefferson, NC: McFarland.

Bell, D.A. (1980). *Brown v. Board of Education* and the interest convergence dilemma. *Harvard Law Review, 93*(3), 518-533.

Bell, D.A. (1992). *Faces at the bottom of the well: The permanence of racism*. New York, NY: Basic Books.

Bonilla-Silva, E. (1997). Rethinking racism: Toward a structural interpretation. *American Sociological Review, 62*(3), 465-480.

Bonilla-Silva, E. (2018). *Racism without racists: Color-blind racism and the persistence of racial inequality in America*. Lanham, MD: Rowman & Littlefield.

Boykoff, J. (2016). *Power games: A political history of the Olympics*. Brooklyn, NY: Verso.

Carter-Francique, A.R. (2017). Is excellence inclusive? The benefits of fostering Black female college athletes' sense of belonging. *Journal of Higher Education Athletics & Innovation, 1*(3), 48-73.

Carter, P.L., & Welner, K.G. (2013). *Closing the opportunity gap: What America must do to give every child an even chance*. New York, NY: Oxford University Press.

Chen, C., & Mason, D.S. (2019). Making settler colonialism visible in sport management. *Journal of Sport Management, 33*, 379-392.

Coakley, J. (2017). *Sports in society: Issues and controversies* (12th ed.). New York, NY: McGraw-Hill Education.

Cooper, J.N. (2012). Personal troubles and public issues: A sociological imagination of Black male student athletes' experiences at predominantly white institutions. *Sociology Mind, 2*(3), 261-271.

Cooper, J.N. (2016). College athletics. In K. Lomotey (Ed.), *Contemporary issues for people of color: Living, working and learning in the U.S.* (pp. 45-51). Santa Barbara, CA: ABC-CLIO.

Cooper, J.N. (2017). A call for a language shift: From covert oppression to overt empowerment. *UConn Today* [Op-Ed]. https://education.uconn.edu/2016/12/07/a-call-for-a-language-shift-from-covert-oppression-to-overt-empowerment/.

Cooper, J.N., Nwadike, A., & Macaulay, C. (2017). A critical race theory analysis of big-time college sports: Implications for culturally responsive and race-conscious sport leadership. *Journal of Issues in Intercollegiate Athletics, 10*, 204-233.

Cooper, J.N. (2019). *From exploitation back to empowerment: Black male holistic (under)development through sport and (mis)education*. New York, NY: Peter Lang.

Cooper, J.N. (2021). *A legacy of African American resistance and activism through sport*. New York, NY: Peter Lang.

Cooper, J.N., Cavil, J.K., & Cheeks, G. (2014). The state of intercollegiate athletics at historically Black colleges and universities (HBCUs): Past, present, & persistence. *Journal of Issues in Intercollegiate Athletics, 7*, 307-332.

Cooper, J.N., Mallery, Jr., M., Macaulay, C.D. T. (2020). African American sport activism and broader social movements. In D. Brown (Ed.), *Sports in African American*

Life: Essays on History and Culture (pp. 97-115). Jefferson, NC: McFarland.

Cooper, J.N., Macaulay, C., & Rodriguez, S.H. (2019). Race and resistance: A typology of African American sport activism. *International Review for the Sociology of Sport, 54*(2) 151-181.

Cooper, J.N., Newton, A., Klein, M., & Jolly, S. (2020). A call for culturally responsive transformational leadership in college sport: An anti-ism approach for achieving true equity and inclusion. *Frontiers in Sociology, 5*(65), 1-17.

Crenshaw, K., Gotanda, N.T., Peller, G., & Thomas, K. (1995). *Critical race theory: The key writings that formed the movement*. New York, NY: The New Press.

Crossroads Ministry. (n.d.) *Continuum on Becoming an Anti-Racist Multicultural Organization* Chicago, IL: Crossroads Ministry. https://philanos.org/resources/Documents/Conference%202020/Pre-Read%20PDFs/Continuum_AntiRacist.pdf.

Cunningham, G.B. (2010). Understanding the under-representation of African American coaches: A multilevel perspective. *Sport Management Review, 13*, 395-406.

Cunningham, G. (2019). *Diversity and inclusion in sport organizations: A multilevel perspective*. New York, NY: Routledge.

Darity, W.A., & Mullen, A.K. (2020). *From here to equality: Reparations for Black Americans in the twenty-first century*. Chapel Hill, NC: University of North Carolina Press.

DeCuir, J.T., & Dixson, A.D. (2004). "So when it comes out, they aren't that surprised that it is there": Using critical race theory as a tool of analysis of race and racism in education. *Educational Researcher, 33*(5), 26-31.

Delgado, R., & Stefancic, J. (2001). *Critical race theory: An introduction*. New York, NY: New York University Press.

Espinoza, O. (2007) Solving the equity–equality conceptual dilemma: A new model for analysis of the educational process. *Educational Research, 49*(4), 343-363.

Fanon, F. (2004). *The wretched of the earth*. New York, NY: Grove Press. (Original work published 1961).

Fay, T., & Wolff, E. (2009). Disability sport in the twenty-first century: Creating a new sport opportunity spectrum. *Boston University International Law Journal, 27*, 231-248.

Feagin, J. (2006). *Systemic racism: A theory of oppression*. New York, NY: Routledge.

Gibson, C. (2020). *Who's highest-paid in your state?* ESPN. www.espn.com/espn/feature/story/_/id/28261213/dabo-swinney-ed-orgeron-highest-paid-state-employees.

Hamilton, D., Darity, Jr., W., Price, A.E., Sridharan, V., & Tippett, R. (2015). *Umbrellas don't make it rain: Why studying and working hard isn't enough for Black Americans*. The Insight Center for Community Economic Development. (p. 1-10). https://insightcced.org/report-umbrellas-dont-make-it-rain

Harper, S.R. (2018). *Black male student-athletes and racial inequities in NCAA Division I college sports*. University of Southern California Race and Equity Center. http://abfe.issuelab.org/resources/29858/29858.pdf.

Harris, C. (1993). Whiteness as property. *Harvard Law Review, 106*(8), 1707-1791.

Harris, O. (2000). African American predominance in sport. In D. Brooks & R. Althouse (Eds.), *Racism in college athletics: The African American athlete's experience* (2nd ed., pp. 37-52). Morgantown, WV: Fitness Information Technology.

Harrison, D.A., Price, K.H., & Bell, M.P. (1998). Beyond relational demography: Time and the effects of surface- and deep-level diversity on work group cohesion. *Academy of Management Journal, 41*(1), 96-107.

Hartmann, D. (2019). The Olympic "revolt" of 1968 and its lessons for contemporary African American athletic activism. *European Journal of American Studies, Special Issue: Race Matters: 1968 as Living History in the Black Freedom Struggle*, 1-24.

Hawkins, B. (2010). *The new plantation: Black athletes, college sports, and predominantly White NCAA institutions*. New York, NY: Palgrave Macmillan.

Hawkins, B., Carter-Francique, A.R., & Cooper, J.N. (Eds.) (2017). *Black athletic sporting experiences in the United States: Critical race theory*. New York, NY: Palgrave Macmillan.

Horne, G. (2017). *The apocalypse of settler colonialism: The roots of slavery, White supremacy, and capitalism in seventeenth-century North America and the Caribbean*. New York, NY: Monthly Review Press.

Horne, G. (2020). *The dawning of the apocalypse: The roots of slavery, White supremacy, settler colonialism, and capitalism in the long sixteenth century*. New York, NY: Monthly Review Press.

Howard, T.C. (2014). *Black male(d): Peril and promise in the education of African American males*. New York, NY: Teachers College Press.

Huma, R., & Staurowsky, E.J. (2020). How the NCAA's empire robs predominantly Black athletes of billions in generational wealth. Riverside, CA: National College Players Association. https://drive.google.com/file/d/1z-97vhcjErrHIvuO3Nu2wUWbG90bFKnm_/view.

Hylton, K. (2010). How a turn to critical race theory can contribute to our understanding of 'race,' racism, and anti-racism in sport. *International Review for the Sociology of Sport, 45*(3), 335-354.

Kendi, I. (2019). *How to be an anti-racist*. New York, NY: One World.

Levenson, M. (2021, February 27). N.B.A. investigating after Jeremy Lin said he was called "coronavirus." *New York Times*. www.nytimes.com/2021/02/27/sports/basketball/nba-jeremy-lin-coronavirus.html.

Martin, L.L. (2015). *White sports/Black sports: Racial disparities in athletic programs*. Santa Barbara, CA: Praeger.

McDowell, J., & Carter-Francique, A. (2017). An intersectional analysis of the workplace experiences of African American female athletic directors. *Sex Roles, 77*, 393-408.

McGee, K. (2021, March 1). "UT needs rich donors": Emails show wealthy alumni supporting "Eyes of Texas" threatened to pull donations. *Texas Tribune*. www.texastribune.org/2021/03/01/ut-eyes-of-texas-donors-emails/.

Miller, S., & Thorbecke, C. (2018, February 18). *UVA's 1st Black female athletic director: "I'm living proof that you can do anything."* ABC News. https://abcnews.go.com/GMA/News/uvas-1st-black-female-athletic-director-im-living/story?id=53063477.

NCAA. (2021, February). *NCAA student-athlete activism and racial justice engagement study*. Indianapolis, IN: National Collegiate Athletic Association. https://ncaaorg.s3.amazonaws.com/research/demographics/NCAARES_SAFallSurvey_ActivismRacialJustice.pdf

Omi, M., & Winant, H. (2015). *Racial formation in the United States* (3rd ed.). New York, NY: Routledge.

Oseguera, L. (2010). Success despite the image: How African American male student-athletes endure their academic journey amidst negative characterizations. *Journal of the Study of Sports and Athletes in Education*, *4*(3), 297-324.

Ray, V. (2019). A theory of racialized organizations. *American Sociological Review*, *84*, 26-53. doi: 10.1177/0003122418822335.

Rosner, S.R., & Shropshire, K.L. (2011). *The business of sports* (2nd ed.). Sudbury, MA: Jones & Bartlett.

Sage, G.H. (1998). *Power and ideology in American sport* (2nd ed.). Champaign, IL: Human Kinetics.

Sage, G.H., & Eitzen, D.S. (2009). *Sociology of North American sport*. New York, NY: Oxford University Press.

Sailes, G. (2010). The African American athlete: Social myths and stereotypes. In G. Sailes (Ed.), *Modern sport and the African American athlete experience* (pp. 55-68). San Diego, CA: Cognella.

Scheurich, J.J., & Young, M.D. (1997). Coloring epistemologies: Are our research epistemologies racially biased? *Educational Researcher*, *26*(4), 4-16.

Scott, D. (2014). *Contemporary leadership in sport organizations*. Champaign, IL: Human Kinetics.

Singer, J.N. (2020). *Race, sports, and education: Improving opportunities and outcomes for Black male college athletes*. Cambridge, MA: Harvard Educational Press.

Smith, E. (2009). *Race, sport and the American Dream* (2nd ed.). Durham, NC: Carolina Academic Press.

Solórzano, D.G., & Yosso, T.J. (2002). Critical race methodology: Counter-storytelling as an analytical framework for education research. *Qualitative Inquiry*, *8*(1), 23-44.

Staurowsky, E. (2007). "You know, we are all Indian": Exploring White power and privilege in reactions to the NCAA Native American mascot policy. *Journal of Sport & Social Issues*, *31*(1), 61-76.

TIDES (2021). The Institute for Diversity and Ethics in Sport. Racial and Gender Report Cards. https://www.tidesport.org/racial-gender-report-card.

Turick, R., Weems, A., Swim, N., Bopp, T., & Singer, J.N. (2019). Who are we honoring? Extending the Ebony & Ivy discussion to include sport facilities. *Journal of Sport Management*, *35*(1), 17-29.

UDHR (1948). *The Universal Declaration of Human Rights*. www.ohchr.org/EN/UDHR/Documents/UDHR_Translations/eng.pdf.

USA Today. (2020, July 18). *These 25 athletic programs raked in the most revenue*. https://www.usatoday.com/story/sports/college/2021/10/13/ncaa-finances-revenue-expense-database-methodology/8432968002/.

Virginia Sports (2021). *Carla Williams Bio*. UVA Athletic Department. https://virginiasports.com/staff/carla-williams/.

Wallerstein, I. (1974). *The modern world system, vol. 1: Capitalist agriculture and the origins of the European world-economy in the sixteenth century*. New York/London: Academic Press.

Wiggins, D.K., & Miller, P. (2003). *The unlevel playing field: A documentary history of the African American experience in sport*. Urbana, IL: University of Illinois Press.

Chapter 5

Adair, D. (2013). Olympic ceremonial, protocol and symbolism. In *Managing the Olympics* (pp. 182-205). London: Palgrave Macmillan.

Ahmad, N., Thorpe, H., Richards, J., & Marfell, A. (2020). Building cultural diversity in sport: A critical dialogue with Muslim women and sports facilitators. *International Journal of Sport Policy and Politics*, *12*(4); 637-653.

Ahmed, S. (2004). Declarations of whiteness: The non-performativity of anti-racism. *Borderlands*, *3*(2).

American Psychological Association, Presidential Task Force on Educational Disparities. (2012). *Ethnic and racial disparities in education: Psychology's contributions to understanding and reducing disparities*. www.apa.org/ed/resources/racial-disparities.aspx.

Anderson, E., & McCormack, M. (2010). Intersectionality, critical race theory, and American sporting oppression: Examining black and gay male athletes. *Journal of Homosexuality*, *57*(8), 949-967.

Armstrong, K.L. (2011). "Lifting the veils and illuminating the shadows": Furthering the explorations of race and ethnicity in sport management. *Journal of Sport Management*, *25*(2), 95-106.

The Aspen Institute (2018). *State of play 2018: Trends and developments*. www.aspeninstitute.org/wp-content/uploads/2018/10/StateofPlay2018_v4WEB_2-FINAL.pdf.

Bonilla-Silva, E. (2006). *Racism without racists: Color-blind racism and the persistence of racial inequality in the United States* (2nd ed.). New York: Rowman & Littlefield.

Camiré, M. (2015). Examining high school teacher-coaches' perspective on relationship building with student-athletes. *International Sport Coaching Journal*, *2*(2), 125-136.

Carter-Francique, A.R. (2020). Intersectionality and the influence of stereotypes for Black sportswomen in college sport. In V.L. Farmer, & E.S.W. Farmer, (Eds.), *Critical race theory in the academy*, (pp. 453-480). Charlotte, NC: Information Age Publishing.

Chapman, T., Dixson, A., Gillborn, D., & Ladson-Billings, G. (2013). Critical race theory. In B. Irby, G. Brown, R. Lara-Aleclo, & S. Jackson, (Eds.), *The handbook of educational theories* (pp. 1019-1026). Charlotte, NC: Information Age Publishing.

Chavous, T.M., Leath, S., & Richardson, B. (2015). African American racial identity: Promoting academic achievement and excellence, resisting stereotypes and the myth of "acting white." In V. Berry, A. Fleming-Rife & A. Dayo, (Eds.), *Black culture and experience: Contemporary issues*, (pp. 3-18). New York, NY: International Academic Publishers.

Choo, H.Y., & Ferree, M.M. (2010). Practicing intersectionality in sociological research: A critical analysis of inclusions, interactions, and institutions in the study of inequalities. *Sociological Theory*, *28*(2), 129-149.

Collins, P.H., & Bilge, S. (2020). *Intersectionality*. (2nd ed.) John Wiley & Sons.

Collins, P.H., & Bilge, S. (2016). *Intersectionality*. Cambridge, UK: Polity.

Crenshaw, K. (1989). Demarginalizing the intersection of race and sex: A black feminist critique of antidiscrimination doctrine, feminist theory and antiracist politics. *University of Chicago Legal Forum*, Vol. 1989, Article 8. Available at: https://chicagounbound.uchicago.edu/uclf/vol1989/iss1/8.

CRIAW. (2009). *Everyone belongs: A toolkit for applying intersectionality*. Ottawa: CRIAW.

Cunningham, G.B. (2020). The under-representation of racial minorities in coaching and leadership positions in the United States. In S. Bradbury, J. Lusted, & J.V. Sterkenburg (Eds.) *'Race', Ethnicity and Racism in Sports Coaching* (pp. 3-21). New York, NY: Routledge.

Dagkas, S. (2016). Problematizing social justice in health pedagogy and youth sport: Intersectionality of race, ethnicity, and class. *Research Quarterly for Exercise and Sport*, *87*(3), 221-229.

de Brey, C., Musu, L., McFarland, J., Wilkinson-Flicker, S., Diliberti, M., Zhang, A., Branstetter, C., & Wang, X. (2019). *Status and trends in the education of racial and ethnic groups 2018* (NCES 2019-038). U.S. Department of Education. Washington, DC: National Center for Education Statistics.

Denham, B.E. (2019). Sports participation and attitudes toward race and ethnicity: A study of twelfth-grade students in the United States. *Sociology of Sport Journal*, *37*(2), 143-151.

DeSensi, J.T., Kelley, D.R., Blanton, M.D., & Beitel, P.A. (2003). Sport management curricular evaluation and needs assessment: A multifaceted approach. *Journal of Sport Management*, *4*, 31-58.

Dill, B.T., & Zambrana, R.E. (2009). Critical thinking about inequality: An emerging lens. In B. T. Dill & R. E. Zambrana (Eds.), *Emerging intersections: Race, class, and gender in theory, policy, and practice* (pp. 1–21). New Brunswick, NJ: Rutgers University Press.

Elassar, A. (2021). A student athlete sparked national change after being disqualified from a volleyball match for wearing a hijab. CNN. www.cnn.com/2021/02/06/us/nashville-volleyball-religious-headwear-rule-trnd/index.html.

Erikson, E.H. (1968). *Identity: Youth and Crisis* (no. 7). W.W. Norton.

Fitzgerald, K.J. (2014). *Recognizing race and ethnicity: Power, privilege, and inequality*. Hachette.

Forsyth, E., & Olson, J. (2013). Challenges in today's interscholastic sport administration. In M.L. Blackburn, E. Forsyth, J.R. Olson & B. Whitehead (Eds.), *NIAAA's Guide to Interscholastic Athletic Administration* (pp. ix-xvi). Champaign, IL: Human Kinetics.

Frank, K. (2007). "Whether beast or human": The cultural legacies of dread, locks, and dystopia. *small axe*, *11*(2), 46-62.

Frazier, S., Holland, B., Nuñez, D., & Bass, G. (2020). *Historic moment: Tyler ISD board votes 7-0 to change names of John Tyler, Robert E. Lee high schools. [website]*. KLTV. KLTV. Last Modified 16 July 2022. Accessed 19 January 2022. https://www.kltv.com/2020/07/16/watch-tyler-isd-board-hold-meeting-renaming-robert-e-lee-john-tyler-campuses/.

Gallagher, G.W. (2020). Robert E. Lee. *Encyclopedia Britannica*. Retrieved January 13, 2021, from www.britannica.com/biography/Robert-E-Lee.

George-Williams, G. (2019). *Love is at the root of resistance: A hermeneutic phenomenological inquiry into the lived experiences of Black college athlete activists* (Doctoral dissertation, Azusa Pacific University).

Giving Compass. (2020). *Elementary school education overview*. Retrieved March 2, 2021, from https://givingcompass.org/article/elementary-school-education/.

Hahn Tapper, A.J. (2013). A pedagogy of social justice education: Social identity theory, intersectionality, and empowerment. *Conflict Resolution Quarterly*, *30*(4), 411-445.

Hallinan, C., & Jackson, S.J. (Eds.). (2008). *Social and cultural diversity in a sporting world*. Emerald Group.

Hammond, Z. (2014). *Culturally responsive teaching and the brain: Promoting authentic engagement and rigor among culturally and linguistically diverse students*. Corwin Press.

Hankivsky, O. (2014). *Intersectionality 101*. The Institute for Intersectionality Research & Policy, SFU, 1-34.

Hankivsky, O., & Cormier, R. (2011). Intersectionality and public policy: Some lessons from existing models. *Political Research Quarterly*, *64*(1), 217-229.

Hanover Research. (2020). *Research Priority Brief: Best Practices in Inclusive Recruiting*. https://wasa-oly.org/WASA/images/WASA/6.0%20Resources/Hanover/Best%20Practices%20in%20Inclusive%20Recruiting%20(1).pdf.

Healey, J. F., & Stepnick, A. (2019). *Diversity and society: Race, ethnicity, and gender*. Sage Publications.

Healey, J.F., Stepnick, A., & O'Brian, E., (2018). *Race, ethnicity, gender, and class: The sociology of group conflict and change.* Sage.

Houston, B.M.W. (2019). *Exceptional recruiting: Identity intersections' impact on decision making for young Black women athletes during the NCAA recruiting process* (Doctoral dissertation, University of Colorado, Colorado Springs).

Hughes, G. (2004). Managing black guys: Representation, corporate culture, and the NBA. *Sociology of Sport Journal, 21*(2), 163-184.

Jones, S.R., & Abes, E.S. (2013). *Identity development of college students.* https://ebookcentral.proquest.com/lib/uccs/detail.action?docID=1123999.

Jowett, S. (2007). Interdependence analysis and the 3+1Cs in the coach-athlete relationship. In S. Jowett & D. Lavallee (Eds.), *Social psychology in sport* (pp. 15-27). Champaign, IL: Human Kinetics.

Kim, G. (2021). Olympic gold medalist Chloe Kim reveals she gets "hundreds" of racist messages a month. *NextShark.* Retrieved 16 September, 2021, from https://nextshark.com/chloe-kim-racist-messages-anti-asian-attacks/.

Lee, D. (2020). The remarkable story of how a teenage runner battled the legacy of Robert E. Lee. *ESPN.com.* Retrieved January 7, 2021, from www.espn.com/espn/story/_/id/30045630/the-remarkable-story-how-teenage-runner-battled-legacy-robert-e-lee.

Lumpkin, A., & Stokowski, S. (2011). Interscholastic sports: A character-building privilege. *Kappa Delta Pi Record, 47*(3), 124-128.

McGovern, J. (2020). The intersection of class, race, gender, and generation in shaping Latinas' sport experiences. *Sociological Spectrum, 41*(1), 96-114. DOI: 10.1080/02732173.2020.1850378

Macon, A.L.F. (2014). Hair's the thing: Trait discrimination and forced performance of race through racially conscious public school hairstyle prohibitions. *University of Pennsylvania Journal of Constitutional Law, 17*, 1255.

Marston, S.B. (2020). Managing fear and fantasy: Cultural politics and gameplay governance in the National Basketball Association, 1990-2006. *Sociology of Sport Journal, 37*(2), 125-132. https://doi.org/10.1123/ssj.2019-0029.

Martin, B.E., Harrison, C.K., Stone, J., & Lawrence, S.M. (2010). Athletic voices and academic victories: African American male student-athlete experiences in the Pac-Ten. *Journal of Sport & Social Issues, 34*(2), 131-153.

Mathews, C.J., Medina, M.A., Bañales, J., Pinetta, B.J., Marchand, A.D., Agi, A.C., & Rivas-Drake, D. (2020). Mapping the intersections of adolescents' ethnic-racial identity and critical consciousness. *Adolescent Research Review, 5*(4), 363-379.

McDonald, M.G. (2020). Once more, with feeling: Sport, national anthems, and the collective power of affect. *Sociology of Sport Journal, 37*(1), 1-11. https://doi.org/10.1123/ssj.2019-0089.

Melnick, J.M., & Sabo, D. (1994). Sport and social mobility among African-American and Hispanic athletes. In Eisen, G., & Wiggins, D.K. (Eds.) *Ethnicity and sport in North American history and culture* (No. 40). ABC-CLIO.

Misawa, M. (2006). Queer race pedagogy in adult higher education: Dealing with power dynamics and positionality of gay students of color. In *Proceedings of the 47th annual Adult Education Research Conference, USA* (pp. 257-262).

Montez de Oca, J., & Suh, S.C. (2020). Ethics of patriotism: NFL players' protests against police violence. *International Review for the Sociology of Sport, 55*(5), 563-587. https://doi.org/10.1177/1012690218825210.

Moraga, J.E. 2018. On ESPN Deportes: Latinos, sport media, and the cultural politics of visibilities. *Journal of Sport and Social Issues 42*(6), 470–497. doi: https://doi-org/10.1177/0193723518797030.

Namkung, V. (2021). *Descriptions of Asian Olympians' bodies are part of trend of dehumanizing Asians in U.S.* NBC News. www.nbcnews.com/news/asian-america/descriptions-asian-olympians-bodies-are-part-trend-dehumanizing-asians-rcna1375.

NFHS (2020). 2018-2019 high school athletics participation survey. National Federation of State High School Associations. www.nfhs.org/media/1020412/2018-19_participation_survey.pdf

NIAAA. (2020). *About the NIAAA.* Retrieved March 20, 2020, from https://members.niaaa.org/page/About.

Northouse, P.G. (2016). *Leadership: Theory and practice.* Sage.

Oates, T.P. (2020). "Where I'm From": Jay-Z's "hip hop cosmopolitanism," basketball, and the neoliberal politics of urban space. *Sociology of Sport Journal, 37*(3), 183-191. https://doi.org/10.1123/ssj.2019-0045.

OED Online. (2020, December). Intersectionality. In *OED Online.* Oxford University Press. Retrieved 14 February 2021.

Page, J.E., & Domingo-Snyder, E.T.B. (June 2016). *Diversity & inclusion at JHMI* [Paper presentation.] Diversity and Inclusion Conference, Johns Hopkins University. www.hopkinsmedicine.org/international/partners-forum/past-presentations/2016/06_PageDomingoSnyder_Trauma_Trust_and_WorldClass_Health_Care.pdf.

Randall. (2018, February 13). *New York Times* writer mistakes Mirai Nagasu for an immigrant. *AsAmNews.* Retrieved 16 September, 2021, from https://asamnews.com/2018/02/13/new-york-times-writer-mistakes-mirai-nagasu-for-an-immigrant/.

Olympic Rings. (2021). The Olympic rings. *International Olympic Committee.* [website] Retrieved April 7, 2021, from www.olympic.org/olympic-rings.

Ortega, G. (2019). Examining the intersection of race and athletics for Latino male student-athletes. *Journal of Hispanic Higher Education, 20*(2), 179-192. https://doi.org/10.1177/1538192719876091.

Oseguera, L. (2010). Success despite the image: How African American male scholar-athletes endure their academic journey amidst negative characterizations. *Journal for the Study of Sports and Athletes in Education, 4*(3), 297-324.

Pickett, M.W. (2009). *The invisible Black woman in the Title IX shuffle: An empirical analysis and critical examination of gender equity policy in assessing access and participation of Black and white high school girls in interscholastic sports* (Doctoral dissertation, University of Miami).

Pickett, M.W., Dawkins, M.P., & Braddock, J.H. (2012). Race and gender equity in sports: Have white and African American females benefited equally from Title IX? *American Behavioral Scientist, 56*(11), 1581-1603.

Rankin, S., & Reason, R. (2008). Transformational tapestry model: A comprehensive approach to transforming campus climate. *Journal of Diversity in Higher Education, 1*(4), 262.

Renn, K.A. (2012). Creating and re-creating race: The emergence of racial identity as a critical element in psychological, sociological, and ecological perspectives on human development. In Wijeyesinghe, C.L. & Jackson III, B.W. (Eds.) *New perspectives on racial identity development: Integrating emerging frameworks, 2,* 11-32. New York: NYU Press

Rodriguez, J.K., Holvino, E., Fletcher, J.K., & Nkomo, S.M. (2016). The theory and praxis of intersectionality in work and organizations: Where do we go from here? *Gender, Work and Organization, 23*(3), 201-222.

Sabo, D. & Veliz, P. (2008). *Go out and play: Youth sports in America.* East Meadow, NY: Women's Sports Foundation.

Schaefer, R.T. (2009). *Race and ethnicity in the United States* (5th ed.). Upper Saddle River, NJ: Pearson.

SEC. (2020). SEC creates council on racial equity and social justice. SEC Sports. www.secsports.com/article/29703422/sec-creates-council-racial-equity-social-justice.

Shen, X., & Tian, X. (2012). Academic culture and campus culture of universities. *Higher Education Studies, 2*(2), 61-65.

Silva, C. (2021). *Asian American Olympians share how anti-Asian hate has affected them.* NBC News. www.nbcnews.com/news/asian-america/asian-american-olympians-share-anti-asian-hate-affected-rcna1474.

Simien, E.M., Arinze, N., & McGarry, J. (2019). A portrait of marginality in sport and education: Toward a theory of intersectionality and raced-gendered experiences for Black female college athletes. *Journal of Women, Politics & Policy, 40*(3), 409-427.

Smith, L.V., Wang, M.T., & Hill, D.J. (2020). Black youths' perceptions of school cultural pluralism, school climate and the mediating role of racial identity. *Journal of School Psychology, 83*, 50-65.

Solorzano, D. G., & Yosso, T. J. (2002). Critical race methodology: Counter-storytelling as an analytical framework for education research. *Qualitative Inquiry, 8*(1), 23–44.

Springer, K. (2005). *Living for the revolution: Black feminist organizations, 1968-1980.* Durham, N.C.: Duke University Press.

Staurowsky, E.J., Watanabe, N., Cooper, J., Cooky, C., Lough, N., Paule-Koba, A., Pharr, J., Williams, S., Cummings, S., Issokson-Silver, K., & Snyder, M. (2020). *Chasing equity: The triumphs, challenges, and opportunities in sports for girls and women.* New York, NY: Women's Sports Foundation.

Stone, D. (2012). *Policy paradox: The art of political decision making.* New York: W. W. Norton & Company.

Syed, M., Juang, L.P., & Svensson, Y. (2018). Toward a new understanding of ethnic-racial settings for ethnic-racial identity development. *Journal of Research on Adolescence, 28*(2), 262-276.

Tate, W. F., IV. (1997). Chapter 4: Critical race theory and education: History, theory, and implications. *Review of Research in Education, 22*(1), 195-247.

Theune, F. (2019). *Brown*, Title IX and the impact of race and sex segregation on sports participation opportunities for Black females. *Sociology Compass, 13*(3), e12661.

Tate, W.F. (1997). Critical race theory and education: History, theory, and implications. *Review of Research in Education 22:* 195-247 https://doi.org/https://doi.org/10.2307/1167376.

Taylor, E., Guy-Walls, P., Wilkerson, P., & Addae, R. (2019). The historical perspectives of stereotypes on African-American males. *Journal of Human Rights and Social Work, 4*(3), 213-225.

Tyler, T.R. (2000). Social justice: Outcome and procedure. *International Journal of Psychology, 35*(2), 117-125.

Vélez, M.M., Nguyen, D.J., & Lee, R.M. (2019). Ethnic-racial identity development in adolescents and young adults. In Barkley, L, Svetaz, M.V. & Chulani, V.L. (Eds.) *Promoting health equity among racially and ethnically diverse adolescents* (pp. 65-84). Cham, Switzerland: Springer.

Veliz, P., Snyder, M., & Sabo, D. (2019). *The state of high school sports in America: An evaluation of the nation's most popular extracurricular activity.* New York: Women's Sports Foundation. www.womenssportsfoundation.org/wp-content/uploads/2019/10/state-of-high-school-sports-report-final.pdf.

Warf, B. (2008). *Time-space compression: Historical geographies.* Routledge.

Watson, B., & Scraton, S. (2018). Re-confronting whiteness. In A. Ratna, A & Samie, S.F. (Eds) *Race, gender and sport: The politics of ethnic 'other' girls and women*, 85-106. London: Routledge.

Way, N., Hernández, M.G., Rogers, L.O., & Hughes, D.L. (2013). "I'm not going to become no rapper": Stereotypes as a context of ethnic and racial identity development. *Journal of Adolescent Research, 28*(4), 407-430.

Wijeyesinghe, C.L. (2012). The intersectional model of multiracial identity: Integrating multiracial identity theories and intersectional perspectives on social identity. *New perspectives on racial identity development: Integrating emerging frameworks, 2,* 81-107. New York: NYU Press.

Wilkins, A.C. (2014). Race, age, and identity transformations in the transition from high school to college for Black and first-generation White men. *Sociology of Education, 87*(3), 171-187.

YCD. (2022). *Resources. [website].* Accessed 19 January. https://ycdiversity.org/get-involved/start-an-inclusion-and-justice-club/.

Zarrett, N., Veliz, P., & Sabo, D. (2020). *Keeping girls in the game: Factors that influence sport participation*. Women's Sports Foundation.

Zayas, R.J. (2018). *Examination of the impact interscholastic athletics has on participating student-athletes from the perspective of the high school principal, athletic director and school counselor*. https://digitalrepository.unm.edu/educ_hess_etds/95. (Doctoral dissertation, University of New Mexico).

Chapter 6

Acosta, V. and Carpenter, L. (2006). Women in intercollegiate sport: A longitudinal, national study. twenty nine year update, 1977-2006.

Ahmed, S. Davis, A.R., Elsey, B., Gibbs, L., & Luther, J. (2019, June). Women's World Cup, NBA/NHL finals, and ultimate Frisbee (No. 111).[audio podcast] *Burn it all down*. www.burnitalldownpod.com/episodes/111.

Alter, C. (2014, April 3). Dudes slam Mike Francesca for blasting Daniel Murphy's paternity leave. *Time*. https://time.com/48225/mike-francesca-daniel-murphy-mets-paternity-leave/.

Anthony, M. (2018, March 10). Geno Auriemma on notion he should coach UConn men: 'I Don't Particularly Think That's A Great Idea.' *Hartford Courant*. www.courant.com/sports/uconn-womens-basketball/hc-sp-geno-auriemma-kevin-ollie-20180310-story.html.

Antunovic, D., & Whiteside, E. (2018). Feminist sports media studies: State of the field. In D. Harp, J. Loke, & I. Bachmann (Eds.), *Feminist approaches to media theory and research* (pp. 111-130). Springer International. https://doi.org/10.1007/978-3-319-90838-0_8.

Aykroyd, L. (2021, April 9). *Women's sports journalists worldwide speak out*. Global Sport Matters. https://globalsportmatters.com/business/2021/04/09/womens-sports-journalists-worldwide-speak-out-stereotypes-opportunities.

Barnes, Katie. (2021a, June 24). *The power of Layshia Clarendon*. ESPN. www.espn.com/espn/feature/story/_/id/31681454/the-power-layshia-clarendon.

Barnes, Katie. (2021b, September 1). *Young transgender athletes caught in middle of states' debates*. ESPN. www.espn.com/espn/story/_/id/32115820/young-transgender-athletes-caught-middle-states-debates.

Bederman, G. (2008) *Manliness and civilization: A cultural history of gender and race in the United States, 1880-1917*. Chicago, IL: University of Chicago Press.

Berri, D. (2006). *The Wages of wins: Taking measure of the many myths in modern sport*. Stanford, CA: Stanford University Press.

Brassil, G.R. (2021, May 29). Sedona Prince has a message for you. *The New York Times*. www.nytimes.com/2021/05/29/sports/ncaabasketball/sedona-prince-ncaa-basketball-video.html.

Brennan, C.. (2021, March 21). Treat NCAA women the same as men or change 'March Madness' to 'Spring Sexism.' *USA Today*. www.usatoday.com/story/sports/christinebrennan/2021/03/21/march-madness-treat-ncaa-women-same-men-call-spring-sexism/4790316001/

Bruce, T. (2015). Assessing the sociology of sport: On media and representations of sportswomen. *International Review for the Sociology of Sport 50*(4-5), 380-84.

Cahn, S.K. (2015). *Coming on strong: Gender and sexuality in women's sport*. Urbana, IL: University of Illinois Press.

Carpenter, L. (2018). Is UConn's women's basketball dominance bad for the sport? Of course not. *The Guardian*. https://www.theguardian.com/sport/2018/mar/30/is-uconns-womens-basketball-dominance-too-good.

Carter-Francique, A.R., & Olushola, J. (2016). Women coaches of color: Examining the effects of intersectionality. In N.M. LaVoi (Ed.) *Women in sports coaching* (pp. 81-94). Routledge.

Collins, P.H. 2009. *Black feminist thought: Knowledge, consciousness, and the politics of empowerment*. New York, NY: Routledge.

Cooky, C., & Messner, M.A. (2018). *No slam dunk: Gender, sport and the unevenness of social change*. Rutgers University Press.

Cooky, C., Messner, M.A., & Hextrum, R.H. (2013). Women play sport, but not on TV: A longitudinal study of televised news media. *Communication & Sport, 1*(3), 203-230. https://doi.org/10.1177/2167479513476947.

Cooky, C., Messner, M.A., & Musto, M. (2015). It's dude time!: A quarter century of excluding women's sports in televised news and highlight shows. *Communication & Sport 3*(3), 261–87.

Cooky, C. and LaVoi, N. (2012). Playing but losing: Women's sports after Title IX. *Contexts 11*(1), 42-46.

Crenshaw, K. (1990). Mapping the margins: Intersectionality, identity politics, and violence against women of color. *Stanford Law Review 43*(6), 1241–1300.

Crocket, H. (2013). "This is men's ultimate": (Re)creating multiple masculinities in elite open ultimate Frisbee. *International Review for the Sociology of Sport, 48*(3), 318-333.

Cruz, M. (2016). Claressa Shields' Endorsements have been slow to come in & her explanation why is depressingly real. *Bustle*. A.R.www.bustle.com/articles/179130-claressa-shields-endorsements-have-been-slow-to-come-in-her-explanation-why-is-depressingly-real.

Cunningham, G.B., Wicker, P., & Walker, N.A. (2021). Gender and racial bias in sport organizations. *Frontiers in Sociology, 6*, 122.

Dator, J. (2021, June 22). *It's time for the NBA to hire a woman as head coach*. SB Nation. www.sbnation.com/nba/2021/6/22/22545098/nba-womens-coach-becky-hammon-dawn-staley-kara-lawson-teresa-weather-spoon.

Davis, A.R. (2021, May 24). Nina King latest of black women AD disruptors." *Global Sport Matters*. https://globalsportmatters.com/culture/2021/05/24/nina-king-duke-tradition-black-women-ads-journey/.

de la Cretaz, Britni. (2018). *The persistence of sex-segregated sports is—like so many things—about men's egos*. Bitch Media.

de la Cretaz, Britni. (2021). *What about the trans athletes who compete—and win—in men's sports?* Yahoo. www.yahoo.com/lifestyle/trans-athletes-compete-win-men-133910920.html.

Dodgson, L. (2020). *Female college athletes from across the US say they've been bullied, manipulated, and psychologically abused by their coaches*. Insider. www.insider.com/players-say-psychological-abuse-college-women-sports-coaches-2020-7.

Dworkin, S.L., & Messner, M.A. (2002). Introduction: Gender relations and sport. *Sociological Perspectives*, 45(4), 347–352. https://doi.org/10.1525/sop.2002.45.4.347.

Elsey, B., & Nadel, J. (2019). *Futbolera: A history of women and sports in Latin America*. Austin, TX: University of Texas Press.

Fink, J.S., Kane, M.J., & LaVoi, N.M. (2014). The freedom to choose: Elite female athletes' preferred representations within endorsement opportunities. *Journal of Sport Management 28*(2), 207–19.

Fischer, M., & McClearen, J. (2020). Transgender athletes and the queer art of athletic failure. *Communication & Sport*, *8*(2), 147-167.

Fletcher, D. (2018). *This is men's derby: Identity, belonging, and community in men's roller derby* (Doctoral dissertation, University of Sheffield).

Gergen, K.J. (2001). *Social construction in context*. SAGE.

Gerretsen, S., Brooks, S.N., Andalis, A., Charhardovali, T., Lofton, R., & Falkner, R. (2021). *NCAA women's basketball head coach hires at HBCUs and Power Five schools from 1984-2020*. Global Sport Institute at Arizona State University (GSI working paper series, volume 5, issue 1). https://globalsport.asu.edu/resources/field-studies-ncaa-womens-basketballhead-coach-hires-hbcus-and-power-five-schools-1984.

Gorn, E.J. (2010). *The manly art: Bare-knuckle prize fighting in America, updated edition*. Cornell University Press.

Grundy, P. (2003). *Learning to win: Sports, education, and social change in twentieth-century North Carolina*. Chapel Hill, NC: University of North Carolina Press.

Haggerty, N. (2015, September 3). The politics of boys playing a "girls" sport. *USA Today High School Sports*. https://usatodayhss.com/2015/the-politics-of-boys-playing-a-girls-sport.

Hardin, M. (2009). The influence of gender-role socialization, media use and sports participation on perceptions of gender-appropriate sports. *Journal of Sport Behavior 32*(2), *207-226*.

Hardin, M., Simpson, S., Whiteside, E., & Garris, K. (2007). The gender war in U.S. sport: Winners and losers in news coverage of Title IX. *Mass Communication and Society*, *10*(2), 211-233. https://doi.org/10.1080/15205430701265737.

Hinchliffe, E. (2021, May 17). 'It changes everything: Renee Montgomery on being the first WNBA player to co-own her team." *Fortune*. https://fortune.com/2021/05/17/renee-montgomery-co-owner-atlanta-dream-kelly-loeffler/.

Hruby, P. (2021, May 20). *Q&A with Dr. Nicole LaVoi of the Tucker Center*. Global Sport Matters. https://globalsportmatters.com/research/2021/05/20/paradox-women-college-sports-dr-nicole-lavoi/.

Hult, J.S. (1999). NAGWS and AIAW: The strange and wondrous journey to the athletic summit, 1950-1990. *Journal of Physical Education, Recreation & Dance*, *70*(4), 24-31. https://doi.org/10.1080/07303084.1999.10605909.

Ignatiev, N. (1995). *How the Irish became White*. New York, NY: Routledge.

Jacobs, J. (2018). Intriguing, but Auriemma says no to men's job. *Connecticut Post*. www.ctpost.com/sports/jeffjacobs/article/Jeff-Jacobs-Intriguing-but-Auriemma-says-no-to-12748403.php.

Jones, A., & Greer, J. (2021). You don't look like an athlete: The effects of feminine appearance on audience perceptions of female athletes and women's sports. *Journal of Sport Behavior*, *34*(4), 358-377.

Jordan-Young, R.M., & Karkazis, K. (2019). *Testosterone*. Harvard University Press.

Kane, M.J. (2016). A Socio-cultural examination of a lack of women coaches in sport leadership positions. In N.M. LaVoi (Ed.) *Women in sports coaching*. New York, NY: Routledge.

Kane, M.J., LaVoi, N.M., &Fink, J.S. (2013). Exploring elite female athletes' interpretations of sport media images: A window into the construction of social identity and 'selling sex' in women's sports. *Communication & Sport 1*(3), 269-298.

Karkazis, K., & Jordan-Young, R.M. (2019, May 3). The myth of testosterone [Op-Ed]. *The New York Times*. www.nytimes.com/2019/05/03/opinion/testosterone-caster-semenya.html.

Karkazis, K., Jordan-Young, R., Davis, G., & Camporesi, S. (2012). Out of bounds? A critique of the new policies on hyperandrogenism in elite female athletes. *The American Journal of Bioethics*, *12*(7), 3-16.

Kimmel, M.S. (1987). Rethinking "masculinity": New directions in research. In M. S. Kimmel (Ed.), Changing men: New directions in research on men and masculinity (pp. 9–24). Sage Publications, Inc.

Killion, A. (2021, March 18). *Get better: Stanford coach reveals gross inequities at NCAA tournament*. San Francisco Chronicle. httpsfchronicle.com/sports/annkillion/article/Get-better-Stanford-coach-reveals-gross-16036715.php.

Knoppers, A., Meyer, B.B., Ewing, M., & Forrest, L. (1991). Opportunity and work behavior in college coaching. *Journal of Sport and Social Issues, 15*(1), 1-20.

Koivula, N. (2001). Perceived characteristics of sports categorized as gender-neutral, feminine and masculine. *Journal of Sport Behavior, 24*(4), 377-393.

Lane, J. (2018). Women are a problem: Title IX narratives in the New York Times and the Washington Post, 1974–1975. *Communication & Sport, 6*(1), 25-40.

Lapchick, R. (2021). Dismal representation of women in sports media, study finds. *ESPN.com*. www.espn.com/espn/story/_/id/32254145/sports-media-remains-overwhelmingly-white-male-study-finds.

LaVoi, N.M., & Baeth, A. (2018). Women and sports coaching." In L. Mansfield, J. Caudwell, B. Wheaton, & B. Watson, (Eds.), *The Palgrave Handbook of Feminism and Sport, Leisure and Physical Education*, (pp. 149-162). London: Palgrave Macmillan UK.

Leong, N., & Bartlett, E. (2018). Sex segregation in sports as a public health issue part II: Sex & gender in the twenty-first century." *Cardozo Law Review* 40(4), 1813-56.

Linehan, M. (2021, September 30). 'This guy has a pattern': Amid institutional failure, former NWSL players accuse prominent coach of sexual coercion. *The Athletic*. https://theathletic.com/2857633/2021/09/30/this-guy-has-a-pattern-amid-institutional-failure-former-nwsl-players-accuse-prominent-coach-of-sexual-coercion/.

Lorber, J. (1994). *Paradoxes of gender*. New Haven, CT: Yale University Press.

Luther, J. (2017, July 12). *A team of their own*. Bleacher Report. https://bleacherreport.com/articles/2721039-girls-travel-baseball-team-mlb-youth.

Luther, J. (2019, July 6). *It's time for women's soccer to break away from FIFA*. HuffPost. www.huffpost.com/entry/fifa-women-world-cup-equal-pay_n_5d1f9720e4b04c481413b849.

Luther, J. (2021, June 11). *How to cover sexual assault in sports: Gendered violence cases challenge sports journalists to consider and reconsider each word they write*. Global Sport Matters. https://globalsportmatters.com/opinion/2021/06/11/guide-cover-sexual-assault-sports-deshaun-watson/.

Macur, J. (2015, August 7). Buccaneers offer women a modern N.F.L. lesson out of the '50s - *The New York Times*. .www.nytimes.com/2015/08/07/sports/football/tampa-bay-buccaneers-womens-movement-shows-that-they-are-the-ones-that-need-help.html.

McClearen, J. (2018). Introduction: Women in sports media: New scholarly engagements. *Feminist Media Studies, 18*(5), 942-945. https://doi.org/10.1080/14680777.2018.1498088.

McClearen, J. (2021). *Fighting visibility: Sports media and female athletes in the UFC*. Urbana, IL: University of Illinois Press.

McKay, J., & Johnson, H. (2008). Pornographic eroticism and sexual grotesquerie in representations of African American sportswomen. *Social Identities 14*(4), 491-504.

Mertens, M. (2021, April). The Title IX loophole that hurts NCAA women's teams. *The Atlantic*. /www.theatlantic.com/culture/archive/2021/04/march-madness-could-spark-title-ix-reckoning/618483/.

Messner, M. (2011). Gender ideologies, youth sports, and the production of soft essentialism. *Sociology of Sport Journal, 28*, 151-170. https://doi.org/10.1123/ssj.28.2.151.

Messner, M.A. (2018). *No slam dunk: Gender, sport, and the unevenness of social change*. Rutgers University Press.

Montgomery, R. (2020). When the W comes back, I won't be there. *The Player's Tribune. https://www.theplayerstribune.com/articles/renee-montgomery-wnba-racial-injustice.*

Morris, J.F., & Van Raalte, J.L. (2016). Transgender and gender nonconforming athletes: Creating safe spaces for all. *Journal of Sport Psychology in Action, 7*(2), 121-132.

Nyong'o, T. (2010).

Oates, T.P. (2009). New media and the repackaging of NFL fandom. *Sociology of Sport Journal, 26*(1), 31-49.

Oliver, B. (2021, July 28). "From player to owner: Renee Montgomery shares her transition to ownership." *Essence*. https://www.essence.com/news/money-career/player-to-owner-renee-montgomery-transition-to-ownership/.

Oriard, M. (2007). *Brand NFL: Making and selling America's favorite sport*. Raleigh, NC: University of North Carolina Press.

Painter, N.I. (2010). *The history of white people*. New York, NY: W.W. Norton.

Pieper, L.P. (2014). Sex testing and the maintenance of western femininity in international sport. *The International Journal of the History of Sport, 31*(13), 1557-1576.

Pieper, L. (2016). *Sex testing: Gender policing in women's sports*. Urbana, IL: University of Illinois Press.

Putney, C. (2009). *Muscular Christianity: Manhood and sports in protestant America, 1880-1920*. Harvard University Press.

Quartz, M.B. (2015, August). Why doesn't Serena Williams have more sponsorship deals? *The Atlantic*. https://www.theatlantic.com/entertainment/archive/2015/08/serena-williams-sponsorship-nike-us-open/402985/.

Ring, J. (2015). *A game of their own: Voices of contemporary women in baseball*. University of Nebraska Press.

Rothenberg, P.S. (2004). *Race, class, and gender in the United States: An integrated study*. Macmillan.

Schultz, J. (2005). Reading the catsuit: Serena Williams and the production of blackness at the 2002 U.S. Open. *Journal of Sport and Social Issues, 29*(3), 338-357. https://journals.sagepub.com/doi/abs/10.1177/0193723505276230.

Schultz, J. (2011). Caster Semenya and the "question of too": Sex testing in elite women's sport and the issue of advantage. *Quest, 63*(2), 228-243.

Scraton, S., & Flintoff, A. (2002). *Gender and sport: A reader*. London; New York: Routledge.

Sobal, J., & Milgrim, M. (2019). Gendertyping sports: social representations of masculine, feminine, and neither-gendered sports among U.S. university students. *Journal of Gender Studies*, *28*(1), 29-44. https://doi.org/10.1080/09589236.2017.1386094.

Soong, K. (2015, August 12). Serena Williams isn't the world's highest-paid female athlete. *Washington Post*. https://www.washingtonpost.com/news/early-lead/wp/2015/08/12/serena-williams-isnt-the-worlds-highest-paid-female-athlete/.

Springer, S. (2018, February 17). What doomed the Boston Breakers? *BostonGlobe.com*. https://www.bostonglobe.com/sports/2018/02/27/what-doomed-boston-breakers/OiNvnLa8cOGaHiBjrczAUK/story.html.

Strauss, E. (2020, February 11). *Why sports can be so toxic to boys and how we unravel that culture*. CNN. www.cnn.com/2020/02/11/health/sports-boys-toxic-parenting-wellness-strauss/index.html.

Staurowsky, E.J. (1998). Critiquing the language of the gender equity debate. *Journal of Sport and Social Issues* *22*(1), 7-26.

Streeter, K. (2021, September 20). The W.N.B.A.'s Seattle Storm are winners. The city should fully embrace them. *The New York Times*. https://www.nytimes.com/2021/09/20/sports/basketball/seattle-storm-stewart-bird-lloyd.html.

Stubbs, R. (2020, November 11). Sam Gordon went viral as a football star. Now she's suing to give more girls a chance to play. *Washington Post*. www.washingtonpost.com/sports/2020/11/11/sam-gordon-girls-football-utah-lawsuit/.

Sullivan, C.F. (2011). Gender verification and gender policies in elite sport: Eligibility and fair play. *Journal of Sport and Social Issues* *35*(4), 400-419.

Tagg, B. (2008). "Imagine, a man playing netball!": Masculinities and sport in New Zealand. *International Review for the Sociology of Sport*, *43*(4), 409-430. https://doi.org/10.1177/1012690208099875.

The Fan Project Report. *The Fan Project*. https://www.thefanproject.co/thefanprojectreport.

Thompson, Becky. (2021, August 6). *Quinn: First out trans Olympian isn't just thinking about medals at Tokyo 2020—"The fight isn't close to over."* CNN. www.cnn.com/2021/08/05/sport/quinn-canada-sweden-spt-intl/index.html.

Thornton, A. (2004). "Anyone can play this game": Ultimate Frisbee, identity and difference. In Wheaton, B. (Ed.) *Understanding lifestyle sports:* Consumption, identity and difference, (pp. 175-196). Routledge.

U.S. Quidditch. (n.d.). Why title 9 3/4 is important. *www.usquidditch.org/about/title-9-3-4*.

Walker, N. (2010, January). The underrepresentation of women in the male-dominated sport workplace: Perspectives of female coaches. Journal of Workplace Rights, 15(1), 47-64. https://doi.org/10.2190/WR.15.1.d.

Walker, N., Bopp, T., & Sagas, M. (2011). Gender bias in the perception of women as collegiate men's basketball coaches. *Journal for the Study of Sports and Athletes in Education*, *5*(2), 157-176. https://doi.org/10.1179/ssa.2011.5.2.157.

Wenner, L.A., & Jackson, S.J. (2009). *Sport, beer, and gender: Promotional culture and contemporary social life*. New York: Peter Lang Publishing, Inc.

West, C., & Zimmerman, D. H. (1987). Doing gender. *Gender & Society*, *1*(2), 125-151.

Chapter 7

Adair, C. (2015). Bathrooms and Beyond. *TSQ: Transgender Studies Quarterly*, *2*(3), 464-468. https://doi.org/10.1215/23289252-2926428.

American Psychiatric Association (1952). *Diagnostic and statistical manual of mental disorders*.

American Psychiatric Association (1968). *Diagnostic and statistical manual of mental disorders* (2nd ed).

American Psychiatric Association (1980). *Diagnostic and statistical manual of mental disorders* (3rd ed).

American Psychiatric Association (1987). *Diagnostic and statistical manual of mental disorders* (3rd ed, revised).

American Psychiatric Association (1994). *Diagnostic and statistical manual of mental disorders* (4th ed).

American Psychiatric Association (2013). *Diagnostic and statistical manual of mental disorders* (5th ed).

Anderson, E. (2002). Openly gay athletes: Contesting hegemonic masculinity in a homophobic environment. *Gender & Society*, *16*(6), 860-877.

Anderson, E. (2005). *In the game gay athletes and the cult of masculinity*. Albany, NY: State University of New York Press.

Anderson, E., & Adams, A. (2011). "Aren't we all a little bisexual?": The recognition of bisexuality in an unlikely place. *Journal of Bisexuality*, *11*(1), 3-22. https://doi.org/10.1080/15299716.2011.545283.

Barra, A. (2013, November 15). The integration of college football didn't happen in one game. *The Atlantic*. www.theatlantic.com/entertainment/archive/2013/11/the-integration-of-college-football-didnt-happen-in-one-game/281557/.

Bible, J., Bermea, A., van Eeden-Moorefield, B., Benson, K., & Few-Demo, A. (2018). A content analysis of the first decade of the *Journal of GLBT Family Studies*. *Journal of GLBT Family Studies*, *14*(4), 337-355. http://doi.org/10.1080/1550428X.2017.1349626.

Block, M. (2021, July 28). *Olympic runner Caster Semenya wants to compete, not defend her womanhood*. NPR. www.npr.org/sections/tokyo-olympics-live-updates/2021/07/28/1021503989/women-runners-testosterone-olympics.

Boren, C. (2018, Feb 25). Transgender wrestler Mack Beggs wins second Texas state girls' championship. *The Washington Post*. www.washingtonpost.com/news/early-lead/wp/2018/02/25/transgender-wrestler-mack-beggs-wins-second-texas-state-girls-championship/.

Bostock v. Clayton County, 590___U.S. (2020).

Boston Athletic Association. (n.d.). *History of the Boston Marathon*. https://www.baa.org/races/boston-marathon/history.

Brown, L.S. (2004). Lesbian identities: Concepts and issues. In Rebecca F. Plante and Michael S. Kimmel (Eds.), *Sexualities: Identities, behaviors, and society* (pp. 171-183). New York: Oxford University Press.

Brown, P. (1990). The name game: Toward a sociology of diagnosis. *Journal of Mind and Behavior, 11*(3-4), 385-406.

Ceatha, N., Mayock, P., Campbell, J., Noone, C., & Browne, K. (2019). The power of recognition: A qualitative study of social connectedness and wellbeing through LGBT sporting, creative and social groups in Ireland. *International Journal of Environmental Research and Public Health, 16*(19), 3636. https://doi.org/10.3390/ijerph16193636.

Chang, C.J., Putukian, M., Aerni, G., Diamond, A.B., Hong, E.S., Ingram, Y.M., Wolanin, A.T. (2020). *Mental health issues and psychological factors in athletes: Detection, management, effect on performance, and prevention* [American Medical Society for Sports Medicine Position Statement]. *Clinical Journal of Sport Medicine, 30*(2). https://doi.org/10.1097/jsm.0000000000000817.

Couillard, E., & Higbee, J. (2018). Expanding the scope of universal design: Implications for gender identity and sexual orientation. *Education Sciences, 8*(3), 147. https://doi.org/10.3390/educsci8030147.

Crenshaw, K. (1993). Demarginalizing the interaction of race and sex: A Black feminist critique of antidiscrimination doctrine, feminist theory, and anti-racist politics. In D. Weisberg (Ed.), *Feminist legal theory: Foundations* (pp. 383-411). Temple University Press.

Davies, R.D., & Davies, M.E. (2020). The (slow) depathologizing of gender incongruence. *The Journal of Nervous and Mental Disease, 208*(2), 152-154. doi: 10.1097/NMD.0000000000001119.

Defense of Marriage Act, Pub. L. No. 104-199, § 110 Stat. 2419. (1996).

Dozono, T. (2017). Teaching alternative and indigenous gender systems in world history: A queer approach. *History Teacher, 50*(3), 425-448. https://www.jstor.org/stable/44507259.

ESPN. (2021, July 2). *Namibia female runners banned from Olympic 400 meters over high testosterone levels*. ESPN. www.espn.com/olympics/story/_/id/31749541/namibia-female-runners-banned-olympic-400-meters-high-testosterone-levels.

Flores, A., Herman, J., Gates, G., & Brown, T. (2016). *How many adults identify as transgender in the United States?* Williams Institute, UCLA School of Law. http://williamsinstitute.law.ucla.edu/wp-content/uploads/How-Many-Adults-Identify-as-Transgender-in-the-United-States.pdf.

Gates, G.J. (2013). *LGBT parenting in the United States*. Williams Institute, UCLA School of Law.

Godfrey, P. (2003). Bayonets, brainwashing, and bathrooms: The discourse of race, gender, and sexuality in the desegregation of Little Rock's Central High. *The Arkansas Historical Quarterly, 62*(1), 42-67. doi:10.2307/40023302.

Goldberg, S., Rothblum, E., Russell, S., & Meyer, I. (2020). Exploring the Q in LGBTQ: Demographic characteristic and sexuality of queer people in a U.S. representative sample of sexual minorities. *Psychology of Sexual Orientation and Gender Diversity, 7*(1), 101-112. https://doi.org/10.1037/sgd0000359.

Goff, S. (2021, June 5). With Mexico in Concacaf Nations League, soccer again confronts homophobic slur at matches. *The Washington Post*. www.washingtonpost.com/sports/2021/06/04/nations-league-mexico-homophobic-slur/.

Greenspan, S.B., Griffith, C., & Watson, R.J. (2019). LGBTQ+ youth's experiences and engagement in physical activity: A comprehensive content analysis. *Adolescent Research Review, 4*(2), 169-185. https://doi.org/10.1007/s40894-019-00110-4.

Griffin, C., et al. (1982). Women and leisure. In Jennifer Hargreaves (Ed.), *Sport, culture and ideology*, 88-116. London: Routledge & Kegan Paul.

Griffin, P. (1992). Changing the game: Homophobia, sexism, and lesbians in sport. *Quest 44*, 251-265.

Griffin, P. (1998). *Strong women, deep closets: Lesbians and homophobia in sport*. Champaign, IL: Human Kinetics.

Hargreaves, J. (2000). *Heroines of Sport: The politics of difference and identity*. London: Routledge & Kegan Paul.

Himmelstein, K., & Brückner, H. (2010). Criminal-justice and school sanctions against nonheterosexual youth: A national longitudinal study. *Pediatrics, 127*(1), 49-57.

Kafer, A. (2016). Other people's shit (and pee!). *South Atlantic Quarterly, 115*(4), 755-762. https://doi.org/10.1215/00382876-3656158.

Kauer, K.J., & Krane, V. (2006). "Scary dykes" and "feminine queens": Stereotypes and female collegiate athletes. *Women in Sport and Physical Activity, 15*(1), 42-55.

Krishnakumar, P. (2021, April 15). This record-breaking year for anti-transgender legislation would affect minors the most. CNN. www.cnn.com/2021/04/15/politics/anti-transgender-legislation-2021/index.html.

Kastanis, A., & Wilson, B. (2014). *Race/ethnicity, gender, and socioeconomic wellbeing of individuals in same-sex couples*. Williams Institute, UCLA School of Law.

Knoester, C., & Allison, R. (2021). Sexuality, sports-related mistreatment, and U.S. adults' sports involvement. *Leisure Sciences*, 1–23. https://doi.org/10.1080/01490400.2021.1895009.

Lawrence et al. v. Texas, 539 U.S. 558 (2003).

Linley, J. L., Nguyen, D., Brazelton, G. B., Becker, B., Renn, K., & Woodford, M. (2016). Faculty as sources of support for LGBTQ College students. *College Teaching, 64*(2), 55-63. https://doi.org/10.1080/87567555.2015.1078275.

Maese, R. (2019, May 1). Court rules Olympic runner Caster Semenya must use hormone-suppressing drugs to compete. *The Washington Post*. www.washingtonpost.

com/sports/2019/05/01/court-decides-against-caster-semenyas-appeal-controversial-rule/.

Messner, M. A. (1995). *Power at play: Sports and the problem of masculinity*. Boston, MA: Beacon Press.

Meyer, I.H. (2003). Prejudice, social stress, and mental health in lesbian, gay, and bisexual populations: Conceptual issues and research evidence. *Psychological Bulletin, 129*(5), 674-697. doi: 10.1037/0033-2909.129.5.674.

Inner strength, inner peace AIDS-stricken Burke at ease with decisions, fate. (1994, November 2). *Milwaukee Sentinel*. p. 1B-2B.

Mink, M., Lindley, L., & Weinstein, A. (2014). Stress, stigma, and sexual minority status: The intersectional ecology model of LGBTQ health. *Journal of Gay and Lesbian Social Services*, *26*(4), 502-521.

Moran, M. (1984, August 6). First women's Olympic marathon to Benoit. *The New York Times*. www.nytimes.com/1984/08/06/sports/first-women-s-olympic-marathon-to-benoit.html.

Morrow, R.G., & Gill, D.L. (2003). Perceptions of homophobia and heterosexism in physical education. *Research Quarterly for Exercise and Sport*, *74*(2), 205-214.

Mosher, D.K., Hook, J.N., Captari, L.E., Davis, D.E., DeBlaere, C., & Owen, J. (2017). Cultural humility: A therapeutic framework for engaging diverse clients. *Practice Innovations*, *2*(4), 221-233. https://doi.org/10.1037/pri0000055.

Movement Advancement Project. (2020). *Equality maps snapshot: LGBTQ equality by state*. www.lgbtmap.org/equality-maps.

Movement Advancement Project, Center for American Progress, & Youth First. (2017, June). *Unjust: LGBTQ youth incarcerated in the juvenile justice system*. www.lgbtmap.org/criminal-justice-youth-detention.

Munce, M. (2021, April 27). Gender-affirming medical treatment for transgender kids would be considered child abuse under Texas Senate bill. *The Texas Tribune*. www.texastribune.org/2021/04/27/texas-senate-transgender-child-abuse/.

Nadal, K.L. (2019). A decade of microaggression research and LGBTQ communities: An introduction to the special issue. *Journal of Homosexuality*, *66*(10), 1309-1316. https://doi.org/10.1080/00918369.2018.1539582.

NCAA. (2021, April 12). *NCAA Board of Governors Statement on Transgender Participation*. www.ncaa.org/about/resources/media-center/news/ncaa-board-governors-statement-transgender-participation.

Nylund, D. (2004). When in Rome: Heterosexism, homophobia, and sports talk radio. *Journal of Sport & Social Issues*, *28*(2), 136-168.

Obergefell v. Hodges 576 U.S. ___ (2015).

Osbourne, D. & Wagner III, W.E. (2007). Exploring the relationship between homophobia and participation in core sports among high school students. *Sociological Perspectives*, *50*(4), 597-613.

Ottosson, D. (2006). *LGBT world legal wrap up survey*. Brussels, Belgium: International Lesbian and Gay Association.

Petty, L., & Trussell, D. (2018). Experiences of identity development and sexual stigma for lesbian, gay, and bisexual young people in sport: Just survive until you can be who you are. *Qualitative Research in Sport, Exercise and Health*, *10*(2), 176-189. DOI: 10.1080/2159676X.2017.1393003.

Picq, M., & Tikuna, J. (2019). Indigenous sexualities: Resisting conquest and translation. In C. Cottet and M. Picq, (Eds.) *Sexuality and translation in world politics* (pp. 57-72). Bristol, England: E-International Relations.

Ronan, W. (2021). *2021 officially becomes worst year in recent history for LGBTQ state legislative attacks as unprecedented number of states enact record-shattering number of anti-LGBTQ measures into law*. Human Rights Campaign. www.hrc.org/press-releases/2021-officially-becomes-worst-year-in-recent-history-for-lgbtq-state-legislative-attacks-as-unprecedented-number-of-states-enact-record-shattering-number-of-anti-lgbtq-measures-into-law.

Rosman, R. (2019, September 27). *Fans cry foul as France cracks down on football homophobia*. Reuters. www.reuters.com/article/us-france-soccer-lgbt-feature/fans-cry-foul-as-france-cracks-down-on-football-homophobia-idUSKBN1WC1ZG.

Russell, S.T., Pollitt, A.M., Li, G., & Grossman, A.H. (2018). Chosen name use is linked to reduced depressive symptoms, suicidal ideation, and suicidal behavior among transgender youth. *Journal of Adolescent Health*, *63*(4), 503-505.

Ryan, C. (2014). Generating a revolution in prevention, wellness & care for LGBT children & youth. *Temple Political and Civil Rights Law Review*, *23*(2), 331-344.

Sabo, D.F. (1994). The politics of homophobia in sport. In Don F. Sabo and Michael A. Messner (Eds.), *Sex, Violence & Power in Sports* (pp. 101-111). Freedom, CA: Crossing Press.

Sanders, J., & Stryker, S. (2016). Stalled: Gender-neutral public bathrooms. *South Atlantic Quarterly*, *115*(4), 779-788. https://doi.org/10.1215/00382876-3656191.

Sandomir, R. (2018, July 23). Rene Portland, 65, long time Penn State basketball coach, dies. *The New York Times*. www.nytimes.com/2018/07/23/obituaries/rene-portland-65-longtime-penn-state-basketball-coach-dies.html.

Srikanth, A. (2021, April 15). Florida's new ban on transgender students in sports would allow schools to subject minors to genital inspections. *The Hill*. https://thehill.com/changing-america/respect/equality/548534-floridas-new-ban-on-transgender-students-in-sports-would.

Sue, D.W., Capodilupo, C.M., Torino, G.C., Bucceri, J.M., Holder, A.M., Nadal, K.L., & Esquilin, M. (2007). Racial microaggressions in everyday life: Implications for clinical practice. *American Psychologist*, *62*(4), 271–286.

The Trevor Project. (2020, August 30). *The well-being of LGBTQ youth athletes.* www.thetrevorproject.org/research-briefs/the-well-being-of-lgbtq-youth-athletes/.

UN Office of the High Commissioner for Human Rights. (2012, September). *Born free and equal: Sexual orientation and gender identity in international human rights law* [HR/PUB/12/06]. www.refworld.org/docid/5065a43f2.html.

USA Hockey Parents. (n.d.). *USA Hockey transgender athlete eligibility policy.* Retrieved September 22, 2021, from www.usahockey.com/parents.

U.S. Government Accountability Office. (2004, January 23). Defense of Marriage Act: Update to prior report (GAO-04-353R).

van Eeden-Moorefield, B., Few-Demo, A., Benson, K., Bible, J., & Lummer, S. (2018). A content analysis of LGBT research in top family journals 2000-2015. *Journal of Family Issues, 39*(5), 1374-1395. https://doi.org/10.1177%2F0192513X17710284.

Williams Institute. (2019, January). *LGBT demographic data interactive.* UCLA School of Law. https://williamsinstitute.law.ucla.edu/visualization/lgbt-stats/?topic=LGBT#density.

Willis, P. (1982). Women in sport ideology. In Jennifer Hargreaves (Ed.), *Sport, culture and ideology*, pp. 117-135. London: Routledge & Kegan Paul.

Chapter 8

AbilityLab. (2021). *Sled hockey.* www.sralab.org/article/sled-hockey.

Adaptive Sports Ohio. (2021). *Interscholastic sports.* https://adaptivesports.dreamhosters.com/interscholastic-sports/.

Allentuck, D. (2019, June 29). Paralympians see a big welcome in a small title change. *New York Times.* www.nytimes.com/2019/06/29/sports/olympics/usoc-paralympians-.html.

Commonwealth Games Federation. (2020). *Para-sports.* https://thecgf.com/our-relevance/para-sports.

Commonwealth Games Federation. (2021). *Where everything counts.* www.birmingham2022.com/the-games/sports/.

CUNYAC. (2017). *CUNYAC launches inclusive and adaptive sports initiative* [Press release]. https://cunyathletics.com/news/2017/12/7/general-cunyac-launches-inclusive-and-adaptive-sports-initiative.aspx.

Fay, T., & Wolff, E.A. (2009). Disability in sport in the 21st century: Creating a new sport opportunity spectrum. *Boston University International Law Journal, 27*, 231-248.

Ferguson, P. (2006). *Infusing disability studies into the general curriculum.* National Institute for Urban School Improvement.

Fernandez, G. (2020, July 7). *Chicago Blackhawks will keep name, pledge to expand awareness of Black Hawk's legacy.* CBS Sports. www.cbssports.com/nhl/news/chicago-blackhawks-will-keep-name-pledge-to-expand-awareness-of-black-hawks-legacy/.

FIFA. (2020, December 3). FIFA celebrates accessibility and inclusiveness in football on International Day of Disabled People. www.fifa.com/football-development/news/fifa-celebrates-accessibility-and-inclusiveness-in-football-on-international-day.

Global Sports Mentoring Program. (2018). U.S. Department of State Sport for Community. https://globalsportsmentoring.org/sport-for-community/.

Hums, M.A., Frederick, E., Pegararo, A., Siegfried, N., & Wolff, E.A. (2020). What's in a name? Examining reactions to Major League Baseball's change from the Disabled List to the Injured List via Twitter. *Baseball Research Journal, 49*(2), 22-32.

Hums, M.A., Moorman, A.M., & Wolff, E.A. (2009). Emerging disability rights in sport: Sport as a human right for persons with disabilities and the 2006 UN Convention on the Rights of Persons with Disabilities. *Cambrian Law Review, 40*, 36-48.

Hums, M.A., Schmidt, S.H., Novak, A., & Wolff, E.A. (2016). Universal design: Moving the Americans With Disabilities Act from access to inclusion. *Journal of Legal Aspects of Sport, 26*(1), 36-51. doi: http://dx.doi.org/10.1123/jlas.2015-0011.

Hums, M.A., Wolff, E.A., & Legg, D. (2019) Leadership in disability sport. In L. Burton, G. Kane, and J. Borland (Eds). *Sport leadership in the 21st century* (2nd ed.). Jones and Bartlett.

IHSA. (2021). *Preliminary/sample schedules for 2021 state final.* www.ihsa.org/documents/tr/2020-21/Sample%20SF%20Schedule.pdf.

Institute for Human Centered Design. (2011). Museum of science: The user expert perspective: Universal design consultation. Boston, MA: Institute for Human Centered Design.

IPC. (n.d.). *Rio 2016 education programme officially added to city schools curriculum.* www.paralympic.org/news/rio-2016-education-programme-officially-added-city-schools-curriculum.

ITF. (2021a). *Honouring outstanding performance.* www.itftennis.com/en/about-us/itf-events/itf-world-champions/past-champions/.

ITF. (2021b). *UNIQLO Wheelchair Tennis Tour.* www.itftennis.com/en/itf-tours/uniqlo-wheelchair-tennis-tour/.

ITF. (2021c). *What we do.* www.itftennis.com/en/about-us/organisation/what-we-do/.

Itoh, M., Hums, M.A., Akiko, N., & Ogasawara, E. (2018). Realizing identity and overcoming barriers: Factors influencing Japanese female Paralympians to become coaches. *International Journal of Sport and Health, 16*, 50-56. https://doi.org/10.5432/ijshs.201630.

IOC. (2020). *Olympic charter.*

Kennedy Jr., T., Jerdee, C., & Henneborn, L. (2019, June 4). 4 ways to improve your company's inclusion practices. *Harvard Business Review*.

Kuzma, C. (2016, Sept. 6). Why the fastest women in the world wheel through Illinois cornfields. *ESPNW*. www.espn.com/espnw/sports/story/_/id/17474397/why-fastest-women-world-wheel-illinois-cornfields.

Kuzma, C. (2021, January 17). There's no hill Tatyana McFadden can't climb. *Women's Running*. www.womensrunning.com/culture/people/tatyana-mcfadden-lessons-in-resilience/.

Lieberman, L. (2021, April 7). *University of Illinois wheelchair basketball program still making Paralympians*. www.teamusa.org/news/2021/april/07/university-of-illinois-wheelchair-basketball-program-still-making-paralympians.

Mackelprang, R.W., & Salsgiver, R.O. (1999). *Disability: A diversity model in human service practice*. Brooks Cole.

National Disability Authority (Ireland). (2020). *What is universal design*? http://universaldesign.ie/What-is-Universal-Design/.

Nixon, H.L. (2007). Constructing diverse sports opportunities for people with disabilities. *Journal of Sport and Social Issues*, *31*(4), 417-433.

O'Brien, C. (2021, August 25). Illini at the Paralympics: McFadden competes in sixth Games, McGrory represents USA for the fourth time. *Daily Illini*. https://dailyillini.com/sports-stories/2021/08/25/illini-at-the-paralympics-mcfadden-competes-in-sixth-games-mcgrory-represents-usa-for-fourth-time/#modal-photo

Passan, J. (2019, February 7). *Major League Baseball to rename Disabled List to Injured List*. ESPN. www.espn.com/mlb/story/_/id/25947020/major-league-baseball-rename-disabled-list-injured-list.

Porter, C. (2016, March 10). *Inclusion programs continue to expand participation opportunities*. NFHS.org. www.nfhs.org/articles/inclusion-programs-continue-to-expand-participation-opportunities/

Portland State University. (2021). *Inclusive rec*. www.pdx.edu/recreation/inclusive-rec#inclusiveprograms.

Pulrang, A. (2019). *How to avoid "inspiration porn."* Forbes. https://www.forbes.com/sites/andrewpulrang/2019/11/29/how-to-avoid-inspiration-porn/?sh=6426f3335b3d.

Shapiro, D., Pitts, B., Hums, M.A., & Calloway, J. (2012). Infusing disability sport into the sport management curriculum. *Choregia Scientific Forum in Sport Management*, *8*(1), http:dx.doi.org/10.4127/ch.2012.0067.

Special Olympics. (2021a). *Special Olympics Unified Champion Schools*. www.specialolympics.org/our-work/unified-champion-schools?locale=en.

Special Olympics. (2021b). *Unified sports*. www.specialolympics.org/our-work/sports/unified-sports.

Toronto 2015. (2015). Para-play demonstration zone training. Toronto 2015.

Toyota. (2021). Meet Team Toyota. www.toyota.com/team-toyota/.

United Nations. (n.d.). *Convention on the Rights of Persons with Disabilities*. www.un.org/development/desa/disabilities/convention-on-the-rights-of-persons-with-disabilities/convention-on-the-rights-of-persons-with-disabilities-2.html.

University of Alabama. (2021). *Adapted athletics*. http://alabamaadapted.com/.

University of Illinois. (n.d.). *Athletics*. https://illinois.edu/athletics/index.html.

University of Iowa. (n.d.). Adaptive and inclusive rec. https://recserv.uiowa.edu/adaptive-inclusive-rec.

University of Louisville Athletics. (2021). By-laws. https://gocards.com/sports/2015/7/21/gen_0721150901.aspx?id=324.

USA Hockey. (2021a). *About disabled hockey*. www.usahockey.com/disabledhockey.

USA Hockey. (2021b). *Disabled section contacts*. www.usahockey.com/disabledhockeysection.

USA Hockey. (2021c). *Diversity, equity and inclusion*. www.usahockey.com/diversityequityandinclusion.

USOPC. (2019, June 20). *US Olympic Committee changes its name to US Olympic and Paralympic Committee*. Team USA. www.teamusa.org/news/2019/june/20/us-olympic-committee-changes-name-to-us-olympic-paralympic-committee.

USOPC. (2020a). *ByLaws of the USOPC Athlete Advisory Council*.

USOPC. (2020b). *Get out and play volleyball*. https://usavolleyball.org/play/.

Wolff, E.A., & Hums, M.A. (2021). Disability inclusion, Olympism and human rights. *International Olympic Academy Journal*, *17-18*, 30-34.

Chapter 9

Abrams, J. (2021, May 27). Ugly N.B.A. fan behavior is back with popcorn toss and spitting incident. *New York Times*. https://www.nytimes.com/2021/05/27/sports/basketball/russell-westbrook-trae-young-spit-popcorn.html.

Belson, K. (2021, March 30). N.F.L. officially adds 17th regular season game. *New York Times*. www.nytimes.com/2021/03/30/sports/football/nfl-adds-17th-regular-season-game.html.

Bemis, T. (2021, April 15). *NFL names Caesars, DraftKings and FanDuel as betting partners*. The Street. www.thestreet.com/investing/nfl-names-caesars-draftkings-and-fanduel-as-betting-partners.

Boren, C. (2021, March 23). Another NCAA tournament player received racist messages and death threats after his team lost. *Washington Post*. www.washingtonpost.com/sports/2021/03/23/kofi-cockburn-instagram-racist-post/.

Brooks, G. (2021, April 25). *Live updates: ESPN Elite Underclassman Camp in Houston*. 247 Sports. https://247sports.com/Article/Texas-Texas-AM-LSU-football-recruiting-Rueben-Owens-Noah-Thomas-Julian-Humphrey-164620231/.

Chu, J. (2018, November 7). *Study: There's real skill in fantasy sports*. MIT News. https://news.mit.edu/2018/hosoi-study-skill-fantasy-sports-1107.

Coakley, J. (2005). Sport in society: An inspiration or an opiate? In D.S. Eitzen (Ed.), *Sport in contemporary society: An anthology*. London: Paradigm.

Collins, T. (2013). *Sport in capitalist society*. New York: Routledge.

Ellenport, C. (2020, April 22). A bold new network, a preposterous idea: How the NFL draft came to TV. *Sports Illustrated*. www.si.com/nfl/2020/04/22/how-espn-televised-nfl-draft-for-the-first-time.

Fantasy Sports & Gaming Association (FSGA). (2019, September 2). *Rise of fantasy football played big part in league's growth*. https://thefsga.org/rise-of-fantasy-football-played-big-part-in-leagues-growth/.

Fantasy Sports & Gaming Association (FSGA). (2020). *Industry demographics*. https://thefsga.org/industry-demographics/.

Football IQ Score (2021). What is the NFL Combine? https://footballiqscore.com/what-is-the-nfl-combine.

Futterman, M. (2021, May 26). Naomi Osaka says she won't talk to journalists at the French Open. *The New York Times*. www.nytimes.com/2021/05/26/sports/tennis/naomi-osaka-french-open-no-interviews.html.

Galluccio, B. (2020, November 23). *NFL player receives death threats after his lost fumble decides game*. Fox Sports Radio. https://foxsportsradio.iheart.com/content/2020-11-23-nfl-player-receives-death-threats-after-his-lost-fumble-decides-game/.

Geier, D. (n.d.). *Medical evaluation critical at NFL Combine*. Dr. David Geier [Website]. www.drdavidgeier.com/medical-evaluation-of-players-critical-at-nfl-combine/.

Get Sports Info. (2021, January 26). *The most popular fantasy sports*. https://getsportsinfo.com/the-most-popular-fantasy-sports-games/.

Globe Newswire. (2021, March 18). *Global sports market report (2021 to 2030)—COVID impact and recovery*. www.globenewswire.com/fr/news-release/2021/03/18/2195540/28124/en/Global-Sports-Market-Report-2021-to-2030-COVID-19-Impact-and-Recovery.html.

Happe, L. (2021, May 20). *Georges St-Pierre vs Oscar de la Hoya: UFC boss Dana White shouldn't have blocked the fight, says Anderson Silva*. DAZN. www.dazn.com/en-US/news/boxing/georges-st-pierre-vs-oscar-de-la-hoya-ufc-boss-dana-white-shouldnt-have-blocked-the-fight-says-anderson-silva/1dfskxca15xhg1fvcmak1azrir.

Harris, L.T., Lee, V.K., Capestany, B.H., & Cohen, A.O. (2014). Assigning economic value to people results in dehumanization brain response. *Journal of Neuroscience, Psychology, and Economics*, *7*(3), 151-163. https://doi.org/10.1037/npe0000020.

Haslam, N. (2006). Dehumanization: An integrative review. *Personality and Social Psychology Review*, *10*(3): 252-264. doi:10.1207/s15327957pspr1003_4.

Healy, D. (2020, November 17). The future of entertainment: How sports betting will change the game. *Rolling Stone*. www.rollingstone.com/culture-council/articles/future-of-entertainment-how-sports-betting-will-change-1089898/.

Hermann, J. (2021, June 5). Naomi Osaka and the language of fame. *New York Times*. www.nytimes.com/2021/06/05/style/naomi-osaka-celebrity.html.

Hilliard, R., & Johnson, C. (2018). Sport fan attitudes and willingness to commit aggressive acts. *Journal of Sport Behavior 41*(3), 305-329

Homewood, B. (2020, March 24). *Athletes association says change of culture needed at IOC*. Reuters. www.reuters.com/article/us-health-coronavirus-olympics-reaction/athletes-association-says-change-of-culture-needed-at-ioc-idUSKBN21B2V9.

Hrdlicka, J., Moretton, G., Hewitt, I., & McNulty, M. (2021, May 30). *Statement from Grand Slam tournaments regarding Naomi Osaka*. Roland-Garros. www.rolandgarros.com/en-us/article/statement-from-grand-slam-tournaments-regarding-naomi-osaka.

Jahan, S., & Mahmud, A.S. (2021). What is capitalism? *The International Monetary Fund*. www.imf.org/external/pubs/ft/fandd/basics/2_capitalism.htm.

Jardy, A. (2021, March 20). Ohio State's E.J. Liddell shares threats, vulgar insults received after Oral Roberts loss. *Buckeye Extra*. www.buckeyextra.com/story/mens-basketball/2021/03/20/ohio-states-e-j-liddell-receives-threats-after-oral-roberts-loss/4780359001/.

Jessop, A., & Brown, T.A. (2019). Big data bust: Evaluating the risks of tracking NCAA athletes' biometric data. *Texas Review of Entertainment and Sports Law*, *20*(1), 1-21. https://papers.ssrn.com/sol3/papers.cfm?abstract_id=3666565.

Kalman-Lamb, N. (2019). Athletic labor and social reproduction. *Journal of Sport and Social Issues*, *43*(6): 515-530. doi:10.1177/0193723519850879.

Kaufman, P. (2008). Boos, bans, and other backlash: The consequences of being an activist athlete. *Humanity & Society*, *32*(3): 215-237. doi:10.1177/016059760803200302.

Kercheval, B. (2021, April 23). *College football spring games 2021: Schedule, TV channels, start times, dates for Power Five conferences*. CBS Sports. www.cbssports.com/college-football/news/college-football-spring-games-2021-schedule-tv-channels-start-times-dates-for-power-five-conferences/.

Kilpatrick, K., Hathaway, E., & Milavec, T. (2016). *#Winning the fan engagement game* [Report]. Gensler. www.gensler.com/gri/win-or-lose.

King, S. (2018). The NCAA says student-athletes shouldn't be paid because the 13th Amendment allows unpaid prison labor. *The Intercept*. https://theintercept.com/2018/02/22/ncaa-student-athletes-unpaid-prison/.

Kisiel, C. (2021, January 27). Loopholes have preserved slavery for more than 150 years after abolition. *The Washington Post*.

Korducki, K.M. (2021, June 6). We are finally starting to revolt against the cult of ambition. *New York Times*. www.nytimes.com/2021/06/06/opinion/Naomi-Osaka-ambition-women.html.

Lapchick, R. (2020). *The 2020 racial and gender equity report card*. Orlando, FL: University of Central Florida. https://www.tidesport.org/racial-gender-report-card.

Larkin, B., Dwyer, B., & Goebert, C. (2020). Man or machine: Fantasy football and dehumanization of professional athletes. *Journal of Sport Management*, *34*(5), 403-416. http://journals.humankinetics.com/view/journals/jsm/34/5/article-p403.xml.

Leimkuehler, M. (2019, April 27). NFL draft in Nashville breaks attendance record at 600,000, league reports. *The Tennessean*. www.tennessean.com/story/news/2019/04/27/nfl-draft-nashville-breaks-attendance-record-league-reports/3602675002/.

Livers v. NCAA. (2017). Memorandum in support of a motion to dismiss. United States District Court Eastern District of Pennsylvania. Civil Action No. 2:17-cv-04271-MMB. https://assets.documentcloud.org/documents/4385598/NCAA-Motion-to-Dismiss-Livers-s-Lawsuit-On.pdf.

Maguire J. (2004). Challenging the sports-industrial complex: Human sciences, advocacy and service. *European Physical Education Review*, *10*(3): 299-322. doi:10.1177/1356336X04044072.

Maine, D. (2021, May 31). *Naomi Osaka withdraws from French Open, will "take some time away" from tennis after controversy over media obligations*. ESPN. www.espn.com/tennis/story/_/id/31543237/naomi-osaka-withdraws-french-open-one-day-fine-threat-harsher-sanctions-skipping-media-obligations.

McCaffrey, M., Fagot, A., Monday, C., Keenan, M., & Panson, S. (2021). *PwC 2021 sports outlook: 2020 changed the game for sports. What's next*. PricewaterhouseCoopers. www.pwc.com/us/en/industries/tmt/assets/pwc-2021-tmt-sports-outlook.pdf.

McGregor, A. (2016, February 25). Constructing the fantasy plantation: The NFL Combine and the language of numbers. *Sport in American History*. https://ussporthistory.com/2016/02/25/constructing-the-fantasy-plantation-the-nfl-combine-and-the-language-of-numbers/.

Melero, S. (2021, June 9). *Tennis Federation president who fined Osaka says he "respects" Roger Federer's withdrawal from the French Open*. Jezebel. https://jezebel.com/tennis-federation-president-who-fined-osaka-says-he-res-1847065296.

Moriello, J. (2020, February 22). *What do players go through at the NFL Scouting Combine?* Sportscasting. www.sportscasting.com/what-do-players-go-through-at-the-nfl-scouting-combine/.

National Football League Operations. (2021a). *The history of the draft*. https://operations.nfl.com/journey-to-the-nfl/the-nfl-draft/the-history-of-the-draft/.

National Football League Operations. (2021b). *College player development*. https://operations.nfl.com/journey-to-the-nfl/nfl-development-pipeline/college-player-development/.

NFL. (2021, May 4). *2021 NFL draft was third most-watched draft ever*. www.nfl.com/news/2021-nfl-draft-was-third-most-watched-draft-ever.

Ornstein, D. (2021, April 24). *English football announces social media boycott to fight racism*. The Athletic. https://theathletic.com/news/football-social-media-abuse-boycott/gnZwFxWnf6If.

Osaka, N. [@NaomiOsaka]. (2021, May 31). [Photo of public statement.] Tweet. https://twitter.com/naomiosaka/status/1399422304854188037/photo/1.

Rhind, D.J.A., Musson, H., Florence, A., Gilpin, P., & Alford, G. (2021). *Census of athletes rights and experiences*. Nyon, Switzerland: World Players Association. https://files.cargocollective.com/c520687/World-Players_CARE-Report-2021-.pdf.

Rhoden, W. (2015, November 25). Fantasy sports' real crime: Dehumanizing the athletes. *New York Times*. https://www.nytimes.com/2015/11/26/sports/football/fantasy-sports-real-crime-dehumanizing-the-athletes.html.

Runstedtler, T. (2018). More than just play: Unmasking Black child labor in the athletic industrial complex. *Journal of Sport and Social Issues*, *42*(3): 152-169. doi:10.1177/0193723518758458.

Schwab, B. (2017). "When we know better, we do better." Embedding the human rights of players as a prerequisite to the legitimacy of lex sportiva and sport's justice system, *Maryland Journal of International Law*, *32*, 5-67. http://digitalcommons.law.umaryland.edu/mjil/vol32/iss1/.

Sleep, S., Thompson, S., & Thomas, M. L. (2019). *The impact of fantasy on the NFL fan: Exploring differences between the fantasy football participant and the traditional fan*. https://digitalcommons.georgiasouthern.edu/cgi/viewcontent.cgi?article=1019&context=amtp-proceedings_2019.

Smith, E. (2014). *Race, sport, and the American dream*. Durham, NC: Carolina Academic Press.

Stutz, H. (2021, April 10). *Increased fan engagement from legal sports betting fuels valuable sports media deals*. CDC Gaming Reports. www.cdcgamingreports.com/commentaries/increased-fan-engagement-from-legal-sports-betting-fuels-valuable-sports-media-deals/.

UCReport. (2021). *ESPN 300 elite underclassmen camp*. https://theucreport.com/uc-espn-camps/.

Varsik, J., Hiegel, M., & Parry, J. (2021, September 1). *Tracker: Name, image, and likeness legislation by state*. Business of College Sports. https://businessofcollegesports.com/tracker-name-image-and-likeness-legislation-by-state/.

West, J.R. (2017, September 29). *The real* Moneyball *effect: Our fetishization of data*. Slate. https://slate.com/technology/2017/09/the-real-moneyball-effect-our-fetishization-of-data.html.

World Players Association. (2017). *Universal declaration of player rights* [Press release]. EUAthletes.org. https://euathletes.org/world-players-association-launches-universal-declaration-player-rights/.

Zaslau, D. (2021, March 22). *WVU basketball players receive death threats on social media following loss to Syracuse*. (2021, March 22). WDTV. www.wdtv.com/2021/03/22/wvu-basketball-players-receive-death-threats-on-social-media-following-loss-to-syracuse/.

Chapter 10

Alexander, H. (2021, July 1). Flag-snubbing U.S. Olympian Gwen Berry is sponsored by "defund the police" advocates Color of Change who applauded the controversial "activist athlete" for her "leadership." *Daily Mail*. www.dailymail.co.uk/news/article-9748123/Gwen-Berry-sponsored-Defund-Police-activists-Color-Change.html.

Anthony, L. (2019, April 18). New coalition announces opposition to proposed Oakland A's ballpark at Howard Terminal. ABC7 News. https://abc7news.com/oakland-as-east-stadium-alliance-howard-terminakl-ballpark-terminal/5258771/.

Berkeley Economic Review. (2019, April 21). *The economics of sports stadiums: Does public financing of sports stadiums create local economic growth, or just help billionaires improve their profit margin?* https://econreview.berkeley.edu/the-economics-of-sports-stadiums-does-public-financing-of-sports-stadiums-create-local-economic-growth-or-just-help-billionaires-improve-their-profit-margin/.

Billings, A., Butterworth, M.L., & Turman, P.D. (2015). *Communication and sport: Surveying the field*. Thousand Oaks, CA: Sage.

Broussard, R., Heath, W., & Barnidge, M. (2021). Incidental exposure to political content in sports media: Antecedents and effects on political discussion and participation. *Communication Review*, *24*(1), 1-21. https://doi-org.ezproxy.ithaca.edu/10.1080/10714421.2020.1853491n.

Brown, R.S. (2004). Sport and healing America. *Society*, *42*, 37-41.

Butterworth, M.L. (2005). Ritual in the sport of "church of baseball": Suppressing the discourse of democracy after 9/11. *Communication and Critical Cultural Studies*, *2*, 107-129.

Callas, B. (2017, September 15). *Forty-nine days later*. Medium. https://medium.com/@bradcallas/forty-nine-days-later-.

Carino, J. (2021, January 19). Trump's basketball legacy: 1-for-14 on White House visits. Will Biden restore a tradition? *USA Today*. www.usatoday.com/story/sports/2021/01/19/donald-trump-basketball-white-house-visits-joe-biden/4219415001/.

CBC Sports. (2019, January 27). *#PayDecker: Women's hockey star to get paid after NHL skills comp success*. Canadian Broadcasting Corporation. www.cbc.ca/sports/hockey/nhl/nhl-all-star-skills-competition-brianna-decker-1.4994353.

Cockrell, J. (2017, February 1). What economists think about financing sports stadiums. *Chicago Booth Review*. https://review.chicagobooth.edu/economics/2017/article/what-economists-think-about-public-financing-sports-stadiums.

Coleman, J. (2020, September 10). *The struggle against a stadium's construction became a battle for the soul of Los Angeles*. The Appeal. https://theappeal.org/sofi-stadium-gentrification-displacement-lennox-inglewood-tenants-union/.

Color of Change. (2021a). *About*. https://colorofchange.org/about.

Color of Change. (2021b, June 21). *Puma joins Color of Change in sponsoring Olympic gold medalist Gwen Berry for 2021 season* [Press release]. https://colorofchange.org/press_release/puma-joins-color-of-change-in-sponsoring-olympic-gold-medalist-gwen-berry-for-2021-season/.

Cooky, C., Council, L.D., Mears, M.A., Messner, M.A. (2021). One and done: The long eclipse of women's televised sports, 1989-2019. *Communication & Sport*, *9*(3): 347-371. doi:10.1177/21674795211003524.

Devereaux, R. (2017, September 28). The NFL, the military, and the hijacking of Pat Tillman's story. *The Intercept*. https://theintercept.com/2017/09/28/pat-tillman-nfl-protest-death-army-disgrace/.

Fischels, J. (2021, June 28). *Gwen Berry changed Olympic trials protest rules last year and is still protesting*. NPR. www.npr.org/2021/06/28/1010995193/gwen-berry-changed-olympic-trials-protest-rules-last-year-and-is-still-protestin.

Fish, M. (2006). *Part one: Tillman's uncertain death*. ESPN. www.espn.com/espn/eticket/story?page=tillman-part1.

FiveThirtyEight. (2020, November 4). *Latest polls: Who's ahead in the District of Columbia?* https://projects.fivethirtyeight.com/polls/president-general/district-of-columbia/.

Garcia, A. (2018, February 24). *NBC's $12 billion investment in the Olympics is looking riskier*. CNN Business. https://money.cnn.com/2018/02/24/media/nbc-olympics-ratings-12-billion-rights/index.html.

Giambalvo, E. (2021, July 1). College athletes unite to launch organization aimed at sustaining empowerment efforts. *Washington Post*. www.washingtonpost.com/sports/2021/07/01/united-college-athlete-advocates-new-group-ncaa/.

Gough, C. (2021, June 24). *Share of sports fans in the United States*. Statista. www.statista.com/statistics/300148/interest-nfl-football-age-canada/.

Hackney, H. (2021, December 25). NCAA Board of Governors unanimously accepts recommendations from Constitution Committee. *Sports Law Expert*. https://sportslawexpert.com/2021/12/25/ncaa-board-of-governors-unanimously-accepts-recommendations-from-constitution-committee/

Hardie, J. (2012, January 24). *Tim Thomas: The ugly truth behind his refusal to meet the president*. Bleacher Report. https://bleacherreport.com/articles/1037288-tim-thomas-the-ugly-truth-behind-his-white-house-refusal.

Hester, M.D. (2005). *America's #1 Fan: A rhetorical analysis of presidential sports encomia and the symbolic power of sports in the articulation of civil religion in the United States* [Unpublished dissertation, George State University].

Heywood, A. (2013). *What is politics?* London: MacMillan Education. www.macmillanihe.com/resources/sample-chapters/9780230363373_sample.pdf.

Hosick, M. (2021, June 30). *NCAA adopts interim name, image and likeness policy*. NCAA. www.ncaa.org/about/resources/media-center/news/ncaa-adopts-interim-name-image-and-likeness-policy.

IOC. (2016). *Editorial use of Olympic properties by media organizations for the 2016 Games*. International Olympic Committee. https://stillmed.olympic.org/Documents/THE%20IOC/IOC_guide_media_web%2029.11.13.pdf.

IOC. (2021a). *Tokyo 2020: Olympic medal count*. (2016, August 21).International Olympic Committee. https://olympics.com/tokyo-2020/olympic-games/en/results/all-sports/medal-standings.htm.

IOC. (2021b). *What is Olympism?* International Olympic Committee. https://olympics.com/ioc/faq/olympic-rings-and-other-olympic-marks/what-is-olympism.

Infield, T. (2020, November 16). Americans who get news mainly on social media are less knowledgeable and less engaged. *Trust*. www.pewtrusts.org/en/trust/archive/fall-2020/americans-who-get-news-mainly-on-social-media-are-less-knowledgeable-and-less-engaged.

Jenkins, S. (2021, June 29). Dan Crenshaw wants Gwen Berry kicked off the Olympic team. How un-American. *Washington Post*. www.washingtonpost.com/sports/olympics/2021/06/29/gwen-berry-dan-crenshaw/.

Jhaveri, H. (2019, January 26). Brianna Decker is going to get her $25K, but not from the NHL. *USA Today*. https://ftw.usatoday.com/2019/01/brianna-decker-25k-prize-money-nhl-all-star.

Johnson, B.K., & Whitehead, J.C. (2000, February). Value of public goods from sports stadiums: The CVM approach. *Contemporary Economic Policy*, *18*(1), 48-58.

JohnWallStreet. (2021, April 26). Super League collapse won't mean end of globalized sports. *Sportico*. www.sportico.com/leagues/soccer/2021/super-league-collapse-globalization-1234628080/.

Kaplan, E. (2019, January 26). Brianna Decker to be paid $25K by CCM for skills competition. *ESPN*. www.espn.com/nhl/story/_/id/25858716/brianna-decker-paid-25k-ccm-skills-competition.

Katsuyama, J. (2021, May 12). *Longtime, loyal Oakland A's fans don't want to see their team leave*. KTVU. www.ktvu.com/news/longtime-loyal-oakland-as-fans-dont-want-to-see-their-team-leave.

Kilgore, A. (2020, September 16). Athlete protests are now celebrated. One Olympian says she's still paying for hers. *Washington Post*. www.washingtonpost.com/sports/2020/09/16/olympian-gwen-berry-anthem-protest/.

Kilgore, A. (2021, June 21). After shaping protest rules in the U.S., Gwen Berry has a new sponsor and an eye on Tokyo. *Washington Post*. www.washingtonpost.com/sports/olympics/2021/06/21/gwen-berry-puma-us-olympic-track-trials/.

Kirby, B. (2018). Trump country: Alabama again tops nation in support for president. *Yellowhammer News*. https://yellowhammernews.com/trump-country-alabama-again-tops-nation-in-support-for-president/.

Kudo, H. (2020, July 27). Learn the story behind Allegiant Stadium. *Sports Illustrated*. www.si.com/nfl/raiders/news/las-vegas-raiders-allegiant-stadium-relocation.

LEAD1 Association. (2018, September 25). *Top 25 congressional staff student-athletes on the Hill contest honorees announced* [Press release]. https://lead1association.com/top-25-congressional-staff-student-athletes-on-the-hill-contest-honorees-announced/.

Lee, T.M.L. (2007). Rethinking the personal and the political: Feminist activism and civic engagement. *Hypatia*, *22*(4), 163-179. www.jstor.org/stable/4640110.

Myers, S.L. (2021, September 29). China is preparing for another Olympics in Beijing, like it or not. *New York Times*. www.nytimes.com/2021/02/19/world/asia/china-olympics-boycott.html.

Neumann, T. (2016, March 1). Why White House visits by champions are a U.S. tradition. *ESPN*. www.espn.com/college-football/story/_/id/14870667/how-white-house-visits-championship-teams-became-american-tradition.

Nielsen. (2020, December 14). *Tops of 2020: Television*. www.nielsen.com/us/en/insights/article/2020/tops-of-2020-television/.

Open Secrets. (2020). *Industry profile: 2020. Annual lobbying on recreation*. Open Secrets. www.opensecrets.org/Lobby/indusclient.php?id=N06&year=2020.

Panja, T., & Smith, R. (2021, April 22). How the Super League fell apart. *New York Times*. www.nytimes.com/2021/04/22/sports/soccer/super-league-soccer.html.

Payne, P. (2019, November 9). President Trump overwhelmingly cheered during Alabama-LSU football game. *USA Today*. www.usatoday.com/story/sports/ncaaf/2019/11/09/president-trump-cheered-overwhelmingly-alabama-lsu-game/2547130001/.

Redihan, E. (2018, February 8). The 1952 Olympic Games, the US, and the USSR. *Process: a blog for American history*. www.processhistory.org/redihan-1952-olympics/.

Reichard, K. (2021a, May 17). After ultimatum, Oakland officials say they will consider A's ballpark plan. *Ballpark Digest*. https://ballparkdigest.com/2021/05/17/after-ultimatum-oakland-officials-say-they-will-consider-as-ballpark-plan/.

Reichard, K. (2021b, July 3). A's Howard Terminal ballpark may come down to tax districts. *Ballpark Digest*. https://ballparkdigest.com/2021/07/03/as-howard-terminal-ballpark-may-come-down-to-tax-districts/.

Rossi, J. (2021, March 30). The 15 cities where your tax dollars paid for billion-dollar stadiums. *Sportscasting*. www.sportscasting.com/taxpayer-money-billion-dollar-stadiums/.

Sage, G. (1998). *Power and ideology in American sport: A critical perspective*. Champaign, IL: Human Kinetics.

Salvador, J. (2021, September 26). Report: Kyrie Irving, NBA anti-vaxxers at odds with NBA protocols, vaccinated players. *Sports Illustrated*. www.si.com/nba/2021/09/26/unvaccinated-nba-players-clash-with-league-covid-19-protocols.

Sanders, J. (2020, January). *Publicly funded stadiums*. The John Locke Foundation. www.johnlocke.org/policy-position/publicly-funded-stadiums/.

Saul Ewing Arnstein & Lehr. (2021). *NIL legislation tracker*. www.saul.com/nil-legislation-tracker#3.

Schad, T. (2020, January 30). Political football: Donald Trump, Michael Bloomberg inject themselves into Super Bowl LIV. *USA Today*. www.usatoday.com/story/sports/Ad-Meter/2020/01/28/super-bowl-donald-trump-michael-bloomberg-mark-new-frontier-ads/4478763002/.

Schneider, M. (2021, May 25). 100 most-watched TV shows of 2020-21: Winners and losers. *Variety*. https://variety.com/2021/tv/news/most-popular-tv-shows-highest-rated-2020-2021-season-1234980743/.

Sharp, R. (2019). Who paid for your stadium? *Global Sport Matters*. https://globalsportmatters.com/business/2019/05/22/who-paid-for-your-stadium/.

Sky Sports Premier League [@SkySportsPL]. (2021, April 18). @GNev2 gives a brutally honest reaction to reports that England's biggest clubs are expected to be part of plans for a breakaway European Super League [Tweet]. Twitter. https://twitter.com/SkySportsPL/status/1383830563300077569?s=20.

Staurowsky, E.J. (2005, November 21-27). Will NFL demand justice for Tillman? *Street & Smith's SportsBusinessJournal*, p. 29.

Staurowsky, E.J. (2016, April 12). *The Power Five and power politics: LEAD1 athletic directors taking their game to Capitol Hill*. Paper submitted to the College Sport Research Institute Conference, Columbia, SC.

Stephens, S. (2017). How did athletes visiting the president at the White House become a tradition? *Rolling Stone*. www.rollingstone.com/culture/culture-sports/how-did-athletes-visiting-the-president-at-the-white-house-become-a-tradition-111073/.

Takala, R. (2021, June 30). *Tom Cotton calls for Gwen Berry to get boot from Olympics: "She should be removed."* Mediaite. www.mediaite.com/news/tom-cotton-calls-for-gwen-berry-to-get-the-boot-from-olympics-she-should-be-removed/.

Terraz, T. (2021, April 16). *(A)Political Games? Ubiquitous nationalism and the IOC's Hypocrisy*. Sports Integrity Initiative.

Thorson, E.A., & Serazio, M. (2018). Sports fandom and political attitudes. *Public Opinion Quarterly*, *82*(2), 391-403. https://doi.org/10.1093/poq/nfy018.

UCAA. (2021). United College Athlete Advocates. *About*. www.ucaa.one/about.

UCAA Letter to NCAA President Mark Emmert. (2021, July 1). https://twitter.com/ucaa_one/status/1410576791693979660/photo/1

University of Minnesota. (2016). *Sociology: Understanding and changing the social world*. https://open.lib.umn.edu/sociology/chapter/14-1-power-and-authority/.

USATF. (2020, December 2). *Olympian, activist Gwen Berry named 2020 Toyota Humanitarian Award recipient* [Press release]. www.usatf.org/news/2020/olympian-activist-gwen-berry-named-2020-toyota-hum.

WARC (World Advertising Research Center). (2020, January 31). *Super Bowl fans reject political campaign ads*. www.warc.com/newsandopinion/news/super-bowl-fans-reject-political-campaign-ads/43177.

Wetzel, D. (2011, September 10). Sports mattered after 9/11 – not as a game, but as a gathering. *Yahoo!Sports*. https://news.yahoo.com/sports-mattered-after-9-11-%E2%80%93-not-as-a-game--but-as-a-gathering.html

Wharton, D. (2021, June 6). Will this be the last time Americans dominate the Olympics? *Los Angeles Times*. www.latimes.com/sports/olympics/story/2021-06-06/will-american-olympic-dominance.

Chapter 11

Ahmed, S. (2018, April 28). When women were forced to choose between faith and football. *The Guardian*. www.theguardian.com/football/blog/2018/apr/28/women-faith-football-hijab-fifa-ban.

Alpert, R.T. (2019). Social justice, sport and Judaism: A position statement. *Quest*, *71*(2), 138-149.

Athletes in Action. (2020). History & financials. https://athletesinaction.org/about/history-and-finances/.

Bain-Selbo, E. (2008). Ecstasy, joy, and sorrow: The religious experience of Southern college football. *Journal of Religion & Popular Culture*, *20*, 2.

Bain-Selbo, E. (2009). From Lost Cause to third-and-long: College football and the civil religion of the South. *The Journal of Southern Religion*, *11*, 1908-1918. Retrieved from http://jsreligion.org/Volume11/Selbo.htm.

Bain-Selbo, E. (2012). *Game day and God: Football, faith,*

and politics in the American South. Macon, GA: Mercer University Press.

Bain-Selbo, E., & Sapp, G. (2016). *Understanding sport as a religious phenomenon*. New York: Bloomsbury.

Baker, W.J. (2007). *Playing with God: Religion and modern sport*. Cambridge, MA: Harvard University Press.

Barnhart, T. (2000). *Southern fried football: The history, passion, and glory of the great southern game*. Chicago: Triumph Books.

Batista, P.J. (2002). Balancing the First Amendment's establishment and free exercise clauses: A rebuttal to Alexander & Alexander. *Journal of Legal Aspects of Sport, 12*(2), 87-116.

Baumgaertner, G. (2019, September 18). Baptism at practice: How college football became a Christian empire. *The Guardian*. www.theguardian.com/sport/2019/sep/18/dabo-swinney-christianity-clemson-football-recruiting.

Belson, K. (2014, August 30). Rams cut Michael Sam, first openly gay player drafted in N.F.L. *New York Times*. www.nytimes.com/2014/08/31/sports/football/rams-cut-michael-sam-first-openly-gay-nfl-draft-pick.html.

Blackman, J. (2010). This lemon comes as a lemon: The lemon test and the pursuit of a statute's secular purpose. *George Mason University Civil Rights Law Journal, 20*, 351-415.

Blair, L. (2014, May 8). NFL team that drafts openly gay player Michael Sam will face boycott, says D.C. lobbyist seeking to ban gays from league. *The Christian Post*. www.christianpost.com/news/nfl-team-that-drafts-openly-gay-player-michael-sam-will-face-boycott-says-d-c-lobbyist-seeking-to-ban-gays-from-league-119382/.

Borden v. School District of East Brunswick, 523 F.3d 153, 3d Cir. N.J. 2008.

Borden v. School District of East Brunswick, 555 U.S. 1212, 2009.

Buck, S. (2017, January 20). When Jesus got 'too feminine,' white dudes invented muscular Christianity. *Timeline.com*. https://timeline.com/muscular-christianity-20d7c88839b9.

Burns, R.D., Schiller, M.R., Fada, R.D., Merrick, M.A., & Wolf, K.N. (2004). Intercollegiate student-athlete use of nutritional supplements and the role of athletic trainers and dietitians in nutrition counseling. *Journal of the American Dietetic Association, 104*, 246-249. doi: 10.1016/j.jada.2003.11.013.

Carter, T. (2012). God does not play dice with the universe, or does he? Anthropological interlocutions of sport and religion. *Religion and Society: Advances in Research, 3*(1), 142-162.

Chamberlain, S. (2018, October 28). *Pittsburgh sports teams pay tribute to synagogue shooting victims*. Fox News. www.foxnews.com/sports/pittsburgh-sports-teams-pay-tribute-to-synagogue-shooting-victims.

Christians in Sport. (n.d.). *History*. www.christiansinsport.org.uk/about/history.

Coakley, J. (2009). *Sports in society: Issues & controversies* (10th ed.). New York: McGraw Hill.

Cohen, S.I.D. (1998, April). Legitimization under Constantine. *PBS: Frontline*. www.pbs.org/wgbh/pages/frontline/shows/religion/why/legitimization.html.

Czech, D.R., Wrisberg, C.A., Fisher, L.A., Thompson, C.L., & Hayes, G. (2004). The experience of Christian prayer in sport: An existential phenomenological investigation. *Journal of Psychology and Christianity, 23*(1), 3-11.

de Blot, P. (2011). Religion and Spirituality. In L. Bouckaert & L. Zsolnai (Eds.), *Handbook of spirituality and business* (pp. 11-17). London: Palgrave Macmillan.

Demarest, G. (1960). Hero worship harnessed. *Journal of Health, Physical Education, Recreation, 31*(5), 30-31.

Dodd, D. (2014). *Parents of Mizzou swimmer who committed suicide: "This has to stop."* CBS Sports. www.cbssports.com/collegefootball/writer/dennis-dodd/24425083/parents-of-mizzou-swimmer-who-committed-suicide-this-has-to-stop.

Dodd, P. (2011a). *The Tebow mystique: The faith and fans of football's most polarizing player*. Englewood, CO: Patheos Press.

Dodd, P. (2011b, December 10). Tim Tebow: God's quarterback. *Wall Street Journal*. http://online.wsj.com/article/SB10001424052970203413304577084770973155282.

Duff, D.R. (2012). *Sports psychiatry: Strategies for life balance and peak performance*. Washington, DC: American Psychiatric Publishing.

Durrett, R. (2012, February 7). Shayne Kelley to help Josh Hamilton. *ESPN.com*. Retrieved from https://www.espn.com/dallas/mlb/story/_/id/7552550/texas-rangers-hire-assistant-help-support-josh-hamilton.

Dzikus, L., Hardin, R., & Waller, S.N. (2012). Case studies of collegiate sport chaplains. *Journal of Sport and Social Issues, 36*(2), 1-27.

Eig, J. (2017, October 26). The real reason Muhammad Ali converted to Islam. *Washington Post*. www.washingtonpost.com/news/acts-of-faith/wp/2017/10/26/the-real-reason-muhammad-ali-converted-to-islam/.

Eschner, K. (2017, December 29). The YMCA first opened gyms to train stronger Christians: Physical fitness was a secondary goal for the movement. *Smithsonian Magazine*. www.smithsonianmag.com/smart-news/ymca-first-opened-gyms-train-stronger-christians-180967665/.

FCA. (2020). *Fellowship of Christian Athletes timeline*. https://timeline.fca.org.

Foster, L., & Woodthorpe, K. (2012). A golden silence? Acts of remembrance and commemoration at U.K. football games. *Journal of Sport & Social Issues, 36*(1), 50-67.

Gillentine, A., Goldfine, B., Phillips, D., Seidler, T., & Scott, D. (2004). Prayer at athletic events. *Strategies, 18*(1), 13-15.

Goldman, L. (2011, December 16). Tim Tebow: How he became the most polarizing athlete in sports. *Business Insider*. http://read.bi/s8cg6y.

Grano, D. (2017). *The eternal present of sport: Rethinking sport and religion*. Philadelphia, PA: Temple University Press.

Gunn, T.J., & Witte, J. (2012). *No establishment of religion: America's original contribution to religious liberty*. New York: Oxford Press.

Hackett, C., & McClendon, D. (2017, April 5). *Christians remain world's largest religious group, but they are declining in Europe*. Pew Research. www.pewresearch.org/fact-tank/2017/04/05/christians-remain-worlds-largest-religious-group-but-they-are-declining-in-europe/.

Hall, D.E. (1994). On the making and unmaking of monsters: Christian socialism, muscular Christianity, and the metaphorization of class conflict. In D.E. Hall (Ed.), *Muscular Christianity: Embodying the Victorian age* (pp. 45-65). Cambridge University Press.

Harkness, G., & Islam, S. (2011). Muslim female athletes and the hijab. *Contexts*, *10*(4), p. 64-65.

Harper, S.R. (2012). *Black male student success in higher education: A report from the national Black male college achievement study*. Philadelphia: University of Pennsylvania, Center for the Study of Race and Equity in Education.

Higgs, R.J. (1995). *God in the stadium: Sports and religion in America*. Lexington, KY: The University Press of Kentucky.

Hodge, S.R., Harrison, L., Burden, J.W., & Dixson, A.D. (2008). Brown in Black and White—Then and now a question of educating or sporting African American males in America. *American Behavioral Scientist*, *51*(7), 928-952.

Huffman, L.T. (2014). *Examining perceived life stress factors among intercollegiate athletes: A holistic perspective* [Doctoral dissertation]. http://trace. tennessee.edu/cgi/viewcontent.cgi?article=4081&context=utk_graddiss.

Hughes, T. (1857). *Tom Brown's schooldays*. London: J.M. Dent and Sons.

Hyndman, M. (2005). Tradition is not law: Advocating a single determinative test for establishment clause cases. *Marshall Law Review*, *31*, 101-136.

Idleman, S.C. (2001). Religious freedom and the interscholastic athlete. *Marquette Sports Law Review*, *12*(1), 296-345.

Judaism. (2022). Retrieved from www.history.com/topics/religion/judaism.

Kaminer, D. (2002). Bringing organized prayer in through the back door: How moment-of- silence legislation for the public schools violates the establishment clause. *Stanford Law & Policy Review*, *13*(2), 267-322.

Kennedy, M. (2017, September 22). Alabama district ends practice of student-led prayer at football games. *American School & University*. www.asumag.com/facilities-management/business-finance/article/20855773/alabama-district-ends-practice-of-studentled-prayer-at-football-games.

KFA. (2018). Fellowship of Christian Athletes and AIA: The difference? *K-Love Fan Awards*. www.fanawards.com/fellowship-of-christian-athletes-aia-difference.

Kingsley, C. (1857). *Two years ago*. Cambridge: Macmillan & Co.

Koppett, L. (1977, March 15). Athletes in Action spreading gospel efficiently. *New York Times*. www.nytimes.com/1977/03/15/archives/athletes-in-action-spreading-gospel-efficiently.html.

Krattenmaker, T. (2010, January 31). Tim Tebow: Cultural warrior? *USA Today*. www.usatoday.com/NEWS/usaedition/2010-02-01-column01_ST_U.htm.

Krattenmaker, T. (2012, January 14). When Tim Tebow loses, does God, too? *USA Today*. www.usatoday.com/news/opinion/story/2012-01-14/tebow-lost-broncos-patriots-god-religion/52566104/1.

Ladd, T., & Mathisen, J.A. (1999). *Muscular Christianity: Evangelical protestants and the development of American sport*. Grand Rapids, MI: Baker Books.

Leonard, W.M. (1998). *A sociological perspective in sport*. Minneapolis, MN: Burgess.

Leung, L.B., Yoon, J., Rubenstein, L.V., Post, E.P., Metzger, M.E., Wells, K., Sugar, C.A., Escare, J.J. (2018). Changing patterns of mental health care Use: The role of integrated mental health services in Veteran Affairs Primary Care. *Journal of the American Board of Family Medicine*, *31*(1), 38-48. doi: 10.3122/jabfm.2018.01.170157.

Lumpkin, P. (2010). *Manhood factories: YMCA architecture and the making of modern urban culture*. Minneapolis, MN: University of Minnesota Press.

Mackintosh, C., & Dempsey, C. (2017). The British Asian Muslim male sport participation puzzle: An exploration of implications for sport development policy and practice. *Journal of Youth Studies*, *20*(8), 974-996.

Maslin, J. (2005, December 15). A massacre in Munich, and what came after. *New York Times*. www.nytimes.com/2005/12/15/books/a-massacre-in-munich-and-what-came-after.html.

Matthews, E. (2013, July 11). Cross banned from mound at Busch Stadium. *USA Today*. www.usatoday.com/story/sports/mlb/cardinals/2013/07/11/st-louis-cardinals-cross-mound-busch-stadium/2509025/.

Matthews-Pillette, R. (2000). Santa Fe Independent School District v. Doe: Adding a brick to the wall of separation between church and state. *Southern University Law Review*, *28*(1), 61-78.

Miller, J.J., Lee, K., & Martin, C.L.L. (2013). An analysis of interscholastic athletic directors' religious values and practices on pregame prayer in Southeastern United States: A case study. *Journal of Legal Aspects of Sport*, *23*, 91-106.

Mirabito, T., Huffman, L., & Hardin, R. (2013). "The chosen one": The *Denver Post's* coverage of Tim Tebow. *Journal of Contemporary Athletics*, *7*(2), 51-68.

MJL. (2018, January). *The Jewish denominations*. My Jewish Learning. www.myjewishlearning.com/article/the-jewish-denominations/.

Modrovich v. Allegheny County, 385 F.3d 397, 2004 U.S. App. LEXIS 20875 (3d Cir. Pa. 2004).

Morrissey, R. (2011, December 7). The Tim Tebow conundrum: Do sports and religion really mix? *Chicago Sun-Times*.

www.suntimes.com/sports/morrissey/9310564-452/the-tim-tebow-conundrum-do-sports-and-religion-really-mix.html.

Murdoch, E. (2014, May 13). Religion and sports collide in NCAA athletic teams. *World Religion News*. www.worldreligionnews.com/religion-news/christianity/religion-and-sports-collide-ncaa-athletic-teams.

Murray, M.A., Joyner, A.B., Burke, K.L., Wilson, M.J., & Zwald, A.D. (2005). The relationship between prayer and team cohesion in collegiate softball teams. *Journal of Psychology and Christianity*, *24*(3), 233-239.

Nye, E. (2019, January 7). *Fellowship of Christian Athletes targets LGBTQ community with statement of faith*. Outsports. www.outsports.com/2019/1/7/18173087/fellowship-of-christian-athletes-gay-lgbt.

Parker, A., & Collins, M. (2012). Sport and Christianity in the 21st century. *Encounters Mission Journal*, *41*, 1-7.

Parker, A., & Weir, J.S. (2012). Sport, spirituality and Protestantism: A historical overview. *Theology*, *115*(4), 253-265.

Perelman, M., & Portillo, V. (2013, August 9). The brutal legacy of the muscular Christian movement. *CounterPunch*. www.counterpunch.org/2013/08/09/the-brutal-legacy-of-the-muscular-christian-movement/.

Peter, J. (2016, September 7). Colin Kaepernick: False rumors of conversion tied to Islamophobia. *USA Today*. www.usatoday.com/story/sports/nfl/49ers/2016/09/07/colin-kaepernick-national-anthem-protest/89975464/.

Popke, M. (2012, August). Pregame prayers under attack at high schools, colleges. *Athletic Business*. www.athleticbusiness.com/rules-regulations/pregame-prayers-under-attack-at-high-schools-colleges.html.

Price, J.L. (2001) *From season to season: Sports as American religion*. Macon, GA: Mercer University Press.

Putney, C. (2001). *Muscular Christianity: Manhood and sports in Protestant America, 1880-1920*. Cambridge, MA: Harvard University Press.

Raney, L.E. (2015). Integrating primary care and behavioral health: The role of the psychiatrist in the collaborative care model. *The American Journal of Psychiatry*, *172*(8), 721-728. doi: 10.1176/appi.ajp.2015.15010017.

Robinson, M. (2014, April 23). Clemson coach Dabo Swinney responds to religion complaint. *USA Today*. www.usatoday.com/story/sports/ncaaf/2014/04/23/clemson-coach-dabo-swinney-responds-to-religion-complaint/8055503/.

Rohan, T. (2019, September 4). Faith, football and the fervent religious culture at Dabo Swinney's Clemson. *Sports Illustrated*. www.si.com/college/2019/09/04/clemson-dabo-swinney-religion-culture.

Rosen, D. (1994). The volcano and the cathedral: Muscular Christianity and the origins of primal manliness. In D.E. Hall (Eds.), *Muscular Christianity: Embodying the Victorian age* (pp. 45-65). Cambridge: Cambridge University Press.

Rothenberg, M. (2017). Sandy Koufax responded to a higher calling on Yom Kippur in 1965. *National Baseball Hall of Fame*. https://baseballhall.org/discover/sandy-koufax-sits-out-game-one.

Saeed, A. (2002). What's in a name? Muhammad Ali and the politics of cultural identity. *Culture, Sport, Society*, *5*(3), 52-72.

Santa Fe Independent School District v. Jane Doe, et al., No. 99-62, (2000); 168 F.3rd 806 (Fifth Cir. 1999).

Schwartz, M. (Reporter) (2011). OTL: Polarizing QB [Television series episode]. In Ebinger, J. (Executive Producer), *Outside the Lines*. ESPN. http://espn.go.com/video/clip?id=6975407.

Shea, C. (2014, October 10). Controversy heats up over exclusionary religious groups. *The Chronicle of Higher Education*, *61*(6), A10-A10.

Slusher, H.S. (1967). *Man, sport, and existence*. Philadelphia: Lea & Febiger.

Smith, D.T. (2014). The Mormon dilemma: How old and new religious divides hurt Mormon candidates in the United States. *Electoral Studies*, *35*, 283-291.

Speich, J. (2001). Santa Fe Independent School District v. Doe: Mapping the future of student-led, student-initiated prayer in public schools. *Albany Law Review*, *65*, 271.

Stampler, L. (2014, September 30). NFL under fire for penalizing Muslim player after end zone prayer. *Time*. https://time.com/3449227/nfl-husain-abdullah-muslim-prayer-touchdown/.

Stevenson, C.L. (1991). The Christian-athlete: An interactionist-developmental analysis. *Sociology of Sport Journal*, *8*, 362-379.

Stone, J., Harrison, C.K., & Mottley, J. (2012). "Don't call me a student-athlete": The effect of identity priming on stereotype threat for academically engaged African American college athletes. *Basic and Applied Social Psychology*, *34*(2), 99-106. doi: 10.1080/019 73533.2012.655624.

Sullivan, S.P. (2010). God in my sporting: A justification for Christian experience in sport. *Journal of the Christian Society for Kinesiology and Leisure Studies*, *1*(1), 9-17.

Tjale, A.A., & Bruce J. (2007). A concept analysis of holistic nursing care in pediatric nursing. *Curationis*, *30*(4), 45-52.

URI. (2020). *Christianity: Basic beliefs*. United Religions Initiative. www.uri.org/kids/world-religions/christian-beliefs.

Waller, S.N. (2016). "Our hope is built on nothing less": Why religion/spirituality matter in the lives of Black male college athletes. In B. Schultz & M.L. Sheffer (Eds.), *Sport and religion in the twenty-first century* (pp. 193-216). Lanham, MD: Lexington Books.

Waller, S., Dzikus, L., & Hardin, R. (2008). Collegiate sports chaplaincy: Problems and promise. *Journal of Issues in Intercollegiate Athletics*, *1*, 107-123.

Waller, S.N., Huffman, L.T., & Hardin, R.L. (2016). The sport chaplain's role in the holistic care model for collegiate athletes in the United States. *Practical Theology*, *9*(3), 226-241.

Watson, N.J. (2007). Muscular Christianity in the modern age: "Winning for Christ" or "playing for glory"? In J. Parry, S. Robinson, N.J. Watson, & M. Nesti (Eds.), *Sport and spirituality: An introduction* (pp. 80-95). New York: Routledge.

Wieting, S.G. (2015). *The sociology of hypocrisy: An analysis of sport and religion*. Burlington, VT: Ashgate Publishing Company.

Wills, M. (2007). Connection, action, and hope: An invitation to reclaim the "spiritual" in health care. *Journal of Religion and Health*, *46*(3), 423-436.

World Health Organization. (1946). *Preamble to the constitution of the World Health Organization as adopted by the International Health Conference*, New York, 19 June-22 July 1946.

Yoonas, Z. (2009, October 14). *Body, mind, and soul: Spirituality may help athletes in coping with the challenges of competition*. www.patheos.com/resources/ additional-resources/body-mind-and-soul.

Yusko, D.A., Buckman, J.F., White, H.R., & Pandina, R.J. (2008). Alcohol, tobacco, illicit drugs, and performance enhancers: A comparison of use by college student athletes and non-athletes. *Journal of American College Health*, *57*(3), 281-290.

Zamanzadeh, V., Jasemi, M., Valizadeh, L., Keogh, B., & Takeghani, F. (2015). Effective factors in providing holistic care: A qualitative study. *Journal of Palliative Care*, *21*(2), 214-227. doi: 10.4103/0973-1075.156506.

Zirin, D. (2014, January 6). *Jovan Belcher's murder-suicide: Did the Kansas City Chiefs pull the trigger?* TheNation.com. Retrieved from www.thenation.com/blog/177787/jovan-belchers-murder-suicide-did-kansas-city-chiefs-pull-trigger#.

Chapter 12

Administration for Community Living. (2021). 2020 profile of older Americans. Washington, DC: U.S. Department of Health and Human Services, Administration on Aging. https://acl.gov/sites/default/files/Aging%20and%20Disability%20in%20America/2020ProfileOlderAmericans.Final_.pdf

Athlete Transition Services. (2021). About the company. Website. https://atscorp.org/about-us/.

Atkinson, J. (2009). Age matters in sport communication. *Electronic Journal of Communication*, 3-4. www.cios.org/EJCPUBLIC/019/2/019341.html.

Aune, T.K., Ingvaldsen R.P., Vestheim O.P., Bjerkeset O., & Dalen, T. (2018). Relative age effects and gender differences in the national test of numeracy: A population study of Norwegian children. *Frontiers in Psychology*, *9*. www.frontiersin.org/articles/10.3389/fpsyg.2018.01091/full.

Barcza-Renner, K., Shipherd, A.M., & Basevitch, I. (2020). A qualitative examination of sport retirement in former NCAA Division I athletes. *Journal of Athlete Development and Experience*, *2*(1), 1-13.

Bercovici, J. (2018). *Play on: How to get better with age*. London: Penguin.

Blinde, E.M., & Stratta, T.M. (1992). The "sport career death" of college athletes: Involuntary and unanticipated sport exits. *Journal of Sport Behavior*, *15*, 3-20.

Borzello, J. (2020a, November 10). Five star Dior Johnson announces he's decommitted from Syracuse. *Twitter*. https://twitter.com/jeffborzello/status/1326294708046487554

Borzello, J. (2020b, February 7). Sophomore 5-star guard Dior Johnson commits to Syracuse. *ESPN.com*. https://www.espn.com/college-football/recruiting/story/_/id/28655676/sophomore-5-star-guard-dior-johnson-commits-syracuse

Brenneman, L. (2019, November 2). *Empower kids, not their delayed puberty*. Global Sport Institute. https://globalsport.asu.edu/blog/empower-kids-not-their-delayed-puberty.

Carroll, C. (2019, July 9). Roger Federer criticizes WTA age rule that limits Coco Gauff. *Sports Illustrated*. www.si.com/tennis/2019/07/09/roger-federer-criticizes-age-rule-cori-coco-gauff

Cervin, G. (2020, August 7). *Not just to counter the history of abuse: Reasons to revise age criteria for elite women gymnasts*. Scroll. https://scroll.in/field/969708/not-just-to-counter-gymnastics-history-of-abuse-reasons-to-revise-minimum-age-as-18-for-women.

Collins, B. (2018, October 1). *Age discrimination suit filed because 16-year-old boy didn't make soccer team*. MPR News. https://blogs.mprnews.org/newscut/2018/10/age-discrimination-suit-filed-because-16-year-old-boy-didnt-make-soccer-team/.

Cosh, S., Crabb, S., & LeCouteur, A. (2013). Elite athletes and retirement: Identity, choice, and agency. *Australian Journal of Psychology*, *65*(2), 89–97. https://doi.org/10.1111/j.1742-9536.2012.00060.x

Crouch, M. (2019, October 16). Inspiring stories from later-in-life athletes. AARP. www.aarp.org/health/healthy-living/info-2019/inspiring-older-athletes.html.

Curtis, M. (2020, November 3). *SU basketball recruit Dior Johnson gets clean slate with new high school team: "Your past is your past."* Syracuse [Website]. www.syracuse.com/orangebasketball/2020/11/su-basketball-recruit-dior-johnson-gets-clean-slate-with-new-high-school-team-your-past-is-your-past.html.

Deffenbach, K., & Thompson, M. (2020). *Coach education essentials: Your guide to developing sport coaches*. Champaign, IL: Human Kinetics.

Dolski, M. (2016, August 2). For gymnasts, age matters—and comes with a cost. *Globe and Mail*. www.theglobeandmail.com/sports/olympics/for-gymnasts-age-matters-and-comes-with-acost/article31200953/.

Duffek, J. (2017, March 19). How to turn your late bloomer into a college recruit. *USA Today*. https://usatodayhss.com/2017/how-to-turn-your-late-bloomer-into-a-college-recruit.

Gewirtz, J. (2021, April 14). Pittsburgh selected to host 2023 National Senior Games. *Sports Travel Magazine*. www.sportstravelmagazine.com/pittsburgh-selected-to-host-2023-national-senior-games/.

Givony, J., & Wojnarowski, A. (2020, April 16). *Top high school player Jalen Green enters NBA/G League pathway*. *ESPN.com*. https://abcnews.go.com/Sports/top-high-school-player-jalen-green-enters-nbag/story?id=70187109#:~:-text=California%20high%20school%20star%20Jalen%20Green%2C%20the%20No.,outside%20of%20the%20minor%20league%27s%20traditional%20team%20structure.\

Gladwell, M. (2008). *Outliers: The story of success.* NY: Little, Brown, and Company.

Godwin, R. (2019, April 7). Age is no barrier: Meet the world's oldest top athletes. *The Guardian*. www.theguardian.com/global/2019/apr/07/age-is-no-barrier-meet-the-oldest-top-athletes.

Goetzel, L. (2020, June 8). *NBA commissioner's comments on older coaches is a lesson to all employers returning to work.* https://www.fisherphillips.com/news-insights/nba-commissioner-s-comments-on-older-coaches-is-a-lesson-to-all-employers-returning-to-work.html#:~:text=NBA%20coach%20Rick%20Carlisle%E2%80%99s%20response%20to%20Silver%E2%80%99s%20comments,healthier%20than%20someone%20in%20their%2030%E2%80%99s%20or%2040%E2%80%99s.

Gray, J., & Plucker, J.A. (2010). "She's a natural": Identifying and developing athletic talent. *Journal for the Education of the Gifted*, *33*(3), 361-380.

Grove, J.R., Lavallee, D., & Gordon, S. (1997). Coping with retirement from sport: The influence of athletic identity. *Journal of Applied Sport Psychology*, *9*(2), 191-203.

Hambrick, D.Z. (2015, September 22). What makes a prodigy? *Scientific American*. www.scientificamerican.com/article/what-makes-a-prodigy1/.

Hansen, A., Perry, J., Ross, M. & Montgomery, T. (2019) Facilitating a successful transition out of sport: Introduction of a collegiate student-athlete workshop, *Journal of Sport Psychology in Action*, *10* (1), 1-9, DOI: 10.1080/21520704.2018.1463329

Hart, J.A., & Swenty, C.F. (2016). Understanding transitions to promote student success: A concept analysis. *Nursing Forum*, *51*(3), 180-185.

Horton, R.S., & Mack, D.E. (2000). Athletic identity in marathon runners: Functional focus or dysfunctional commitment? *Journal of Sport Behavior*, 23, 101.

Howard, B. (2020). *2020-2021 NFHS handbook*. Indianapolis, IN: National Federation of State High School Associations. www.nfhs.org/media/4119446/2020-21-nfhs-handbook_10-1.pdf.

Interdonato, S. (2017, November 25). Saugerties phenom lighting up Section 9—as a 7th grader. *Times Herald-Recorder.* https://amp.recordonline.com/amp/16967892007 .

Interdonato, S. (2020, July 17). Former Saugerties hoops star Dior Johnson picks Syracuse. *Times Herald Record.* www.recordonline.com/story/sports/high-school/basketball/2020/02/08/former-saugerties-hoops-star-dior-johnson-picks-syracuse/111795368/.

Jane Doe, next friend of John Doe v. Ladue Horton Watkins High School. (2018). No. 4:18-CV-01637 JAR. www.leagle.com/decision/infdco20181004791.

Joyner, P.W., Lewis, J., Mallon, W.J., Kirkendall, D., Rehan, D., Fagerberg, A., Mills, F.B., & Garrett, W. (2020). Relative age effect: Beyond the youth phenomenon. *BMJ Open Sport & Exercise Medicine*, 6:e000857. doi: 10.1136/bmjsem-2020-000857.

Kerr, R., Barker-Rutchi, N., Schubring, A., Cervin, G., & Nunomura, M. (2015, February). Coming of age: Towards best practice in women's artistic gymnastics. LEaP Research Report No. 37. Lincoln, New Zealand: Lincoln University. https://core.ac.uk/download/pdf/35469692.pdf.

Kidd, V.D., Southall, R.M., Nagel, M.S., Reynolds II, J.F., Scheyett, A.M., & Anderson, C.K. (2018). Profit-athletes' athletic role set and post-athletic transitions. *Journal of Issues in Intercollegiate Athletics*, *11*, 115-141.

Lally, P. (2007). Identity and athletic retirement: A prospective study. *Psychology of Sport and Exercise*, *8*(1), 85-99.

Lavallee, D. (2005). The effect of a life development intervention on sports career transition adjustment. *The Sport Psychologist*, *19*(2), 193-202.

Lavallee, D., & Robinson, H.K. (2007). In pursuit of an identity: A qualitative exploration of retirement from women's artistic gymnastics. *Psychology of Sport and Exercise*, *8*(1), 119-141.

Leitch, W. (2019, April 3). The era of the old athlete is over. *New York Magazine*. https://nymag.com/intelligencer/2019/04/the-era-of-the-old-athlete-is-over.html.

Lindemann, E. (1965). Symptomatology and management of acute grief. In H.J. Parad (Ed.). *Crisis intervention: Selected Readings* (pp. 10-11). New York, NY: Family Service Association of America.

Little League. (2021). *Little League divisions by age*. https://www.littleleague.org/play-little-league/determine-league-age/?gclid=Cj0KCQiA88X_BRDUARIsACVMYD-8BKtm1Ss97XhJcamyMXESmnsiiDs5gTP_IciTaLj_Xw0hh0aK85IaAj8aEALw_wcB.#agechart

Lovell, B. (2012, Winter). Eighteen years old and ready for driving, cigarettes and war, but not basketball: Why the NBA is committing a foul on the age eligibility rule. *Journal of Civil Rights and Economic Development*, *2*(26), 415-448.

McCann, M. (2020, November 18). NBA ban of prep-to-pro jump draws scrutiny from Congress. *Sportico*. www.sportico.com/law/analysis/2020/legality-of-age-restrictions-1234616861/.

McCarthy, K. (2020, September 24). Tiny surf dude! Boy aged FOUR wows crowds with his skills as he rides the waves off Devon. *The Daily Mail*. www.dailymail.co.uk/news/article-8767407/Tiny-surf-dude-Boy-aged-FOUR-shows-skills-rides-waves-Devon.html.

Meehan, W.P., & Landry, G.L. (2015). Tackling in youth football. *Pediatrics*, *136*(5), n.p. https://pediatrics.aappublications.org/content/136/5/e1419.

Miller, A. (2020, October 7). In Europe, you don't play high school or college sports. Some think U.S. should follow suit. *Post and Courier*. www.postandcourier.com/sports/in-europe-you-dont-play-high-school-or-college-sports-some-think-u-s-should/article_92ad84ba-a5c8-11e8-86ae-df88215ac3a1.html.

Moon, D. (2017, March 19). Still rollin'. *NSGA.com.s*. https://nsga.com/still-rollin/.

Mumm, T. (2021, June 3). What the Ducks are getting in Oregon commit Dior Johnson. *Sports Illustrated*. www.si.com/college/oregon/recruiting/ducks-getting-a-supreme-leader-in-dior-johnson.

Myerberg, P. (2016, February 3). Recruiting's color wheel: Redshirt, greenshirt, grayshirt, blueshirt. *USA Today*. www.usatoday.com/story/sports/ncaaf/recruiting/2016/01/31/college-football-recruiting-red-shirt-greenshirt-grayshirt-blueshirt/79603750/.

National Senior Games Association. (2021). *About*. https://nsga.com/history/.

NCAA. (2018). *After the game*. www.ncaa.org/student-athletes/former-student-athlete.

Nowinski, C., & Cantu, R. (2019, November). *Flag football under 14: An education campaign for parents: A white paper*. Boston, MA: Concussion Legacy Foundation. https://concussionfoundation.org/sites/default/files/2021-02/Flag_Under_14_White_Paper_110119.pdf.

O'Donnell, R. (2019, August 8). *How elite high schoolers are skipping college and to get to the NBA*. SB Nation. www.sbnation.com/college-basketball/2019/8/8/20753788/nba-draft-college-basketball-recruiting-lamelo-ball-rj-hampton.

Olympic Channel. (2018, September 11). Ageism is the new sexism, says trailblazer for women's rights in sport. www.olympicchannel.com/en/stories/news/detail/50-years-later-kathrine-switzer-is-fighting-a-new-discrimination/.

Parkes, C.M. (1971). Psycho-social transitions: A field for study. *Social Science & Medicine*, *5*(2), 101-115.

Petrin, K. (2016, November 16). This 91 year old won't stop running. *St. Louis Magazine*.

Pietruszkiewicz, N. (2021, May 23). *How Phil Mickelson stunned golf by becoming the oldest major champion*. ESPN. www.espn.com/golf/story/_/id/31497332/how-phil-mickelson-stunned-golf-becoming-oldest-major-champion.

Redd, M.J., Fukuda, D.H., Beyer, K.S., & Oliviera, L.P. (2018). No observable relative age effects in professional surfers: A constraints-based evaluation. *International Journal of Exercise Science*, *11*(6), 355-363.

Robert Barker, Dennis Allocco, & Michael Pilla v. National Collegiate Athletic Association et al. (2020). Supreme Court of the State of New York County of New York. www.courthousenews.com/wp-content/uploads/2020/01/robert-ncaa.pdf.

Rohrs-Cordes, K. & Paule-Koba, A.L. (2018). Evaluation of an NCAA sponsored online support group for career-ending injured collegiate athletes transitioning out of sports. *Journal for the Study of Sports and Athletes in Education*, *12*(3), 200-219.

Schlossberg, N.K. (1981). A model for analyzing human adaptation to transition. *Counseling Psychologist*, *9*(2), 2-18.

Smith, A.B., & Hardin, R. (2018). Female student-athletes' transition out of college competition. *Journal of Amateur Sport*, *4*(2), 61-86.

Smith, A.B., & Hardin, R. (2020). The transition experiences of Division I and III collegiate athletes. *Journal of Athlete Development and Experience*, *2*(3), 142-161.

Sports Engine. (2018, November 7). There's more than just red shirts in college sports. www.sportsengine.com/article/theres-more-just-red-shirts-college-sports.

Stark-Mason, R. (2018). The one and done dilemma. *NCAA Champion Magazine*. www.ncaa.org/static/champion/the-one-and-done-dilemma/.

Stokowski, S., Paule-Koba, A.L., & Kaunert, C. (2019). Former college athletes' perceptions of adapting to transition. *Journal of Issues in Intercollegiate Athletics*, *12*, 403-426.

Stoltenburg, A.L., Kamphoff, C.S., & Lindstrom Bremer, K. (2011). Transitioning out of sport: The psychosocial effects of collegiate athletes' career-ending injuries. *Athletic Insight*, *3*, 115-133.

Tandon, K. (2019, July 8). Cori Gauff's Wimbledon run prompts look at WTA's age restrictions rule. *Tennis*. www.tennis.com/pro-game/2019/07/coco-gauff-cori-wta-age-restriction-rules-wimbledon-halep-federer-rafa/83327/.

Tayrose, G.A., Beutel, B.G., Cardone, D.A., & Sherman, O.H. (2015). The masters athlete: A review of current exercise and treatment recommendations. *Sports Health*, *7*(3), 270-276. https://doi.org/10.1177/1941738114548999.

U.S. Olympic Committee (2019). *Athlete career education program*. www.teamusa.org/athlete-resources/athlete-career-and-education-program.

Walker, M. (2020, September 18). Huge 6-year-old dominates opponent in viral football video. *New York Post*. https://nypost.com/2020/09/18/monstrous-6-year-old-dominates-opponents-in-viral-video/.

Warehime, S., Dinkel, D., Bjornsen-Ramig, A., & Blount, A. (2017). A qualitative exploration of former college student-athletes' wellness. *Physical Culture and Sport Studies and Research*, *75*(1), 23-34.

Weiss, R.S. (1976). Transition states and other stressful situations: Their nature and programs for their management. In G. Caplan & M. Killilea (Eds.), *Support systems and mutual help: Multidisciplinary explorations* (pp. 213-232). New York, NY: Grune & Stratton.

Winner, E., & Drake, E. (2018). Giftedness and Expertise: The Case for Genetic Potential. *Journal of Expertise*, *1*(2), 1-7.

Wrady & Michel, LLC. (2015, August 10). Age discrimination rears its head in the NFL. Wrady & Michel Employment Blog. www.wmalabamalaw.com/employment-law-blog/2015/august/age-discrimination-rears-its-head-in-the-nfl/.

Wylleman, P., Alfermann, D., & Lavallee, D. (2004). Career transition in sport: European perspectives. *Psychology of Sport and Exercise*, *5*, 7-20.

Chapter 13

Acosta, V.R., & Carpenter, J.L. (2014). *Women in intercollegiate sport: A longitudinal, national study thirty-seven year update 1977-2014*. Unpublished manuscript. Retrieved March 18, 2021, from www.acostacarpenter.org/2014%20Status%20of%20Women%20in%20Intercollegiate%20Sport%20-37%20Year%20Update%20-%201977-2014%20.pdf.

Carmichael, S. & Hamilton, C.V. (1967). *Black power: The Politics of liberation in America*. New York, NY: Vintage.

Bennett, L. (1975). *The shaping of Black America: The struggles and triumphs of African Americans, 1619-1990s*. Chicago:

Johnson Publishing.

Buzuvis, E.E. (2015). Barriers to leadership for women in college athletics. In E. Comeaux (Ed.), *Introduction to Intercollegiate Athletics* (pp. 272-284). Baltimore, MD: John Hopkins University Press.

Fanon, F. (1963). *The wretched of the earth.* New York: Grove Press.

Hawkins, B.J. (2010). *The new plantation: Black athletes, college sports, and predominantly White NCAA institutions.* New York: Palgrave MacMillan Press.

Leonard, Wilbert M. (1987). Stacking in college basketball: A neglected analysis. *Sociology of Sport Journal*, *4*(4): 403-409.

Mapping Police Violence. (2020). Police violence map. Retrieved October 22, 2020, from https://mappingpoliceviolence.org.

NCAA. (2020a). *NCAA demographics database*. Retrieved January 4, 2021, from www.ncaa.org/about/resources/research/ncaa-demographics-database.

NCAA. (2020b). *Presidential pledge*. www.ncaa.org/about/resources/inclusion/ncaa-presidential-pledge.

NCAA Office of Inclusion. (2021). *National Collegiate Athletic Association*. Retrieved March 12, 2021, from www.ncaa.org/about/resources/inclusion/office-inclusion-staff.

Stangl, J.M., & Kane, M. (1991). Structural variables that offer explanatory power for the underrepresentation of women coaches since Title IX: The case of homologous reproduction. *Sociology of Sport Journal*, *8*(1), 47-60.

U.S. Department of Justice. (2018). *2018 hate crime statistics.* Retrieved October 22, 2020, from https://ucr.fbi.gov/hate-crime/2018/topic-pages/incidents-and-offenses.

TIDES (2021). The Institute for Diversity and Ethics in Sport: Making Waves of Change. Retrieved September 8, 2021, from Home | TIDES (tidesport.org)

Chapter 14

Adler, N. (1986). *International dimensions of organizational behavior*. Boston: Kent.

Armstrong, K.L. (2013). Cultural essence and sport consumption: Marketing organizational charisma. *Innovative Marketing*, *9*(1), 62-71.

Bartol, K.M., Martin, D.C., & Kromkowski, J.A. (2003). Leadership and the glass ceiling: Gender and ethnic group influences on leader behaviors at middle and executive managerial levels. *Journal of Leadership and Organizational Studies*, *9*(3), 8-18.

BBC. (2020, July 13). *Washington Redskins to drop controversial team name following review.* www.bbc.com/news/world-us-canada-53390944.

Brown, J. (2016). *Inclusion: Diversity, the new workplace & the will to change.* Publish Your Purpose Press.

Bumbaca, C. (2020, September 3). ESPN report details more on Washington NFL team's toxic culture with interviews from four former female staffers. *USA Today*. www.usatoday.com/story/sports/nfl/washington/2020/09/03/washington-nfl-teams-toxic-culture-detailed-further-espn-report/5700870002/.

Carmeli, A., & Spreitzer, G.M. (2009). Trust, connectivity, and thriving: Implications for innovative behaviors at work. *Journal of Creative Behavior*, *43*(3), 169-191.

Carr-Ruffino, N. (2009). *Managing diversity: People skills for a multicultural workplace* (8th ed.). Custom Publishing.

Cook, A., & Glass, C. (2013). Glass cliffs and organizational saviors: Barriers to minority leadership in work organizations? *Social problems*, *60*(2), 168-187.

Cox, T. Jr. (1994). *Cultural diversity in organizations: Theory, Research & Practice.* Berrett-Koehler.

Cox, T. Jr. (2001). *Creating the multicultural organization.* John Wiley & Sons.

Davis, D.R., & Maldonando, C. (2015). Shattering the glass ceiling: The leadership development of African American women in higher education. *Advancing Women in Leadership*, *35*, 48-64.

Deal, T.E., & Kennedy, A.A. (1982). *Corporate cultures: The rites and rituals of corporate life.* Addison-Wesley.

Ely, R.J., & Meyerson, D.E. (2000). Theories of gender in organizations: A new approach to organizational analysis and change. *Research in Organizational Behavior*, *22*, 103-151.

Ferdman, B.M. (2014). The practice of inclusion in diverse organization. In B.M. Ferdman & B.R. Deane (Eds.), *Diversity at work: The practice of inclusion.* Jossey-Bass.

Greenwell, M. (2018, December 20). *Mark Cuban's plan for cleaning up his #MeToo mess: Hire a woman to do it for him.* Deadspin.com. https://deadspin.com/mark-cubans-plan-for-cleaning-up-his-metoo-mess-hire-1831228538.

Hall, E.T. (1981). *Beyond culture.* Doubleday.

Hatch, M.J., & Schultz, M. (1997). Relations between organizational culture, identity and image. *European Journal of Marketing*, *31*, (5/6), 356-365.

Izzo, J., & Vanderwielen, J. (2018). *The purpose revolution: How leaders create engagement and competitive advantage in an age of social good.* Berrett-Koehler.

Jenkins, S. (2020, September, 10). *Every sponsor Dan Snyder and the Washington Football Team nearly lost due to name change controversy.* Sportscasting. www.sportscasting.com/every-sponsor-dan-snyder-and-the-washington-football-team-nearly-lost-due-to-name-change-controversy/.

Jhaveri, H. (2020, August 1). Why is the NHL so afraid of saying Black Lives Matter? *USA Today*. https://ftw.usatoday.com/2020/08/nhl-so-afraid-of-saying-black-lives-matter.

Kilgore, A. & Allen, S. (2020, July 13). Washington's name change happens fast, but it was decades in the making. *Washington Post*. www.washingtonpost.com/sports/2020/07/13/washingtons-name-change-happened-fast-it-was-decades-making/.

Lussier, R.N., & Kimball, D.C. (2014). *Applied sport management skills.* Human Kinetics.

Mezirow, J. (1997). Transformative learning: Theory to practice. *New Directions for Adult and Continuing Education*, *74*, 5-12.

Moskovitz, D. (2018, March 23). A used condom, screaming, and porn: There's so much more to how bad harassment was at the Dallas Mavericks. *Deadspin*. https://deadspin.com/a-used-condom-screaming-and-porn-theres-so-much-more-1823256222

Ng, E.S., & Sears, G.J. (2017). The glass ceiling in context: The influence of CEO gender, recruitment practices and firm internationalizing on the representation of women in management. *Human Resources Management Journal, 27*(1), 133-151.

Northouse, P.G. (2004). *Leadership: Theory and practice* (3rd ed). Sage.

NOW. (2020, July 17). Washington's football team must change its toxic culture—not just its [Press release]. https://now.org/media-center/press-release/washingtons-football-team-must-change-its-toxic-culture-not-just-its/

Ortiz-Lytle, C. (2020, August 30). NHL team loses season ticket holders over support for Black Lives Matter. *Washington Examiner*. www.washingtonexaminer.com/news/nhl-team-loses-season-ticket-holders-over-support-for-black-lives-matter.

Park, D.C., & Huang, C.M. (2010). Culture wires the brain: A cognitive, neuroscience perspective. *Perspectives on Psychological Science, 5*(4) 391-400.

Pittinsky, T.L., Shih, M., & Trahan, A. (2006). Identity cues: Evidence from and for intra-individual perspectives on stereotyping. *Journal of Applied Social Psychology, 36*, 2215-2239.

Quinn, R.E, & Spreitzer, G.M., (2005). Entering the fundamental state of leadership: A framework for the positive transformation of self and others. In Burk, R. & Cooper C. (Eds.), *Inspiring leaders*. Routledge.

Schein, E.H. (1992). *Organizational culture and leadership* (2nd ed.). Jossey-Bass.

Shaw, S., & Frisby, W. (2006). Can gender equity be more equitable?: Promoting an alternative frame for sport management research, education, and practice. *Journal of Sport Management, 20*, 483-509.

Testa, M.R, & Sipe, L.J. (2013). The organizational cultural audit: Countering cultural ambiguity in the service context. *Open Journal of Leadership, 2*(2), 36-44.

Thomas, D.A, & Ely, R.J. (1996, September/October). Making differences matter: A new paradigm for managing diversity. *Harvard Business Review, 74*(5), 79-90.

Tsui, A.S., & O'Reilly, C.A. (1992). Being different: Relational demography and organizational attachment. *Administrative Science Quarterly, 37*, 549-579.

Ushe, N. (2021, July 1). Washington Football Team fined $10m following investigation into toxic workplace culture. *People*. https://people.com/sports/washington-football-team-fined-10m-following-investigation-toxic-workplace-culture/.

Vohra, N., & Chari, V. (2015). Inclusive workplaces: Lessons from theory and practice. *Journal for Decision Makers, 40*(3), 324-362.

Whitinui, P. (2020, July 14). Washington Redskins finally agree: Dismantling racist team mascots is long overdue. The Conversation. https://theconversation.com/washington-redskins-finally-agree-dismantling-racist-team-mascots-is-long-overdue-142618.

Williams, C.L. (2013). The glass escalator, revisited: Gender inequality in neoliberal times. *Gender and Society, 27*(5), 609-629.

Wingfield, A.H. (2009). Racializing the glass escalator: Reconsidering men's experiences with women's work. *Gender and Society, 23*(1), 5-26.

Chapter 15

Agyemang, K.J., Singer, J.N., & Weems, A.J. (2020). "Agitate! Agitate! Agitate!": Sport as a site for political activism and social change. *Organization, 27*(6), 952-968.

Allen, S. (2016, December 6) NBA teams visit the African American Museum while in D.C. to play the Wizards. *The Washington Post*. Retrieved on January 14, 2022 from www.washingtonpost.com/news/dc-sports-bog/wp/2016/12/06/nba-teams-visit-the-african-american-museum-while-in-d-c-to-play-the-wizards/

Anti-Defamation League. (2021). *Our mission*. www.adl.org/who-we-are/our-mission.

Armstrong, K.L., & Jennings, M.A. (2018). Race, sport, and sociocognitive "place" in higher education: Black male student-athletes as critical theorists. *Journal of Black Studies, 49*(4), 349-369.

Athlete 365. (2021). *Rule 50 explained*. International Olympic Committee. https://olympics.com/athlete365/rule-50-resources/.

Athlete Ally. (2016). *Athlete equality index*. https://aei.athleteally.org

Blackburn-Dwyer, B., & McMaster, A. (2018, February 7). *18 times politics trumped sport in Olympic Games' history*. Global Citizen. www.globalcitizen.org/en/content/history-political-activism-olympics-rio/.

Boring, E.B. (1963). *History, Psychology and Science*. New York, NY: Wiley.

Bryant, H. (2019). *The heritage: Black athletes, a divided America, and the politics of patriotism*. Boston, MA: Beacon Press.

Calamur, K. (2016, June 4). Muhammad Ali and Vietnam. *The Atlantic*. www.theatlantic.com/news/archive/2016/06/muhammad-ali-vietnam/485717/.

Carlos, J., & Zirin, D. (2011). *The John Carlos story: The sports moment that changed the world*. Chicago, IL: Haymarket.

Carter-Francique, A.R. (2022). Black sportswomen's activism in the era of Muhammad Ali. In J. L. Conyers and Christel N. Temple (Eds.), *Muhammad Ali and Africana Cultural Memory, (Chapter 12)*. New York, NY: Anthem Press.

Carter-Francique, A., Gill, E., & Hart, A. (2017). Converging interests: Black scholar-advocacy and the black college athlete. In B.J. Hawkins, A.R. Carter-Francique, & J.N. Cooper (Eds.), *Critical race theory: Black athletic sporting experiences in the United States* (pp. 85-119). New York, NY: Palgrave Macmillan.

Cavil, J.K. (2015). Early athletic experiences at HBCUs: The creation of conferences. *The athletic experience at historically Black colleges and universities: Past, present, and persistence (pp.* 19-58). Lanham, MD: Rowman & Littlefield.

Coakley, J. (2017). *Sports in society: Issues and controversies*

(12th ed.). New York, NY: McGraw-Hill Education.

College Football Hall of Fame. (2021). *Home Page*. www.cfbhall.com/.

College Sport Research Institute. (2021). *Conference, report, journal*. University of South Carolina. www.csri.org/.

Comstock, D. (1982). Power in organizations: Toward a critical theory. *The Pacific Sociological Review, 25*(2), 139-162.

Cooper, J.N. (2012). Personal troubles and public issues: A sociological imagination of Black athletes' experiences at predominantly White institutions in the United States. *Sociology Mind, 2*(3), 261.

Cooper, J.N., Macaulay, C., & Rodriguez, S.H. (2019). Race and resistance: A typology of African American sport activism. *International Review for the Sociology of Sport, 54*(2), 151-181.

Cooper, J.N., Mallery Jr, M., & Macaulay, C.D. (2020). African American sport activism and broader social movements. In D.D. Brown (Ed.), *Sports in African American life: Essays on history and culture*, (pp. 97-115). Jefferson, NC: McFarland & Company, Inc. Publisher.

Cunningham, G.B., Dixon, M.A., Singer, J.N., Oshiro, K.F., Ahn, N.Y., & Weems, A. (2021). A site to resist and persist: Diversity, social justice, and the unique nature of sport. *Journal of Global Sport Management, 6*(1): 1-19.

Davis, A. (2019, September 26). Sixty years ago she refused to stand for the anthem. *Zora*. https://zora.medium.com/sixty-years-ago-she-refused-to-stand-for-the-anthem-cf443b4e75c7.

Denver Broncos. (2021, April 26). *Broncos name China Jude as vice president of diversity, equity & inclusion*. Denver Broncos News: Homewww.denverbroncos.com/news/broncos-name-china-jude-as-vice-president-of-diversity-equity-inclusion.

The Drake Group. (2020). *Athlete rights, positions and issues*. www.thedrakegroup.org.

Edwards, H. (1979). The Olympic project for human rights: An assessment ten years later. *The Black Scholar, 10*(6-7), 2-8.

Edwards, H. (2010). Social change and popular culture: Seminal developments at the interface of race, sport and society. *Sport in Society, 13*(1), 59-71.

Edwards, H. (2016, November 3). *The fourth wave: Black athlete protests in the second decade of the 21st century* [Keynote address]. North American Society for the Sociology of Sport conference, Tampa, FL.

Edwards, H. (2017). *The revolt of the Black athlete*. Urbana, IL: University of Illinois Press.

Edwards, H. (2018, May 22). *It is time: From protest to policies, programs, and progress*. Institute for the Study of Sport, Society and Social Change, San José State University. www.sjsu.edu/wordstoaction/legacies/edwards/it-is-time.php.

Estrada, S. (2018, February 28). Golden State Warriors' trip to African American museum outshines Trump's refusal for White House visit. *Diverse Inc. News*. www.diversityinc.com/golden-state-warriors-trip-african-american-museum-outshines-trumps-refusal-white-house-visit/.

Greenwood, R. & Hinings, C.R. (1988). Organizational design types, tracks, and the dynamics of strategic change. *Organization Studies, 9*, 293-316.

Greiner, l.E. (1967). Patterns of organizational change. *Harvard Business Review, 45*, 119-130.

Hartmann, D. (2003). *Race, culture, and the revolt of the Black athlete: The 1968 Olympic protests and their aftermath*. Chicago, IL: University of Chicago Press.

Hartmann, D. (2009). Activism, organizing, and the symbolic power of sport. *Journal for the Study of Sports and Athletes in Education, 3*(2), 181-194.

Haslett, D., & Smith, B. (2019). Disability sport and social activism. In *The Routledge Handbook of Disability Activism* (pp. 197-208). London, UK: Routledge.

Hill, C.E. (2018, October 15). Jerry Jones, Dallas Cowboys staying extra day in D.C. to visit African American museum. *Fort Worth Star Telegram*. www.star-telegram.com/sports/nfl/dallas-cowboys/article220069980.html.

Institute for the Study of Sport, Society and Social Change. (2021). *Educational toolkits*. San José State University. https://www.sjsu.edu/wordstoaction/index.php.

Intergroup Resources. (2012). *Primers: Power*. www.intergroupresources.com/power/.

Jackson, J.H. (2017). *SJSU: Home to the Sociology of Sport. SJSU Washington Square*. Retrieved on January 13, 2022 from https://blogs.sjsu.edu/wsq/2017/01/20/sjsu-home-to-the-sociology-of-sport/.

Kaufman, P., & Wolff, E.A. (2010). Playing and protesting: Sport as a vehicle for social change. *Journal of Sport and Social Issues, 34*(2), 154-175.

Kikulis, L., Slack, T. & Hinings, C.R. (1992). Institutionally specific design archetypes: A framework for understanding change in national sport organizations. *International Review of Sociology of Sport, 27*, 343-370.

Kimberly, J.R. (1980). The life cycle analogy and the study of organizations: Introduction. In J.R. Kimberly & R.H. Miles (Eds.), *The Organizational Life Cycle*, 1-14. San Francisco, CA: Jossey-Bass.

Ladson-Billings, G. (1995). Toward a theory of culturally relevant pedagogy. *American Educational Research Journal, 32*(3), 465-491.

Ladson-Billings, G. (2008). Yes, but how do we do it? Practicing culturally relevant pedagogy. In W. Ayers, G. Ladson-Billings, G. Michie, & P.A. Noguera (Eds.), *City kids, city schools: More reports from the front row* (pp. 162-177). New York, NY: The New Press.

Lankes, C. (2021, June 3). *How George Floyd's death reignited a worldwide movement*. DW. www.dw.com/en/how-george-floyds-death-reignited-a-worldwide-movement/a-56781938.

Le Poidevin, O. (2020, June 9). *George Floyd: Black Lives Matter protests go global*. BBC. www.bbc.com/news/av/world-52967551.

LoRé, M. (2020, May 19). The importance of sports amid the coronavirus pandemic continues to be emphasized. *Forbes*. www.forbes.com/sites/michaellore/2020/05/19/the-importance-of-sports-amid-the-coronavirus-pandemic-continues-to-be-emphasized/?sh=1e24b51930f6.

Lorsch, J. (1986). Managing culture: The invisible barrier to strategic change. *California Management Review, 28*, 95-109.

Maxouris, C., Hanna, J., & Almasy, S. (2020, May 28). *Prosecutors do not announce charges in George Floyd's death but say "justice will be served."* CNN. www.cnn.com/2020/05/28/us/minneapolis-george-floyd-thursday/index.html.

Merriam-Webster. (n.d.). *Power.* In Merriam-Webster.com dictionary. Retrieved January 14, 2022, from https://www.merriam-webster.com/dictionary/power.

Mills, C.W. (1959). *The sociological imagination.* New York, NY: Oxford University Press.

Montville, L. (2017). *Sting like a bee: Muhammad Ali vs. the United States of America,* 1966-1971. New York, NY: Doubleday Publishers.

Move United (2021). *Redefining disability podcasts and Move United magazine.* www.moveunitedsport.org.

National Museum of African American History and Culture (NMAAHC) (n.d.) Home page. Smithsonian. Retrieved on January 14, 2022 from https://nmaahc.si.edu.

Parenti, M. (1995). *Democracy for the few* (6th ed.). New York, NY: St. Martin's Press.

Peck, R. (Director). (2016). *I am not your Negro.* Magnolia Pictures.

Peters, T. (1990). Get innovative or get dead. *California Management Review, 33,* 9-26.

Pettigrew, A.M. (1980). *The awakening giant.* Oxford, UK: Basil Blackwell.

Pettigrew, A.M. (1987). Context and action in the transformation of the firm. *Journal of Management Studies, 24*, 649-670.

Purnell, L. (2000). A description of the Purnell model for cultural competence. *Journal of Transcultural Nursing, 11*(1), 40-46.

Purnell, L.D. (2016). The Purnell model for cultural competence. In Inter*vention in Mental Health-Substance Use* (pp. 57-78). CRC Press.

Race Equity Tools. (2020). Glossary: Power. www.racialequitytools.org/glossary.

Sage, G.H. (1998). *Power and ideology in American sport: A critical perspective* (2nd ed.) Champaign, IL: Human Kinetics.

Shinn, P. (2019, October 23). *Tommie Smith to accept Hall of Fame honor for his 24 year old self.* Team USA. www.teamusa.org/news/2019/october/23/tommie-smith-to-accept-hall-of-fame-honor-for-his-24-year-old-self.

Slack, T., & Parent, M.M. (2006). *Understanding sport organizations: The application of organizational theory* (2nd ed.). Champaign, IL: Human Kinetics.

Smith, T., & Steele, D. (2008). *Silent gesture: The autobiography of Tommie Smith.* Philadelphia, PA: Temple University Press.

Special Olympics (2021). *Unified champion schools.* www.specialolympics.org.

Suddler, C. (2021 May 25). George Floyd changed the world of athlete activism. *The Washington Post.* www.washingtonpost.com/outlook/2021/05/25/george-floyd-changed-world-athlete-activism/.

Taylor, D.B. (2021 March 28). George Floyd protests: A timeline. *The New York Times.* www.nytimes.com/article/george-floyd-protests-timeline.html.

Theberge, N., & Donnelly, P. (Eds.) (1984). *Sport and the sociological imagination.* Fort Worth, TX: Texas Christian Press.

TIDES: The Institute for Diversity and Ethics in Sport. (n.d.). Racial & Gender Report Cards . University of Central Florida. Retrieved on January 12, 2022 from www.tidesport.org/racial-gender-report-card.

Tracy, M. (2017 May 24). African-American museum wins new fans: Athletes. *The New York Times: Sports.* Retrieved on January 14, 2022 from https://www.nytimes.com/2017/05/24/sports/national-museum-african-american-history-culture-nba-athletes.html.

Tucker Center for Research on Girls and Women in Sport. (2021). *SHECANCOACH Project.* University of Minnesota. https://www.cehd.umn.edu/tuckercenter/default.html

Whitener, M. (2021). A history of athletes and activism. *Yardbarker.* www.yardbarker.com/general_sports/articles/a_history_of_athletes_and_activism/s1__32219363#slide_1.

Wilterdink, N. and Form, W. (2021, December 14). *Social change.* Encyclopedia Britannica. Retrieved on January 12, 2021 from https://www.britannica.com/topic/social-change.

Wimbledon. (2021). The Wimbledon lawn tennis museum and tour. www.wimbledon.com/en_GB/museum_and_tours/index.html.

Women's Sports Museum. (2021). Home. www.womenssportsmuseum.org/.

World Health Organization [WHO]. (2020, March 11). *WHO Director-General's opening remarks at the media briefing on COVID-19.* www.who.int/director-general/speeches/detail/who-director-general-s-opening-remarks-at-the-media-briefing-on-covid-19---11-march-2020.

Wulf, S. (2019, January 30). *Athletes and activism: The long, defiant history of sport protests.* The Undefeated. https://theundefeated.com/features/athletes-and-activism-the-long-defiant-history-of-sports-protests/.

Zirin, D. (2005). *What's my name, fool? Sports and resistance in the United States.* Chicago, IL: Haymarket Books.

Zirin, D. (2007). *Muhammad Ali handbook.* MQ Publications.

Zirin, D. (2014 December 19). Interview with Ariyana Smith: The First athlete activist of #BlackLivesMatter. *The Nation.* Retrieved on January 14, 2022 from https://www.thenation.com/article/archive/interview-ariyana-smith-first-athlete-activist-blacklivesmatter/

Zucker, L.G. (1983). Organizations as institutions. In S.B. Bachrach (Ed.), *Advances in organizational theory and research* (vol. 2, pp. 1-43). Greenwich, CT: JAI Press.

Zucker, L.G. (1987). Institutional theories of organization. *Annual Review of Sociology, 13*, 443-464.

GLOSSARY

ableism—Inequitable treatment of people with disabilities typically based on stereotypes and lack of information.

activism—Engagement in intentional actions to disrupt oppressive systems; techniques used by individuals and groups to challenge inequitable situations.

advocacy—A declaration of support or recommendation for a specific policy or cause.

age discrimination—Discrimination based on age.

age microaggression—A subtle expression of prejudice based on age.

ageism—Prejudice or discrimination against an individual based on their age.

ally—Someone who stands up for or advocates alongside another person to advance their interests.

allyship—A situation in which member(s) of dominant social groups align themselves with a marginalized social group or individuals to actively protest systemic oppression and move toward a more equitable power system.

anti-racism—Promoting racial equality and equity through concerted policy replacement efforts.

apolitical—Not connected to politics, or not connected to any particular political party.

assimilation—A process in which members of an underrepresented group or culture adopt and accept the values, behaviors, and beliefs of the culture of the majority group, often at the expense of their cultural distinctiveness.

athlete prodigy—An athlete who exhibits athletic skills and accomplishments that are advanced for their age.

athlete retirement—A transition an athlete goes through when they stop competing at a particular level. This transition does not necessarily mean that a person no longer participates or trains but generally signals a process of change in their athletic career.

athletic identity—The level to which a person identifies with the role of being an athlete, both cognitive and socially.

authority or legitimate authority—Influence or power exercised over a group of people who have given their approval for its use or accept it as being appropriate.

best practices—Strategies and actions sport managers can use as models to develop an inclusive organization.

bias—A prejudice for or against a group of people. Bias can be **implicit** (unconscious), meaning you are not aware of having a certain preference or attitude toward something, someone, or a group of people. Bias can also be **explicit** (conscious), meaning that you are aware of certain preference or attitude toward something, someone, or a group of people.

bonding social capital—A value developed through social networks between relatively homogenous groups of family, neighbors, and close friends, where the interaction and familiarity are strong and help a person get by or cope.

bourgeoisie—*see Marxist*

bridging social capital—Relationships developed between socially heterogeneous groups, where social ties and bonds may be looser and more diverse. These bridging networks provide individuals with the potential to reach a broader set of resources.

capitalism—An economic system of private ownership where owners control property in accord with their individual or organizational interests; goods are produced in markets in accordance with economic principles such as supply and demand.

charismatic authority—Influence deriving from extraordinary personal qualities that leads followers to remain loyal to the influencer.

Civil Rights Act of 1964—Law that prohibits discrimination on the basis of race, color, religion, sex, or national origin; also strengthened voting rights and led to school desegregation.

civilizational racism—The prevalence of multiple societies reproducing racist beliefs, laws, rules, structures, institutions, and treatment toward groups deemed as subordinate based on their race.

colonization—Exploitation, usually by a nation "conquering" (invading) and land-grabbing other nations, that is centered on inequality and contempt, is perpetrated through force, and systematically denies the humanity of the exploited people.

coming out—A process with multiple layers that involves recognizing and accepting one's sexual orientation or gender identity and making decisions about how, whether, and when to share that information with others.

commodity—Goods in a capitalist system that can be bought or sold; in a sports economics framework, the athlete (who can be paid or unpaid) effectively sells labor-power to an employer for a wage, salary, or other form of compensation (e.g., an athletic scholarship).

constitutional growth delay (CGD)—Delayed puberty.

counter-spaces—Recognizable sites where a positive academic racial climate for non-White people can be established and maintained and deficit ideas can be challenged.

Criteria for Inclusion—A tool that sport managers can use to assess how inclusive their sport organization is when it comes to disability.

critical theory—Conceptual framework that analyzes the role of power and power dynamics of social structures and the interplay with individual and groups' culture, values, and morals.

cultural capital—Assets, such as behaviors, objects, and skills that can demonstrate cultural competence and influence social status.

cultural competencies—Ability to collaborate effectively among multiple cultures while respecting the cultures of the other people.

cultural diversity—The presence of different cultural (ethnic, racial, and other types of culture) groups within an organization or place.

cultural homogeneity—Preponderance of cultural sameness represented within a group.

cultural masking—Covering or hiding stigmatized aspects of authentic cultural identity, cultural orientations, lifestyles, values, or behaviors to conform to organizational cultural norms.

cultural myopia—A narrow-mindedness, shortsightedness, inability, and/or unwillingness to acknowledge elements of culture.

cultural pluralism—A value based on an appreciation for and encouragement of cultural diversity through simultaneously acknowledging cultural distinctions, promoting cross-cultural relationships, and encouraging the maintenance of the unique cultural identities of subgroups.

cultural plurality—Preponderance of cultural differences represented within a group.

decolonization (or decolonizing)—Shifting power from colonial invaders into the hands of the Indigenous people in colonized territories; emancipatory strategies to equalize the imbalance in power. Remnants of colonization linger where power is centralized into the hands of a few.

deep-level diversity—A group's or organization's practices that welcome people with differences in characteristics, backgrounds, and cultures, in a way that results in feelings of inclusion.

developmental model—A sociological model positing that school sport participation has a positive effect on social mobility through better student-athlete performance academically and on the field.

disability—An impairment, visible (e.g., amputee, person using a wheelchair) or invisible (e.g., post-traumatic stress disorder, traumatic brain injury), that affects activities and interactions.

discrimination—Actions against a group of people (as distinct from *prejudice*, which refers to biased thinking) based on a shared characteristic such as (but not limited to) age, religion, health, race, sexual orientation, or national origin.

disinformation—False information that is intended to mislead; can be false information issued by authorities or political enemies to influence public opinion.

diversity, equity, and inclusion (DEI)—Programs and policies that encourage representation and participation by often marginalized people, including people of different genders, races, ethnicities, abilities and disabilities, religions, cultures, ages, and sexual orientations and people with diverse backgrounds, experiences, skills, and expertise. Beyond having diverse representation, equity means providing access and opportunity for all, and inclusion is the atmosphere that welcomes the differences of the people.

diversity—Representatives of multiple racial, gender, ethnic, sexual orientation, language, age, nationality, religious beliefs, ability, backgrounds, skills, and experiences. Diversity is often looked to when assessing whether an organization is actively creating multicultural acceptance or is content to promote those who have always been in power.

equality—The same treatment for all, while not acknowledging or adjusting for existing disparities.

equity—A state of fairness and justice sought through policies and practices that address access opportunities along with outcomes.

evangelical athlete—An athlete who identifies with a conservative form of Protestant Christianity.

fantasy sports—A quickly growing realm of play featuring virtual teams populated by real players of professional sports whom the fantasy players pick and draft when selecting their fantasy team; players' teams face off against other virtual teams, with the outcome depending on how the real players perform in actual games in a given day or week.

femininity—The traits or characteristics typically associated with being female. Traditionally, masculinity and femininity have been conceptualized as opposite ends of a single dimension, with masculinity at one extreme and femininity at the other.

feminism—The advocacy of women's rights to promote equality of the sexes.

First Amendment—The First Amendment of the United States Constitution provides for protections against government intrusion into the establishment or exercise of religion; it also protects freedom of speech, freedom of the press, and freedom of assembly, as well as the right to petition the government when a perceived injustice or wrong has occurred.

gender—The state of being female, male, or nonbinary in relation to the social and cultural roles that are considered appropriate for men and women.

gender binary—The idea that gender is strictly an either/or option of male/man/masculine or female/woman/feminine based on sex assigned at birth, rather than a continuum or spectrum of gender identities and expressions.

gender identity—A person's deep-seated, internal sense of who they are as a gendered being (e.g., cisgender, transgender, nonbinary, genderqueer).

gender verification testing or sex testing—Invasive testing by athletic organizations to attempt to determine one's sex. This testing has only been aimed at policing the category of women. The actual procedure has ranged from genital examinations to hormonal testing.

gender-typing—The process by which someone becomes aware of their gender and adopts values and attributes that society has deemed to be characteristics of one gender or another. Gender-typing of sports refers to ideas about the sport itself being perceived as masculine or feminine, and then emphasizing characteristics that would affirm that designation.

gentrification—A process whereby construction projects are built in lower income neighborhoods, resulting in those living there being pushed out or displaced in favor of projects that financially benefit the wealthy.

goals—The broad statements regarding what the organization wants to achieve.

high-performance sports—A term used to refer to college sports and Olympic sports, where the players are often reduced to commodities.

horizontal social mobility—The transition of an individual from one social group to another on the same level.

in-groups—Social groups a person identifies with; most people have several such groups, including some they wouldn't necessarily identify.

inclusion—The atmosphere when deep-level diversity is embedded within an institution and organization to the extent that all diverse groups seeking harmonious coexistence feel safe, welcomed, valued, embraced, and supported, with full access to opportunities.

individual racism—Interpersonal acts of prejudice stemming from racial bias that cause harm to an individual or group.

Industrial Revolution—A movement in the 18th and 19th centuries that marked a shift from farming societies to urban, mechanized forms of industry in Europe and the United States.

institutional racism—Organizations reinforcing racialized hierarchies and prejudice in policies and practices (e.g., racial bias in hiring, evaluation, retention, and promotion), whether or not they are aware they are reinforcing them.

institutional sexism—A product of the system of patriarchy. It is reflected in institutional policies and practices, and it functions to discriminate against women.

intergenerational social mobility—The difference between individuals' social positions at particular points in their lives and those of their parents.

intersectionality—The interconnected nature of often-marginalized social categorizations such as race, class, and gender, which together create overlapping and interdependent systems of discrimination or disadvantage; or the theoretical approach originally coined by Kimberlé Crenshaw that explains this premise.

intersex—Individuals born with variations in sex characteristics, including chromosomes, hormones or genitals, that are atypical in either a female or male body.

intragenerational social mobility—Short-term mobility within a single generation.

leadership—An interpersonal and behavioral process whereby an individual influences and motivates others to achieve certain goals.

linking social capital—Relationships with people in positions of influence within formal institutions.

male practice player—On some women's teams, coaches will allow male players to practice with the team throughout the season.

Marxist (Marxism)—Philosophy of Karl Marx, a 19th century German philosopher, that criticizes capitalism and structural class systems; in a capitalist mode of production, tensions arise between the small number of owners who own the means of production (the **bourgeoisie**), and the larger number of workers who produce goods and services (the **proletariat**).

masculinity—The traits or characteristics typically associated with being male. Traditionally, femininity and masculinity have been conceptualized as opposite ends of a single dimension, with masculinity at one extreme and femininity at the other.

mechanistic dehumanization—Treating people as objects with no emotion or rights.

meritocracy—A theory that those who work hard and follow the rules will be rewarded on the basis of their merit and, conversely, that people in positions of power have earned it through work; the concept assumes equitable backgrounds for everyone.

microaggression—Brief and commonplace verbal, behavioral, or environmental slights, intentional or unintentional, that communicate hostile, derogatory, or negative attitudes toward marginalized people.

monocultural—The normalizing of one common culture.

multicultural—The normalizing of multiple diverse cultures.

muscular Christianity—A philosophical movement that started in the mid-1800s that focused on patriotism, self-discipline, moral, and physical strength. Organizations such as the Young Men's Christian Association (YMCA) used sport as a vehicle to promote this belief system.

national identity—A strong sense of belonging to a particular nation that carries with it some measure of commonality.

nonbinary—Gender identities that are neither female nor male, existing outside the gender binary.

objectives—Specific, measurable, achievable, realistic, and time-bound action items that propel the organization to accomplish the stated goals.

organizational climate—The metaphoric "temperature" of an organization relative to how it feels to work there (e.g., warm or accepting, cold or unwelcoming).

organizational culture—The collective norms, values, expectations, behaviors, belief systems, and artifacts (images, symbols, narratives, etc.) that define and represent the charisma or personality of an organization.

patriarchy—A society or system in which men dominate women, hold all authority and power, and fiercely hang onto it through a wide variety of strategies.

personal culture—A person's accumulation of learned behaviors, beliefs, and attitudes that represent groups they identify with and symbolic expressions of what each group thinks, values, says, and does.

politics—Activities through which people make, preserve, and change the general rules under which they live.

polycultural—Consisting of a number of cultural or ethnic groups.

positionality—The power inherent in a person's immediate respective social position that influences the difference in what individuals have access to in society.

power—The ability to influence others or impose one's will to get what one wants.

prejudice—The beliefs, thoughts, feelings, and attitudes someone holds about a group; such prejudgments typically originate outside actual experience.

privilege—Social benefit based on a dominant group characteristic; often invisible and may be present whether or not members of the dominant group realize it.

proletariat—*see Marxist*

race—The social and political construction of group differences/categories based on phenotypical and cultural characteristics with the initial purpose of creating a human hierarchy that positions White people of European descent as the most superior and Black people of African descent as the most inferior.

racism or racialized social systems—Multiple interlocking systems that place people in categories of race that inherently involve domination, oppression, exploitation, objectification, and dehumanization.

redlining—The systematic denial of services to racial minorities; best known as government practice to keep neighborhoods segregated in the 20th century; the practice perpetuates economic inequalities.

relative age effect (RAE)—Athletes who are born earlier within a sport age qualification timeframe have a longer time to develop physically and emotionally compared to athletes who are born later; the benefits of an early start can have a positive impact on long-term performance.

settler colonialism—The process of geographical, sociocultural, economic, political, and military domination by people of European descent of non-European people and their native lands and cultures across the world.

sex assigned at birth—The sex (female or male) assigned to a child at birth.

sexism—Prejudice, stereotyping, or discrimination, typically against women, on the basis of sex.

sexual behavior—The variety of different ways human beings engage in sexual activities.

social capital—A benefit of social networks, consisting of trust and reciprocity, that results in coordination and cooperation for mutual benefit.

social change—A process guided by individual and group action to alter current rules of behavior, social organizations, and value systems.

social class—A large grouping of people across society who share an economic position based on their income and inherited wealth, job or career, level of education, and social connections.

social construct or social construction—An idea that has been created and agreed upon by society and can present as fixed—such as race or gender—despite it actually being flexible.

social identity theory—The concept that groups influence their members' self-concepts and self-esteem, when people categorize themselves as members of that group and identify strongly with it.

social identity—A person's sense of who they are, based on their association with social groups.

social justice—Efforts to correct the relationship balance of society's distribution of fairness and access to opportunities, as applied to marginalized groups and individuals.

social mobility—The movement of people between different positions within the system of social stratification, resulting in changes to their social environment and living conditions.

social movement—A loosely organized but sustained campaign in support of a social goal, typically either the implementation or the prevention of a change in society's structure or values.

social return on investment (SROI)—The social, environmental, and economic value that is being created by an organization.

social stratification—Ranking of people by economic or cultural attributes such as education or income.

societal racism—Embedded systems of racist cultural norms across and within a given geopolitical area.

sociological imagination—The ability to shift from one mindset to another to connect an individual's personal troubles and society's public issues.

soft influence or soft power—A type of influence that shapes preferences through appealing messages (and messengers) rather than coercion; it can involve developing networks, building relationships, and educating decision makers about a particular perspective or set of facts.

sport chaplain—A professional who ministers to a sport community's administrators, athletes, coaches, staff, and other stakeholders.

sport for development and peace—The use of sports as a vehicle to meet international development objectives such as youth development, health promotion, gender equity, social inclusion, and conflict prevention.

sport managers—Administrators in charge of the daily operations or governance of a sport organization.

sports industrial complex or athletic industrial complex—A socioeconomic concept that recognizes sport as a social institution intertwined with other social and economic institutions.

stereotype—Widely held societal beliefs, expectations, and generalizations applied to individuals who share common characteristics or a social group like ethnicity, race, social class, and nationality.

stereotype threat—Self-editing behavior felt by a person from a marginalized group when that person is worried about confirming negative stereotypes about members of their group.

strategic plan—A dynamic document or framework containing analyses, strategies, and tactics addressing where an organization is, where it wants to go, and how it plans to get there.

surface-level diversity—Differences among group members in overt biological characteristics that are typically reflected in physical features.

SWOT analysis—An analysis of the strengths (internal conditions that are favorable to organizational success), weaknesses (internal conditions that are unfavorable to organizational success), opportunities (external conditions in the environment that are favorable to organizational success), and threats (external conditions in the environment that are unfavorable to organizational success).

systemic discrimination—Discrimination that is embedded in the policies, practices, habits, and traditions of organizations that are often taken for granted, have a negative impact on marginalized people, and often are perpetuated even when there is no intent to discriminate.

technology—The use of scientific knowledge through machinery or processes to achieve practical goals of social or individual importance.

thriving—A state of being in individuals who feel a sense of purpose, excitement, and vitality for their work, leading to job satisfaction and workplace innovation.

Title IX—The 1972 educational amendment that prohibits institutions receiving federal funding from discriminating or excluding anyone from educational opportunities based on sex.

transactional leadership—Leadership that focuses on the exchanges (such as rewards and punishments, and informational, personal, physical, and financial resources) that occur between the leaders and their followers.

transformational leadership—Process whereby a leader engages with members of the organization and creates connections that inspire and raise the level of motivation and morale among the leader and the followers.

transgender—Having a gender identity or expression that differs from what was assigned at birth. Cisgender refers to having a gender identity or expression that matches assigned sex at birth.

treatment discrimination—When perceptions about an individual's identity markers like race and gender are used, consciously or unconsciously, to treat an individual employee as if they cannot handle the job.

universal design—A method to ensure that an environment is as inclusive as possible, for both physical and intangible access and use.

vertical social mobility—Changes of significant improvement or descent of the social class position.

zero-sum model—As applies to sport participation's effect on social mobility, a sociological model that says when youth spend time on sport, it takes away time better spent on academics, hindering school performance and social mobility.

INDEX

Note: The italicized *f* and *t* following page numbers refer to figures and tables, respectively.

S

Y

Z

ABOUT THE EDITORS

Drexel University Office of Communications

Ellen J. Staurowsky, EdD, is a professor of sports media in the Roy H. Park School of Communications at Ithaca College. She is internationally recognized as an expert on social justice issues in sport, including college athletes' rights, the exploitation of college athletes, gender equity and Title IX, and the misappropriation of American Indian imagery in sport.

Staurowsky is coauthor of *College Athletes for Hire: The Evolution and Legacy of the NCAA Amateur Myth* and editor of *Women and Sport: Continuing a Journey of Liberation and Celebration*. She regularly works with the National College Players Association and has coauthored several of their reports, including "How the NCAA's Empire Robs Predominantly Black Athletes of Billions in Generational Wealth." She has worked with the Women's Sports Foundation on several research projects and served as lead author on "Chasing Equity: The Triumphs, Challenges, and Opportunities in Sports for Girls and Women."

Staurowsky is currently a senior writer for *Legal Issues in College Athletics* and *Sports Litigation Alert*. She has been a columnist with *College Sports Business News* and the *Women in Coaching* blog, and she is cofounder and editor of the *LGBT Issues in Sport: Theory to Practice* blog.

Courtesy of Missouri State University.

Algerian Hart, PhD, is the associate dean of the graduate college and a professor of kinesiology at Missouri State University. He is president of the North American Society for the Sociology of Sport (NASSS) and has served on the organization's diversity and conference climate committee. He also serves on the inclusion committee for the North American Society for Sport Management (NASSM).

Hart is a peer reviewer for the Higher Learning Commission, is a faculty evaluator for the American Council on Education, and serves on the editorial review boards for the *Journal of Athlete Development and Experience* and the *Sociology of Sport Journal*. He has written extensively on the topics of marginalized populations in education and student-athlete advocacy, and he is the author of *The Student Athlete's Guide to College Success.*

ABOUT THE CONTRIBUTORS

Ketra L. Armstrong, PhD, is a University of Michigan (UM) diversity and social transformation professor and a professor of sport management in UM's School of Kinesiology. She is also the school's director of diversity, equity, and inclusion; the director of the Center for Race and Ethnicity in Sport; and UM's NCAA faculty athletics representative. Her scholarly interests are the social psychology of race, ethnicity, and gender and the implications for sport. She is a fellow in the National Center for Institutional Diversity, the North American Society for Sport Management, and the National Academy of Kinesiology. Dr. Armstrong is the former president of the National Association for Girls and Women in Sport and a former Division I collegiate student-athlete, coach, and administrator.

Courtesy of San Josê State University.

Akilah R. Carter-Francique, PhD, is the executive director for the Institute for the Study of Sport, Society, and Social Change (ISSSSC) at San José State University. She is also an associate professor at SJSU in the department of African American studies. Her scholarly endeavors and field of focus encompass the intersection of sport, society, and social justice, including issues of diversity, social movements, and the dynamics of social change and development. Dr. Carter-Francique served as the 2018-2019 president of the North American Society for the Sociology of Sport (NASSS), currently serves as a member of Laureus "Sport for Good" Research Council in the United States, and is the coeditor of *Athletic Experience at Historically Black Colleges and Universities: Past, Present, and Persistence* and *Critical Race Theory: Black Athletic Experiences in the United States.*

Courtesy of University of Massachusetts-Boston.

Joseph N. Cooper, PhD, is the Dr. J. Keith Motley endowed chair of sport leadership and administration (SLA) and special assistant to the chancellor for Black life at the University of Massachusetts Boston. As the inaugural endowed chair for the UMass Boston SLA program, he has established a unique program whose mission is to cultivate equity-minded, character-driven, and transformational leaders who will positively improve society through sport. His research focuses on the intersection of race, gender, sport, education, and culture, with a focus on how sport contributes to holistic development and collective uplift. He is the author of *From Exploitation Back to Empowerment: Black Male Holistic Under (Development) Through Sport and (Mis)Education* and *A Legacy of African American Resistance and Activism Through Sport.*

Courtesy of Michael T. Davis Photography.

Amira Rose Davis, PhD, is an assistant professor of history at Penn State University, where she focuses on the intersection of race, gender, sports, and politics. Named a Mellon Emerging Faculty Leader by the Institute for Citizens and Scholars, Dr. Davis is the author of the forthcoming book *"Can't Eat a Medal": The Lives and Labors of Black Women Athletes in the Age of Jim Crow.* Davis provides sports commentary for public venues such as NPR, ESPN, and BBC and has bylines in *Washington Post* and *The New Republic,* among other places. A member of the American Studies Association's Sports Caucus, Dr. Davis also serves on the advisory board of the Jackie Robinson Museum and the Arthur Ashe Legacy Foundation. Dr. Davis is the cohost of the feminist sports podcast *Burn It All Down.*

Courtesy of Sonia Strohl.

Kiera D. Duckworth, PhD, is the training manager for the City of Rochester and is the founding consultant at Birch Consulting Group. She has spent her career in education and public service teaching about social issues and advocating for more LGBTQ-inclusive spaces and policies. She holds a doctoral degree in sociology from State University of New York at Buffalo, specializing in sexuality and gender in society. Dr. Duckworth has worked to successfully implement policies protecting transgender students and employees in both institutions of higher education and municipalities. She consults with colleges, K-12 school districts, and businesses regarding their inclusion policies and strategizes how to create more inclusive professional and learning climates.

Courtesy of University of Georgia.

Billy Hawkins, PhD, is a professor at the University of Houston in the department of health and human performance. He is the author of several peer-reviewed articles and books. He is the Global Intersectionality of Education, Sports, Race, and Gender series editor for Peter Lang Publishers, and he serves on the editorial board of Lexington Press. He also serves on several journal editorial boards. Dr. Hawkins received the College of Liberal Arts and Social Sciences Distinguished Faculty Award at the University of Houston. He is a North American Society for the Sociology of Sport (NASSS) research fellow and a recipient of the NASSS Service Excellence Award. He is also a recipient of the Robert Maynard Hutchins Award for his research on intercollegiate athletics.

Robin Hardin, PhD, is a professor in the sport management program housed in the department of kinesiology, recreation, and sport studies at the University of Tennessee. He earned his PhD in communications from the University of Tennessee (2000). He also earned a master's degree in communications (1996) as well as a master's degree in sport studies (1998) from Tennessee. He earned his bachelor's degree in communications and political science from East Tennessee State University (1993). He has more than 100 scholarly publications in the profession's top journals and has made more than 150 scholarly presentations. He is a former editor of *Sport Management Education Journal* (2018-2021). He retired in 2008 after 20 years of service in the Tennessee National Guard and is a veteran of Operation Desert Storm (1991-1992).

Courtesy of Kymoroa Jaxson Photography.

Beau Manierre Houston, PhD, is the athletic director and climate and culture coordinator at Gateway High School in Aurora, Colorado. She oversees interscholastic sports and physical education and supports ROTC. She is a research fellow at the Center for Critical Sport Studies at UCCS and was recently named a Moonshot Edventures Fellow. Previously, she served as an assistant coach and physical education instructor at the United States Air Force Academy and a head coach at Southern University in Louisiana. She was an All-American hurdler at the University of Alabama, where she earned marketing and sports administration degrees. She is a member of the North American Society for the Sociology of Sport (NASSS) and serves on the equity committee for the Colorado High School Athletic Association (CHSAA).

Courtesy of University of Louisville College of Education and Human Development.

Mary A. Hums, PhD, is a professor of sport administration at the University of Louisville. In 2009, she was named a NASSM Earle F. Zeigler lecturer, the organization's most prestigious academic honor. She was invited to White House events, including the 2015 White House Presidential Reception celebrating the 25th anniversary of the Americans with Disabilities Act. In 2014, she received the NASSM Diversity Award. She has worked four Paralympic Games, the Olympic Games, and the Parapan American Games. Hums coauthored Article 30.5 of the 2006 UN Convention on the Rights of persons with Disabilities. Her research interests are policy development in sport organizations regarding inclusion of people with disabilities and also sport and human rights.

Courtesy of John Noltner / APeaseOfMyMind.net.

Luca Maurer, MS, is the founding director of the Center for LGBTQ Education, Outreach, and Services at Ithaca College. He also teaches sociology and received the Faculty Excellence Award, Ithaca College's highest academic honor, in 2018. Among his numerous publications, he coauthored *The Teaching Transgender Toolkit*, an award winning book about the lives and experiences of transgender people that was later featured in the pages of *National Geographic*. He received the American Psychological Association's Division 44 Distinguished Contribution to Education and Training Award in 2017. He has served on the editorial boards of the *American Journal of Sexuality Education*, *The Prevention Researcher*, and *Transgender Studies Quarterly*. The American Association of Sex Educators, Counselors and Therapists has designated him a certified sexuality educator, counselor, and supervisor.

Courtesy of Ithaca College Office of Communication.

Timothy Mirabito, PhD, is an assistant professor of journalism and sports media at Ithaca College in Ithaca, New York. His research agenda focuses on mythology, framing, and language use surrounding sport and sport figures. He earned his PhD at the University of Tennessee, where he worked with faculty that have been on the leading edge of research surrounding religion and college athletics. He serves on the editorial board of the *Sport Management Education Journal* (SMEJ) and is an active member of the International Association of Communication and Sport (IACS).

Jeffrey Montez de Oca, PhD, is a professor of sociology and founding director of the Center for the Critical Study of Sport at the University of Colorado at Colorado Springs. He is the past president of the North American Society for the Sociology of Sport and author of *Discipline and Indulgence: College Football, Media, and the American Way of Life During the Cold War* (Rutgers University Press, 2013).

Courtesy of BGSU Marketing.

Amanda L. Paule-Koba, PhD, is a professor of sport management at Bowling Green State University. Dr. Paule-Koba is a leading scholar examining athlete development and issues in intercollegiate sport (such as academic clustering, transitioning, and the athlete experience). Her research investigates contemporary prevailing problems or issues that affect athletes in collegiate sport. Dr. Paule-Koba is also the cofounder and coeditor of the *Journal* *of Athlete Development and Experience (JADE)*, which focuses on research that puts the athletes at the center of the equation and prioritizes people over profits. Dr. Paule-Koba has presented research at international, national, and regional conferences; coauthored two textbooks; and published her research in leading academic journals.

Courtesy of Temple University.

Michael Sachs, PhD, is a professor emeritus in the department of kinesiology at Temple University in Philadelphia, Pennsylvania. He received his PhD in sport psychology from Florida State University. Michael is coeditor of the recently published *Performance Excellence: Stories of Success From the Real World of Sport and Exercise Psychology* (2020) and *Applied Exercise Psychology: The Challenging Journey From Motivation to Adherence* (2018). His research interests focus upon exercise psychology, particularly motivation and adherence, excusercise, exercise addiction, exercise identity, and the psychology of running. Michael is a past president of both Association for Applied Sport Psychology (AASP) and Division 47, the Society for Sport, Exercise and Performance Psychology, of the American Psychological Association (APA). He is certified by AASP as a Mental Performance Consultant (CMPC).

NaRi Shin, PhD, is an assistant professor of sport management in the department of educational leadership at the University of Connecticut. She won the North American Society for Sport Management (NASSM) 2019 Student Research Competition with her dissertation on the 2018 Pyeongchang Winter Olympic Games and its impact on the host community's globalization and development. She has been serving as a member of the diversity and inclusion committee for NASSM since 2020. She was a faculty fellow for the Institute for Peace and Conflict at Texas Tech University, and her lines of research include sport for development and peace movement. Her research has been published in the *Journal of Sport Management, Communication and Sport; International Review for the Sociology of Sport*; and many other journals in the wider sport studies.

Eli A. Wolff, MA, directs the Power of Sport Lab, a platform to fuel and magnify creativity, diversity, connection, and leadership through sport. Wolff's work has been at the intersection of research, education, and advocacy in and through sport, with a focus on sport and social justice, diversity, disability, and inclusion. Wolff has cofounded Disability in Sport International, Athletes for Human Rights, the Olympism Project, and Mentoring for Change. Wolff is also an instructor with the sport management program at the University of Connecticut, an instructor with the sport leadership program at University of Massachusetts at Boston, and cofounder and advisor to the Sport and Society initiative at Brown University.